Elisabeth Schöndorf

Against the Odds

Successful UN Peace Operations –
A Theoretical Argument and Two Cases

Nomos

Diese Arbeit ist im Rahmen des kulturwissenschaftlichen Forschungskollegs
SFB 485 „Norm und Symbol. Die kulturelle Dimension sozialer und politischer
Integration" der Universität Konstanz entstanden und wurde auf seine
Veranlassung unter Verwendung der ihm von der Deutschen Forschungs-
gemeinschaft zur Verfügung gestellten Mittel gedruckt.

Die Deutsche Nationalbibliothek verzeichnet diese Publikation in
der Deutschen Nationalbibliografie; detaillierte bibliografische
Daten sind im Internet über http://dnb.d-nb.de abrufbar.

Die Deutsche Nationalbibliothek lists this publication in the
Deutsche Nationalbibliografie; detailed bibliographic data
is available in the Internet at http://dnb.d-nb.de.

Zugl.: Konstanz, Univ., Diss., 2009

ISBN 978-3-8329-5636-3

1. Auflage 2011
© Nomos Verlagsgesellschaft, Baden-Baden 2011. Printed in Germany. Alle Rechte,
auch die des Nachdrucks von Auszügen, der fotomechanischen Wiedergabe und
der Übersetzung, vorbehalten. Gedruckt auf alterungsbeständigem Papier.

List of Contents

List of Figures, Tables, and Boxes

List of Abbreviations

ACABQ	Advisory Committee on Administrative and Budgetary Questions
CA	Constituent Assembly
CB	Cognitive Biases
CC	Constitutional Commission
CEP	Community Empowerment Programme
CHDR	Center for History, Development, and Reconciliation
CIC	Center on International Cooperation
CivPol	United Nations Civilian Police
CNRT	Conselho Nacional de Resistência Timorense
DAC	District Advisory Council
DSRSG	Deputy Special Representative of the Secretary General
DTA	Deputy Transitional Administrator
EC	Executive Council
ECHA	Executive Committee on Humanitarian Assistance
ECHO	European Commission's Humanitarian Aid Office
ECPS	Executive Committee on Peace and Security
ETTA	East Timorese Transitional Administration
EU	European Union
EUMM	European Union Military Mission
Falintil	Forças Armadas De Libertação Nacional de Timor Leste (Armed Forces for the National Liberation of East Timor)
FAO	Food and Agriculture Organization
FRAP	Falintil Reinsertion Assistance Program
Fretilin	Frente Revolucionária do Timor-Leste Independente (Revolutionary Front for an Independent East Timor)
FRY	Former Republic of Yugoslavia
GA	General Assembly
GoC	Government of Croatia
GPA	Government and Public Administration Unit
GPPi	Global Public Policy Institute
HC	Humanitarian Coordinator
HCA	Head of Civil Affairs
HDZ	Hrvatska Demokratska Zajednica (Croatian Democratic Union)
HQ	Headquarters
HR	Human Rights
ICRC	International Committee of the Red Cross

ICTY	International Criminal Tribunal for the former Yugoslavia
IDP	Internally Displaced Persons
IMF	International Monetary Fund
IMTF	Integrated Mission Task Force
INGOs	International Non-governmental Organizations
	Instruction in Peacekeeping Operations
IO	International Organization
IPA	International Peace Academy
JEN	Japan Emergency NGOs
JIC	Joint Implementation Committee
JNA	Jugoslav National Army
MILOPS	Military Operations
MSF	Médecins Sans Frontières
NATO	North Atlantic Treaty Organization
NC	National Council
NCC	National Consultative Council
NGO	Non-governmental Organization
NRC	Norwegian Red Cross
OCHA	Office for the Coordination of Humanitarian Affairs
OSCE	Organization for Security and Co-operation in Europe
Oxfam	Oxford Committee for Famine Relief
PA	Principal-Agent-Problems
PD	Path Dependence Deficiencies
P-5	The five permanent members of the Security Council
RC	Resident Coordinator
RSK	Republika Srpska Krajina
SC	Security Council
SFRY	Socialist Federal Republic of Yugoslavia
SG	Secretary-General
SOP	Standard Operating Procedure
Spc	Special political committee
SRSG	Special Representative of the Secretary-General
STACTA	Secretariat of the Transitional Administrator for the Coordination of the Transfer of Authority
TA	Transitional Administrator
TC	Tight Coupling of Complex Interactions
TOKTEN	Transfer of Knowledge through Expatriate Nationals
TPF	Transitional Police Force
UN Doc.	United Nations Document
UN	United Nations
UNAIDS	The United Nations Joint Programme on HIV/AIDS

UNCRO	United Nations Confidence Restoration Operation
UNDFS	United Nations Department of Field Support
UNDG	United Nations Development Group
UNDP	United Nations Development Programme
UNDPA	United Nations Department of Political Affairs
UNDPI	United Nations Department of Public Information
UNDPKO	United Nations Department of Peacekeeping Operations
UNDPO	United Nations Department of Peace Operations
UNHCR	United Nations High Commissioner for Refugees
UNICEF	United Nations International Children's Emergency Fund
UNITAR POCI	United Nations Institute for Training and Research Programme of Correspondence
UNMIH	United Nations Mission in Haiti
UNMIK	United Nations Mission in Kosovo
UNMIS	United Nations Mission in Sudan
UNPOS	United Nations Office for Project Services
UNPRO-FOR	United Nations Protection Force
UNTAC	United Nations Transitional Authority in Cambodia
UNTAES	United Nations Transitional Administration in Eastern Slavonia, Baranja, and Western Sirmium
UNTAET	United Nations Transitional Administration in East Timor
UNTAG	United Nations Transition Assistance Group, Namibia
UNV	United Nations Volunteers
WFP	World Food Programme
WHO	World Health Organization

"Was ist eine tragische [Handlung]? [...] Das ist dann der Fall, wenn die in ihr agierenden Figuren mit einer gewissen Zwangsläufigkeit in ein Geschehen verwickelt werden, das in die Katastrophe führt. Da ein solcher Weg selten ohne Zutun der Figur selber angetreten wird, lässt sich das Geschehen dialektisch auffassen: Es wird sowohl durch verantwortliches Handeln der Figur als auch durch Widerfahrnisse unberechenbarer Art bestimmt. Der tragische Charakter dieses Vorgangs wird gesteigert, wenn eine paradoxe Gegenstrebigkeit zwischen Handeln und Widerfahren besteht, d.h. wenn sich die katastrophalen Ereignisse jedem planenden Eingriff verschließen, aber gerade durch das planende Vollbringen zurechenbarer Taten heraufbeschworen werden [...]."[1]

1   Söring, Jürgen. 1982. *Tragödie: Notwendigkeit und Zufall im Spannungsfeld tragischer Prozesse.* Stuttgart: Klett-Cotta, p. 36.

Abstract

The thesis explores an alternative explanation for the success and failure of complex UN peace operations. The suggested perspective focusses on organizational and behavioral processes. I start with the assumption that UN missions operate under unfavorable conditions: they are constrained by political considerations of member states, by rigid institutional rules and scarce resources of the UN, and they face adverse on-the-ground conditions in the form of local hostility and low capacities. I argue that, under these "ill-structured" conditions, peace operations develop organizational pathologies. The more virulent these pathologies become, the more likely failure is. I argue further that "fit" coping behavior of the decision-makers of the mission can attenuate these pathologies and make a mission succeed "against the odds."

I specify my argument by falling back on concepts from administrative science and organizational theory, including concepts from organizational psychology: Integrating the concepts of cognitive biases, of principal-agent interactions, of tight coupling of complex interactions, and of path dependency into a coherent model, I make stipulations on the existence of pathologies and coping strategies. I examine the argument by analyzing the most complex mission type of the UN, namely transitional administrations: in these extreme cases, ill-structured conditions can most likely be assumed. In specific, I examine the missions in Eastern Slavonia (UN-TAES, 1996-1998) and East Timor (UNTAET, 1999-2002). Both were notably successful ventures and hence, observations of coping behavior shall be possible, too. To reconstruct the transitional management process and to find evidence in support of my propositions, I conduct expert interviews particularly with (senior) mission staff and analyze primary and secondary sources.

I am able to demonstrate that pathologies that are well known to classic administrative science and organizational theory are also operating in international peace operations. Most striking is the persistence of principal-agent problems – they occur regularly in both cases. Even more, I am able to show how both missions successfully coped with the huge challenges they were facing and I identify a vast range of such contingency strategies. There are patterns in which a successful coping strategy fits which type of pathology; these patterns partly correspond with theoretical recommencations, partly the recommendations have to be modified. It shows that coping also depends on the availability of certain advantages, particularly authoritative power, sufficient resources, a clear political end state, and determined leadership to put the other advantages to good use. In fact, the leaders of the missions often had to fall back on informal arrangements and at most critical points of the transition process, they had to break, or at least ignore, the rules in order to implement their mandates successfully.

"[Transitional civil administrations] face challenges and responsibilities that are unique among United Nations field operations. No other operation must set and enforce the law, establish customs services and regulations, set and collect business and personal taxes, attract foreign investment, adjudicate property disputes and liabilities for war damage, reconstruct and operate all public utilities, create a banking system, run schools and pay teachers and collect the garbage – in a war-damaged society, using voluntary contributions, because the assessed mission budget, even for such 'transitional administration' missions, does not fund local administrations itself. In addition to such tasks, these missions must also try to rebuild civil society and promote respect for human rights, in places where grievance is widespread and grudges run deep. [...] Beyond such challenges lies the larger question of whether the United Nations should be in this business at all [...] [given] evident ambivalence about civil administration among United Nations Member States and within the Secretariat [...]."[2]

I. Introduction

When in September 1999, the Security Council authorized the UN Transitional Administration in East Timor, the international community engaged in an unprecedented task: for the first time in its history, a UN peace operation was to build a state from scratch. However, the road to the independence ceremony of May 2002 was rocky, fraught with dilemmas and tough decisions: UNTAET's leadership struggled with various challenges, which emanated either from the political caveats or from the adverse situation on Timorese ground. A fault of consequence was the premature foreclosure of East Timorese from their very own transition process: Being subject to Indonesia's pressure, to inadequate rules and routines of the UN Department of Peacekeeping Operations, and to internal turf wars, the mission came to assume a Timorese *terra nullis*. As consequence, a policy path was locked in that forestalled the pursuance of local ownership. Exacerbating Timorese frustration, the well-equipped international administration missed out on early improvements to the locals' impoverished lives.

A combination of ambiguous principals at the international level, of misperceptions and automatisms within the UN system pushed UNTAET on a wrong track. Despite its comparatively broad political support and abundant resources, UNTAET was close to becoming a failure early on.

---

2 United Nations, "Report of the Panel on United Nations Peace Operations," UN Doc. A/55/305 – S/2000/809, 21 August 2000, para. 77. Available online at www.un.org/peace/reports/peace_operations, last access on 6 March 2009. The document is also known as the "Brahimi report." For an overview of the document symbols and the symbol structure of UN documents, see UN Dag Hammarskjöld Library, "United Nations Documentation: Research Guide." Available online at http://www.un.org/Depts/dhl/resguide/symbol.htm, last access on 6 March 2009.

1. Bound to Fail? Inherent Problems of UN Peace Operations

Are UN peace operations tragic? By definition, a tragedy has a noble protagonist who becomes enmeshed in an "intrinsicate knot"[3] of challenging situations and ill-fated actions that make them prone to defeat and disaster. Hope is distorted, ambition frustrated.

Peace operations in general and transitional administrations in specific are ambitious tools used by the international community to stabilize territories that experience horrifying conflicts – and some of their fundamental features strikingly resemble those of a classic tragedy indeed.[4] The challenges and responsibilities are extreme: they are confronted with post-conflict hostility, low human capacity for reconstruction, and poor local infrastructure. At the same time, they are highly complex missions striving for a multitude of ambitious goals in a short timeframe while struggling with dilemmas of governance and legitimacy. All of these features are *inherent* to the nature of their objectives and institutional genesis – and is thus *inevitable*. The question of interest is how these adverse scope conditions determine the performance of a mission. Is it doomed to failure? The first fundamental proposition of the thesis specifies this thought and argues that the inherent "ill-structured" conditions and challenges of a complex UN peace operation translate into the development of organizational pathologies during the transition process. The more complex and demanding the mission is designed, the more likely pathologies develop. Since transitional administrations represent the most extreme design of a peace operation, I assume pathologies to develop most likely in these cases. The focus of the study is therefore put on this type of mission.

The academic literature on UN transitional administrations approaches them from two perspectives: macro-studies discuss the political conditions and particularly the question of legitimacy,[5] and they identify quantifiable variables explaining the performance of an operation, such as local hostility, capacity, and international commitment at large.[6] The micro-perspective comes to the fore in single case studies about individual missions which focus on particular aspects in the process of post-conflict reconstruction. The majority of these studies emphasize specific tech-

---

3   Ibid. 1992. *The Tragedy of Antony and Cleopatra.* Edited by Raimund Borgmeier. Stuttgart: Reclam, Act V, scene II.
4   Cf., e.g, Rotberg, Robert. 2003. *When States Fail. Causes and Consequences.* Princeton: Princeton University Press.
5   E.g., Zaum, Dominik. 2007. *The Sovereignty Paradox: The Norms and Politics of International State Building.* Oxford: Oxford University Press; Chesterman, Simon. 2004. *You, the People: The United Nations, Transitional Administration, and State-Building.* Oxford: Oxford University Press, chapter 4.
6   E.g., Doyle, Michael W. and Nicholas Sambanis. 2000. "International Peacebuilding: A Theoretical and Quantitative Analysis." *American Political Science Review* 94:4, pp. 779-801; Doyle, Michael W. and Nicholas Sambanis. 2006. *Making War and Building Peace: United Nations Peace Operations.* Princeton: Princeton University Press.

nical-administrative and policy-oriented issues.[7] I attempt to integrate the two research rationales by adding the process dimension to the macro-perspective, as well as by putting the micro-perspective in the greater political and institutional context: taking into account the intricate macro-conditions of a UN transitional administration, I set out to analyze their effect on the transition process. Assuming that these conditions are "ill-structured," that means that they induce complexity, uncertainty and ambiguity, as well as time pressure, I argue that they are very likely to result in pathologies: the mission develops behavioral patterns that undermine its very objectives. In the worst-case scenario, such inadequate decision-making and behavior becomes virulent and propels ultimate failure. As a matter of fact, there are no instances where transitional administrations of the international community have experienced complete successes.

However, there are two cases where transitional administrations have experienced at least partial successes, namely the missions in Eastern Slavonia and in East Timor. A crucial explanatory approach accounting for these exceptions, and the second fundamental proposition of the thesis, relates to the mission's coping behavior during the ongoing transition management: I argue that the capacity of these missions to develop contingency strategies prevented, reduced, or contained the pathologies that had ensued from the mission's ill-structured conditions. A resumption of the introductory narrative, which has described how UNTAET was teetering on the brink of disaster, serves as preliminary evidence for the argument: in this situation, the head of the mission, in a heavily discussed move, decided to start over. Going for a genuine power-sharing arrangement, he changed the complete set up of the transitional approach. It resulted to be a critical move for UNTAET's mandate achievement. – And this type of contency or coping strategy you would never find in any rule book.

The general research goal of the study is to build a theory on how the conditions and inherent characteristics of complex peace operations of the UN produce pathological setbacks – and how a mission can get to terms with them. With this approach, the study is deeply realistic in that it accepts the fact that a mission is permanently precarious: the burden of peace operations rests in the impending impotence to alleviate people from suffering and to build them a better future. At the same time, the study is genuinely optimistic as it focuses on those factors and processes that may help a mission to control its precariousness and even avert foreboding tragedies.

Summarizing the above considerations, I ask the following research questions: what effects do ill-structured conditions have on the management of a UN peace operation; what kind of organizational pathologies develop; and how can they suc-

---

7   Cf. Bonacker, Thorsten. 2008. *Sozialwissenschaftliche Konflikttheorien: Eine Einführung.* Wiesbaden: VS Verlag für Sozialwissenschaften, p. 4.

cessfully be coped with? I specify my argument by falling back on theories of a different discipline, namely organizational research and administrative science where the analysis of pathological phenomena is a primary subject. The selection of the theoretical lenses to be applied is based on considerations of complementarity. All of them make statements about pathologies and failure, but they do so at four different analytical levels: individual, inter-actors, organizational, and temporal. Thus, the theoretical framework can identify four pertinent patterns of pathologies: problems are perceived in a cognitively biased way,[8] the processing of a problem furthers dilemmatic principal-agency situations of flawed commitment by either party,[9] political, financial, time, or institutional pressure leads to a tight coupling of complex interactions that may bind resources for the adequate handling of a given problem,[10] or the organization locks itself into a previous policy without consideration of additional factors.[11] While pathologies may not be avoidable under ill-structured conditions, their virulence can be attenuated by appropriate coping strategies. This said, the propositions on coping strategies in the realm of the theoretical literature use to be of an idealized as well as very generic nature, notoriously appearing as an aphorism on the last page of a given study.

The empirical goals of the thesis are to examine how the assumed pathologies materialize, to find evidence for their virulence, and to identify strategies of coping that reduces, contains, or even avoids them.

I will analyze emerging pathologies and how they were coped with by studying the UN operations in East Timor and in the Croatian region of Eastern Slavonia.[12] While no transitional administration or complex UN peace operation has been a raving success story, these two missions stand out though: they are the two most successful (interim administration) missions the UN has ever deployed. This positive score on the dependent variable (*performance*) is assumed to allow for ob-

---

8   Bazerman, Max. 2002. *Judgement in Managerial Decision Making*. 5. ed. New York: John Wiley & Sons; Dörner, Dietrich. 2004. *Die Logik des Misslingens. Strategisches Denken in komplexen Situationen*. 2nd ed. Reinbek: Rohwolt; Schulz-Hardt, Stefan. 1997. *Realitätsflucht in Entscheidungsprozessen. Von Groupthink zum Entscheidungsautismus*. Göttingen: Verlag Hans Huber.

9   Ackerloff, Russell L. 1970. *A Concept of Corporate Planning*. New York: Wiley; Fama, Eugene F. 1980. "Agency Problems and the Theory of the Firm." *Journal of Political Economy* 80, pp. 288-307; Ross, Stephen A. 1973. "The Economic Theory of Agency: The Principal's Problem." *American Economic Review* 63, pp. 134-139; Seibel, Wolfgang. 1996. "Successful Failure. An Alternative View on Organizational Coping." *American Behavorial Scientist* 39, pp. 1011-1024; Seibel, Wolfgang. 2008. "Moderne Protektorate als Ersatzstaat: UN-Friedensoperationen und Dilemmata internationaler Übergangsverwaltungen." *Politische Vierteljahresschrift*, special issue, pp. 499-530.

10   Perrow, Charles. 1993. *Complex Organizations*. 3rd ed. New York: McGraw-Hill.

11   Pierson, Paul. 2000. "Not Just What, but When: Timing and Sequence in Political Processes." *Studies in American Political Development* 14, pp. 72-92; Thelen, Kathleen. 1999. "Historical Institutionalism in Comparative Politics." *Annual Review Political Science* 2, pp. 369-404.

12   On the case selection, see Chapter III.

servations of valuable coping behavior. By means of an in-depth qualitative within-case study design, I reconstruct the causal interactions leading to pathologies, their effects, and how they were coped with, to trace and explain the positive outcomes of these inherently ill-fated missions. I will reveal evidence that the two missions, which had their very own "flavors" and differed in several respects – such as their purposes (reintegration in Eastern Slavonia, state-building in East Timor), geographic location (Europe, Asia), and personal style of their leaders (bold Jacques-Paul Klein in Eastern Slavonia, diplomatic Vieira de Mello in East Timor) – displayed similar coping strategies that were decisive in the missions' ultimate success.

2. Why this Book?

There are two criteria for the relevance of a scientific piece of work: theoretical and real world relevance.[13] The study lives up to both. First, by contributing to knowledge accumulation through the transfer of theories from disciplines of political and management science to a field that is partly under-theorized, partly occupied by international relations scholars. Second, by identifying hitherto unrecognized factors and processes which contribute to the success or failure of a most important instrument of the international community to restore peace and stability.

The theoretical relevance comes with a scientific perspective on UN-operated transition processes that complements existing studies and delivers a crucial microfoundation to their claims. It delivers a new set of concepts – ill-structured conditions, pathologies, and coping strategies – that allows for a cohesive analysis of causal processes. Eventually, the thesis also strives to benefit from inter-disciplinarity by applying theories from administrative science to under-studied aspects of a topic that has been generically located in the realm of international relations.

What is new about the perspective of pathologies and coping as explanatory concepts for the performance of complex peace operations rests in a fivefold argument on theory and method. First, it does not reiterate macro-factors as explanatory variables,[14] but treats them as scope conditions. It looks at the effects that these conditions have on the mandate implementation process. Second, it explains that,

---

13   King, Gary et al. 1994. *Designing Social Inquiry: Scientific Inference in Qualitative Research*. Princeton: Princeton University Press.
14   The most prominent and influential quantitative study is Doyle and Sambanis 2000. They developed the concept of the "peacebuilding triangle," arguing that the three factors of local hostility, local capacity and international will determine the performance of peace operations. "Their study was in fact distributed to peacekeepers and -builders on-the-ground, accompanied by a headquarter request to 'maximize the triangle'." Personal discussion with a former UN official.

under largely unfavorable conditions, complex peace operations will necessarily develop pathologies that are likely to affect their overall performance. This trajectory of what I call "ill-structured conditions," "pathologies," and, possibly resulting, "accidents," represents a whole new set of explanatory constructs for *failure*. Third, by arguing that pathologies do not necessarily lead to failure but, depending on the coping capabilities of a mission, can be attenuated, or even eliminated, the framework will offer a new explanatory concept for the *success* of a mission. Again, it does not stop at the macro-level by looking at, say, local hostility or international will,[15] but instead sheds light on the behavior of the mission itself. The theoretical scheme that I aim at developing provides a link between independent macro-variables and the outcome. Fourth, as these constructs represent emergent phenomena *per se,* they call for a method of study that looks at the entire transition process and that takes interactions between different components of the mission and different actors involved in the transition into account. Thus, the theoretical framework prescribes a holistic method of analysis that allows tracing causal processes. Eventually, the research perspective that I apply lays the ground for a different understanding of the performance of a mission: contrary to existent studies that conceptualize success nearly explicitly as effectiveness, a focus on coping strategies that looks at how adequately a mission puts its means to good use, implies a relational concept of success, the ratio being "means/effect". In terms of practical recommendations, "fit" coping should not only lead to (relatively) effective but to (relatively) efficient results. I add the term *relative* in brackets since I am reluctant to be suggestive of the existence of a "recipe for success" – which does not exist. What does exist, however, is good and bad coping with problems.

The second criterion for scientific relevance is answered by the very topic of the study. UN peace operations are a most important and frequently used instrument to restore peace and stabilit in war-torn territories. Frequently, decision-makers in peace operations have to resolve matters of the life or death of people in some of the most miserable places in the world. The number of such operations and the need for them is steadily increasing, yet they continue to be marred by mismanagement and failure. The book reprocesses a highly visible and politically sensitive topic from a new angle, aiming at providing appropriate analysis and recommendations that transcend the usual calls for better resources and more political backing.

---

15   Cf. Doyle and Sambanis 2006.

3. *Structure*

The remainder of the book is organized in six parts.

Background: Peace Operations of the United Nations

The chapter that follows introduces to UN peace operations and interim administrations. After providing an overview of the development of the UN fallback system for peace and a political and historical contextualization, I describe the crucial features, stages, and actors of UN-led missions.

Theoretical Framework

The goal of this chapter is to build a theoretical model for the analysis of the case studies. First, I outline the ill-structured conditions that are inherent to complex UN operations. They refer to local challenges in the post-conflict territory as well as to political and institutional constraints. I will discuss four concepts of organizational pathologies that I deem fruitful for the analysis of the challenges to complex UN peace operations: cognitive biases, principal-agent problems, tight coupling of complex interactions, and path dependence deficiencies. Each conceptual perspective also makes more or less explicit recommendations for coping with the respective pathologies which I am also going to summarize. That said, it will remain an empirical issue which type of recommended strategy are applied to which kind of problems, what other coping strategies are put forward, and which ones are eventually successful. The chapter concludes with an elaboration on the selection of cases that suit the purpose of the study.

Reconstruction and Analysis of the Cases

This pivotal part of the thesis deals with the in-depth empirical reconstruction and detailed analysis of the UN Transitional Administration in Eastern Slavonia, Baranja, and Western Sirmium (UNTAES) and of the UN Transitional Administration in East Timor (UNTAET). The empirical reconstructions of the cases are structured in three parts, respectively. First, I will give an overview of the conditions on-the-ground – of the territory and its people, the history and the conflict that triggered the international intervention. Second, I reconstruct the planning phase of the international administration – the negotiations for the peace agreement, the set up of the mandate, and the processes of designing, financing, and staffing the mission. During these two stages, the specific ill-structured conditions for the operation materialize. The third part deals with the operative parts – deployment, implementation, and termination. I attempt a narrative reconstruction of these processes, focussing on the development of organizational pathologies and how the missions came to terms with them.

The subsequent analyses draw together the conditions under which UNTAES and UNTAET operated, the pathologies that developed, and if and how they were coped with, and interprets these processes in light of the theoretical framework.

Results

The chapter "Success Against the Odds: Findings" summarizes the results of each case, identifies patterns, interprets, and contrasts them. Building on the empirical findings of the case study, I also specify my theoretical framework and I discuss a conceptualization of the dependent variable that lends itself to better comparability of different cases.

Conclusion

The last part of the thesis entails a critical discussion of the results and an outlook on future inquiries that could build on the research contribution of this study. I conclude with a personal résumé.

II. Background: Peace Operations of the United Nations

The role of the UN in the maintenance of peace and security has developed from traditional "buffer missions" by a handful of Blue Helmets to the assumption of a temporary government role by transitional administrations. The latter are a most "complex, costly, and risky"[16] mission type. This chapter presents the historical evolution of UN peace operations and their discerning features and purposes, the usual life cycle of such a mission, and the major actors and actor groups that are involved in planning and implementation.

1. Political and Historical Context

Since 1948, the UN have been involved in peace operations.[17] The original mission type of traditional peacekeeping involves "the deployment of military units and

---

16 United Nations, "Report of the Panel on United Nations Peace Operations," UN Doc. A/ 55/305 – S/2000/809, 21 August 2000, para. 77.
17 The generic phrases of "peace operations," "peace support operations," and "peace missions" refer synonymously to any international preventive, enforcing, peace keeping, or post-conflict mission. The specific termini for different kinds of missions are: preventive diplomacy, peacemaking, peaceenforcement, peacekeeping, and peacebuilding. According to the Agenda for Peace, set up in 1992 by then-Secretary General Boutros-Ghali, preventive diplomacy refers to "action to prevent disputes from arising between parties, to prevent existing disputes from escalating into conflicts and to limit the spread of the latter when they occur." UN Secretary-General, "Report of the Secretary-General pursuant to the statement adopted by the Summit Meeting of the Security Council on 31 January 1992," UN Doc. A/47/277-S/ 24111, 17 June 1992, para. 20. Closely related to the concept of preventive diplomacy, peacemaking is defined as diplomatic action in order "to bring hostile parties to a negotiated agreement through such peaceful means as those foreseen under Chapter VI of the UN Charter." UN Doc. A/47/277-S/2411, para. 20. Peaceenforcement can support peacemaking. As sketched out in "An Agenda for Peace," peace enforcement involves the coercive, yet impartial, use of force in terms of civil and military sanctions. The latter are employed beyond use in self-defense. Peaceenforcement operations are granted Chapter VII authorities and are conducted in environments of imperfect consent. Cf. UN Doc. A/47/277-S/2411, para. 44; McDonald, Brian. 2001. *On the Road to Peace: The Implementation of the EU Special Support Programme for Peace and Reconciliation.* Monaghan: ADM/CPA Peace Programme. Peacekeeping operations usually monitor and observe the compliance with a peace agreement. "[A] monitoring and observer mission is an interim arrangement used in violent conflicts with the consent of the host government. In these conflicts, there is no formal determination of aggression. The purpose is to monitor a truce and help negotiate a peace through the presence of military and civilian observers." Doyle and 2000, p. 781. Peacebuilding missions have more dimensions, particularly in the civilian realm, than traditional peacekeeping missions. Cf. Paris, Roland. 2004. *At War's End: Building Peace After Civil Conflict.* New York: Cambridge University Press, p. 38. See also UN Department of Peacekeeping Operations and UN Department of Field Operations. 2008. *United Nations Peacekeeping Operations. Principles and Guidelines.* Capstone Doctrine. New York: United Nations. Available

civilian officials in order to facilitate the negotiated settlement of a conflict."[18] Operating under Chapter VI of the UN Charter, they are employed *with the consent* of the belligerent parties and only use force in self-defense.[19] Typically, they establish a buffer zone and "assist the demobilization and disarmament of military forces"[20] in an impartial, non-combatant manner.

For decades, traditional peacekeeping was only selectively supplemented with civilian elements.[21] A fundamental transformation of UN missions came after the end of the Cold War with two seminal changes in the international security paradigm. On the one hand, the doctrine of the "Responsibility to Protect" has been gaining momentum since the mid-1990s.[22] Based on the proposition that state sovereignty[23] can no longer act as a barrier to intervention in the face of violations

online at http://pbpu.unlb.org/pbps/Library/Capstone_Doctrine_ENG.pdf, last access on 6 March 2009.

The terminology on peace operations is far from unanimous and is considerably blurred. "For policymaking and applied research [there has been] a confusion of terminology. There has been a seemingly endless elaboration of new concepts and definitions. Definitions are contested, vary, and terminology passes in and out of fashion. Terminology has proliferated as policy and research in each arena has passed through phases, usually in direct relation to events and state institutional interests. Researchers have been partly to blame for this, but we have suffered the consequences." Taylor, Mark B. and Jennings, Kathleen M. 2004. *In Search of Strategy: An Agenda for Applied Research on Transitions from Conflict.* Fafo-report 480, p. 6. Observing the astonishingly inconsistent use of terms, part of the problem is that the pivotal concepts are quite general, "Categories such as peace-building and state-building capture a wide range of cases – a strategy that can result in 'conceptual stretching,' when the meaning of concepts are broadened to the point when they can become vague and amorphous." Ibid. In what follows, I will clarify my use of the notions for this analysis of peacekeeping, peacebuilding, and interim, civil or transitional administrations. For an overview UN peace operations since 1948, see the official website of UN DPKO at http://www.un.org/Depts/dpko/dpko/overview.shtml.

18 Doyle and Sambanis 2000.
19 Cf. ibid. Since they represent a development not envisioned in the Charter, consent-based missions are sometimes referred to as 'Chapter six-and-a-half.' More robust missions short of enforcement have been dubbed 'Chapter six-and-three-quarters' and are also sometimes referred to as 'grey area' peacekeeping." Page-Fortna, Virginia. 2004. *Peace Time: Ceasefire Agreements and the Durability of Peace.* Princeton: Princeton University Press, p. 270, fn. 4.
20 Doyle and Sambanis 2000, p. 781.
21 The most prominent example of early multidimensional peacekeeping is the UN's involvement in Congo from 1960 to 1964. E.g. Dobbins et al. 2005, pp. 5-28.
22 For a comprehensive overview, see Evans, Gareth. 2008. *The Responsibility to Protect: Ending Mass Atrocity Crimes Once and for All.* Washington, DC: Brookings Institution Press.
23 Cf. Monteiro, Antonio. 2003. "Additional Remarks." In: Nassrine Azimi and Chang Li Lin, eds., *The United Nations Transitional Administration in East Timor (UNTAET): Debriefing and Lessons, Report of the 2002 Tokyo Conference.* London: Martinus Nijhoff Publishers for UNITAR, pp. 235-241, p. 235, "A simple reading of the United Nations Charter immediately reveals how much the international community was focused on the respect for the sovereignty of States in 1945. This principle emanates from a long established international practice and, generally, aims to shield countries from foreign interference. Article 2, paragraph 7 clearly states that 'nothing contained in the present Charter shall authorize the United Nations to intervene in matters which are essentially within the domestic jurisdiction of any state or

of human rights and humanitarian norms that threaten international peace and security, the doctrine favors more intrusive international actions. Examples of the practical impact of this new perspective include NATO's bombing campaign in Yugoslavia in 1999 and the military intervention in East Timor. More tellingly, it has encouraged intervening states to focus on mechanisms that guard against the recurrence of violence and even to orchestrate transitions from conflict to peace.[24]

On the other hand, the Security Council has broadened its interpretation of "threats to international peace and security" to include economic, social, humanitarian, and ecological fields. This change of approach manifested itself in documents such as the 1992 *Agenda for Peace* on preventive diplomacy, peacemaking, and peacekeeping by Secretary-General Boutros-Ghali, his *Agenda for Development* of 1994, and the 1995 *Supplement to an Agenda for Peace*, where he re-emphasized the mutual conditioning of development and security. The same tune is echoed in the UN High-Level Panel Report on Threats, Challenges, and Change, *A More Secure World: Our Shared Responsibility* of 2004, or the European Security Strategy Paper *A Secure Europe in a Better World* of 2003, which both call for a holistic view on peace and security.[25]

In line with this new orientation, UN peacekeeping observed a transformation from traditional military emphasis towards "multidimensional"[26] mission designs

shall require the Members to submit such matters to settlement under the present Charter.' However, it is immediately followed by the wording that 'this principle shall not prejudice the application of enforcement measures under Chapter VII,' opening the door to a possible Security Council intervention."

24 In what has come to be known as his Chicago Speech, former British Prime Minister Tony Blair outlined the key aspects of this doctrine, "Non-interference has long been considered an important principle of international order. But the principle must be qualified in important respects. Acts of genocide can never be a purely internal matter. When oppression produces massive flows of refugees which unsettle neighboring countries then they can properly be described as 'threats to international peace and security.'" Speech of British Prime Minister Tony Blair to the Chicago Economic Club, 22 April 1999. Available online at http://www.pbs.org/newshour/bb/international/jan-june99/blair_doctrine4-23.html, last access on 6 November 2005. As Blair emphasised, "In the past, we have talked too much of exit strategies, but having made a commitment we cannot simply walk away once the fight is over." Ibid. See also International Commission on Intervention and State Sovereignty. 2001. Responsibility to Protect. Report of the ICISS. Availaibly online at http://www.iciss.ca/report-en.asp, last access on 2 March 2009.

25 United Nations, "Report of the Secretary General's High-level Panel on Threats, Challenges and Change, A More Secure World. Our Shared Responsibility," UN Doc. A/59/565, 2 December 2004. Available online at http://www.un.org/secureworld/, last access on 2 March 2009; European Union, "Report of the European Council on a Secure Europe in a Better World," presented by Javier Solana, EUHR for CFSP – European Council, Thessaloniki, 20 June 2003. Available online at http://ue.eu.int/ueDocs/cms_Data/docs/pressdata/en/reports/76255.pdf, last access on 2 March 2009.

26 Multidimensional peacekeeping, according to Doyle and Sambanis, "Includes a mix of strategies to build a self-sustaining peace, ranging from those of traditional peackeeping operations to more multidimensional strategies for capacity expansion (e.g., economic reconstruction) and institutional transformation (e.g., reform of the police, army, and judicial

that include more actors, such as international and particularly regional organizations ("regionalization of peacekeeping"),[27] and more complex tasks involving peace-building and even state-building activities.[28] Decisively promoted by then UN Secretary-General Boutros Boutros-Ghali,[29] *peace-building* operations com-

system; elections; civil society rebuilding)." Doyle and Sambanis 2000, p. 781. Today, peacekeeping is frequently used in an all-encompassing manner, blurring the usage of what is properly termed peacemaking and peaceenforcement, as well as peacebuilding. Contrary to that everyday speech, peacekeeping technically refers to the non-coercive but still military dominated use of force, and is the counterpart to peace enforcement with a slightly longer-term horizon as it is also directed at conflict prevention once peace has been attained (during, post-conflict, pre-potential conflict).

27 Daase, Christopher. 1999. "Spontaneous Institutions: Peacekeeping as an International Convention." In: Helga Haftendorn et al., eds., *Imperfect Unions: Security Institutions over Time and Space*. Oxford: Oxford University Press, pp. 223-258, p. 256. See also Rivlin, Benjamin. 1992. "Regional Arrangements and the UN System for Collective Security and Conflict Resolution: A New Road Ahead?," *International Relations* 11:2, pp. 95-110; Weiss, Thomas, ed. 1997. *Beyond UN Subcontracting: Task-Sharing with Regional Security Arrangements and Service Providing NGOs*. London: Macmillan.

28 Cf. Pippard, Tim. Undated. *East Timor and the Challenge of UN Transitional Administration*. Available online at: http://www.una.org.uk/UN%20and%20Conflict%20Programme%20Briefs/East%20Timor.htm, p. 2, last access on 27 November 2008. "By the end of the 1990s, the doctrinal quarters of peace operations increasingly converged on ideas for comprehensive, political missions. The UK established a Joint Defence Centre to develop high-level joint strategic doctrine, promote civil-military operations with multiple actors, and provide long-term conceptual assessment. The NATO peace operations manual was redrafted in this light and circulated to member states for comment. Most notably, the US created its May 1997 Presidential Decision Directive-56 process. Initiated after an internal review of the Somalia experience and first tested in Haiti, it was built on five central pillars: an executive committee for unified management; a political-military implementation plan; US interagency rehearsals; after-action reviews; and interagency training. It was an American document for better co-ordination in Washington, and its sound principles needed to be internationalized. In spring 1999, this doctrinal step was taken through development of a genuinely international concept of operations for exercising executive and legislative authority in transition, at all levels of a mission – operational (national) and tactical (district). A draft was presented at the US Chairman of the Joint Chiefs seminar on peace operations at the US Army Peacekeeping Institute in June. It was subsequently debated later in the month at a meeting of Force Commanders and Special Representatives of the UN Secretary-General." Chopra, Jarat. 2002. "Building State Failure in East Timor." *Development and Change* 33:5, pp. 979-1000, pp. 985-986. See also Chesterman 2004, pp. 1-3; Pugh, Michael. 1995. "Peacebuilding as Developmentalism: Concepts from Disaster Research." *Contemporary Security Policy* 16:3, pp. 320-346., p. 321.

29 The term peacebuilding entered the scene in 1992 with "An Agenda for Peace" by then Secretary General Boutros Boutros-Ghali who further developed the term in "An Agenda for Development" of 1994. UN Secretary-General, "An Agenda for Peace. Preventive Diplomacy, Peacemaking, and Peacekeeping," UN Doc. A/47/277-S/24111, esp. para. 2; Ibid., "An Agenda for Development," UN Doc. A/48/935, 6 May 1994. Available online at http://www.un.org/Docs/SG/agdev.html, last access on 6 March 2009. The Utstein study by the Norwegian government defines peacebuilding as an attempt "to encourage the development of conditions, attitudes and behavior that foster and sustain social and economic development that is peaceful, stable and prosperous." Smith, Dan. 2003. *Getting their Act Together: Toward a Strategic Framework for Peacebuilding*. Synthesis report of the joint Utstein Study

prise civilian and developmental activities as well as the promotion of democracy as key elements of post-conflict engagement by the international community. They focus on the provision of security, the establishment of the socio-economic and political foundations of sustainable peace, and on the furthering of reconciliation, of "a healing of the wounds of war and injustice."[30]

In a historical window of opportunity in the early and mid-1990s,[31] the Security Council consented that transitional administrations become a new tool for post-conflict reconstruction. The creation of this most encompassing type of mission represented the apogee within the UN "fallback system for peace."[32] Defined by DPKO as "a transitional authority established by the Security Council to assist a country during a government regime change or passage to independence,"[33] transitional administrations pursue peacekeeping and peacebuilding tasks with a strong political component. Being non-coercive in nature,[34] they usually have a robust mandate and engage in a multitude of cooperative relations to achieve their mandate.

While their authority exceeds that of other mission types, they vary in the type of authority that they are endowed. Following a classification by Michael W. Doyle, transitional administrations may have monitoring/facilitation, administrative, executive, or supervisory authority.

In case of monitoring or facilitation authority, the mission observes, reports, and provides assistance at the request of the parties to help on their part. "So it leaves let's call it sovereignty for lack of a better term very much in the hands of the

of Peacebuilding, The Royal Norwegian Ministry of Foreign Affairs, p. 10. On a most general level, peacebuilding activities fall under four main headings: providing security, establishing the socio-economic foundations of long-term peace, establishing the political framework of long-term peace, and generating reconciliation. Cf. Smith 2003, p. 10. Resulting from these complex tasks are the imperatives of responsiveness, adaptability, as well as sustainability to any peacebuilding operation. The challenges of peacebuilding culminate when the conflict has resulted in a complete breakdown of government institutions.

30 Smith, Anthony L. 2004. *Timor-Leste: Strong Government, Weak State.* Singapore: Institute of Southeast Asian Studies, p 10.

31 For a similar argument on the post-Cold War surge of peacekeeping see Lipson, Michael. 2005. "Transgovernmental Networks and Nonproliferation: International Security and the Future of Global Governance." *International Journal* 61:1, pp. 179-198.

32 Wesley, Michael. 1997. *Casualties of the New World Order: The Causes of Failure of UN Missions to Civil Wars.* Basingstoke: Macmillan, pp. 1-15. See also Coicaud, Jean-Marc. 2007. *International Organizations as a Profession and Distribution of Power: The Importance of Human Resources Management for the Success of UN Reform.* Speech by the Head of United Nations University (4 January 2007). Available online at http://www.unitarny.org/mm/File/Presentation%20by%20Jean-Marc%20Coicaud.pdf, last access on 15 March 2009; Barnett, Michael and Finnemore, Martha. 1999. "The Power, Politics, and Pathologies of International Organizations." *International Organization* 53:4, pp. 699-732.

33 UN Department of Peacekeeping Operations and UN Department of Field Operations 2008, p. 99.

34 Cf. Chapter II.1 for the difference between transitional administrations and military occupations.

locals."[35] Examples are the UN Transition Assistance Group (UNTAG) in Namibia, the UN Mission in Haiti (UNMIH), or the UN Protection Force (UNPROFOR) in parts of Bosnia-Herzegovina and Croatia. In the second case, the UN is the administering authority, but the domestic actors and organs remain the ultimate legislative and executive authorities. This role was assumed, for instance, in Cambodia from 1992 to 1993: the international community had the authority for administering a single function, and in this case, all issues with regard to the election were transferred to the control of UNTAC.[36] "Executive authority" denotes a case in which the UN administration is given the authority to execute a given peace agreement. The UN administration cannot go beyond the agreement, but it can digress considerably in its interpretation. An exemplary case is the mission in Eastern Slavonia. Eventually, "supervisory authority" implies that the UN has full executive, legislative, and administrative power: sovereignty is being transferred completely to the international community, who may delegate functions if it wishes but does not need to do so. This most comprehensive form of authority has been given to the transitional administrations in Kosovo and East Timor.

For the purpose of this study, cases are relevant where the UN has been in charge of managing the transition process and possessed full executive authority.[37] I therefore dismiss the type of monitoring/facilitation for my approach to interim administrations.[38]

In order to enforce the political authority they are endowed, UN transitional administrations usually have robust mandates, meaning that the peacekeeping forces are granted the authority to challenge anyone who attempts to block their mission, and to use force if necessary. In discerning a robustly mandated UN mission from military occupation,

---

35 Interview with Michael W. Doyle, Harold Brown Professor at Columbia University in the School of International and Public Affairs and Columbia Law School, Assistant Secretary-General and Special Adviser to United Nations Secretary-General Kofi Annan from 2001 to 2003, New Haven/Connecticut, 11 September 2006.
36 Later on, border monitoring was included as well.
37 Cf. Caplan, Richard. 2005. *International Governance of War-Torn Territories: Rule and Reconstruction*. Oxford: Oxford University Press, p. 86, "Perhaps the most distinctive feature of an international territorial administration is the establishment of interim structures with broad responsibility for the management of public assets and the provision of public services – some of the core functions of a modern government. While only in Kosovo and East Timor was it deemed necessary to create and maintain such structures more or less from scratch, all international administrations exercise at least extensive oversight of indigenous administrative bodies [...]".
38 For a similar argumentation, see e.g. Croissant, Aurel. 2006. "International Interim Governments, Democratization, and Post-Conflict Peace-Building: Lessons from Cambodia and East Timor." *Strategic Insights* 5:1. Available online at http://www.ccc.nps.navy.mil/si/ 2006/Jan/croissantJan06.asp, last access on 6 March 2009. The types of authority have impications for the processing of the operation, too. Cf. Caplan 2005, pp. 254-255.

There is a significant difference: military occupation entails the occupation of sovereign territory by a state or group of states acting jointly and without the authorization of the United Nations or a similar body, as with the Allied occupation of Germany and Japan after the Second World War and the US-led occupation of Iraq […]. By contrast, an international administration is under the control of, and answerable to, an international body.[39]

In the cases of interest for the thesis, this international body is the UN.[40]

2. Stages and Actors

Authority and purpose of a peace operation are written down in the mandate and reflected in its organizational structure and implementation style. The following paragraphs describe the "life cycle"[41] of a UN mission. They also introduce to the

39 Ibid., p. 3. "The UN Charter, it may be said, provided a kind of 'negative authorization' for the Allied occupation of Germany and Japan (and other 'enemy states') with Art. 107: 'Nothing in the present Charter shall invalidate or preclude action, in relation to any state which during the Second World War has been an enemy of any signatory to the present Charter, taken authorized as a result of that war by the governments having responsibility for that action.'" Ibid., p. 4. Obviously, though, in the framing of the spoiling 'host,' as it was Serbia in the case of Kosovo, there would be a great resemblance between a military/NATO-backed UN administration and a coercive foreign occupation and indeed, many of the challenges for the external actors may be similar.

40 In certain circumstances, it can also refer to an ad hoc organization such as the Peace Implementation Council in the case of Bosnia-Herzegovina, which will have authorized or sanctioned its establishment.

41 I discern these four stages by building on suggestions by practitioners as well as by the political science heuristic of policy cycles. Using the policy cycle terminology, these stages are equivalent to agenda setting, policy formulation, implementation, and termination. Cf., e.g., Müller, Ragnar and Schumann, Wolfgang, "The Policy Cycle." Available online at http://www.dadalos.org/politik_int/politik/policy-zyklus.htm, last access on 28 November 2008; Howlett, Michael and M. Ramesh. 2003. *Studying Public Policy: Policy Cycles and Policy Subsystems.* Toronto: Oxford University Press. During agenda setting, the process by which problems are identified and the basic policy structure for their management is sketched; policy formulation or formation refers to the specification of the "problem management tools"; policy implementation consists in the way of how the relevant bodies put these policies into effect; and termination is defined as the "premeditated cessation of a public activity or entity." Daniels, Mark Ross. 1997. *Terminating public programmes: an American political paradox.* Armonk: Sharpe, p. 5. The theoretical contributions on termination are relatively young; the most important authors being Behn, Robert D. 1976. "Closing the Massachusetts Public Training Schools." *Policy Sciences* 7:2, pp. 151-171; Ibid. 1977a. "The False Dawn of the Sunset Laws." *Public Interest* 49, pp. 103-118; Ibid. 1978. "How To Terminate a Public Policy: A Dozen Hints for the Would Be Terminator." *Policy Analysis* 4:3, pp. 393-413; Brewer, Garry D. 1978. "Termination: Hard Choices – Harder Questions." *Public Administration Review 38:4,* pp. 338-344; DeLeon, Peter. 1978a. "Public Policy Termination: An End or a Beginning." *Policy Analysis* 4, pp. 369-392; Ibid. 1987. "Policy Termination as a Political Phenomenon." In: Dennis Palumbo, ed., *The Politics of Program Evaluation.* San Francisco: Sage, pp. 173-202; and Kauffmann, Herbert. 1976. *Are Government Organizations Immortal?* Washington, DC: Brookings Institution Press; Kaufman, Herbert. 1987.

major actor groups that are involved at the respective stages. It almost goes without saying that "no single department or agency can be expected to devise and implement, on its own, all the elements of a comprehensive peace strategy."[42]

Negotiating, Mandating, and Planning of a Transitional Administration

Negotiations on the settlement of a peace agreement are usually conducted by representatives of the parties to the conflict and one or more third parties. Third parties, such as neighbor states, regional hegemons or "superpowers", or international organizations, play a crucial role in negotiations. Apart from assuming a mediating role, "Third parties are able to enforce the terms of a peace agreement that the combatant parties would agree to, but would otherwise be unable to effectively guarantee."[43] The peace agreement sets the structural as well as the procedural provisions, i.e. *what* is going to happen and *how* peace is to be brought about and maintained.[44] The peace agreement is the basis for the subsequent UN mandate.

The body that mandates any UN peace operation is the Security Council of the UN.[45] The Security Council is the highest institution in the UN system. According to Article 24 in Chapter V of the Charter, it has a "primary responsibility for the maintenance of international peace and security."[46] Since the UN's inception in

Time, Chance, and Organizations: Natural Selections in a Perilous Environment. Chatham: Chatham House. In the 1980s the debate even stagnated and only since the late 90s a new interest in the termination process can be observed. The more recent contributions include Daniels 1997; Frantz, Janet E. 1992. "Reviving and Revisiting a Termination Model." *Policy Sciences* 25:1, pp. 175-186; Geva-May, Iris. 2004. "Riding the Wave of Opportunity: Termination in Public Policy." *Journal of Public Administration Research and Theory* 14:3, pp. 309-333.

42 UN Secretary-General, "No Exit without Strategy: Security Council Decision-making and the Closure or Transition of United Nations Peacekeeping Operations," UN Doc. S/2001/394, 20 April 2001, para. 21. For an illustrative graph of the "UN peace operations bureaucacy and its environemnt," see Benner, Thorsten et al. 2007. *Learning to Build Peace? United Nations Peacebuilding and Organizational Learning: Developing a Research Framework.* DSF-Forschung No. 9, p. 29.

43 Ouellet, Julian. 2004. "Procedural Components of Peace Agreements." In: Guy Burgess and Heidi Burgess, eds., *Beyond Intractability.* Boulder: Conflict Research Consortium, University of Colorado. Available online at http://peacestudies.conflictresearch.org/essay/procedural_peace_agree/?nid=1397, last access on 15 March 2009, p. 3. In making this argument, he refers to Walter, Barbara. 1997. "The Critical Barrier to Civil War Settlement." *International Organization* 51:3, pp. 335-364.

44 Cf. Ouellet 2004.

45 United Nations. 1945. *Charter of the United Nations and Statute of the International Court of Justice.* New York: United Nations, Chapter V, Art. 24.

46 "The Security Council's usual means for maintaining peace and security are promoting settlement through mediation and/or arbitration, deploying peacekeeping forces, securing ceasefires imposing economic sanctions, and ordering collective military action." Aall, Pamela et al. 2000. *Guide to IGOs, NGOs, and the Military in Peace and Relief Operations.* Washington, DC: United States Institute of Peace Press, p. 35.

1945, the Council has authorized over 60 peace operations[47] – which were subject to the era's power politics during the Cold War and which are still bound by political interests and resource constraints today. Thus, the composition of a substantial resolution represents an intricate bargaining process that needs a qualified majority of nine out of 15 members of the Council, requiring the "Permanent Five (P-5)", the United States, the United Kingdom, France, Russia, and China, to vote affirmatively for it.[48] The process itself is, however, rather hard to retrace since bargaining positions, strategies, and arguments are generally put *sub rosa*: in fact, the meeting types of "informal consultations" and "private" and "closed meetings," which are not open to the public or the media, are formally acknowledged procedures.[49] Besides, informal talks in the UN's East River cafeteria may be as essential as the official negotiation settings.

> After a resolution is passed by the Security Council, the planning ensues in the Secretariat[50] where its Department of Peacekeeping Operations (DPKO) assumes a pivotal role.[51] Headed by an Under-Secretary-General, DPKO leads on administrative, financial, political, logistic, and policy analysis matters of UN-led operations.[52]

---

47 Cf. UN Department of Peacekeeping Operations, "List of Operations." Availabe online at http://www.un.org/Depts/dpko/list/list.pdf, last access on 21 December 2008.

48 Cf. UN Charter, Chapter V, Art. 27.

49 Bailey, Sidney and Daws, Sam. 1998. *The Procedure of the UN Security Council*. Oxford: Clarendon Press, p. 21. "In specific: official records [of private and closed meetings] are kept […], but the Council may decide that only one copy of the verbatim record is made by the Secretariat, and kept by the Secretary-General, to be viewed only by those who attended the meeting, and others given specific permission. Whatever is decided on the issuing of verbatim record, an official communiqué is always issued by the Secretary-General after the close of the meeting. […] There are no provisions in the Rules of Procedure of the Council for non-members to request permission to attend private meetings. In addition, there are 'informal consultations.' There has been some argument over the status of informal consultations, and whether they may properly be described as 'meetings' of the Council, but their existence per se is not in doubt." Ibid., pp. 21-22.

50 The administrative organ of the UN works for all of the other UN organs, administering their programs. "Of the six principal organs, only the Secretariat can be said to have essentially a supporting role, implementing those decision made by the political organs." Shimura, Hisako. 2001. "The Role of the UN Secretariat in Organizing Peacekeeping." In: Ramesh Thakur and Albrecht Schnabel, eds., *United Nations Peacekeeping Operations: Ad Hoc Missions, Permanent Engagement*. Tokyo: United Nations University, pp. 46-56, p. 46. The Secretariat is headed by the Secretary General as the 'chief administrative officer' of the UN. "However, under the Charter, the Secretary-General has been considered to play a larger political role than his counterpart in the League of Nations or in most international organizations. […] Even so, the role of the Secretary-General and the Secretariat in organizing and managing peacekeeping operations can be said to be unusually prominent […]." Ibid. On the UN predecessor of the League of Nations see, e.g., Walters, Francis P. 1952. *A History of the League of Nations*. London: Oxford University Press.

51 Up to the late 1980s, peace operations were organized by six officials at the UN Office of Special Political Affairs. By initiative of Secretary-General Boutros-Ghali, the specialized agency of DPKO was created only in 1992.

In 2007, DPKO was restructured and a new Department of Field Support (DFS) was established. DFS now leads on the administration and management of field personnel, procurement, information, communication technology, and finances for peace operations.[53] Also involved is the Department of Political Affairs (DPA). DPA provides "advice and support on all political matters to the Secretary-General in the exercise of his global responsibilities under the Charter relating to the maintenance and restoration of peace and security."[54] The Department also leads in activities that are related to "early warning, preventive diplomacy, peacemaking, post-conflict peace-building, electoral assistance, counter-terrorism, and the provision of substantive support to policy-making organs."[55]

The budget plans for the mission are reviewed by the Advisory Committee on Administrative and Budgetary Questions (ACABQ), a subsidiary organ of the General Assembly. The 16-member body examines and reports on the proposed mission budget that was submitted by the Secretary-General to the General As-

52 In accordance with the purposes and principles enshrined in the Charter of the United Nations, the DPKO is dedicated to assisting the Member States and the Secretary General in their efforts to maintain international peace and security. The Department's mission is to plan, prepare, manage, and direct UN peacekeeping operations, so that they can effectively fulfil their mandates under the overall authority of the Security Council and General Assembly, and under the command vested in the Secretary-General. DPKO provides political and executive direction to UN peacekeeping operations, and maintains contact with the Security Council, troop and financial contributors, and parties to the conflict in the implementation of Security Council mandates. The Department works to integrate the efforts of UN, governmental and non-governmental entities in the context of peacekeeping operations. DKPO also provides guidance and support on military, police, mine action, and other relevant issues to other UN political and peacebuilding missions. UN Department of Peacekeeping Operations, "Mission Statement." Available online at http://www.un.org/Depts/dpko/dpko/info/page3.htm, last access on 3 December 2008.

53 DPKO underwent its first major transformation in the aftermath of the so-called "Brahimi report" of 2000. In an attempt to confront the challenges of current peacekeeping, the Secretary-General initiated a Panel on UN peace operations, "composed of individuals experienced in various aspects of conflict prevention, peacekeeping, and peace-building, to assess the shortcomings of the existing system and to make frank, specific and realistic recommendations for change." United Nations, "Report of the Panel on United Nations Peace Operations," UN Doc. A/55/305-S/2000/809, 21 August 2000, p. viii. The report also explicitly addresses the challenge of transitional civil administration.

54 UN Department of Political Affairs, "About DPA." Available online at http://www.un.org/Depts/dpa/about_dpa/fr_dpa_mission.htm, last access on 3 December 2008.

55 Ibid. Maintenance responsibilities include "monitoring, analyzing and assessing political developments throughout the world; identifying potential or actual conflicts in whose control and resolution the United Nations could play a useful role; recommending to the Secretary-General appropriate actions in such cases and executes the approved policy; assisting the Secretary-General in carrying out political activities decided by him and/or mandated by the General Assembly and the Security Council in the areas of prevention, control and resolution of conflicts, including post-conflict peace-building; providing the Secretary-General with advice on requests for electoral assistance received from Member States and coordinating implementation of programmes established in response to such requests; providing the Secretary-General with briefing materials and supporting him in the political aspects of his relations with Member States." Ibid.

sembly. The ACABQ is usually very strict in the review of the budget plans. With the budget eventually approved, DPKO continues with detailed operational planning, implementation and supervision of the mission.

Implementing the Mandate

The mandate is specified by a mission implementation plan, identifying sub-goals, activities, and benchmarks for the implementation process.[56] The specifics of developing implementation guidelines are very much empirical questions and will be outlined for UNTAES and UNTAET in the case studies.

A recommendation that mandates usually point out is cooperation with other UN agencies and programmes, with the international financial institutions, donor states, international and regional institutions, as well as with international and local NGOs. By means of cooperation, the transitional administration is assumed to take advantage of the specialized knowledge and resources of the respective partners at the nexus of security, peace, and development.[57] However, due to diverging rationales and interests, counterproductive frictions emerge as likely.

The institutions that UN missions frequently cooperate with on-the-ground include, most prominently, the UN country team, the UN agencies, such as UNDP[58] and UNHCR,[59] OCHA,[60] bilateral organizations in the field of develop-

---

56 For more on the operational planning for peace missions, see Richter, Bastian. 2008. "Planning and Deployment of UN Peacekeeping Operations – Interactive Guide." Presentation, ZIF. Available online at http://www.zif-berlin.org/de/analyse-und-informationen/veroeffentlichungen.html, last access on 15 March 2009.

57 Cf. UN Doc. S/2001/394, para. 21, "It is essential to ensure that all key parts of the United Nations system are fully engaged in a collaborative and constructive fashion."

58 As the world's largest multilateral source of grant funding for development cooperation, the UNDP, founded in 1965, also has high stakes in peace support operations. Highly active at the operational level, the program's foci are on poverty elimination, environmental regeneration, job creation, ad the advancement of women. In support of these goals, "UNDP is frequently asked to assist in promoting sound governance and market development and to support rebuilding societies in the aftermath of war and humanitarian emergencies. [...] In administering its programs, UNDP draws on the expertise of developing country nationals and NGOs the other specialized agencies of the UN system, and research institutes in every field." Aall et al. 2001, p. 42.

59 The initial aim of the institution, established in 1951, was to manage post-World War II refugee streams in Europe. Yet, with the broadening of the refugee problem, UNHCR's mandate expanded, too. Primarily, UNHCR provides protection, food, shelter, medical attention, and other types of relief to refugees, asylum seekers and so-called internally displaced people.

60 Established in 1998 as a successor to the DHA by the Secretary-General Kofi Annan, the functions of OCHA's emergency relief coordinator (ERC) are focused in three core areas, "policy development and coordination functions in support of the Secretary-General, ensuring that all humanitarian issues, including those that fall between gaps in existing mandates of agencies such as protection and assistance for internally displaced persons are addressed,

ment aid, the international monetary institutions, particularly the World Bank Group[61] and the IMF, and regional organizations, especially OSCE,[62] NATO, and EU, as well as the ICRC and some large international NGOs, for instance Oxfam, Caritas, or Médecins Sans Frontières. Missions are also urged to support the emergence and maintenance of local NGOs and to cooperate with them. The most crucial – and often most difficult – partner on-the-ground is the host nation.

The crucial "mechanism" that coordinates all these different actors and activities and determines the course of action is the the head of the mission. As Special Representative of the Secretary General (SRSG), he or she is endowed with comprehensive authority.[63] "[S]pecial representatives are conceived as surrogates for the Secretary-General, essentially as extensions of his person who do what the

advocacy of humanitarian issues with political organs, notably the Security Council; and coordination of humanitarian emergency response, by ensuring that an appropriate response mechanisms is established, through IASC (*Inter-agency Standing Committee; author*) consultations, on-the-ground. [...] OCHA discharges its coordination function primarily through the IASC, which is chaired by the ERC, with the participation of all humanitarian partners, including the Red Cross Movement and NGOs. IASC's task is to ensure interagency decision making in response to complex emergencies, including need assessments, consolidated appeals, field coordination arrangements, and the development of humanitarian policies." Aall et al. 2000, pp. 44-45.

61 "The World Bank Group is composed of four different organizations; the International Bank for Reconstruction and Development (IBRD), the International Development Association (IDA), the International Finance Corporation (IFC), and the Multilateral Investment Guarantee Agency (MIGA). The IBRD and the IDA, combined, make up the World Bank. [...] The World Bank offers loans, advice, and an array of customized resources to more than a hundred developing countries and countries in transition. It does this in a way that maximizes the benefits, and cushions the shocks, to poorer countries as they play a greater part in the world economy. The World Bank uses its money and staff, and coordinates with other organizations, to help each developing country achieve a stable, sustainable, and equitable growth. The main focus is on helping the poorest people and the poorest countries, but for all its client the bank emphasises the need for investing in people, particularly through basic health and education protecting the environment, supporting and encouraging private-sector development; strengthening the ability of the governments to deliver quality services, efficiently and transparently; and promoting reforms to create a stable macroeconomic environment, conducive to investment and long-term planning." Ibid., pp. 45-46.

62 Until the Paris Summit of 1990, the then-Conference on Security and Cooperation in Europe functioned as a series of meetings and conferences, setting norms and commitments and reviewing their implementation. Responding to the new challenges of the post-Cold War era, the OSCE has been established as a primary instrument in its region for early warning, conflict prevention, crisis management, and post-conflict rehabilitation in Europe. "Its bodies and institutions take a cooperative approach to a wide range of security-related issues, including arms control, preventive diplomacy, confidence- and security-building measures, human rights, election monitoring, and economic security." Ibid., pp. 78-79.

63 For an overview of the hitherto poorly studied field of the role of SRSGs, see Fröhlich, Manuel et al. 2006. "Mapping UN Presence. A Follow-Up to the Human Security Report." *Die Friedenswarte. Journal of International Peace and Organization* 81:2, pp. 13-23. This being said, the UN also fails to maintain a systematic database on the performance and impact of SRSGs.

Secretary-General would and could do if he were personally present."[64] Their competences are derivates of the administrative and political powers of the Secretary-General. Former Secretary-General Kofi Annan described the functions of his SRSGs as follows.

> First, you are, in a very real sense, the personification of the United Nations in the country or region in which you serve. Second, you are leaders of a peace process, the international community's links and main interlocutors with the parties. Third, you are the head of a peacekeeping operation or a political or peacebuilding mission, in which management is a key requirement. And fourth, I count in many of you to be the unifying force of all United Nations activities in their field – the political leader of the United Nations team in the country or region where you serve.[65]

In the case of UN transitional administrations, SRSGs are wearing two hats: not only are they the head of the mission but also the Transitional Administrator that governs an entire territory with comprehensive legislative and executive powers over a certain time period. These responsibilities make a SRSG in part diplomat, administrator, and politician accountable to different constituencies[66] and obliged to engage in "constant negotiation with a wide range of actors."[67] For all these requirements, however, the SRSG is not equipped with specific guidelines. To the contrary, the mandate, which is the basis as well as the limitation of his or her actions, is usually a document of vague language. It is left to the SRSGs and their team to translate "the overall direction for the mission from New York into day-to-day decision-making on-the-ground."[68] The SRSG is granted "wide latitude."[69] This implies that the leadership style of a mission – an important factor for success[70] – is primarily a matter of the personality of the SRSG and the quality of his or her team.[71]

---

64 Puchala, Donald J. 1993. "The Secretary-General and his Special Representatives." In: Leon Gordenker and Benjamin Rivlin, eds., *The Challenging Role of the UN Secretary- General: Making "The Most Impossible in the World" Possible.* Westport: Praeger, pp. 81-97, p. 82.
65 UN Secretary-General, "Speech of the Secretary-General, Dialogue 'Vital to Success of UN Missions, Says Secretary-General in Remarks to Seminar of Special Representatives.'" Press Release, UN Doc. SG/SM/7760, 2 April, 2001. See also Puchala 1993, pp. 84-85.
66 Cf. Peace Implementation Network 1999. *Command from the Saddle: Managing United Nations Peace-building Missions.* Fafo report 266. Available online at http://www.fafo.no/ pub/rapp/266/266.pdf, last access on 15 March 2009, p. 13; Fröhlich et al. 2006, p. 9.
67 Peck, Connie. 2004. "Special Representatives of the Secretary General." In: David M. Malone, ed., *The UN Security Council. From the Cold War to the 21st Century.* Boulder: Lynne Rienner, pp. 325-339, p. 327.
68 Ibid.
69 Puchala 1993, p. 94.
70 Cf. Doyle, Michael. 2007. "The John W. Holmes Lecture: Building Peace." *Global Governance* 13:1, pp. 1-15, p. 7.

Termination and Withdrawal

Termination comprises three aspects: arranging for its own liquidation; handing over authority and, in cases of transitional administrations, governance functions to the local stakeholders, i.e. its successors as a government;[72] and handing over remaining stabilization and reconstruction tasks to a supporting international follow-on mission.[73] There are, however, no standard checklists or benchmarks for these activities.[74] The baseline for termination must be that an inappropriate termination will not put previous achievements at risk.[75] A carefully designed and implemented exit strategy that operates a deadline thoughtfully is key.

> [W]e must be very careful, when we talk about exit strategies, not to confuse them with exit deadlines. We agree that it is highly preferable that peacekeeping operations have an end state, and not be absolutely open-ended. But an exit strategy must be directed towards a defining overall objective, not an arbitrary, self-imposed, artificial deadline. [...] Artificial deadlines give hope to warlords, to criminals and to corrupt officials that they can outlast the international community.[76]

Going in line with this statement of former US ambassador to the UN, Richard Holbrooke, during an Open Security Council Meeting, the "term 'exit strategy' should never be allowed to mean a hasty or arbitrary departure from a strategically stated goal" and rather "should mean the implementation of a comprehensive sett-

---

71 "Appointed on an ad hoc basis, in exceptional circumstances, an SRSG's role could be said to be defined by its lack of definition. SRSGs must act with ingenuity and flexibility consistent with a policy framework generally received from the Security Council and often characterized by only a weak consensus concerning the UN's role. In such a context, individuals matter greatly, and the success or failure of UN initiatives can rest on an SRSG's performance." Peace Implementation Network 1999, p. 29. On this note, the SRSG also has a say in composing the immediate leadership team which comprises one to two Deputy SRSGs, the Force Commander, and the Head of Police.

72 The new national government is installed by means of democratic elections. Cf. Lyons, Terrence. 2002. *Postconflict Elections: War Termination, Democratization, and Demilitarizing Politics.* Working Paper No. 20, Institute for Conflict Analysis and Resolution. Fairfax: George Mason University.

73 An exit strategy must "include coordinating, planning and preparing the political groundwork for a successor mission, a systematic handover of responsibilities to local authorities and other partners or a joint UN system effort to move from post-conflict priorities to a peacebuilding process." United Nations. 2003. *Handbook on UN Multidimensional Peacekeeping.* Available online at http://pbpu.unlb.org/Pbps/library/Handbook%20on%20UN%20P-KOs.pdf, last access on 15 March 2009.

74 Cf. UN Department of Peacekeeping Operations 2008, p. 8.

75 Cf. UN Doc. S/2001/394.

76 United Nations, "Meeting of the Security Council," UN Doc. S/PV.4223, 15 November 2000, p. 4. See also Hollingworth, Larry. 2003. "Resolutions, Mandates, Aims, Missions, and Exit Strategies." In: Kevin McCahill, ed., *Emergency Relief Operations.* New York: Fordham University Press, pp. 267-283.

lement."[77] The ultimate goal must be stability and good governance. Hence, the international intervention must cease without the internationals' departure triggering a return to the very issues that had caused the intervention in the first place.

---

77   Ibid. See also Rose, Gideon. 1998. "The Exit Strategy Delusion." *Foreign Affairs*, pp. 56-67.

III. A Theoretical Perspective: Complex UN Peace Operations as pathological Organizations

The ultimate goal of theoretical research, be it in philosophy, science, or mathematics, is the construction of systems, i.e. theories.[78]

The present study builds a comprehensive theoretical framework for the analysis of complex peace operations by making use of promising theoretical perspectives from a different discipline: from four different yet complementary administrative science perspectives, I deduce four general hypotheses on the performance of complex missions.

1. State of the Art

Its theoretical approach makes the present study an exception in the bulk of peace-keeping literature and of literature on transitional administrations in specific. Most contributions are merely descriptive and deal with peace operations in an idiosyncratic way. For example, prominent contributions on the East Timor instance include single within-case studies, such as *The East Timor Report* by the King's College[79] or Joel Beauvais' comprehensive *Benevolent Despotism*.[80] Their value rests in the thick description of a given case and the detailed information revealed. Their disadvantage is that they are atheoretical and fail to contribute to theory

---

78 Bunge, Mario. 1974. *Treatise on Basic Philosophy, Vol. I.* Dodrecht: Reidel Publishing Company, p. v.
79 Conflict Security & Development Group at King's College (CSDG). 2003. *A Review of Peace Operations: A Case for Change. East Timor Report.* London: King's College. In the remainder of the book, I will quote the study as CSDG, "East Timor Report.".
80 Beauvais, Joel C. 2001. "Benevolent Despotism: A Critique of UN State-building in East Timor." *International Law and Politics* 33, pp. 1101-1178. On transitional administrations in general, see Berdal, Mats and Caplan, Richard. 2004. "The Politics of International Administration." *Global Governance* 19/1, pp. 1-5; Caplan, Richard. 2002. *A New Trusteeship? The International Administration of War-Torn Territories.* Adelphi Paper No. 341. Oxford: Oxford University Press for the International Institute for Strategic Studies; Ibid. 2005; Chesterman 2004; Croissant 2006; Mortimer, Edward. 2004. "International Administration of War-torn Societies." *Global Governance* 10/1, pp. 7-14. For a historically comparative perspective on transitional administrations, see Owen, John M. 2002. "Foreign Imposition of Domestic Institutions." *International Organization* 56:2, pp. 375-409; Shain, Yossi and Linz, Juan J. 1995. *Between States: Interim Governments and Democratic Transitions.* Cambridge: Cambridge University Press; Wilde, Ralph. 2001. "From Danzig to East Timor and Beyond: The Role of Territorial Administration." *The American Journal of International Law* 95/3, pp. 583-606.

development which is one of the important characteristics of scientific work.[81] Another strand of contributions consists of studies which use a systematizing perspective but who do not apply well-established theories. They are guided by some general hypotheses and apply and/or generate low-range concepts. Their advantage is that their basic theoretical guidance results in more systematic and more comparable analyses and they contribute to a theoretically informed understanding of peace operations. Some of these studies are also engaging in theorybuilding. However, these studies remain at an intra-disciplinary level. Cases in point are *Making War and Building Peace* by Michael Doyle and Nicholas Sambanis who identify three macro-variables and develop a theory explaining successful peacebuilding, or Roland Paris' *At War's End* which systematically generates an argument about the sequencing of peacebuilding tasks.[82]

The present study aligns with a small number of recent contributions that are seeking for more innovative theoretical perspectives to the intricate topic. Examples include Michael Lipson's transfer of the organizational theoretical "Garbage Can Model" to explain the evolution of peacekeeping, Nancy Roberts' discussion of "wicked problems" for peace resolution, Anna Herrhausen's application of co-operation theories for the de- and prescription of inter-agency collaboration in the field, Michael Barnett and Martha Finnemore's reflections about the organizational culture that influences the operation of a mission, or discussions of concepts of learning as done by Rainer Breul for the headquarter level and by Lise Morjé Howard for the field level.[83] The disadvantage of such approaches may rest in the risk of transferring irrelevant theories to the topic of field operations and in a liability to interpret data exclusively in accordance to their theoretical lenses – which is the affliction of deductive research. The great advantage, still, comes with the application of well-established theories, a systematic and consistent procedure, the comparability of results, and the consistent accumulation of knowledge.

81 Cf. King, Keohane, and Verba 1994, p. 14.
82 Doyle and Sambanis 2006; Paris 2004.
83 Barnett, Michael and Finnemore, Martha. 2004. *Rules For the World. International Organizations in Global Politics*. Ithaca: Cornell University Press; Breul, Rainer. 2005. *Organizational Learning in International Organizations: the Case of UN Peace Operations*. Konstanz: University of Konstanz; Howard 2008; Roberts, Nancy. 2000. "Wicked Problems and Network Approaches to Resolution." *International Public Management Review, the e-journal of the IPMN* 1:1. Herrhausen, Anna. 2007. *Coordination in United Nations Peacebuilding*. Discussion Paper SP IV 2007-301. Berlin: Wissenschaftszentrum Berlin für Sozialforschung; Lipson, Michael Lipson. 2007b. "A Garbage Can Model of UN Peacekeeping." *Global Governance* 13:1, pp. 79-97.

This being said, why are theories worthwhile at all?[84] Stoker describes the usefulness of theories as

> [helping] us to see the wood for trees. Good theories select out certain factors as the most important or relevant if one is interested in providing an explanation of an event. Without such a sifting process no effective observation can take place.[85]

The argument points to the pivot position of theories in scientific research agendas as the structuring agent of observations. It makes also explicit that it is impossible to thoroughly separate theory and empirical perception: every statement, be it formal-theoretical, descriptive, or trivial, necessarily operates on the basis of a specific set of assumptions about "how the world works."

> Theorizing intellectualizes perceptions. It is not just that theory helps us to identify that which is significant. Any event may involve multiple happenings that appear to be meaningful: [...] events are multidimensional and theorists have to decide what they plan to explain from the array of multiple games embedded in any single situation. Theorists have to generate speculations or hypotheses about which of the games is to take precedence.[86]

Modifying this quote, well-established political theories are well-founded speculations about how games are being played. In this vein, the study will make well-founded speculations about factors influencing the performance of transitional administrations, applying theoretical concepts that make statements about trajectories of unfavorable or ill-structured conditions, the (inevitable) development of pathologies, and how such pathologies can still be coped with, so that they do not necessarily lead to accidents and failure.[87]

2. "Ill-Structuredness:" UN Peace Operations' Constraints and Challenges

Complex UN peace operations and transitional administrations are challenging ventures. *Qua* purpose and *qua* institutional background, they operate under ad-

---

84 A theory should be a causal argument of generic character on a specified population or domain ("*Objektbereich*") and needs to comprise a set of plausible assumptions and abstract concepts as well as causal mechanisms in order to deduce hypotheses. Cf. Schöndorf, Elisabeth. 2005. *Der Vergessene Hegemon. Die Vereinigten Staaten und die Europäische Integration.* Konstanz: University of Konstanz. The definition is based on King et al. 1994, Beyme, Klaus von. 1992. *Theorie der Politik im 20. Jahrhundert: Von der Moderne zur Postmoderne.* 2nd ed. Frankfurt a.M.: Suhrkamp, p. 11, and Zürn, Michael. 1992. *Interessen und Institutionen in der internationalen Politik. Grundlegung und Anwendungen des situationsstrukturellen Ansatzes.* Opladen: Leske + Budrich, p. 29.
85 Stoker, Gerry. 1995. "Regime Theory and Urban Politics." In: David Judge et al., eds., *Theories of Urban Politics.* London: Sage, pp. 54-71, p. 16.
86 Cf. Rosamond, Ben. 2000. *Theories of European Integration.* Basingstoke: Palgrave, p. 5.
87 Cf. Reason, J. T. 1997. *Managing the Risks of Organizational Accidents.* Burlington: Ashgate Publishing.

verse, complex, and ambiguous conditions as well as under intense time pressure. Within the Security Council, tough decisions have to be made by actors with, at times, greatly differing interests. And even if (vague) compromises are reached and mandating resolutions signed, the risk of obstruction *ex post* is not eliminated. Both vagueness and obstruction can become pathological and may have the most virulent effects on a mission.

UN peace operations are run by the UN Secretariat – which, in theory, could profit from synergies by its various departments if they cooperated. Yet, the contrary is often the case, and "bureaucratic territorialism" may negatively affect a mission in the field – for instance if significant information is not processed at the headquarters level. Eventually, the financing procedures, controlled by the General Assembly and its ACABQ, should ideally be flexible and abundant for a venture as complex and precarious as a transitional administration – but in reality, rules are extremely rigid and resources are regularly much lower than recommended by experts. This, as well as recruitment procedures, is not likely to change any time soon.

In addition, local circumstances are far from conducive to controlled proceedings: the level of hostility is usually still high when a mission goes in – while the mission itself is still not well established. Nonetheless, the trust and support of the local populace needs also to be won, basic infrastructure must be rebuilt, and locals need to be trained in order to gain capacities.

In accordance with the organizational theory scholars MacGrimmon und Taylor, I call the sum of these constraints and challenges "ill-structuredness."[88] On this basis, the fundamental argument of the thesis is that ill-structured conditions make UN missions prone to develop counterproductive pathologies. The conceptual framework shall theoretically inform the argument of the emergence of pathologies, their virulence, and of potential coping strategies by outlining four different explanatory approaches. The following paragraphs focus on the dimensions of ill-structuredness, explain them, and organize them systematically.

2.1 Local Hostility

The level of local hostility denotes the intensity of the conflict that is still ongoing, perpetrated by local and regional spoilers. The term "spoiler" has been defined by Stephen J. Stedman as "leaders and parties who believe the emerging peace threaten their power, world view, and interests and who use violence to undermine attempts

---

88 MacGrimmon, Kenneth R. and Taylor, Ronald N. 1983. "Decision Making and Problem Solving." In: Marvin D. Dunnette, ed., *Handbook of Industrial and Organizational Psychology.* New York: John Wiley & Sons, pp. 1397-1453.

to achieve it."[89] Going in line with Doyle and Sambanis,[90] local hostility can be specified via the number, coherence, and hostility of factions,[91] war duration, war type,[92] and deaths and displacement.[93] The existence of a comprehensive peace agreement is an indicator that the most extreme phase of the violence has been overcome, and that at least some rudimentary support for the mission is available.

2.2 Local Capacity

Important indicators for local capacity, according to Doyle and Sambanis, are economic development and the per capita GDP of a given (conflict-ridden) territory. I would even include further criteria, such as the degree of formal education and qualification of the people.

In post-conflict societies, the level of these indicators is typically rather low,[94] as is the local infrastructure (transport, economy, finance, information, administration, education). In some places, a UN mission even has to start from scratch: it needs not only to build new institutions but also the buildings in which these new public and private institutions are to be located and the roads by which to get to them. An additional intricacy relates to reliability and loyalty:

> How do you identify 'the locals' with whom you're dealing? In countries in transition, you often have a completely dysfunctional structure. You have either no government at all or a government which is ridden with problems, where there is virtually no real competence left – totally corrupt, inept – and which is very hard to accept as counterpart. So, your search may have to go beyond the regime, or what is left of it, and into society to find your partners.[95]

---

89 Stedman, Stephen J. 1997. "Spoiler Problems in Peace Processes." *International Security* 22:2, pp. 5-53, p. 5.
90 Doyle and Sambanis 2000; 2006. See also Doyle, Michael. 2002. "Strategy and Transitional Authority." In: Donald Rothchild et al., eds., *Ending Civil Wars: The Implementation of Peace Agreements*. Boulder: Lynne Rienner, pp. 71-88.
91 Doyle 2002.
92 I equal this dimension with "source(s) of conflict", as in Doyle and Sambanis 2006.
93 Doyle and Sambanis 2006.
94 Cf., e.g., Caplan 2005, p. 147.
95 Interview with Professor Dirk Salomons, Director of the Program for Humanitarian Affairs at the School of International Public Affairs, Columbia University, New York, 20 September 2006. He served in management, policy advisory, and peace building functions in several organizations of the UN system.

2.3 Precarious Member State Support

Besides the challenges at the local level, a UN mission faces inhibiting conditions at the international level. This relates to the precarious commitment of member states. Considering the comprehensiveness of complex missions and of transitional administrations in particular, they obviously are highly expensive missions. At the same time, the latter are also among the most politically sensitive ones, and in an organization that tries to bring together extremely diverging interests, such strong commitments by the UN are not likely to happen frequently. In fact, "evident ambivalence about civil administration among United Nations Member States and within the Secretariat"[96] exists. On that background, the Secretariat is confronted with a dilemma:

> To assume that transitional administration is a transitory responsibility, not prepare for additional missions and do badly if it is once again flung into the breach, or to prepare well and be asked to undertake them more often because it is well prepared. Certainly, if the Secretariat anticipates future transitional administrations as the rule rather than the exception, then a dedicated and distinct responsibility centre for those tasks must be created somewhere within the United Nations system. In the interim, DKPO has to continue to support this function.[97]

In the words of the former Head of DPKO, the support of member states to UN peacekeeping is "brittle."[98] "The reserve of good will required to keep the organization going in adversity is simply not there. One or two major peacekeeping failures, whatever the reasons, and support for the whole system could evaporate."[99]

2.4 Rules for United Nations Peace Operations

The rules of the UN's organization for peace operations make up their own subsystem of "intrinsicate knots,"[100] since there is a variety of different actors and rationales that have a stake in the process. I am concentrating on two aspects: the financial rules and provisions for peace operations and the rules and routines of engagement in such ventures.

The rules for UN peace operations are strict on both their equipment and their actions. First, the financing of the operations is subject to a rigid division of assessed

---

96   UN Doc. A/55/305 – S/2000/809, para 77.
97   Ibid., para. 78.
98   Guéhenno, Jean-Marie. 2005. *Statement by Jean-Marie Guéhenno*. Statement by Under-Secretary-General for Peacekeeping Operations to the Challenger Project, 2 March 2005. Available online at http://www.un.org/Depts/dpko/dpko/articles/article020305.htm, last access on 4 December 2008.
99   Ibid.
100 Cf. Chapter I.

and voluntary contributions. Corresponding with the institutional division of the UN, the Security Council can only dispose over budgets that relate to threats to security, while social and economic issues fall in the scope of the Economic and Social Council. The costs relating to the genuine peacekeeping components of a mission and to its support are covered by the assessed budget, i.e. the regular UN budget out of annual member states contributions.[101] The ACABQ-supervised budgeting procedure is very strict and does allow for merely minimal deviations.[102] However, in transitional administrations and in multidimensional peace operations in general, the agenda entails much more than "only" the genuine peacekeeping tasks. The funding modality of these humanitarian and developmental activities is voluntary contributions, raised in an *ad hoc* manner from member states and international or regional organizations, such as the EU. "Without those voluntary contributions, peacekeeping operations initiated by the Security Council would be doomed to failure."[103]

Second, there is a "holy trinity"[104] of DPKO mission imperatives: impartiality, state consent, and minimum use of force. Impartiality indicates "that the peacekeepers are not intended to favor one combatant over another; there is no designated aggressor, and the peacekeeping forces are to implement their mandate without discrimination."[105] State consent and the minimal use of force refer to the permission of the major parties to the conflict to the intervention, while the latter is allowed to use force in self-defense or in defense of the mandate only. However, in Chapter

---

101 "The current financing authority for peacekeeping and peacebuilding does not give the Security Council the scope or control required to ensure an integrated response. The definition of 'peace and security' as conceived in chapters VI and VII of the UN' Charter places economic and social stability largely outside the Security Council's reach. The Security Council has no authority to impose any expenditure on the Member States of the UN beyond the traditional military/administrative intervention model. In other words, while assessed contributions from either peacekeeping accounts or the regular budget will normally cover the core costs of the typical missions headed by SRSG's, they by no means provide all the tools and resources required to complete the mission successfully." Salomons, Dirk and Dijkzeul, Dennis. 2001. *The Conjurers' Hat: Financing United Nations Peace-building in Operations Directed by Special Representatives of the Secretary-General.* New York: Center on International Cooperation, New York University and the Programme for International Co-operation and Conflict Resolution, Fafo Institute for Applied Social Science, p. 13.
102 See Chapter II.2.3.
103 Salomons and Dijkzeul 2001, p. 13.
104 Cf. Diehl, Paul F. 2008. *Peace Operations.* Cambridge: Polity Press; Bellamy, Alex J. et al. 2004. *Understanding Peacekeeping.* Cambridge: Polity Press.
105 Diehl 2008, p. 7.

VII mandates, the situation deviates and an intervention can be staged even without the consent of the parties to the conflict and peace may be "enforced".[106]

All of those rules are vital to UN ventures: member states need planning dependability for the money and the personnel they invest, and the peacekeeping rules render operations calculable and are an important source of legitimacy. The complex and dynamic realities on-the-ground, however, may at times require more flexible elements and belie the usefulness of these institutions. In their book *Rules for the World*, Michael Barnett and Martha Finnemore exemplarily analyze the problems that may manate from inadequate rules. Reconstructing the UN failure in Rwanda, they show how the bureaucratic politics and culture with its standard operating procedures and principles translated into dysfunctional action – and to the ultimate disaster that the Rwandan mission has come to be known for.[107]

2.5 Capacities for United Nations Peace Operations

With the rise of international peacekeeping after the Cold War, the DPKO has been notoriously overloaded. The already low level of staff coverage was even reduced by about one quarter following the dramatic setbacks of the mid-1990's failures in Somalia, Srebrenica, and Rwanda, when UN peacekeeping was losing international support. This was the time when the two missions that are in the focus of this study went operational. Today, numbers have been rising again, but given the likewise increasing number of peace operations, missions' strain is still a major issue. "The UN peacekeeping system is simply overloaded by the current surge of mission activity, and unless we raise our game, the possibility of a major breakdown is there."[108] At the same time, the procedures for recruiting are cumbersome, "Staffing is the biggest problem the UN have, getting the right people in a mission

---

106 Cf. UN Department of Peacekeeping Operations 2008, p. 43, "The Security Council may take enforcement action without the consent of the main parties to the conflict, if it believes that the conflict presents a threat to international peace and security. This, however, would be a peace enforcement operation. It may also take enforcement action for humanitarian or protection purposes; where there is no political process and where the consent of the major parties may not be achievable, but where civilians are suffering. Since the mid-1990s, enforcement action has been carried out by ad hoc coalitions of Member States or regional organizations acting under United Nations Security Council authorization."
107 Barnett and Finnemore 2004, chapters 2 and 5.
108 Guéhenno 2005. At the time of writing (2005-2008), four more (large) missions were deployed, putting even more pressure on the system.

doing the right thing."[109] A major benchmark in the restructuring of the system was the so-called Brahimi-Report.[110] Efforts are ongoing as well as they continue to be resisted.[111] "The UN Member states have said they do not want the UN preparing for running countries and we should not develop a dedicated capacity in that area."[112]

2.6 Time Pressure and Complexity of the Challenges

Eventually, the sheer time pressure and complexity under which a transitional administration operates constitutes a challenging condition. "[Transitional adminis-

---

109 Interview with Dr. Christine Coleiro of the UN Institute for Training and Research Programme of Correspondence Instruction in Peacekeeping Operations (UNITAR POCI), Washington, DC, 1 December 2006. Dr. Coleiro is author of the book *Bringing Peace to the Land of Scorpions and Jumping Snakes: The Legacy of the United Nations in Eastern Slavonia and Transitional Missions* and conducted extensive local field research while UNTAES was operational.

110 "Eine von UN-Generalsekretär Kofi Annan eingesetzte Reformkommission unter Leitung des ehemaligen algerischen Außenministers Lakhdar Brahimi (Brahimi-Panel) legte 2000 einen umfangreichen Katalog von Reformvorschlägen vor. Viele dieser Vorschläge wurden zwischenzeitlich umgesetzt. Die UN sind heute deutlich besser aufgestellt als noch vor zehn Jahren. […] Einige wichtige Reformempfehlungen des Brahimi-Panel scheiterten aber an Vorbehalten von Mitgliedstaaten oder auch an sekretariatsinternen Widerständen. Zudem ging das Panel im Jahr 2000 noch von der Annahme aus, dass pro Jahr maximal eine neue große Friedensoperation durch das Sekretariat ausgeplant und implementiert werden müsse. Die Realitäten sind bekanntlich andere. Vor diesem Hintergrund bekennt die Führungsspitze der im UN-Sekretariat für die Führung der Friedensoperationen zuständigen Abteilung für friedenserhaltende Maßnahmen (Department of Peacekeeping Operations – DPKO) unumwunden, dass Belastungsgrenzen erreicht und in Teilen überschritten sind. Die Personalstärke des DPKO liegt derzeit bei rund 650 Mitarbeitern, darunter 60 militärische Spezialisten/Stabsoffiziere und 20 Polizeioffiziere. Für die Analyse, Planung und Führung von 18 Operationen mit fast 100.000 Missionsangehörigen im Einsatz ist dies ein sehr gestreckter Ansatz. Erschwerend kommt hinzu, dass unterhalb des UN-Hauptquartiers keine stehende Kommandostruktur existiert. Hauptquartiere für neue Missionen müssen fallweise und zumeist kurzfristig aus dem Boden gestampft werden. Häufig bleibt nicht die Zeit für die notwendige Vorausbildung. Und die Qualität des militärischen, polizeilichen und zivilen Personals in den Stäben entspricht nicht immer den Erfordernissen. Viele der zivilen Stabsstellen in den neuen Missionen bleiben derzeit unbesetzt, weil qualifizierte Bewerber fehlen. Sorge bereitet auch das konzeptionelle Vakuum, in dem »multidimensionales, robustes Peacekeeping« derzeit stattfindet. Die UN praktizieren es, ohne dass hierzu ein solides Einvernehmen zwischen Truppenstellern, Sekretariat und Sicherheitsrat über die wesentlichen Rahmenbedingungen besteht. Es fehlt an wichtigen Grundlagendokumenten, an Standardisierungs- und Durchführungsvorschriften und an Einsatzverfahren." Huhn, Walter. January 2006. *UN Peacekeeping – Entwicklungen und Tendenzen.* Available online at http://www.europaeische-sicherheit.de/Ausgaben/ 2006/2006_01/02_UN/2006,01,02,02.html, last access on 4 December 2008.

111 Cf, e.g., Varwick, Johannes, ed. 2006. Die *Reform der Vereinten Nationen: Bilanz und Perspektiven.* Berlin: Duncker und Humblot.

112 Interview with a senior staff member of the UN DPKO's Best Practices Section, New York, 15 September 2006.

tration] implies institution-building, which is what makes transitional missions so complex and difficult to achieve in a short time frame."[113] Virtually every situation that a peace operation must deal with is subject to high time pressure. In fact, peace operations are subject to a *multitude* of timetables:

> Militant groups are often standing-off uneasily waiting for an opportunity to seize a speedy victory rather than engage in the tortuously slow work of compromise and reconciliation. Local people are impatient for security and normality to return to their lives. Peacekeepers and parachuted civil administrations are working through their allotted time before their successors begin their own steep learning curves. The major financial contributors are nervously watching the meter tick, knowing that each day represents millions of dollars in costs to their taxpayers. And the international community, fed by a frenetic media, finds it hard to maintain focus for long as it is beckoned to switch its attention to the next urgent situation.[114]

The general preference of the Security Council is to keep missions as short as possible; extensions are ceded only on grounds of severe security concerns. The Secretariat may also develop a tendency to push towards the direction of quick accomplishment, as it has only limited organizational capacity to operate such a comprehensive missions – especially as the number of peace operations has been steadily increasing.

Summing up, the diverse challenges and constraints can be assigned to two arenas.[115] First, the local conditions on-the-ground that the mission is required to transform and, second, the institutional and political conditions that result from the character of a transitional administration as a Security Council-mandated, General Assembly-budgeted, and Secretariat-operated entity which means that it is subject to various and partly conflicting imperatives. These conditions constitute a situation where a mission is loaded with intricate dilemmas even before it starts to operate.

113 Coleiro, Christine. 2002. *Bringing Peace to the Land of Scorpions and Jumping Snakes: The Legacy of the United Nations in Eastern Slavonia and Transitional Missions.* Clemensport: Canadian Peacekeeping Press Publications, p. 95. For a discussion of the connection between time pressure and stress, see Kahn, R. L. and Boysière, P. 1992. "Stress in Organization." In: Marvin D. Dunette and L. M. Gough, eds., *Handbook of Industrial and Organizational Psychology*, Vol. III, 2nd ed. Palo Alto: Consulting Psychologists Press, pp. 571-650.

114 Rich, Roland and Newmann, Edward. 2004. "Introduction: Approaching Democratization Policy." In: Ibid., eds., *The UN Role in Promoting Democracy. Between Ideals and Reality.* New York: United Nations University Press, pp. 3-31, p. 21.

115 The divide is an analytical one: in reality, they are intertwined.

3. From Ill-Structured Conditions to Organizational Pathologies ... to Failure?

Its ill-structured conditions make the "organization"[116] transitional administration prone to dysfunctional behavior, i.e. "behavior that undermines the [organization's] stated objectives"[117] and confront it with notorious challenges. This may become a severe obstacle to living up to the mandate. For instance, from the perspective of the theory of tight coupling, the high time pressure induced by the ticking clocks of donors and the Security Council may lead to an overdue focus on getting things done as soon as possible instead of getting things right. This refers in particular to having the local population owning the transition process – which is hard enough anyway since many locals will not be able to take on tasks in the transitory structures due to their poor education. Yet, the perspective of tight coupling of complex interactions is not the only one under scrutiny. There a three other theories and each is providing a different general hypothesis on the causal process linking ill-structured conditions and inclination towards failure.

On this note, a massive external shock can obviously prevent a successful accomplishment of the mandate as well. That factor, however, is not the explanatory concept that I am interested in. My goal is to analyze how the *inherent* characteristics of a transitional administration mission and of its immediate environment translate into dysfunctional organizational pathologies – and how they can be favorably dealt with.[118]

Transferring them from their original application areas of economic firms and public administrations, concepts of organizational theory and administrative science yield valuable descriptive, explanatory, and prescriptive potential for the study of pathologies and coping of UN peace operations. Rather than providing an exhaustive overview of the extensive research on organizational pathologies and fail-

---

116 With its specified goals, the regulated division of work among the participating actors, transitional administration defines itself as an organization. Cf. Schreyögg, Georg. 1999. *Organisation. Grundlagen moderner Organisationsgestaltung.* 3rd ed. Wiesbaden: Gabler, p. 10. In fact, it is a very complex organization indeed: its tasks are interdisciplinary in substance, it is subject to *politeli*, i.e. multiple and possibly contradicting goals, there are a large number of variables to be considered in the organization's management, and they are connected. "Changes of one variable affect the status of many other, related variables [and it is thus; ES] difficult to anticipate all possible consequences of a given situation." Funke, Joachim. 1991. "Solving Complex Problems: Exploration and Control of Complex Social Systems." In: Robert J. Steinberg and Peter A. Frensch, eds., *Complex Problem Solving: Principles and Mechanisms.* New Jersey: Lawrence Erlbaum Assoc., pp. 185-222, p. 187. See also MacGrimmon and Taylor 1983; Dörner 2004.

117 Barnett and Finnemore 1999, p. 716. These objectives, the "publicly proclaimed mission of the organization," are fixed in the mandate. Ibid.

118 For a similar argumentation, see Barnett and Finnemore 1999, p. 716. For the development of the concept "pathology" in the organizational context see Deutsch, Karl. 1963. *The Nerves of Government: Models of Political Communication and Control.* Glencoe: The Free Press.

ure, I chose four generic theories that, given the preliminary evidence on the characteristics of multidimensional UN missions, seem relevant to their analysis as they recognize the complexity, uncertainty, and adversity of their conditions as well as the limits to the rationality of actors. Accordingly, the foundation of each of the theories is the bounded rationality expectation which holds that there is no rationally optimal reaction to ill-structured problems, and that under stressful conditions, the decision-making actors are likely to fall back on dysfunctional behavior.[119]

Countering pathologies' negative implications on the performance of a transitional administration, I argue that missions are, in principle, capable of coping with these dysfunctionalities. Some initial thoughts on what may be "fit" strategies for avoiding, reducing, or containing pathologies are provided by the pertinent contributions on organizational pathologies and will be discussed in the remainder of this chapter.

3.1 Organizational Pathologies

[Transitional civil administrations] face challenges and responsibilities that are unique among United Nations field operations. No other operation must set and enforce the law, establish customs services and regulations, set and collect business and personal taxes, attract foreign investment, adjudicate property disputes and liabilities for war damage, reconstruct and operate all public utilities, create a banking system, run schools and pay teachers and collect the garbage – in a war-damaged society, using voluntary contributions, because the assessed mission budget, even for such 'transitional administration' missions, does not fund local administrations itself. In addition to such tasks, these missions must also try to rebuild civil society and promote respect for human rights, in places where grievance is widespread and grudges run deep. [...].[120]

119 The theorem of bounded rationality was developed by Herbert A. Simon in his Nobel Prize-winning work. It includes: Simon, Herbert A. 1957. *Models of Man: Social and Rational.* New York: The Free Press; Ibid. 1976. *Administrative Behavior. A Study of Decision-Making Processes in Administrative Organizations*, 3rd ed. New York: The Free Press; Ibid. 1979. "Rational Decision Making in Business Organizations." *American Economic Review* 69, pp. 493-513; Ibid. 1982. *Models of Bounded Rationality*. Cambridge: MIT Press; Ibid. 1991. "Bounded Rationality and Organizational Learning." *Organizational Science* 2:1, pp. 125-134. Other relevant contributions include: March, James G. 1978. "Bounded Rationality, Ambiguity, and the Engineering of Choice." *The Bell Journal of Economics* 9:2, pp. 587-608; March, James G. and Simon, Herbert A. 1958. *Organizations*. New York: Wiley; Lindblom, Charles. 1959. "The Science of Muddling Through." *Public Administration Review* 19, pp. 79-88; Ibid. 1965. *The Intelligence of Democracy*. New York: Macmillan; Radner, Roy. 1975a. "A Behavioral Model of Cost Reduction." *The Bell Journal of Economics* 6:1, pp. 196-215; Ibid. 1975b. "Satisficing." *Journal of Mathematical Economics* 2, pp. 253-262; Tversky, Amos and Kahnemann, Daniel. 1973. "The Framing of Decisions and the Psychology of Choice." *Science* 211, pp. 453-458.
120 UN Doc. A/55/305 – S/2000/809, para 77.

This quote of the Brahimi-report[121] clearly points out the various tasks, actors, and interests involved, as well as the sheer adversity of a post-conflict situation. Transitional administrations operate under conditions of complexity, uncertainty, and time pressure. For decision-makers, these conditions imply that they "often lack important information on the definition of the problem, the relevant criteria," as well as the necessary time and resources to explore the available information. Nonetheless, "even under these circumstances, actors need to make decisions – and they do."[122] Proponents of behavioral organizational theory argue that "actors fall back on simplifying, selective, and habitualizable decision rules."[123] In the language of the theorem of bounded rationality, this means that actors "satisfice": they take "the shortcut of setting an adjustable aspiration level and [end] the search for alternatives as soon as one is encountered that exceeds the aspiration level."[124] These simplifying strategies and the action rationale may be useful in certain instances, but under certain circumstances, they are likely to produce pathological patterns.

I look at pathologies on different levels of analysis, in line with the different conceptual lenses applied. Concepts of cognitive biases are suitable for analyzing the behavior of unitary actors, principal-agent problems denote dysfunctions in interpersonal or intergroup dealings, Charles Perrow's theory about the tight coupling of complex interactions points to pathologies that emanate from the very systemic character of a complex organization, whereas the theory of path dependency captures deficiencies that develop at a macro-level over time, implying a temporal dimension. By designing the theoretical framework in this way, I do not treat the different theories and the hypotheses as rivalling approaches, but rather as complementary lenses that help in delivering a holistic account of pathologies operating in peace missions.

Reasoning on the meta-theoretical conditions of the very integration of these different ideas of pathologies, including their proposed causal mechanisms, into *one* theoretical framework, specific criteria of theorybuilding must be adhered to.

---

121 On this seminal assessment study of UN peace operations, cf. fn. 1.
122 Cf. Bazerman 2002, p. 5.
123 Ibid.
124 Plümper 1996, p. 182. Gigerenzer and Todd illustrate the idea with the following example of fire-fighter commanders making life-and-death decisions under high time pressure, "Rather than surveying all of the alternative courses of action to combat the flames in, say, a basement of a four-story apartment building, they seem to pick one possible action, play it quickly through in a mental simulation, and if it works well enough – that is, if its outcome exceeds a predetermined aspiration level for success – they act it out without ever considering other alternatives. If the outcome of the mental simulation does not meet their aspiration level, they go on to the next alternative, repeating the simulation process until a satisfactory course of action is found." Gigerenzer and Todd 1999a, pp. 13-14. See also Klein, Garry. 1998. *Sources of Power. How People Make Decisions.* Cambridge: MIT Press. Obviously, the study deals with more aggregate phenomena.

These criteria were proposed by Imre Lakatos in his *Methodology of Scientific Research Programmes* and further developed by Bennett, Dessler, and Moravcsik.[125] The relevant criteria to combine and integrate perspectives are logical coherence and multi-causal consistency.[126] Logical coherence means that the concepts must not have contradictory hard core assumptions. Since the meta-theoretical foundation of all approaches rests within the bounded rationality theorem,[127] logical coherence is no obstacle here. Furthermore, the theoreticcal framework to be built lives up to the criteria of multicausal consistency, since each of them focuses on a different analytical level, and they supplement each other in the study of pathological phenomena in the transitional management of multidimensional UN peace operations. Furthermore, the application of the different theories also allows for different ontological perspectives: while the theories of cognitive biases and the principal agent problem explain pathologies with a focus on agency, the theories of tight coupling and path dependency focus more on structural aspects. While the structure-agency debate is one of the most prominent and important ones in the social sciences,[128] structure and agency explanations are analytically complementary, and, in fact mutually dependent, as elaborated by Anthony Giddens in his structuration approach.[129] Real world phenomena usually embrace both driving forces – as does the present study.

3.1.1 Cognitive Biases

Ever and anon, the information deficits of the transitional administration and its planning agency DPKO abounded. For instance, in late 1999, no seeds were ordered for the upcoming season: an entire agricultural cycle was lost. If the information had been available, it was either ignored or omitted amidst the multitude of challenges at the

125   Lakatos, Imre. 1970. "Falsification and the Methodology of Scientific Research Programmes." In: Imre Lakatos and Alan Musgrave, eds., Criticism and the Growth of Knowledge: Proceedings of the International Colloquium in the Philosophy of Science, London 1965. Cambridge: Cambridge University Press, pp. 91-196; Bennett, Andrew. 2003. "A Lakatosian Reading of Lakatos: What Can We Salvage from the Hard Core?" In: Colin Elman and Miriam Fendius Elman, eds., *Progress in International Relations Theory. Appraising the Field.* Cambridge: MIT Press, pp. 455-494; Dessler, David. 2003. "Explanation and Scientific Progress." In: ibid., pp. 381-404; Moravcsik, Andrew. 2003. "Liberal International Relations Theory. A Scientific Assessment." In: ibid., pp. 159-204.
126   Cf. Schöndorf 2005, p. 114.
127   See Chapter II.2.1.
128   Cf., e.g., Dessler, David. 1989. "What's at Stake in the Structure-Agency Debate?" *International Organization* 43:3, pp. 441-473.
129   Giddens, Anthony. 1984. *The Constitution of Society. Outline of a Theory of Structuration.* Cambridge: Polity Press. See also Crozier, Michel and Erhard Friedberg. 1977. *L'Acteur et Le Système: Les Contraintes de l'Action Collective.* Paris: Seuil.

early, confusing stages of the mission. The distressing consequence was that in the hard-to-reach rural districts, people were starving, some even dying.[130]

At the individual level,[131] behavioral decision theory identifies pathological behavior as "cognitive biases" – impairing judgments and choices, and potentially leading to failure or, as the above example of the case study about the mission in East Timor illustrates, directly to humanitarian catastrophe.[132] The general hypothesis issued from this perspective is that ill-structuredness increases the probability that a mission succumbs to pathological cognitive biases – which increase the probability of overall mission failure, in turn. Specifying the causal process denoted by this theoretical perspective, the underlying mechanism that operates the behavioral patterns consists of the trajectory of flawed information gathering and situative misperception, deficient information processing and misinterpretation, and ensuing inadequate decision-making and actions. Cognitive biases may occur at any stage within the trajectory. In a worst-case scenario, every stage is flawed, and failure lurks around the corner. The more, the more frequent and the more virulent cognitive biases occur, the more likely the mission will be inclined to fail. In the following, I give an overview of the most pertinent and potentially pathological patterns of behavior.[133]

Ignoring Problems

On ignoring problems, "Psychologists have studied people's aversion to ambiguity and uncertainty. Results indicated that uncertainty beyond a particular level creates considerable anxiety. One way of obviating or reducing this anxiety is simply to ignore the more uncertain parts of the decision environment."[134] Cyert and March have identified this phenomenon in cases of business firms:

> Some business firms avoid uncertainty by neglecting to consider sources of uncertainty. To some extent this neglect may be due to an inability to consider all the potential

130 Observation on the early stage of deployment of the UN Transitional Administration in East Timor. Cf. Chapter V.3.1.
131 "Individual" does not exclusively refer to a "natural" person but may also denote a unitarily acting organization. The difference to the pathologies at the systemic or organizational level is that the latter result from the organizational set up itself and can thus only be observed in an organization. Cf. Perrow 1993.
132 Bazerman 2002 provides a comprehensive overview of cognitive bias research.
133 While bounded rationality and satisficing are important concepts to the argument and differentiate from rational decision-making, they still make no systematic statements of the type of the emerging cognitive biases. This gap had prominently been filled by Kahnemann and Tversky in their early 1970s contributions.
134 MacGrimmon and Taylor 1983, p. 1403. See also Adorno, Theodor W. et al. 1950. *The Authoritarian Personality*. New York: Harper; Rockeach, Milton. 1960. *The Open and Closed Mind*. New York: Basic Books.

sources of uncertainty, but when it occurs for major influences [...] on the firm's decisions, then probably an avoidance strategy is being used.[135]

In a peace operation, a pertinent trajectory would consist in the ongoing neglect of issues that are "too hot a potato" to touch, that are too political. In both cases under scrutiny, I will be able to detect such patterns.

Defensive Avoidance

"Is it realistic to hope to find a better solution?"[136] If, under conditions of ambiguity and bounded rationality and assumed that no more information may be available from previously unused sources, the answer to that question is "No," then we can speak of defensive avoidance.

> The temptation for defensive avoidance [in the form of procrastination, buck passing, or bolstering] is especially strong whenever a difficult policy decision is to be made [...]. When prime conditions for defensive avoidance are present, [...] [decision makers are] likely to make an ill-considered decision bolstered by shared rationalizations and a collective sense of invulnerability to threats of failure.[137]

When this strategy becomes dominant, the decision maker tries to avoid negative feedback to – potential or real – shortcomings of his or her decisions. "Hear no evil," as the saying goes.

Generating only Few or Insufficient Alternatives

Uncertainty may be minimized by considering only a few alternatives, which are manageable for the decision-maker. In the extreme case, the decision-maker will only generate one option in order to deal with the given problem. In cases of organizations, this "parsimonious" generating of alternatives may also be produced by organizational filtering systems. "When information flows to the decision maker, these filters simplify, select, and interpret information either by pre-designed

---

135 MacGrimmon and Taylor 1983, p. 1403, referring to Cyert, Richard M. and March, James G. 1963. *A Behavioral Theory of the Firm*. Englewood Cliffs: Prentice Hall.

136 Janis and Mann 1977, p. 70.

137 Ibid., p. 107. See also Janis, Irving L. 1972. *Victims of Groupthink: A Psychological Study of Foreign-Policy Decisions and Fiascoes*. Boston: Houghton Mifflin; Peterson, Randall S. et al. 1998. "Group Dynamics in Top Management Teams: Groupthink, Vigilance, and Alternative Models of Organizational Failure and Success." *Organizational Behavior and Human Decision Processes* 73:2/3, pp. 272-305.

procedures and/or by oversight before transmitting it to the decision maker."[138] This filtering process does not eliminate the problem of an uncertain environment. It only reduces the uncertainty a decision maker may perceive. "Filters operate as external devices for information structuring"[139] in the process of generating alternatives. There are different mechanisms that lead to inadequate generation of alternatives to a given problem: a narrow focus on a pre-preferred alternative or "decision autism," the exclusive use of familiar sources for the gathering of information, arguments by analogy, stereotyping, filtering by prioritizing short-run values, focussing on controllable factors, overconfidence, escalation, and reverting to routines.

The symptom of "decision autism" refers to a very limited analysis of the alternatives, which is not objective or candid. The evaluation is biased and the advantages of the preferred alternative are exaggerated as opposed to its potential pitfalls.[140] Aspects of the problem that might not be solved by preferred alternatives are omitted or at least underestimated and only aspects that correspond with the decision maker's preferences of potential alternatives are further processed.[141]

Decision-makers display a clear preference for sources in the provision of information or in the generation of alternatives that are familiar.[142]

> The implications of such source preferences [for alternative generation] seem rather direct. Sources perceived [...] as conveying information which has led to successful decision making in the past should be sought, and sources seen as less profitable should be avoided. Resistance by the decision maker to new sources of information, or sources that have been previously supplying information perceived as of low quality would seem to be difficult to detect and overcome.[143]

For worse, however, adherence to familiar sources that is not reflected upon may lead to inappropriate or biased information depending on the decision problem.

Stereotyping seeks to "simplify the environment [...] by assuming elements subject to variability are in fact certain or subject to completely predictable dynamic behavior."[144] When stereotyping, the decision-maker adopts interpretation

---

138 Stanbury, William T. et al. 1977. *Uncertainty in Policy Analysis: Perception, Specification, and Coping Strategies: Discussion Papers 77-59.* Berlin: Wissenschaftszentrum Berlin, Internationales Institut für Management und Verwaltung, p. 81.
139 Ibid.
140 See Schulz-Hardt 1997.
141 See ibid., p. 101.
142 Cf. MacGrimmon and Taylor 1983, p. 1420, "Multiple sources of information in the decision environment also contribute to the complexity and influence the way in which decision-makers aggregate information. The value of the information depends heavily on its relevance to the decision and its reliability. In complex environments, a decision maker can reduce the amount of information he must process by selecting information from relevant and reliable sources and by ignoring information from other sources."
143 Ibid., p. 1421. See also March 1958.
144 Stanbury et al. 1977, p. 60.

schemes for the analysis of alternatives which refer to predetermined categories. For example, by predicting dire consequences, he may categorically rule out certain alternatives. This may also be used as a *rhetorical* strategy during evaluation processes.

When filtering by prioritizing short-run values, the cognitive bias consists of evaluating alternatives in terms of their fruitfulness for resolving what appear to be *urgent* problems.[145]

A focus on controllable factors can be a useful simplifying strategy, but it can lead to pathological situations when factors are omitted that are uncontrollable yet crucial.

Furthermore, unrealistically positive views of one's self and unrealistic optimism are regular findings across a wide range of fields, "including academia, business, medicine, and the military."[146] Overconfidence becomes pathological if it strongly impairs judgement in a risky situation.[147]

Escalation or sunk cost effects refer to "the tendency for people to escalate commitment to a course of action in which they have made substantial prior investments of time, money, or other resources."[148] Ideally, one would not have his decision be influenced by considerations of past in-recoverable investment decisions. In reality, however, people often behave the opposite, "throwing good money after bad."[149]

Eventually, reverting to routines can become pathological. Routines describe the extent of the institutionalization of a set of procedures to which the decision-makers refers to in generating alternatives to a given decision-problem:

> *Auch und gerade in Krisensituationen und angesichts tiefgreifender Umbrüche neigen die korporativen Akteure [...] dazu, ihre Optionen im Rückgriff auf habitualisierte und bewährte Deutungsschemata zu strukturieren, um die anstehenden Entscheidungssit-*

---

145 Holsti, Ole R. 1979. "Theories of Crisis Decision Making." In: Paul Gordon Lauren, ed., *Diplomacy. New Approaches in History, Theory, and Policy.* New York: The Free Press, pp. 99-136, p. 104.

146 Roberto, Michael A. 2002. "Lessons from Everest: The Interaction of Cognitive Bias, Psychological Safety, and System Complexity." *California Management Review* 45:1, pp. 136-158, p. 142.

147 For more on the phenomenon, see Bazerman 2002; Russo, J. Edward and Schoemaker, Paul J. H. 1989. *Decision Traps: The Ten Barriers to Brilliant Decision Making and How to Overcome Them.* New York: Fireside.

148 Roberto 2002, p. 139.

149 For more on the phenomenon, see Staw, Barry M. and Ross, Jerry. 1989. "Understanding Behavior in Escalation Situations." *Science* 246, pp. 216-220; Arkes, Hal R. and Blumer, Catherine. 1985. "The Psychology of Sunk Cost." *Organizational Behavior and Human Decision Processes* 35, pp. 124-140; Brockner, Joel. 1992. "The Escalation of Commitment to a Failing Course of Action." *Academy of Management Review* 17, pp. 39-61.

uationen auf diese Weise kognitiv zu vereinfachen und handhabbar zu machen (standard operating procedures).[150]

In the peacekeeping context, a sad case in point was an episode in the ill-fated Rwandan mission:

> Force Commander Dallaire communicated to headquarters that he had received fresh evidence of a plot by extremists to scuttle the Arusha Accords by massacring civilians and killing peacekeepers and that he intended to seize weapons in the basement of President Habyarimana's party headquarters in order to stop the plot. DPKO overruled Dallaire's plan and insisted that he use consent-based tactics. The contrast between these extraordinary predictions of violence and DPKO's standardized response has led many scholars and investigators to wonder how DPKO could ever have believed that such a response was appropriate.[151]

Unconflicted Adherence

Unconflicted adherence describes the situation when, after the problem has been identified, alternatives generated, and evaluation efforts been made, it is still possible that no decision is made and that the status quo is unconflictedly adhered to. In this case, the level of aspiration referring to the necessity of change, of making a decision, is not met.[152]

Incrementalism

When the decision-maker reasons that a situation requires some sort of change, and perceives the risks of not changing to be relatively high while he perceives, at the same time, the risks of change to be fairly low, then "un-conflicted change" is the strategy of choice.

> Unconflicted change is often the dominant pattern when an executive adopts a very crude satisficing strategy. Once an executive realizes that there is something wrong about his current policy he focuses on a salient alternative that differs only slightly from the policy to which he is committed, which he believes will patch up the defect. Seeing nothing's grossly wrong with it if the one that mediates 'incrementalism.' The original policy in turn runs into trouble, yet another modification that seems to be free of serious

150 Olk, Thomas. 1996. "Wohlfahrtsverbände im Transformationsprozess Ostdeutschlands. " In: R. Kollmorgen et al., eds., *Sozialer Wandel und Akteure in Ostdeutschland. Empirische Befunde und theoretische Ansätze.* Opladen: Leske + Budrich, pp. 179-216, p. 201.
151 Barnett and Finnemore 2004, p. 140.
152 Janis and Mann 1977, pp. 72-73.

risks is uncritically adopted. […] Thus he makes a series of incremental changes without ever canvassing or evaluating the full range of available alternatives.[153]

Summing up, under ill-structured conditions, the rationality[154] of decisions decreases relatively: decisions are cognitively biased. The actor *is* still capable of making decisions by means of simplifying, selective, and framing decision rules, as well as by habitualization.[155] However, these decision-making biases can become pathological when they do not fit the situation and exacerbate the original problem, i.e., when the "alignment between strategic choices and critical contingencies in either environmental (external) or organizational (internal) contexts"[156] is not consistent.

3.1.2 Principal-Agent Dilemmas

'The mission was effectively run by about ten percent of the people. Maybe 50, 60 percent of people were simply collecting their salary and not doing any great harm, and the rest were positively dangerous, who you had to keep out.' Consequently, there was a work overload for these ten percent, a waste of resources, and a hard time implementing the mandate. It is questionable anyway if a mission should be labelled a success if there is such a small range of 'success bringers.' [157]

A virulent manifestation of ambiguous international support was the 'Chinese Chapter VII' provision, with the crucial P5 member cutting the robustness of the mission. This debilitation carried the risk of impairing the mission's safety as well as its credibility vis-à-vis local spoilers and the population in general. With the 'Chinese Chapter VII,' the consistency of military action was severely challenged. [158]

---

153 Ibid., p. 73. See also ibid., pp. 56-57. The likelihood of adopting the strategy of unconflicted change largely depends of the commitment and/or lock-in of the policy maker to his earlier courses of action. "The more committed the decision maker, the greater the stress when a challenging communication or event motivates him to search for a better course of action." Ibid.

154 Under the assumption of complete and perfect information, intransitive preferences, and accurate assessments of the decision-maker's risk preferences and values, a rational decision-making process is logically expected to lead to the inter-subjectively optimal outcome. Cf. Bazerman 2002.

155 Seibel, Wolfgang, "Das Deutsche Regierungssystem," lecturing material for BA-seminar at the University of Konstanz, on file with author.

156 Ensign, Prescott C. 2001. "The Concept of Fit in Organizational Research." *International Journal of Organizational Theory and Behavior* 4:3/4, pp. 287-306, p. 288. In the case study analyzes, I will allow for the discussion of both approaches to the conceptualization of fit, *ex ante* and *ex post*.

157 Observation on the UN Transitional Administration in East Timor.

158 Observation on the UN Transitional Administration in Eastern Slavonia.

In complex organizations – such as a transitional administration – division of work becomes necessary: one part or actor of the organization (the "agent") performs services for the good of another part or actor within the organization (the "principal"). The principal is conceptualized as the one who orders actions, the agent the one executing them. As indicated in the above examples, taken from the case studies of the transitional administrations in East Timor and Eastern Slavonia used in this thesis, the dysfunction may rest on both sides: agents, such as the international field staff working in a mission who are free riding, and the principals, such as powerful member states who are not interested in ceding (too much, in their opinion) military power to the UN.

The principal-agent approach to the analysis of organizational frictions was developed within the research tradition of microeconomic organization analysis. It explains success and failure of organizations in terms of problematic information asymmetries between those in charge of the organization, i.e. the principals, and the agent.[159] The agent may hide information on its actions, intentions, "true colours," commit moral hazard, and be prone to adverse selection, and to holding up.[160]

For the present study, the general hypotheses deduced from this theory holds that ill-structured conditions induce pathologically deviant agent behavior, and the more frequent these behavioral patterns occur and the more virulent they are in their quality, the more likely failure becomes. The mechanisms of the causal process consist in the trajectory of opportunism, purposeful misinformation, or defective action, so that the inherent delegation risks may lead to organizational failure if the agent starts to act strategically in his private interest. The agent does not care (any longer) for the effective or even efficient performance of the principal and the organization.[161]

However, the interest of the principal can too lead to deficiencies and failure. Accordingly, when looked at the causal trajectory from this perspective, the general hypothesis is that ill-structured conditions induce pathologically deviant principal behavior, and the more frequent these behavioral patterns occur and the more vir-

159 Cf. Fama 1980; Eisenhardt, Kathleen M. 1989. "Agency Theory: An Assessment and Review." *Academy of Management Review* 14:1, pp. 57-74; Milgrom, Paul and Roberts, John. 1988. "An Economic Approach to Influence Activities in Organizations." *American Journal of Sociology* 94, supplement, pp. 154-179; Picot, Arnold et al. 2000. *Organisation: Eine Ökonomische Perspektive*. Stuttgart: Schäffer-Poeschel; Picot et al. 1996. *Die grenzenlose Organisation*. 2nd ed. Wiesbaden: Gabler; Ross 1973; Rauchhaus, Robert. 2006. *Principal-Agent Problems in Conflict Management: Moral Hazards, Adverse Selection, and the Commitment Dilemma*. Paper presented at Annual meeting of the American Political Science Association, Pennsylvania Convention Center, Philadelphia.
160 Cf. Goldberg, Victor P. 1976. "Regulation and Administered Contracts." *Bell Journal of Economics and Management Science* 7:2, pp. 426-448.
161 It is assumed that the interests of the principal are congruent with the interests of the organization.

ulent they are in their quality, the more likely failure becomes. While this perspective is not included in the original approach,[162] the gap has been closed by Meyer and Zucker and Seibel.[163] I draw especially on Seibel, whose contribution I deem particularly relevant for the context of UN operations: his concept of successful failure holds that principals continuously mobilize resources for permanently failing organizations since they are interested in failure and in ignorance about failure. He argues that under conditions of scarce human, organizational, and financial resources and simultaneous entrapment in self-binding previous commitment, principals have an interest in an organization that continuously addresses problems, without being able to solve them, and they also have an interest in ignorance of the pertinent failure on part of other actors – other principals, agents, addressees – involved.[164] As long as no definitive disaster results, principals sustain this causal trajectory, tolerating the limited failure of problem-solving. In fact, this "successful failure" consideration might even become a valuable approach to dealing with an over-load of work, as the threshold for further demands of efficiency enhancement remain low. Likewise, ignorance about failure allows the principals to continue their way of "resource protection" without losing face or eventually adopting a costly new policy. In the context of the UN, this may lead, however, to fig leaf missions that propagate an ambitious mandate but are not in the position to live up to it.[165] In sum, the intricacies of the principal-agent dilemmas describe a lack of commitment to the stated organizational goals.

3.1.3 Tight Coupling of Complex Interactions

Multidimensional UN peace operations are restricted to two separate tracks of funding, assessed and voluntary contributions. The former are to be spent on peacekeeping issues and on the mssion only. The latter is for the so-called peacebuilding tasks. As the name indicates, voluntary contributions have to be raised – and this costs time. The consequence for the mandate implementation process is that important non-military

---

162   This omission was prominently criticized by Perrow. Cf. Perrow, Charles. 1986. *Complex Organizations: A Critical Essay*. New York: McGraw-Hill, p. 12.
163   Meyer, Marshall and Zucker, Lynne. 1989. *Permanently Failing Organizations*. Newbury Park: Sage; Seibel 1996.
164   Seibel, Wolfgang. 1992. *Funktionaler Dilettantismus. Erfolgreich scheiternde Organisationen im 'Dritten Sektor' zwischen Markt und Staat*. Baden-Baden: Nomos Verlagsgesellschaft (published Habilitationsschrift); Seibel 1996.
165   The concept of successful failure makes me think of a phrase by Friedrich Nietzsche in *Menschliches, Allzumenschliches*, "Was wisst ihr davon, was könntet ihr davon wissen, wie viel List der Selbst-Erhaltung, wie viel Vernunft und höhere Obhut in solchem Selbst-Betruge enthalten ist [...] – und wie viel Falschheit mir noch noth tut, damit ich mir immer wieder den Luxus meiner Wahrhaftigkeit gestatten darf?" Nietzsche, Friedrich. 1900. *Menschliches, Allzumenschliches*, Vol. 1, 8th ed. Friedrich Nietzsche: Werke. Leipzig: Naumann, p. 14. It nicely captures the nature of the causal mechanism at work.

challenges, such as reconciliation programmes or economic reconstruction, cannot be started early on. In East Timor in particular, this had immediate consequences as the mission appeared not to deliver. Combined with bad communication, it sharply reduced the originally high input-legitimacy.[166]

So far, human deficiencies and self-interested obstructers have been discussed. Yet, there are also genuine *organizational* causes for accidents and failure. I am going to focus on the disadvantages of subjecting complex organizational interactions to tight coupling. This potential cause for organizational pathologies was identified by Charles Perrow in his seminal work on "normal accidents."[167]

Complex interactions denote the interplay of different variables and processes that go on in an organization. They are inherently difficult to perceive and to comprehend as well as poorly predictable. Tight coupling refers to high interdependence within the organization under high centralization and rigidity. "Each part of the system is tightly linked to many other parts and therefore a change in one part can rapidly affect the status of other parts."[168] In this situation, there is very little organizational slack available and "a problem in one area quickly triggers failures in other aspects of the system."[169] In systems with these two features, "Things will go wrong not as a result of random, unpredictable, and exogenous shocks, attacks and incursions, but as the consequence of a complex string of events, antecedent conditions and small but cumulative defects and deficiencies in operating systems."[170] Transitional administrations experience a typical instance of tight coupling in the rigid financing regulations that keep them from investing their abundant mission funds into peacebuilding policies. The above-cited paragraph on the case study on UNTAET illustrates the cause.

The general hypothesis under this theoretical perspective is that ill-structured conditions make it more likely for the mission to pathologically enmesh itself in

166 Observation on the UN Transitional Administration in East Timor.
167 Perrow, Charles. 1984. *Normal Accidents: Living with High-risk Technologies.* New York: Basic Books.
168 Marais, Karen et al. 2004. *Beyond Normal Accidents and High Reliability Organizations: Lessons from the Space Shuttle.* ESD External Symposium, March 2004, Cambridge, p. 1.
169 Roberto 2002, p. 147. In contrast, loosely coupled systems "have fewer or less tight links between parts and therefore are able to absorb failures or unplanned behavior without destabilization." Marais et al. 2004, p. 1.
170 Weir, David. 2004. "Disaster Management After September 11: A 'Normal Accident' or a 'Man-made Disaster'? What Did We Know, What Have We Learned?" In: Gabriele G.S. Suder, ed., *Terrorism and the International Business Environment: The Security-Business Nexus.* Cheltenham: Edward Elgar Publishing, pp. 201-216., p. 202. See also Marais et al. 2004, p. 2, "When the system is interactively complex, independent failure events can interact in ways that cannot be predicted by the designers and operators of the system. If the system is also tightly coupled, the cascading of effects can quickly spiral out of control before operators are able to understand the situation and perform appropriated corrective actions. In such systems, apparently trivial incidents can cascade in unpredictable ways and with possibly severe consequences."

contradictory decisions that, the more frequently and virulently they occur, increase the probability of failure. As Perrow rests within the tradition of the functionalist paradigm, the causal mechanism that operates this type of pathology consists in the *spillover* of problems from one area to another, thus leading to the accumulation of (minor) accidents. The more, the more frequent, and the more virulent problems spill over, the more likely major accidents and failure become.

3.1.4 Path Dependence Deficiencies

As result of the combination of Indonesian pressure, the exclusion of experts from other parts of the UN system, the extensive analogy to another UN mission, and under the impression of standard routines of the department in charge, UNTAET was under a stereotyping terra nullis assumption, implying that they would operate the transition on their own, that there was nothing they could build on. A policy path was locked in that deferred the integration or participation of East Timorese, foreclosing consistent pursuance of local ownership.[171]

This example from the case study on the UN administration in East Timor points to the virulence of inadequately persisting assumptions and policies, running counter to the imperatives of the mandate that should have guided the mission in the first place.

Path dependency denotes the phenomenon of self-reinforcing institutions – organizations, technologies, rules, norms, or cognitive frames. It is a concept relevant in economics, institutional sociology, and historical institutionalism. The original idea by Paul David and Brian Arthur deals with the paradox of the persistence of sub-optimal technologies.[172] "[C]ertain technologies, for idiosyncratic and unpredictable reasons, can achieve an initial advantage over alternative technologies and prevail even if in the long run the alternatives would have been more efficient"[173] due to positive feedback effects. The moment a certain institutional formation establishes itself is called "critical juncture": at this point, the path is set for an institutional development that still responds to changing environmental conditions but "in ways that are constrained by past trajectories."[174] The path is "locked in"; if it is not conducive to the goals of the organization in question, a dysfunctional pathology will develop out of this trajectory. In the context of peace operations, one scenario may be the unreflected transplantation of structures and routines from one mission to another, completely different one.

171 Observation on the UN Transitional Administration in East Timor.
172 David, Paul. 1985. "Clio and the Economics of QWERTY." *American Economic Review* 75:2, pp. 332-337; Arthur, Brian. 1989. "Competing Technologies, Increasing Returns, and Lock-in by Historical Events." *Economic Journal* 99:394, pp. 116-131.
173 Thelen 1999, pp. 384-385.
174 Ibid., p. 387.

The general hypothesis deduced from the path dependency theory holds that ill-structured conditions increase the probability that the mission sets out on an inappropriate path that is not conducive to transitional management and, as a result, is pathologically locked-in in this situation, thus inclining the mission towards failure. The (reproductive) causal mechanisms that sustain the trajectory fall into two categories:[175] incentive structures or coordination effects and distributional effects of institutions. The first mechanism rests on the functional idea of self-reinforcing legitimation: once a certain formation is in place, the diverse participating actors adapt their behavior to the institutional positive and negative incentives. The second feedback concept is similarly functional and, according to Thelen, denotes that "institutions are not neutral coordinating mechanisms but in fact reflect, and also reproduce and magnify, particular patterns of power distribution in politics."[176] Only another critical juncture can bring about change of the adopted path and produce a new prevailing pattern.

The general causal process that operates behavioral patterns of defunct path-dependency consists in the trajectory of flawed information gathering and situative misperception, deficient information processing and misinterpretation, and ensuing inadequate decision-making and actions.

3.2 Coping Strategies

In a world characterized by complexity, uncertainty, ambiguity, as well as by ongoing time pressure, the assumption of thorough problem solving becomes obsolete. The concept that in this world supercedes "rational" trouble-shooting is coping. A successful coping strategy prevents, reduces, or contains problems, dilemmas, pathologies. The term strategy does thus not convey the technical meaning as it has in game theoretical applications but, in following Janis and Mann, George, and Etzioni,[177] denotes "basic types of search and choice procedures."[178] The further specification of coping strategies will be one of the major empirical challenges of this study: they will be identified inductively. In order to craft some orientation

175 Cf. Ikenberry, G. John. 1994. *History's Heavy Hand: Institutions and the Politics of the State*. Paper presented at Conference on New Institutionalism, 14-15 October 1994, University of Maryland.
176 Thelen 1999, p. 394, referring to Ikenberry 1994.
177 Janis and Mann 1977; George, Alexander 1974. "Adaptation to Stress in Political Decision Making: The Individual, Small Group, and Organizational Contexts." In: George V. Coelho et al., eds., *Coping and Adaptation*. New York: Basic Books, pp. 176-245; Etzioni, Amitai. 1968. *The Active Society: A Theory of Societal and Political Processes*. New York: The Free Press.
178 Janis and Mann 1977, p. 415. For the concept of coping, see also Lazarus, R. S. et al. 1974. "The Psychology of Coping: Issues of Research and Assessment." In: George V. Coelho et al., eds., *Coping and Adaptation*. New York: Basic Books, pp. 249-315.

for the empirical search for coping strategies, I am using the existent – yet scarce – contributions and recommendations that I find in the literature on how to deal with cognitive biases, principal-agent-problems, tight coupling of complex interactions, and path-dependence-induced pathologies.

3.2.1 Coping with Cognitive Biases

Diverse contributions have punctually identified recommendations and empirical observations on the prevention, reduction, or containment of the pathologies resulting from cognitive biases. The following strategies appear applicable to the context of transitional administrations:[179] acquiring experience and expertise, communication, sequential pursuing of goals, and vigilance.

According to the aphorism coined by Oscar Wilde, "Experience is just the name we give our mistakes." In the context of peace operations, experience consists of individual and organizational lessons learned from past missions. But also the transfer of knowledge from other UN bodies or from other actors that are involved in peacekeeping and peacebuilding may also add expertise. The objective must be to garner individual as well as institutional knowledge such as to be better prepared for dealing with pathologies. Individual knowledge can be won by recruiting personnel with pertinent experience, i.e. experience resulting from their participation in previous missions or experience that relates to their profession. The latter becomes the more necessary the more specialized the duties are, for instance if the person works in legal affairs. In case individual knowledge is generalized, aggregated, and (electronically) fixed, we speak of institutional knowledge.[180] The agency that is responsible for developing and storing such institutional knowledge of peace operations is the DPKO's Best Practices Unit.

It would be particularly useful for peace operations to discern explicitly between knowledge of facts ("know that") and rules ("know how", for instance cause-effect relationships, heuristics, "recipes," routines, norms, standards).[181] A variation of the facts necessitates a variation of the rules that were learned in a previous mission.

---

179 Cf. Cyert and March 1963; Bazermann 2002.
180 For a detailed outline of the relationship between individual and organizational knowledge and learning cf. March, James G. and Olsen, J.P. 1979. *Ambiguity and Choice in Organizations*. Bergen: Universitetsforlaget.
181 Schreyögg 1999, p. 535. See also Kogut, B. and Zander, U. 1992. "Knowledge of the Firm, Combinative Capabilities, and the Replication of Technology. Organization." *Science* 3, pp. 383-397; Sackman, Sonja A. 1992. "Culture and Subcultures. An Analysis of Organizational Knowledge." *Administrative Science Quarterly* 19, pp. 140-161.

Experience and expertise, however, can only be put to good effect if properly applied and communicated.[182] Communication within a given complex organization is crucial for the identification of misperceptions, deficient information processing, and interpretation. It is defined as "any process whereby decisional premises are transmitted from one member of an organization to another",[183] either into the direction of the decision-makers or downwards from the decision-center to other parts of the organization.[184] Channels of communication can be formal, i.e. fixed in the organizational structure and obligatory, and informal, i.e. built around social relationships. In peace operations, informal communication can become even more important than formal communication channels, as the latter has a chance of being less politicized, thus adding transparency. That said, it is important to note that communication results in different trajectories: an organization's internal culture of communication can aggravate or mitigate pathologies. If organizational communication is characterized by transparency and the regular and open interchange of arguments, cognitive biases (such as overconfidence, defensive avoidance, unconflicted change, and the ignorance of problems, for example) can certainly be reduced.

The sequential pursuit of goals ("fractionalization") has been described by Amitai Etzioni as a useful strategy in coping with cognitive biases: the conflict potential of concurring goals is attenuated by the temporal disentanglement of their pursuance. "Instead of spreading a single intervention over time, it treats important judgments as a series of sub-decisions and may or may not also stagger them in

---

182 Cf. Simon 1976, p. 155, "The information and knowledge that has a bearing on decisions arises at various points in the organization. Sometimes the organization has its own 'sensory organs' – the intelligence unit of a military organization, or the market analysis section of a business form. Sometimes individuals are recruited and installed in positions for the knowledge they are presumed already to possess – a legal division. Sometimes the knowledge develops on the job itself – the lathe operator is the first one to know when his machine breaks down. Sometimes the knowledge is knowledge of other decisions that have been made – the executive turns down one request for expenditure of funds because he knows that he has already committed these funds to another use. In all these cases particular individuals in the organization are possessed of information that is relevant to particular decisions that have to be made. An apparently simple way to allocate the function of decision-making would be to assign to each member of the organization those decisions for which he possesses the relevant information. The basic difficulty in this is that not all the information relevant to a particular decision is possessed by a single individual. If the decision is then dismembered into its component premises and these allocated to separate individuals, a communication process must be set up for transmitting these components from the separate centers to some point where they can be combined and transmitted, in turn, to those members in the organization who will have to carry them out." See also Barton, L. 1990. "Crisis Management: Selecting Communications Strategy." *Management Decision* 28:6, pp. 5-8.
183 Ibid.
184 Of course, communication proceeds as well horizontally.

time".[185] This allows the organization in question to "relate turning points in the decision process to turning points in the supply of information."[186]

Generally, the vigilance of actors is crucial for increasing the chances of "fit" decision-making. As suggested by Janis and Mann, a vigilant decision-maker displays the following characteristics to the best of his ability and within his information-processing capabilities:

> [The decision-maker] thoroughly canvasses a wide range of alternative courses of action; surveys the full range of objectives to be fulfilled and the values implicated by the choice; carefully weighs whatever he knows about the costs and risks of negative consequences, as well as the positive consequences, that could flow from each alternative; intensively searches for new information relevant to further evaluation of the alternatives; correctly assimilates and takes account of any new information or expert judgment to which he is exposed, even when the information or judgment does not support the course of action he initially prefers; re-examines the positive and negative consequences of all known alternatives, including those originally regarded as unacceptable, before making a final choice; makes detailed provisions for implementing or executing the chosen course of action, with special attention to contingency plans that might be required if various known risks were to materialize.[187]

Furthermore, other strategies that helped to cope with cognitive biases have been identified in (non-prescriptive) empirical observations. For instance, a manipulation of performance criteria and the recourse or establishment of myths and artificial "legends of legitimation" can effect the temporary containment of a deteriorating situation: facing conflicts or ambiguities in the course of a decision's implementation, the actors in charge are likely to revert to manipulation strategies implying "*[m]angelnde bzw. beschönigende Erfolgskontrolle; dadurch Fortsetzung fehlgehender Handlungen.*"[188] Similar to the manipulation strategy, legends of legitimation are characterized by the evocation of established organizational practices or normative patterns which help to make decisions acceptable.[189] The strategies of manipulation and building organizational legends may be subsumed under the more general phenomenon of "framing." Framing refers to the communicated presentation, most often linked with norm appellations of a given object, e.g. a decision,

---

185   Etzioni, Amitai. 1989. "Humble Decision Making." *Harvard Business Review* 67, pp. 122-126, p 125.
186   Ibid.
187   Janis and Mann 1977, p. 11.
188   Schulz-Hardt 1997, p. 103. See also Meyer and Zucker 1989; MacGrimmon and Taylor 1983, pp. 1403-1404. For early findings on the issue cf. Festinger, Leon. 1957. *A Theory of Cognitive Dissonance.* Stanford: Stanford University Press; Ibid. 1964. *Conflict, Decision, and Dissonance.* Stanford: Stanford University Press.
189   Cf. Meyer, John W. and Rowan, Brian. 1977. "Institutionalized Organizations: Formal Structure as Myth and Ceremony." *The American Journal of Sociology* 83:2, pp. 340-363.

influencing its perception and acceptance by the "target actors."[190] However, at the end of the day, these coping strategies do not promise to mitigate the problems of cognitive biases in the long term.

3.2.2 Coping with Principal-Agent Dilemmas

Suggestions for reducing, containing, or preventing the pathologies resulting from agent opportunism point to supervision and control (hierarchy), extending the organizational information system, threats of sanctions, especially threats of losing one's reputation, the creation of positive incentives for agents, and generally for an organizational culture that emphasizes the commonness of goals and values.

The narrower the span of control in a given entity, the more likely the principal discloses deviant agent behavior, but it also implies more supervising actors. Control can consist of the supervision of behavior and control of outputs. For both forms of control, the fundamental structure of the relationship between the principals and agents in consideration defines the opportunities for such control.[191] A helpful supplement to a control structure is the extension of the information system: the more information the principal can get via additional information channels, the less he or she is vulnerable to agent defection. Another strategy for coping with deviant agent behavior rests on the setting of incentives. Incentives can consist of threats of sanctions: the graver the sanction for deviant behavior, the higher the opportunity cost for an agent to hazard the required course. In addition, the sanctioning of an agent who has been caught has a preventive impact vis-à-vis other spoilers. Sanctions can also be positive in that agents are rewarded for complying and productive behavior, be it in monetary or non-monetary terms.[192] The classic elaboration of Chester Barnard holds that:

> An organization can secure the efforts necessary to its existence [...] either by the objective inducements it provides or by changing states of mind. [...] We shall call the

190 See, e.g., Entman, Robert M. 1993. "Framing: Toward Clarification of a Fractured Paradigm." *Journal of Communication* 43:4, pp. 51-58; Goffman, Erving. 1974. *The Presentation of Self in Everyday Life*. New York: Double Day.
191 Cf. Hall, Richard. 1972. *Organizations: Structure and Process*. Englewood Cliffs: Prentice-Hall.
192 For a formal justification of the argument, see Laffont, Jean-Jacques and Martimort, David. 2002. *The Theory of Incentives. The Principal-Agent Model*. Princeton: Princeton University Press. The first attempt to define a theory of incentives was the seminal *Functions of the Executive*. Barnard, Chester I. 1938. *The Functions of the Executive*. New York: Wiley.

process of offering objective incentives 'the method of incentives;' and the process of changing subjective attitudes 'the method of persuasion.'[193]

The most obvious way to avoid agent defection is to prevent it by making the organization's goals and wishes the goals and wishes of the agent. Under the assumption of sanity, an actor who identifies with the overall purpose of the entity he belongs to will not act against it.

The disadvantage of all of these potential coping strategies is that they are expensive and add to the complexity of the organization. The crucial elements that remain to be built up within the organization or the respective groups are trust and solidarity.[194]

Concerning the pathology of principal-induced "successful failure", hardly any recommendations have been developed in the literature. The several risks this kind of fig leaf-policy entails – "above all the risk of de-legitimization and an ensuing loss of even the limited amount of resources that are indispensable for 'keeping the system going'"[195] – will make further research in this area a worthwhile venture. Seibel tentatively points to the role of ideologies that may frame and thus mitigate the dilemmatic nature of the principal's behavior. Non-framing coping strategies that emphasize preventive action are suggested by Rouleau, Gagnon, and Cloutier. They argue that a pathological organization needs to promote "better and pro-active methods to ensure accountability of actions (and thus discourage inconsistency between what is said and what is done), improved information flows, and open and frank discussions (and eventual agreement) on what the organizations' priorities and values are, and should be."[196] Generally, they propose generic incremental strategies in dealing with the phenomenon of sustained successful failure.[197]

---

193 Ibid., p. 142. He further elaborates, "The specific inducements that may be offered are of several classes, for example; a) material inducements; b) personal non material opportunities; c) desirable physical conditions; d) ideal benefactions. General incentives afforded are, for example: e) associational attractiveness; f) adaptation of conditions to habitual methods and attitudes; g) opportunity of enlarged participation; h) the condition of communion." Ibid.

194 Cf. Kramer, Roderick M. and Tylor, Tom R. 1995. *Trust in Organizations. Frontiers of Theory and Research.* Thousand Oaks: Sage; Heisig, Ulrich and Littek, Wolfgang. 1995. "Wandel von Vertrauensbeziehungen im Arbeitsprozess." *Soziale Welt* 46, pp. 282-304.

195 Seibel, Wolfgang. 2007. *The 'Responsibility to Protect' and Modern Protectorates – UN Peace Operations as Successfully Failing Venture.* Paper Prepared for the Conference "The New Protectorates: International Administration and the Dilemmas of Governance", Cambridge University, 6-8 June 2007, p. 13.

196 Rouleau, Linda et al. 2008. "Revisiting Permanently Failing Organizations: A Practice Perspective." *Les Cahier de Recherche du GéPS* 2:1. Available online at web.hec.ca/geps/GePS-08-01.pdf, last access on 15 March 2009, p. 30.

197 "It is our general contention that small, systematic and sustained efforts have better potential to yield results than more radical approaches, which are more likely to provoke resistance, and lead to actions that exacerbate rather than remedy the situation at hand." Ibid., p. 31.

3.2.3 Coping with Tight Coupling of Complex Interactions

The recommendations that Charles Perrow gives in order to cope with the intricacies of a tightly coupled complex system and to make them safer consist of the (obvious) reduction of complexity and elements of tight coupling in the organizational designs and redundancies and other safety measures. That can be achieved, for instance, by decomposing a complex system into subunits that are in turn connected by monitored links.[198] However, Perrow issues bleak predictions for the effectiveness of such measures since respective efforts will probably lead to more complexity. Less pessimistic suggestions are made by other authors who emphasize the creation of organizational slack and organizational learning.

The theoretical discussion of organizational slack goes back to contributions by Chester I. Barnard and James D. Thompson, who found that the use of slack resources was essential for protecting the core of the organization under dynamic environmental conditions.[199] Applying the concept of slack to the purpose of this study, I define the coping strategy as the attenuation of conflict through excessive resources, which mitigates contests for scarce resources or which functions as a compensation payments for actors that got a bad deal.

Organizational slack is "important for organizational adaptation and innovation – two often cited requirements for organizations of the future."[200] Likewise important for adaptive and innovative behavior is the learning ability of the organization. Organizational learning, defined as a collective process driven by groups of individuals entailing cognitive change through the questioning of the means and/or ends of addressing problems,[201] can proceed incrementally and in a "big bang" fashion, i.e. following shock, and its subject can be facts as well as procedures. Coping with the vulnerabilities of complexity, "fit" learning would refer to increased probability and speed of identifying dysfunctions and how to adequately deal with them by applying previously learned, and if necessary, modified lessons. An efficient solution that allows for learning how to deal with the vulnerabilities of complexity would be the establishment of formal systems for feedback of mistakes. In general, learning and implementing what has been learned are two fun-

---

198 Cf. Perrow, Charles. 1999. "Organizing to Reduce the Vulnerabilities of Complexity." *Journal of Contingencies and Crisis Management* 7:3, pp. 150-155.
199 Cf. Rust, Kathleen. 2002. *Organizational Slack and Performance: The Interactive Role of Workforce Changes.* Paper to be presented in the Strategic Management Track of the Midwest Academy of Management Conference, p. 4. For the classic contributions on the issue, see Barnard 1938; Thompson, J. 1967. *Organizations in Action.* New York: McGraw-Hill.
200 Lawson, M. 2001. "In Praise of Slack: Time Is of the Essence." *Academy of Management Executive* 15:3, pp. 125-135, p. 25.
201 Cf. Benner et al. 2008. "Learning to Learn? UN Peacebuilding and the Challenges of Building a Learning Organization." *Journal of Intervention and State-building* 2:1, pp. 43-62, p. 18.

damentally different things: only if the so-called theories-in-use of a peace operation change as consequence of learning can we speak of successful coping.

3.2.4 Coping with Path Dependence Deficiencies

Recommendations for un-locking an unfavorable path address the role of political or institutional entrepreneurs.[202]

Following the definition by John Kingdon, these entrepreneurs are "advocates willing to invest their resources – time, energy, reputation, financial resources – to promote a position in return for anticipated future gain in the form of material, purposive, or solidary benefits."[203] Building upon the idea of the garbage can decision-making model,

> The linkage between problems to be solved and the solutions promoted by influential actors are independent from each other, and are instead driven by contingent configurations of opportunities to take a decision and time sequences, rather than by rational calculation of means and ends. According to Kingdon, policy entrepreneurs are waiting for 'windows of opportunity' to insert a preferred combination of different 'streams' (the politics stream, the policy or solution stream, and the problem stream) in a political decision-making process. These streams are combined in accordance with the opportunity as such and the respective institutional setting that defines the space in which the 'streams' can be coupled. Successful policy entrepreneurs are connecting those 'streams,' thus shaping the dominant public discourses and, consequently, the public policy agenda in a way that favors the acceptance and ultimate implementation of the policy solution they advocate.[204]

Hence, entrepreneurs fulfill a double task: on the one hand, they are initiators and agenda-setters; on the other hand, they are coordinators and managers. They enact a structuring influence in both rolls on problem perception, political decisions, and the implementation thereof.[205] On that note, it is important to add:
The policy entrepreneur concept is not a leadership theory in the conventional sense. Policy entrepreneurs have no 'followers' and they are not necessarily located in a senior hierarchical position. They are rather networkers than superiors and their particular skills reside in their ability to engage others in collective action by boundary spanning activities that glue together human resources, support, and

---

202 Seibel, Wolfgang et al. 2006. This is in fact the only recommendation for active action that I have identified; the broad range of studies on path dependence restricts itself to the analysis of causes, mechanisms, and effects – and not on how to cope with them.
203 Seibel et al. 2008, p. 9.
204 Ibid., referring to Kingdon, John W. 1995. *Agendas, Alternatives, and Public Policies.* New York: Harper Collins. See also Roberts, Nancy and King, Paula. 1996. *Transforming Public Policy. Dynamics of Policy Entrepreneurship and Innovation.* San Francisco: Jossey-Bass.
205 For this phenomenon of structuration cf. Giddens 1984.

commitment from a variety of arenas for the purpose of promoting a particular political project. The role of a policy entrepreneur can be assumed, for instance, by someone outside the formal hierarchical order, which also means that their role may vanish once the goal has been achieved and the project is done.[206]

The exceptional position of the SRSG in a UN mission relates very much to his or her qualities as a political or institutional "entrepreneur" – how capable is a SRSG to connect different "streams" of problems and solutions and, if necessary, bring about a critical juncture. Leadership ist "one major cause of successful policy outcomes and an important mechanism to overcome gridlock and uncontrollable events."[207]

3.2.5 Conclusion

"Good" coping is assumed to prevent, reduce, or contain the negative impacts of pathologies, and is defined by its "fit." For the purpose of the study, I specify "fit" as an emergent phenomenon that consists in the process of arriving at the desired performance by a favorable match of coping strategies to developing organizational pathologies.[208] Evidently, the *ex post facto* perspective is not in line with a prediction goal. This, however, is not the purpose of this study anyway. I intend to explore successful coping strategies and to generate hypotheses based on these observations. The recommendations deducted from the pertinent literature serve as helpful guidelines for exploration and observation.

One important condition for fit coping, deduced from the theoretical considerations above, seems to be the leadership style. As discussed by almost all approaches, the leader of an organization is in the pivot position to enact valuable coping strategies. He does so in a political and in a managerial function: he sets the agenda – for instance when it comes to a change of policy following the detection of shortcomings of the mission – as well as coordinates the agenda's implementation – for instance concerning the monitoring of personnel. Theoretically, the person taking over as SRSG/Transitional Administrator can be expected to prove a crucial factor for a mission's capacity of fit coping.

---

206 Seibel et al. 2008, p. 10. For policy entrepreneur's social networking capacity cf. Fligstein, Neil. 2001. "Social Skill and the Theory of Fields," *Sociological Theory*, 19:2, pp. 105-125.
207 Seibel, Wolfgang et al. 2006, p. 21. See also Janis, Irving L. 1989. *Crucial Decisions: Leadership in Policymaking and Crisis Management*. New York: The Free Press/Collier Macmillan Publishers, pp. 3-4.
208 Cf. Ensign 2001. On that note, there is one last important remark to make on the conceptualization of coping for this study: obviously, coping does not exclusively apply to pathologies *per se* but is also applicable to external shocks, i.e. events external to the mission itself. A case in point may be coping with natural catastrophes. My focus, however, is another.

In conclusion, one should note that the literature is not as coherent as I have presented it here by neatly distinguishing between pathological trajectories and coping strategies. The state of the art is much more scattered: I collected a wide range of singular statements and to supplement them with contributions from other strands of literature, such as to create an analytical framework that seems apt for the study of pathologies and coping at the subject of post-conflict transitions managed by complex UN missions.

As *coping with pathologies in transitional administrations* has not yet been subject to academic analysis, the study shall retain a partly explorative character. This implies an openness to include observations that are not covered by either background theory. Particularly the coping behavior applied and its fit remains an empirical question.

4. Case Selection and Method of Analysis

The argumentative structure of this study is threefold. First, complex UN missions operate under ill-structured conditions that produce organizational pathologies. By selecting two highly complex missions, namely transitional administrations, the observation of pathologies will be very likely. Second, the more frequent and virulent these pathologies become, the more likely are accidents and ultimate failure to occur. By selecting two transitional administrations that have been judged relative successes, I trace the factors, processes and mechanisms that were responsible for the unlikely positive outcome. The third part of my argument consists of the general hypothesis about the causes: I argue that the respective coping behavior of the missions makes the difference, ultimately preventing ill-fated and pathological missions from failure. The case selection, design, and the methods of data selection and analysis of the study correspond with its theoretical argument.

For the narrower research purposes of the study, I need two selection criteria – the population and the dependent variable's value – for which I have chosen transitional administrations and successful cases, such as to be able to observe fit coping strategies. The first criterion assures that we talk about the right population of cases. Starting from the definition of UN transitional administrations presented in the second part, there are six cases that fit the criteria: the UN Transitional Authority in Cambodia (UNTAC, 1992-1993), the UN Transitional Administration in Eastern Slavonia (UNTAES, 1996-1998), the UN Mission in Kosovo (UNMIK, since

1999), the UN Transitional Administration in East Timor (UNTAET, 1999-2002),[209] the operation in Bosnia, and the UN Mission in Somalia (UNOSOM II, planned in 1993).[210]

The second criterion refers to the dependent variable (*performance*): as explained, in order to identify valuable coping strategies – as the hypothesized *explananda* – it is most promising to look at successful transitional administrations. Screening most pertinent comparative studies on UN transitional administrations[211] as well as the concluding reports of the Secretary-General on those missions, the administrations in Eastern Slavonia and East Timor stand out: UNTAES has been called the "most successful of all post-Cold War UN- or US-led nation-building missions," and the even more comprehensive Transitional Administration in East Timor, which set out to build a new state while managing the transition to independence, furthered "deep and significant"[212] successes. Analogous with the success-criterion is the exclusion of failing missions. I do also exclude missions that have, at the time of writing, not yet terminated. I hence exclude the mission in Bosnia: besides not being a success story, it was not a UN-operation,[213] and neither has it terminated. It thus lies outside the goal population of the study. This holds true for UNMIK as well. At the time that I conducted the expert interviews for this study, it was difficult to anticipate when and if, at all, UNMIK would end. As I explain below, I am interested in the overall process of transition including its termination – hence, the Kosovo mission is not considered in this study. The per-

---

209 As for prominent case study literature on UNTAET see Beauvais 2001; Chesterman, Simon. 2002. *Justice Under International Administration: Kosovo, East Timor and Afghanistan.* New York: International Peace Academy; Chopra, Jarat. 2000. "The UN's Kingdom of East Timor." *Survival* 42:3, pp. 27-39; Conflict Security & Development Group at King's College 2003; Suhrke, Astri. 2001. "Peacekeepers as Nation-builders: Dilemmas of the UN in East Timor." *International Peacekeeping* 8:4, pp. 1-20; on UNTAES see UN Department of Peacekeeping Operations 1998; Coleiro 2002; Boothby, Derek G. 2003. "The Successful Application of Leverage in Eastern Slavonia." In: Jean Krasno et al., eds., *Leveraging for Success in United Nations Peace Operations.* Westport: Praeger, p. 117-140; Ibid. 2004. "The Political Challenges of Administering Eastern Slavonia." *Global Governance* 10:1, pp. 37-51.

210 Scholars dispute on whether to include the UN Operation in Mozambique (ONUMOZ, 1992-94) in this class of cases. Based on the argument made in Doyle 2002, I do not consider ONUMOZ a transitional administration.

211 Especially Howard, Lise Morjé. 2008. *UN Peacekeeping in Civil Wars.* Cambridge: Cambridge University Press, p. 297; Dobbins et al. 2005.

212 Howard 2008, p. 297.

213 Bosnia is also "a tricky case since it 'transitional administration' qualities developed over time out of mission creep, bringing about extended powers for the Office of the High Representative (OHR). Moreover, the international mission in Bosnia is not a UN mission like the other cases (the OHR reports to the Peace Implementation Council (PIC) which comprises 55 states). The OHR was endorsed by the UN Security Council, but not authorized in the first place." Elges, Reinhold. 2004. *International State-building – Time to Reconsider.* POWI 04, Graduiertenkonferenz: Neue Impulse für die Politikwissenschaft in Österreich, 2004, p. 14.

formance of the mission in Cambodia is ambivalent: a few months after the deployment of UNTAC, its mandate was revised and narrowed so significantly by the SRSG and the Secretary-General that the relative success that has been attributed to the mission is questionable. While the narrow mandate had been fulfilled, it was the tricky parts that had been omitted – and were not implemented at all. I do not count, accordingly, the mission as a success.[214] A special case is UN-OSOM II as it, in methodological terminology, constitutes a so-called negative case:[215] the mission had been planned as a transitional administration but was never implemented. As I am interested in the very process of transitional management, I neglect this case.

UNTAES and UNTAET are widely acknowledged as the most successful ventures of complex UN peace operations so far.[216] In addition to this, the cases of UNTAES and UNTAET are also chosen because they represent terminated missions. This implies that I am going to be able to study the entire transition process and even give an account of the situation on-the-ground after the mission withdrew. Furthermore, while there are lots of accounts and articles on the mission in East Timor, surprisingly few analyzes of UNTAES exist.[217] Given the fact that it is praised as possibly the most successful UN mission ever, a detailed examination promises insight in successful coping strategies.

If the relative success of the two missions depended on their superior coping behavior, I shall be able to trace it. This being said, the rival hypothesis, which holds that their success must be attributed to conducive external circumstances, will be taken into account as well. Still, preliminary evidence from other case studies and reports suggests that there *were* severe problems of hostility (particularly UNTAES), capacity (particularly UNTAET), the common intricacies of a post-conflict territory such as destroyed infrastructure and grievances in the local population, as well as the institutional constraint of a scant personnel situation at headquarters and in the field.

---

214 For corresponding evaluations see, e.g., Van der Lijn, Jaïr. 2009. *If only There Were a Blueprint! Factors for Success and Failure of UN Peace-Building Operations.* Netherlands Institute of International Relations 'Clingendael.' Clingendael Security and Conflict Programme (CSCP). Available online at http://www.clingendael.nl/publications/2009/20090218_joup_lijn3.pdf, last access on 16 March 2009.

215 Cf. Mahoney, James and Goertz, Gary. 2004. "The Possibility Principle: Choosing Negative Cases in Comparative Research." *American Political Science Review* 98:4, pp. 653-669.

216 On UNTAES see, e.g., Chesterman 2004; Coleiro 2002; Binnendijk, Hans et al. 2006. *Solutions for Northern Kosovo: Lessons Learned in Mostar, Eastern Slavonia, and Brcko.* Washington, DC: National Defense University; UN Department of Peacekeeping Operations, Lessons Learned Unit. 1998. *The United Nations Transitional Administration for Eastern Slavonia, Baranja and Western Sirmium (UNTAES), January 1996-1998: Lessons Learned.* Available online at http://www.pbpu.unlb.org/pbu/library/UNTAES.pdf, last access on 10 January 2007, on UNTAET see, e.g., Chesterman 2004; Dobbins et al. 2005; Smith 2004.

217 The most pertinent exceptions are Coleiro 2002, Boothby 2003, and Boothby 2004.

A matter of fact, the extrapolarization capacity of the study with its qualitative within-case analyses is obviously limited. Again, this is not the goal anyway: in the first place, I aspire to make statements on these particular cases and to contribute to theory-building. The method by which this shall be achieved is the so-called process tracing approach. Process tracing is a method that calls for the systematic collection and analysis of non-quantitative data on the basis of a preliminary analytical roster or a research questionnaire of "structured" and "focused" questions.[218]

> From the statistical (and survey) research model, this method borrows the device of asking a set of standardized, general questions of each case. These standardized questions [...] must be carefully developed to reflect adequately the research objective and theoretical focus of the inquiry. Using a set of general questions is necessary to assure acquisition of comparable data from the several cases. [...] The method also requires that comparison of cases be 'focused;' that is, undertaken with a selective theoretical focus. Not all the theoretically interesting aspects of a case can be usefully addressed in a single study.[219]

The method allows for an iterative process of data collection, data analysis, and data abstraction, thus generating categories, concepts, hypotheses, or theories.

As the term suggests, the method is about the identification and theoretical interpretation of causal *processes*. I attempt a reconstruction and an analysis of the processes that connect the explanatory factors of ill-structuredness, different kinds of pathologies, and coping strategies and link it to the dependent variable *performance*. A careful mapping of the processes should allow me to explore the extent to which the observations coincide with prior, theoretically derived expectations about driving factors and mechanisms.[220] Still, the method of process tracing leaves

---

218 Cf. Gläser, Jochen and Laudel, Grit. 2004. *Experteninterviews und qualitative Inhaltsanalyse als Instrumente rekonstruierender Untersuchungen.* Wiesbaden: VS Verlag für Sozialwissenschaften, "Die dem Text entnommenen Informationen werden den Kategorien des Analyserasters zugeordnet und relativ unabhängig vom Text weiterverarbeitet, d.h. umgewandelt, mit anderen Informationen synthetisiert, verworfen usw." See also Mayring, Philipp. 1993. *Qualitative Inhaltsanalyse: Grundlagen und Techniken.* Weinheim: Deutscher Studien Verlag.

219 Bennett and George 1997b, p. 3. The rationale adheres to the scientific criteria of better comparability and knowledge accumulation. They further emphasize that "it is important to recognize that a single historical event can be relevant for research in a variety of theoretical interests. [...] Treatment of [the event of interest] in a case study must be selectively focused in accord with the type of theory that the investigator is attempting to develop." Ibid.

220 "The outcomes of concern to policy researchers typically involve complex chains of events unfolding over time, which defy accurate characterization through regression analysis, with its more static snapshots of co-variation." Steinberg, Paul. 2004. *New Approaches to Causal Analysis in Policy Research.* Paper presented for the panel "Multi-Methods in Qualitative Research," Annual Convention of the American Political Science Association, 2-5 September 2004, pp. 1-2. Process tracing is thus an opportune method for the study of causal

much for the researcher to specify – contrary to quantitative methods where fixed standards and procedures are available and need to be adhered.

I specify and adapt the method for my research purpose as follows: for each case, a historical reconstruction of the transitional process will be elaborated, focusing on the main lines of policies. I will make sure that the case studies are arranged in kind by asking the same structured and focussed questions about ill-structured conditions, pathologies, accidents, and coping strategies for each case.[221] Process tracing also requests to check the theoretically suggested evidence throughout the case studies.[222] I will introduce such "mini-checks" in the form of a summarizing and evaluating chapters at the end of each transitional phase. Subsequent to the reconstruction, I will analyze the empirical evidence in terms of the theoretical lenses and present the respective ill-structured conditions, pathologies, accidents, and coping strategies, as well as further findings. Every relevant trajectory will be looked at separately, interpreted according to the theoretical framework, and summarized in table form. On the basis of this analysis, I will be able to abstract out observations, come to theoretically relevant statements, and find answers to the research questions.

As the case studies will reveal, the findings on pathologies and coping strategies extend into several branches of organizational theory, management, and political science. On account of this broad spectrum, not every aspect will be elaborated in detail. Nonetheless, once relevant evidence surfaces in the analysis, I will include it in the discussion.

The data[223] being analyzed via process tracing stems from secondary literature, especially descriptive case studies,[224] primary sources, such as UN documents, press releases, mission reports, and reports by DPKO and other organizations involved such as the World Bank, and from expert interviews. Interview with experts,

processes with dimensions of complexity, interaction, and sequence. Such processes can be better represented in a qualitative, narrative case study than in a quantitative study that uses regression analysis builds on correlation.

221 For a similar application of the structured and focussed questionnaire approach see the study on *UN Peacekeeping and Civil Wars* by Lise Morjé Howard of 2008.

222 Cf. Checkel 2005.

223 One should keep in mind that contrary to everyday speech and contrary to quantitative analysis, "data" in qualitative analysis does not signify sets of numbers but sets of words, "The first thing that characterizes qualitative analyzes is that it analyzes a distinctive form of data, namely language and texts." Gibbs, Graham. 2002. *Qualitative data analysis: Explorations with NVivo*. Buckingham: Open University Press, p. 1.

224 For a justification of and considerations for the use of secondary material, see Heaton, Janet. 1998. "Secondary Analysis of Qualitative Data." *Social Research Update* 22. Available online at http://www.soc.surrey.ac.uk/sru/SRU22.html, last access on 25 November 2008. Drawing together the relevant secondary literature on the cases to be examined, I build upon established findings and analyze them through the perspective of my theoretical framework, thus using this verbal data "from a different perspective, [examining] concepts which were not central to the original research." Ibid., p. 2.

especially with former members of the missions,[225] are supposed to uncover information necessary for the reconstruction of the deficiencies and coping capabilities of UN interim administrations. As I focus on the main lines of the transition policy and as I am particularly interested in information provided by the major decision-makers, I selected primarily mission officials who served in senior positions. Questioning these experts by means of semi-standardized and mostly open questions, I strive for a comprehensive coverage of relevant issues.[226] While I modify the individual questionnaire according to the respondent's position within the transition process, I will continue to adhere to the imperatives of "structured" and "focused" organization.[227] The evidence of the expert interviews in the form of direct and indirect quotes will be used extensively throughout the text and in the footnotes. These verbal data pieces are crucial components of the cases' reconstructions.

The case studies follow the same structure and entail two generic parts: reconstruction and analysis. Reconstructing the cases, I will start with an overview of the background facts on the country and its history, the conflict and previous UN involvement, of the situation post conflict, as well as of the ensuing peace agreement negotiations and the planning and designing of the mission. I will continue with the reconstruction of the transition process on-the-ground: I am going to explore the implementation of the transitory provisions, describing how the mission was run, and closing with a reconstruction of the termination process. In the analysis, I structure the previous observations according to the different lenses applied: for each perspective, I am going to discuss the evidence on pathologies and how they were being coped with.

225 "Interviews mit Experten – also mit Personen, die sich – ausgehend von spezifischem Praxis- und Erfahrungswissen, das sich auf einen klar begrenzbaren Problemkreis bezieht, die Möglichkeit geschaffen haben, mit ihren Deutungen das konkrete Handlungsfeld sinnhaft und handlungsleitend zu strukturieren [können] [...]durch die offene Gesprächsführung und die Erweiterung von Antwortspielräumen [den] Bezugsrahmen des Befragten bei der Fragebeantwortung miterfassen, um so einen Einblick in die Relevanzstrukturen und die Erfahrungshintergründe des Befragten zu erlangen." Schnell et al. 1999. *Methoden der empirischen Sozialforschung*. 6th ed. München: Oldenbourg, p. 355.
226 Expert interviews can tentatively guarantee that "alle forschungsrelevanten Themen auch tatsächlich angesprochen werden." Bogner, Alexander et al. 2002. *Das Experteninterview: Theorie, Methode, Anwendung*. Opladen: VS Verlag für Sozialwissenschaften, p. 45.
227 Questionnaire on file with the author.

IV. Case Study on the UN Transitional Administration in Eastern Slavonia, Baranja, and Western Sirmium

The first case study reconstructs and analyzes the post-conflict transition in Eastern Slavonia. From 1996 through 1998, the international community invested a great deal in a comprehensive transitional administration that was supposed to reintegrate the Serb-occupied territory into Croatia.

During the Balkan Wars from 1991 to 1995, Serbia occupied the former Croat regions of Eastern Slavonia, the Baranja, and Western Sirmium. Having witnessed extremely brutal battles, murder, rapes, and lootings, the fighting in Eastern Slavonia were amongst the most gruesome of the conflict between the two ethnicities. Only when the international community got involved, under the leadership of the United States, did the conflict move towards a settlement. A peace agreement for the region was settled in 1995 during the Dayton process. Yet, despite its high interest in the peaceful reintegration of the region into Croatia, the United States did not want to run another consummate peace operation and thus requested the UN to operate a comprehensive stabilization and reconstruction mission. Under the so-called "Basic Agreement," the UN was given the responsibility of deploying a transitional administration in order to reintegrate Eastern Slavonia into Croatia, reconciling differences within a multiethnic society.

The Basic Agreement required the Security Council to set-up a transitional administration to govern the region for a period of two years. UNTAES was deployed in January 1996. This was only five months after the massacre of 8,000 Bosnians by the Serbian military, police, and paramilitary troops in Srebrenica – when 400 armed Dutch peacekeepers were present but did not intervene, representing one of the most horrifying disasters in the history of UN peacekeeping.[228] This constellation had bleak implications: not only was there enormous pressure for the UN to succeed, as another failure might have marked the end of UN peace operations once and for all, but also because Eastern Slavonia was a likely candidate for failure as war crimes, perpetrated by both parties to the conflict, furthered extremely high levels of hostility. Besides, the infrastructure was destroyed and the local economy was hitting rock bottom. In this situation, UNTAES was supposed to build joint Croat-Serb institutions – an almost impossible thing to do. Being aware of these ill-structured conditions, the international community and the United States in particular provided comprehensive political and financial support for UNTAES. The prominent interest of the United States to have a success story was reflected in the

---

228 For a detailed chronology of the events, see Blom, Hans J.C. and Romijn, P. 2002. *Reconstruction, Background, Consequences and Analyzes of the Fall of a Safe Area.* Amsterdam: Netherlands Institute for War Documentation.

staffing of the position of the SRSG with an American air force general and career diplomat.

Still, the ill-structured conditions triggered pathological obstacles for the mission. The local population played waiting games and boycotted the mission; UNTAES struggled with the often conflicting but tightly coupled imperatives of the mandate, as well as with regulations that impeded their mission, and it experienced friction with cooperation partners. At the end of the day, UNTAES was able to cope successfully with most of the emerging pathologies by tough negotiations. In particular, it established itself as the agenda-setter vis-à-vis both local obstructers and New York headquarters, not shying away from changing course, and applying a generally proactive course. According to my interviewees, an outstanding factor of the mission's proactiveness and ultimate success was the SRSG and his leadership style.

1. Background

The territory of the former Yugoslavia has been a highly instable region for centuries. During the last 100 years, the rivalry between Serbs and Croats represented one of its greatest conflicts. Following the death of Josip Tito in 1980 and of collapse of the Communist system in 1989, conflicts between the different ethnicities in the former Yugoslavia increased and culminated in a war fuelled by hatred. Tens of thousands of people were killed, men tortured, women raped, houses burnt, and livelihoods destroyed for years to come.

1.1 History of the Region

Today, the territory then known as Eastern Slavonia, the Baranja, and Western Sirmium[229] is the easternmost Croatian *županije* (county) of Vukovar-Syrmia and Osiek-Baranja, with the main cities being Vukovar, Beli Manastir, and Vinkovci.[230] It comprises a total area of 3,400 square kilometres and its Western boundary is identical to the 1992 ceasefire line, when fighting in the area between the Croats and the Serbs came to a halt.

In the former Yugoslavia, the region was one of the wealthiest in the country. Called the "granary of Croatia," it also disposed over large manufacturing and

---

229 As choosing the Croat or the Serb names for the regions would have been perceived as partisan, the UN decided to use the Latin version of the name.

230 Croatia consists of 22 counties. The Baranja is located between the Drava and Danube rivers, Eastern Slavonia and Western Sirmium south of the Drava. In the following, Eastern Slavonia, Baranja and Western Sirmium will be referenced by the term "Eastern Slavonia".

industrial sites and oilfields.[231] After the war, the economy of the region was in crisis, and at the time UNTAES came in, unemployment rates were extremely high.[232]

Prior to the war, nearly 200,000 people inhabited the region, with Croats making up about 45 percent of the population, Serbs around 25 percent, and Hungarians, Slovaks, Ruthenians, and others accounting for the remaining 21 percent.[233] Population estimates for 1995, after cessation of the hostilities, range from 150,000 to 175,000 people spread across a core of urban settlements and about 100 villages. At this point in time, the Serbs accounted for about 85 percent of the population, and the Croat share diminished to only eight percent.[234]

---

231 Contrary to other socialist states, a significant amount of the land was privately owned.
232 "Croatia's cross national product for 1994 was estimated to be about US$2,000 per capacity. Industrial production dropped since 1991 by at least 40 percent. Triple-digit inflation levels in the years immediately following the conflict have stabilized since 1994. Traditional procurement sources and markets for Croatian goods in the former Yugoslavia have been disrupted by the war in the Region. Tourism, a key sector of the economy, has witnessed deep decline since fighting began in the area. The official unemployment rate has hovered around 17 percent. An active stabilization program has been instituted through the introduction of restrictive financial and income policies, structural adjustment and rationalization of the tax structure. However, microeconomic restructuring initiated three ears ago [1992; ES] with passage of the Law on Transformation of the Croatian Economy and Establishment of a Privatization Fund, has been slow." United Nations Task Force to Establish the Transitional Administration in Sector East. 1995. *Background Report on the Region of Eastern Slavonia, Baranja and Western Sirmium* Zagreb, December 1995, para. 16. The report is on file with the author. In the remainder of this study, I will refer to the report as "UN Task Force 1995."
233 Government of the Republic of Croatia, "Report of the Republic of Croatia on the Implementation of the Framework Convention for the Protection of National Minorities, pursuant to Article 25, paragraph 1 of the Framework Convention for the Protection of National Minorities of the Council of Europe, COE Doc. ACFC/SR(1999)005, received on 16 March 1999," pp. 5-11. The report quotes the 1991 census of the State Bureau of Statistics as well as the Department for Analysis of Office for Displaced Persons and Refugees, and is available online at
    http://www.coe.int/t/e/human_rights/minorities/2._framework_convention_(monitoring)/
    2._monitoring_mechanism/3._state_reports_and_unmik_kosovo_report/1._first_cycle/PD
    F_1st_SR_Croatia_en.pdf#xml=http://www.search.coe.int/texis/search/pdfhi.txt?query=fr
    amework+convention+state+report+croatia+1999&pr=Internet_D2&prox=page&order=
    500&rprox=750&rdfreq=500&rwfreq=500&rlead=500&rdepth=250&sufs=1&order=r&
    mode=&opts=&cq=&sr=&id=484a78ab1d, last access on December 1, 2008.
234 Cf. UN Task Force 1995, para. 10. "Half of the Serb population have been living in Eastern Slavonia since prior to the war; the other half comprises Serbs displaced from the Krajina and other areas formerly controlled by Serbs." Human Rights Watch. 1997. *Croatia*. Available online at http://www.hrw.org/reports/1997/croatia/Croatia-02.htm#P134_26389, last access on 29 January 2009. All of these figures are, however, approximate numbers since the enormous and complex streams of refugees makes them hard to estimate. Cf. Government of the Republic of Croatia, "Report of the Republic of Croatia on the Implementation of the Framework Convention for the Protection of National Minorities." There is no accurate data available for the total number of people in Eastern Slavonia or for the number of original residents who remained in Eastern Slavonia. The Croatian government estimates

The sharp distinction between ethnicities, population groups, and nationalities today appears to be less ambiguous than is justified. For centuries, the Balkans has seen more migration – voluntary and forced – of diverse population groups, it has seen empires rise and fall, boundaries change, and minorities and majorities alternate across regions, than hardly any other region in the world.[235] The course of the development of the Croat nation, as well as that of the Serb, was determined between 800 and 1600. Around 800, Frankish Emperor Charlemagne conquered large parts of what today constitutes Croatia, incorporating it into the Western Empire,[236] while the major portion of today's Serbia remained with the Eastern Empire, delimited by the river Drina.[237] Croatia's first formal appearance in the annals was in the tenth century, when King Tomislav united the regions of central Croatia, Slavonia, and parts of Dalmatia and Bosnia into the Kingdom of Croatia.[238] The first Serbian state was founded in 1166 – and was absorbed into the Ottoman Empire after the defeat in the Battle of Kosovo in 1389.[239] In 1526, the Ottomans extended their rule in the Balkans, inducing a new territorial split: the eastern territories became Ottoman, while Croatia and Hungary were aligned with the Hapsburg Em-

that there are 88,000 ethnic Serbs in Eastern Slavonia. Government of Croatia, "Foreign Ministry Statement on the Documents Program in the Danubian Region and on the Status of Serbs and Other Minorities in Croatia," Zagreb, 6 February 1997. Others suggest considerably higher numbers for the current population of Serbs in Eastern Slavonia. See, e.g., Randal, Jonathan. 1997. "Last Serb Outpost in Croatia Is Sceptical Reintegration Will Succeed," *Washington Post*, 11 February 1997. 120,000 Serbs currently live in Eastern Slavonia, of which half are displaced.

235 For instance, Thracians around 2000 BC, Illyrians around 800 BC, Greeks around 700 BC, Romans in 34 BC, Huns 375 AD, Avars around 500 AD, Slaws around 600 AD– just to name the most crucial- all left their mark, which was constantly changing. Cf. Domini, Mirjana. 2000. "National Minorities in the Republic of Croatia." *Central Europe Review* 2:19. Available online at http://www.ce-review.org/00/19/domini19.html, last access on 15 March 2009, "Natural-geographic, economic, traffic and ethnic entities (units, totalities) were criss-crossed with boundaries while the parts of nations have become minorities in the established territory/state communities." For a detailed overview, see Ćirković, Sima. 1999. "Zur Ethnogenese auf dem Gebiet des ehemaligen Jugoslawien." In: Dunja Melcic, ed., *Der Jugoslawien-Krieg: Handbuch zu Vorgeschichte, Verlauf und Konsequenzen*. Opladen: Westdeutscher Verlag, pp. 14-27.

236 The Slovenes lost against the Franks in 748 and became Christianized, as were the Croats. Cf. Magas, Braka. 2007. *Croatia through History. The Making of a European State*. London: Saqi Books.

237 Cf., e.g. Pavlowitch, Stefan K. 2002. *Serbia: The History behind the Name*. London: Hurst.

238 "This new state prospered for nearly 100 years, but it was not a strong state. Croatia had no central city as a center of gravity for ecclesiastical and secular power. Consequently, Croatia fell prey to the expansionism of Venice and Hungary, [...]. However, independence was later restored to Croatia under the rule of King Krešimir IV (r. 1058-1074) and Croatia enjoyed another brief period of prosperity. Over these two centuries Croatia, for the most part, existed as an independent state and it is from this experience that all future aspirations for Croatian independence emanated." Coleiro 2002, p. 51.

239 Cf., e.g., Mazower, Mark. 2000. *The Balkans. A Short History*. London: Random House.

pire.[240] In the following years, the Hapsburgs built a large military frontier called *Krajina*. The region was primarily inhabited by Serbs who were granted settlement rights in the territory under the condition that they defend it.

Croatia was part of the Hapsburg Empire and the subsequent Austro-Hungarian Kingdom unto the latter's collapse in 1918.[241] That very year, Croatia proclaimed its independence, joining a union with Montenegro, Slovenia, and Serbia, which had become independent in 1878 following the Ottoman defeat in the Russo-Turkish war. Together, they formed the Kingdom of Serbs, Croats, and Slovenes. This development was also the logical endpoint of the longstanding desire of the Balkan peoples to self-determination: riding the waves of the nationalist currents all over Europe, the movement of the so-called *Illyrism*, which strived for a pan-Slavic state, gained momentum. However, the newly found Kingdom could not live up to the intricate task of balancing the manifold nationalist interests. Eventually, the hegemonic claims of Serbia prevailed within the kingdom.

The dominance of Serbia increased over the years. As a result, nationalist tensions resurfaced sharper than ever: The 1920s and 1930s witnessed killings of major leadership figures on both sides. The nationalist rivalry weakens the state and makes it eventually easy prey to Axis occupation in 1941. During the occupation, a pro-fascist Croatian terrorist movement emerged. Being in close ranks with the Axis, the so-called *ustaše* movement declared the Independent State of Croatia (NDH). "[T]his regime committed genocide against Jews, Serbs, Gypsies, and Croatian antifascists who lived in Croatia and Bosnia and Herzegovina, which became a part of the new Croatian state under the patronage of Germany." [242] In retaliation, the Serbs in the NDH soon formed two (antagonistic) groups:

> One part joined Dragoljub Mihailovic and his pro-monarchist forces (commonly known as the *cetniks*), while the other fought on the side of the communist-led partisans, commanded by the Croat Josip Broz Tito. Tito's army consisted of Serbs, Croats, Muslims, and other ethnic groups. During the war, the *cetniks* committed ethnic cleansing and massacres in Bosnia and Herzegovina against the Muslims, while in Dalmatia they terrorized the Croat population. Yugoslavia's Muslims were also divided between those who supported the *ustaše* and those who fought on the side of the multiethnic partisans. The unsolved national question that had preoccupied the interwar Kingdom of Yu-

---

240 In 1102, the *Pacta Conventa* ("Agreed Accords") between the Croatian nobility and King Coloman of Hungary, disputed then and now, brought Croatia under the personal reign of the Hungarian king.

241 Solely Croats in Herzegovina remained under Ottoman rule, until 1878.

242 Center for History, Democracy and Reconciliation (CHDR). 2008. *The Shared History and the Second World War and National Question in ex Yugoslavia*. International conference, Tres Culturas Foundation, Seville (Spain), 31 January-2 February 2008. Available online at http://www.centerforhistory.net/index.php?option=com_content&task=view&id=22&Itemid=49, last access on 30 January 2009.

goslavia erupted into full-scale civil war and ethnic cleansing during the Second World War.[243]

After the war had ended, the Tito partisans were able to get the upper hand and took control of Yugoslavia.[244]

Tito's Yugoslavia

For more than thirty years, Tito was able to contain the explosive tensions among the different Yugoslav peoples. Under his rule, ethnic nationalism was suppressed and the Socialist Federal Republic of Yugoslavia (SFRY)[245] promoted a joint Yugoslavian vision, while the constitution formally recognized six main peoples: Croats, Slovenes, Serbs,[246] Bosnians, Montenegrins, and Macedons. The Serbs in the Krajina-territories continued to live on Croat soil though.

Despite ongoing containment efforts, the strife for national self-determination and an argument about which form of government should be used remained a constant issue. After Tito's death in 1980, the authority of the state began to wane, tensions in the multiethnic state increased and economic failures of the old system became virulent. Socialism as a major integrating factor lost its appeal.[247]

> At the end of the 1980s, the disintegration of the communist system resurrected the ghosts of World War Two and opened a Pandora's Box of competing historical narratives and revisionism. Rekindled hatreds and fears, most related to the trauma of World War Two, were spread by nationalist politicians who sought to occupy the vacuum created by the collapse of communism, which played a leading role in Yugoslavia's violent destruction in the 1990s.[248]

These developments culminated in the advance of nationalist-separatist movements and parties in the six Yugoslav republics, particularly in Croatia, Slavonia, and Bosnia Herzegovina. Starting in 1991, the secession of Croatia and Slovenia trig-

---

243 Ibid.
244 At the end of World War Two, the Tito partisans committed crimes against Croats, Serbs, and Muslims who had allegedly collaborated with the Axis occupiers. Ibid.
245 The People's Republic of Yugoslavia, founded in 1946, was renamed in 1963 to include a socialist supplement.
246 "Tito also shrewdly recognized the threat to Yugoslavian unity posed by a strong Serbia, the largest of the country's republics. When piecing together post-World War Two Yugoslavia, Tito deliberately divided Serbia into two non-contiguous provinces – Vojvodina in the north and Kosovo in the south – to reduce the republic's power. The resulting gerrymandering left one-third of the Serbian population outside their own province and an Albanian majority firmly in place." CNN, "Biography of Slobodan Milosevic." Available online at http://www.cnn.com/resources/newsmakers/world/europe/milosevic.html, last access on 30 January 2009.
247 "[T]he fall of the USSR weakened the glue that had held together the diverse, mutually antagonistic ethnic groups of the former Soviet bloc." Ibid.
248 CHDR 2008.

gered the Yugoslav Wars and marked the disintegration of the SFRY.[249] The complex historic sequences, which I have sketched merely superficially, provided both Serbs and Croats with sufficient latitude of interpretation to construct their own national pasts – so as to justify war and atrocities against one another.[250]

1.2 Nationalist Tensions and Conflict Leading to UN Intervention

When Josip Tito – the key integration figure – died, the tensions that had been contained for decades gained ground, eventually materializing in full-scaled civil war. Some of the cruellest battles occurred between the Serbs, under Slobodan Milosevic, and the Croats, led by Franjo Tudjman.

After Tito's death, the persistent feelings of nationalism, religious differences, and ethnicity were *instrumentalized* by the warmongers, multiplying the dissonances for the profane purposes of power.[251] In Croatia, the newly founded radical-nationalist party *Hrvatska Demokratska Zajednica* (Croatian Democratic Union, HDZ) won the parliamentary election in April 1999. On 30 May 1990,[252] its leader Tudjman became President of Croatia and soon declared the independence of the Republic of Croatia. In early January 1991, he started to organize the Croatian National Army. In Serbia, the desire for a reunified homeland resurged after the collapse of multiethnic Yugoslavia, and a nationalistic movement emerged. Its populist politician Milosevic knew how to ride this wave.[253] Having been the leader

---

249 The successive "Federal Republic of Yugoslavia" was a federation in the territory of the two remaining republics of Serbia (including the autonomous provinces of Vojvodina, Kosovo and Metohija) and Montenegro, founded in April 1992. As of February 2003, the entity was transformed into the "Union of Serbia and Montenegro" and the name "Yugoslavia" was officially abolished. In June 2006, Montenegro and Serbia respectively declared their independence. The last remnants of the former Yugoslav federation thus ultimately evaporated. Chandler, David. 2000. "Western Intervention and the Disintegration of Yugoslavia: 1989-1999." In: Philip Hammond and Edward S. Herman, eds., *Degraded Capability: the Media and the Kosovo Crisis*. London: Pluto Press, pp. 15-30.

250 Cf. Ćirković 1999. See also Todorova, Maria. *Balkan Identities. Nation and Memory*. New York: NYU Press.

251 The following paragraphs focus on the developments in Croatia and Serbia.

252 Baumgartner and Baumgartner describe this day as key in the conflict to come. Baumgartner, Ilse and Baumgartner, Wolfgang. 1997. *Der Balkan-Krieg der 90er: Fakten, Hintergründe, Analysen, Zukunftsperspektiven*. Berlin: Verlag für Wissenschaft und Forschung.

253 „Milosevic was a minor political figure in 1987 when an incident occurred that thrust him into prominence. On 24 April, Milosevic was summoned to help calm a riotous crowd of Serbs outside the town hall in Kosovo Polje. The Serbs claimed to have been mistreated by the Albanian majority and barred from entering the town hall by baton-wielding police. Milosevic silenced the Serbian crowd, telling them, 'No one will ever beat you again,' and invited them into the hall to voice their grievances to the Communist party delegates. Afterward, Milosevic shaped the issues of alleged Albanian mistreatment of Serbs and a widespread sense of economic deprivation into concrete political goals. In 1989, he inspired

of the Serbian Communist Party since 1987, Milosevic became the elected President of the Republic of Serbia in December 1990, dominating the central government of transitioning Yugoslavia.

Claiming to be the legitimate heir of the Yugoslav Republic and motivated by increasing nationalism, Serbia strived for hegemonic power, occupying more and more territories that were formally Croat-controlled. Supported by atrocities committed by paramilitary groups, Serbia eventually seized the strategically important Eastern Slavonian region, including Vukovar, the capital.

When Croatia and Slovenia declared independence from the SFRY in the spring of 1991, the Serbian-led government in Belgrade decided to use military force to keep the country together – under Serbian leadership.[254] At the end of June, rebel Serb forces, supported by the JNA, the army of the former Yugoslav Republic, began major military offensives in the Krajina, the Croat territories with Serb majorities or strong minorities.[255] At that time, Serbia became motivated massively by nationalism and declared the "Serb War" with the goal of establishing a "Greater Serbia," striving to make the Krajina territories a single associated state. The *"Republika Srpska Krajina,"* self-proclaimed in 1991, included the "Serbian Autonomous Oblast of Krajina," an extensive territorial strip along the border of Bosnia and Herzegovina of Croatia, and the "Serbian Autonomous Oblast of Eastern Slavonia, Baranja and Western Srem." For Serbia, the region was of high strategic importance, providing it with a buffer zone in the event of a Croatian attack. Plus, the territory was wealthier than the average in Yugoslavia. The capture proceeded cruelly: the Croat population was systematically expelled or killed, their possessions looted or burnt.[256]

Nichts sollte mehr an jene erinnern, die noch vor wenigen Wochen hier gelebt hatten. Dieser im 'Namen der Nation' durchgeführte Vernichtungsfeldzug ging in seiner Radikalität weit über 'kriegerische' Ziele hinaus. Systematisch und durchaus von oben

violent Serbian demonstrations that drove the constitutionally elected leaders of both Vojvodina and Kosovo out of office. Milosevic had begun building a Greater Serbia." CNN, "Biography of Slobodan Milosevic."

254 Immediately before the declaration, the first armed clashes between Croats and Serbs occurred among their respective police corps!

255 "Die Serben in Kroatien begründen ihren Krieg mit dem Ziel mit militärischen Mitteln vollzogener Abspaltung von Kroatien und später mögliche Integration ihres Gebietes ins serbische (großserbische) Mutterland mit der Unabhängigkeitserklärung Kroatiens. Es sei ihnen nicht möglich, in einem unabhängigen, von Tudjman geführten Kroatien die Rechte der serbischen Minderheit zu leben, da zu befürchten sei, daß dieses Kroatien die Rechte der serbischen Minderheit massiv verletzen würde, und es gelang der Krajina Serben, zumindest vorläufig, sich die volle politische und militärische Unterstützung der Volksgemeinschaft im serbischen Mutterland zu sichern." Baumgartner and Baumgartner 1997, p. 71.

256 Cf. Rathfelder, Erich. 1999. "Der Krieg an seinen Schauplätzen." In: Dunja Melcic, ed., *Der Jugoslawien-Krieg: Handbuch zu Vorgeschichte, Verlauf und Konsequenzen.* Opladen: Westdeutscher Verlag, pp. 345-363, 350.

gewollt wurden rechtsfreie Räume geschaffen, in denen sich die durch nationalistische Phrasen aufgestachelte Kriminellen austoben konnte.[257]

These legal vacuums were seized by a multitude of paramilitary groups. Representing a repository for criminals and waifs of all kinds, and led by notorious warmongers, they proceeded with outmost brutality. There were the "Scorpions" and the "Jumping Snakes", and the "Tigers," under the command of local gangster Zeljko Raznjatovic, also known as Arkan.[258] There were the "White Eagles," under the command of Mirko Jovic,[259] and the "*Cetnics*," led by Vojislav Seselj, a Serb ultranationalist who was eventually prosecuted at the UN International Criminal Tribunal for the former Yugoslavia (ICTY) at the Hague.[260]

The violence mounted in the siege of Vukovar. The main city in the region was nearly destroyed between 27 August and 18 November 1991 by arguably the most brutal battle of the Balkans war.[261] During the atrocities, about 4,700 people of a former population of 44,369 inhabitants were killed: approximately 1,700 Croatians and 3,000 Serbs. 2,097 Croatians and 7,200 Serbs were wounded, and 100 Serbs and 3,000 Croats were still missing at the time UNTAES was deployed.[262] As the Croatian army was nearly non-existent at the time of the surge, the city was largely abandoned to its fate.

In the following years, Tudjman was able to set up a powerful national army and in 1995 succeeded in a counter strike. In May and August 1995, Croatia – in op-

---

257 Rathfelder 1999, p. 350. "Am 2. August wurde in Dalj ein Massaker an Kroaten verübt (80 Tote, Mönnesland). Aber auch auf der kroatischen Seite kam es später zu Übergriffen und willkürlicher Ermordung serbischer Zivilisten, so in Gospić (Lika) und in West- und Ostslawonien." Ibid.

258 Their "manning level" varied between 50 and 1000 men.

259 In 2004, Jovic became a candidate in the Serbian Presidential election, calling for "a Christian, Orthodox Serbia with no Muslims and no unbelievers." Velikonja, Mitja. 2003. *Religious Separation and Political Intolerance in Bosnia-Herzegovina*. College Station: Texas A&M Press, p. 268.

260 "Prozess gegen Serben-Führer Seselj eröffnet." *Sueddeutsche Zeitung*, 7 November 2007. Available online at http://www.sueddeutsche.de/ausland/artikel/934/141627/, last access on 30 January 2008. On the militia groups see, e.g., Coleiro 2002; Tanner, Marcus. 1997. *Croatia – A Nation Forged in War*. New Haven: Yale University Press.

261 "Im November spitzte sich der Kampf um Vukovar zu. Frische Truppen aus Serbien bei gleichzeitiger Reorganisation der Kommandostruktur, der Einsatz von Artillerie, die große Teile der Stadt dem Erdboden gleichmachte, führte schließlich zum Sieg der Serben in diesem ungleichen Kampf. Die serbischen Freischärler – Seselj-Tschetniks und Arkan-Truppen – zogen am 18. November zusammen mit den reguläre Einheiten in die völlig zerstörte Stadt ein. Der von dem amerikanischen Nachrichtensender CNN aufgenommene Marsch der Serben mit dem Lied 'Wir schlachten die Kroaten ab' schockierte die Öffentlichkeit der Welt. Nach dem Massaker an mindestens 261 Patienten des Krankenhauses von Vukovar (Ovcara), der Verhaftung und Internierung von Tausenden, der Ungewissheit über deren Schicksal ging ein Ruck durch die Bevölkerung." Rathfelder 1999, pp. 350-351.

262 The numbers are taken from a power point presentation ("UNTAES") about the state of the mission by SRSG Klein. The presentation is on file with the author. In the remainder of this study, I will refer to the presentation as Klein, "UNTAES".

erations "Flash" and "Storm" – recaptured large parts of the Serb-occupied territories in the Krajina, with Eastern Slavonia and its associated regions remaining
the last Serbian stronghold on former Croatian territory. In the months that followed, several thousand Serb refugees fled eastwards from the Krajina and Western
Slavonia.

1.3 Summary and Assessment

The social climate throughout the disbanding SFRY was characterized by deeply-
rooted conflict.[263] Additionally, opportune warmongers fuelled the hatred and the
ongoing military and paramilitary occupation of the burnt and looted territory rendered the common populace in constant fear of attack: at this time the *Armija Re-
publica Srpska Krajina*, the Slavonia Baranja Corps, the Serbian *milicija*, and
paramilitary groups[264] remained active in Eastern Slavonia. As the UN stated,
"There is, in this Serb-controlled area, [...] an element of lawlessness [...]."[265] On
the Croatian side, as well, the HDZ and the police were "very difficult to co-operate
with,"[266] striving to reduce the number of Serbs in Eastern Slavonia from pre-war
14 percent to post-war five percent of the population. The Report of the Secretary-
General points out that "the Croatian Government has, in the recent past repeatedly
stated its preparedness to embark on military action to achieve the reintegration of
the territory."[267]

Croats were traumatized by Serbian atrocities and many of the Serbs who ended
up in the region were destitute refugees.[268] In fact, the various streams of refugees
complicated the settlement of hostilities: everywhere throughout the Balkans, people were either still on the run, or they desired to return to a home that meanwhile
had been occupied by other families.[269] "It is estimated that 80,000 Croats were
displaced from Serb-controlled areas during the war and approximately that number of Serbs took their place in the Region. Of the 70,000 Serbs who went to Sector

---

263 Cf. UN Secretary General, "Report of the Secretary General on Croatia pursuant to Security
     Council Resolution 1025," UN Doc. S/1995/1028, 13 December 1995, para. 4, "After four
     years of hostilities and prolonged tension, deep-rooted mistrust prevails and each party
     perceives the other to have broken agreements and committed acts of aggression.".
264 The composition of the "Arkan Tigers" varied between 300 and 1000 men, the "Scorpions"
     comprised of 200-250 men, and the "Jumping Snakes" were the smallest group with
     around 50-60 men.
265 UN Doc. S/1995/1028, para. 4.
266 Interview with Dr. Gerard Fischer, Head of Civil Affairs, UNTAES, New York, 21 Novem-
     ber 2006.
267 UN Doc. S/1995/1028, para. 4.
268 "Eastern Slavonia was the scene of heavy fighting, particularly around the urban centres of
     Vukovar, Vinkovci, and Osijek." UN Task Force 1995, para. 9.
269 Cf. Coleiro 2002, p. 68.

East after 1991, 5,000 [were] refugees from Bosnia, 50,000 displaced persons from Western Slavonia and 15,000 from the Krajina."[270] Accordingly, massive population movements were expected to continue throughout the transition period, representing "enormous problems of housing, property compensation, economic reconstruction, and rehabilitation in an environment in which reconciliation and confidence building will need to be fostered at every level."[271]

Another aspect of the significant refugee problem was the "brain drain:" those who had the possibility to flee from the region into Western Europe did so. These people were, however, those that were the most capable and hence the most needed ones in helping to re-build the region.

2. Negotiations, Mandate, and Planning for the Transitional Administration

Determined not to repeat the UN Protection Force in Bosnia's dreadful failure, the international community pushed the parties to the conflict towards a clear peace settlement and endowed UNTAES with consummate executive authority under Chapter VII of the UN Charter. The Security Councilalso provided the mission with sufficient financial means. However, on the other hand, the mandate suffered from typical vague language, leaving the mission's leadership to cope with ambiguity. Likewise typical were problems that occurred in the staffing of the civilian parts of the mission, where no proper recruitment process was in place, and in the financing of the peacebuilding parts of the mission. All of these problems effected delays in the implementation of the mandate, whose deadline had been calculated tightly.

2.1 UN Engagement in the Balkans Prior to 1996

The UN had been active in the area for several years. Following unsuccessful European appeasement attempts, the UN involvement in the Balkan conflict began in September 1991 when the Security Council imposed an arms embargo on Yugoslavia.[272] The international involvement intensified with the deployment of the UN Protection Force (UNPROFOR). UNPROFOR, however, was a major failure and was eventually replaced by the UN Confidence Restoration Operation for Croatia (UNCRO).

---

270 UN Task Force 1995, para. 3.
271 UN Doc. S/1995/1028, para. 6.
272 "Yugoslavia" denotes the former Socialist Federal Republic of Yugoslavia and its republics. The embargo was fixed in UN resolution 714. UN Security Council, "Resolution on the Socialist Federal Republic of Yugoslavia." UN Doc. S/1991/713, 25 September 1991.

As the conflict broke out on a massive scale in late 1991, the Council decided to establish the UNPROFOR peacekeeping mission.[273] It was responsible for three demilitarized "safe-haven" areas, one of them roughly denoting the region of Eastern Slavonia, Baranja, and Western Sirmium ("UNPROFOR Sector East").[274] In March 1995, however, the largely unsuccessful UNPROFOR was replaced. "Sector East" was taken over by UNCRO.[275] Based on Security Council resolution 990, "It

273 Cf. UN Security Council, "Resolution on the Socialist Federal Republic of Yugoslavia," UN Doc. S/1992/743, 21 February 1992. "Initially established in Croatia as an interim arrangement to create the conditions of peace and security required for the negotiation of an overall settlement of the Yugoslav crisis, UNPROFOR's mandate was to ensure that the three 'United Nations Protected Areas' (UNPAs) in Croatia were demilitarized and that all persons residing in them were protected from fear of armed attack." UN Department of Peacekeeping Operations. 1996. *United Nations Protection Force: Profile*. Available online at http://www.un.org/Depts/dpko/dpko/co_mission/unprof_p.htm, last access on 30 January 2009. "In the course of 1992, UNPROFOR's mandate was enlarged to include monitoring functions in certain other areas of Croatia ('pink zones'); to enable the Force to control the entry of civilians into the UNPAs and to perform immigration and customs functions at the UNPA borders at international frontiers; and to include monitoring of the demilitarization of the Prevlaka Peninsula and to ensure control of the Peruca dam, situated in one of the 'pink zones.' In addition, UNPROFOR monitored implementation of a cease-fire agreement signed by the Croatian Government and local Serb authorities in March 1994 following a flare-up of fighting in January and September 1993. In June 1992, as the conflict intensified and extended into Bosnia and Herzegovina, UNPROFOR's mandate and strength were enlarged in order to ensure the security and functioning of the airport at Sarajevo, and the delivery of humanitarian assistance to that city and its environs. In September 1992, UN-PROFOR's mandate was further enlarged to enable it to support efforts by the United Nations High Commissioner for Refugees to deliver humanitarian relief throughout Bosnia and Herzegovina, and to protect convoys of released civilian detainees if the International Committee of the Red Cross so requested. In addition, the Force monitored the 'no-fly 'zone, banning all military flights in Bosnia and Herzegovina, and the United Nations 'safe areas' established by the Security Council around five Bosnian towns and the city of Sarajevo. UNPROFOR was authorized to use force in self-defense in reply to attacks against these areas, and to coordinate with the North Atlantic Treaty Organization (NATO) the use of air power in support of its activities. Similar arrangements were subsequently extended to the territory of Croatia. UNPROFOR also monitored the implementation of a cease-fire agreement signed by the Bosnian Government and Bosnian Croat forces in February 1994. In addition, UNPROFOR monitored cease-fire arrangements negotiated between Bosnian Government and Bosnian Serbs forces, which entered into force on 1 January 1995. In December 1992, UNPROFOR was also deployed in the former Yugoslav Republic of Macedonia, to monitor and report any developments in its border areas which could undermine confidence and stability in that Republic and threaten its territory." Ibid.
274 In specific, the "Sector East" comprised of the municipalities (opstine) of Beli Manastir, Vukovar, parts of Osijek (east of Osijek city), plus certain villages in the far Eastern part of Vinkovci. "On the Croatian side of the confrontation line, towns and zupanjas (counties) of Osijek and Vinkovci (in absentia of Vukovar) are centres of governance." UN Task Force 1995, para. 4.
275 The other operative areas of UNPROFOR were taken over by the United Nations Preventive Deployment Force (UNPREDEP), being responsible for the former Yugoslav Republic of Macedonia (FYROM), and a downscaled UNPROFOR mission that was now restricted to Bosnia and Herzegovina. They operated under the single command of the UNPF. "Observers were also stationed in the Prevlaka peninsula. The new mandate included: (a) performing the functions envisaged in the cease-fire agreement of 29 March 1994; (b) facili-

was decided that UNCRO should be an interim arrangement to create the conditions that would facilitate a negotiated settlement consistent with the territorial integrity of Croatia and which would guarantee the security and rights of all communities living in Croatia."[276] A few months later, however, Croatia's military operations Flash and Storm effectively brought about the reintegration of Western Slavonia and the Krajina region and thus "eliminated the need for United Nations troops in those areas and their withdrawal was initiated."[277] The last territory with an unresolved status was Eastern Slavonia,[278] which was still controlled by the remaining *Republika Srpska Krajina* (RSK) administration. Under increasing international and particularly US pressure, "The Government of Croatia and the Croatian Serb leadership agreed to resolve the issue of Eastern Slavonia through negotiation."[279]

2.2 Negotiations to Reach the Erdut Agreement

The distribution of power between Serbs and Croats shifted, and the US' strong interest in the settlement of the Balkan Wars was the fundamental political parameter for the negotiation of the peace agreement. The Basic Agreement, also known as the Erdut Agreement, was a rather concise document, where both parties consented to the reintegration of a multiethnic Eastern Slavonia into Croatia. That said, it remained ambiguous on some crucial issues, such as the transitional administration's concrete competences.

Local and International Dynamics

After the successful Croat military operations Flash and Storm, the strategic landscape in the region changed dramatically: Tudjman was now in a very powerful

tating implementation of the economic agreement of 2 December 1994; (c) facilitating implementation of all relevant Security Council resolutions; (d) assisting in controlling, by monitoring and reporting, the crossing of military personnel, equipment, supplies and weapons, over the international borders between Croatia and Bosnia and Herzegovina, and Croatia and the Federal Republic of Yugoslavia (Serbia and Montenegro) at the border crossings; (e) facilitating the delivery of international humanitarian assistance to Bosnia and Herzegovina through the territory of Croatia; and (f) monitoring the demilitarization of the Prevlaka peninsula." UN Department of Peacekeeping Operations, "Croatia: United Nations Confidence Restoration Operation." Available online at http://www.un.org/Depts/dpko/dpko/co_mission/uncro.htm, last access on 30 January 2009.
276 Ibid.
277 Ibid.
278 For this region, the mandate of UNCRO remained essentially unchanged.
279 Ibid.

position. On strategic grounds, Milosevic eventually made the crucial decision to give up Eastern Slavonia.

> Tudjman was in a position to play the prima donna, but instead he made it clear that he had only one non-negotiable objective in these talks – the reintegration of Eastern Slavonia. [...] There was never any ambiguity in Tudjman's message, there could be no peace agreement without agreement on Eastern Slavonia, and if Eastern Slavonia could not be returned to Croatia peacefully, then he would conquer it. However, [...] Eastern Slavonia was on the Serbian border making a military victory less predictable than Tudjman would have liked.[280]

On the Serb side, Milosevic initially wanted a UN mission to protect the pro-Serbian status quo in the region. However, with a Croatian military attack on the horizon and thus a potential change in the status quo, he changed his strategy and asked for two things, which would allow him to keep looking strong. "First, Milosevic did not want the reintegration of Eastern Slavonia to result in a mass exodus of Serbs. That would have been a sure sign of his failure to protect Serb interest in the Balkans;"[281] after his reluctance to counter-strike Flash and Storm, this issue immediately affected his political survival. Secondly, he asked that he not be linked to the agreement, "In fact, Milosevic initially insisted that he could not negotiate Eastern Slavonia because it was an issue for the local Serbs."[282]

On the international scene, there was a consensus that quick and comprehensive action was needed to resolve the issue of Eastern Slavonia without further bloodshed. The United States were the driving force for action. At the same time, however, Washington was reluctant to deploy its soldiers in Eastern Slavonia. No country really wanted to shoulder the lion's share of the burden for the resolution of the situation.

> After the two major attacks on Serb-held positions in Croatia, and the subsequent expulsion of the Serb minority, international observers in general and the United States in particular did not want to risk a third offensive that might spark an all-out war between Croatia and Serbia. In addition, 'The international community did not wish to see a resumption of conflict in Eastern Slavonia just at the time when the Dayton Peace Agreement was able to bring war to an end in Bosnia' (Boothby 1998, p. 11). Viewed in this larger context, there was considerable momentum on all levels to reach a peace agreement. It is necessary to note, however, that foreign countries, and especially the United States, viewed Eastern Slavonia and its problems as merely peripheral to the more important peace process in Bosnia.[283]

The original plan for Eastern Slavonia was to be "a joint Russian-American cooperative effort: they would come in, stabilize the situation, and then re-integrate

280 Coleiro 2002, p. 66.
281 Ibid.
282 Ibid.
283 Howard 2008, pp. 229-230.

Eastern Slavonia into Croatia."[284] But with the United States and large parts of the alliance becoming bound to Bosnia, Secretary of State Albright pressured the UN to take on the lead on a mission in the region.[285] This idea, in turn, was initially strongly opposed by Boutros-Ghali, as well as by Franjo Tudjman – the UN had heavy baggage from its recent failure with UNPROFOR, the shock from its failures in Somalia and Rwanda had not yet been overcome, and UN peacekeeping was at that time teetering on the brink of collapse. For Tudjman, the UN was not acceptable as a peacekeeping force as it had proven its weakness with SFOR and could not guarantee the reintegration of Eastern Slavonia into Croatia. Yet, Washington's position was unambiguous and it could eventually make both the UN and Croatia comply with its preferences: the deal that resulted was that the US would provide strong support for the UN mission, and, regarding Croatia, a compromise was made with Tudjman that the head of the mission would be American.

The Erdut Agreement

The situation in Eastern Slavonia was solved in the course of the Dayton peace process, which primarily focused on Bosnia, in a peripheral agreement named after the village where it was signed, Erdut. Calling for an UN-governed transitional period, the agreement outlined the goal of reintegrating the region into Croatia. While being rather short and concise, the Erdut agreement, for the sake of its quick resolution, left out some crucial points concerning, for instance, the future status of Serbs in the territory. It also left what it actually meant to have the UN govern a territory in vague terms.

After a dialogue about the future status of the region had started in August/ September 1995 among UNCRO,[286] the Croatian government, and the local Serbs in Eastern Slavonia, the peace negotiations gained momentum in late 1995. The UN was directly involved in the negotiations through its Special Envoy, the UN Representative to the International Conference on the Former Yugoslavia, Thorvald Stoldenburg.[287] The major differences that needed to be dispelled were "the

---

284 Telephone interview with Ambassador Jacques-Paul Klein, SRSG/TA, UNTAES, 19 July 2007.
285 Cf. The Washington Post, "UN's Normal Decorous Diplomatic Discourse Takes Beating in Dispute, 16 December 1995.
286 The initial talks were undertaken jointly with UNPF, the coordinating body for UN operations in the former Yugoslavia.
287 "The United States was clearly the main international power arbitrating the end of the conflict in Croatia and Bosnia. The UN and the Contact Group – including France, Germany, Russia, the United Kingdom, and the United States (and later Italy) – were kept informed

length of the transitional period, UN representation in international structures which may administer the region, composition of an International Force, type, and location of police formations and, the holding of an election or a referendum at the end of the transition."[288]

After about two weeks of negotiations and considerable pressure on Tudjman and Milosevic, an UN-operated transitional administration for the region with the purpose of reintegrating the region into Croatia was agreed upon.[289] Complying with "Milosevic's insistence that Serbia had nothing to do with this deal, the agreement was signed by the local Serb leadership."[290] In fact, "Ironically, the key issue there was that Milosevic was prepared to do that deal, he was prepared to sell out the Serbs in Eastern Slavonia."[291]

The results were put on record in a short and general peace agreement, the Basic Agreement on the region of Eastern Slavonia, Baranja, and Western Sirmium, signed in the village of Erdut on 12 November 1995. The 14-Points Agreement allowed for a transitional period of twelve months, extendable "at most to another period of the same duration if so requested by one of the parties."[292] The signing parties – Milan Milanovic, Head of the Serb Negotiating Delegation, and Hrvoje Sarinic, Head of the Croatian Government Delegation, requested the Security Council "to establish a Transitional Administration, which shall govern the Region during the transitional period in the interest of all persons resident in or returning

about negotiations on Eastern Slavonia and the larger Dayton Agreement, but aside from the United States, they were not directly involved in the talks, much to their dismay. Holbrooke explained that he found it more complicated to keep the Europeans, as well as the UN, directly involved in the discussions, and therefore all but excluded them during the Bosnia negotiations. The official negotiators for Eastern Slavonia were Peter Galbraith, US Ambassador to Croatia, and Thorvald Steoltenberg [...]. However, in actuality, the major breakthrough on the negotiations occurred in Dayton, Ohio, between Tudjman, representing the Croatian government, and Milosevic, representing the Serb minority." Howard 2008, p. 230. See also Holbrooke, Richard C. 1998. *To End a War*. New York: Random House.

288 UN Task Force 1995, para. 700.
289 Cf. UN Security Council, "Security Council Resolution on proposal for termination of the mandate of the UN Confidence Restoration Operation in Croatia," UN Doc. S/RES/1025 (1995), 30 November 1995. In Eastern Slavonia, the real trade-off was getting Milosevic and Tudjman to agree to the Erdut agreement. They did so under great pressure. Number one, it was getting Tudjman to agree with there being a transitional authority within the sovereign territory of Croatia – at least on the books. And number two, persuading Milosevic that the interest of the Serb population would be adequately protected by this mission whose endpoint would be re-integration into Croatia. So, it took a lot of movement there. Interview with Michael W. Doyle, New Haven, 11 September 2006. While UNTAES was operational, Mr. Doyle conducted extensive local field research. The negotiations became the first step on the road to Dayton where, by mediation of the US government, the peace agreement for Bosnia was hammered out. The negotiation process ended with the signing of the Dayton Accords in Paris on 14 December 1995.
290 Coleiro 2002, p. 67.
291 Telephone interview with a senior UN official, 26 October 2006.
292 Basic Agreement on the Region of Eastern Slavonia, Baranja and Western Sirmium, para. 1.

to the Region"[293] as well as an International Force to be deployed during the transition. Other major features included "demilitarization of the Region, establishment, and training of a temporary police force, observance of human rights, election to local bodies and recognition of the right to return for those original from the area, and the right to stay for those currently living here."[294] What it did not mention, however, was the right of return for displaced Serbs, as well as the details of the process of reintegration into Croatia:

> They didn't get into many details. There was the need to get an agreement in the short term. This tension was reflected in the peacemaking framework from the very start. An ideal treaty would have much more details spelt out. The Erdut Agreement was one of the shortest peace treaties ever.[295]

The advantage of being short and relatively vague was the speed of consent. The disadvantage was the ensuing interpretative ambiguity that might have become virulent in the implementation process: while the Serbs saw the future status of the region as an issue yet to be decided and wanted a long-term mission to secure their physical as well as their economic survival in the region, the Croatians took the agreement as an instrument enabling the quick reintegration of Eastern Slavonia into Croatia. Accordingly, Croatia was strongly in favor of a mission that was as short as possible. Given these diametrically opposed preferences, getting local acceptance and support for the mission was going to be a tightrope walk: action perceived by one party as favoring the other could result in the reluctant party possibly boycotting the mission. Being sceptical of the UN's capacity to protect their safety, many Serbs had already fled the region. To get legitimation by both parties, the UN had to find a middle ground in living up to contradicting expectations.[296]

Certainly, an advantage of the negotiations for the agreement was that it provided for the early involvement of local stakeholders: on a political level, the Serbs and the Croats were consulted early in the process that lead to the Basic Agreement as the local actors on-the-ground. A subsequent letter from the Secretary-General to the Security Council also recommended the establishment of a "transitional council," chaired by the Transitional Administrator and including "one representative each of the Government of Croatia, the local Serb population, the local Croat population, and other local minorities."[297] In the course of action, the idea of this in-

293 Ibid., para. 2. Peter W. Galbraith, United States Ambassador to Croatia, and Thorvald Stoltenberg, United Nations Mediator, witnessed the signing of the agreement.
294 UN Task Force 1995, para. 72.
295 Interview with Professor Michael W. Doyle, former UN Assistant Secretary-General, New Haven, 11 September 2006.
296 Telephone interview with a staff member of STACTA, UNTAES, 10 January 2007.
297 UN Doc. S/1995/1028, para. 14.

stitution was not exactly followed, but at least it materialized in the form of regular meetings at the senior level.[298]

With the Erdut Agreement being signed, the framework for the transitional administration was provided. When the UNCRO mandate ended, on 15 January 1996, the UN Transitional Administration for Eastern Slavonia was scheduled to take over.[299] At the same time, the *de facto* rule by the RSK was bound to end: the RSK consented to its transformation into the "Secretariat" or "Executive Council" of the Serb Region. "[T]he quid pro quo between Tudjman and Milosevic signified an acceptance of the state of affairs. [...] chances were that at a political level there would be a reasonable degree of cooperation."[300]

2.3 Mandating UNTAES

Resolution 1037 authorized an international interim administration, to be led by the UN, to govern the territory of Eastern Slavonia for a transitional period and to reintegrate the territory into Croatia. Besides stabilizing the region and bringing humanitarian relief, UNTAES was specifically supposed to set up a new and multiethnic administration, including a transitional police force, and to further reconciliation between the formerly warring parties. Drafted in January 1996, the resolution was the most intrusive mandate the UNSC had ever passed, representing a remarkable convergence among the P-5. It was also one of the best-equipped missions of all time. In spite of these favorable semblances, the numbers of troops, police, civilian personnel, and resources granted to the mission did not meet the initial recommendations or requests of the Secretary-General. Another factor that constrained the prospects of success was a tight deadline: the mission had a maximum of two years to implement its mandate and to create sustainable structures.

Background Documents

UNTAES was based on three documents, the Erdut or Basic Agreement, the Background Report on the Region of Eastern Slavonia, Baranja, and Western Sirmium,

---

298 See Chapter IV.3.2.1.
299 Cf. UN Doc. S/RES/1025 (1995). Following the Dayton Agreements, which the Erdut Agreement was a part of, the Security Council restructured the UN activities in the region. They comprised, apart from UNTAES, three new missions: the UN Mission in Bosnia and Herzegovina (UNMIBH), and, within it, the UN International Police Task Force (UNIPTF), and the UN Mission of Observers in Prevlaka (UNMOP).
300 Coleiro 2002, p. 67.

and the Report of Secretary-General Kofi Annan pursuant to UNSC resolution 1025.

The peace process in Eastern Slavonia benefited from the fact that both parties to the conflict signed the peace agreement. The goals stipulated in the mission's mandate were based on and repeated the Erdut Agreement's imperatives. The second document on which the mandate referred was the Background Report on the Region of Eastern Slavonia, Baranja, and Western Sirmium, written by the UN Task Force to Establish the Transitional Administration in Sector East. Finalized in December 1995, it entailed an overview of the geo-political situation of the region as well as a discussion of the tasks and objectives of the Transitional Administrator. The SRSG of UNCRO appointed his Head of Political and Humanitarian Affairs, Gerard Fischer, to be Chairman of the "Task Force to Establish the Transitional Administration in Sector East."

> The Task Force has been considering a number of organizational frameworks for the Transitional Administrator, which essentially attempted to capture the core tasks as outlined in the Agreement to be accomplished by a Joint Commission process. Collection of information on the Region, dissemination of information on the Basic Agreement and relevant Security Council Resolutions, as well as the establishment of a continuous follow-up mechanism in the form of meetings with local authorities and community leaders have been some of the key activities of the Task Force. Vukovar has been identified as a possible location for the Transitional Administrator.[301]

The third important document, the Secretary-General's Report Pursuant to Resolution 1025 overlaps with the Background Report.[302] It summarizes and cements the previous documents, outlining the basic parameters of the mandate to be drafted in more detail. Specifying the purpose of peaceful reintegration of the Region into the Croatian constitutional and legal system, the Report states:

> By the end of the transitional period, the region should be demilitarized and secure under the sovereign control of the Government of Croatia; it should also be multiethnic in character, with all displaced persons enjoying the right to return freely to their homes. Free and fair local elections would have been held within this period. Provisions would also have been made for interested countries and organizations to take appropriate steps to monitor and report on respect of human rights in the region on a long-term basis.[303]

In regards to the military, the Secretary-General and his Secretariat drafted a Concept of Operations, emphasizing the necessity of a robust Chapter VII mandate.[304] For civilian tasks, the Report of the Secretary-General called for eight

---

301 UN Task Force 1995, para. 77.
302 UN Doc. S/1995/1028.
303 Ibid.
304 "Lighter options, involving forces of lesser strength operating under a Chapter VI mandate, are not considered by my military advisers to be feasible ways of ensuring implementation of the agreement." UN Doc. S/1995/1028, para. 9.

"Implementation Committees" as major transitory implementation mechanisms, "wherein Serb and Croat leaders, along with UNTAES officials, would work out detailed institutional reform programs."[305] The composition of the committees was supposed to be determined in consultation with the parties.

UNTAES' Mandate

UNTAES' mandate did not only represent one of the most complex mandates the UN had ever passed to that date, but also endowed the UN mission with unprecedented governing authority and military robustness. All three features reflected the generally high international support and political will for comprehensive crisis management. However, as an indicator of the precariousness of international support, even this exceptional mission suffered from the reluctance of single member states to grant the UN too much latitude: following an intervention by P-5 member China, the military robustness of the mission was restrained.

Recurring to the above mentioned documents, the UNSC entrusted UNTAES with the peaceful reintegration of the region into Croatia: the UN Transitional Administration in Eastern Slavonia was to "supervise and facilitate the demilitarization [...]; monitor the voluntary and safe return of refugees and displaced persons [...]; contribute, by its presence to the maintenance of peace and security" and "assist in implementation of the Basic Agreement."[306] The rather clear military mandate was supplemented with complex civilian duties. Its tasks related to the Secretary-General's report and referred the restoration of public services, including "water sanitation, energy supply, public transport, communications, waste disposal, health and educational facilities", as well as overseeing the "rebuilding of houses",[307] (re)establishing the civil administration, managing the refugee issue, assisting with economic development, and organizing elections. Furthermore, UNTAES was asked to monitor the respect of human rights, to establish an "active public affairs element,"[308] and to run a UN CivPol with the primary goal of recruiting and training a new multiethnic local police force.

The Security Council voted unanimously in favor of the mission, with the strong support of the United States, the "lone superpower" at that time.[309] "There was a

---

305   Howard 2008, p. 242.
306   UN Security Council, "Resolution on the Situation in Croatia," UN Doc. S/RES/1037 (1996), 15 January 1996, para. 10.
307   Ibid., para. 11.
308   Ibid., para. 12.
309   For an argument based on game-theory of how the former may be explained as an effect of the latter, see Voeten, Erik. 2001. "Outside Options and the Logic of Security Council Action." *American Political Science Review* 95:4, pp. 845-858.

basic consensus that Eastern Slavonia should remain a part of Croatia, and that its ethnic minority Serb population should be protected and reintegrated into Croatian government and society."[310] This position did not change over the course of the transition.

In order to live up to the comprehensive mandate, the mission was given full executive authority. While this meant that UNTAES was indeed supposed to be the government of the region for a transitional period,

> Theoretically, the authorities in Zagreb, possibly also Belgrade, could say, 'No, you're exceeding your authority and you have to stop now.' That is: the transitional administration can use its digression to execute the agreement but it can't go beyond what's in the agreement. Still, it can interpret what the agreement means.[311]

The strong mandate and the mission's considerable latitude were possible because of Eastern Slavonia's status as a region:

> Eastern Slavonia is very different from most other missions because it's a region, it's not a country, and that had much impact on how the UN could establish a transitional mission. It's a lot easier because we are not talking about sovereignty. You couldn't administer a country but you could administer a region.[312]

UNTAES was also granted a robust mandate under Chapter VII of the UN Charter. The authorization of the use of armed force without parties' consent whenever it "may be necessary to maintain or restore international peace and security"[313] featured a specific restriction: due to Chinese pressure in the UNSC, UNTAES was only allowed to use its force if the freedom of the mission's movement was at stake ("Chinese Chapter VII").[314]

By UN standards, UNTAES' mandate was a prototype of conciseness. In parallel to the character of the Erdut Agreement, it left – for political reasons – some crucial notions in vague terms. The person in charge of drafting the mandate was Julian Harston, a UK career diplomat with lengthy experience in the UN, who had also

---

310 Howard 2008, p. 235. "The mission's main supporter on the Council was the United States, even though the United States was reluctant to provide the funding to the mission requested by the Secretary-General. While there was some concern that in Security Council debates Russia might press for greater concession to the Serbs, in the end 'the Russian Ambassador told the Serbs that there was 'no light' between their view and the west's view on the issue of Eastern Slavonia' (unlike in Bosnia, where Council opinions were divided)." Ibid.

311 Interview with Professor Michael W. Doyle, former UN Assistant Secretary-General, New Haven, 11 September 2006.

312 Interview with Dr. Christine Coleiro, UNITAR POCI, Washington, DC, 1 December 2006.

313 Charter of the UN, Chapter VII, Art. 42.

314 The decisive introductory paragraph of the Security Council resolution read as follows, "Determined to ensure the security and freedom of movement of the personnel of the United Nations peacekeeping operation in the Republic of Croatia, and to these ends, acting under Chapter VII of the Charter of the United Nations." UN Doc. S/RES/1037 (1996), (italics in original). See e.g. Boothby 2004, p. 45; Doyle and Sambanis 2006, p. 17. The Chinese refused a full Chapter VII authorization.

been involved in Great Britain's decolonization process in the 1960s and 1970s. Harston and his team worked out major parts of the mandate on-the-ground, with input from UNPROFOR and UNPF. The rationale in drafting the document consisted in the principles of simplicity[315] and feasibility – and a touch of cynicism. "We deliberately did not put in the mandate words which would suggest some kind of special treatment for the remaining Serbs. The mandate simply said that it had to be handed-over. Full stop. We deliberately wrote a very much uncomplicated mandate – which made it possible to achieve it."[316]

Rationales of simplicity and feasibility, however, are not necessarily synonymous with conciseness and certainty: on the contrary, the mandate left room for interpretation. As mentioned above, there was no mention of special treatment or status of the Serbs in the region. In accordance with the less clear Erdut Agreement, it did not define the meaning of the verb "to govern," nor did it specify the tasks to be accomplished in reintegration. The issue of how to deal with this considerable interpretative vacuum was left up to the mission.

2.4 Planning Process

UNTAES entailed many military, civilian, and particularly political functions. Despite its core political mandate, the mission was not operated by DPA but, due its strong military component, by DPKO, which the mission's basic structure was modelled after. Contrary to the case of the transitional administration in East Timor, this decision to put DPKO in the driver's seat did not have negative consequences as it fit the local constellation and priorities well. The financing and staffing of the highly complex mission, however, suffered from (predictable) problems. The financing procedure of peacebuilding actions was not covered by assessed contributions, which meant that money had to be raised ad hoc via voluntary contributions, implying both planning uncertainty for the mission's leadership, as well as a general delay in the mandate implementation process.[317] There was also no proper roster to identify civilian staff at the low and mid-levels: not enough staff with appropriate qualifications was hired here.

At the top level, staffing decisions were made based on political rationale, and the decision of who to post in the key position of the SRSG was influenced by the United States. Eventually, Jacques-Paul Klein was chosen to lead the mission. Klein had excellent diplomatic contacts and "hot wires" to Washington and to NA-

---

315   The mandate "was essentially to return Eastern Slavonia to Croatia within two years." Telephone interview with Julian Harston, senior UN official, 26 October 2006.
316   Ibid.
317   Cf. Chapter II.2.3.

TO. He also had a flamboyant personality that often clashed with UN headquarters in New York. However, for Eastern Slavonia, Klein turned out to be the right man for the job, and he initiated a range of audacious and eventually successful measures. Klein's pro-active personality and credibility also fit the case because the planning process and the mandate remained inconclusive on various issues, deferring these details to the SRSG in order for them to elaborate on mission structure and transition strategy specifications.

Mission Design

In 1996, when the mission was being designed as a transitional administration, it was the first UN mission to be given executive authority. In that respect, UNTAES was an innovation, yet the mission's design followed the conventional blueprint of a multidimensional peace operation.

The mission's staffing used standard recruitment rosters – which were not supplemented by criteria that fit the special nature of the transitional administration mission, such as identifying institution-building or public administration experts, or providing training. Likewise constraining the mission, "The Security Council provided only about half of what had been requested in terms of numbers of military troops and hardware"[318] and far less funding than the UN-Secretariat had previously suggested. "The basic design, senior positions, and staffing tables of the mission were defined before UNTAES came into the picture."[319]

The head of the mission was called the Transitional Administrator and Special Representative of the Secretary-General (SRSG)[320] and was endowed with comprehensive competences. "[T]he Transitional Administrator alone would have executive power and he would not have to obtain the consent of either the [Transitional; ES] Council or the parties for his decisions."[321] In addition, the Transitional Administrator had the "legislative power to enact regulations for carrying out the functions attributed to him by the agreement."[322] Complying with the deal that had been struck with Tudjman, the SRSG was American. Through mediation by As-

---

318 Howard 2008, p. 234.
319 Telephone interview with Ambassador Jacques-Paul Klein, SRSG/TA, UNTAES, 19 July 2007.
320 The meanwhile common term was originally coined in these days. "One of the titles they had was 'Governor General' but I said that this is too silly. We had 'Special Representative' but that was not good enough. And then the National Security Advisor at the time said, 'Look, if it's a transitional administration, why don't we call you Transitional Administrator?' Still, the title don't mean much, it's the authority that counts." Ibid.
321 UN Doc. S/1995/1028, para. 14.
322 Ibid., para. 17. "[…] the validity of such regulations would expire at the end of the transitional period, unless the Croatian authorities decided otherwise." Ibid.

sistant Secretary of State for European and Canadian Affairs, Richard Holbrooke, and Secretary of State, Madeleine Albright, Jacques-Paul Klein,[323] a career member of the Department of State's Senior Foreign Service and retired Major General of the US Air Force, was suggested as Transitional Administrator. After Klein had personally assessed the mission's chances of success in an on-site visit and the US had reconfirmed their strong political support for the UN mission, he eventually agreed to take on the job.[324]

Box 1: Jacques-Paul Klein

Ambassador Jacques-Paul Klein had spent most of his career in the US Senior Foreign Service of the Department of State.

Born in 1939 in Alsace, a region bordering Germany in the northeast of France that used to be fiercely contested for centuries, he was raised in World War Two. After the war ended, he and his mother immigrated to the United States, settling in Chicago. Klein entered the Foreign Service in 1971. His tour of duty led him frequently back to Europe and particularly to the two Germanies. In 1996, UN Secretary-General, Boutros Boutros-Ghali selected him to serve as Transitional Administrator for UNTAES with the rank of Under-Secretary-General.

During his duty in Eastern Slavonia, Klein proved to be a straightforward and outspoken leader who got the reputation as caring about the common man on the streets and engaging dedicatedly in confidence-building and reconciliation. At the same time, he lived up to his reputation of being a flamboyant enfant terrible – at least this is what it must have seemed to people at New York headquarters – who stubbornly adhered to his own way.

In a move that was allegedly unfortunate for UNTAES, Klein pulled out of Eastern Slavonia in August 1997 and became Principal Deputy High Representative for Bosnia and Herzegovina. In August 1999, he became Special Representative of the Secretary-General and Coordinator of UN Operations in Bosnia and Herzegovina with the rank of Under-Secretary-General.

In July 2003, the UN Secretary-General called on him to serve as his Special Representative and Coordinator of UN Operation in Liberia where he oversaw the transition from Charles Taylor's rule to the election of President Johnson-Sirleaf. Soon, however, Klein encountered trouble: within the mission he was accused of making a divide between "his" people with whom he had worked with in the Balkans and the others whom he had not known before, but also concerning cooperation partners, particularly NGOs which felt excluded, and concerning local power brokers for whom he was too bullying. What was far more, re-qualified US documents revealed last year that Klein was having a personal relationship with a local woman. "A number of staff interviewed by [U.N. investigators] expressed concern that the Local Woman was passing information […] to Mr. Taylor."[325] As consequence of the affair, Klein had to resign and in April 2005 left Liberia.

This story contrasts the praises that he likewise earns and points out the ambiguity that came along with his persona. Still, in Eastern Slavonia, he and his special leadership style apparently contributed very much to the mission's ultimate success.

His support structure consisted of a Force Commander, UN Military Observers, a Deputy Transitional Administrator, and an Administration Unit that was responsible for managing the mission itself, the Civil Affairs Unit, the UN Civilian Police

---

323 See Box 1.
324 "We actually did an initial analysis of the lay and the land of Eastern Slavonia as we got there." Telephone interview with Ambassador Jacques-Paul Klein, SRSG/TA, UNTAES, 19 July 2007.
325 Lynch, Colum. 2008. "US Officials Divulge Reports on Confidential UN Audits", *Washington Post*, 17 February 2008, p. 20.

Unit, and the Office of the Transitional Administrator, which consisted of Public Affairs, Legal Affairs, and a Political Unit.[326]

Figure 1: Organizational Chart of UNTAES

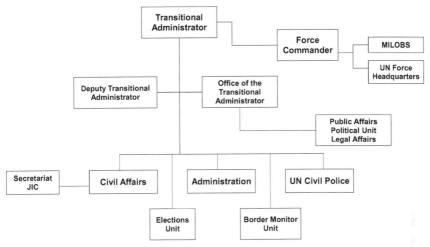

Source: Klein, "UNTAES."

Caption: MILOBS: Military Operations; JIC: Joint Implementation Committee

The large civil affairs component featured four pillars: Field Offices – in Vukovar, Vinkovci, Ilok, Beli Manastir, Darda, and Erdut; three Liaison Offices outside of Eastern Slavonia – in Borovo, Beli Manastir, and Osijek; an Economic Reconstruction and Coordination Unit; and a Secretariat for the (Joint) Implementation Committees. The staffing table of the civilian side of the mission was elaborated at DPKO, in accordance with the department's mandate. The process involved senior UNTAES staff, including Klein, his First Deputy Derek Boothby, who at the time was Director of the Europe Division at DPA, the Head of UNTAES Civil Affairs and then-Head of the UNTAES Task Force, Gerard Fischer, and the Director of Administration of DPKO, Souren G. Seraydarian.[327] 317 international

---

326 Cf. Gravelle, Robert J. A. R. Undated. *The United Nations Transitional Administration in Eastern Slavonia, Baranja, and Western Sirmium (UNTAES): A Successful Mission*, p. 4. The document is on file with the author.

327 In fact, Seraydarian, who was the former Chief Administrator Officer (CAO) of the UN Mission in Haiti (UNMIH), a leading member of the political mission of the United Nations in South Africa in 1994, and a former staff member of the United Nations Industrial Development Organization (UNIDO), succeeded Boothby during the course of the mission.

civilian staff and 686 local staff were authorized for the civilian part of the mission.[328]

UNTAES' military and police forces reached large numbers – but not as many as were envisioned by the Secretary-General in his suggestion to the Security Council. Two crucial preconditions for successful military action consisted in the facts that the mission could fall back on two battalions that were already present in and familiar with the region, and that it had full NATO backing throughout the transition period.

The Secretary-General had suggested deploying 9,000 troops, but the Security Council-authorized military force merely totalled 5,700 uniformed personnel, including "5,000 troops, 100 military observers, and 600 civilian police."[329] The main reason behind this significant reduction was that Washington, who had the lion's share of financing the military troops, had signalled that they would not pay for more than 5,000. Eventually, the deployed numbers added up to 2,346 troops, 97 military observers, and 404 civilian police only. Coping with these limited possibilities, the designated Transitional Administrator engaged in talks with other potential troop contributors. As a Russian and a Belgian battalion had already been in the region as part of UNCRO and, hence, would be readily available when the mission started, the Transitional Administrator succeeded in getting them to stay on. Having the support of the Russian forces was an additional advantage in that it lent the mission credibility vis-à-vis the Serbs. In fact, a Russian general was selected as Deputy Force Commander – a novelty in UN mission history.[330] Eventually, the largest combat units were being provided by Russia, Belgium, Jordan, and Pakistan.[331] Belgian Major General Schoups held the position of Force Com-

---

328   Cf. UN Department of Peacekeeping Operations, "Eastern Slavonia, Baranja and Western Sirmium: Facts and Figures." Available online at http://www.un.org/Depts/dpko/dpko/co_mission/untaes_p.htm, last access on 25 February 2009.

329   Ibid. Eventually, the maximum strength on-the-ground, counted on October 31, 1996 amounted to "5,561 uniformed personnel including 5,009 troops, 457 civilian police and 95 military observers." Ibid.

330   "I went to Moscow and met with Foreign Minister Primakov. I said, 'Look, I got a difficult problem here: the Serbs are really suspicious of the UN. I would like to have a battalion of Russians, if you can spare them.' He agreed, pointing to a Russian parashoot battalion in the region, coming out of Czechia. I continued and told him that I would also like to have a Russian general to be a Deputy Force Commander.' And he said, 'Are you serious? I thought you are an American?!' And I said, 'No, Mr. Primakov, I was born in Alsace, I am a European first. So my roots are very much here, and I understand the situation, better than most Europeans.' He said, 'All right – we'll give you one.' So we had a Russian Deputy Force Commander and a Russian battalion." Telephone interview with Ambassador Jacques-Paul Klein, SRSG/TA, UNTAES, 19 July 2007.

331   Other troop contributing countries included Argentina, the Czech Republic, Slovakia, Poland, and Ukraine.

mander.[332] Schoups adapted the NATO command and control structure for UNTAES, in fact staffing "key positions on all shifts with Belgian military personnel. According to the General Accounting Office of the United States, "This ensures a unity of command and direct communications links to NATO."[333] UNTAES operated under the umbrella of promised NATO support if it was needed. "NATO commanders in Bosnia received explicit authorization from the North Atlantic Council to provide close-air support and, if circumstances made it necessary, to evacuate UNTAES personnel."[334] Despite the cutbacks in personnel, at the mission's peak, there were 34.2 soldiers per thousand inhabitants – the highest ratio ever in a complex UN peacekeeping mission.[335]

The inclusion of the local actors, both Croats and Serbs, was supposed to proceed via two transitional structures: the "Executive Council" and the Joint Implementation Councils (JICs). First, the Serb RSK was to be transformed into an Executive Council (EC) for the region, with Serbian Deputy Ministers for each resort in Belgrade. "That was the deal with Tudjman, that there would be a Serb representative of every one of the ministries at the senior level."[336] The idea was "to work with what was still around, and not to impose completely new structures."[337] The second

---

332 "Now, we needed the NATO countries, but nobody volunteered as everyone else in NATO was in Bosnia. I went to see NATO General Joulwan and I said 'George, can't you spare a battalion from some country?' And he said that this is not going to happen, that they are over-taxed, over-whelmed, over-everything. However, he said that the Belgians weren't planning in Bosnia and that they might be interested. So I went to see the Belgian Prime Minister, de Haan, and I said, 'Mr. Prime Minister, I have a problem here, it's not easy, it's a linguistic problem, it's a religious problem, it's a historic problem.' And he said, 'Who the hell do you think you're talking to? What do you think I have here in Belgium?' That meant that he understood the situation. And he said, 'Look, I'm gonna help, I will give you one battalion.' I said, 'Good, if that's the situation, then I would select a Belgian as a Force Commander. Do you have a good general?' You have to know Europe is full of generals what I call tin soldiers: they dress like soldiers, they play soldiers, they go to War Academy, they do war games, but when it comes to shooting, they wet their pants. Because Europe has not had a war for over 40 years and that's a really long time. So he said, 'Yes, I have one, his name is Schoups. He's very, very good, he's not of the most friendly sort, but he's solid.' So I interviewed Schoups, and the Prime Minister was absolutely right, he was a very tough soldier." Telephone interview with Ambassador Jacques-Paul Klein, SRSG/TA, UNTAES, 19 July 2007. Schoups was succeeded by his countryman Major-General Willy Hanset.
333 United States General Accounting Office, National Security and Internal Affairs Division, "United Nations: Limitations in Leading Missions Requiring Force to Restore Peace." Report to Congressional Committees, 27 March 1997. Available online at http://www.gao.gov/archive/1997/ns97034.pdf, last access on 25 February 2009.
334 Dobbins et al. 2005, p.114. "Coming on the heels of the recent NATO air strikes in operation 'Deliberate Force' in Bosnia, the threat of NATO air strikes was very credible, providing additional military backing for the operation." Howard 2008, p. 238. See also UN Department of Peacekeeping Operations, Lessons Learned Unit 1998, para. 32.
335 Cf. Dobbins et al. 2005, p. 114.
336 Telephone interview with Ambassador Jacques-Paul Klein, SRSG/TA, UNTAES, 19 July 2007.
337 Interview with Dr. Christine Coleiro, UNITAR POCI, Washington, DC, 1 December 2006.

transitional structure was an arrangement that was intented to function as a nucleus for the region's future multiethnic public service. The JICs – stipulated in the Secretary-General's Report, designed by the UNTAES Head of Civil Affairs, and elaborated at DPKO[338] – ought to include all ethnic groups present in the region, thus providing a forum for reconciliation policies. Thirteen committees were planned, each with numerous sub-committees, the crucial linkages among them consisting of "political considerations of reintegration and administrative procedures for implementation."[339] That said, no local actors were involved in the planning of the mechanism that was supposed to guarantee their ownership in the transitional process. The planning took place at UN headquarters in New York.

Recruiting

"In contrast to the military component, each civilian component of the operation had to be recruited individually,"[340] which ran into the problem of having inadequate staffing rosters.[341] At the top level, however, more scrutiny was used in the hiring process.

Staffing at the senior level normally does not run through standard DPKO staffing rosters but is subject to political considerations. Jacques-Paul Klein was selected following American pushing and Croatian demands. His deputy was Derek Boothby, also an American, who had been working at the UN for a long time. While Boothby did not have much mission experience, he had detailed knowledge of the personalities and procedures of the UN headquarters in New York – contrary to Klein and thus complementing the qualifaction set of the mission leadership. As mentioned above, the Force Commander and his Deputy were selected by the Transitional Administrator, with consent of the Security Council. The person formerly in charge of the Task Force became Head of Civil Affairs.

As the planning agency, DPKO had to struggle with a shortage in personnel at the lower levels. "The UN was always short of people as people were needed

---

338 "It is my understanding that the idea and development of the concept of the JICs were primarily the design of the Head of Civil Affairs. The initial thinking on these aspects that went into the Secretary-General's report to the Security Council of 12 December 1995 was carried out in the Department of Peacekeeping Operations [...]." Written interview with Derek G. Boothby, DSRSG/DTA, UNTAES, 5 February 2007.
339 Gravelle undated, p. 4.
340 Dobbins et al. 2005, p. 115.
341 "The DPKO has a service for personnel, they pre-select candidates either from the roster or from people who had applied for the jobs on the basic of specific job descriptions, and then they select let's say three, four people, and then it's up to the mission to select one out of the list that is submitted from New York." Telephone interview with Souren G. Seraydarian, DSRSG/DTA, UNTAES, 16 January 2007.

somewhere else too."[342] And especially at that time, "DPKO had its hands more than full with the UNPROFOR situation in Bosnia and Croatia and the major changes that would be required by the Dayton Accord."[343] Compounding the recruiting process for the transitional administration, the standard DPKO staffing roster did not contain criteria that would have suited the new and extraordinary international interim government mission type. Consequently, people with public services and civic administration knowledge and skills were hardly identified:[344] "UNTAES had almost no-one on staff with experience in town administration (budgeting, finance, education, hospitals, energy supply, etc)."[345] For civil affairs, there were even "no generic job descriptions at that time."[346] In order to overcome these shortcomings, civilian staff that had just finished other multi-dimensional missions, for instance in Cambodia, South Africa or UNPROFOR, were asked to join the mission.[347]

Eventually, in staffing the UN Civilian Police Force for Eastern Slavonia (UN CivPol), a different yet typical problem came up:

> Donor countries cannot send their national police with the same flexibility through which they can commit their military since police men are needed for their own country's public security. Typically, national police are stretched thin in their own country and, unlike in the military, there are no police reserve units. Consequently, finding the numbers of police required for a CivPol mission is difficult. This also means that the selection standards for police suffer because the UN has to take all the police it can get, whether they meet the required criteria or not.[348]

---

342 Telephone interview with Souren G. Seraydarian, DSRSG/DTA, UNTAES, 16 January 2007.

343 Written interview with Derek G. Boothby, DSRSG/DTA, UNTAES, 5 February 2007.

344 "We should have had – from the very beginning – staff who had specific experience of public services and civic administration." Ibid.

345 Telephone interview with Souren G. Seraydarian, DSRSG/DTA, UNTAES, 16 January 2007.

346 Interview with Dr. Gerard Fischer, Head of Civil Affairs, UNTAES, New York, 21 November 2006. "I think it's only two or three years ago that there is a generic job description for civil affairs." Ibid.

347 "For the civilian staff we took people who were just finishing. Cambodia was finishing at that time, South Africa was finishing at that time – so we took qualified people. And Cambodia was very important because it was a transitional administration at the beginning." Telephone interview with Souren G. Seraydarian, DSRSG/DTA, UNTAES, 16 January 2007.

348 Coleiro 2002, p. 95.

Financing

As is common for multidimensional operations, UNTAES' financing consisted of assessed contributions, which were instantly available to UNTAES, and voluntary contributions, which UNTAES had to raise *ad hoc*.

The assessed budget totalled $575 million and was earmarked exclusively for peacekeeping activities and expenses directly related to the mission.[349] In fact, there is not much room for digression, as the budget is extremely detailed. It is built around four blocks: procurement, staffing, transportation, and communication gear. The ACABQ does not allow for more than five percent of the money allocated to one resource to be spent on another. "And all this requires regular reporting: once the budget has been approved, every six month you have to do a detailed overview of expenditures that goes to the General Assembly through the ACABQ, which can be very, very tough."[350]

All peace*building* activities have to be paid for using voluntary contributions.[351] Voluntary contributions, however, have to be *raised*, and that requires time – to the degree that in the early and crucial months of the mission, not enough money for quick reaction projects targeted at civilian needs was available.[352] This notorious obstacle was overcome in part through timely initiatives by the designated mission leadership, who procured pledges of international support. They appealed to donors for projects of "reconstruction and economic revitalization," backed by the Transitional Administrator's persistent visits to capitals and organizations, especially in Europe and in the US.[353] Additionally, two donor conferences were held in Zagreb on 6 December 1996 and 3 March 1997. Despite the fact

---

349 "The General Assembly decided on 7 June 1996 to appropriate $94,269,700 gross ($93,073,300 net) for UNTAES for the period of 15 January through 30 June 1996 (Resolution 50/242). The Assembly also appropriated, as an ad hoc arrangement, an additional $64,769,700 gross ($64,036,200 net) for UNTAES for the same time period. On 4 December 1996, the Secretary-General, in a report to the General Assembly, estimated the cost for the maintenance of UNTAES and the liaison offices at Belgrade and Zagreb for the one-year period 1 July 1997 to 30 June 1998 at $274,993,600 gross ($265,657,900 net), representing a 0.7 percent decrease to the previous budget due mainly to reduced requirements for helicopters. The budget provides for the deployment of 100 military observers, 556 civilian police, 477 international staff, 721 local staff and 100 United Nations volunteers. In resolution 51/153 of 20 January 1997, the Assembly decided to appropriate $140,484,350 gross ($136,087,550 net) for maintaining UNTAES from 1 July 1996 through 30 June 1997." UN Department of Peacekeeping Operations 1997.
350 Interview with Professor Dirk Salomons, New York, 20 September 2006.
351 Cf. Chapter II.2.3.
352 "[...]it would have been very valuable indeed for the Transitional Administrator to have authority to spend, on his own decision, significant money for quick reaction projects; it would have been much better to have the mission leadership fully involved in pre-mission planning [...]." Written interview with Derek G. Boothby, DSRSG/DTA, UNTAES, 5 February 2007.
353 Klein, "UNTAES."

that the Council was not in line with the number of troops and funding requests of the Secretary-General, UNTAES was one of the best-equipped UN missions of all time.[354]

2.5 Summary and Assessment

The Erdut Agreement nailed down the conflict parties to a settlement on the status of Eastern Slavonia. However, the cost of proceeding quickly resulted in omitting specifications on some crucial aspects, such as the refugee issue. In general, the agreement made extensiv use of vague language. The mandating resolution of the Security Council was not much better: while elaborating somewhat on each of the points of the agreement,[355] crucial definitions were evaded. There was no explanation of what governing entailed: the mandate stipulated identifying "how various aspects of local government worked and to oversee their functioning"[356] but this was not informative for the implementers.[357] This confusion implied the risk of recurring disputes with the two parties to the conflict over the interpretation of the mandate.

The sheer comprehensiveness and complexity of the mission's mandate is striking.[358] Juggling peacekeeping and peacebuilding tasks, the mission was responsible for acting as a government by: building new institutions, promoting reconciliation, managing the refugee problem, recruiting multiethnic staff for the new political and administrative structures, guarantee security, promote human rights, create and

---

354 On this note, a senior UNTAES official made the remark that "one should write a thesis about to what extent the lobby an African nation has vis-à-vis the Balkans or the Kosovo in particular. These missions have the amount of money, efforts, meetings, et cetera. to get the regions in a situation we would never have considered in Burundi or Rwanda. It has many reasons. One reason is that the European countries don't want any more, say, Kosovars in their respective countries. So we have to create something that we keep them happy in their own place. OK, very cynical, very simplified, but very often this is the case. If you work in the DRC and four million people are dying in the last five to seven years and still 120 people are being killed, you just know that the lobby is not very powerful..." Interview with a senior UNTAES official.

355 Some of the elaborations consisted in mere cross-references to the Report of the Secretary-General.

356 Boothby 2004, p. 41.

357 "Such tasks may be described as supervision and oversight – but they are not governing, which implies the direction and control over the actions and affairs of a community." Ibid.

358 "The magnitude and complexity of these tasks should not be underestimated." UN Doc. S/1995/1028, para. 6. The Head of Civil Affairs reflects, "When you look at the history of peacekeeping you had the traditional peacekeeping missions where you were sitting along a ceasefire line and there were maybe two political advisors that draft reports, saying, 'Well I think I saw some guys moving from the left to the right although they were not supposed to move from the left to the right.' And that's it – there was no sanction, it was not proactive. And then all of a sudden we had Croatia. And everything was in there." Interview with Dr. Gerard Fischer, Head of Civil Affairs, UNTAES, New York, 21 November 2006.

train a multiethnic police, and organize elections. While the mandate's authors strived to make the objectives achievable, the long list of tasks was squeezed into a rather tight timeframe. The mission was also assigned the role of the coordinator for the various international and local organizations and agencies in the region. An important advantage was the mission's substantial authority that was eventually put to good use by its leadership. Likewise important was NATO's "over-the-horizon"-backing, and the UN forces' robust mandate, somewhat impaired by Chinese intervention though.

The most constraining issue in the mission's further planning was cumbersome recruitment: the overloaded DPKO's rules did not fit the mission's requirements, and staffing decisions were eventually made in an ad hoc manner. As for the military, some of the usual difficulties in deployment were avoided in the run-up to the mission through the "annexation" of two former UNCRO battalions. Still, the funding provisions were potentially unreliable: the inflexibility of the rules did not match the complex and dynamic nature of the interim administration mission. Furthermore, "Inadequate pre-mission planning was one of the weaknesses."[359]

> The field staff such as the Transitional Administrator, deputy, civil affairs, border monitoring and force commander, plus the chief negotiator should go in for at least two weeks and all should be sitting there saying, 'This is how we are going to do this, this is what we need, this is the staffing table, this is how we find these people, with competences,' so that when you hit the ground, everyone knows their job.[360]

Decisions concerning the mission's physical set up and the crafting of detailed benchmarks were left up to the Transitional Administrator and his team.

An innovative feature was the integrated structure of the mission: the Transitional Administrator was responsible for civilian as well as for UN military components, and the UN appealed to bilateral and international agencies and organizations to comply with his coordination efforts. In this regard, UNTAES was very much ahead of its time.[361]

---

359 Written interview with Derek G. Boothby, DSRSG/DTA, UNTAES, 5 February 2007. "We did not get any guidelines or templates from DPKO." Telephone interview with Ambassador Jacques-Paul Klein, SRSG/TA, UNTAES, 19 July 2007.

360 Telephone interview with Dr. Robert J.A.R. Gravelle, Head of the JIC Secretariat and Head of STACTA, 11 August 2007.

361 "It would be useful to have more standard operation procedures, especially the integrated model – which we had and which I gave them for all other missions. And they are finally learning to use it, now other missions are using it. There is a model – just fill in the blanks." Telephone interview with Dr. Robert J.A.R. Gravelle, Head of the JIC Secretariat and Head of STACTA, 11 August 2007. After his UNTAES appointment, he served in the UN CivPol Support Group in Croatia.
For the elaboration of the integrated approach, see Eide, Espen B. et al. 2005. *Report on Integrated Missions: Practical Perspectives and Recommendations.* Independent Study for the Expanded UN ECHA Core Group, May 2005.

The transition process in Eastern Slavonia featured poorly-structured conditions that left the mission with bleak prospects of being able to hit the ground running and implement its comprehensive mandate: the high level of hostility among the factions, adversity towards the mission, a lack of local capacity due to post-war brain-drain were compounded by a a short time to plan, and the usual problems in financing and staffing a multidimensional mission.

As could be expected, pathologies were emerging. Cognitive biases occurred in the form of design lapses that remained unsolved, tunnel visions of international officers who were supposed to lead the JICs, or stereotyping images on local (non-existent) civil society organizations. Principal-agent dilemmas emerged on various levels as well, in the form of, for instance, a mandate-weakening obstruction of China, the boycotts by the actual "agents of transition," i.e. the local leaders and populace, who took advantage of the precariousness and uncertainty of the mission, or in form of the difficult relationship between the cautious headquarters in New York and the (occasionally adventurous) mission leadership. Likewise, the pathology of tight coupling was observable, for instance, when the delays ran the risk of being exploited by local paramilitary groups or when budgeting provisions obviated the mission from quick reaction projects. Furthermore, a pathological tendency of path dependency developed within the JICs. At the end of the day, a determined change of course prevented major accidents.

The ability to "fitly" cope with emerging pathologies holds for the transitional management in general: cognitive biases could often be corrected; problems caused by principl-agent dilemmas attenuated or contained by the cagey and well-informed mission leadership; tight couplings could, in many cases, be straightened out by creating financial, organizational, or time slack.

3.1 Deployment

During its early days, UNTAES struggled with unfavorable conditions caused by planning deficits, deployment delays, and an instable and hostile situation on-the-ground. Damned to succeed, the mission's leadership was able to engage in a relatively thorough analysis of the situation, it outlined an implementation plan, took on pressing security and humanitarian issues, and it was eventually able to frame UNTAES as a determined actor that would not suffer from the same powerlessness as UNPROFOR or UNCRO.

3.1.1 Arriving in Eastern Slavonia

UNTAES' arrival in Eastern Slavonia was initially challenged by Serbs who were hostile to the mission and who wanted to prevent it from gaining ground. Besides, it started to suffer from a very typical UN shortcoming – lame deployment.

Due to the strong presence of Serb military and militia in the Region and because Belgrade kept on obstructing substantial communication between the local Serbs and UNTAES,[362] the UN mission pitched its initial headquarters in Zagreb. For its first two to three months, UNTAES worked from there. Yet, as its military component was gaining strength,[363] the Transitional Administrator insisted that there be a single, joint UNTAES headquarters in the regional capital of Vukovar, where the civilian, military, and police leadership could all be located, and where the mission would be able to make its presence and forcefulness be felt.

> The Croatian government in Zagreb offered UNTAES premises in Osijek, just outside the Serb enclave, as headquarters for UNTAES. This was declined as the Transitional Administrator rightly considered that to accept such premises would send the wrong message to the Serbs. Instead, it was decided that the UNTAES headquarters should be in Vukovar, and the best site was the one that was occupied by the Serb military. One of the first acts of UNTAES, to demonstrate that UNTAES was made of sterner stuff than UNCRO, was to give firm notice to the Serb military that they should quit within weeks and take their weapons with them. It was largely only with their departure that UNTAES could turn its attention to the Serb civilian administration.[364]

Early on, its military strength proved to be key for UNTAES' progress, signalling an increasing threat to Belgrade's grip on the region. "We moved in over 5,000 troops in six weeks. That was a record. We moved them in not by American Air Force; we did it through private commercial contractors from the region."[365] The first troops were directly deputized to the guard of a strategically important oilfield near Osijek.[366]

> [Headquarters were] co-housed with all of the other UNTAES units, in a field in the back of the Yugoslav People's Army headquarters in Vukovar [...]. The troops engaged actively with the local population (unlike the peacekeepers in neighboring Bosnia). The battalions were joined in a central location and generally went out on foot patrol, but also in UN vehicles, with the intent of keeping a high, but not aggressive, UN profile. The troops would patrol, guns pointing up, with orders not to intimidate or harm the local population, 'We wanted to give the impression of a strict, no-nonsense peace-

---

362 "There was little contact with the Serbs in Eastern Slavonia as the local Serb government officials were under the control of Belgrade." Written interview with Derek G. Boothby, DSRSG/DTA, UNTAES, 5 February 2007.
363 It was at least stronger than the 1,000 troops of the preceding UNCRO mission.
364 Written interview with Derek G. Boothby, DSRSG/DTA, UNTAES, 5 February 2007.
365 Telephone interview with Ambassador Jacques-Paul Klein, SRSG/TA, UNTAES, 19 July 2007. See also Dobbins et al. 2005, p. 114.
366 See Chapter IV.3.3.4.

keeping force that would provide security to the local Serb population after their forces disarmed.'[367]

The deployment of the military staff was completed by June 1996.[368] Delays during this stage were due substantially to the slow deployment of the civilian support components that were responsible for the mission's logistics. These shortcomings, in turn, resulted from a delay in the approval of the budget for UNTAES personnel – sufficient funds were not available until July 1996. As a consequence, in July only half of the scheduled civilian staff was deployed.

> Some components arrived several months after the establishment of the Mission head-quarters. The Chief Administrative Officer did not arrive in the Mission until four months after deployment and for the first six months, the Mission did not have a chief finance officer. The main body of the integrated support services arrived eight months after the beginning of the mandate and three months after the full deployment of the military force. Because of the civilian staff shortage, those on-the-ground initially had to work double shifts.[369]

The situation was somewhat mitigated by the fact that the mission could, from day one, fall back on personnel from the former UN presence in the area. "This meant that, in addition to a smaller military contingent of UNCRO, there were several UN international civilians at Erdut with a small logistic, communications and administrative organization."[370] While the civilian deployment was ongoing, the mission could become operational in June 1996. "As of 31 May 1996, total strength stands at 5,349 uniformed personnel, consisting of 4,849 troops, 99 military observers, and 401 civilian police."[371]

3.1.2 Setting up the Mission

During its deployment, UNTAES was challenged with the coordination of a multitude of demands, while at the same time struggling with the issue of how to interprete the vague language of its mandate, particularly on what "governing" actually meant.

---

367 Howard 2008, p. 238, also referring to her interview with Derek Boothby on April 7, 2001.
368 "It took some four months for the battalions to reach full strength in personnel and equipment, the Jordanian and Pakistani battalions and heavy armour having to be brought by ship to Rjeka, in western Croatia, then driven overland to Eastern Slavonia." Written interview with Derek G. Boothby, DSRSG/DTA, UNTAES, 5 February 2007.
369 UN Department of Peacekeeping Operations, Lessons Learned Unit 1998, para. 16.
370 Written interview with Derek G. Boothby, DSRSG/DTA, UNTAES, 5 February 2007.
371 UN Department of Peacekeeping Operations. "Eastern Slavonia, Baranja and Western Sirmium: Brief Chronology." Available online at http://www.un.org/Depts/DPKO/Missions/untaes_e.htm, last access on 25 February 2009. The Transitional Administrator declared the full deployment on 20 May.

The implementation of the governing functions began sluggishly. One hitch was the sheer workload of these early days: as with any new operation, the first five to six months were spent establishing the mission, "building up the arrival of personnel, finding suitable places for living and office accommodation, setting up communication transport and administrative capacities."[372] Another issue was the "interpretation gap" between the vague language of the mandate and how it was supposed to translate into concrete action. Particularly problematic was the specification of what "governing" was supposed to imply. The parties to the conflict each had their own opportunistic interpretation of what governing meant: the Croats' interpretation consisted of full-fledged "authoritative control over all aspects of local government,"[373] while the Serbs wanted it to mean a minimal approach in adhering to the status quo. Thus, the mission leadership had to engage in substantial work vis-à-vis the local actors, but also vis-à-vis its staff, who had little experience with public services and institutions. For the time being, the general mission staff obtained some documents that served to clarify the mandate. There was also at least one one-day seminar where one of the negotiators from Dayton came down and told about the background issues and thinking, but it was neither obligatory for staff to attend, nor were the documents widely distributed.[374]

For the overall good of the mission's progress,[375] the leadership soon made a stern attempt to elaborate a consistent approach to the implementation of the mandate, setting up a strategy and mission benchmarks.[376] Its overarching rationale was

---

372 Written interview with Derek G. Boothby, DSRSG/DTA, UNTAES, 5 February 2007. "Our first tasks were to find a site for the construction of an UNTAES headquarters in Vukovar, take on the necessary construction work using containers, find suitable places for the incoming UNTAES troops to establish their battalion headquarters and living facilities and gradually build up the civilian and police components." Ibid.

373 Boothby 2004, p. 40.

374 Telephone interview with a field officer, UNTAES, 10 January 2007. Sources who asked not to be named are listed anonymously. In the remainder of the study, they will be referred to by function only.

375 This positive interpretation was found in all relevant interviews the author conducted on UNTAES.

376 Cf. UNTAES, "Mission Brief" by Transitional Administrator Klein, on file with the author. The benchmarks were identified by UNTAES negotiator Robert Gravelle, who laid out a forerunner to the now gone standard mandate implementation plans, "In fact, everyone in New York takes credit for it. But it's nonsense, we had the first one. It was done in Eastern Slavonia when Gravelle said, 'Why don't we lay out what we need to do and what the benchmarks are so that we can measure every two or three months how we are doing.' That was the first time and then we did it in Bosnia as well. And one day someone came from headquarters and said, 'Oh, this looks good, can we take this with us?' And then they started teaching it in New York and now every UN mission is doing it." Telephone interview with senior staff member, UNTAES.

to keep Eastern Slavonia a multiethnic place.[377] Accordingly, the message that UNTAES wanted to get across to the Serb residents was that it "can do nothing about the past, but together we can help build the future."[378] These goals were not an easy task, "Many Serbs had great fears that once we left, the Croats would come and take their revenge."[379] In order to avoid this scenario, the following benchmarks were identified: the first major step was demilitarization. After that, the focus was to shift towards the civil administration implementing its major task of bringing about a phased reintegration of the region into Croatian administrative structures, accompanied by displaced persons measures, economic reconstruction, and the set up of a human rights monitoring mission. The elections, which were supposed to complete the political reintegration process, were scheduled no later than 30 days before the mission ended. The final tasks consisted of the preparation of drawing-down the military and establishing post-UNTAES monitoring institutions.

3.1.3 Demilitarization

The demilitarization policy addressed the RSK/EC's army and the paramilitary forces in the region, but also the local population, as individual households possessed massive numbers of small arms. The most challenging task was the demilitarization and expulsion of the paramilitary groups that were still operating in Eastern Slavonia: in a well-planned and determined action, that was not approved by headquarters and that was legally disputable though, UNTAES flexed its muscles and forced the paramilitary to leave. This action was indicative for the proactiveness of the mission and its leadership. After the completion of the demilitarization phase, UNTAES fully established itself as a credible actor, in terms of impartiality and robustness.

"At the beginning of the UNTAES mission, it was recognized that the first step of transfer would be to prise authority out of the hands of the local Serbs and into

---

377 According to the Transitional Administrator, the mission imperative was, "How do we keep the population here? How do we continue to maintain Croatia a multiethnic place? The Croats would have liked nothing better than to cleanse Eastern Slavonia. Period. But you have to remember these Serbs had been there for four, five hundreds years. They were form the *Vojna Krajina*. They were the militia that guarded the frontier against the Ottomans. And most of them were innocent: there were also people in Eastern Slavonia who had nothing to do with the damn war, this insanity that Milosevic had created." Telephone interview with Ambassador Jacques-Paul Klein, SRSG/TA, UNTAES, 19 July 2007.

378 Written interview with Derek G. Boothby, DSRSG/DTA, UNTAES, 5 February 2007.

379 Ibid. "This meant that some of the Serbs left and moved to Former Yugoslavia. In addition, there many Serbs who were displaced from the Croatian ethnic cleansing of Krajina and were living in houses left empty by Croats who had fled westwards in 1991. The arrival of Croatian government authority would mean the return of former owners, and therefore the eviction yet again of Serb occupants." Ibid.

the hands of UNTAES."[380] In accordance with the Basic Agreement, the Transitional Administrator announced the demilitarization of the region immediately after the mission's full military deployment on 21 May.[381]

> [T]he civilian and military leadership of UNTAES made it very clear to the Yugoslav generals, and directly to Yugoslav authorities in Belgrade, that UNTAES would draw up a disarmament plan with deadlines. Part of that plan was that the Serb military could withdraw their weapons to Yugoslavia as they wished, but any weapons still in the region by end-July would be impounded by UNTAES. Step by step, the Serbs withdrew their tanks and artillery, often at night so as to minimize the effect on local Serb morale. In order to allow the FRY military withdrawal to take place without losing face, UNTAES was firm but deliberately took no overt actions to force the withdrawal or otherwise create any military embarrassment.[382]

Between March and June 1996, UNTAES monitored the removal of 93 tanks, 11 armoured personnel carriers, 35 anti-tank systems, 107 artillery pieces, 123 mortars, and 42 anti-aircraft guns. On 26 August, General Schoups noted "remarkable progress in opening up Eastern Slavonia due to successful demining."[383] This success was also attributed to close consultation between UNTAES and the commander of the RSK army, General Dushan Loncar, who also agreed to participate in stabilization measures even after the demilitarization process.[384] UNTAES cultivated this cooperation through consistent efforts in order to portray an image of impartiality, "When Croatian police attempted to enter Eastern Slavonia in contravention to the Basic Agreement, UNTAES faced them down, forcing them to leave the region. This provided UNTAES with crucial credibility with the ethnic Serb community."[385]

Another measure solidifying UNTAES' credibility vis-à-vis the local Serbs was how it dealt with members of the former Serb military. As the Transitional Administrator recalls,

> The Serbs came in to see me. They said, 'Well, many of us are gonna be demobilized. But we're in needs here, we live here, that's where we were born, we wanna stay here, we don't wanna go to Serbia.' – I said, 'But what do you propose to do?' – 'Well, we need to find a way to regularize our position with the Croatian government.' So what we proposed was that we took an engineering battalion of Serbs and made them a

380 Ibid. "In Eastern Slavonia, the mandate was to demilitarize in 30 days. And when they got there that was going to be the first thing they took care of." Interview with Dr. Christine Coleiro, UNITAR POCI, Washington, DC, 1 December 2006.
381 Cf. UN Department of Peacekeeping Operations, "Eastern Slavonia, Baranja and Western Sirmium: Brief Chronology.".
382 Written interview with Derek G. Boothby, DSRSG/DTA, UNTAES, 5 February 2007.
383 UN Department of Peacekeeping Operations, "UNTAES."
384 Cf. Dobbins et al. 2005, p. 116, "[…] not only did Loncar cooperate with demilitarization, he also agreed to stay in Eastern Slavonia after demilitarization, accompanied by 450 troops, to reassure local Serbs that they had not been abandoned."
385 Dobbins et al. 2005, pp. 116-117.

civilian company, PMT: and they became a private demining company, demining the zone between Eastern Slavonia and the rest of Croatia.[386]

Obviously, Tudjman fiercely opposed this proposal – but with a purposefully cynical argument, Klein convinced him to comply.[387]

Vis-à-vis the paramilitary groups, demilitarization could not proceed as straightforwardly. The forces had created areas outside the law, and particularly the "Scorpions,"[388] occupying the profitable oilfield near Djelatovci, had no incentive to disband. "[The oilfield] was controlled by Arkan's people, about 250 of them. And one third of the money was going to Belgrade, one third to the RSK and one third into their own pockets."[389] Klein's efforts to convince Milosevic to halt the paramilitary threat remained unheard. In this situation, the Transitional Administrator asked his Force Commander to do an assessment on "how many hostiles are in the territory, how well armed are they, how much money are they making – and how do we take this on."[390] The assessment took about two to three months and furthered the result that, it would, in fact, be possible for UNTAES to force the militias out. On this basis, Klein kicked off negotiations[391] and he got Arkan to agree to his withdrawal. However, at the literal last minute, Arkan reneged on his promise and tried to play waiting games. Determined not going to be "son-of-UNCRO,"[392] the Transitional Administrator decided to confront them,[393] "ordering the Jordanian battalion to descend on the region in full forces, in tanks and armed personnel carriers."[394] Klein recalls his actions on that day:

> Jockin [Chief of Staff, UNTAES; ES] called me and he said, 'Well, it doesn't seem that they are willing to leave.' I said, 'Will you tell him that they have time till midnight, that they can leave the easy way or the hard way. The easy way is they drive away themselves, the hard way is that we gonna drive them away.' By about ten thirty or eleven at night, Arkan showed up. Unfortunately we didn't have a warrant for him to arrest. He said, 'Let these people go. We won't cause you any trouble.' And we said,

386 Telephone interview with Ambassador Jacques-Paul Klein, SRSG/TA, UNTAES, 19 July 2007.
387 "I said, 'Mr. President, would you rather have Serbs get blown up on demining or Croats?' – 'Oh, Serbs.' – 'OK, so you understand me now.' That's how it works, that's the real world. And they did, they started the demining, with tanks, with everything you can imagine, we tried every technique there is." Ibid.
388 "A tough paramilitary force under Arkan had its base at Erdut and presented a significant problem." Written interview with Derek G. Boothby, DSRSG/DTA, UNTAES, 5 February 2007.
389 Telephone interview with Ambassador Jacques-Paul Klein, SRSG/TA, UNTAES, 19 July 2007.
390 Ibid.
391 With a sticks and carrots tactic, Klein used the international military power at hand as a threat while additionally baiting them with 1,500,000 Deutsch Marks. Ibid.
392 Boothby 2004, p. 39.
393 Cf. ibid., pp. 39-40. UNTAES was eager to show its military robustness.
394 Howard 2008, p. 239.

'Ok, no weapons, no rage, you will take your private vehicles and personal goods.' And then he left. What he didn't know is that at both sides of the road we had Belgian commandos in the bushes, Ukrainian helicopters above them, and the Jordanian infantry behind them. And we managed to secure the oilfields.[395]

The next day, Tudjman was informed.

I called Tudjman, who had his birthday at that day, the next morning and I said, 'Mr. President, I wanna wish you a happy birthday, and also, as a birthday present, I want you to know that we have secured the Djelatovci oilfields. They're heavily mined but we are in control of it and you can send a representative down tomorrow to look them over.' He replied, 'You know what I have always liked about you is that you have a wonderful sense of humor. I know the UN is incapable to do anything like this and would never dare.' I said, 'Mr. President, not only did we dare, it's done.'[396]

Headquarters in New York, however, was upset about the unauthorized action,[397] which had a legal side, too, since the "Chinese Chapter VII" did not clearly safeguard the action.

I had a telegraph from New York saying, 'Congratulations for successfully securing the Djelatovci oilfields. However, this headquarter was very, very, very upset that you had undertaken this action without prior coordination and staff planning by headquarters.' Now, had we done that, the operation would have been on the front pages of all the newspapers before it had ever happened. And people would have gone killed in the process.[398]

What helped Klein deal with this situation was the insights and cooperation of a DPKO staff member who mediated and mitigated the precarious situation.

One DPKO staff member was smart enough to call me up and he said, 'Listen, I have to report to the Council. What questions do you want me to ask you?' And I said, 'All right, you will have to discuss this, this, and this – and we will give you the answers.' And so, he looked good and we looked good.[399]

Apart from the essential security gains, the seizure of the oil fields also had positive consequences for the economic reconstruction of the area through UNTAES.[400] That being said, the paramilitary threat was not yet eliminated. Over the following couple of weeks, aggressors would at night "infiltrate the border and fire in the UNTAES peacekeeping troops. Klein gave the instructions to fire back at the at-

395 Telephone interview with Ambassador Jacques-Paul Klein, SRSG/TA, UNTAES, 19 July 2007.
396 Ibid.
397 "Kofi Annan, at the time the Under Secretary-General for Peacekeeping, was away, so Klein informed Marrack Goulding, who informed the important parties at UN headquarters, but not quickly enough to call the intervention off." Howard 2008, p. 239, fn. 53.
398 Telephone interview with Ambassador Jacques-Paul Klein, SRSG/TA, UNTAES, 19 July 2007.
399 Ibid.
400 I am going to explore this aspect in Chapter IV.3.3.4.

tackers, always using a heavier calibre weapon. While the nightly exchanges escalated for a time, by the end of about three weeks the challenges faded away. The 'Scorpions' were simply outgunned."[401]

The last stage of the demilitarization process included a weapons-buy-back programme, "designed to purchase weapons from the local population."[402] Although the mandate did not explicitly include the demilitarization of the population, "the Transitional Administrator interpreted his instructions to demilitarize the region and ensure civil law and order as including initiatives to reduce the numbers of weapons in the hands of the population."[403] That being said, the UN is not allowed to purchase weapons. UNTAES could only begin their program after convincing the Croatian government to formally convey its acquisition and to provide the necessary funds to do so. After this issue was settled, the program began within two weeks.[404] The first one to register his weapon was the SRSG himself, intending to set an example.[405] After the collection, obsolete weapons were destroyed by UNTAES, while newly manufactured weapons were transferred to the HV.[406] The program ended relatively successfully on 19 August 1997. "[It] provided a carrot that made the introduction of gun registration and the handover of heavier weaponry much easier to achieve."[407] That being said, the demilitarization process was accounted for by Belgrade and intended mainly for the Serb army – getting the cooperation of the *local* Serb population and their leaders in institution-building, and particularly in setting up a joint police force, was still a hard deal.[408] In this situation, "We insisted that someone from the region, a Serb, is designated as Assistant Minister of Internal Affairs in Zagreb."[409]

401 Howard 2008, p. 239.
402 Gravelle undated, p. 3.
403 Dobbins et al. 2005, p. 117.
404 It set out on October 2, 1996.
405 "I was actually the first one to go in and I said, 'Here is my nine millimeter which I wish to register.' It was registered and the others followed." Telephone interview with Ambassador Jacques-Paul Klein, SRSG/TA, UNTAES, 19 July 2007.
406 In numbers, the buy-back program looked as follows: 9,709 rifles, 774 A/T rocket launchers (reuse) and 5,638 A/T rocket launchers (dispos), 14,845 grenades, 1,991,700 ammunition, 116 mortar rounds, 6 A/aircraft missiles (shoulder), and 5 kg TNT were seized. Klein, "UNTAES."
407 Dobbins et al. 2005, p. 117.
408 "Furthermore, while Tudjman had his reasons for supporting the Basic Agreement and agreeing to a UN transition mission, its implementation required his bureaucracy to support the principles of the Basic Agreement and to cooperate with the transitional administration. Such cooperation was not forthcoming." Coleiro 2002, p. 93.
409 Telephone interview with Souren G. Seraydarian, DSRSG/DTA, UNTAES, 16 January 2007.

3.1.4 Humanitarian Action

Besides demilitarization, the other pressing task was the quick provision of humanitarian aid and the resettlement of refugees and of the internally displaced.[410] Throughout the years of war, Eastern Slavonians suffered tremendous losses and traumas, and had been scattered across the Balkans. In joint efforts with international partners, UNTAES took on the humanitarian challenges. Occasionally, the diverging objectives and purposes of the actors involved produced results that were counterproductive to the achievement of the mission's mandate.

"[A]bout 30,000 Croats had in the aftermath of Vukovar been forced to leave and there was an equal number of Serb ethnic people that had come in from other areas where they had been thrown out from Sector North [of UNPROFOR]."[411] To accomplish these challenges, UNTAES could rely on multiple UN agencies and programs that were present in the mission's area, among them UNHCR, UNICEF, the WFP, and WHO.[412] UNHCR had an especially prominent role as the lead agency who oversaw the repatriation of returning refugees and IDPs. In addition, various non-UN organizations, including the Office of the High Representative of IFOR, the OSCE, the ICRC, and the IOM, as well as international and local NGOs assisted in humanitarian aid coordination.[413]

In particular UNHCR's approach to the refugee issue at times foiled UNTAES' efforts to manage the multiethnic character of the region.

> You had a Serb community that was now dealing with the Croatian state and government in Zagreb. So, if you look at the balance of power, the Serbs at this point were really at the disadvantage. The civil service in Zagreb did everything to undermine the Serbs so that they would be so frustrated that they would just leave. That was a concerted effort. The ultimate goal, from a political standpoint, is to, first, have all the mechanisms that are going to protect the rights of a minority group, and then open this up. UNHCR didn't see this. UNHCR was just interested in 'We have so many refugees, they all have to come here – let's get it going, we need to move.' And UNTAES was saying, 'No, if you do that, people will pack up and go back to Yugoslavia – because they are going to be harassed, they are not going to have work, they're not gonna get the pension, they are not gonna be able to negotiate.' So, this would have produced ethnic cleansing,

---

410 On the importance of the refugee issue for public security, see Caplan 2002, p. 36.

411 Interview with Dr. Gerard Fischer, Head of Civil Affairs, UNTAES, New York, 21 November 2006.

412 Their funds were provided by the revised consolidated inter-agency appeal of 1 March 1996. The then-Department of Humanitarian Affairs issued an appeal for the territories of the former Yugoslavia, including the region. However, the revised financial target for the entire area, covering calendar year 1996, amounted to $825 million. "As of 29 April 1996, total funds available for the operation stood at $291 million, leaving a shortfall of $534 million." UN Department of Public Information. 1996. *United Nations Transitional Administration for Eastern Slavonia, Baranja and Western Sirmium. Information Package.* New York: United Nations, p. 9.

413 As of April 1997, 25 NGOs and IOs were operating in the region. Klein, "UNTAES."

basically, if they had opened up Eastern Slavonia to Croats before the Serbs had the protections they needed.[414]

In addition, the Croats were resolute in not providing support to alleviate the situation of the Serbian refugees in the region, as an example on the reconstruction of houses for Serb refugees illustrates:

> When you look at the demographic composition of the villages: it's not clear. You have in Vukovar an agglomeration of Croats, an agglomeration of Serbs, and then an agglomeration of Croats again, or vice versa. And what can be noted is that of course if Croats pay for their reconstruction, they pay for their own people. And if we discovered where this was the case – and of course this was the case – then you go to the ministry of reconstruction, talk to the guy and say, 'We have evidence here that there is this and that problem.' You can't do that. But then he'd go, 'Our money is limited, whe political pressure', et cetera. Very often we took it back to the donor; and the donor would have money for 20 Serb houses to be re-built in the area. But again, this is not cast in iron. You have to sort of find out the concept.[415]

Connected with the refugee management were human rights issues. Human Rights figured prominently in the mandate and human rights officers had been formally included in UNTAES' budget. However, "No human rights unit was established until mid-1997."[416] An observer attributes this failure to the "weak or non-existent" human rights professionalism available at DPKO at that time, "There was no involvement of the HCHR/CHR until early 1997, when it was agreed that the HCHR/CHR should take on the role of giving professional direction and support to these human rights units."[417]

414 Interview with a former UN staff member, 1 December 2006. He adds, "Now, UNTAES never managed to get all the instruments they should have had."
415 Interview with Dr. Gerard Fischer, Head of Civil Affairs, UNTAES, New York, 21 November 2006.
416 Martin, Ian. 1998. "A New Frontier: The Early Experience and Future of International Human Rights Field Operations," *Papers in the Theory and Practice of Human Rights* 19, University of Essex. Available online at http://www.essex.ac.uk/rightsinacutecrisis/report/martin.htm, last access on 25 February 2009. Ian Martin has been a human rights activist and is currently SRSG of the United Nations mission in Nepal.
417 Ibid. He continues in fn. 32, "These arrangements were described in the Secretary-General's report (UN document S/1997/115, 7 February 1997, p.10-11) as follows: 'The unit would report to the UN High Commissioner for Human Rights through the head of the follow-on mission. The UN High Commissioner for Human Rights would select and train qualified human rights personnel in consultation with UN Headquarters in New York. He would further ensure that the Human Rights Unit received all necessary guidance to enhance its capacity to carry out effective human rights work. The High Commissioner would further support the Unit by providing assistance in formulating, developing and implementing advisory services and technical cooperation projects aimed at strengthening national human rights institutions and the administration of justice.'"

3.1.5 Summary and Assessment

The sluggish deployment of the civilian staff and of the "government part" of the mission was a consequence of the hampered pre-mission planning as well as of the rigid coupling of the complex planning and deployment processes that would have required more flexibility. Additionally, the mandate-implementation gap created the space for a range of access points for potential spoilers. Luckily, the UNTAES' leadership found ways to cope with this: damned to succeed, the Transitional Administrator and his team engaged in uncompromising actions towards local spoilers and elaborated a strategy with consistent benchmarks for the implementation of the generic mandate.[418] They even went as far as omitting HQ in their tactical military planning for the sake of surprise and, thus, of effectiveness. In those early days, UNTAES was able to establish and frame itself as a strong actor, building credibility not only vis-à-vis potential militant obstructers but also vis-à-vis the local population of both ethnicities. With smart moves, the leadership managed to play the conflict parties off against each other (further examples follow in the next chapter.) On other occasions, when its counterparts appeared trustworthy, the mission established working relationships with the two sides in the process, thus preempting obstruction and further increasing its credibility.

Specific problems occurred in the humanitarian and human rights sphere. First, working together with UNHCR – which was requested to comply with the Transitional Administrator on paper – on the refugee issue was difficult: the divergent perspective and rationale of the humanitarian organization resulted in actions that countervailed UNTAES' efforts. Second, under the poorly structured conditions of the stressful deployment phase and with no templates available, the neglect of human rights components may have been unavoidable.

That said, after the first couple of months, "We really controlled the territory. And I think this gave us some flexibility, and we really wanted to perform and wanted to do this – also because of the UNPROFOR failure just before."[419]

3.2 Implementation of the Mandate

UNTAES had two purposes: reconciling the formerly warring parties as a precondition to multiethnic governance of the region, and reconstructing the public institutions and governing the region over an interim period. The difficulty consisted

---

418 "The strategy was written down in the plan that I gave to Klein, saying, 'This is how we should reintegrate these things and the agreements that we need.' But that was it – we learned as we went along." Telephone Dr. Robert J.A.R. Gravelle, Head of the JIC Secretariat and Head of STACTA, 11 August 2007.
419 Telephone interview with a field officer, UNTAES, 10 January 2007.

in the fact that the former was only possible as soon as the basic needs were met, while basic services, in turn, could only be provided for in cooperation with and among the local population and potentates. The necessity-turned-philosophy that ensued from these tightly coupled problems was that Croats and Serbs had to co-operate if the mandate was to be achieved.[420] But they did not – and engaged in boycotts and waiting games instead. The following chapters describe UNTAES' attempts to live up to the multiple challenges in the police and the civil adminis-tration sector and how it coped with emerging pathologies.

3.2.1 The Reintegration Process in Police and Civil Administration

The (re-)building of the police and administrative institutions represented UN-TAES' primary civilian tasks. In both sectors, the hostility of the former warring parties and their reluctance to reconcile put the implementation of the mandate regularly at risk. The official financing procedures also contributed to delays and had constraining effects. Although it could do nothing about the loss of time, UN-TAES could prevent major accidents. It coped through innovations, for instance by training future police officers or by actively engaging in the identification of additional donors to finance necessary programs or equipment, and through making full use of its disciplinary power.

3.2.1.1 UN Civilian Police and the Transitional Police Force

UNTAES' civilian police force was entrusted with the maintenance of security and public order in the territory as well as with the composition, training, and subse-quent monitoring of a multiethnic local police force. Resulting from the sheer scope of tasks, as well as from its own diversity, UNTAES' CivPol faced various patholo-gies. However, major accidents were prevented by innovative actions and by using the full authority of its mandate.

From the outset, CivPol faced obstacles. "The Secretary-General estimated that 600 UN CivPol would be necessary" for the 24/7-job, but the component "never received adequate funding, and the force came to a maximum strength of only 455 international officers, many of whom were not adequately qualified."[421] In addi-tion, the CivPol component encountered specific functional and political problems.

---

420   Cf. Dobbins et al. 2005, p. 115.
421   Howard 2008, pp. 245-246. Some of them were even found guilty on heavy misconduct charges. Cf. Lessons Learned Unit 1998, para. 60.

Besides notorious shortages of personnel and equipment,[422] the use of arms was problematic: international guidelines ban the police from carrying them,[423] but that often reduces their credibility towards local spoilers.[424] In this situation, "The Transitional Administrator sought an alternative solution,"[425] arranging for "a Polish Special Police Group of some fifty strong to join UNTAES in order to provide security for visiting VIPs and for any special operations that might be required."[426] And this Special Police Force, of course, *was* carrying weapons. Likewise increasing the mission's credibility was the military component's ability to exhibit and execute its robustness: its display of military strength ath the oilfields and the accomplished demilitarization program lent the mission respect and credibility early on.

A typical problem of international police relates to its cultural dimension: from day one, officers from a multitude of countries are to work hand-in-hand. "There were 20 contributing countries for CivPol in UNTAES. The differences in policing methods and social behavior can be a great source of tensions within CivPol units."[427] Fortunately, they did not have a major negative effect in this case since they were relatively well contained. In fact, due to the UNTAES integrated system, the civilian police component could very early "establish a presence in all the local police stations and begin monitoring local police."[428]

The first steps in the set up of the henceforth-called Transitional Police Force (TPF) were taken in July 1996.[429] "Particularly in light of the fact that the outbreak of fighting in the region in 1991 had been among the police themselves,"[430] the TPF was assumed to convey great significance for the future of the reintegration

---

422 "[U]nlike the military, which deploys with all its equipment and logistics, police turn up with nothing but their uniforms, and sometimes not even that. This means that the UN has to outfit them, equip them and deploy them with some form of logistical support." Coleiro 2002, p. 95.

423 Boothby 2004, p. 43.

424 On the importance of credibility-building cf. Doyle, Michael W. and Müller, Jan. 1998. "Anatomie eines Erfolges. Die UN-Mission in Ostslawonien." *Internationale Politik* 53:6, pp. 34-38, p. 37.

425 Boothby 2004, pp. 43-44.

426 Ibid. In fact, this was the very police group that made the first arrest of an indicted war criminal, "Before any similar arrest by NATO-led troops in Bosnia – by apprehending the former mayor of Vukovar and delivering him to the International Criminal Tribunal in The Hague." Ibid.

427 Coleiro 2002, p. 95.

428 Ibid., p. 97. "As the UNTAES police presence grew, UNTAES police were placed in the local police (*milicija*) stations to monitor the activities of the *milicja*." Written interview with Derek G. Boothby, DSRSG/DTA, UNTAES, 5 February 2007.

429 Klein, "UNTAES."

430 Boothby 2004, p. 43. "In the view of the common local man, when you had a problem, you didn't go to the police. *They* were the problem, *they* were the agents of state terror." Telephone interview with Ambassador Jacques-Paul Klein, SRSG/TA, UNTAES, 19 July 2007.

process,[431] allowing the Serb police officers to have a primary position as role models.[432]

CivPol's strategy for the reintegration of the local police envisioned three stages: initially, only incumbent Serb officers should be recruited. Croat officers could then be introduced gradually; the first ones were introduced into the force in September 1996.[433] In the third stage, the "responsibility for [the] management and operational control [of the TPF]," by which time should have reached its desired ethnic composition,[434] "was transferred to the Croatian Ministry of Interior and [it] became part of the Croatian Police Force."[435] The first problem that emerged was the recruitment of suitable officers:

> Many of the first Serb TPF candidates were former militiamen who had no understanding of police functions and were only seeking temporary employment. These candidates had no interest in the training programme because they had already decided to leave Eastern Slavonia and to move to FRY at a later date. A lot of time and effort was wasted on these candidates.[436]

After a mediocre recruitment process, an ensuing recalcitrance among the designated police officers continued to challenge the mission. A useful countermeasure was the external training of police contingents: taking the aspirants out of the region, the first TPF training courses started out in Budapest at the Hungarian Police Academy.[437] "Initially, the atmosphere [among the 20 Croat and the 20 Serb police officers; ES] was strained, but as the course progressed the officers began to interact with each other. The foreign context facilitated the ice-breaking process."[438] Little by little, a kind of community spirit evolved.

> The fellow who was in charge of that brought with him 50 T-shirts and 50 blue jeans, and he distributed them to the whole group, so that you could not see who is who. I think it took three days before they sort of co-operated. But, you know, they went out together after work… And that was amazing to see. But again an observation: this is

---

431 "The TPF was very important to give confidence to both Croats and Serbs." Telephone interview with Souren G. Seraydarian, DSRSG/DTA, UNTAES, 16 January 2007.

432 "Initially the Serbs were extremely hostile to these changes. Wearing the Croatian crest the 'Hrvatska,' which they associated with the Ustaŝe, on their uniform and having it stamped on their citizenship papers was intolerable. Even the Serb community at large was facing this deeply emotional dilemma, because they too needed Croatian documents. So it was important that the TPF officers would lead the people by their own example." Coleiro 2002, p. 98.

433 Cf. ibid., p. 99.

434 The aspired composition was 40 percent Croat, 40 percent Serb and 20 percent other ethnic minorities. The numbers were based on results on ethnic composition of the 1991 census in the FRY. Cf. ibid.

435 Ibid.

436 Ibid.

437 Interview with Dr. Gerard Fischer, Head of Civil Affairs, UNTAES, New York, 21 November 2006.

438 Coleiro 2002, p. 98.

possible with people who are used to discipline. And they were policemen. Civilians are more complicated to streamline into this direction.[439]

Their positive experience with this multiethnic programme had some police training officials[440] come up with the idea of importing the approach to Eastern Slavonia. This move, however, bore a substantial risk as it meant bringing Croat police officers in the region when such an action could still be highly provocative vis-à-vis the local Serbs. The conflict potential was very clearly perceived within UNTAES, and while many opposed the idea, the Transitional Administrator preferred the potential gains to the potential losses and saw it as a measure of enormous symbolic emanation. "If the initiative succeeded, if the people could see Serb and Croat officers train together, it would kick-start the difficult psychological transition from hostility to cooperation."[441] Wisely enough, Klein and heads of ICITAP[442] realized that "in order to succeed, the people needed to be part of the process."[443] Accordingly, they "visited the mayors of all the villages through which the Croat police officers would be transported on their way to Erdut, to explain what they were doing and why it was so important for the Serb community to cooperate."[444] Finally, the first Croatian police officers arrived, escorted by UNTAES soldiers. By the third week, however, UNTAES no longer considered this necessary and the safety of the Croats was left to the TPF officers, who were all Serbs."[445]

CivPol encouraged the Serbs and Croats to conduct joint patrols. This was an excellent suggestion because it also addressed some of the ethnic concerns between the TPF and the local community. When officers took action against offenders of their own ethnicity it was not perceived as ethnic harassment. [...] However, it should also be said that in some cases the TPF officers refused to get involved in crimes committed by members

---

439 Interview with Dr. Gerard Fischer, Head of Civil Affairs, UNTAES, New York, 21 November 2006. "Policemen, like firemen, all get along because they have certain professional characteristics that are very similar. So, we worked that." Telephone interview with Ambassador Jacques-Paul Klein, SRSG/TA, UNTAES, 19 July 2007. On this note, a further "support technique" for reconciliation was having the officers socialize "by drinking beer and smoking cigarettes." Interview with Dr. Gerard Fischer, Head of Civil Affairs, UNTAES, New York, 21 November 2006.
440 This approach was pushed particularly by the International Criminal Investigative Training Assistance Programme (ICITAP), a programme of the US Department of Justice's Criminal Division involved with the development of "professional and transparent law enforcement institutions that protect human rights, combat corruption," directed at "[reducing] the threat of transnational crime and terrorism." For more information see the Official Homepage of the US Department of Justice, available online at http://www.usdoj.gov/criminal/icitap/. ICITAP was cooperating in the training of police officers throughout Croatia, starting in 1995.
441 Coleiro 2002, p. 98.
442 See fn. 440.
443 Coleiro 2002, p. 98.
444 Ibid.
445 Ibid.

of their own ethnicity for fear of being seen as traitors. Here CivPol had to demand professionalism and insist that the officers perform their duties.[446]

When the second phase started in September 1996,[447] much more upheaval was expected, but the risk of emotions running high was successfully contained.

> One of the reasons for this relatively peaceful transition was that UNTAES, and therefore CivPol, had both the power and the determination to control the situation. [...] This power emanated from both the mandate, through which UNTAES had operational control of the TPF, and the Memorandum of Understanding, which gave CivPol extensive rights to monitor and conduct investigations."[448]

Still, singular instances occurred where "TPF officers refused to get involved in crimes committed by members of their own ethnicity for fear of being seen as traitors. Here CivPol had to demand professionalism and insist that the officers perform their duties."[449] In cases where the misconduct of officers was more serious, CivPol dismissed the officers in question, "In fact, 18 officers were dismissed as a result of these minor incidents."[450] Ejections from the force also resulted from Serb refusals to adopt the Terms of Conduct standards of the Croatian police. "Efforts were constantly made to move the standard and conduct of the Transitional Police Force toward those of the Croatian police."[451] Those Serbs who were unwilling to accept them had to drop out.

> It was crucially important that CivPol maintained its control over the TPF [...], because the change in balance of power was having a destabilizing effect within the TPF and in the community at large. Thus, CivPol issued a directive requiring CivPol's approval and presence during home visits by TPF officers. As a result of this directive, the Commissioner let the TPF know that evidence would be weighed in favor of the resident. It also helped to regain local confidence in the TPF.[452]

Other pressing issues emerged; particularly concerning salaries, the terms of conduct, and also concering the uniforms the officers wore. First, the uniform issue inherently entailed symbolic importance but was compounded by a pending question of funding. As the old uniforms of the Serb *milicija* could not be accepted as TPF uniforms and as Serb officers were not willing to wear the Croatian uniforms,[453] a compromise had to be found at a time when there was still a stalemate on both sides. "[T]he only place they could meet to have these talks was an area

---

446 Coleiro 2002, p. 100.
447 In this phase, the original Serb police chief was replaced by a Croat police chief.
448 Coleiro 2002, p. 100.
449 Ibid.
450 Ibid.
451 Boothby 2004, p. 43.
452 Coleiro 2002, pp. 100-101.
453 "Wearing the Croatian crest the 'Hrvatska,' which they associated with the Ustashe, on their uniform and having it stamped on their citizenship papers was intolerable." Coleiro 2002, p. 98.

on the border between Eastern Slavonia and Osijek, called 'No-Man's-Land.' This was a small parcel of land surrounded by mines and guarded by Croats and UNTAES forces on one side and Serbs and UNTAES forces on the other."[454] They eventually agreed to wear neutral uniforms. A "bland dark blue uniform" was picked from a readily available commercial catalogue of US police equipment.[455]

> After a week or two, maybe a month, everyone had the same uniform and caps. Those are things that you can discuss endlessly; but it sort of works out, you now. You have to, hopefully, appeal to the smarter ones who say, 'This is a symbol for something, but let's forget about the symbol for a time.'[456]

The financial bottleneck[457] regarding the uniform funding was handled informally, too, with the Transitional Administrator himself drawing on his connections to the US Department of Justice and convincing them to make the purchase.[458] Obviously, however, "It was inevitable that the Serbs would have to adopt the Croatian uniform when the TPF became part of the Croatian Police Force, and CivPol had to persuade the Serbs to accept this reality and the inevitability of reintegration."[459] The financial bottleneck regarding salaries and operational equipment became a subject of tough political negotiation between UNTAES and the GoC.

> At first, the Croatian government balked at paying money to Serb police but eventually accepted the argument that because the region was regarded in Zagreb as part of Croatia, they had a certain responsibility to help UNTAES establish and maintain acceptable law and order. An additional argument, not articulated but silently recognized, was that by providing money for the Transitional Police Force, Zagreb could expedite or delay monthly payments, thereby exerting leverage over UNTAES acceptance of Croats in place of Serbs.[460]

A discussion on the currency of the salaries broke out, "The Croats refused to pay in Yugoslav *dinars*, and until UNTAES forced the acceptance of the Croatian currency into the region, the Serb police refused to be paid in Croatian *kuna*."[461] The

---

454 Ibid. "This indicated the extent to which the tremendous hostility and suspicion still prevailed and how precarious these negotiations were." Ibid.
455 Cf. Boothby 2004, p. 43. Initially, the Croats had suggested a black uniform – which was, however, quickly rejected by the Serbs who pointed out associations with fascism.
456 Interview with Dr. Gerard Fischer, Head of Civil Affairs, UNTAES, New York, 21 November 2006.
457 Appeals to the Croat government were in vain: they were not willing to pay for non-Croat uniforms.
458 Cf. Boothby 2004, p. 43.
459 Coleiro 2002, p. 98. "Klein placed the following argument before the Serb community, 'What would you prefer, a Croat policeman in your village or a Serb policeman? ... Well, then one of our men must join and put on the Croatian uniform.'" Ibid.
460 Boothby 2004, p. 43.
461 Ibid. Discussions on the payment currency emerged throughout every sector; pension payment was particularly concerned. Cf. Chapter IV.3.2.2.

interim solution that ultimately emerged, tolerated by UNTAES, was payment in German Marks.[462]

> Through patience and persuasion, and on the basis of the existing rapport between UNTAES and the Serb community, the advantages of an integrated police force became apparent, and peer pressure to resist change began to recede. This shift in attitude was critically important because, ultimately, an integrated, multiethnic police force could only be successful if supported by the people.[463]

A veritable indicator of the positive impact of the TPF was the increasing numbers of reports taken to the police by the population.[464] In spite of this overall progress, the TPF remained overshadowed by the persistent fragility of the daily working relationship of the officers.

3.2.1.2 Civil Administration

The overarching goal of UNTAES was to reintegrate the residual RSK structure into the Croatian administrative and legal system while preserving the rights of the Serb community.[465] Approximately 800 international civil servants and about 1,700 locals worked towards this goal. At the strategic level, the cooperation among the international and local actors consisted of regular meetings, while the JICs were the main mechanisms at the operational level. In the JICs, the reluctance of both parties to the conflict to work together in the transitory structure was a major problem. Not only did the local officers represent challenges to the mandate's implementation: the international civilian staff in the JICs succumbed collectively to cognitive biases, focusing on the factors and processes that were easiest to deal with, i.e. issues that were more of a technical and less of political nature. After nine months into the mission, the SRSG demanded a comprehensive re-design of the JIC's approach in order to stop this inefficient policy. This *rupture* and its effects were decisive for the further course of the mission.

---

462 Cf. Boothby 2004, p. 43.
463 Coleiro 2002, pp. 98-99.
464 Ibid., p. 102, referring to an interview she conducted with Gerard T. Beekman, CivPol Deputy Chief of Staff.
465 Cf. ibid., pp. 103-104.

Strategic and Operational Mechanisms for Reintegration

UNTAES established cooperation mechanisms on the strategic and operational levels, creating fora for Serbs and Croats to meet and to exchange their arguments peacefully. It was also a means for pushing the mission's transition agenda.

At the strategic level, the goal of reintegration was pursued during regular meetings between

> the Head of the Mission, myself [DSRSG Seraydarian; ES], our Chief of the Political Unit, the Force Commander, and the Minister of Justice of Croatia, the Minister of Interior of Croatia, the President and the Minister of Foreign Affairs. We regularly met in order to work things out in small detail; the transfer of authority was step-by-step. Sometimes, we met twice in a week and sometimes we didn't meet in three weeks – it depended on where we stood with the process. We had ups and downs.[466]

This roller coaster ride owed to diverging interests of the two parties to the conflict and to internal divides. Although UNTAES had a thumbs-up from the Croatian government as Tudjman was eager to demonstrate his commitment to human rights and democracy in order to claim his place in Europe,

> his administration officials were deeply sceptical of the capacity of UNTAES to realize its mandate as well as hostile to the idea of a multiethnic society in the region: they preferred to wait for UNTAES' mandate to run out so they could work out the details of the reintegration on their own terms and without foreign interference.[467]

On the Serb side, the Executive Council was also divided:

> There were those who had short-term goals in Eastern Slavonia, i.e., they were marking time until they moved to Serbia. Many knew that they would be indicted for war crimes if they stayed on; having no future in Croatia, they did not care about the fate of the local Serb community. Then there were those who believed that Eastern Slavonia would always be an autonomous region distinct from Croatia; therefore, they felt no urgency to negotiate the terms of reintegration. Few […] understood the situation and recognized the importance of the JICs.[468]

In fact, the civilian affairs side of the RSK was rather frail,

> What they found, when they arrived, is that the local administration existed only on paper, and that the region had been ruled really by the JNA. And when Milosevic cut the deal, he pulled out – as he was supposed to – the JNA, which meant that there was

---

466 Telephone interview with Souren G. Seraydarian, DSRSG/DTA, UNTAES, 16 January 2007.

467 Coleiro 2002, p. 105.

468 Ibid., p. 104. "Needless to say that neither the Croats understood the mandate as the Security Council had intended it. [...] So, maybe you had two or three months to highlight the obligations of the Croatian state, what it means, integration; and at the same time you had to convince them that there was not much leverage for them." Interview with Dr. Gerard Fischer, Head of Civil Affairs, UNTAES, New York, 21 November 2006.

really no real authority in Eastern Slavonia. What existed was there on paper, but the persons were extremely weak.[469]

Another factor that complicated the process was the unequal negotiating capacity of Serbs and Croats. "The Serb negotiating teams were neither career administrators nor politicians and were no match for the seasoned Croat administrators who were sent to negotiate on behalf of the Croatian government."[470] In order to level the playing field, UNTAES officials advised Serb negotiators on basic negotiation techniques.

At the operational level, the main mechanism for the shift in authority was, apart from the mission itself, the RSK/EC structure complemented by the JICs. The latter consisted of representatives from all ethnic groups in the region.[471]

> We came in and said, 'Yes, we have executive authority, but in reality we let RSK run it – as they had run it for five years.' We did think of setting up – or simply taking over – a UN person in charge of each RSK ministry. But we didn't. And I think that was smart. In Eastern Slavonia, we left the structures intact. It was a pass-through situation. We tried to respect, as much as possible, their political structure, so they had ownership over the process. For a while, they thought they would become a state, but within a year of us being there, it became… it lost significance.[472]

Thus, UNTAES opted to go for a "facilitator role"[473] in making the RSK/EC structure "more and more hollow until it finally evaporated."[474] The region was then to be integrated into regular Croatian municipalities.

---

469 Interview with Professor Michael W. Doyle, former UN Assistant Secretary-General, New Haven, 11 September 2006.

470 Coleiro 2002, p. 105. "There was a sort of a power mismatch: it was arranged that the negotiations would be at one time on the Croatian side and the next time on the Serbian side – but Serbs sometimes even couldn't afford to get to the location. They were often, I'd say, appointed a little bit above their capacity, whereas the Croatians often were well-trained and had the backing of the whole government. So, those were negotiation issues that impacted a lot." Telephone interview with a staff member of STACTA, UNTAES, 10 January 2007.

471 Cf. Dobbins et al. 2005, p. 115.

472 "We tried to respect, as much as possible, their political structure so they had ownership over the process. For a while, they thought they would become a state but within a year of us being there, it lost significance and their structure looked more and more hollow." Interview with a UNTAES staff member, Washington, DC, 1 December 2006. "It was extremely important to Klein. And that not only was he aware of the continuity that had to go on after the mission ended but he felt the mission has to be a continuation of what there was originally. I mean Klein had the power to go there, establish a totally international government and rule like a king. He had that kind of power. But Klein went there and did nothing of the sort. […] You know, what they found in place they tried to keep in place." Telephone interview with a field officer, UNTAES, 10 January 2007.

473 Ibid.

474 Ibid. "At the time that we were there with the negotiations, the Serbs had Deputy Ministries of Education, Healthcare, Security, and Administration in Zagreb. Now, we wouldn't tell them anything or show them any papers or whatever. The point was that symbolically, they

133

There were around 25 municipalities in Croatia. Eastern Slavonia came to constitute three or four. So, for Croatia it was just a question of re-establishing those municipalities. But they ended up exactly like the municipality of Zagreb, the municipality of Vukovar being just a regular municipality. And we couldn't really argue with this. We'd say, 'That is fine, the administrative structure looks like any other municipality structure in Croatia – except there should be some minority guarantee.'[475]

However, at the end of the day, the approach might have been too optimistic, "I think the Serbs and the UN maybe understood fairly late how little influence the Serbs would have eventually. There would be no Serb political structure."[476]

UNTAES also wanted to preserve continuity among regular workers, regular local capacities – despite intense controversies over its stance. For example, the US ambassador in Croatia expressed his view towards Klein that he wanted him to "get rid off them all."[477] However, the Transitional Administrator stuck to the adopted course:

I said, 'Peter, who of them is the government, who are the civil servants, who are the judges?' I said that what I intended to do is go in and have a nice sort of meeting with them and say, 'Look, you will all retain your positions and your places as long as you do what the hell I tell you to do. And the day you don't, you're fired. I have a full mandate of the Security Council to govern here.'[478]

The ultimate goal was to establish confidence, to have the locals "buy in." – "And how do you get that? By saying, 'Well, if the people already have these leaders, and if these people are already in certain offices, we're gonna tell them we respect that, and we're just going to keep things as they are."[479]

The capacity of the local population in terms of their professional qualification, knowledge, and skills in the former Yugoslavia were relatively high compared to

were there." Telephone interview with a staff member of STACTA, UNTAES, 10 January 2007. "And there, again, after a while, the Croats were cooperating. And to make this even stronger we convinced Tudjman and his gang in November 1996 that he would have to accept Deputy Ministers of Serb ethnicity that would be based in Zagreb – and of course, they were very unhappy with this proposal. But with the assistance of the Contact Group and with the assistance of a statement by the Security Council which came out 5 January 1997, it was a done deal. And then the next problem was to find six Serbs who would go to Zagreb. But subsequently it worked; they had an apartment, they had security, they spent in the beginning maybe one day in Zagreb and drove for the evening back out; and after three, four months, they even settled down, you know. The level of tension reduced and nothing happened to them, at least nothing really bad... I guess, they were beaten up once..." Interview with a senior staff member of UNTAES, New York, 22 November 2006.

475 Telephone interview with a staff member of STACTA, UNTAES, 10 January 2007.
476 Ibid.
477 Telephone interview with Ambassador Jacques-Paul Klein, SRSG/TA, UNTAES, 19 July 2007.
478 Ibid.
479 Interview with a UNTAES staff member, Washington, DC, 1 December 2006.

the standard environment of peace operations.[480] "[I]n many instances, the people that were working there were better than our crew."[481] Occasionally, however, local and international staffs' different socializations became obvious. For instance, "When you talked to them about capitalism: they couldn't understand how the state could not take care of everything. They had been a communist country – and there were many things they didn't understand."[482] The former RSK structure had been functioning relatively well in a technocratic sense, but they had no experience with the policy processes of a democratic political system and some of them remained very hostile towards forthcoming change.[483] Eventually, the UN tried to increasingly handpick moderate Serb proponents, aiming to build them up as new strong local leaders of the Serbs, putting them into the transformed EC structure.[484] One straightforward exclusion criteria for both sides consisted of the sorting out of perpetrators of severe war crimes.[485]

Around April and May 1996, the JICs were set up.[486] As suggested by the mandate, they amended the RSK/EC structure. The chairmanships of the 15 bodies were assigned to UNTAES Civil Affairs officers.[487] In the beginning, the approach was minimalist and aimed at mere peaceful interaction, so "that they could sit in one and the same room and loosen up and forget about sort of the difficulties that have arisen as a result of the war."[488] Nonetheless, these initial meetings were extremely difficult and both sides obstructed the process, making all kinds of manoeuvres in

---

480 "In terms of administration, it worked all in all very well. The Yugoslavs had one of the most efficient, professional police forces in Europe." Telephone interview with Ambassador Jacques-Paul Klein, SRSG/TA, UNTAES, 19 July 2007.

481 Interview with Dr. Gerard Fischer, Head of Civil Affairs, UNTAES, New York, 21 November 2006.

482 Interview with a former UNTAES staff member, Washington, DC, 1 December 2006.

483 "The former Yugoslavia had only begun to develop rudimentary non-state institutions and that weakness passed on to its successor entities." UN Task Force 1995, para. 52.

484 Cf. Doyle and Sambanis 2006, p. 229.

485 "The most important thing was to have a background-checking on whether they were on any list of war criminals during the war. So, we checked back with The Hague, with the ICT for the Former Yugoslavia, with local authorities, and neighborhoods on whether these people were involved in raping, killing, or in whatever violations of human rights. We used also the international police as well as civilian people to do background checking." Telephone interview with Souren G. Seraydarian, DSRSG/DTA, UNTAES, 16 January 2007. "You're dealing with the devil sometimes, but that is what you have to work with. And so that's what Klein did." Interview with Dr. Christine Coleiro, UNITAR POCI, Washington, DC, 1 December 2006.

486 Telephone interview with Dr. Robert J.A.R. Gravelle, Head of the JIC Secretariat and Head of STACTA, 11 August 2007.

487 The civil affairs officers were usually grouped as P3 or P4.

488 Interview with Dr. Gerard Fischer, Head of Civil Affairs, UNTAES, New York, 21 November 2006.

order to avoid talking to each other. Only through UNTAES' ongoing mediation efforts did the former opponents continue the talks.[489]

> [E]ach side mistrusted and hated the other. In most cases, initial meetings, designed to introduce each delegation, were foiled by one delegation not showing up until several hours after the designated hour and the other delegation refusing to wait for its counterpart, or no delegation appearing at all. Once the meetings actually took place, the difficulty arose whereby one side would not speak directly to the other but only through the UNTAES civil affairs officer designated to chair individual committees. Another problem was that one delegation would send persons at the ministerial level to discuss a specific sector of reintegration while the other sent technical experts. This proved cumbersome as one party or the other did not have the authority to make decisions but had to seek political guidance in each specific issue discussed.[490]

At the top of each committee, there was a Serb counterpart and a Croat counterpart to the international head of the JIC. The key person on the Croatian side was the Director of the Office for Transitional Administration of the GoC, Ivica Vrkic.

> Tudjman had one person responsible for Eastern Slavonia whom I dealt with on a daily basis, Mr. Vrkic. He was very, very good. He was one of the few Croats who could actually drive his own car in Eastern Slavonia without being harmed. He was respected and so he was a key person.[491]

The staffing of the JICs was community work by UNTAES, Croats, and Serbs. Due to their differing preferences,[492] at times, things were not moving.[493] In addition, their approaches to recruitment differed, "From the Croatian side it was a lot more centralised: we would just call up Zagreb and they'd say, 'Well, this is the person.' On the Serb side, it was a little more political: they would have their own political games on who gets a sit in the JIC."[494]

The people who were eventually appointed often did not support the implementation of the mandate. In renitent cases, the Transitional Administrator used his executive authority and fired them.

---

489   Coleiro 2002, p. 105. "This could only have happened in the context of UNTAES because the mediator was a crucially important player. The UNTAES chair had enough integrity and power to sustain the process. One Serb member of the Human Rights JIC confirmed, 'The human element is very important in negotiation. I really appreciated the coordinating role of UNTAES in this process. I had the impression that we were all back in school again.'" Ibid.

490   Gravelle undated, p. 5.

491   Telephone interview with Ambassador Jacques-Paul Klein, SRSG/TA, UNTAES, 19 July 2007.

492   "We would ensure that the people, the Serbs, were qualified. Same with the Croats. We were not bringing in unqualified people here. We were not in a quota system here. Either you're qualified or you're not. And they were qualified." Telephone interview with Dr. Robert J.A.R. Gravelle, Head of the JIC Secretariat and Head of STACTA, 11 August 2007.

493   Telephone interview with a staff member of STACTA, UNTAES, 10 January 2007.

494   Ibid.

By the way, the first person I fired was a judge, the Head of the Supreme Court of Eastern Slavonia. He came to me and said, 'I don't know who you are or what you think your mandate is, but the law is the law, and I am the law here.' Et cetera. And I said, 'Well, Mr. Chief Justice, I'm afraid that I have just fired you. You're no longer anything. And I'll have your Deputy to replace you. We are the law here, we have the mandate from the Security Council, and we are going to govern. And we are not tolerating any interference based on Serbian political tricks.' So he was out. And it sent a clear message: do your job, stay the hell out of politics and you'll survive – play politics, oppose the administration and you'll be gone. You don't share power with criminals. You need a democratic group of interlocutors. And you still have to understand what your mandate is.[495]

Often, however, firing was not the ultimate solution to the problem since someone else who was even worse would replace the first ill-suited person, or the replacement would be substantially delayed.[496] "What we have probably missed or not put enough effort on would be this postponing of bringing people together and to get them to work together again."[497] Similar to discussions in the police sector, the issue of salary payment for those working in the transitional structures required lengthy negotiations. The Croatian negotiators dabbled in various sleights of hand:

They didn't find their records, they had not paid taxes previously, they hadn't contributed to this fund, to that fund, et cetera. There are constantly stalling techniques. And of course, if you would go to a Croat he would say, 'Oh I cannot take this guy, he's a war criminal.' You know, this is the first thing you will get. And we said, 'You should not cooperate with a war criminal. But *if* you say this guy is a war criminal: give me evidence, and give me evidence within a week.' And of course, in 90 out of 100 cases there was absolutely no evidence about anything. For instance, we had one guy who said, 'I cannot sit with this person on one table because during the war this person provided logistic support to the enemy.' I said, 'Can you be more specific, what does logistic support to the enemy mean?' And the reality was: it was a woman who brought soup to her father who was in the defense force.[498]

Eventually, UNTAES and the Croatian government agreed on financing from two sources: the major source being the Croatian government itself, pledging about six million *kuna*[499] per month; the other consisting of the gains from the Djelatovci oilfield that UNTAES had recaptured in the early days of its mission.[500]

---

495 Telephone interview with Ambassador Jacques-Paul Klein, SRSG/TA, UNTAES, 19 July 2007.
496 "You have to understand one thing: nothing happens the time and the day when you think it should happen. It all happens significantly with serious delays." Interview with Dr. Gerard Fischer, Head of Civil Affairs, UNTAES, New York, 21 November 2006.
497 Ibid.
498 Ibid.
499 At the time, the amount equalled about 1 million Deutsch Marks.
500 Telephone interview with Souren G. Seraydarian, DSRSG/DTA, UNTAES, 16 January 2007.

The general issue of refugees strongly affected the capacity-building efforts of UNTAES and the progress made by the JICs. Many qualified people who sought their future in mainland Croatia or Serbia or even abroad had left the region.[501] The problem related particularly to the local Croats: many of them were chased from their positions and eventually fled when the RSK declared its authority over the Region in 1991.

> The problem was that they didn't have qualified people. In Yugoslavia, the tendency was for Croats to be in administrative roles, even in government. The major part of all the civil service in former Yugoslavia had a lot of Croats. The ministries, people with power were Serbs; but the people who actually ran the bureaucracy were mostly Croats. And they knew how to work a system, and they were very good at that.[502]

Yet, as power shifted increasingly towards the Croats in the course of the transition, Zagreb – with a *quid pro quo* attitude – started to exploit its new position of strength and advanced a discrimination policy against ethnic Serbs in its future Croat province. "You had a Serb community that was now dealing with the Croatian state and government in Zagreb. If you look at the balance of power, the Serbs at this point were really at the disadvantage. The civil service in Zagreb did everything to undermine the Serbs so that they would be so frustrated that they would just leave. That was a concerted effort."[503] As early as mid-1996, Civil Affairs tried to bring the Croats to begin a policy of reconciliation – "which they didn't."[504] Eventually, UNTAES wrote the reconciliation policy. The Croats endorsed it, but then again, it took another year until they adopted it[505] – and much longer until they finally implemented parts of it.[506] UNTAES could occasionally identify some key Serbs who were qualified as well as idealistic enough to stick out those difficult times for the purpose of a peaceful, multiethnic Eastern Slavonia.[507] In addition, UNTAES

---

501   "It was very confusing: there was Flash and Storm which created Serb refugees, there was the invasion of Eastern Slavonia which created Croat refugees… Originally, they should all have been *displaced* people, but eventually, when they all became individual states, the problem was one of *refugees* because their legal status changed… It was a mess. It was humongous." Interview with a former UNTAES staff member, 1 December 2006.
502   Ibid.
503   Ibid.
504   Interview with Dr. Gerard Fischer, Head of Civil Affairs, UNTAES, New York, 21 November 2006.
505   "It was September 1997 – a year later – when we basically forced the Croats to announce that they had a reconciliation policy." Ibid.
506   "It took them probably another five years before parts of these reconciliation policies are being implemented or are being considered as useful." Ibid.
507   "Many people had left. That's true. But not everyone had left. For instance, there was a man, Stanimirovic, who was a psychiatrist; he stayed through the whole thing. He was a very solid, decent man who was trying to do the best for his people." Telephone interview with Ambassador Jacques-Paul Klein, SRSG/TA, UNTAES, 19 July 2007.

organized training courses. Similar to what was done for the TPF,[508] a training course for teachers – Serbs and Croats and other minorities such as Hungarians and Ruthenians – and other professional groups were set up. "We took a bunch of them and went to Strasbourg."[509]

> We had workshops with them – doctors, teachers, pharmacists, lawyers – and we were sitting in some nice environment to discuss the possibilities of how to lower the tensions, if you wish. And again: in many other conflicts you have a much greater diversity of hatred – here there were people who studied together, they went together at universities in Zagreb, in Sarajevo, in Belgrade... The academia is not that huge in these countries. So, whoever was in human rights, whether it was Serb or Croat, they knew one another, from previous years. And they had the same teachers, the same philosophy, there was not great divergence. But the political instruments were stronger than their intellectual capacity to counterattack the political structures at that time.[510]

In sum, the JICs proceeded slowly, "There is no magic stick how you can make this work."[511] If the "chemistry" between the mediator – "we had singled out good people [to do that; ES], and then subsequently, some of them became good and others mediocre and others were very bad and we had to replace them"[512] – and the group was fine, things had a chance to work out. Often, however, that was not the case and the sides did not have balanced negotiation skills. "The UN person was often a substantive expert. For example, in the human rights sector we had a Swedish human rights lawyer who knew the law in and out, and in other areas, public utilities, we had somebody who really knew those things. However, all of them did not have much negotiation skills."[513]

As result of the persistent recalcitrance, the JICs did not live up to their task of managing the process of transition in their respective sectors, monitoring and (where necessary) administering governmental process in these areas for several months.[514]

Besides recruitment for the JICs, UNTAES hired local people to work within its own structure. UNTAES personnel conducted the recruitment of UN people, i.e. those being paid with UN salaries.[515] Initially, however, the local staffs were

---

508 See Chapter IV.3.2.1.1.
509 Interview with Dr. Gerard Fischer, Head of Civil Affairs, UNTAES, New York, 21 November 2006.
510 Ibid. "We also worked to arrange meetings between lawyers, doctors, schoolteachers, dentists et cetera." Written interview with Derek G. Boothby, DSRSG/DTA, UNTAES, 5 February 2007.
511 Interview with Dr. Gerard Fischer, Head of Civil Affairs, UNTAES, New York, 21 November 2006.
512 Ibid.
513 Telephone interview with a staff member of STACTA, UNTAES, 10 January 2007.
514 Coleiro 2002, p. 104.
515 Telephone interview with Souren G. Seraydarian, DSRSG/DTA, UNTAES, 16 January 2007.

merely drivers and interpreters, "[A] lot of the local staff were not in political positions, most of them were service support, logistic support positions, whether they were drivers, local secretaries, administrative assistants, mechanics, communication people, workers, you know, to build cantonments, sides and so on."[516]

3.2.2 Redesign of the Reintegration Process and Accelerated Action

The slow progress in the first couple of months made the SRSG decide to redesign the JIC approach. "We realized that this transition was really not going fast enough in many areas and we would have to hand over authority rather quickly."[517] The reluctance of the local JIC officers and the narrow focus on controllable factors of the international field staff resulted in inertia that put the timely termination of the transition process at risk. On the other hand, institution-building and reconciliation processes took their time and, during the first months of the mission, it was not self-evident that a wrong path was being taken. Yet, when the effects of the slow progress were beginning to show and an overly "minimal steps policy" began to stall the process, the SRSG and his senior leadership team decided to implement a comprehensive *rupture*. This structural, procedural, and personnel redesign of the JICs was remarkable because it took place after almost half of UNTAET's mission was already up.

In addition to restructuring the JICs, the mission adopted a harder negotiation pace vis-à-vis the GoC and hammered out a range of binding agreements that were supposed to lay the legal foundations for the preservation of a multiethnic Eastern Slavonian society.

3.2.2.1 Restructuring the Joint Implementation Committees

In October 1996, Klein appointed a new Head of the JIC Secretariat. The person formerly in charge had come from the WFP and did not have pertinent experience in negotiation and mediation. His successor was better versed in negotiation tactics and put them to good use in the dealings with Croatia. Furthermore, the original 15 JICs were reduced to 13 and assigned to three categories: political, political-administrative, and technical. The first sub-component consisted of the JICs for Human Rights, for Refugees and Displaced Persons and for Elections. The political-administrative category was comprised of the Civil Administration, Education and Culture, and the Health JICs. The JICs on Agriculture, Railways, Roads, Utilities,

---

516 Ibid.
517 Telephone interview with a staff member of STACTA, UNTAES, 10 January 2007.

and Municipal Services formed the technical component. After this structural re-arrangement, the new director went on to evaluate the effectiveness of the reintegration process so far, conducting a review of all committees.

> When I made my assessment on it, I said, 'Listen, what we are doing here is we are not getting stuck in building roads or railroads – we don't do that, you know, I am not in the roadbuilding business. What we need to do is concentrate on the reintegration process: how are we going to reintegrate the public institutions or private institutions that are already existing within Croatia.' So, I called in all the chairmen of all the Implementation Committees and I asked a common thing, 'What have you done, what can you put on the table, what has been agreed to, what is still outstanding?'[518]

The chairs of the JICs were subsequently asked to forward summaries of their respective sector's activities. "This summary included general principles; process for reintegration and mediation; priority issues; issues mediated; issues currently under discussion; outstanding issues; and time frames for implementation of reintegration programs."[519] Furthermore, the chairs were requested "to outline the process by which meetings were conducted, agendas set, agreements reached and implemented, and obstacles to mediation identified,"[520] in order to find out about obstacles and obstructions to the overall goal of reintegration. The analyses showed that one generic flaw was the excessive occupation of many JICs with technical instead of substantial issues.[521] Obviously, organizational-technical issues are less likely to be subject to political arguments and thus easier to work through.

The Joint Implementation Committees

On the *technical* JICs, the review identified a rationale to their approaches that was highly specified and subject matter-related. Although this was not a disadvantage in itself, it was not conducive to the establishment of an overall strategic perspective. Such a perspective would have been "required if the reintegration process was to be completed within the time frame of the UNTAES mandate."[522] Additionally, the issue of territorial integrity was a primary obstacle in the negotiations between the JICs of Municipal Service and of Utilities. Besides, the technical JICs were not free of ideologically motivated disputes either.

> An example about railway: we opened the transport way connection from Vinkovci to Novi Sad via Vukovar. So, you had the head of the Croatian railway, the head of the

---

518 Telephone interview with Dr. Robert J.A.R. Gravelle, Head of the JIC Secretariat and Head of STACTA, 11 August 2007.
519 Gravelle undated, p. 5.
520 Ibid.
521 Cf. ibid.
522 Ibid., p. 6.

Vinkovci area, and the one of the Novi Sad area, and the one who was in charge of Vukovar. And when the locomotive first went in, they stareted a discussion about the flag on the train, like, 'Oh, there has to be a Croatian flag on the train.' But well, when there is a Croatian flag, there also has to be a Serb flag, because otherwise, they would put the train on fire or whatever. So we agreed that they would have the flag as long as they are in the Croatian area [laughs]. And then we agreed that in the Vukovar municipalities, there would be the UN flag, which was supposed to be the largest flag, and then you would have the Serb flag *and* then the Croatian flag. And then the Hungarians said, 'Why not our flag?' I remember we even had to postpone a meeting for ten hours because we couldn't agree – but you can't make the decision for them. You can be a catalyst in helping them to make a decision. And then, if it doesn't work: you have to give them some space where they have a chance to negotiate, to find out what can be acceptable. And if they can't reach that, then you say, 'Listen, we don't postpone this meeting any more, either a UN flag or no other flag.' And then the Serbs said, 'Ah, when Tudjman is hanging out there, we also want the face of Milosevic being…' It gives you headaches.[523]

Emotional involvement was even higher in the *political-administrative* JICs. Together with a lack of political guidance and will on the Croatian side and the renitence of the Serb delegations with respect to maintaining the region's integrity, every issue turned contentious and prohibited the JIC from performing its supposed tasks.

For the people in the Education and Culture JIC, "The emotional issues included curriculum, employment security, language, and preservation of cultural sites."[524] Within the Civil Administration JIC, a major obstacle was the "long-term integration concerns in terms of identification of functional areas at the central, county, and municipal levels established according to the constitutional system of the Republic of Croatia. The second major issue was the documentation of persons."[525] In the Health JIC, work even stopped for a while. The delegations could not agree on the mode of representation, they had a hard time elaborating an integrated health insurance plan,[526] and employment security was an overarching issue for the local Serbs.[527] The latter was particularly virulent in the health sector because of the abhorrent war atrocities that had happened in the Vukovar hospital. In order to alleviate the difficult negotiation process, UNTAES brought about the replacement of the former Director of the Vukovar hospital, who was held in high regard by the Croatian population, but "antagonized the Serb delegation. It was

---

523 Interview with a senior staff member of UNTAES, New York, 22 November 2006.
524 Gravelle undated, p. 6.
525 Ibid.
526 "However, on 6 September 1996, the President of the Executive Council in the UNTAES Region agreed to reintegrate the region into the Croatian health insurance system. Despite these endorsements, proposals from either party were not forthcoming." Ibid., p. 8.
527 In fact, ten JICs placed employment security as their first priority. But since there was no consistent policy on this matter, "it had been difficult to mediate the issue and arrive at a consensus […]." Ibid., p. 7.

determined that she was on the Croat delegation for political purposes and to ensure, through her presence, that the Serbs would not negotiate, therefore bringing the JIC to a halt. Her removal would lessen the friction between the two delegations."[528] In addition, the Serb delegation was "instructed to negotiate in good faith and cease its opposition to health insurance reintegration and make concrete suggestions in this matter."[529]

The problems encountered by the *political* JICs were somewhat different in nature: they did not suffer as much from obstructions. For example, the Human Rights JIC made good progress in establishing mechanisms for monitoring human rights violations, and the chair was purportedly "extremely diligent and professional in his approach."[530] The shortcomings, particular in the JIC on Returns and Displaced Persons, rather consisted of the lack of an overall strategic policy of the region as a whole. In part, this was due to the fact that the political JIC was co-chaired by UNHCR, which was allegedly not only reluctant to share responsibility but even followed a different rationale in organizing refugee returns.[531]

> [I]t was recommended, that the Transitional Administrator and High Commissioner of UNHCR reach agreement on an overall strategy in this regard. As well, to ensure that co-operation between UNHCR and UNTAES was enhanced, the OIC JIC would approach the UNCHR Regional Representative to reach some understanding on preparing an agenda prior to JIC meetings. It was believed that co-operation in this matter would improve relations between UNTAES and UNHCR.[532]

Eventually, the JIC was substituted by a Joint Working Group and "its progress was enhanced but it did not facilitate a large two way return as was first envisaged."[533]

Finally, the Election JIC, which was taken out of the formal JIC hierarchy to report directly to the Head of Civil Affairs and the Transitional Administrator, "functioned in an efficient and effective manner whereby it identified its principles, implementation plan, and time frames."[534]

---

528 Ibid., p. 9.
529 Ibid.
530 Ibid. "This JIC was scheduled to continue after the UNTAES mandate expired [...]." Ibid.
531 "Additionally agendas for meeting were not set in advance. One major flaw in the process was that it had not defined its principles or implementation process. It continued to focus on individual returns ad an overall strategic plan was not formulated." Ibid., p. 7.
532 Ibid., pp. 9-10.
533 Ibid.
534 Ibid., p. 6.

"[I]n order for benchmarks to be adhered to,"[535] the Secretariat was, on the one hand, entrusted with more monitoring capacities, on the other hand, it was also instructed to provide the JICs with more comprehensive support.[536]

> The JIC Secretariat became actively involved in JIC meetings on a periodic basis and acted as mediator when the need arose to assist in resolution of impasses. The JIC Secretariat then received from the Chairs a weekly work schedule outlining meetings and informal discussions between delegations and the Chair. This allowed the JIC Secretariat to follow and monitor progress. The JIC Secretariat provided resources in the areas of guidance, mediation interface, and became available to provide possible avenues of solution to problems impeding the reintegration process. The weekly OIC JIC meeting was then held on a bi-weekly basis. The agenda for this meeting focused on issues identified in agendas that would be discussed by each Chair. This allowed for common concerns to be discussed, avenues of mediation proposed, and agenda items identified. This assisted in identifying patterns or themes that emerged across the wider spectrum of the JIC reintegration strategy.[537]

In order to monitor the implementation, "A schematic chart was developed for each JIC with required letters of principle defined, processes by which issues were identified and prioritized, methodologies of implementation, issues agreed upon, outstanding issues and critical paths established."[538]

3.2.2.2 "Hard-Nosed Approach"

"Eventually Klein said, 'It's not going fast enough. We need a hard-nosed approach.'"[539] Parallel to the *rupture* in the JIC process, UNTAES started to pursue a more rigid course in its dealings with the local Serbs who were still boycotting most of UNTAES's policies as well as with the Croatian government, which was responsible for guaranteeing a multiethnic society in Eastern Slavonia after the exit of the UN. The SRSG decided to accelerate a number of issues that were fundamental for the efficient management of reconciliation and institution-building efforts.[540] First and foremost, these concerned the policy on civic documents and the

---

535   Ibid., p. 10.
536   "Each Chair welcomed the visible support of the JIC Secretariat in identifying realistic attainable goals." Ibid.
537   Ibid.
538   Ibid.
539   Telephone interview with a staff member of STACTA, UNTAES, 10 January 2007.
540   "For us, being the first transitional administration, there was no model to go through; we had to do it the best we could because we were the first. And we learned a lot." Telephone interview with Dr. Robert J.A.R. Gravelle, Head of the JIC Secretariat and Head of STAC-TA, 11 August 2007.

establishment of employment security.[541] The core document that was hammered out in the negotiations with the GoC was the so-called Affidavit on Serb employment rights and the Annex to the Affidavit that specified implementation benchmarks. The Affidavit was also the basis and argument for the negotiations on further social, economic, and security issues that followed. UNTAES would regularly refer to the Croatian commitments that were fixed in this crucial document.

Document Policy

The open question of citizenship was highlighted as a major obstacle to effective measures. Thus, the establishment of documentation centres that issued citizenship papers, identity cards and other personal documents became a core activity of UNTAES.[542] This challenge was multilayered because the Serbs did not want to adopt Croatian citizenship, and Croats, likewise, did not want Serbs to enjoy the same rights as Croatians. However, Serbs had to accept the Croatian documents either way: those who wanted to remain in the region had to carry documents certifying their citizenship in order to be granted legal and constitutional rights,[543] and those who wanted to leave could only do so with a valid passport – to be issued by the Croatian government.[544] In this deadlock situation, the Transitional Administrator and the Head of Civil Affairs, negotiating with some of Tudjman's closest assistants on the matter, triggered a change in law[545] and the Croatian Ministry of the Interior was ready to issue 110,000 *domovnicas*, transitory identity documents. Despite this massive effort, many Serbs simply either did not know about the necessity of obtaining a *domovnica*, they did not want to adopt Croat citizenship, or they did simply not believe that the Croatian government would be cooperative in the processing of their requests:

541 The constant negotiations at the senior level and the mediation efforts at the operational one were likewise continuing.
542 The implementing entity was UNTAES Civil Affairs.
543 "Without documentation, every person in the region was without any legal or constitutional rights. This effectively made him/her a non-person who could not purchase or sell property, have protection under the law, nor entitled to any public services, education, or protection by the state." Gravelle undated, p. 9.
544 "Some people wanted to leave and couldn't." Telephone interview with Ambassador Jacques-Paul Klein, SRSG/TA, UNTAES, 19 July 2007.
545 "So I called the Minister and I said, 'Off the record: you would like every Serb to leave tomorrow morning if they could, right? But that won't happen. You know that and I know that. However, there are some who legitimately want to leave and can't.' – 'Why not?' – 'They don't have Croatian passports. And to get a Croatian passport they have to serve in the Croatian army.' – 'That's crazy.' – 'I know, Mr. Minister, that's crazy, but that's your law…' Within a week the Sabor [Croatian Parliament; ES] changed the law. So, any Serb in Eastern Slavonia who applied for a Croatian passport could get them and leave." Ibid.

145

Two days later, I met with all the Serbs and I said, 'I have to advise you that now you have to become leaders and you have to pay attention, because that is your future.' And we did discuss with them all the questions involved, such as, 'Do I have to become Croat, do I have to give up my Serb citizenship?', et cetera. Some solutions were found, some solutions were not found. Four or five hours we sat. And then I asked three of these guys, 'You are the key leaders: will you support the citizenship policy?' And one of the guys said to me, 'You know, Mr. Fischer, do you really think the Croats will give me the *domovnica*?' I said, 'Well, they are obliged.' And he said to me, 'If you can give me the *domovnica* in 24 hours, I will convince my people to take it.' I said, 'Anyone else who wants to go for this option?' When two other guys put their hands up, I sent my deputy to the office to get the three domovnicas. You know, there is always the element of surprise… You go nowhere telling them, 'You *have* to take this or that.' You can say, 'You have to take the following circumstances into account and this is what is in for you.' And there you come to the importance of talking to people, of informal dealings.[546]

Accordingly, "It was recommended that all efforts be undertaken to ensure persons were properly informed of the need for documentation and the consequences of not doing so. In order to build confidence in the local population, all local officials were strongly urged to make a public demonstration of their sincerity by taking out documentation with full media coverage."[547] UNTAES Public Affairs, for example, produced a Questions and Answers brochure containing "comprehensive explanations of relevant regulations and requirements,"[548] and the local UNTAES offices were deeply involved in drafting the information in and distributing the *domovnicas*.[549] With the goal of obtaining an ultimate guarantee for the local Serbs, UNTAES also tried to secure them dual citizenship. The SRSG accordingly approached President Milosevic:

When I went to Milosevic one time I told him, 'You know, Mr. President, we are almost there now: the population is stable, I think they want to stay, they have property, the Croats have guaranteed their rights, including religion. Now there is one caveat: they are still very nervous about their future citizen status, but we could fix that. If you gave them dual nationality, they would have a passport and they would know that they had a place to go when things turn badly.' And he only said, 'That's their problem.'[550]

---

546 Interview with Dr. Gerard Fischer, Head of Civil Affairs, UNTAES, New York, 21 November 2006.
547 Gravelle undated, p. 9.
548 UN Department of Peacekeeping Operations 1997.
549 "We should issue documents for Serbs – and so, off we went and set up some documentation offices; everyday we would convoy in some Croatian immigration or documentation officers, and they would give Serbs Croatian documentation of citizenship so that they could stay after the UN left because right now they either had a temporary Serb ID or a Red Cross ID." Telephone interview with a field officer, UNTAES, 10 January 2007.
550 Telephone interview with Ambassador Jacques-Paul Klein, SRSG/TA, UNTAES, 19 July 2007.

The *domovnica* policy was eventually successful, indicated by its growing acceptance by the local Serbs.[551] In fact, "To many young people who accepted the passports it was a ticket to the free world because the Croats had visa valid for most of the European countries."[552]

Affidavit and Annex to the Affidavit

Employment security emerged as a major concern for the remaining Serbs[553] and thus constituted a pivotal topic for the mission's overall approach to reintegration.[554] "So, I came up with a process by which all the different types were linked,"[555] the former Head of the JIC Secretariat recalls. This process started on 2 December 1996, when he met with delegates of the Croatian Transitional Administration in Osijek. During these discussions, "The Croatians unwittingly stated that all public employees in the region would retain their employment status."[556] Knowing the importance of this statement, UNTAES was eager to have it formalized on paper. Further talks ensued:

> UNTAES was told that such a written guarantee could not be undertaken as public employees in the UNTAES region were to become Croatian citizens and as citizens their rights would automatically be protected. This stance by the Croatians confirmed that the rights of public employees in the region were at risk. The UNTAES response was to press the Croatian representative in charge of coordinating the transition from the UN to Croatia in the matter of a written guarantee. UNTAES recommended that such a written declaration would facilitate the smooth reintegration of public enterprises

---

551 Interview with Dr. Gerard Fischer, Head of Civil Affairs, UNTAES, New York, 21 November 2006.
552 Ibid. He continues, "And I meet sometimes people in Stockholm who walk up to me and say, 'Do you remember me? You know, I was in Vukovar, took up the Croatian passport at your office.'"
553 "Two things that they wanted: they wanted autonomy for the region, to keep it Serb, and they wanted to keep their jobs. Well, on the first thing: we had to give the Executive Council, ran by Stanimirovic, a wake up call, saying, 'You lost the war, it's never gonna happen, you will never have autonomous status within the Republic of Croatia. But what we can do is to ensure that your social, economic, and human rights all are adhered to.' And then, what I came up with is that these are the same things that are running across every issue: employment security, education security, minority rights et cetera. What I did then, I wrote out a plan for Klein, he agreed to it, and then I said, 'What we have to do is to give the Croatian interlocutor these documents and have the government of Croatia to agree that these people have at least employment rights.'" Telephone interview with Dr. Robert J.A.R. Gravelle, Head of the JIC Secretariat and Head of STACTA, 11 August 2007.
554 "Once agreement was reached on employment rights, it was a matter of persistence until other rights could be guaranteed." Gravelle undated, p. 10.
555 Telephone interview with Dr. Robert J.A.R. Gravelle, Head of the JIC Secretariat and Head of STACTA, 11 August 2007.
556 Gravelle undated, p. 10.

and send a signal to the local population that Croatia wished to foster reconciliation in the region.[557]

Eventually, the Croatian representative "agreed that such a statement would be beneficial to peaceful reintegration."[558] Now, UNTAES wanted to see things through before the Croatian window of opportunity would close again, but a juristic hurdle was still in its way. "The UNTAES Legal Affairs Unit wished to review this document and stated that [the review of a Declaration; ES] would take up to three weeks."[559] In order to circumvent the impending delay,[560] the negotiators played a trick by labelling the document an Affidavit instead of a Declaration, which implied a different review procedure. Thus, "Legal Affairs was bypassed."[561] The Croatian government signed the "Affidavit" on 16 December 1996.

The next step was to ensure its implementation. In order to bring such a guarantee on track, the Government of Croatia was asked to indicate the conditions and guarantees the Affidavit cover. Here, UNTAES adopted a policy that was as smart as it was necessary: it established itself as the agenda-setter in the process.[562]

> So I laid out 18 areas that they needed to have agreed – because I knew they had a hidden agenda, and I had a hidden agenda. And I said, 'What we're gonna do is this: we're gonna write the agreement, I am the authority to write and sign. We're gonna present to them agreements that we want them to sign. There is no negotiation here, they can change a word or two but that's it. They are not gonna change a damn thing.'[563]

---

557 Ibid., pp. 10-11. UNTAES composed a draft declaration within twenty-four hours.
558 Gravelle undated, p. 11.
559 Ibid. "One of the problems was that I wanted to call it a declaration, but the UN legal advisor was, 'Well, I have to have a look at it, calling it a declaration it has to go to the Parliament…' This would have taken too long." Telephone interview with Dr. Robert J.A.R. Gravelle, Head of the JIC Secretariat and Head of STACTA, 11 August 2007.
560 "And I looked at Klein and said, 'Jacques, we don't have time to do this. These are political agreements here, let the lawyers straight them up later.'" Ibid.
561 Gravelle undated, p. 11.
562 "I wrote to Klein, 'We don't have time to negotiate it, we got a two year mandate, and we are already almost a year into it." Telephone interview with Dr. Robert J.A.R. Gravelle, Head of the JIC Secretariat and Head of STACTA, 11 August 2007.
563 Ibid. Cf. also Gravelle undated, p. 11, "To ensure that negotiations would result in a positive manner and to allow the least amount of manoeuvering by the Government of Croatia, it was decided that any agreement reached would have to be presented as a final draft at any initial meeting. This meant that the UN was not negotiating but rather presenting a document for signature. Negotiating techniques were adapted to the rule that the Croatians would only be allowed to revise the wording but never to negotiate the terms."

The negotiation process that followed was a constant bouncing back and forth of arguments. Ultimately, an agreement was reached.[564]

A final request addressed to the Croatian Government was a formal and visible declaration that the Serbs that were qualified to remain in their jobs would be able to do so, arguing "that in order for educational reintegration to be completed some form of guarantee was required that students attending educational institutions in the region would be able to continue to do so and that certificates acquired would have to be recognized."[565] After various meetings with highly emotional contributions, the Croatian government eventually agreed to the requests of equal acknowledgement of exams.[566] Pointing to these arrangements, the Croatian delegation was, in turn, quick to declare itself a spearhead of democracy and proponent of human rights. UNTAES did not interfere. The Annex was signed on 14 February 1997.

With the agenda and the implementation guidelines in place, written agreements needed to materialize through the adoption of the guidelines by the local Serbs. Yet, the local leadership still "refused to believe that Croatia could be made to comply and they were reluctant to advise their workers of these documents."[567]

---

564 "The Croatian government began by stating that this document was not necessary as Croatian laws already existed to provide its citizens with employment rights. UNTAES responded that for reconciliation purposes the Government of Croatia should be willing to put these rights in writing as these were not rights to be given to a special group but those of all citizens. Therefore, signing a document that only stated existing law was not prejudicial to their legislation. The Special Advisor indicated that if this was the case then why not just state that all residents of the region were to be treated as equal citizens. UNTAES then pointed out that the residents of the region were not citizens as most did not have documents, and to facilitate better relations a document outlining guarantees under existing law would further the process of reintegration. The Croatians then demanded that certain rights and conditions as presented could not be agreed to as they were already addressed in some of the clauses. These were removed and eight clauses were agreed to. These included: the years 1991-1996 to be counted as pensionable time; that all employees who fulfil work requirements are guaranteed continuation of employment; that those medically unfit were guaranteed pensions; that employees at retirement age would be guaranteed pensions; that workers whose positions became redundant or whose position were no longer required would receive retraining or re-education for other positions; that employees not possessing Croatian citizenship were guaranteed issuance of temporary work permits; that employees accepting work contracts have 30 days to make application for documents in order to remain employed." Ibid., pp. 11-12.

565 Ibid., p. 13. UNTAES leaders emphasized that "children should not suffer the consequence of five years of war conditions." Ibid.

566 "The agreement reached in writing declared that certificates issued in schools of the region during the period 1991-1997 were to be validated, recognized, and replaced by the appropriate Croatian certificate. [...] This agreement also recognized that those public employees who had receiving educational certificates during this period, they could not be released from their employment by the Government of Croatia under the condition that they were not qualified." Ibid.

567 Ibid., p. 12.

When I went to Beli Manastir, I said, 'We can guarantee jobs here.' But they all got up and said, 'Oh no, no, we are all going to quit.' And I got up, I was fed, and said, 'If you want to commit collective suicide, be my guest. I don't care. Croats will take your jobs if you don't take them. But we have already agreed with Croat ministers on your job, pensions and everything. Each of you will get an individual contract. You have 48 hours to make up your mind. So, go and talk to your family. And remember: people sitting here won't provide you the money for housing, for food, put your children to school et cetera – they already have a job, they don't care about you.'[568]

Promoting its policy, UNTAES also extended its public information campaign that had started with the *domovnica* policy, addressing workers and residents about their enforceable rights. "Meetings between workers and UNTAES were held and the appropriate Croatian authorities attended to publicly state that Croatia would live up to its commitments."[569] Eventually, by means of a referendum, "99 percent accepted contracts with the public institutions or private enterprises."[570]

3.2.3 The UNTAES Agreements and STACTA

The signing of the Affidavit and the Annex of the Affidavit marked a "shift from an inclusive mediating approach to a very hard-nosed negotiation approach,"[571] supposed to prevent the situation from becoming instable.[572] Based on these documents, UNTAES and the GoC started various rounds of negotiations on diverse socio-political, economic, and security-related questions, as diverse as vehicle registration, pensions, currency, or electricity provisions. The negotiations were conducted by two new transitory institutions, the so-called "Radic-Commission", directed by Croatian Vice-Prime Minister, and UNTAES's newly created "Secretariat of the Transitional Administrator for the Coordination of the Transfer of Authority" (STACTA), which was supposed to efficiently coordinate the negotiation process in the remaining short amount of time. The resulting body of agreements has been called the "UNTAES Agreements" and set a legal framework for the rights and duties of the GoC and of the non-Croatian population in the region after the UN-guided transition period ended.

---

568 Telephone interview with Dr. Robert J.A.R. Gravelle, Head of the JIC Secretariat and Head of STACTA, 11 August 2007.
569 Gravelle undated, p. 12.
570 Telephone interview with Dr. Robert J.A.R. Gravelle, Head of the JIC Secretariat and Head of STACTA, 11 August 2007.
571 Telephone interview with a staff member of STACTA, UNTAES, 10 January 2007.
572 "We didn't want the situation to become instable. The fear was that the Serbs, once the Tribunal had formed, would all run away, or that they would run away and burn the place for." Telephone interview with Ambassador Jacques-Paul Klein, SRSG/TA, UNTAES, 19 July 2007.

As of April 1997, new transitional institutions emerged. The short-changed Croats[573] created the "State Commission for the Establishment of the Constitutional Legal Order of the Republic of Croatia in the Regions of Osijek-Baranja and Vukovar-Srem Counties Currently under UNTAES Administration" that was going to be "the senior and only interlocutor between the Government of Croatia and UNTAES."[574]

> The Commission consisted of nine members and Dr. J. Radic, Vice-Prime Minister and Minister of Development and Reconstruction was named as its head. This became known as the Radic Commission. The aim of the Commission was to coordinate those Croatian State bodies dealing with UNTAES and to provide one point of contact between the Government of Croatia and UNTAES.[575]

Bundling forces, UNTAES created a counter chief interlocutor institution, the STACTA. It was "to resolve all major outstanding issues and other projects designated by the Transitional Administrator,"[576] and also had the "responsibility for overseeing the compliance of all agreements reached."[577] The first meeting between the Radic Commission and STACTA was at the Vukovar HQ on 6 May 1997. "At this meeting, four major issues to be resolved through negotiation were tabled by UNTAES. These were: the Amnesty Law, Pensions, Vehicle Registration Program and Judicial reintegration."[578] Again, the provision was that UNTAES acted as the agenda-setter and the Croatian government was conceded little discretion in amending the agreements.[579] In addition, UNTAES introduced a tight decision-making schedule. "It was established that UNTAES would present issues at each subsequent meeting and that those previously presented had to be resolved within one week."[580]

The following paragraphs give an illustrating overview of the agreement negotiations between STACTA and the Radic Commission, which went on for about nine months, over the reintegration of public enterprises and institutions, economic

---

573 "Then in March, after we got the Affidavit [laughs], Tudjman said, 'Hey, wait a minute, my ministers just signed things that shouldn't be signed.'" Telephone interview with Dr. Robert J.A.R. Gravelle, Head of the JIC Secretariat and Head of STACTA, 11 August 2007.

574 Ibid.

575 Gravelle undated, p. 13.

576 Ibid., p. 14.

577 Ibid., p. 17. This meant that in cases of non-compliance, STACTA had to gather all information necessary from other units and to establish a compliance strategy in close cooperation with the Radic Commission. The head of STACTA was Dr. Robert Gravelle. As explained, he was also crucially involved in the negotiations of the UNTAES agreements.

578 Ibid., p. 14.

579 "We said, 'OK, every week we are going to sign an agreement,' and, 'This is what I want you to sign next week.'" Telephone interview with Dr. Robert J.A.R. Gravelle, Head of the JIC Secretariat and Head of STACTA, 11 August 2007.

580 Ibid. The person in charge of the process was Gravelle. The Head of Civil Affairs was also heavily involved.

issues, judicial reintegration, returns, municipalities and elections, as well as of the subsequent implementation approaches.

Vehicle Registration

The first topic they tackled was the reintegration of the registration mechanism into the responsibility of the Croatian Ministry of the Interior.

> The difficulty was that regional vehicles carried Serbian registration and displayed Republic of Srpska Krajina plates. As the RSK was an illegal entity, plates and registration would become invalid once the region was reintegrated into Croatia. UNTAES believed that vehicle registration and the issuance of Croatian plates would signal a *de facto* recognition by local residents that Croatian sovereignty was at hand. To assist in getting the local residents to register their vehicles, STACTA was able to negotiate an agreement whereby the cost to individuals would be minimal.[581]

On May 23, UNTAES and the GoC signed an Agreement on Vehicle Registration that included special conditions for residents.

> It was agreed that those registering vehicles would have to provide proof of residency or citizenship; proof of ownership; that technical inspections of vehicles would be phased in with regional technical certificates being recognized until Croatian technical inspections were held; that registration, technical and inspection fees and road taxes would be waived for the first year; that RSK plates could be retained; and that insurance costs would be reduced so that six months insurance fees would be purchased for the price of three months.[582]

With implementation on the horizon, UNTAES announced its intention on television, radio shows, and town-hall meetings, and tried to accommodate the population's objections and doubts, in particular the more radical local Serbs. The latter, not willing to accept the "roadmap" for the region, were trying to postpone decisions at each imaginable opportunity:

> And we talked this trough and they said, 'Well, the insurance is so expensive, we can't afford this.' – 'Okay.' So, we went to this insurance company in Croatia and made a deal with them: they pay for one year but they would have insurance for two years, plus they would not have to pay the fee for the license plate. They would also be able to keep their Serb license plate if they cross over to Novi Sad. Everything was done. I think they had nine months to change the license plate and we had maybe five or six places open, with opening hours from seven in the morning to ten in the evening, six days a week. You know, really everything was made possible so that nobody could say, 'I didn't have the time.'[583]

---

581 Gravelle undated, p. 10.
582 Ibid.
583 Interview with Dr. Gerard Fischer, Head of Civil Affairs, UNTAES, New York, 21 November 2006.

After more than eight months of negation and information, only "a very small amount"[584] had registered. Yet, UNTAES was still holding strong, and when there were only nine days to go, the resistance slowly started to crumble, "They realized, finally, that there is absolutely no more extension to that."[585] In the last three days, an excessive rush to the offices began, "We had lines that we had to open to two o'clock in the morning – in order to facilitate them. It was the last three days."[586] Reflecting on those days during which everyone was edgy, the Head of Civil Affairs made the point that this "is so significant for, I would not say the region, but for people who do not want to face reality. So with all the good intentions from the international community, it was not sufficient. Only in the last moment, maybe something happens,"[587] but it might also have gone wrong.

Pension Services and Rights

Repeating previous behavioral patterns, the Croats fiercely objected to paying pensions to inhabitants of Serb ethnicity, "They sent in their pension people, and they said, 'No, we can't do pensions.'"[588] When the UNTAES' leadership kept on pushing, the Croat negotiator, who was the Director of the Croatian Invalid and Pension Fund, reverted to the "argument" that he did not have the authority to make the final decision. "So I dismissed them. I said, 'I am not talking to you, I am gonna have to see Tudjman.' And this is when Radic came in, and I said to him that we need to have these agreements signed."[589] According to the Head of STACTA,

> Radic then ordered the director to reach an agreement with UNTAES. Within three days, UNTAES was able to complete the process and on 29 May, Radic signed on behalf of the Croatian government and the Transitional Administrator signed on behalf of the UN. The provisions included agreement that the Croatian Pension fund would abide by the Affidavit and the Annex; that new offices would be opened in the UNTAES region; a joint working group would implement the pension fund organization into the region, that those eligible for pensions would be able to register for Croatian benefits, and that within thirty days of being registered, pensioners would begin receiving benefits.[590]

584 Ibid.
585 Ibid.
586 Ibid.
587 Ibid.
588 Ibid.
589 Telephone interview with Dr. Robert J.A.R. Gravelle, Head of the JIC Secretariat and Head of STACTA, 11 August 2007.
590 Gravelle undated, p. 10.

Employment Security

On employment security, specifics remained to be sorted out, such as insurance for Serb employees. The Head of Civil Affairs recalls an illustrating example,

> For instance, a Serb who was fighting against the Croats becomes now a Croat. He lost a leg during the war. – Now, he is he entitled to invalid insurance from the Croatian side? A very complicated legal issue: to convince the Croatian insurance company to afford a combatant who was siding against the Croatian state a subsidy for the rest of his life... You know, there is a political dimension in it which is not easy to conquer. But whenever we found some of these particularities, we would immediately go and see the Croatian institutions and talk to them.[591]

Resembling the JIC experience, the negotiations for the health sector were at risk of a stalemate. During emotional discussions, the Croatian Minister of Health refused to sign a document that allowed Serbs to be employed in the Croat health system.[592] Thus, the Transitional Administrator and his STACTA Head changed their tactics,

> Klein and I went to see the Minister of Health and said, 'Look, you have to do this, your government signed it.' – 'No, I won't do it.' So, Klein looked at me – we made this up before – and said, 'If he's not going to have signed this in ten minutes then we get the hell out of here and then we go to see Tudjman.' So Klein walked out of the door, and the Minister of Health went, 'Where are you going?' – 'We are leaving.' And Klein comes back and looks him straight in the eye, 'And I will change your name.' – 'What do you mean, change my name?' – 'I am gonna call you Mr. Mandate.' – 'What do you mean?' – 'Well, because of you we gonna have to tell the Security Council that you are not going along with the agreements and so, we gonna have the mandate extended another year. So, we call you Mr. Mandate.' Then we got on the plane and we went back to Vukovar. The next morning, he gets the call from Tudjman, saying that this guy is not longer one of his ministers. So, Klein called me and told me that Tudjman got a new Minister of Health – and we flew back there and got it signed.[593]

Specifically, the agreement, signed on 6 June 1997, stated that the hospital in Vukovar and the health centre in Beli Manastir would be supported financially by the Croatian Ministry of the Interior.[594] However, implementation was put on hold for several months, and UNTAES had to get involved in another agreement re-

---

591 Interview with Dr. Gerard Fischer, Head of Civil Affairs, UNTAES, New York, 21 November 2006.
592 "The Minister of Health said never in his lifetime would he sign the agreement; he didn't care about the Affidavit and the Annex." Telephone interview with Dr. Robert J.A.R. Gravelle, Head of the JIC Secretariat and Head of STACTA, 11 August 2007.
593 Ibid.
594 "Additionally, once reintegration was completed, the Ministry would be responsible for all operational costs related to the provision of health services in the UNTAES region." Gravelle undated, p. 12.

garding work contracts in the health sector.[595] This agreement was signed on 19 November 1997. At the end of the day, "The Croatian National Health Service integrated the medical facilities in the region, full financing was obtained, and 300 previously unrecognized Serb health diplomas were recognized."[596]

Education Directives and Admissions

Education was an equally difficult sector to settle. A multitude of sub-issues needed to be sorted out individually, such as, "Is your secondary school diploma as good as the Croat one? Is your certificate from medical school as good as the Croat one?"[597] Awkward situations resulted when, for example, UNTAES employees found out that a discussion over degrees from *the same* university broke out.[598]

The Head of Civil Affairs led the first round of negotiations, adopting a rather consent-oriented approach. Vis-à-vis the hard-nosed Minister of Education, Mrs. Vokic, however, his efforts were not crowned with success. In August, STACTA took over. With a stricter reference to the Affidavit and the Annex in the negotiations, the talks accelerated. In an open meeting, with media present, the Minister called for UNTAES to remove itself from the reintegration process as the Croatian government considered UNTAES an impediment. The Minister stated that if only the UN would leave then the Serbs and Croats could come to a peaceful solution to all problems. STACTA stated to the Minister that the UN was mandated to reintegrate the region into the Republic of Croatia and that no reintegration of the education systems would take place until certain educational guarantees were made. Immediately after the open meeting, STACTA met with the Minister and indicated that private discussions were called for and that a concentrated effort was required if reintegration was to take place prior to the new school year. The Minister agreed and STACTA then directed the Serb delegation to meet with its Croatian counterpart to come to an agreement on the curriculum and syllabus, textbooks, and national minority subjects. The Minister directed her representatives to com-

---

595 "Conditions included permanent work contracts for those who had medical qualifications; notification of qualifications by the government to be completed within four weeks; state medical examination to be firmly scheduled for those requiring them; costs of notification to be reimbursed by the Ministry; the provision of health services to all residents irregardless if they were in possession of Croatian health cards; and twelve month contract to employees awaiting state examinations and once passed, permanent contracts to be issued." Ibid.

596 Howard 2008, p. 244.

597 Interview with Dr. Gerard Fischer, Head of Civil Affairs, UNTAES, New York, 21 November 2006.

598 "One day we sat at a table and I said, 'But didn't *both* of you go to the University of Belgrade?' They were trying to push each other in the corners, to humiliate each other." Ibid.

promise if reasonable demands were made. Both delegations were directed to remain in negotiations until an agreement was reached.

In sum, five documents on education issues were signed. The first was the Declaration on Educational Certificates of 12 March 1997. At a meeting of top-level employees on 4 August, the Agreement on the Distribution of Principal Positions, the Declaration on Minority Education Rights, and the Decision on Curriculum Content were determined, followed by a Letter of Agreement by the Ministry of Education three days later.[599]

> [B]y the end of UNTAES, textbooks describing a distorted history of the conflict had been recalled, school signs were issued in both Cyrillic and Latin letters, and many Serb teachers' education diplomas had been recognized. Disagreements persisted, however, over the content of textbooks and exams, school registration, and the recognition of education diplomas.[600]

Currency

With Eastern Slavonia being reintegrated into Croatia, its currency also had to change. This implied that those who had money and saving accounts in *denar* had to be able to convert it, at a decent rate, into *kuna*. However, Serbs did not want to accept "*ustaše* money," while Croats were not willing to lose money on ostensibly unfavorable exchange rates.[601]

Two factors were essential in having Croats and Serbs overcome their initial objections to UNTAES' currency policy: first, the support of other international actors: specifically the World Bank, which "shipped in and financed this – to some extent,"[602] and more general "the international community [which; ES] was behind

---

599 "UNTAES and the minister met again on 4 August with the head of each delegation and the obstacles were quickly removed and a curriculum acknowledging minority subjects and translated textbooks were agreed to. UNTAES insisted that both delegations initial the agreed to clauses and this was complied with. The Minister and STACTA then returned to their private meeting where STACTA tabled the final agreement for the reintegration of the educational systems. The agreement called for neutral names for schools in the region; that the existing functional schools could not be closed or amalgamed until the whole system was reviewed in consultation with the minority group affected; that minorities in the region had a right to be educated in educational institutions in the languages and script pertaining to each minority; and that a moratorium on the teaching of history referring to the former Yugoslavia and its former constituent republics during the period 1989-1997 was to be in effect for five years. After further discussions the Minister signed on behalf of the government." Gravelle undated, pp. 14-17.

600 Howard 2008, p. 243.

601 The negotiating Head of Civil Affairs remembers the Central Bank director arguing, "We cannot do that, we have no money…" Interview with Dr. Gerard Fischer, Head of Civil Affairs, UNTAES, New York, 21 November 2006.

602 Ibid.

it."[603] Thus, "The Croats had very many difficulties in not agreeing to that."[604] The second factor was the linkage of the currency to the pension issue, proposed to Jacques-Paul Klein by his Head of Civil Affairs.[605] The Transitional Administrator recalls:

> I went to see Franjo Tudjman and I said, 'Mr. President, I wanna start changing the currency now.' He shouted at me, 'You should have started that seven months ago, you wasted time!' And I said, 'Mr President, everything in the plan has its place and its time. Now is the time and here is what I propose. We have about 28,000 pensioners and I suggest paying them in *kuna*. And *you* will pay those *kuna*.' And he said that he was not going to pay 'any Serb nationalist, Serb rebel anything.' – 'My own school teachers don't get pensions, my soldiers don't get pensions.' Et cetera. And I said, 'We're trying to do a job here. And now my feeling is this: if we pay pensioners in *kuna*, they can either reject it or accept it. If they accept it, they will go to the local grocery store and go to buy candy for the grandchildren. The grocer will say that he is not accepting any Croat *ustaše* money, and then the old grandmother will take her umbrella and hit him over the head. And then he will take her money. And she'll get her candy. And over time we will have established the *kuna*.' And he said, 'Oh, that's not bad, that's not bad, I like it.' And he told Kustovic, who was the Prime Minister at that time, to work with me on this. When I met with Kustovic, he said to me, 'I hope you have something nice to say to my family – because tomorrow I will be a dead man. The newspaper won't announce that President Tudjman did this, the newspaper will say that Prime Minister Kustovic authorizes payment of pensions to Serbs in Eastern Slavonia.' I told him that it won't be that serious, we would work that out. And it worked.[606]

One remaining fear was that Milosevic would manipulate the process from Belgrade "in terms of inflating the account."[607] However, by that time, the reality on-the-ground was already changing:

> The interesting thing was when you went to the market in Vukovar in the beginning of May, you could already change into *kuna*. The market is much faster. People know that if you want to make money, you can't be stupid – and the *kuna* became increasingly accepted.[608]

Eventually, Milosevic complied, launching the respective instructions, "And it worked."[609] On that note, an important and initially risky measure was the opening of a Saturday market in the Eastern Slavonian borderland that was intended to help residents buy daily goods, introduce the *kuna*, and help foster reconciliation, "An-

---

603 Ibid.
604 Ibid.
605 He, in turn, lauded his aide "who was a very good economist and made the right moves." Ibid.
606 Telephone interview with Ambassador Jacques-Paul Klein, SRSG/TA, UNTAES, 19 July 2007.
607 Interview with Dr. Gerard Fischer, Head of Civil Affairs, UNTAES, New York, 21 November 2006.
608 Ibid. "These local structures," he adds, "are not so bad." Ibid.
609 Ibid.

other example of encouraging the local Serbs to recognize their future was the opening of a Saturday market in the 'No-Man's Land' between Eastern Slavonia and the adjacent Croatian territory. This permitted trade and market stalls between Serbs and whoever wished to come across from the Croatian side."[610] A further communal level measure was the introduction of a bus service connecting all major Croatian cities.[611]

UNTAES "oversaw the transition of the monetary and financial systems" and also "assisted in developing the registration process for small businesses, and in securing guarantees for formerly socially owned enterprises so that the government, under the guise of privatization, would not unilaterally terminate or sell Serb-owned enterprises."[612] The mission could even make for some financial slack in the creation of the local civil service by seizing the Djelatovci oilfields and using the money for reconstruction efforts:

> Taking over those oilfields was really important because it allowed UNTAES to pay the salaries of teachers, sanitation workers, civil service workers. Thus, they did not depend on Zagreb, which meant that Serbs were to hold on to their civil sector jobs in ways that they may not have been able to unless UNTAES would have been responsible for their payment. UNTAES gave the money to Zagreb only on the condition that Zagreb actually paid the Serb servants.[613]

Electricity Provision

The talks on electricity provision started with a Croat lie: while the Croats claimed to serve the Vukovar grid, in reality it was Belgrade who was doing it. When the Transitional Administrator and his chief negotiator found out,

> We went right away to Belgrade to talk with Milosevic and we said, 'Croatia here says that they are providing the electricity for Vukovar and the UNTAES region.' He said, 'Yes, that's right.' I said, 'No, it is not. So if you wanna pull one over, you should: they don't have the grid, you do. So why don't you come up and embarrass them? Say that they don't have the grid but that you do.' And he did, he supplied electricity free.[614]

Essential as this was, it could only be an interim arrangement: in the long term, Croatia needed to take over. Yet, the rationale of Tudjman's government, as described by the Head of STACTA, was to wear down the Serb majority in Vukovar

610   Written interview with Derek G. Boothby, DSRSG/DTA, UNTAES, 5 February 2007.
611   Cf. Howard 2008, p. 243.
612   Ibid., p. 244.
613   Interview with Professor Michael W. Doyle, former UN Assistant Secretary-General, New Haven, 11 September 2006.
614   Telephone interview with Dr. Robert J.A.R. Gravelle, Head of the JIC Secretariat and Head of STACTA, 11 August 2007.

by denying them electricity, "He knew he couldn't force them out physically, so he said, 'We don't provide them so they will leave.'"[615] The tough negotiations that followed took more than three weeks:

> You had a wide spectrum of problems. The Croats said, 'We will only use these generators,' which were very expensive and which of course were only for the benefit of the Croats. And then we forced them, literally, to buy electricity from Novi Sad. At the end of three weeks negotiation they finally agreed. But they did not want to have it become public, so the billing had to come from the Croats and not from Novi Sad. You know, there are all of these mechanisms that you have to create, and to be fairly innovative and creative, to satisfy the political imperatives.[616]

Amnesty Law

Despite ongoing efforts, UNTAES did not accomplish an agreement on the amnesty law for Serbs that chose to continue living in the region.

> We were pushing for an amnesty for Serbs who didn't commit war crimes. We wanted Croatia to sign that into effect so that Serbs felt safe to stay because almost all Serbs had somehow been asked to contribute to the war efforts. For example, I had a landlord who had been a nurse. So, of course, he had treated Serb soldiers. But he was nervous that once Croatians came back they would put him into prison – because he had a uniform, as a nurse. And he ended up leaving, he lives in Serbia today. We pushed for the amnesty law for people like this man to stay, to feel comfortable to stay. Croatia wouldn't sign it, because it felt it was politically impossible. You know Croatian soldiers saying, 'How can we let these Serbs go? They have blood on their hands.' Now, actually, one day we were sitting around the office and we were thinking about how we could gonna pressure them. We found out that Klein knew somebody at IMF – and Croatia had just applied for an IMF loan. So we called IMF and asked, 'Can you hold back on that loan until they sign amnesty?' They said yes. Then we called Zagreb and said that they would not get the money until they signed. For about a week, it went back and forth. Finally Croatia said, 'We don't care, we don't need the money.' Still, you know, we used as many pressure tools as possible. This was most on the Croatian side but we also had to do that on the local Serb side, of course.[617]

---

615 Ibid.
616 Interview with Dr. Gerard Fischer, Head of Civil Affairs, UNTAES, New York, 21 November 2006.
617 Telephone interview with a staff member of STACTA, 10 January 2007. "The difficulties with the Amnesty Law were seen as part of a pattern of 'administrative discrimination' against the Serb population, characterized by arbitrary decisions and deliberate misinformation supplied to Serbs, especially in the part of lower-ranking bureaucrats. It was to this type of discrimination that the UNTAES civilian administration devoted much of its attention. Administrative discrimination was also combined with low-level harassment, which increased with greater freedom of movement in the region. Throughout the duration of UNTAES there were reports of hate speech against Serbs in the media, harassment, intimidation, physical assault, killings of Serbs, and looting of Serb property. These human rights

Box 2 gives an overview of the STACTA agreements.

Box 2: Agreements Concluded between UNTAES and the Croatian Government[618]		
Affidavit on the Rights of Public Employees		16 December 1996
Annex to the Affidavit		14 February 1997
Public Enterprises and Institutions		
Roads	Letter of Agreement by Hrvatske Ceste	21 March 1997
Radio/TV	Letter of Agreement by Hrvatska Radiotelevizija	2 April 1997
Post/Tele	Letter of Agreement by Hrvatska Pošta i Telekomunikacije	9 May 1997
Water	Letter of Agreement by Hrvatske Vode	22 May 1997
Railway	Letter of Agreement by Hrvatske Zeljeznice	6 June 1997
Electricity	Letter of Agreement by Hrvatska Elektro Privreda	22 July 1997
	Declaration on Maintenance of Electrical Supply	17 June 1997
Forestry	Letter of Agreement by Hrvatske Šume	25 June 1997
Education	Letter of Agreement by Ministry of Education	7 August 1997
	Agreement on the Distribution of Principal Positions	4 August 1997
	Declaration on Educational Certificates	12 March 1997
	Declaration on Minority Education Rights	4 August 1997
	Decision on Curriculum Content	4 August 1997
Fuel	MOU on INA/NIK Reintegration	18 June 1997
Police	MOU on Restructuring the Transitional Police Force	June 1997
	MOU on Restructuring of the Fire Brigades	28 November 1997
Health	Agreement on Regional Health Services	6 June 1997
	Agreement on Regional Health Services	3 December 1997
Pensions	Agreement by Croatian Pension Fund on Pension Services	29 May 1997
Vehicles	Agreement by Ministry of Interior on Vehicle Registration	23 May 1997
Taxation	Joint Statement on Reintegration of Tax Department	4 September 1997
Employment	Joint Statement on Reintegration of the Employment System	11 September 1997
Welfare	Joint Statement on Reintegration of the Social Welfare System	11 September 1997
Records	Agreement on Recognition and Hand-over of Record Books	25 September 1997
Economic		
MOU on Agricultural Trade/Barter		11 October 1996

violations were not considered by UNTAES to be serious, high-level abuse, as in times of war, but they were recognized as damaging to the peace process." Howard 2008, p. 248, referring to UN Secretary-General, "Report of the Secretary-General on the United Nations Transitional Administration for Eastern Slavonia, Baranja and Western Sirmium," UN Doc. S/1997/767, 2 October 1997, para. 37.

618   Klein, "UNTAES.".

Agreement by Ministry of Economy on Agricultural Trade/Barter	19 March 1997
TA Directive on Reintegration of the Payment System (ZAP)	18 July 1997
MOU on Introduction of Croatian Customs System and Annex of Goods	May 1997
Others	
Agreement on the Joint Working Group on Returns	23 April 1997
Organization of the Joint Council of Municipalities	23 Ma 1997
Certification of Elections	22 April 1997
Declaration on Conditions for Judicial Reintegration	30 September 97

Additionally, UNTAES had the GoC sign a Letter of Intent "on all the promises they said they will do, in order to guarantee [UNTAES'; ES] departure."[619] The UNTAES leadership had been pushing for such a document since they were sceptical "about the Croats being able to sustain their provinces."[620]

3.2.4 Summary and Assessment

The overall approach to reintegration consisted in a progressive shift in authority from the residual RSK/EC structures to the Croatian government, with UNTAES in the role of the facilitator. The mission operated its approach using two different processes, one was focused on clear legal agreements, and the other one was focused on institution-building, with reconciliation and confidence-building side-effects.[621]

First, UNTAES implemented the cooperative JIC mechanism. Constrained by continuing recalcitrance and mistrust between Serbs and Croats, inhibiting institutional provisions, and an overwhelming workload, reintegration turned out to be too slow. What ensued was a comprehensive and, in fact, gutsy redesign effort, which was proceeded in a rational manner, identifying priorities and benchmarks and imposing more control elements on the JICs. "I'd say that it was typical for anybody in UNTAES, to get the big picture."[622] The restructuring and the set-up

---

619 Telephone interview with Souren G. Seraydarian, DSRSG/DTA, UNTAES, 16 January 2007.
620 Ibid. They expressed this concern also towards the Security Council. Ibid.
621 "The JICs had a second purpose, which was simply confidence-building. And STACTA didn't have any of that. So, it's interesting looking afterwards which one would have worked in the long term, and maybe, the JICs would have worked much better. For instance, the first two meetings we had were just about getting to know each other again; and by the third meeting they were drinking *rakia* together and slapping each other on the back and, 'Oh, you remember then...' and so on. And that was very positive for the general reconciliation because they would go back to their communities and give a positive feedback. Also, we tried to have a general reconciliation programme. But these people that we brought together, these were the ones who had power in the community." Interview with Dr. Gerard Fischer, Head of Civil Affairs, UNTAES, New York, 21 November 2006.
622 Telephone interview with a field officer, UNTAES, 10 January 2007.

of STACTA was all the more remarkable. "There was no model to go through. We had to do it the best we could because we were the first."[623] One useful measure was, for instance, the external training for the aspiring police officers that took them out of the region:

> One of the formulas that I realized is working is that you take them out of this environment. If you see destruction and the influence of the various political streams – there is no ambiance or environment for these kinds of negotiations. When you take them out, you have a chance of success: at least while they're out they're cooperative and seeking a solution. But all this is not provided under the mandate, it's not part of the mission's objective, because it lacks finance.[624]

While the JICs continued to be a valuable tool for reintegration and reconciliation purposes,[625] it was the UNTAES Agreements that helped push the process forward. "In STACTA, we went through all the JICs, one by one by one, to basically make sure there was an agreement in place before the UN left. But instead of mediating, as in the JICs, we took on an arbitration role or even, I'd say, a negotiation role."[626]

The negation processes encountered recurring obstructing patterns.[627] "The Croats wished to negotiate rather [than] make decisions and sign agreements."[628] The Serbs were not easy to deal with either, some of them opposing reintegration *per se*, and the rest remaining sceptical of UNTAES' power to achieve substantial agreements with the Croatian government on their sustained rights. While the Croatians wanted to move forward as fast as possible, the Serbs opted for delaying and maintaining the status quo at any opportunity they had.[629]

---

623 Telephone interview with Dr. Robert J.A.R. Gravelle, Head of the JIC Secretariat and Head of STACTA, 11 August 2007. "We learned a lot," he adds. Ibid.
624 Interview with Dr. Gerard Fischer, Head of Civil Affairs, UNTAES, New York, 21 November 2006.
625 Again, "The JICs never had full authority. Eastern Slavonia was just another region that was absorbed into Croatia." Telephone interview with a staff member of STACTA, UNTAES, 10 January 2007.
626 Ibid.
627 "One has to realize one thing: the moment somebody co-operates, he or she will know that they are accountable to their society. So there is this consideration, 'Am I doing right if I negotiate, is there another option, what happens if we don't cooperate?'" Interview with Dr. Gerard Fischer, Head of Civil Affairs, UNTAES, New York, 21 November 2006.
628 Gravelle undated, p. 14.
629 "I'd say that obviously, you can imagine what the parties' interests were. For the Croatians, it was to get as little as possible, and for the Serbs to get as much as possible. So, Croats wanted it more fast, Serbs more slow, and the UN kind of had to find a middle way. So, there might well have been very sensitive issues on either side. And what is interesting now that I'm thinking of it, they were often different, and it took a while to discover that. For Croatia, I think, it was the national [pride] issue: the whole idea of winning and getting everything back, in one piece. For Serbs, it was more, I think, an issue of surviving somehow. I think that was a problem: that there was the assumption that we were negotiating with two parties, and mediating between two parties, that had equal interests. But most likely not: one side was interested in jobs and surviving and the other side was interested in getting

The coping style that emerged vis-à-vis the recurring obstructions from both sides was reflected in a very proactive, sometimes hard-nosed, sometimes risky, sometimes innovative tactics. Being pro-active was typical of the mission's approach. "I told my people, 'Don't let them stop you, keep moving keep crossing.' All in all, our concern was to get things done as much as we can: the language issue, the education curriculum, the religious issues et cetera. Get it done now."[630] The same held true for the implementation of the agreements:

> Literally, his people would go out there. For instance, if a Serb comes to them and say, 'I applied for the job, and I couldn't get it, and I know I couldn't get it because of the Croats,' one of the UNTAES people would actually go with that person to the office and make the case. And that's how hands-on they were.[631]

The idea or necessity triggering this policy of being pro-active lay in the fact that "we saw that if we didn't lock these agreements in, we would have a real problem. We were really sure that once we were gone, this little OSCE monitoring mission could not really control the Croats."[632]

---

executive authority." Telephone interview with a staff member of STACTA, UNTAES, 10 January 2007. "There are all sorts of tricks – that you have four meetings in four times you have four different people for different excuses." Interview with Dr. Gerard Fischer, Head of Civil Affairs, UNTAES, New York, 21 November 2006.

630   Telephone interview with Ambassador Jacques-Paul Klein, SRSG/TA, UNTAES, 19 July 2007. Similar another senior UNTAES staff member who adds, "There were all these incredibly idiotic ideas like of taking a language test at the universities, i.e. Croatian universities, for Serbs. They tried, but when we heard about it, we stopped it. We may not have stopped all abuse, by no means – you can only stop what you hear, and they may probably come up with another iteration of problems. But I think we were fairly alert here." Interview with a senior staff member of UNTAES, 22 November 2006.

631   Interview with Dr. Christine Coleiro, UNITAR POCI, Washington, DC, 1 December 2006. UNTAES' standard reaction to the Serbian sceptics and obstructionists was a combination of sticks and carrots: a constant pressure – "if you want to establish some guarantees for your future in the region you have to do it now" – was accompanied by substantive efforts to present them with sufficient options.

632   Telephone interview with Ambassador Jacques-Paul Klein, SRSG/TA, UNTAES, 19 July 2007. See also Coleiro 2002, p. 109, "Consensus was often reached in the eleventh hour without much time to give the documents all the legal attention necessary. Furthermore, because of reluctance on the part of the Croat officials to commit too much to paper, the text of the agreements was frequently lacking in specificity. This was also due to the Serb perception that a nebulous agreement would allow them to manipulate its implementation to their advantage. UNTAES had made incredible progress by the mere fact that it created a forum for discussion, it brought the two sides together and it negotiated agreements on all the areas indicted in its mandate. However, the test of validity of the agreements within the Croatian legal and administrative system was that of implementation and, by the time these agreements were signed, the UNTAES mandate was running out and there was no time left to monitor implementation. Responsibility for implementation now rested with the Government of Croatia. However, it would be the OSCE follow-on mission, invited by the Croatian Government to oversee and monitor the implementation of the reintegration commitments that inherited the task to ensure Croat compliance as stated in the UNTAES Agreements."

These lurking problems notwithstanding, the mission earned credibility among not only the high-level negotiation partners[633] but also with the population at large. The relationship with the local population is one subject covered by the following chapter.

3.3 Running the Mission

Not only is the transitional administration a powerful governance institution for a war-torn territory, it is in itself a highly complex organization that needs internal management. Correspondingly, the senior management of a mission has internal and external leadership responsibilities: as SRSG, Klein was the head of a UN mission, needing to set up and keep the mission running, motivate, support, direct and control his field staff, make strategic decisions, manage and lead his people, coordinate cooperation with other organizations in the field, and be accountable for the mission vis-à-vis the Secretariat and the Security Council in New York. As Transitional Administrator with executive authority, Klein was the governor of the territory. In order for UNTAES to deal with the local leaders so that they would support the UN's transitional management, the mission leadership had to achieve highly political goals and was responsible for the local population's wellbeing, making critical decisions about their future.[634]

The following chapters focus on pathological patterns and coping approaches by UNTAES in its relationship to the local population, in its capacity-building efforts, its cooperation with other organizations, in how it managed its funds and resources, and in its leadership style.

3.3.1 Relation to Local Population

One feature of UNTAES that various observers and people involved in the mission have stressed unanimously is its remarkable people-orientation.[635] In its outreach

---

633 "We were accepted as a valid third party, I guess because of the process being effective and being locally owned. We were able to maintain the authority, in a positive way, and we were never challenged the way we were in other missions." Telephone interview with a field officer, UNTAES, 10 January 2007.

634 That said, one should note that a UN operation is accountable to the Security Council only; the accountability to a local populace is no legal obligation, but a decrease in acceptance and local legitimacy might, one, diminish the chances of success as local cooperation is essential for it, and two, it might agitate claims of neo-colonialism.

635 "'We're going to come in and the first thing we're going to establish is confidence.'" Interview with Dr. Christine Coleiro, Washington, DC, 1 December 2006, recalling Klein's approach.

to the population, UNTAES relied on diverse instruments, from "endless townhall meetings to explain what was going on,"[636] to village meetings, radio[637] and TV[638] shows, and printed media. UN soldiers, police, and civilians were also used as information multipliers. While UNTAES stands out as an exemplary case of public relations activities, the tragedy is that it was still not enough: nationalist propaganda and reluctance to accept the mission continued to persist.

Townhalls and Churches

In TV and radio shows, senior UNTAES staff took calls from people and answered their questions. Deputy SRSG Boothby recalls:

> As Deputy Transitional Administrator, I participated in many town and village meetings, personally telling sceptical (and sometimes very difficult) audiences that they did not have good options, but the least bad option was that they should stay on their land rather than fleeing to Serbia. Part of my 'sermon' was to tell them bluntly that UNTAES would not be there forever and that indeed time was short so it would be in their best interest to help us to help them.[639]

After a troublesome start – in the first weeks, there were "only attacks on the UN mandate, from either side, like, 'You're not protecting us, you're forcing us...'"[640] – people made increasing use of the instrument, "actually talking about real issues."[641] UNTAES also distributed its own newspaper. It was published in the local languages and got "hand-carried, from house to house, by our CivPol; because I

---

636 Telephone interview with Ambassador Jacques-Paul Klein, SRSG/TA, UNTAES, 19 July 2007.
637 "[...] UNTAES radio was functional within weeks of the establishment of the mission, largely because its operators were able to rely on staff and equipment from UNPROFOR Radio in Zagreb. This relationship did not continue for long, however, because the local staff in Zagreb was unwilling to move to Vukovar. The UNTAES public affairs office subsequently reached an agreement with Radio Vukovar, whereby UNTAES Radio could operate from the Radio Vukovar facilities, utilize its equipment, technicians and engineers, but remain separate from the somewhat biased Radio Vukovar productions. The original Radio UNTAES broadcasts lasted only fifteen minutes per day, but these were quickly increased to seven hours daily. During the April 1997 elections, UNTAES radio sponsored twelve hours daily of programming, which reported on the elections, and on technical aspects of voting procedures." Howard 2008, pp. 251-252.
638 "[...] UNTAES TV was operational from February to July 1997. Its half-hour broadcasts on Saturday nights dealt with practical themes, such as registering to vote, obtaining citizenship and other documents, and employment opportunities." Ibid., p. 252.
639 Written interview with Derek G. Boothby, DSRSG/DTA, UNTAES, 5 February 2007.
640 Interview with Dr. Gerard Fischer, Head of Civil Affairs, UNTAES, New York, 21 November 2006.
641 "It was only after four, five, six weeks that people started actually to talk about real issues, [that means; ES] to show preparedness to accept the mandate." Ibid.

wanted the population to know what was going on not from the propaganda,"[642] as the Transitional Administrator emphasized. However, in spite of various public campaigns, in the judgement of the Head of Civil Affairs, the efforts were not comprehensive enough. He even identified media control as one of the most deficient aspects of UNTAES:

> Where I believe that we failed was control of the media. We could have been much stricter on hate messages, on both sides. On the Croatian television, you could see every day at seven o'clock how horrible the Serbs had been, for half an hour. And with the mandate we had we could have said that we wanted to screen for one year all the programmes that they put out. And I am a firm believer that they would have had to accept it. Equally on the Serb side. Same thing with newspapers: we made once an attempt where we brought local journalists from either side together and gave them a workshop on how we expect them to report – and I am not saying influencing the reporting but cleaning the reporting. And, you know, it was accepted; but the mentality of course did not change. And you could see it from all the radio and TV programmes: HDZ had the power and they were horrible.[643]

Supplementing its media activities, the mission used its different command structures of the military, civilian police, and civil affairs[644] for information purposes.

> In every sector of Eastern Slavonia we had one of our battalions, Jordanian, Pakistani, Belgian, and Russians. And they were collecting information. And then we had Civilian Police, who were doing the same thing, in almost every village. And then you have your Civilian Affairs people, on the civilian side of the mission, who are always out there. In other words, we have area coordinators, town coordinators, and village coordinators.[645]

---

642 Telephone interview with Ambassador Jacques-Paul Klein, SRSG/TA, UNTAES, 19 July 2007.

643 Interview with Dr. Gerard Fischer, Head of Civil Affairs, UNTAES, New York, 21 November 2006.

644 "The public affairs unit was really huge within UNTAES, because they did a lot of explaining to the people what UNTAES is about. You know, UNTAES was all over it: it would do radio, and newsletter, and publications, and info-cafés – just getting the people informed, getting them on board. They did a good job. They don't do that everywhere. For instance, in Liberia they tried to do it but it wasn't half the success as it was in Eastern Slavonia. The unit itself was not as highly motivated as the public affairs in Eastern Slavonia. But in Eastern Slavonia, UNTAES, the people that Klein had – and I think it triggled down – were really motivated. People would do things that really were not even in their job description. For example, when there was this girl, an aid of Klein would go and went to get the girl a passport. They wouldn't give it to her, so she went there and she waited in the line with this girl for two hours and then came in into the office and argued with the official. She just went and took care of it herself. It was like fighting for family, so committed. But it was small: the mission itself was compact." Interview with Dr. Christine Coleiro, UNITAR POCI, Washington, DC, 1 December 2006.

645 Telephone interview with Ambassador Jacques-Paul Klein, SRSG/TA, UNTAES, 19 July 2007.

The leaders of UNTAES even became regular churchgoers:

> I remember we went every Sunday to all churches that they had. I am not a Christian myself, but anyway. There were so many churches you cannot believe: Serb, Croatians, Protestants, Catholics, Orthodox, Ruthenians et cetera. We went there and we went through – or stood through – the ceremonies which took an hour or two. And afterwards, we had lunch with these guys and there we got many good ideas. The philosophy behind that was: people in a post-conflict situation look for something more than natural. They may not be the best Orthodox or Croats or Catholics or whatever, but there was some sort of a fundamental basis of … relatively good people, let's say. You could use that as a sort of starting point.[646]

Obviously, "These kinds of guidelines you don't get in the mandate, you know, 'Go to church every Sunday and eat all of the strange food.'"[647] Informal practices like these developed as the mission went along. Senior UNTAES staff also went to see the patriarch in Belgrade, as well as numerous Serb and Croat bishops, trying to get their support. In the end, however, it was not possible to bring both sides together. In fact, the religious leaders were the most renitent, "The one singular community that we were unable to bring together was the respective church authorities, the Croatian Catholics and the Serbian Orthodox."[648]

Klein is said to have made the people of Eastern Slavonia feel that they were not forgotten by the world, by promoting international support and drawing attention to Eastern Slavonia. For instance, "He would invite Madeleine Albright and she would come, several times, and even Clinton came. He had this good skill of selling ideas."[649] The Head of Civil Affairs remembers an anecdote that is said to be typical for Klein:

> Vukovar was horribly looking and destroyed and everything. And he said, 'We have to do something for kids. These kids haven't seen any merry-go-round, they haven't seen elephants.' And we had one guy in Public Affairs to whom Klein said, 'Bill, get me an elephant; get me a merry-go-round, ketchup, sausages, mustard!' And this guy was American also and he contacted Ramstein, in Germany, and they managed to get all that. And Klein had a children's day. You know, in a destroyed world, these are all signals that it is improving. And at this dimension, he was excellent. You know, he was looking at these details – where he had all of us laughing – like, 'But make sure there is enough ketchup! And the sausages and the small bred…' And for each of the kids he had a little gift. So, he was very personal. Of course, it was like he was the king [laughs].

---

646 Interview with Dr. Gerard Fischer, Head of Civil Affairs, UNTAES, New York, 21 November 2006. "Also, Klein would regularly go to Church – not because he was so religious but in order to see and talk to the local people, to find out what their concerns and thoughts were." Ibid.

647 Ibid. "So, that was one of the informal mechanisms that was very good," he adds. Ibid.

648 Written interview with Derek G. Boothby, DSRSG/DTA, UNTAES, 5 February 2007.

649 Interview with Dr. Gerard Fischer, Head of Civil Affairs, UNTAES, New York, 21 November 2006.

And this was the other side: that he was the viceroy of this. Anyway, I think this was probably very important in certain stages.[650]

3.3.2 Capacity-building

Capacity-building in Eastern Slavonia was hampered by ongoing recalcitrance and reluctance of the former parties of the conflict to cooperate. At the same time, however, people had a relatively high level of formal education. Hence, the pivotal challenge for capacity-building consisted of reconciliation-building and identifying people who were ready to participate in the new multiethnic structures.

> In the Balkans, you have no culprits, you have only victims. The mindset is that, 'We are right, the others are wrong.' Through history, through all the wars that this region has seen, you had never the preparedness to say, 'Well, maybe *we* also did something wrong, maybe *our* policy is not right.' It was a one-party state since Yugoslavia was created and prior to that, it wasn't a cradle of democracy either. There is absence of such a tradition and you have a very thin pool from where you can start.[651]

Obviously, there were also the hard-liners, those who attempted to block the mission.

> Here, the only advice I could see and give at that moment is that you have to be relentlessly tiring them out. There is no fine skill of carrots that you can offer them. But you can – I don't want to use the word 'threaten' – but you can tell them that they are obliged under the word of the Security Council to co-operate. And that may fail: the person may be sick, the person may not show up, the person may disappear, may be replaced... There are all sorts of tricks. You have four meetings and four times you have four different people for different excuses.[652]

Capacity-building in Eastern Slavonia did not resemble the capacity-building of most other missions which were deployed in developing countries and where the level of education was substantially worse, "You cannot come and administer a country that has been a lead nation among the non-aligned states. You would take away a lot of that pride. And in many instances, the people that were working there were better than our crew."[653] Hence, the provision of support became UNTAES' capacity-building policy. For instance,

> When they wanted to organize something, for example a conference, they wouldn't know how to do it logistically. It was those things that the UN helped them out with. It

---

650 Ibid.
651 Interview with a senior UNTAES official, 22 November 2006.
652 Interview with Dr. Gerard Fischer, Head of Civil Affairs, UNTAES, New York, 21 November 2006.
653 Ibid.

is also a more diplomatic way of support. And capacity-building has to be done very diplomatically.[654]

Likewise, a focus was put creating civil society institutions, particularly local NGOs.[655] The Task Force Report outlined:

> Local non-governmental organizations in Sector East are virtually non-existent with the exception of the local Red Cross Society. Some NGOs visit the Sector from Belgrade such as the Anti-War Campaign. In Croatia, groups such as the Local Democracy Network in Osijek, Anti-War Campaign and Open Eyes have been quite active, especially in Osijek and Vinkovci. A few international NGOs are present in Sector East.[656]

In the following months, UNTAES provided locals with the know-how for the set up and maintenance – financing that is – of an NGO.[657] Yet, as demand increased, so did abuse: the majority of the NGOs that had emerged had done so just in order to siphon off funding. Observing the severe malpractice, the Transitional Administrator drew his conclusion and closed them off not only from the UNTAES meetings but also from cooperation in general.[658]

Besides basic support, consulting, and the creation of civil society organizations, UNTAES acted as a facilitator of the involvement of other relevant organizations. For example, in the field of civil affairs, "A human rights training seminar sponsored by the Council of Europe and a local NGO was conducted by the JIC on Human Rights at Osijek, Croatia. Delegates to all JICs were invited to the seminar, the first such training for middle-level civil servants in the region and its immediate environs."[659]

3.3.3 Cooperation with International and Local Organizations

About 25 international and non-governmental organizations were operating in the region. They helped achieve the complex mandate.[660] Their cooperation was rather smooth. According to observers, an important factor that contributed to this result

---

654 Interview with Dr. Christine Coleiro, UNITAR POCI, Washington, DC, 1 December 2006.
655 UNTAES had to realize quickly that there simply were no proponents of civil society. "Initially, they were a bit naïve and they thought, 'We just go and help the local organizations.' However, there was none to speak of." Ibid.
656 UN Task Force 1995, para. 52-53.
657 "These people did not know how to set up their local NGOs." Interview with an UNTAES staff member, 1 December 2006.
658 See below.
659 Interview with Dr. Gerard Fischer, Head of Civil Affairs, UNTAES, 21 November 2006.
660 "Wisely, in the 1990s, peacekeeping operations began to delegate particular functions to the international agencies. Their support is crucial. They also helped with regards to the political support." Interview with Professor Michael W. Doyle, former UN Assistant Secretary-General, New Haven, 11 September 2006.

consisted of the regular meetings between the mission and the other organizations. A close observer of UNTAES recalls,

> There is a lot of variation in how good cooperation in peace operations is. It was always a good sign when the meetings were full. And in Eastern Slavonia, they most often were. Whereas in Cambodia, for instance, meeting rooms were often almost empty. When all the representatives from all the various organizations working there on-the-ground were there, then you just knew: this is going to work out.[661]

Stressing good leadership as making a difference, he credits Klein with enabling cooperation to function.[662] "There are always frictions, but it went along very well: UNTAES was very homogenous. But if the chain of command gets split, then you have competition at the top – and then you have a competition at the bottom."[663]

Cooperation Partners

A multitude of UN agencies and organizations were active in the region, especially on humanitarian and human rights issues. The major players included UNHCR, UNICEF, WHO, WFP, EU/EUMM, OSCE, MSF, ICRC, ECHO, NRC, CARE, and JEN. UNICEF, for instance, conducted mine-awareness and media campaigns.[664] Furthermore, the World Bank, who was of particular importance in currency negotiations,[665] and the IMF played a central role in the region. "And then you have of course these contact groups, bilateral donors, et cetera; they have to make them interested in particular areas to help you to go along with them. It is extremely important that one has these networks."[666] Overall, the cooperation with the UN and bilateral agencies was working, "UNHCR was well, the Japanese Emergency Network, JEN, was doing well, the demining people from Germany were doing well. It was an all around effort and everyone could see the results, and especially the local population."[667] In addition, UNTAES entertained beneficial relations with the Office of the High Representative of the NATO-led multinational Implementation Force (IFOR) for Bosnia and Herzegovina on humanitarian aid

---

661   Ibid.
662   Ibid.
663   Interview with Dr. Christine Coleiro, UNITAR POCI, Washington, DC, 1 December 2006. "The more competition you are going to have, the less effective you are going to be in the field. But this is a reality in the field, unfortunately. If you have a spreading out of the chain you are going to have a lot of competition – competition will start out at the top before it starts out at the bottom, but it will triggle down all the way." Ibid.
664   Cf. Coleiro 2002, p. 91, referring to UN Department of Peacekeeping Operations 1997.
665   See Chapter IV.3.2.3.
666   Interview with Dr. Gerard Fischer, Head of Civil Affairs, UNTAES, New York, 21 November 2006.
667   Telephone interview with Dr. Robert J.A.R. Gravelle, Head of the JIC Secretariat and Head of STACTA, 11 August 2007.

coordination. Its close link to NATO, in the form of guaranteed "over the horizon"-forces, worked well and was sustained by joint training units.

Other organizations active in Eastern Slavonia were the ICRC, the IOM, the OSCE, as well as the EU.[668] While the ICRC and the IOM worked on humanitarian and refugee needs, the OSCE was mainly involved in organizing and overseeing the elections.[669] The EU was informally "affiliated"[670] with UNTAES. The head of the EU office at Vukovar was the *de facto* deputy to the UNTAES Head of Civil Affairs, "Whatever process he had, I had to sort of approve it."[671] The specific advantage of this kind of working relationship was that UNTAES Civil Affairs also had money from the EU for peacebuilding necessities, such as rebuilding the school system. "That was fantastic because it never went through the UN channels."[672] Besides, at the international level, UNTAES also had a good rapport with the Commission of the EU.

On the non-profit side, there were about twenty international NGOS (MSF, CARE, Oxfam, etc.) in the field, which played a vital role in mobilizing resources,

All these NGOs are really important participants. They often do more local re-building than any international official can do. And they often have more expertise. You know, UN people would not know how to do it. *They* knew how to do it; there was really a lot of expertise.[673]

Often, however, frictions occurred because of UNTAES and the NGOs' diverging mandates, which were already very heterogeneous. The Transitional Administrator came forward with a pointed categorization:

Most of them were young people, with cell phones and fax machines – war groupies who would go where the action is. But they wouldn't deliver anything. The second group were well-meaning groups, Christians, Jews, Moslems: they want to do the right thing but they don't know what the hell they're doing. And then the third group consisted of the large international NGOs, OXFAM, CARE et cetera, and they actually knew what they were doing and they did it well.[674]

668 Cf. UN Department of Peacekeeping Operations. 1997. *Croatia: UNTAES.* Available online at http://www.un.org/Depts/DPKO/Missions/untaes_b.htm, last access on 18 February 2009.
669 See Chapter IV.3.4.2.
670 Interview with Dr. Gerard Fischer, Head of Civil Affairs, UNTAES, New York, 21 November 2006.
671 Ibid.
672 Interview with a senior UNTAES staff member, 22 November 2006.
673 Interview with Professor Michael W. Doyle, former UN Assistant Secretary-General, New Haven, 11 September 2006.
674 Telephone interview with Ambassador Jacques-Paul Klein, SRSG/TA, UNTAES, 19 July 2007. Regarding the second group, the Head of Civil Affairs cites another example. "We had an incidence where Caritas from Rheinland-Pfalz came and had this fantastic pro-gramme – which we were totally unaware of – where they only rebuilt Catholics' houses. You know, with the best of intentions, but with no political sensitivity." Interview with Dr. Gerard Fischer, Head of Civil Affairs, UNTAES, New York, 21 November 2006.

This being said, one needs to consider that NGOs have their own agendas, too. "They are still very independent organizations. What you have to do is to make sure that they understand your mandate, what you are trying to, and to get them help you do that, and not working on something at cross-purposes."[676]

Coordination Mechanisms

The major mechanism for UNTAES' coordination of the various actors in the field was regular executive meetings. This was something that, at least in the late 1990s, was not standard for complex peace missions.

> We had structured meetings. One of my deputies numbered them. You do that all the time: the first thing you do in the morning is the staff meeting, even on Saturdays. A staff meeting is 25 to 30 people: your military, all your battalion commanders, the heads of all your organizations, logistics, communication, administration, engineering et cetera. In addition, EU and OSCE key personalities attended. Then once a week you have a meeting with all the other heads of the UN family. And then the third type of meetings would be with the NGOs, on a regular basis. The Head of Civil Affairs chaired the meetings with the NGOs and my Deputy chaired the meetings with the other UN organizations. I would stop by once in a while.[677]

---

675 Howard 2008, pp. 239-240. On the difficulties of UN independent intelligence capacities and further arguments on its un-desirability, see Chesterman, Simon. 2006. *Shared Secrets: Intelligence and Collective Security*. Lowy Institute Paper 10. Sydney: Lowy Institute for International Policy.

676 Telephone interview with Ambassador Jacques-Paul Klein, SRSG/TA, UNTAES, 19 July 2007.

677 Ibid.

While certain NGOs did not come to these meetings, most of them attended,[678] taking advantage of the transparency that was thus created. Even though "at the end of the day, Klein couldn't care much about what these people said. If he wanted to change, he would change. But he played the transparency card very well."[679]

Eventually, UNTAES was very active in *off-* the-ground cooperation, too. Not only vis-à-vis the Friends of the Secretary-General, but regarding a range of other states:

> It's really important that the neighboring states are cooperative. Klein spent a lot of his time on the plane, in Austria, in Germany, in France. He really played up that he is, by heritage, an Alsatian. So, whenever he'd go to France, he'd speak French and would refer to it as 'My home-country,' and whenever he went to Germany, he would speak German and said the same thing. And he played up, building up neighborhood support. Really important.[680]

At the international level, UNTAES also organized donor cooperation for financial support. "That was another important facet of this mandate that you had to be innovative. The mission does not have the funding for peacebuilding. And here again we had extremely good assistants."[681] These assistants will be introduced below.

3.3.4 Raising and Managing Resources

Financial management is a precarious feature of any complex peace operation, from where pathologies regularly emanate. While UNTAES was sufficiently equipped with assessed contributions for peacekeeping and directly mission-related expenses,[682] it suffered from constraints for peacebuilding activities.

> We had financial constraints. One of the problems the UN always faces is that the UN has money for peacekeeping, it's called assessed budget for peacekeeping, but you can't use that money outside the UN. This means that you always have to have a donor

---

678 "The door was open." Interview with Dr. Gerard Fischer, Head of Civil Affairs, UNTAES, New York, 21 November 2006. "Right from the start we were working together." Telephone interview with Dr. Robert J.A.R. Gravelle, Head of the JIC Secretariat and Head of STAC-TA, 11 August 2007.

679 Interview with a senior UNTAES staff member, 22 November 2006.

680 Interview with Professor Michael W. Doyle, former UN Assistant Secretary-General, New Haven, 11 September 2006.

681 Interview with Dr. Gerard Fischer, Head of Civil Affairs, UNTAES, New York, 21 November 2006.

682 These resources were sufficiently available, for example, "When we wanted to set up a field office it was like 'boom' – we got the money and everything immediately, within a week or two." In addition, "We never felt under-resourced in terms of security." Telephone interview with a field officer, UNTAES, 10 January 2007.

conference, voluntarily contributions, and establish trust funds, so that donors come in.[683]

The mission had to find innovative takes on procurement by raising voluntary funds through different channels.[684] However, raising voluntary funds conveyed four major hitches: delay and uncertainty, earmarking, and donor fatigue. UNTAES did not have instant access to money for quick reactions projects,[685] "For example, the ability to immediately authorize the expenditure of $250,000 for the quick construction of a school or equipping a clinic." Such projects, if "started without delay and quickly completed, can have enormous positive impact in a local community,"[686] but delay and uncertainty about the programmes may trigger early frustration. Earmarking denotes the fact that donors often do not want their money to go to a UN trust fund but prefer to spend it bilaterally for specific projects, telling the mission what they want the money to be spent on.[687] The problem that ensues is, one, inflexibility for the mission, and, two, donors watching out for prestigious projects and abandoning less visible but nonetheless crucial measures. Finally, almost every mission will face the phenomenon of donor fatigue sooner or later, i.e. ceasing money, patience, and attention of the backers,[688] who are incessantly moving to the next hot spot. "And once you get donor fatigue – then, what do you do? The UN has no back-up for that."[689] What follows from these difficulties is a high degree of uncertainty and precariousness of all peacebuilding-related activities.[690]

Facing the challenges, UNTAES organized two donor conferences promoting financial commitments. Their nominal success was enormous. At the first donors'

---

683 Telephone interview with Souren G. Seraydarian, DSRSG/DTA, UNTAES, 16 January 2007.
684 "[...] you had to be innovative." Interview with Dr. Gerard Fischer, Head of Civil Affairs, UNTAES, New York, 21 November 2006.
685 "A UN operation will never have the flexibility for its leadership to be able to implement a project that needs doing urgently." Written interview with Derek G. Boothby, DSRSG/ DTA, UNTAES, 5 February 2007.
686 Ibid. He continues, "It would have been very valuable indeed for the Transitional Administrator to have authority to spend, on his own decision, significant money for quick reaction projects."
687 "The problem is that we were always having our necks in the hands of the donors. We could not do something without their consent." Telephone interview with Souren G. Seraydarian, DSRSG/DTA, UNTAES, 16 January 2007.
688 "Donors have a very short span of attention; they want to see quick and dirty results. That is what it comes down to at the end. Because new crises come up somewhere else; and donors have to go to their parliamentarians and have to make an argument that they spend x million dollars in a particular country." Interview with a senior UNTAES staff member, 22 November 2006.
689 Interview with Dr. Christine Coleiro, UNITAR POCI, Washington, DC, 1 December 2006.
690 "And we still have this concept. In my last mission, in Liberia, it was the same thing. Until the money came in it took a long time. The UN does not allow using UN money for these purposes, for peacebuilding." Telephone interview with Souren G. Seraydarian, DSRSG/ DTA, UNTAES, 16 January 2007.

meeting on 6 December 1996, UNTAES raised $37.3 million in pledges via the support of the EU, the United States, Germany, Italy, Belgium, Sweden, the Netherlands, and Great Britain.[691] For instance, the EU signalled its willingness to spend a total of 10.1 million Euro on reconstruction, de-mining efforts for civilian purposes, refugee settlement, and reconstruction; $9.7 million came from USAID for economic reconstruction projects; Belgium agreed to invest $1 million for the Port of Vukovar, $1.5 million for other UNTAES projects, and $0.4 million for school heating; Sweden was involved in providing fuel for humanitarian purposes and projects relating to schools; and Norway was active in a program that distributed vitamins to children in the region.[692] The second donor conference was also held in Zagreb, on 14 March 1997, and was attended by almost 200 representatives of governments, NGOs, international organizations, as well as the GoC and local authorities. "Donors present confirmed their pledges [...] made at the first Donors' Meeting [...]. Additional pledges of $21.8 million were made by the United States, Norway, Belgium, Italy and other parties."[693] Including the results from fundraising activities other than the conferences,[694] a total of $76.8 million was raised between January and December 1996.

Besides these fundraising activities, financial cooperation with *European institutions* –particularly the EU but also the Council of Europe – was crucial. For instance, "The election was paid by the Europeans."[695] As said, relations with the EU office on-the-ground were working, and money for peacebuilding projects could come in over EU channels and thus did not need consent of the UN.[696] The downside of it was, however, that it took a long time until the money arrived, "The process of getting funds from the EU is a lengthy one. Particularly when you propose things in July – because, in August, Brussels is closed, and you get things only in October, when you're lucky."[697]

An important funding mechanism was the Transitional Administrator himself, who put his connections and contacts to fruitful use and engaged in constant efforts to visit potential donors in Europe and the United States. "Klein went out and got his own funding."[698] The Head of Civil Affairs made the point that Klein "made a lot of things moving which in other missions would never, never happen."[699] The

---

691 Klein, "UNTAES.".
692 Cf. ibid.
693 UN Department of Peacekeeping Operations 1997.
694 The EU, Norway, Belgium, USA, Italy, UNHCR, ICRC, IFRC and various NGOs pledged $17.7 million.
695 Interview with Dr. Gerard Fischer, Head of Civil Affairs, UNTAES, New York, 21 November 2006.
696 Ibid.
697 Ibid.
698 Interview with Dr. Christine Coleiro, UNITAR POCI, Washington, DC, 1 December 2006.
699 For instance, the international financial institutions do normally not give money to a *region*.

UNTAES leadership also eventually obtained an agreement with the Croatian government to assume the expenses of the regional civil service and pensions.

> They did not agree very enthusiastically, they were very adamant from the very beginning to include all the people in the pension fund; because there demography was such that there were a lot of people older than 60 and not having the chance to get a job in this destroyed environment. So, there was a big push to make them accept that. Again, they came up with all kinds of tricks, like not paying and delaying or excluding people from payment. But a strong mandate allowed us to hold them to their commitment under the implementation of the mandate – which you don't have in other missions.[700]

In fact, this issue had initially been perceived as one of the greatest challenges to the mission, and the agreement was a considerable success.[701] In sum, despite the comparatively comfortable equipment, the mission "by far couldn't finance all those things that we wanted to finance."[702]

3.3.5 Leadership Style and Relation to New York Headquarters

The leadership style of Jacques-Paul Klein and his senior management team turned out to be adequate for the constellation in Eastern Slavonia. By a variety of observers, this was pointed out as one crucial factor for success. At the end of the day, Klein's proactive and, at times, provocative decisions were crowned with success, yet his leadership was at times also risky.

Mandate as "Floor"

UNTAES' leadership adopted a very active and pushy approach to completing its mission. The central figure, SRSG and Transitional Administrator Klein, was given executive authority. "Klein was very forceful and exerting executive authority

---

700 Interview with Dr. Gerard Fischer, Head of Civil Affairs, UNTAES, New York, 21 November 2006.
701 "The biggest problem was who was to pay the the salaries for the local community officers. I mean, this was not big money, it was about six million *kuna* a month. Still, somebody had to pay them. The Croats said, 'We will not pay the Serbs the salary,' and then we said, 'OK, then you mean that you will accept that Belgrade will pay the salaries. They will be very happy, because this means that they will remain Serbs, not Croats.' And this negotiation went on and on and on. Eventually they said, 'OK, you're right, actually, we don't want to get any help from Belgrade, we want to do that from Zagreb.'" Telephone interview with Souren G. Seraydarian, DSRSG/DTA, UNTAES, 16 January 2007.
702 Interview with Dr. Gerard Fischer, Head of Civil Affairs, UNTAES, New York, 21 November 2006.

when it was needed."[703] Described as a charismatic and energetic person,[704] Klein furthered his credibility through close links to Washington and NATO:

> Klein was in constant contact with Washington. It's a UN operation, he is working for the Secretary-General of the UN, but he was on the phone every other day to the State Department and the Department of Defense to make sure Washington's backing. And that's because the only actor that Tudjman listened to was the United States. For the long term, Tudjman was worried about admission to the EU, but in terms of day-to-day, he wanted to get in to NATO first. Thus, Washington could pressure him in ways that no one else could. Klein knew that. And Klein knew that if he'd got into real trouble, he would have NATO forces, they would back him up. And Klein is a US Two-Star-General who also was a long-serving official within the NATO Secretariat. So, he knew NATO very well and they knew him.[705]

He was able to strike the right tone towards the likes of Tudjman, Milosevic, and other hardliners in the region, "He has a good way of talking to leaders: very straightforward, very clear, incorruptible. He was accused of being too close to the Serbs, too close to the Croats, but I have never seen anything in this direction, and I think nobody else has."[706] He and the mission earned themselves a reputation of being fair.[707] Furthermore, Klein had "a very good insight in sort of the political gaming that is necessary to do in these circumstances."[708] And he was "all over the damn place:"[709] constantly, "I was shuttling between Zagreb-Belgrade-Zagreb-Belgrade. In a way, I became the middleman for messages between Milosevic and

---

703 Telephone interview with a staff member of STACTA, UNTAES, 10 January 2007.
704 "Klein's leadership is very special. He is a man who is extremely talented, he is very good in starting up a mission, and he is full of himself: after 20 minutes when you see him you say, 'I will never be able to say anything' [laughs]. He is a great leader, or at least, let's say he was a great leader for this particular mission. This man is best when he is new in the area, when he has to rely to some extent on his closest staff. The moment he thinks he knows the whole thing better than anyone else in the mission, he disregards everybody's advice because he thinks he has the best instincts." Interview with a senior UNTAES staff member, 22 November 2006. He adds, "He is dynamic, he is hard working, day and night, 22 hours a day, and he expects that everybody else is doing the same. There was some sort of a leadership dimension that was very positive in this mission. He is a fantastic, charismatic kind of guy." Ibid.
705 Interview with Professor Michael W. Doyle, former UN Assistant Secretary-General, New Haven, 11 September 2006.
706 Ibid.
707 Telephone interview with a field officer, UNTAES, 10 January 2007.
708 Interview with Dr. Gerard Fischer, Head of Civil Affairs, UNTAES, New York, 21 November 2006.
709 Telephone interview with Ambassador Jacques-Paul Klein, SRSG/TA, UNTAES, 19 July 2007.

Tudjman."[710] At the same time, his style was strongly oriented towards the common people.[711] "He is not a humble person, but he had one thing that many others don't have: he is very much down to earth and he knows what people need when they suffer."[712]

Klein was proactive in his dealings with the local leaders as well as New York headquarters.

On the one hand, friction emerged over his and his senior staff's arbitrary actions, e.g. when UNTAES took the Djelatovci oilfields. While being conscious of the consequences if their unilateral actions would have gone wrong, UNTAES' senior staffs were stern in their proactive course. The internally coined wording was that "it's easier to seek forgiveness than permission."[713] New York, however, definitely "objected to not being consulted."[714] As regards to Klein's persona, "There were, as there is all the time within the UN, elements of grudges of the work that he did."[715] It goes without saying, "If Klein had failed, there'd be no one there to protect him. He had gone beyond the mandate. But as he succeeded, they could all take credit for that. Thus, acting strong is a risky road for a SRSG to take, but those are the kind of trade-offs they face."[716] At the same time, DPKO "was over-

710 Ibid. He continues, "And I finally got tired of it because, as I finally told the Serb foreign minister, Milosevic and Tudjman would in fact speak to each other every other day, 'Other people don't know that but I know that, so why am I used as a messenger here?' By the way, there was never an attack on Franjo Tudjman in Serb newspapers. There were attacks on the Croats, Ustaŝe, this, that. The same on the Croat site: attacks on Serbs, Orthodox, fanatics, Cetniks, but not on Milosevic. They always looked out for each other. They weren't stupid." Ibid.

711 "If the mission gave particular emphasis to any of the Committees it would be those aspects that were going to have build confidence for the mission, build confidence for the integration process, provide some kind of healing process because both sides have suffered – at that point it was that both sides had suffered tremendously." Interview with Dr. Christine Coleiro, UNITAR POCI, Washington, DC, 1 December 2006.

712 Interview with Dr. Gerard Fischer, Head of Civil Affairs, UNTAES, New York, 21 November 2006.

713 Telephone interview with Dr. Robert J.A.R. Gravelle, Head of the JIC Secretariat and Head of STACTA, 11 August 2007. "Many of the actions that we did – we did them and then we would inform New York. Rather than the contrary. We were known for that. New York would feel that Jacques and I had that reputation." Telephone interview with Souren G. Seraydarian, DSRSG/DTA, UNTAES, 16 January 2007.

714 Interview with Professor Michael W. Doyle, former UN Assistant Secretary-General, New Haven, 11 September 2006.

715 Interview with Dr. Gerard Fischer, Head of Civil Affairs, UNTAES, New York, 21 November 2006, adding that this is nothing unusual.

716 Interview with Professor Michael W. Doyle, former UN Assistant Secretary-General, New Haven, 11 September 2006.

whelmed, it was tired, it was not in the business of making very many decisions."[717] Headquarters thus accepted the "proactiveness of Jacques Klein and the team around him who decided, 'That's the way we're gonna do it.'"[718] Senior UNTAES personnel were not overly appreciative of headquarters capacities, "Don't expect much from headquarter. They are generally people that have never been in the field and don't know very much."[719] This being said, regarding *formal* interaction via the mission briefings to the Security Council,[720] UNTAES maintained an open reporting style:

> What is important in a mission is that you stick very much to the truth when you report back to New York. And again, I can claim from the experience of many missions that we have often these 'Good News Missions' where you only send reports that please the Security Council, the Secretary-General, and the DPKO. But this is a leadership question. You know, some people just want to cover their asses and say, 'Everything is fine.' But in the end, it may come out that it wasn't so fine. I am not saying that people are lying in their reports but they may not talk about all the problems that you have in a mission and only talk about the successes. For instance, you do not report on those issues where you haven't found a solution, and you say, 'Let's not report now, let's report maybe in a week, maybe we can fix it.' And then maybe you don't fix it, and maybe you still don't report. This is a very sensitive issue. I have been in missions, where I saw reports as they had been prepared and sent to New York and where I thought, 'I cannot be in the same mission. There is nothing that I recognize.'[721]

Managing the Mission

There was a fair share of division of labor between the Transitional Administrator and his deputy.[722] While the cooperation among the senior mission staff was rocky

---

717 Telephone interview with Julian Harston, senior UN official, 26 October 2006. "I'm not saying they're not interested, but when there are 18 missions and let's say five have pressing issues for the Under-Secretary-General to answer, and with all the time differences, and until he gets the inputs from his desk officers and from his advisors: it's gone. I mean it's not realistic to expect that they can back you up in a certain instance." Interview with senior UNTAES official, 23 November 2006.

718 Telephone interview with Julian Harston, senior UN official, 26 October 2006.

719 Interview with senior UNTAES official, 23 November 2006, who adds, "In fact, most people in charge there have never been on a UN mission, never served overseas. So, to go to them with any kind of serious question, you're wasting your time.".

720 "And, of course, the Security Council is important, too. And that's why, every couple of months, they go back and brief the Security Council to make sure support is there." Interview with Professor Michael W. Doyle, former UN Assistant Secretary-General, New Haven, 11 September 2006.

721 Interview with a senior UNTAES staff member, 22 November 2006.

722 From January 1996 until April 1997, this position was held be Derek Boothby. "As the mission developed, my [Derek Boothby's; ES] role changed to represent the Transitional Administrator as necessary, coordinate the day-to-day work of the civilian elements of the

at times, it always remained solid and furthered positive results.[723] The Head of Civil Affairs reflects:[724]

> Klein and myself, we were at the office at half past six in the morning every day and never left before nine, ten o'clock in the evening. There were a lot of things that we checked, and what I didn't see, he would see and vice versa. There was a good cooperation. But there were many frictions, too. When I summarize this, it wasn't as if Klein saw everything and had the answer to everything, or as if I did. These were results from discussions and dialogues. Still, I have the feeling that we, because of the dialogues that we had with everyone, we could iron out what was a problem. That doesn't mean that we ironed out all problems in time, that's not what I try to claim. But I think there was a very proactive feeling. And you had to be aware that you had to propose with Klein. You know, I had sometimes discussions with Klein where he fired me four times and hired me five times, because we wouldn't be eye to eye on the issues. But this didn't mean we were antagonists.[725]

The chain of command of the mission was very clear *and* flexible in terms of allowing the operational staff considerable latitude:[726]

> Obviously, we reported to UN headquarters, but my sense was that we had a lot of authority in the field to manage all these things ourselves. So, that felt flexible – for the size of it. It might have been partly an outcome of a good structure, but it also could

mission, chairing staff meetings and discussions, provide the political guidance on police issues, and maintain the reporting channel to UNHQ New York. I also worked with the local Serb authorities and with the Croatian government on specific issues or difficulties as they arose, such as the special arrangements for weapons buyback." Written interview with Derek G. Boothby, DSRSG/DTA, UNTAES, 5 February 2007. In April 1997, Boothby was succeeded by Souren G. Seraydarian, for whom a similar work sharing arrangement with the Transitional Administrator was in place, "We divided tasks between the head of the mission and myself. And since he was also negotiating with the EU, going to New York, et cetera, I would say that at least 30 percent of the time I was in charge of the mission. On the other hand, when Jacques-Paul Klein was there he took more care of the military side and some of the political side, and I took more care about the civil affairs side, the logistic support side, the administration, i.e. the day-to-day operation of the mission; and of course, the report-writing afterwards et cetera." Telephone interview with Souren G. Seraydarian, DSRSG/DTA, UNTAES, 16 January 2007. Both DSRSGs had extensive field experience from previous appointments.

723 "We worked well as a core group. And then we went to Bosnia, and then three of us went to Liberia and did it there. We know what we are doing in missions. But that needs years and years and years of experience." Telephone interview with Dr. Robert J.A.R. Gravelle, Head of the JIC Secretariat and Head of STACTA, 11 August 2007.

724 "Dr. Gerard Fischer was responsible for the more detailed aspects of working with the local Serb administration in Vukovar." Written interview with Derek G. Boothby, DSRSG/DTA, UNTAES, 5 February 2007.

725 Interview with Dr. Gerard Fischer, Head of Civil Affairs, UNTAES, New York, 21 November 2006.

726 "I was quite impressed, at my level of information, with the flexibility. And at the time, I felt it has most to do with the structure, with the organizational set-up and also the size and authority of the mission, compared to the territory. So, we were able to transfer information back and forth. [...] I think we were able to apply the lessons; it's like a task force that's up to do a task and that had the right size and resources to do it." Telephone interview with a field officer, UNTAES, 10 January 2007.

have been an outcome of a good leadership that we were able to learn relatively quickly and adjust to new and ever-changing conditions.[727]

Relative to other missions, UNTAES did not face much staff misconduct. However, the mission still had some internal struggles. A problem in the early days was that the US State Department, which had pushed the nomination of Jacques-Paul Klein as Transitional Administrator, also pushed to nominate other senior mission staff. Thus, Klein initially brought a couple of people from the State Department with him. "At the beginning, it was a battle about the terms at stake, the State Department versus the UN."[728] Fortunately, Klein quickly realized that this was dysfunctional, "He quickly learned that this was a UN mission and, eventually, his senior people were all UN."[729]

The other, graver problem that UNTAES had was that most of the approximately 250 civil affairs staff, the number including UNVs, had previous peacekeeping mission experience but none or poor experience in public services and civil administration. "They would have wished to have had more professional people in the row. They would have wanted people who knew how to offer specific services and they didn't have that. That was one of the problems. It's a question of resource."[730] Exceptions to the rule also occurred, though.[731] Adding to general lack of specialists' professional knowledge, mediation and negotiation were also lacking:

> Each JIC officer should have had a training course in negotiations. As I said, they might know about railroads or human rights or whatever, but they absolutely didn't know how to mediate. The lack of negotiation skills is a big weakness of the UN system – and often, we need to send out people very quickly and so there is no time for training. This is a basic thing. So, once it was decided to have JICs, it would have been clear to me

---

727 Ibid.
728 Telephone interview with Dr. Robert J.A.R. Gravelle, Head of the JIC Secretariat and Head of STACTA, 11 August 2007.
729 Ibid.
730 Interview with Dr. Christine Coleiro, UNITAR POCI, Washington, DC, 1 December 2006. "We should have had – from the very beginning – staff who had specific experience of public services and civic administration." Written interview with Derek G. Boothby, DSRSG/DTA, UNTAES, 5 February 2007. "Many of the staff were not the best ones, but there is not much that you can do about. The vast majority of them had previous mission experience but this doesn't mean much: it doesn't guarantee you that this person is adequately prepared to do this type of job." Interview with Dr. Gerard Fischer, Head of Civil Affairs, UNTAES, New York, 21 November 2006. This is, in fact, a problem not likely to change within the current system anytime soon.
731 "We had also a number of very good people that were very capable. We had some people in engineering that knew how to run an electricity grid; we had people with experience in transport: road, rail." Interview with Dr. Gerard Fischer, Head of Civil Affairs, UNTAES, New York, 21 November 2006. He adds," I have been in many missions and I think this mission was by far not the worst in terms of capacity at this time." Ibid.

to say, 'Yes, we need experts and that are the functional tasks they need to carry out.' Like, 'It's this and this – so let's train them for two days.' But it wasn't that way.[732]

In addition, "For each of the JICs, especially on the more technical ones like the human rights, it might have been good to have a one-day seminar to make sure that all parties could say, 'OK, we're talking about the same thing'."[733] Some training courses were provided especially for civil affairs officers. They remained scarce, however.[734] Not all skills that would have been required for a transitional administration could be assembled, and Klein is said to have "'fired many staff members' who were not of high calibre."[735] At the same time he made sure that he "hire[d] good people and then let them do their jobs,"[736] ensuring that they were motivated and kept a hands-on attitude, thus compensating for other shortcomings.

Leave of the SRSG

In a rather unexpected course of action, Klein left the mission in August 1998. Upon nomination by the Government of the United States and by the Dayton Peace implementation Council's Steering Board, he became Principal Deputy High Representative for Bosnia and Herzegovina in Sarajevo.[737] His departure six months before the end of the mission was neither well received nor understood by his staff or the local population.[738]

---

732 Telephone interview with a staff member of STACTA, UNTAES, 10 January 2007.
733 Ibid.
734 "Civil officers are good, equipped people, they do work hard – but they have to be trained. We needed them to know about human rights, legal affairs, concerning property rights; they also need to know how to deal with ministers, because civil affairs officers meet ministers often, so they need to know how to monitor. And they need a job description. – But there wasn't any." Interview with Dr. Gerard Fischer, Head of Civil Affairs, UNTAES, New York, 21 November 2006.
735 Howard 2008, p. 245, quoting Klein.
736 Ibid., p. 34.
737 Klein recalls the situation, "The problem that I had is that I was called by Albright in August. She said, 'I want you to go to Bosnia, I need you in OHR.' I said, 'What the hell is OHR? What do you want me to do there?' – 'Well, you'll be the Deputy.' – 'I don't like Deputy, I don't do Deputy well.' She said, 'No, the Europeans have said that there will be a European as the High Representative, but an American will be the Deputy.' So I left in August 1997 to go to Bosnia, but by that time, the mission was finished. It was only another three months, it was done." Telephone interview with Ambassador Jacques-Paul Klein, SRSG/TA, UNTAES, 19 July 2007.
738 "Now, there are two sides to the story: Klein told me he was very disappointed he had to leave. He'd tell me, 'It's like having a canvass where you paint two thirds of it, and then you're just about getting finished the last third of it and they pull you away.' However, when I went to Bosnia and met him there, he introduced me to someone who had worked with him in Eastern Slavonia and to whom I said, 'It was such a pity that Klein had to leave, he

The tragedy of the situation is that Klein left before the mission ended. Not only was the mission too short but he left before the mission ended. And so, the first year was lost because the Serbs didn't want to negotiate and when it got serious and they really started negotiate, then Klein left. And Klein was the only person in the mission who had leverage with Tudjman. He had a way of talking to Tudjman. So, they lost their best advocate and negotiator in the last three months. The UNTAES agreements, which had been difficult to negotiate, fell short in the end: they didn't have the legal power and clarity to be implemented without ambiguity. And ambiguity is a great friend of Croat bureaucracy, because then, they could manipulate the agreements. They needed an extra year and they needed Klein – in my opinion. And had they done that, I think, they would have managed to put in place a much more effective legislation. Just in the end, it wasn't so.[739]

This development was a great shock to the local Serbs in particular:

People were shocked. They thought Klein would never leave them. I was there a year later after he left and, you know, he still was being god: people talking about him, telling something he said, what he wore, and how he did this and how he did that, and so on. He was a great hero for them – just a very rare incidence. He knew how to do it, in that environment he really knew how to handle it. And he did a great job and sincerely cared about them. And so they thought, 'If he cares about us so much he will never leave us.' So, his leave was a huge shock.[740]

Klein was succeeded by William Walker, also a US citizen. Again, the State Department pushed for the position to be filled by an American.[741] Walker's leadership style was "completely different"[742] though, and in fact may have been "too blunt for the Balkans."[743]

was so good.' And the guy said, 'Klein *wanted* to leave.' So, no one really knows. The tragedy is: Klein *did* leave." Interview with a former UNTAES staff member, 1 December 2006.

739 Ibid.
740 Ibid.
741 "The United States is committed to seeing the UNTAES, UNTAES mandate successfully completed in Eastern Slavonia. The United States calls on the Republic of Croatia and the local Serb community in Eastern Slavonia to work closely with UNTAES to ensure that this mandate is successfully completed. We expect that Ambassador Klein's position in Eastern Slavonia will be filled very shortly. That's a high priority position for us." US State Department, "News Briefing," Wednesday, 2 July 1997, FDCH Political Transcripts.
742 Interview with Dr. Gerard Fischer, Head of Civil Affairs, UNTAES, New York, 21 November 2006.
743 Interview with a former UNTAES staff member, 1 December 2006. "The local 'political heroes' of the time were very *macho*. And Klein fit right in: he wore this jacket, he came from the military – he had that. Walker, on the other hand, was polite... different. Probably, he would listen more. But anyway, it's really unfair to judge him because I would hate to follow an act like Klein. And you really don't have a chance to establish yourself in three months. How are you going to build confidence in three months with these people? He didn't have a chance to do that." Ibid.

3.3.6 Summary and Assessment

UNTAES implemented its mandate relatively successfully. This positive result is attributed to: a general willingness to be proactive, setting the right priorities,[744] dealing with local leaders in the right tone (Klein often dealt with problematic issues directly at the top level, which turned out to be very effective), communicating the mission to the local population, an active donor policy, the courage to change underperforming institutions, a strong mandate, international support, and the abundant peacekeeping resources.[745] While important steps towards reconciliation and reintegration were taken, a range of issues were left incomplete, such as thorough capacity-building and economic reconstruction.

UNTAES was able to demonstrate "a gradual and steady tightening of control"[746] and its strong appearance earned the mission credibility in the eyes of the Croats. Being respected by the Croats lent it credibility with the minority Serb population. While it was important to preserve the continuity of the mission's structures and to present Croatia with a guarantee of the UN's continuing presence in the region, it was set in the UNTAES Agreements that the local population should participate in the process. "And talking openly with people and convincing them of the mandate and its purposes is already something that is maybe more powerful than formal integration mechanisms towards finding a solution."[747] The mission wanted the message that "we can do nothing about the past, but together, we can build the future" to come across.[748] However, capacity-building in a narrower sense was not a priority, due to rigid time constraints and uncertain funding. "There were many drafts for reports of the Secretary-General that spelled out what's really needed, and some of them did talk about capacity-building and training but in reality, there wasn't a whole lot of that. Let's say, maybe, the mission was too short for that."[749] Economic reconstruction was a similar case. While it was included in the mandate, it was not a priority:

> It was too far reaching. It's not clear in my mind who could have possibly done this. I was first thinking maybe a different organization, but that was complicated, too. The political outcome was so clear, unlike many of the other missions, and for that reason,

744 "Without first establishing security and firm law and order under UNTAES control, nothing would have been possible (a lesson that appears to have escaped USA in Iraq in 2003)." Written interview with Derek G. Boothby, DSRSG/DTA, UNTAES, 5 February 2007.
745 "It really made such a difference that we – 6,000 people, including soldiers – were covering an area of maybe 2,600 square kilometres." Telephone interview with a former field officer, UNTAES, 10 January 2007.
746 Written interview with Derek G. Boothby, DSRSG/DTA, UNTAES, 5 February 2007.
747 Interview with Dr. Gerard Fischer, Head of Civil Affairs, UNTAES, New York, 21 November 2006.
748 Telephone interview with Ambassador Jacques-Paul Klein, SRSG/TA, UNTAES, 19 July 2007.
749 Telephone interview with a staff member of STACTA, UNTAES, 10 January 2007.

I think, it was correct to be relatively narrow on administrative tasks: we knew what would happen afterwards, and then it was up as well to the parties whether they wanted to have an economic future.[750]

The whole issue of differing time horizons of the various objectives was reflected in many activities. For instance, when Klein cut off the abusive local NGOs, "What he didn't realize is that when you go to a place that has no capacity you are going to have to weigh it out until they start to learn."[751] Problems also occurred in co-operating with humanitarian institutions. While in comparison to sustainability-oriented actors, UNTAES' time horizon was short and was put under considerable time pressure by the Security Council. The time pressure increased with the non-availability of guidelines. "You know, you go in hitting the ground running. You don't have six months to learn what is going on. We learned as we went along."[752] Crucial decisions were made by the mission's senior staff,[753] "We made the decisions on-the-ground. New York never told us how to run the mission – we told them how we were going to do it."[754] Treating the mandate "as floor," as DSRSG Boothby conceptualized the approach,[755] the Transitional Administrator used his comprehensive authority in a very proactive manner.

There are mandates and they make a difference. They set the broad frame of what you can do. And if you radically violate them, you'll get all sorts of protests. Because people claim it's not authorized. And that will constrain what you do. But beyond that, there is an awful lot of ambiguity, also built in into the language. So, how do you operate? How do you read the spirit of the agreement? What you do and how capable you are can make a big difference in how things happen. You know, arguably in Cambodia, there was enough authority to remake the police and to be much more proactive in general. But Hun Sen was a powerful person who resisted that, and UNTAC SRSG Akashi had a ceiling view on the mandate: it was the most he could do. Klein, on the

---

750 Ibid.
751 Interview with a former UNTAES staff member, 1 December 2006.
752 Telephone interview with Dr. Robert J.A.R. Gravelle, Head of the JIC Secretariat and Head of STACTA, 11 August 2007. "For us, being the first Transitional Administration, there was no model to go through; we had to do it the best we could because we were the first. And we learned a lot." Ibid.
753 On his own and his senior staff mates' professional experience, the Transitional Administrator summarizes, "I had 30 years of US air force military experience, from Lieutenant to General. I had 32 years of State Department experience, from being a plain Foreign Service Officer to Ambassador. And then my Deputies, who are key to this, were experienced and brilliant guys like Souren Seraydarian, Gerard Fisher, Robert Gravelle, and Jack Greenberg. For instance, Greenberg, an Australian, is one of the brightest people I know: he can sit down and in ten minutes draft you a brilliant, distinct speech. Those are the people you depend on. Don't ever have the illusion that you are doing that by yourself. That would be the worst mistake you can make. It's your staff who can make you or who break you." Telephone interview with Ambassador Jacques-Paul Klein, SRSG/TA, UNTAES, 19 July 2007.
754 Telephone interview with Dr. Robert J.A.R. Gravelle, Head of the JIC Secretariat and Head of STACTA, 11 August 2007.
755 Cf. Boothby 2004.

other hand, had a floor view on his mandate: it was the minimum he should do. So, he was always out there to try to do more. He had no authority, for example, to seize the oilfields. But: it was not unreasonable, and it was very helpful for this mission.[756]

At the end of the day, Klein was given the long leash, "People in headquarters want a success. And when they see a really good Special Representative – unless the person is violating all sorts of international norms – they will approve. And if you're succeeding, you'll get blessed."[757]

3.4 Termination

In Security Council resolution 1037, UNTAES was supposed to operate for one year, with the option of extending another year if the parties to the conflict and the P-5 consented to it. With careful coordination of support, this option was settled upon in late 1996. As of April 1997, the termination phase started, including elections, planning for mission drawdown, and arranging for the following mission. During this period, priorities shifted and additional tasks and pathologies surfaced, such as recurrent attempts at manipulation and obstruction of deadlines and elections, decreasing political leverage of the transitional administration, and the run of good staff. A number of pathologies could not be contained, yet others were dealt with relatively successfully – for instance, by flexible management of election dates or by creating economic (non-political) leverage.

3.4.1 Extension of the Mandate

Due to the constant delyas by the local conflict parties, the Security Council extended UNTAES' mandate. The original resolution stated that the mission would be deployed for a one-year period but that, if necessary, it could continue for another year – at most. "The costs of the way it was negotiated and the dealing with the states put a deadline: UNTAES had two years and that was it."[758]

---

756 Interview with Professor Michael W. Doyle, former UN Assistant Secretary-General, New Haven, 11 September 2006.
757 Ibid. He adds, "Headquarters will give most Special Representatives a long leash – if they're successful."
758 Interview with Dr. Christine Coleiro, UNITAR POCI, Washington, DC, 1 December 2006. The appraisal by the Head of Civil Affairs was that "Croatian government would not have cooperated on that." Interview with Dr. Gerard Fischer, Head of Civil Affairs, UNTAES, New York, 21 November 2006. Likewise, Washington was also not in favor of an ongoing engagement. Cf. Koinova, Maria. 1996. "Stoyanov: An End to a Divisive Political Culture?" *Pursuing Balkan Peace* 45, 12 November 1996. Available online at http://www.hri.org/news/balkans/pbp/1996/96-11-12.pbp.html, last access on 18 February 2009.

Arguing over the Deadline

The clear-cut peace agreement notwithstanding, the two parties to the conflict attempted to impair the framework. Tudjman wanted the mission to have an even shorter timeframe, "Tudjman wanted us out the first year: we were just there seven, eight months, and he had been trying to push us out."[759] However, the Serbs wanted UNTAES to stay as long as possible, anxious to maintain the status quo.[760]

Paradoxically enough, both parties obstructed their very objectives: the Croatians were *de facto* elongating UNTAES' stay because of various tactics to delay the mission, e.g. on documents or employment security issues,[761] while the Serbs put their stake in future official structures at risk by stubbornly ignoring deadlines and refusing to work within multiethnic structures. "They thought, 'Great, we'll end up like Cypress. We will have our own autonomy and the UN protection. Why would we need to negotiate?'"[762] Only after the first year was over did UNTAES' hard-nosed approach made the Serbs comprehend that this was not going to occur.[763] In the course of the transition, the local Serbs in Eastern Slavonia also lost the support from the mainland. While Belgrade had initially been pressing for an extension of the mandate[764] so that they at least had a kind of buffer zone on their western border, "Somewhere half way through the mission they gave that up and said to the locals, 'Listen, we don't spend political capital on you anymore because it's not gonna be a Serb outpost. We're gonna take care of you if you come home

---

759 Telephone interview with Ambassador Jacques-Paul Klein, SRSG/TA, UNTAES, 19 July 2007. When UNTAES eventually left, the Deputy SRSG Seraydarian recalls Tudjman commented on the announcement, "I remember Tudjman telling me when I was leaving, 'Mr. Seraydarian, we love you, we love you very much, and we are so happy that you are leaving now.'" Telephone interview with Souren G. Seraydarian, DSRSG/DTA, UNTAES, 16 January 2007.
760 There was a shift of emphasis from the former to the latter aspect across time, since the status quo and the perception of the status quo were changing.
761 See Chapter IV.3.2.3.
762 Interview with a former UNTAES staff member, Washington, DC, 1 December 2006.
763 "Klein would tell them, 'We are out here at the end, whether you negotiate it or not.'" Ibid.
764 "Meeting on 8 November with Jacques Klein, head of the UN transitional administration in Eastern Slavonia, Serbian President Slobodan Milosevic asked that the UN mandate in the area be extended by a full year, AFP reported. Federal Yugoslavia sent a letter to the Security Council officially requesting a year-long extension of the mandate and saying that a shorter mandate could threaten regional stability through the prospect of a mass exodus of tens of thousands of Serbs." In principle, Croatian President Tudjman agreed to an extension, but wanted to limit it to an additional six-months period only. As Reuters reported, Tudjman met with local Serb leaders for the first time on 9 November to discuss the timeline issue. Sito Sucic, Daria. 1996. "Bosnia's Presidency Members Disagree Over Cabinet..." *Pursuing Balkan Peace* 45:12. Available online at http://www.hri.org/news/balkans/pbp/ 1996/96-11-12.pbp.html, last access on 18 February 2009.

to Serbia.'"[765] Eventually, they even "signed a normalization agreement with Croatia and set up embassies."[766]

Extension of the Mandate

Delays took their toll though. Given the persistent political tension and recalcitrance, the Transitional Administrator called on the Security Council to extend the mandate. Not only did Klein want a pro forma extension, he also required the Council to send a strong, explicit signal to Croatia that it had to support the UN mission.[767] The difficult part was convincing Croatia to agree; this was fundamental to the *executive* authority nature of the mission. Preparing the political ground for the desired resolution, "Steps were taken to pre-empt any opposition from Zagreb."[768] This was done in personal talks between Klein Tudjman and by "keeping ambassadors in Zagreb well briefed, so that they could report to their respective capitals, and by similar efforts to UNHQ in New York so that the Secretary-General and DPKO could talk with the relevant ambassadors on the Security Council, the support of all concerned was obtained by persuasive argument."[769] An addition, potential EU membership was used as an incentive to encourage Tudjman to comply, "The Croats saw their future also in Europe and they did not want to expand their nationalisms and anti-Serb movement, i.e. they didn't want to burn all the bridges to Europe."[770] Eventually, "There was little, if any, opposition in the Se-

---

765 Telephone interview with a staff member of STACTA, UNTAES, 10 January 2007.
766 Ibid.
767 "With mandate extension, you have to be clever. Normally, the Security Council does the new mandate when the old mandate expires. But I said, 'I need a very powerful political statement from you.' And they agreed and actually extended the mandate of UNTAES four months ahead of schedule. This sent Tudjman a clear message, 'If you screw up war, it might even take longer. So, if you want the UN out of here, cooperate.'" Telephone interview with Ambassador Jacques-Paul Klein, SRSG/TA, UNTAES, 19 July 2007.
768 Written interview with Derek G. Boothby, DSRSG/DTA, UNTAES, 5 February 2007. "The fact that the Transitional Administrator was an American was certainly very helpful in securing US attention to the need to extend the UNTAES mission." Ibid.
769 Ibid.
770 Telephone interview with Souren G. Seraydarian, DSRSG/DTA, UNTAES, 16 January 2007. They also had an eye on entering NATO's Partnership for Peace Programme. "Meanwhile in Croatia, Deputy Defense Minister Vladimir Zagorec and Bell Helicopter officials signed a $15-million deal to purchase ten helicopters for the Croatian military, Hina reported on 31 October. Defense Minister Gojko Susak said Croatia intends to fully introduce a Western military structure and weapons by the year 2005. In Washington, Susak discussed with US officials Croatia's desire to join NATO's Partnership for Peace program. He said Croatia's admission to the program was postponed at the latest NATO meeting although the US supports its membership. Admission will depend on the situation in Bosnia-Herzegovina [...]. Susak also said Washington would support the termination of the UN mandate in eastern Slavonia – the last Serb-held part of Croatia – in mid-July next year." Sito Sucic,

curity Council,"[771] also because the mission was doing fairly well overall.[772] Security Council Resolution 1120 (1997) extended UNTAES' mandate until 15 January 1998.[773]

In August 1997, four months before the operation was supposed to end, an internal memo rated the mission as being on track. "'It is a successful mission so far.'"[774] That being said, the memo excerpt defined "success" in terms of short-term goals only – and not in terms of the long-term inpact of the mission's achievements. "'So far, the mission's success is short-term compliance with requested benchmarks.'"[775]

Short-term vs. Long-term Focus

As almost any mission, UNTAES struggled with a tension between imperatives for short-term benchmark achievement and the longer-term sustainability of the mission's efforts.

The tight deadline exacerbated this tension as it constituted constant time pressure.[776] On the other hand, the deadline was also judged to be an advantage, especially among the senior mission staff and the non-civil affairs staff. "Many crucial things happened because we had a strong Security Council mandate and because there was an end date: you could not postpone indefinitely, and you could not introduce the things at the last day, because you wanted to see how it worked and how it sort of moulded with the society."[777] This perspective mirrored the Transi-

Daria. 1996. "Croatia Buys US Military Helicopters." *Pursuing Balkan Peace* 45, 12 November 1996. Available online at http://www.hri.org/news/balkans/pbp/1996/ 96-11-12.pbp.htm, last access on 18 February 2009.

771 Written interview with Derek G. Boothby, DSRSG/DTA, UNTAES, 5 February 2007.

772 "By the autumn of 1996, the UNTAES mission was recognized as going fairly well. As has been said before, success has many fathers – it is failure that is an orphan." Ibid. It was also important that by that time, the negotiations for the UNTAES Agreements had already started.

773 On that note, it was never an issue to change the mandate's substantial content; it was only its length that was discussed.

774 The internal memo for the Transitional Administrator was cited on telephone by its author. Telephone interview with a staff member of STACTA, UNTAES, 10 January 2007.

775 "'So far the mission's success is short-term compliance with requested benchmarks.'" Ibid.

776 "Governance, elections, the councils, all those things. We had a very tough time delineating." Telephone interview with Ambassador Jacques-Paul Klein, SRSG/TA, UNTAES, 19 July 2007.

777 Interview with Dr. Gerard Fischer, Head of Civil Affairs, UNTAES, New York, 21 November 2006. He adds, "I think it is very good that there are deadlines for mandates. And deadlines are there to be kept and a mission is time-limited: it is not an ever-evolving and ongoing process. I mean Kosovo is this example where the mandate was decided in June 1999 and they still haven't changed the mandate but nobody remembers the mandate any

tional Administrator's "Getting Things Done"-attitude.[778] At the operational level and among a wide range of civil affairs staff,[779] in contrast, the attitude was more sustainability-oriented. They argued that the issue was "whether the re-integrated structures will be accountable to the local population. And will they be able to redress in assemblies. So, not only: will they be accountable to an outside body like the UN but to the locals. And will they be able to address these issues.'"[780] Accordingly, the proponents of this view thought the deadline to be more of a constraint than an advantage.

> When we were in the middle of it, it felt very constraining, especially in the field. I think we had two elections, national and local, that one year, at very short notice. So it felt like things happened very quickly and I'd say, at the time, I was thinking that there must be people who are more qualified than I to do this, in the sense that for each of the issues, there must be an expert. But *I* had to make an expert opinion, as a young graduate. Obviously, there were other people who talked on that, too. But I felt that maybe, on issues like that we could have spent more time debating, also in other fora. You might have had an international conference on the issue, bringing in experts. We were just like, 'Let's find out, let's go, do it!' So, that, I think, was a constraining factor.[781]

For many other agencies, UNTAES' timeframe must have seemed short and inadequate. At times, it even was an obstacle to cooperation at times, for instance to cooperation with UNHCR:

> UNHCR had a huge mandate in terms of returning refugees and displaced persons; and we often had very harsh debates with them. We said, 'We need to have these people returned now!' And they said, 'Take it easy, it's a long process – we're gonna be here the next ten years.' Whether they wanted us to go or not – I'm not sure. But certainly, their time focus was so different that we felt that they were not being effective and slow. And they probably felt that we were not being careful. As for cooperation with other actors, I think, that was probably the most difficult.[782]

It was, however, obvious from the very start of the mission that the Security Council would not invest lots of time and resources to UNTAES:

> Eastern Slavonia was never one of the more important items on the Security Council's agenda, paling in comparison to the Bosnia crisis. From 1995 to 1997, many resolutions

longer." He adds that the strict mandate deadline was "absolutely" part of the success of UNTAES.

778 "Klein really was like boom, boom, boom, 'Let's get out of here.'"Telephone interview with a staff member of STACTA, UNTAES, 10 January 2007.

779 Ibid.

780 Ibid. On the other hand, however, towards the Croats, another attempt for a deadline extension "might have turned things sour. The Croats had a tremendous pressure from the refugee people." Telephone interview with Ambassador Jacques-Paul Klein, SRSG/TA, UNTAES, 19 July 2007.

781 Telephone interview with a field officer, UNTAES, 10 January 2007.

782 Ibid.

addressed the territories of the former Yugoslavia, but few were concerned with Eastern Slavonia. By 1998, the focus of the Council had shifted decisively to Africa, with almost half of all resolutions concerning conflicts of the continent.[783]

Precarious Leverage

It was determined that UNTAES' deadline would not be extended: the crucial benchmarks had been achieved.

> We came up with the key ingredients that would allow Serbs to stay there. Far from perfect, but: they were they. There was a judiciary system with Serbs amongst the judiciary and a police of 8,000 people of which 4,600 were Serbs, in this area. So, every fifth person was a police man; but better to have them this way under control than having them outside.[784]

The Serbs eventually ended lobbying for an extension, "They knew. We explained them, 'It's over, we're gone.'"[785] But when the withdrawal date came closer, the mission came to face a typical problem of fixed deadlines, namely a constant decrease in political leverage:

> In July, when we knew and when they knew that we had only six months left, we had no leverage anymore. Political leverage was gone. So, Klein went to Washington and met with Albright, Secretary of State. He said right away, 'We need more leverage but we can't be extended. So here is what you should do.' And Albright comes out in CNN and she said, 'We expect the Croats to keep their word because all agreements are linked to IMF loans.' So we had them economically. When time was running out, we needed some leverage – and we got economic leverage.[786]

3.4.2 Elections

[T]he Security Council underlined that it was in the best interest of the Serb community to collect their citizenship documents, to participate fully in the elections, and to take part in Croatian political life as equal citizens. It called upon all residents of the region to follow wise leadership, to stay in the region, and to take up their future as citizens of the Republic of Croatia. The Council urged the Government of Croatia to redouble its efforts to ensure the completion of the necessary technical preparations for the holding of elections. At that time, the Council expressed serious

---

783 Howard 2008, p. 235.
784 Interview with Dr. Gerard Fischer, Head of Civil Affairs, UNTAES, New York, 21 November 2006.
785 Telephone interview with Dr. Robert J.A.R. Gravelle, Head of the JIC Secretariat and Head of STACTA, 11 August 2007.
786 Ibid.

concern that no progress had been made concerning the future of displaced persons in the region and the establishment of equal treatment with respect to housing, access to reconstruction grants, loans and property compensation.[787]

A crucial milestone in the process of "clear[ing] the path for the two-way return of all displaced persons"[788] was the elections. When the Transitional Administrator announced that they be held on 13 April 1997,[789] Secretary-General called it UN-TAES' most critical phase:

> Success will be determined by the extent to which the Serb leadership and people demonstrate wisdom and realism and by the will and ability of Croatia to meet all technical requirements for the holding of free and fair elections. Long-term success will be determined by the Croatian authorities' commitment to reconciliation and to ensuring that those Serbs who are currently residents in the region will enjoy equal rights as Croatian citizens. UNTAES is encountering challenges in all these areas.[790]

The Erdut Agreement required the scheduling of free and fair elections of all local governmental bodies no later than 30 days before the end of the mission.[791] However, neither the Basic Agreement not the Report of the Secretary-General was specific on the technical aspects of implementation. Thus, "UNTAES and the two sides were faced with many further negotiations before elections could be held."[792] Eventually, ten political parties and about 1,000 individual candidates ran in the election. A new Serb political party, the Independent Democratic Serb Party (SDSS), was formed. An important aspect of the elections was that they signalled to the local Serbs that they would have a stake in the future development of the region. "It gave the Serbs a sense that they were going to have representation in the Sabor. We negotiated with the Croats and there would be x number of Serb delegates sitting in the Sabor representing Eastern Slavonia."[793] In addition, the Serb community had been ceded to vote on a "Joint Municipalities Council."[794]

---

787 UN Security Council, "Security Council urges Completion of Preparation for 13 April Elections on Eastern Slavonia, Baranja, Western Sirmium." Press Release, UN Doc. SC/6334, 7 March 1997.
788 UN Department of Peacekeeping Operations 1997.
789 The Transitional Administrator decided to have the regional elections coincide with the Croatian national elections scheduled for April 13.
790 UN Department of Peacekeeping Operations 1997.
791 Cf. Basic Agreement, Art. 12.
792 Howard 2008, p. 253. Eventually, it was the Election JIC that engaged in developing election principles, an implementation plan, and a rough time frame. Local Electoral Commissions (LECs) were appointed by the Joint Implementation Committee on Elections (JIC) and assisted by UNTAES Election Officers. The JIC on Elections appointed an Electoral Appeals Commission composed of Serb and Croat jurists and chaired by an UNTAES-appointed international judge. A Media Experts Commission (MEC) was appointed with a similar composition to monitor equitable access of all registered parties and candidates to the media. Cf. UN Department of Peacekeeping Operations 1997.
793 Telephone interview with Ambassador Jacques-Paul Klein, SRSG/TA, UNTAES, 19 July 2007.
794 Cf. Gravelle undated, p. 4; UN Task Force 1995, para. 108.

Extension of the Election Deadline

The constant and notorious delays by the Croats presented UNTAES with recurrent challenges. In this situation, Klein decided to extend the election date as long as necessary, dealing with the issue at the top level:

> I called the Minister of Administration and I said, 'Mr. Minister, you probably thought that Sunday is Election Day?' – 'And that is today.' – 'That is true, but election day is not only today, election day will also be on Monday, on Tuesday, and on Wednesday – until every Serb who is eligible to vote will have voted. And the longer it takes to get those ballots here, the more Serbs will be registered to vote. You understand me?' As they realized the situation, they flew in helicopters, literally, with the ballot. And that's the kind of thing that you have to do.[795]

His staff also welcomed this decision:

> So he extended the election by one day, on the day that we thought that they were playing with us. What I want to say is that Klein looked at the result, not at the procedure. And that is very important: what is the desired result? And he didn't want to have this election to be a failure. And had he sort of said, 'We now close the various places where you can vote', maybe 200,000 Serbs may not have been able to vote. And that was not the intent. So he extended it by one day.[796]

It was also important that "during the transitional period, the Croatian Government authorized the presence of international monitors along the international borders of the region to facilitate the free movement of persons across existing border crossings."[797] On polling day, UNTAES, in cooperation with OSCE, opened 193 polling stations in the region and 75 external poll locations for Croats living outside the region and other displaced persons that had not been able to return yet.[798] To allow these populations to vote, the election was postponed to 14 April.[799]

---

795 Telephone interview with Ambassador Jacques-Paul Klein, SRSG/TA, UNTAES, 19 July 2007. "I told Tudjman, 'If you want us to get out of here, you gotta compromise.' And Tudjman was smart enough to comply, but some of his ministers were sabotaging and undermining. For example, on election day, they didn't deliver all the ballots and they didn't deliver the right ballots." Ibid.

796 Interview with a senior official, UNTAES, 22 November 2006.

797 UN Department of Peacekeeping Operations 1997.

798 "Within the UNTAES region, over 150 UNTAES observers were deployed to all polling stations as static monitors. In addition, 30 OSCE observer teams, observers from the Council of Europe and diplomats visited numerous polling stations during the elections. No intimidation, violence or electoral improprieties were observed before, during or after the elections." Ibid.

799 At one polling station outside the region, people could even cast their votes until 15 April. Ibid.

Results

"According to the final results, 130,716 votes were cast of which 72,835 were in the region and 58,331 were cast by Croat and other displaced persons outside the region. This total figure represents some 90 percent of all eligible voters."[800] This was beyond expectation.[801] In a statement made on 22 April, the Transitional Administrator summarized the achievement of the elections as being free, fair, open, and successful.[802] That said, the organization of the elections could have been much better,

> The elections division had trouble recruiting staff, and thus came to rely heavily on UN Volunteers. The UN Volunteers often ad more experience in elections monitoring than the regular Secretariat staff allotted to UNTAES, which created some tension between the two groups. There were also other staffing problems, since some important contracts

800 Klein, "UNTAES." "Residents currently living in the region voted at 193 polling station including 30 polling locations for absentee voting for the authorities outside the region. Over 56,000 displaced persons elsewhere in Croatia cast absentee ballots in 75 polling locations with 645 polling stations. The final number of voters inside the UNTAES mandate area was over 71,000, of which fewer than 1,000 voted in absentia for authorities to be elected in their former places of residence." Ibid.

801 Ibid. "The Transitional Administrator certified the elections on 22 April, and the results have been accepted by all major parties. The newly formed [SDSS] won an absolute majority in 11 of the 28 municipalities. In the symbolically important city of Vukovar, SDSS and the [HDZ] each won 12 out of 26 seats. Discussions have commenced between them on a coalition city administration. The elections opened the way for rapid progress on practical aspects of reintegration. On 24 April, the Croatian Government adopted the recommendations of a Joint Working Group of UNTAES, UNHCR and Croatia on the return of displaced persons which provide for equal treatment and equal rights for all affected. The final report of the Electoral Appeals Commission stated that all complaints presented were duly considered but dismissed and, therefore, did not impact on the free and fair character of the elections. By a letter dated 29 April 1997, the Secretary-General communicated the election results to the President of the Security Council (S/1997/343)." Ibid.

802 "The successful holding of free, open, and fair elections in the region was a historic milestone in the peaceful reintegration of the region, the success of the UNTAES mandate and in creating conditions for reconciliation and return. It should be recalled that 18 months ago, the region was an area of military hostility with 17,000 soldiers and numerous heavy weapons deployed in expectation of war. There was a real possibility of renewed hostilities with unforeseeable consequences. Instead, UNTAES had succeeded in bringing stability and progress in peaceful reintegration of the region. The mission succeeded in demilitarizing the region, opening-up economic and human contacts. Obtaining comprehensive political, cultural and employment guarantees for residents in the region, attracting $70 million in international assistance and processing the return of displaced persons. Looking ahead after the elections, the next step is reconciliation and return. The key aspects are economic reconstruction and revitalization; the provision of orderly and secure housing arrangements; strong and wise political guidance and leadership; and continuing international support for bilateral efforts between Croatia and the Federal Republic of Yugoslavia. UNTAES is looking forward to working with the new Joint Council of Municipalities which, for the first time in six years, will give Serbs a legal voice within the Croatian political system and will genuinely represent the concerns of the people. UNTAES continues to make extraordinary progress in its mandate and in forming the bridge for normalization between Croatia and the Federal Republic of Yugoslavia." UN Department of Peacekeeping Operations 1997.

expired just prior to the elections, leading to the departure of severely key elections personnel.[803]

3.4.3 Devolution and Arrangements Following UNTAES' Withdrawal

Aiming at a controlled exit, UNTAES engaged simultaneously in the planning for mission drawdown and for the follow-on arrangements. The greatest obstacle for the devolution process was to leave good international field staff behind. That said, most of them had already started to look for other employment opportunities. A successor mission was supposed to be run by OSCE. The problem was that the Organization was still relatively inexperienced in running missions in post-conflict territories. Besides, the OSCE mission's competences were sharply restricted.

In extending the mandate, Resolution 1120 outlined a plan for the gradual devolution of executive responsibility of civil administration in the region. "The Council also endorsed the plan for restructuring UNTAES and for a drawdown of the UNTAES military component by 15 October 1997."[804] The planning for the restructuring of the mission started in April 1997. "The military drawdown was on schedule, as was CivPol and the border monitoring component."[805] On the civilian side, the gradual handover across sectors continued to proceed – under the condition that UNTAES would maintain executive authority until 15 January 1998. Thus, Croatian authority was severely restricted until that date:

> We always gave them, whenever we reintegrated an enterprises or institution back into Croatia, *administrative* authority, never *executive* authority. We were in control. We would continue to have executive authority until midnight, January 15, 1998. […] What we did is we said, 'OK, you are now reintegrated. You have a minister here, which is Croatian, and a deputy minister, who is Serb: work on it. We will monitor to ensure that your rights are upheld and that the agreements are upheld that they had signed. And we said to the Croats, 'Now you have administrative control within the UNTAES region – but we have executive authority until the day we leave.' So if they did something wrong, we could step in right away. We never devolved any executive authority to them until the day we left.[806]

One of UNTAES' internal problems was that civilian staff left prematurely. Starting to look for new jobs in new missions, they quit their jobs in Eastern Slavonia as soon as they had found an assignment.

After UNTAES' withdrawal, two international missions took over in order to guarantee the achievements of the preceding mission, supervise compliance with

---

803 Howard 2008, pp. 254-255.
804 Written interview with Derek G. Boothby, DSRSG/DTA, UNTAES, 5 February 2007.
805 Telephone interview with Dr. Robert J.A.R. Gravelle, Head of the JIC Secretariat and Head of STACTA, 11 August 2007.
806 Ibid.

the agreements, and complete tasks that had not been fulfilled in due time by UN-TAES: a civilian OSCE mission and a police support group (UNPSG), under the leadership of former UNTAES Deputy SRSG, Seraydarian. UNPSG had the ability to execute interim authority, comprising about 400 people, including 150 police officers. Its task was to "guarantee the adherence to the achievements of UNTAES, for one year."[807] In addition, it was entrusted with completing some of the refugee and war crimes issues. "We had one action which had not been completed in UN-TAES' time which we then completed in the UNPSG time. That was the dealing with refugees and the question of war crimes: who is a war criminal, who will be sent to The Hague, who is going to be brought before local courts?"[808] OSCE's mission was operational in June 1997, taking advantage of its overlap with UN-TAES. "The OSCE fielded an international staff of 250 to protect human rights and national minorities, assist in the implementation of legislative agreements, and assist with the two-way refugee return programs. While the OSCE operation was fairly small, it managed to exert disproportionate influence because it had the backing of the EU."[809] This represented valuable political leverage as Croatia was eager to join the Union. OSCE's mission was problematic in its weak mandate: it was clear from the beginning that it would merely be allowed to monitor, under article 11 of the OSCE regime.[810] "When the OSCE came to take over and monitor the implementation, the agreements were being abused, and those at the OSCE found themselves without the power to make sure implementation was done in the spirit of the way they were negotiated: they didn't have the legal influence."[811] Unfortunately, OSCE's previous activities in the region[812] did not result in a consistent mission design that could have helped the organization to take on a new task.

> You know, the OSCE... I mean they are very nice people, getting very nice salaries. But in terms of production, delivering, doing something: very, very difficult. We call them the *Organization of Seriously Confused Europeans*. They never get up to do any-

---

807 Telephone interview with Souren G. Seraydarian, DSRSG/DTA, UNTAES, 16 January 2007.
808 Ibid.
809 Howard 2008, p. 256.
810 "There was no chance for an executive mandate." Interview with Dr. Gerard Fischer, Head of Civil Affairs, UNTAES, 21 November 2006.
811 Interview with Dr. Christine Coleiro, UNITAR POCI, Washington, DC, 1 December 2006.
812 "What I actually can say on this is that I was actually quite impressed that already in mid-1997, an OSCE commissioner for national minorities had a seminar in the region to discuss the post-UNTAES phase. That is a year and a half before. It's a special function in the OSCE to look at minorities. And so, they were thinking about minorities; and they had all the right political parties involved to think this through. And based on that, I would have thought that maybe they would have conferred that into their planning of the mission that then started in January 1998. But they didn't. Whether it was a lack of resources, or because it was a new type of mission for them, or lack of international attention to the mission – I don't know." Telephone interview with a field officer, UNTAES, 10 January 2007.

thing, but then they wanted to do everything all of a sudden: suddenly they wanted the police thing, they wanted to do education, in Kosovo. But the OSCE never had the infrastructure or the personnel to take these things on.[813]

The OSCE mission was a compromise between the pressure to get out and to declare success, and the need to have a long-running impact, but in the end, it "did not totally fulfil what it was supposed to do."[814] UNTAES's leadership had seen this coming and negotiated as many issues as possible and locked them in.[815] Furthermore, "Some good people stayed,"[816] changing hats from UNTAES to OSCE. "That meant that there was a continued expertise available."[817] That said, most of them left even before the first mission was over:

> As far as working ourselves out of the job: that is a problem. Because once people knew the mission was closing, they started leaving. Only ten to twelve percent of the UN is permanent UN staff, 85 or 90 percent are six months or one-year contractors. So, when you are on a contract and you start realizing that you will be out of the job in four months, you quickly try to find something else. And that causes a major, major disturbance. And I asked Kofi Annan once, I said, 'Kofi, why at the end of a mission you break teams up? No one gives a damn where they go, no one says let's sign them up for this mission or that place. No one even cares, these people have to go up themselves and find a new position.' And he said, 'You're right, that's one of our biggest failings. We don't take care of our people.'[818]

In addition, the "hat change" took place primarily at the mid- or working level. Thus, the people who had negotiated the agreements were no longer there to monitor their long-term implementation.

> It is a flaw that the people who are going to implement are not the same people that have negotiated the mechanisms. The people who negotiate things are saying, 'Oh, well I am not gonna be the one who has to make sure it happens; somebody else, the poor bloke, is going to come and has to take care of that. So, as long as it looks good on paper I can go out here with glory, I don't really have to worry about how good it is.' So the

813 Interview with a senior UNTAES staff member, 23 November 2006.
814 Interview with Dr. Gerard Fischer, Head of Civil Affairs, UNTAES, New York, 21 November 2006.
815 "I can't really think of anything that we deferred. We saw that if we didn't lock these agreements in, we would have a real problem. We were sure that once we were gone, this little OSCE monitoring mission could not really control the Croats." Telephone interview with Ambassador Jacques-Paul Klein, SRSG/TA, UNTAES, 19 July 2007. Furthermore, the agreements were set up without an end date, "They are still valid. There is no end date." Telephone interview with Dr. Robert J.A.R. Gravelle, Head of the JIC Secretariat and Head of STACTA, 11 August 2007.
816 Interview with Professor Michael W. Doyle, former UN Assistant Secretary-General, New Haven, 11 September 2006.
817 Ibid.
818 Telephone interview with Ambassador Jacques-Paul Klein, SRSG/TA, UNTAES, 19 July 2007.

fact that the people who negotiate and the people who implement are two different entities is an inherent flaw.[819]

OSCE would have probably liked more overlap – in terms of personnel and in regards to a more gradual take-over of functions.[820] This might have also mitigated the considerable time pressure in the set up phase of the mission. As of 16 October 1998, OSCE took over police monitoring, too.[821] In 1999, the OSCE mission merged with the Croatia OSCE office and continued its presence in the region.

3.4.4 After UNTAES

UNTAES lived up to the tasks stipulated by its mandate and has indeed been praised as one of the UN' greatest successes. Long-term success, however, is inherently more difficult to achieve and to measure, and its accomplishment remains ambiguous.

Evaluating UNTAES

As stated in the introductory chapter of this study, "UNTAES was the most successful of all post-Cold War UN- or US-led nation-building missions."[822] Shortly after the mission ended, DPKO declared on its website:

> Today, more than 90 percent of the residents who were present at the time of signing the Basic Agreement remain in the region. More than 112,000 have Croatian documents. Fields are being planted, children are going to school, and the mood of the region has begun to look for the future and not the past. There is hope and there is determination to work for a better future.[823]

819   Interview with a staff member, UNTAES, 2 December 2006.
820   Telephone interview with a field officer, UNTAES, 10 January 2007. "From some OSCE people, I got a sense that it would have been very good if we could have transferred more knowledge – either some of us staying on, some of the functions overlapping, or some of the OSCE people coming in earlier." Ibid.
821   OSCE, "Report of the OSCE Mission to the Republic of Croatia on Croatia's progress in meeting international commitments since September 1998," 26 January 1999. Available online at http://www.osce.org/documents/mc/1999/01/1049_en.pdf, last access on 18 February 2009.
822   Dobbins et al. 2005, p. 123.
823   UN Department of Peacekeeping Operations 1997. Even Tudjman took his hat off. "When I left," SRSG Klein recalls, "I went to see Tudjman and he said, 'You know, I was really much opposed to this UN business, I had no respect for the UN after IFOR, and I was very reluctant to allow a UN mission you come in here. But you did a good job. By that, I mean we could have done that militarily, we could have taken Eastern Slavonia, and we could have beaten them, because at that time we had good equipment and American help. That

In terms of mandate implementation, "We didn't have very many failures, I mean, we did the plan and then we had to get out of there."[824] However, the mandate's evaluation standard is in itself of a limited perspective, i.e. does not take into account broader and longer-term measurement criteria.[825] As a staff member notes, "We were probably not strong enough in ensuring some long-term validity."[826] That means that a mandate can be successfully implemented – as was done by UNTAES – but the overall strategic and long-term goal for the conflict-ridden territory in question is not achieved. Another senior staff member recalls:

> Last April I went to Zagreb for DPKO to meet with these Croats that I dealt with in 1996. But not all of them were there: some of them have disappeared, some are in The Hague. But the interesting thing was to discuss with them how long you need in your mind to shift from conflict/post-conflict to relative forgiveness. And I think the international community in general expects that this mind-shift is taking place within the mandate of a mission.[827]

The OSCE and other independent organizations such as Human Rights Watch criticize anti-Serb discrimination and an ongoing Serb exodus from Eastern Slavonia.[828] 150,000 Serbs received their *domovnizas*, but many of them left the region again. These were in particular "people who had a family, who were better educated and who could not see that they would have an advantage of staying in Croatia, because the atmosphere was very hostile."[829] While in big city centres, like Zagreb or other major cities, "the atmosphere has now changed a bit,"[830] while in Vukovar and its surroundings, "neither the Croats have returned, and many of the Serbs have left."[831] Eastern Croatia remains economically weak. "The region has achieved nowhere near the high level of pre-war economic activity that it used to en-

said, it would have costed four or five thousand Croat lives and maybe three or four times as many Serbs. So, the fact that you did it without that violence and did it peacefully is to the credit of the UN and to your personnel.'" Telephone interview with Ambassador Jacques-Paul Klein, SRSG/TA, UNTAES, 19 July 2007.

824 Ibid.
825 A senior staff member adopts a similar stance,"I am not saying that the mission was successful but the mission went well in the implementation, and they had these two years and everything that was set out in the mandate was accomplished. I mean, I have many reservations about what is happening now, ten years later in the UNTAES region, but here we are." Interview with Dr. Gerard Fischer, Head of Civil Affairs, UNTAES, New York, 21 November 2006.
826 Telephone interview with a staff member of STACTA, UNTAES, 10 January 2007.
827 Interview with Dr. Gerard Fischer, Head of Civil Affairs, UNTAES, New York, 21 November 2006.
828 "[…] societal-level reconciliation remains at bay, even though there are new Croatian civil society organs that are devoted to protecting human rights and national minorities." Howard 2008, p. 258.
829 Interview with Dr. Gerard Fischer, Head of Civil Affairs, UNTAES, New York, 21 November 2006.
830 Ibid.
831 Ibid.

joy."[832] This observation does not hold for Eastern Slavonia only, but is encountered throughout the post-war Balkan territories:

> [T]he exodus of Serbs from Eastern Slavonia has been just one in a series of population transfers in the region, involving both Serbs and Croats alike. This phenomenon is of course not specific to Eastern Slavonia. Real or perceived concerns about personal security, discrimination by local authorities and miserable economic prospects are characteristics common to all of the parts of ex-Yugoslavia that have experienced violent conflict. [...] Eastern Slavonia represents just one small piece of the damaged fabric of society in former Yugoslavia. Sadly, like most of the other conflict-ridden areas of the former Yugoslavia, few are bullish on the region's prospects for renewal in the short term.[833]

To end on a more optimistic note, there have also been positive developments.

> Freer and fairer elections than ever before took place after Tudjman's death in December 1999. The January 2000 elections ushered in a new government and a completely new political agenda [...]. The new government began a process of formal reconciliation with Croatia's Serbs. In 2000 and 2001, constitutional amendments fundamentally changed the balance of power in Croatia, granting less power to the President, and more to the Parliament. In the 2003 parliamentary elections, the relatively new Serb party from Eastern Slavonia, the Independent Democratic Serbian Party, won three seats in the 152-seat Parliament. [...] [W]hile societal reconciliation remains a slow process, many legal reforms have been instituted in recent years.[834]

Even more important, peace has been maintained. "There is no doubt that the UN's efforts in Eastern Slavonia have left the region better off than had there been a less-effective international presence."[835]

3.4.5 Summary and Assessment

After the well-prepared mandate extension in late 1996, UNTAES accelerated its actions, and by the time it was preparing to leave, security in the region had been stabilized. On the civilian side, the agreements were arranged to reintegrate every public sector in order to preserve Serb minority rights. For the Serbs, elections were

---

832 Howard 2008, p. 258. See also World Bank. 2007. *Croatia – Living Standards Assessment.* Available online at http://www.worldbank.hr/WBSITE/EXTERNAL/COUNTRIES/ECAEXT/CROATIAEXTN/0,,contentMDK:21192606~pagePK:141137~piPK:141127~theSitePK:301245,00.html, last access on 15 March 2009.
833 Walker, Christopher. Undated. "Conflict Continues to Simmer on the Eastern Side of Croatia." *Conflict Resolution Journal.* Available online at http://www.sipa.columbia.edu/cicr/research/journal/archive/features/croatia.html, last access on 18 February 2009.
834 Howard 2008, p. 257.
835 Ibid. For an inventory of the effectiveness of peace operations, see Page-Fortna, Virginia. 2008. *Does Peacekeeping Work? Shaping Belligerent's Choices after Civil War.* Princeton: Princeton University Press.

an important cornerstone, giving them a sense of influence. Nevertheless, until the very last day, Serbs tried to keep UNTAES in the region.

> In fact, even getting them to vote was difficult, getting them to register to vote was difficult, getting them to take the *domovnica* was difficult. They just didn't get it. What they were hoping for was kind of a permanent UN occupation. I mean, they kept telling you, 'We love you, stay here! Five years, ten years!'[836]

In order for more to be done on longer-term projects, an even stronger mandate might have been the key,

> Personally I would have liked to see a stronger mandate; and I think less Serbs would have left. This becomes a very basic indicator for me, whether Serbs stayed or not. Obviously, economic development has never really come back to the area and so, maybe, they would have left anyway, but they left for political and discrimination reasons in the first place."[837]

Yet, long-term orientation and an even more flexible deadline arrangement were luxuries that the international community could not afford. It "was not prepared to stay for the ten years that it usually takes to launch a peacebuilding process."[838] The question of withdrawal is "not only a question of resources but also of attention: there are an awful lot of other conflicts to be looked at."[839]

Unfortunately, the OSCE mission may not have fulfilled what it was supposed to do. That might also relate to the fact that communication between UNTAES and OSCE was not as good as it could have been. UNTAES staff was only marginally involved in the planning of the ensuing arrangements. In fact, it is unusual for UN personnel to be formally involved in the planning of another organization's planning processes. What UNTAES staff *did* do, "We helped them out on what the agreements were, how we were doing it, we prepared them, gave them copies of

---

836 Telephone interview with Ambassador Jacques-Paul Klein, SRSG/TA, UNTAES, 19 July 2007. "One of the things was that the local Serbs didn't think that we would ever leave. First of all they didn't want us because they thought we were pro-Croats, then we got them all their rights et cetera. and they loved us, then when we were about to leave they said, 'You can't leave.' – 'Yeah, actually we can, and we are. Watch.'" Telephone interview with Dr. Robert J.A.R. Gravelle, Head of the JIC Secretariat and Head of STACTA, 11 August 2007.

837 Telephone interview with a staff member of STACTA, UNTAES, 10 January 2007.

838 Interview with Professor Michael W. Doyle, former UN Assistant Secretary-General, New Haven, 11 September 2006. In fact, he adds, "Ten years are the minimum, in my view, under good conditions, to engage in a thorough peacebuilding reconstruction. And it's rarely ever done."

839 Ibid.

the agreements, this is what we were doing, this is the police training et cetera."[840] Another part of the problem was that many UNTAES staff left early, and from the Serb perspective, "there was this typical feeling of let-down,"[841] aggravated by Klein's surprising leave.[842]

In the complicated world of peace operations, despite its known shortcomings UNTAES counts as one of the UN's greatest successes. It concluded with an implementation record that is rare for UN missions and created mechanisms that allowed Serb minorities to be integrated in Croatia.

> On a scale from one to ten we did eight. Number one: we managed the political tension. Number two: it was – and I guess number one might be a consequence of number two – an inclusive process for nearly a year, where the different parties, the political interests, were brought forward. And the place was small enough so that the general public knew what was going on, they knew the people they were in. So it felt like a locally owned process. It wasn't Belgrade and Zagreb negotiating. That was probably the second biggest thing, that it was locally owned. They felt they were part of the process; they were able to go on the street and to demonstrate and it had an impact.[843]

4. Analysis: The Transitional Management Process

Analyzing the conditions and UNTAES' transitional management, I break down the findings of the case reconstructions according to the concept specification that I elaborated in the theoretical framework.

UNTAES encountered high levels of hostility but also relatively high levels of capacity in Eastern Slavonia. It operated with a background of high but still ambiguous international support, as well as of sufficient but frequently inadequate resources and manpower. Typically for transitional administrations, the mission was to implement a highly complex mandate under a tight time schedule. Various pathologies and threats to a successful mandate implementation developed, but UNTAES found ways to cope with most of them.

---

840 Telephone interview with Dr. Robert J.A.R. Gravelle, Head of the JIC Secretariat and Head of STACTA, 11 August 2007. In line with this statement by the chief negotiator, another UNTAES staff member recalls that "[I thought] that it was surprisingly limited [...] when we had one OSCE person come in – I think during the last month or the last few weeks of STACTA – who was supposed to sort of gather information. And it was very limited what came out of that." Telephone interview with a staff member of STACTA, UNTAES, 10 January 2007.
841 Interview with Dr. Gerard Fischer, Head of Civil Affairs, UNTAES, New York, 21 November 2006.
842 "Nothing really happened anymore, at least not as dramatic as during Klein's time." Ibid.
843 Telephone interview with a staff member of STACTA, UNTAES, 10 January 2007.

4.1 Ill-Structured Conditions: Challenges, Constraints and Dilemmas

UNTAES encountered relatively favorable parameters as far as local capacities and political/financial international supports were concerned. The local hostility level, on the other hand, remained high throughout the entire transition period and triggered many pathological patterns that UNTAES had to cope with.

Local Hostility

On basis of the Erdut agreement, the security situation was stable but far from relaxed: hostility between the ethnic factions remained high and some paramilitary enclaves continued to exist. Divided by a century-long history of rivalry and recalcitrance, Serbs and Croats were characterized by comparatively high coherence. The coherence was owed mainly to each ethnic group's strong, populist leaders.

When UNTAES was deployed, the Vukovar area was still too insecure for the mission to settle there. For different reasons, both Serbs and Croats were highly sceptical of the mission and, at the outset, did not support their policies.

Local Capacity

While Croatia maintained a comparatively high economic level, the war destroyed much of the infrastructure, industries laid idle, and the living standard decreased sharply: during the war, Croatia's GDP per capita dropped from $7,870 to $6,620.[844] Fortunately, basic services were restored relatively quickly and roads remained intact.

An outstanding challenge, overshadowing the entire transition process, was the difficult management of the return of the refugee and the IDPs: the enormous flows of refugees triggered frustration and violence. Besides, a major "brain drain" away from the region had set in. The level of education and capacities in the former Yugoslavia had been rather high, and Croats, in particular, were well-versed in running public institutions. That said, neither Croats nor Serbs had a history of democracy. For the last 45 years, they had been living within a socialist system and had not been familiar with the new democratic "rules in town."

---

844 Cf. Global Property Guide, "Croatia." Available online at http://www.globalpropertyguide.com/Europe/Croatia/gdp-per-capita, last access on 15 March 2009.

International Support

As indicated by the comprehensive and robust mandate, international support was high, but it conveyed the clear imperative of short-term success. International support was inherently ambiguous. First, member states in general do not want the UN to routinely operate state-building or even state-running missions and keep an eye on such comprehensive missions as UNTAES. Second, donors did not want to pay for an infinitely long mission and a tight time frame was set, "Eastern Slavonia was never one of the more important items on the Security Council's agenda, paling in comparison to the Bosnia crisis."[845] Third, the attention span of the Security Council was also inherently limited. Hence, the time was ticking for the mission from day one and the political will driving the mission was of a precarious nature.

United Nations Capacities

In 1996, UNTAES' mission was the most comprehensive challenge the UN had ever taken on. In this situation, resources, personnel capacities, and expertise were not adept at the new tasks. Staffs with experience in administration and public administrations were virtually not available, and the specification of a mandate implementation plan was left for the mission leadership to come up with.

United Nations Rules and Funding

The mission was relatively well resourced. However, the budget was not as large as was requested by the Secretary-General. Even more, the assets for peacebuilding had to be raised *ad hoc*, implying an additional workload for the mission. Rules of engagement translated into constraints of UNTAES' actions, particularly concerning the enactment of its robust mandate.

Time Pressure and Mandate Complexity

The pressure for UNTAES was immense: the mission was initially scheduled to last only one year, and the non-compliance of the two parties to the conflict – despite the peace agreement – compounded the situation. Within a tight timeframe, UNTAES was supposed to perform various peacekeeping and peacebuilding tasks, including demilitarization, refugee return, security maintenance, establishment of

845   Howard 2008, p. 235.

a Serbo-Croat police force, reconciliation and minority protection, elections, in-stitution-building, and -transformation.

4.2 Pathologies and Coping Strategies

In the beginning, the high level of local hostility caused pathological challenges in the form of principal-agent dilemmas: Serbs and Croats, the indispensable agents of transition, constantly tried to change the status quo in their favor. UNTAES – put in the position of the principal by the peace agreement – was not able to elim-inate the obstructions from both actors, and (minor) accidents occurred. At the end of the day, however, UNTAES was able to contain and attenuate a range of the emerging dilemmas and stalemates, putting negotiation tactics and appropriate communication to good use. Another challenge that emerged as a consequence of the ongoing hatred and hostility but also from the high workload of international civilian officers was the lock-in of useless procedures. If it had not been for a resolute redesign of large parts of the civil affairs on the SRSG's initiative, UN-TAES' chances for success would have decreased significantly. The resoluteness of the SRSG and his proactive yet integrating leadership quality was decisive for the positive impact of a range of coping strategies. Cognitive biases and the pathol-ogy of tightly coupling complex processes emerged as well, but less virulently so. Against the odds, UNTAES prevented major accidents and was able to cope with contingencies.

In what follows, I structure the case study observations on pathologies and con-tingency strategies according to the study's theoretical framework as well as ac-cording to the mission's timeline of deployment, implementation, and termina-tion.[846]

4.2.1 Cognitive Biases

The trade-offs involved in its mandate made it difficult for UNTAES and its deci-sion-making actors to avoid cognitive biases. Simplifying behavior, avoiding vir-ulent issues without conflict, and focussing on controllable issues were the most pertinent strains that UNTAES suffered from.

---

846 Where I do not indicate a coping strategy, successful avoidance or containment of the pathology did not occur.

4.2.1.1 Deployment

During the days of its deployment, UNTAES struggled with the cognitive biases of focussing on controllable factors, procrastination, and inadequate routines that materialized in inadequate recruiting decisions, delays, and unnoticed design lapses.

Inappropriate Peer Recruitment

The SRSG/Transitional Administrator wanted to make sure that the personnel he knew and deemed good was aboard. Hence, he brought some people from the US State Department with him to the UN mission. However, by people he was familiar with, he did not conceive of the tensions that were programmed to occur between the two entities. A turf war was about to break out.

By showing vigilance and responsiveness to his senior leadership team, Klein was able to prevent impending rivalries and internal partisanship by quickly readjusting to negative feedback.

Mandate-Implementation Gap

The gap between the vague text of the mandate and concrete implementation measures produced confusion for the international field staff who procrastinated during the early days when no one knew what to do. The result was a delay of implementation.

Fortunately, the delay was not exacerbated into failure. Early on, the senior mission staff decided on a coherent – though not exhaustive – implementation approach, creating a strategy with benchmarks and therefore orientation for their staffs.

Table 1: Ill-Structuredness, Cognitive Biases, Accidents, and Coping Strategies

	Ill-Structuredness	Pathology	Accident	Coping
Deployment	UN Rules, Mandate Complexity	Inappropriate Peer Recruitment	(Internal Fights)	Vigilant and Responsive Feedback Adjustment
	Mandate Complexity, Insufficient UN Capacity	Mandate-Implementation Gap	(Confusion, Delay)	Benchmark-Setting
	UN Routines, Time Pressure	Design Lapse	Neglect of HR Issues	-
Implementation	UN Routines, Insufficient UN Capacity	Continued Lack of Guidance	(Implementation Insecurity)	Floor Approach
	High Local Hostility, Mandate Complexity, Time Pressure	Individuals' Tunnel Visions	Wrong Priorities	-
	Mandate Complexity, Insufficient UN Capacities, UN Rules	Narrow Focus on Political and Administrative Responsibilities	Neglect of Economic Reconstruction	Singular Measures for Economic Kick-off
	UN Rules, Ambiguous Intern. Support, Time pressure	Contradiction between Short-term and Long-term Priorities	(Internal Tensions)	Open Communication within Mission
	Low Local Civil Society Capacity, UN Rules and Routines	Stereotype about Local NGOs	(Waste of Time and Effort)	Hand-picking Trustworthy Locals for Civil Society Advancement
	Local Socio-cultural System, UN Rules	Imposition Trap	Questionable Sustainability of Institution-building	Maintenance of Institutional and Personal Continuity
Termination	No Observation	No Observation	No Observation	No Observation

Design Lapse

A pathology that was poorly coped with was the omission of the designated Human Rights unit. For the first time, the mandate formally required the assignment of human rights officers. However, the mission was not designed accordingly: the component was omitted. After a great delay, the shortcoming was made up for in mid-1997, i.e. six months before the mission ended.

Table 1 summarizes the ill-structured conditions triggering cognitive biases, the accidents they produced, and the coping strategies that were applied. Where accidents are put in brackets, this means that they did not become virulent: fit coping mitigated negative effects of organizational pathologies.

4.2.1.2 Mandate Implementation and Mission Management

When UNTAES started to tackle the core issues of its mandate, above all, the complexity and vagueness of the mandate made the mission succumb to biases and neglects in the implementation of tasks. For instance, the threat of a lack of guidance, the slow-moving economic reconstruction, and tensions about priorities all had their reason in the ambiguous and occasionally contradicting aims of the mandate. The pathology of individuals' tunnel visions was a result of the sheer complexity of the mandate, which created a climate where JIC officers focussed on manageable technical issues and neglected the substantial ones. That said, fitting coping mechanisms were able to prevent most of the emerging pathologies from becoming harmful.

Continued Lack of Guidance

Despite the widely hailed clarity of the mandate, "There were many aspects that were either unclear or totally absent."[847] The lack of guidance became particularly virulent with regards to the governmental part of the mandate. Given the considerable lack of guidance from headquarters, UNTAES leadership decided to adopt a generically proactive "floor approach" in implementing the mandate. "There are broadly two ways of interpreting a mandate–either as a ceiling or as a floor. If the mandate is taken as the ceiling, the leadership, when faced with an action, often poses the question 'Is it in the mandate? If not, we shouldn't do it.' But if the mandate is taken as the floor, the question is posed differently, 'Is there anything in the mandate to say that we should not do it? If not, let us proceed.'"[848] Determinedly, UNTAES went for the latter option.

Individuals' Tunnel Visions

The behavior of UNTAES officers that presided over the JICs was less decided. In a highly politicized environment where they had to work together with Serb and Croat officers, the international staff tended to focus heavily on controllable tech-

847 Boothby 2004, p. 48.
848 Ibid., p. 48-49.

nical matters while defensively avoiding conflict-ridden issues with political or ideological implications. Ongoing recalcitrance between Croats and Serbs working in the JICs aggravated their poor performance on substantive matters. The overall consequence was a very slow progress. The "tunnel visions" of JIC officers eventually led to a lock-in of inadequate civil affairs procedures.[849]

Narrow Focus on Political and Administrative Responsibilities

A thorough pursuit of regional economic reconstruction was not possible. UNTAES maintained a relatively narrow focus on administrative and security-related tasks, widely neglecting economic reconstruction, knowing that Croatia would take over soon. Understandably, the unemployed population's discontent grew. Individual measures, such as siphoning off the Djelatovci oilfield revenues, provided funds for kicking off some economic reconstruction efforts, but there was no coherent approach.

Contradiction between Short-Term and Long-term Priorities

The emphasis on short-term stabilization had repercussions on intra-mission discussions as well. The diverging views led to internal tensions between the office of the Transitional Administrator and civil affairs time and again, and the sustainability-oriented concerns of civil affairs officers and of cooperation partners from the development field had to step back. At the end of the day, plain and open communication prevented an escalation: the disputes among the senior staff took place on a basis of openness and trust. Allegedly, knowing how to deal with the Transitional Administrator's personality was a crucial asset.

Stereotype about Local NGOs

In its dealings with NGOs, UNTAES displayed what I called in the theoretical framework a stereotyping behavior.[850] When UNTAES wanted to start cooperating with local NGOs, only slowly did it realize that in the previously communist country, no organized civil society existed in the first place. As a consequence, time and effort was lost. This loss was limited however, since the mission adjusted quickly and started to advance the creation of local NGOs.

849 The resulting path dependence pathology will be discussed in Chapter IV.4.2.4.
850 Cf. Chapter III.2.2.1.

Imposition Trap

Eventually, like any peace operation that sets out under the "standard" liberal model, UNTAES ran the risk of starting with wrong assumptions and imposing inadequate institutions.[851] While contrary to most other post-conflict contexts, the level of education in Eastern Slavonia was rather high, the populace of the region was still inexperienced with the ways of a liberal democracy.

UNTAES tried to get around the gap between its aspirations and reality: civil affairs began training a very "thin pool"[852] of people, providing forms of support other than conventional capacity-building, such as the promotion of NGOs, and facilitating the involvement of other specialized organization, for instance, putting the Council of Europe in charge of human rights training.

4.2.2 Principal-Agent Dilemmas

The Serb and Croat agents of transition severely hampered the transitional management process by boycotting and constantly delaying UNTAES' policies and requests. At the international level, commitment problems of principal member states also became pathological in that they caused the mission notorious hitches. They materialized in the form of reduced robustness, resources, and decreasing member states' attention.

4.2.2.1 Deployment

During the first couple of months of 1996, UNTAES faced a challenging security situation while struggling with constraints on its military latitude as well as the slow and partly inadequate recruitment of field staff.

The Chinese Chapter VII

Indicating the ambiguity of international support for the operation, a decision on the mission's design weakened the authority of UNTAES: P-5 member China enforced a limitation on the mission's robustness. The "Chinese Chapter VII" carried

---

851 As the Head of Civil Affairs noted on the "imposed" institutions, "They have to be definitely right for the setting." Interview with Dr. Gerard Fischer, Head of Civil Affairs, UNTAES, New York, 21 November 2006.
852 Ibid.

the risk of impairing the mission's safety as well as its credibility vis-à-vis local spoilers and the population in general. In fact, "credibility is the single most important resource in arguing and depends on both impartiality and consistency."[853]

Coping with the deliberate constraint, UNTAES went for a "floor approach." Already proven useful for coping with the lack of implantation guidance, the "floor approach" was a useful strategy for coping with the member state-imposed constraint. The mission's leadership under Klein was constantly de-coupling the mission from headquarters' political liabilities, while simultaneously framing its legally ambiguous military actions as having been self-defense and thus, within the mandate.

Questionable Reeling of Pivotal Croatia

Despite the peace agreement, dealings with the GoC continued to be cumbersome and started to affect the chances for a controlled transition: Croatia was eager to quickly take over in Eastern Slavonia and was still capable of "solving" the Eastern Slavonia issue militarily. The difficulty was to have Croatia in but at the same time not constraining the mission by an unrealistically short timeframe.

In this situation, the very mandate design proved to be useful: resolution 1037 stated a one-year timeframe, which dangled a quick reintegration to Croatia, but at the same time inserted the flexible element of a one-year mandate extension option. This implied a time slack on which the UN could eventually fall back.

Inadequate Staff Qualifications

The ambiguous member state support of the transitional administration was also reflected by the deficient staffing process: there was no interest in developing "dedicated capacity in that area [of running states]."[854] As consequence, many of the staff would not fit their job descriptions. "That does not mean that these people are not well-intentioned, it doesn't mean that they don't work hard. But it's the same thing as if you would have a brain-surgeon to become a podiatrist. You know,

853 Rittberger, Berthold and Schimmelfennig, Frank. 2006. "Explaining the Constitutionalization of the European Union." *Journal of European Public Policy* 13:8, pp. 1148-1167, p. 1159. See also Elster 1992, pp. 18-19.
854 Interview with a senior staff member of UN DPKO, 15 September 2006.

he would do as good as he can, but he would just not be in the position to do the job."[855] That being said, the lack of capacity-building qualifications was not too severe since both, Serbs and Croats, were well versed in running public services and did not have to be trained in basic administration skills.

4.2.2.2 Mandate Implementation and Mission Management

Throughout the transition process, UNTAES continued to encounter obstructions by Croats and Serbs at multiple levels: there were top-level political constraints, spoiling actions by individuals in the TPF and in the JICs of the general population, but also extremist agitations by hard-line spoilers.

I will give an outline of the general pathological patterns that UNTAES faced in these obstructions, the coping strategies that they were contrasted with, and complement this outline with examples from various policy sectors where the pathological pattern repeated itself.

Serbian Boycotts

The Serb minority recurrently engaged in boycotts: the local Serb leadership blocked UNTAES' reconciliation and institution-building efforts over its first year. "The first year was completely wasted."[856] It was "mainland Serbia" negotiating the Erdut agreement – the local Eastern Slavonian Serbs were only formally involved, and did not support the treaty; but without their participation, there would be no mandate implementation.

Coping with this obstacle, UNTAES tried to allow the Serbian minority access to the Croatian government. For instance, an Eastern Slavonian Serb was appointed as Assistant Minister of Internal Affairs in Zagreb early on in the transition process, thus promoting Serb ownership as well.

855 Interview with Dr. Gerard Fischer, Head of Civil Affairs, UNTAES, New York, 21 November 2006. "UN missions don't have a problem of not filling positions – but often they don't have people with sufficient experience." Telephone interview with Souren G. Seraydarian, DSRSG/DTA, UNTAES, 16 January 2007.
856 Interview with Dr. Gerard Fischer, Head of Civil Affairs, UNTAES, New York, 21 November 2006.

Table 2: Ill-Structuredness, Principal-Agent Problems, Accidents, and Coping Strategies

	Ill-Structuredness	Pathology	Accident	Coping
Deployment	Ambiguous Support	Chinese Chapter VII	(Credibility Loss)	"Floor Approach," Framing of Actions towards HQ
	Local Hostility	Questionable Reeling of GoC	(Precarious Mandate Implementation)	Designing a "Janus Deadline"
	Ambiguous International Support, UN Rules and Routines	Inadequate Staff Qualifications	Precarious Mandate Implementation of Administrative Mandate	Staff Motivation
Implementation	Local Hostility, Time Pressure	Minority Boycotts	Delay, Perpetuation of Status Quo, Obstruction of Mandate Implementation	Minority Buy-In, Maintenance of Structural and Agency Continuity, Co-Opting (Moderate) Local Leaders
	Local Hostility, Time Pressure	Majority Waiting Games	Delay, Hindrance of Serb Integration, Obstruction of Mandate Implementation	Browbeating Backed by Interorganizational Linkage, Institutionalization of Talks, Making Commitment Felt, Bridging through Interim Solutions
	Local Hostility, Time Pressure	Ongoing Majority Waiting Games	Delay, Hindrance of Serb Integration, Obstruction of Mandate Implementation	Harder Negotiation Pace, Creating Negotiation Support Agency
	Local Hostility, Time Pressure	Stalemate on Security Policy	Delay, Obstruction of Mandate Implementation	Creating Win-Win Situation, Pacification of Unemployed Veterans through Large Police Service
	Local Hostility, Time Pressure	Stalemate on Employment Policy	Delay, Obstruction of Mandate Implementation	Blaming
	Local Hostility Time Pressure	Stalemate on Health Policy	Delay, Obstruction of Mandate Implementation	Exclusion of Provocative and Reckless Figures

Local Hostility, Time Pressure	Stalemate on Currency Policy	Delay, Obstruction of Mandate Implementation	Issue Linkage Policy, Organizational Slack through Interorganizational Linkage, Browbeating backed by International Community, Trust-building via Communal Level Measures
Local Hostility, Time Pressure	Stalemate on Electricity Policy	Delay, Obstruction of Mandate Implementation	Playing Parties to the Conflict Off against Another
Local Hostility, Time Pressure	Stalemate on Amnesty Law Policy	Delay, Obstruction of Mandate Implementation	Cross-Cutting and Informal Deals, Browbeating through Interorganizational Linkage
Local Hostility, Time Pressure	Stalemate on Reconciliation Policy	Delay, Obstruction of Mandate Implementation	Agenda-Setting Policy
Local Hostility, Time Pressure	Fractionalization Dynamics and Hidden Agendas of Civil Administrators and TPF Officers	Obstruction of Mandate Implementation	Using Local Political Leverage, Singling Out Reliable Local Leaders, External Training and Reconciliation Workshops (Evoking Sense of Community, Providing Informal Get Together), Prompt Delinquent Dismissal, CivPol Monitoring MoU
Local Hostility	Pathology of Population Mistrust and Defection	Delay	Public Information Campaign, Hands-On Attitude of International Staff, Generic People-Orientation Approach with Reach-Out Efforts
Mandate Complexity, Necessity of Cooperation to Implement Complex Mandate	Frictions in International Cooperation	(Inconsistent Mandate Implementation)	Exclusion of Spoilers, "Transparency Card"
Precarious Local Capacities	Fake NGOs	Waste of Money and Effort, Civil Society Development on Hold	Exclusion of Spoilers
UN Rules, Mandate Complexity	Dilemma between Rule Following and Efficacy	(Tension between Different Mandate Goals, Risk of Sanctions)	"Seeking Forgiveness rather than Permission," Good Informal Relationships, Open Reporting Style
Mandate Complexity, UN Capacities	Frictions in International Cooperation	(Inconsistent Mandate Implementation)	Regular Staff and Interagency Meetings at All Working Levels
Mandate Complexity, Time Pressure	Over-performance	Missed Opportunities for Reconciliation	(Capacity Limits)

Termination	Local Hostility, Time Pressure	Fox'n'Geese	Precarious Mandate Achievement	Coordination of International Mandate Extension Support
	Local Hostility, Time Pressure	Fragile Reconciliation	Precarious Protection of Minority Rights	Anti-discrimination Agreements and Implementation Guarantees
	Local Hostility, Time Pressure	Election Obstruction	(Precarious Exit)	Flexible Extension of Election Deadline
	Local Hostility, Time Pressure	Deadline Exploitation	(Precarious Exit)	Adapted Framing of the Mission towards Parties to the Conflict

Croatian "Waiting Games"

On the other hand, the GoC and local Croat leaders tried to engulf the transitional administration in delays and constantly initiated "waiting games." At the outset, the GoC resisted UNTAES' calls for more financial and policy support, especially in cases where local Serbs would have been among the profiteers. Particularly affected policy fields included employment security, education, and currency. As a result, the reintegration processes ran the risk of massive procrastination.

Coping with impending obstruction, the SRSG/Transitional Administrator put his authority to good use from the start. He forced a policy of tough negotiation upon the top level, being unafraid to browbeat the obstructing parties. "We used as many pressure tools as possible, most on the Croatian side."[857] His contacts in Washington and NATO were essential. "He was on the phone every other day to the State Department or to the Defense Department to make sure Washington's backing. Tudjman [would] only listen to the United States."[858] Besides, "Klein knew NATO very well and they knew him."[859] This phenomenon of inter-organizational links to "important and powerful suppliers of scarce resources"[860] has been studied as a crucial organizational strategy for reducing environment uncertainty.[861] Furthermore, "Klein had a good way of talking to the leaders,"[862] and was

857 Telephone interview with a staff member of STACTA, UNTAES, 10 January 2007.
858 Interview with Professor Michael W. Doyle, former UN Assistant Secretary-General, New Haven, 11 September 2006.
859 Ibid.
860 Provan, Keith G. 1982. "Interorganizational Linkages and Influence over Decision Making." *Academy of Management Journal* 25, pp. 443-451, p. 444.
861 Ibid., p. 443. Further important studies include Aiken, Michael and Hage, Gerald. 1968. "Organizational Interdependence and Intraorganizational Structure." *American Sociological Review* 33:6, pp. 912-930; Van de Ven, Andrew H. 1976. "On the Nature, Formation and Maintenance of Relations among Organizations." *Academy of Management Review* 1:4, pp. 24–36.
862 Interview with Dr. Gerard Fischer, Head of Civil Affairs, UNTAES, New York, 21 November 2006.

committed to the issues at stake, "I was all over the damn place, constantly, I was shuttling between Zagreb-Belgrade-Zagreb-Belgrade."[863] He made his presence and his commitment felt and visible. Under structural aspects, regular meetings at the top level were established where not only strategic issues were decided, but elaborated in small detail,[864] thus reducing ambiguity.

Croatian Reluctance to End the "Waiting Games"

While UNTAES was able to achieve some partial success, Croats tried to circumvent commitments whenever possible.

Facing ongoing "waiting games," UNTAES eventually answered with harder negotiation techniques – changing from an incremental, consensus-oriented *ductus* to a hard-nosed negotiation approach – and established the supporting STACTA institution. The parallel creation of STACTA and the Radic Commission accelerated the transition process, as both Croatia and UNTAES came to speak with one voice, in one single forum, respectively. What was even more, UNTAES established itself as the agenda-setter, pushing the GoC to make commitments, while letting the latter frame itself as a benevolent power and as a democratic state ready to join the EU. Having doubts about Croatian goodwill post-UNTAES, the international negotiators pushed for as many written agreements as they could possibly get.

A range of examples illustrates how political obstructions by Serbs and Croats materialized.

Stalemate on Security Policy: The GoC refused to integrate former Serbian combatants into the military through a regularizations agreement. Hence, the crucial issue of military reintegration depended upon Tudjman's goodwill. Coping with bleak prospects, the SRSG/TA created a (admittedly cynical) win-win-situation, suggesting that Serbs to do the most dangerous jobs in the Croatian army. In addition, UNTAES triggered the creation of a large police service, "Every fifth person was a policeman, but better to have them this way under control than having them outside."[865] The idea was worthwhile in the short-term, but in long run, this approach became extremely expensive and might have caused disputes, as Serbs would probably be the first to be removed from the Croatian Ministry of the Interior.

Stalemate on Employment Policy: Croats fiercely resisted granting employment security rights to Serbs living in Eastern Slavonia, In particular, the hard-line Croatian Mi-

863 Telephone interview with Ambassador Jacques-Paul Klein, SRSG/TA, UNTAES, 19 July 2007.
864 Telephone interview with Souren G. Seraydarian, DSRSG/DTA, UNTAES, 16 January 2007.
865 Interview with Dr. Gerard Fischer, Head of Civil Affairs, UNTAES, New York, 21 November 2006.

nister of Health denied employment status to Serbs within the Croat health system. The implication of this policy was the *de facto* ethnic cleansing of Serbs as they would not be able to make their livings in the region. Getting the Croats' agreement, Klein and his chief negotiator threatened to blame the Minister for the impending mandate extension which the latter was not ready to shoulder.

Stalemate on Health Policy: UNTAES coped with the stalemate on health policy by pushing the replacement of the Director of the Vukovar hospital in the Croatian negotiation delegation. This intervention at the top political level thus lessened frictions with the Serb counterparts and had the talks going again.

Stalemate on Currency Policy: A stalemate occurred in the negotiations about the region's future currency. Both sides refused, for different reasons, to agree to have the *kuna* as the official means of payment. In a smart move, UNTAES directly linked the currency issue to the pension issue and could thus foster a deal. Furthermore, UNTAES had the World Bank weigh in. The interorganizational linkage created financial slack: the World Bank financed the Croat losses on unfavorable exchange rates. Even more, the conditional involvement of the World Bank as well as of the EU imposed a "shadow of the future"[866] on Croatia to continue to cooperate with the international community. Given the possibility of a future in the international and particularly in the European community, Croatia had to comply. Last but not least, UNTAES adopted individual measures that curbed the local trade structures – where the *kuna* was accepted soon.

Stalemate on Electricity Policy: As both sides refused to provide an electricity grid to Eastern Slavonian during the interim period, the population was put on the brink of another disaster. UNTAES coped with this situation by playing both sides off against one another, having the Serbs run the grid during the precarious transition time.

Amnesty law stalemate: Croats were determined not to grant Serbs amnesty. Yet, without an amnesty law, nearly all Serbs were fair game, making a multiethnic society obsolete. In reaction, Klein made a crosscutting and informal deal once again, making use of his good connections to the IMF, where Croatia was just about to apply for a loan, and asked them to refuse the grant until a law was signed.[867] The good cooperation between Klein, the IMF, and Washington, who backed the deal, was essential.

Stalemate on reconciliation policy: UNTAES pushed GoC towards accepting a policy of reconciliation. While the latter had agreed to move forward, it was far from showing any real commitment to doing so. Reconciliation was put on hold. Coping with the stalemate situation, UNTAES eventually moved to set the agenda and wrote the reconciliation policy paper itself, which the GoC was to adopt. The outcome was mixed though, since the policy's implementation was delayed and operated half-heartedly.

Fractionalization Dynamics

Compounding matters, a divide emerged between the top Croat political level – which came to agree with UNTAES – and the mid-level Croat bureaucrats – who continued trying to obstruct the peace process.

---

866 Cf. Axelrod, Robert. 1984. *The Evolution of Cooperation.* New York: Basic Books.
867 "'You won't get the money until you sign.'" Telephone interview with Ambassador Jacques-Paul Klein, SRSG/TA, UNTAES, 19 July 2007.

In order to cope with the resulting delays and stalemates, the leadership of UNTAES decided to give direct feedback to the GoC, using its political leverage to have the spoiler's superior handle the problem.

The fractionalization problem was particularly virulent within the JICs, where the local civil administrators openly displayed their non-commitment to the reintegration roadmap. While the JICs provided a platform for communication and exchange of ideas, they were also susceptible to the emergence of new hostilities. In fact, Serbs and Croats did not delegate their best bureaucrats but their most partisan ones instead. UNTAES could not prevent Serbs and Croats working in the JICs from engaging in games of tit-for-tat. "There are all sorts of tricks."[868] As consequence, there was not much progress. For senior positions, UNTAES tried to cope with the problem by getting hold of people who were reputable and mutually accepted individuals and who also complied with UNTAES' ideas. Furthermore, external workshops for public administrators were offered, for instance in Strasbourg – with limited success, though. In general, the mission's recruitment approach was careful and minimalist. Possibly, a more comprehensive and determined approach at reconciliation would have been more rewarding.

The pathological problem was repeated in the TPF: the ongoing recalcitrance among Serb and Croat applicants was the TPF's biggest problem. There were individual yet recurrent offences within the TPF. While Serb and Croat offences balanced each other out at the beginning, Croat officers committed more offenses the faster the reintegration date approached. In addition, the sponsor, i.e. the GoC, initially refused to pay for salaries, uniforms, etc. Hence, the crucial police sector reform was extremely fragile. In the cases of severe offences, UNTAES dismissed the delinquent. The good thing was that this sent strong signals. The bad thing was that the dismissed officers' successors would not necessarily be any better. In addition, UNTAES decreed the directive to conduct TPF home visits only if they were monitored by CivPol. A positive side-effect of this measure was that it contributed to the recreation of "local confidence in the TPF."[869]

On a general level, a range of reconciliation measures were taken. First, UNTAES arranged for external training and reconciliation courses for the TPF: similar to the civil affairs workshops, taking the applicants out of the region and into a different environment created better chances for the development of a corporate sense. Normally, such measures would go under the header of capacity-building, but with capacities relatively high, their main objective was reconciliation. Second, having them wear the same clothes, even though their "uniform" consisted merely of identical jeans and T-shirts, further evoked a sense of community. Third, UN-

---

868 Interview with Dr. Gerard Fischer, Head of Civil Affairs, UNTAES, New York, 21 November 2006.
869 Coleiro 2002, p. 100.

TAES officials also made sure that there was time for informal get together – "where they could smoke a cigarette together and maybe chat a little." Fourth, back in Eastern Slavonia, a comprehensive CivPol monitoring presence started to supervise the new TPF forces. And eventually, Croatia complied with the financing request, going along with joint pressure from UNTAES, the UN Security Council, and the Contact Group for Croatia.

That said, some troops from the former Serb *milicija* tried to get into the TPF as a means of earning an income, yet had no interest in long-term employment in the region. For UNTAES, this was a waste of time and effort.

Local Population's Mistrust and Defection

Pathological obstacles were observable outside the transitional structures too, as large parts of the population refused to commit to the transition requirements. UNTAES encountered mistrust from both the Croat and Serb populaces: Croats wanted UNTAES out and Serbs refused to accept UNTAES as the agent of change. For instance, the Serbs were not willing to have their vehicles re-registered, which was one of the benchmarks identified in the roadmap for the region. Again, delays, "waiting games," and refusals to adapt to UNTAES policies ensued.

To cope with widespread mistrust, UNTAES installed registration offices and engaged in comprehensive public information campaigns, particularly vis-à-vis the Serbs – however, without much success. Only on the very last day of the term did Serbs started to realize that there was no alternative, and started to register their cars. Facilitating the process, UNTAES worked "until two o'clock in the morning."[870] Generally, UNTAES sustained a very proactive and interactive approach towards the population, materializing in its enormous outreach efforts. The latter comprised a multi-language newspaper, constant efforts by regular staff (military, police, civilian) to provide information, as well townhall meetings, village meetings, and radio and TV shows where senior staff participated, but also just talking to people in the streets, attending mass and going to lunch afterwards to "eat strange food."[871] The mission's bottom line came to be, "How you're going to take care of the people."[872] Orientation towards the people was fostered decidedly by the Klein, who had a good sense for "what people need when they suffer."[873] For instance, he would also use his contacts and have high-profile personalities fly in to Eastern

870 Interview with Dr. Gerard Fischer, Head of Civil Affairs, UNTAES, New York, 21 November 2006.
871 Ibid.
872 Interview with a former UNTAES staff member, 1 December 2006.
873 Interview with Dr. Gerard Fischer, Head of Civil Affairs, UNTAES, New York, 21 November 2006.

Slavonia to make the people feel that they were not forgotten by the world, or he would organize a children's party with informal US Air Force support. In addition, the mission's robust appearance vis-à-vis Serbs and Croats fostered the mission's credibility and impartial image.[874] Despite its successes, UNTAET did not succeed in convincing the clerical leaders of either side though. This was unfortunate since religious leaders as major identity figures could have played a primary role in reconciliation.

Frictions in International Cooperation

Cooperation can be an important coping strategy to manage an overwhelming task spectrum, but it may also be a source of problems: it creates new issues, requires more planning, and implies more monitoring. As a general rule of thumb, the higher the number of cooperation partner, the higher the probability of frictions – and UNTAES cooperated with a very high number of actors.[875] Negative consequences included a waste of time, energy, and resources, and the damaging effects of diverging interests. An example of this was the cooperation with UNHCR: UNHCR's rationale was to return as many refugees as possible as soon as possible, while UNTAES reckoned that this might prove to be a destabilizing factor for its reconciliation work. UNTAES' fear was entitled, "Return does not necessarily entail reconciliation and, in practice, the return of refugees has contributed to new tensions between ethnic communities, as well as within them. In Croatia, laws introduced by the former Tudjman regime which discriminated against non-ethnic Croats have exacerbated tensions and frustrated the process of return in war-torn areas."[876] A second example is a cooperation issue with a NGO: a conflict between goals emerged with the Catholic NGO "Caritas Rheinland-Pfalz," which engaged in building houses for Catholics. This meant that they were building houses for Croats only.[877]Obviously, this thwarted UNTAES' reconciliation goals.

To cope with the risk of misunderstandings and counterproductive agendas, the SRGS/Transitional Administrator established regular meetings, at first informally, later institutionalizing them. While executive staff meetings took place every weekday, even on Saturdays (chaired by Klein or DSRSG), the meetings with the

---

874 On this note, UNTAES also faced down the Croatian police when it attempted to enter Eastern Slavonia during the demilitarization phase – which conformed to the Erdut Agreement.

875 Many of them had been active in the region before, others were just entering the scene.

876 Blitz, Brad K. 2003. "Refugee Returns in Croatia: Contradictions and Reform." *Politics* 23:3, pp. 181-191, p. 181.

877 Interview with Dr. Gerard Fischer, Head of Civil Affairs, UNTAES, New York, 21 November 2006.

directors of other UN bodies took place once a week (mostly chaired by DSRSG). In addition, periodical meetings with NGO representatives took place, chaired by the Head of Civil Affairs, and Klein would drop by once in a while, too. "Meetings were full – that was a good sign."[878] Furthermore, the mission tried to provide for a climate of transparency. "Klein played the transparency card very well."[879]

Fake NGOs

A related difficulty consisted of the behavior of emerging local NGOs. The delegations sent to these new "agents" did not always proceed well: particularly the recently founded local NGOs abused their funds. There was too much money and too little control.

Rather harshly, Klein reacted by excluding all local NGOs from cooperation with UNTAES.

Dilemma between Rule Following and Efficiency

UNTAES acted in different roles: it was not only the transition's "principal" vis-à-vis local "agents," but, in an inverse perspective, it was the "agent" to its "principal" in New York. In its dealings with headquarters, UNTAES was constantly in a difficult situation between New York's request for formal adherence to a strict interpretation of the peacekeeping rules on the one hand, and effective actions and credibility on the other hand. DPKO's institutional interest consisted in the adherence to its principles and political primers – but in many cases, the very stance countervailed field level efficacy. For instance, the prior information of DPKO would have undermined the taking of the Djelatovci oilfields. Still, DPKO did not approve of UNTAES's "floor" approach and frictions became inevitable.

In most of these situations, the mission coped by acting on the rationale of "seeking forgiveness rather than permission."[880] This meant that the senior mission staff traded for their own accounts. In addition, UNTAES maintained good informal relationships with single HQ officers who attenuated the tensions. That said, if anything would have gone wrong, the senior staff would have been replaced. Also, UNTAES did a good job of maintaining a good formal relationship with head-

---

878 Interview with Professor Michael W. Doyle, former UN Assistant Secretary-General, New Haven, 11 September 2006.
879 Interview with Dr. Gerard Fischer, Head of Civil Affairs, UNTAES, New York, 21 November 2006.
880 Telephone interview with Dr. Robert J.A.R. Gravelle, Head of the JIC Secretariat and Head of STACTA, 11 August 2007.

quarters in New York, delivering regular and open reports: UNTAES was no "window-dressing good news mission".[881]

Over-performance

UNTAES was a positively proactive mission, but a crucial pathological trajectory consisted in a side-effect of these efforts, namely over-performance. Given the numerous delays and the steady display of Serb and Croat reluctance to adapt to the mission, UNTAES ended up doing too much of the work itself. In hindsight, reconciliation might have occurred faster through the allocation of joint responsibility from the mission's beginning, letting UNTAES stay in the background.

The pathology of over-performance is probably a regular in complex missions. At the end of the day, however, overperformance meets is "natural" limits in the inherent constraints of a mission's resources, capacities, and attention.

4.2.2.3 Termination

During the termination phase, pathological patterns revolved around local obstructions of the mission deadline and the benchmarks that should have been reached by then. UNTAES was able to attenuate many dilemmatic situations by creating organizational slack and by creating new sorts of leverage.

Fox'n'Geese

The mandate extension needed the agreement by the GoC. This formal provision gave the Croats an opportunity for obstruction. UNTAES, however, could prevent this. Its leadership made cautionary provisions to have the international community's support for a mandate extension guaranteed. "By keeping ambassadors in Zagreb well briefed so that they could report to their respective capitals, and by similar efforts to headquarters in New York so that the Secretary-General and DPKO could talk with the relevant ambassadors in the Security Council,"[882] the international community was well informed about the situation and the necessities in Eastern Slavonia and enabled to speak with one voice vis-à-vis Croatia. Eventually, the mandate was extended without any disputes.

---

881   Interview with Dr. Gerard Fischer, Head of Civil Affairs, UNTAES, New York, 21 November 2006.
882   Written interview with Derek G. Boothby, DSRSG/DTA, UNTAES, 5 February 2007.

Fragile Reconciliation

As the end of the mission came closer, UNTAES had a reason to increasingly doubt the Croatian respect for the Serb minority in the region.

Attempting to curb Serb discrimination, UNTAES negotiated with the Croats regarding the Serb quota in future political representation and institutions by fixing the number of seats in the Sabor, creating a Joint Council of Municipalities, and by signing a range of anti-discrimination agreements and implementation guarantees.

Election Obstruction

Furthermore, Croats continued to obstruct the elections by violent attempts to hinder Serb refugees from participating.

Coping with these obstacles, Klein used his authority effectively and extended the election deadline for as long as necessary, i.e. until all Serbs in the region were able to vote. In addition, UNTAES made sure that there would be international monitors on the region's borders.

Exploitation of the Deadline

Eventually, both Croats and Serbs tried to exploit the mission's deadline in their favor. An unambiguous deadline has consummate advantages, but at the same time conveys the pertinent pathology of abuse by spoilers.

Confronting the manipulations by the Serbs, who were hoping to end up as a "second Cypress," UNTAES adopted a stern position towards them, holding that there would be no extension at all. In fact, "It is always the weaker parties, the minorities who are in favor of a longer international presence."[883] Towards the Croats, UNTAES tried to ensure that its achievements remain sustainable and reminded the GoC of future prospects.[884] Besides, the international community was planning two post-mission arrangements, the PSG and an OSCE civilian successor mission, maintaining as much continuity in personnel as possible.

---

883 Interview with Professor Michael W. Doyle, former UN Assistant Secretary-General, New Haven, 11 September 2006.
884 Cf. Axelrod 1984.

4.2.3 Tight Coupling of Complex Interactions

In post-conflict peace operations, mishaps are a regular occurrence and accidents in one area can quickly lead to the collapse of other parts of the system. Failure lurks just around the corner. UNTAES coped with pathologies of tight coupling of complex interactions mainly by innovative ways of creating different forms of slack.

4.2.3.1 Deployment

During the first few months, UNTAES was enmeshed in an "intrinsicate knot" of unfavorable conditions. They involved the local security situation, the inert deployment process, member states' ambiguous support, and inflexible financial provisions, which all translated into pathologies that threatened the mission.

Precarious Credibility

The risk for a major accident surfaced at the very beginning of the operation: paramilitary groups were still acting strong around Vukovar while, due to usual delays in deployment, UNTAES was not yet fully operational. It needed to evade to Zagreb. The negative consequence was that UNTAES could not be in the spot where it was most urgently needed and faced a serious challenge to its credibility.

Coping with this accumulation of unfavorable circumstances, the determined UNTAES leadership conducted provident planning measures, omitted HQ information, successfully enacted its robust mandate and surprised the shorttaken spoilers. The flight of the Serb *milicija* and paramilitary had the additional side-effect of establishing UNTAES' credibility. The Chapter VII mandate and the thorough analysis and planning by the mission's leadership were essential for putting this decision into action.

No Money, No Action

UNTAES was facing obstacles "from within," too. In the first place, the budgeting divide for multidimensional UN peace operations implied delays, uncertainty, and earmarking. For instance, there was no money available for quick reaction projects on peacebuilding related issues. Hence, no early reconciliation measures could be installed.

There was a need to be innovative and UNTAES installed two successful donor conferences. Likewise, Klein would directly lobby at governments in Europe and in Washington. "He made a lot of things moving which in other missions would never, never happen."[885] UNTAES would also very much involve the EU, a then new actor in the international peace operations scene. The EU enormously contributed to the financing of peacebuilding-related tasks. However, while the EU did not have a security-development divide in funds, the inherent pathology of this institution was that the approval of funds was highly bureaucratic and thus took quite a long time. The most important measure to alleviate the financial impediments was that UNTAES could eventually go after the UNSC suggestion and make the GoC assume the expenses' lion share for the transitional regional civil serve and for the related pensions.

Impeding Regulations

A range of specific legal regulations for UN missions counteracted effective mandate implementation, such as the regulations on weapon purchasing, on UNCivPol equipment, or on the labelling of treaties. First, the widespread distribution of weapons amidst army, paramilitary, and population made comprehensive demilitarization a *sine qua non* for further mandate implementation. However, the UN is not allowed to purchase weapons – which would be a potential means for immobilization.

With international support, the UNTAES leadership could convince GoC to do the purchase – by its own funds. The deal was that the HV was allowed to take the newer weapons for their own use. In its efforts to disarm Serbs, UNTAES was able to initiate a positive spillover process: its strong stance vis-à-vis the Croats lent the mission credibility and it had the Commander of the RSK army cooperate with UNTAES' Force Commander. This not only helped build up trust but also facilitated the demilitarization process enormously.

Second, the strict international law provision that UNCivPol must not carry arms was counterproductive. The "absolute prerequisite"[886] security depends to a high degree upon the international mission's perception by potential obstructers. It is obvious that the latter are more likely to spoil the peace and reconstruction process if they deem the mission weak. Unarmed police forces contribute to such an image.

UNTAES coped by creating a sort of organizational slack: the mission wangled a stronger image by asking headquarters for a Special Tasks police force – which

885 Interview with Dr. Gerard Fischer, Head of Civil Affairs, UNTAES, New York, 21 November 2006.
886 Salomons 2005.

was allowed carrying weapons – and having them mingle with "normal" UN-CivPol, thus creating a more favourable, stronger public image.

Third, when trying to lock the GoC in on their concessions on Serbs' employment status by having them sign a corresponding declaration, the formal UN provisions on the review of national declarations would have put the process on hold. Possibly, this would have gambled away GoC's agreement.

Quickly moving, UNTAES circumvented the UN regulations by titling the document an *Affidavit* instead of a *Declaration*.

Mission, interrupted

A similar kind of pathology was the interruption of the mission by the slow deployment of civilian staff. As consequence of the slow recruitment standard operating procedures,[887] civil affairs started delayed and there was also no civilian support for the military component. Accordingly, UNTAES could not "hit the ground running."[888] In addition, the situation implied an immense workload for those civilian staff that was already on-the-ground. A delayed start of the very essential governing/administrative duties resulted.

Coping with the shortages, UNTAES contacted former UNCRO personnel who were still in the region and informally hired them. They also took over their "logistic, communication, and administrative"[889] equipment. While the delay problem persisted, it was at least attenuated. In addition, the deployment of troops was outsourced: private contractors from nearby countries such as Russia and the Ukraine were successfully in charge of shipping and flying the multinational troops in.[890]

4.2.3.2 Mandate Implementation and Mission Management

Different mission imperatives contradicted each other or, at least, conveyed trade-offs. Compounding the transitional administration's inherent fragility, effective measures and political imperatives were often thought not to be in sync. In addition,

---

887 Cf. Chapter II.2.3.
888 Telephone interview with Dr. Robert J.A.R. Gravelle, Head of the JIC Secretariat and Head of STACTA, 11 August 2007.
889 Interview with Dr. Gerard Fischer, Head of Civil Affairs, UNTAES, New York, 21 November 2006.
890 "The military deployment was a record." Telephone interview with Ambassador Jacques-Paul Klein, SRSG/TA, UNTAES, 19 July 2007.

the red tape for financing, recruitment, and implementation policies continued to slow things down.

Table 3: Ill-Structuredness, Tight Coupling, Accidents, and Coping Strategies

	Ill-Structuredness	Pathology	Accident	Coping
Deployment	Ambiguous Internat. Support	Precarious Credibility	(Security Risk for the Mission)	Vigilant Planning, Enacting Robustness, Creating Surprise Slack by Non-Compliance to Formal Rules
	UN Funding Rules	No Money, No Action	No Quick Implementation Projects, Peacebuilding Put on Hold, Delay	Raising Local Revenues, Donor Conferences, Direct SRSG/TA Lobbying, and Including New, Potent Donors
	UN Rules	Impeding Regulations	(Precarious Mandate Implementation)	Financial Slack by Creating Win-Win Situation, Positive Spillover Process through Cooperation with Local Military Key Figure, Creating Organizational Slack by Having Special Forces Mingle with CivPol, Circumventing Regulation through new Labelling of Treaties
	UN Recruitment Rules, Insufficient UN Capacity	Mission, interrupted	Delay	Falling Back on UN Personnel and Equipment Present in Region Plus Outsourcing of Troop Deployment to Local Contractors
Implementation	Mandate Ambiguity, Local Hostility	Lost in Interpretation	Delay	Bridging through Interim Solution
	Mandate Complexity, UN Rules	No Money, No Action	Precarious Financing of Civil Servants/ Instruction-building	Proactive Creation of Revenues
	Mandate Complexity, Local Hostility	Conflict of Goals	Rejection by Locals	Adopting Facilitator Role and Incremental Structural Transformation
	Local Hostility	Ongoing Extremist Propaganda	Precarious Reconciliation	-
	Local Hostility, Time Pressure	Risk of Unintended Provocation	(Security Risk)	Extensive Information and Consultation of the Minority
	Ambiguous Int. Support, Mandate Complexity, Time Pressure	Contradicting Imperatives for Institution-building	(Precarious Mandate Achievement)	Floor Approach and Promoting Staff Proactiveness
Termination	Ambiguous Internattional Support	Deadline Liability	(Croat Spoiling)	Economic Leverage Backed by Powerful Member State Plus Plain Communication vis-à-vis Population
	Ambiguous Support, Local Hostility	Precariousness of Controlled Exit	(Putting Mandate Achievement at Risk)	Gradual Mission Downsizing while Retaining Authority
	UN Rules and Routines	On the Leave	Risking Mandate Achievement	Convincing Staff to Change Hats
	UN Capacity, UN Rules	Moving Chairs	Risking Mandate Achievement	-

227

Lost in Interpretation

A problem that became pathological for UNTAES was the contradiction between the need to foster a comprehensive mandate that found consensus in the Security Council and the need to have a clear mandate that guided the mission unambiguously. This tension was "solved" in favor of the former, as it is easier for member states to agree and find consensus on a vague mandate that leaves space for individual interpretation than engaging in over-determined commitments that are much more binding in nature. Yet, the logic of Security Council negotiation has a direct and constraining impact on the mission: first, it takes time for the mission leadership to devise a mandate implementation plan, and second, the mandate's (necessary) vagueness about governing duties gave the local conflict parties opportunities to insert their own interpretations. Obviously, this countervailed UNTAES's implementation plans and resulted in a local reluctance, particularly by Serbs, to adopt UNTAES's transition policy. "Lost in interpretation," the reintegration process was hampered.

Generally spoken, just as the fox is not the most trustworthy one to watch your geese, the parties to the conflict are not the ones you would usually pick for decision-making roles in a complex and fragile venture. Yet obviously, they are at the same time the most crucial actors to a transition's success. In Eastern Slavonia, much depended upon the GoC's stance, for instance the establishment of the TPF, which was a crucial issue for the overall transition. Its funding was made dependent upon Croatia's goodwill. Thus, UNTAES got ensnared in waiting games and delays. For the time being, UNTAES managed the equipment shortages informally. From a US police equipment catalogue, neutral uniforms were picked and Klein could eventually convince the US Justice Department to do the purchase. Klein's connections were essential for this move. As regards salary payment, the unresolved currency issue hampered the negotiations. Again, UNTAES suggested an interim solution and arranged for a Croat salary payment in German Marks – which was the unofficial currency in the Balkans at that time anyway. Thus, by de-emphasizing his initial position on Croat TPF payment and refocusing on his real underlying interest, namely security and reconciliation, Klein created a win-win situation – which is the definition of the negotiation strategy of "bridging."[891]

891 Cf., e.g., Pruitt, Dean G. 2001. "Achieving Integrative Agreements." In: Ira G. Asherman and Sandra Vance Asherman, eds., *The Negotiation Sourcebook*. Amherst: HRD Press, pp. 187-196. Butler, John K. 1996. "Two Integrative Win-Win Negotiation Strategies." *Simulation & Gaming*, 27:3, pp. 387-392.

No Money, No Action

A pathology that related very specifically to the mission's nature as a transitional administration consisted in the non-availability of money for paying the salaries of the local civil servants: neither was it included in the UN budget, nor would the GoC pay for it – at least, that was the stance at the outset. The financing of civil servants and thus institution-building put on hold.

Kicking off, UNTAES assigned the revenues yielded by the taken Djelatovci oilfield for the civil servant payment.[892]

Conflict of Goals

The tight temporal and organizational coupling of various tasks conveyed the risk of a conflict of objectives. For instance, UNTAES was trapped with the tricky challenge of simultaneously aborting the Serb administrative structure and building the new local Croat administration, while not offending any of the conflict parties.

On that background, UNTAES decided to go for an incremental transformation of the RSK into the EC and to act as a facilitator in the overall transition process.

Further pathologies that UNTAES was facing consisted of ongoing extremist propaganda using the media infrastructure that UNTAES was simultaneously re-building, the risk of unintended provocations, the pathological gap between tasks and capacities, and the tension between participation and efficacy.

Ongoing Extremist Propaganda

While UNTAES was making good use of the media, other actors were good at its instrumentalization, too. "You could see from all the radio and TV programmes: HDZ had the power and they were horrible."[893] In a sadly paradoxical in a sense, the media infrastructure was just too good for a post-conflict country – and this was where UNTAES did too little about. UNTAES would have had the power to reduce hard-line Croat and Serb propaganda, but there had been no firm pushes into that direction. The consequence was ongoing hatred.

892 Diehl lists this strategy in his suggestions for innovative mission financing. Diehl 2008, p. 115.
893 Interview with Dr. Gerard Fischer, Head of Civil Affairs, UNTAES, New York, 21 November 2006.

Risk of Unintended Provocation

At the same time, UNTAES had to take care not to foment recalcitrant emotions: after the success of the multiethnic training abroad, UNTAES considered to conduct the same training class within the region. The conceivable risks, however, was that bringing Croat officers back in region at that early date might provoke Serbs who would possibly turn to violence.

Recognizing this risk, UNTAES extensively informed and involved local Serb leaders so that they felt important – and eventually supported the plan which could be implemented relatively smoothly.

Contradicting Institution-building Imperatives

Eventually, one must not forget that the newness, workload, and time pressure implied by the mandate as well as local parties' non-cooperation and reluctance rendered the mission in a persistently precarious situation: even minor efficiency failures or credibility losses would have impaired their international and local support, respectively. At the same time, UNTAES was supposed to adhere to the limits that were set by its institutional and political context. Thus, UNTAES had to work under conditions of constricted latitude and enormous international pressure.

Coping with this typical yet pathological precariousness, Klein and his immediate team interpreted the mandate "as floor." Likewise, he ceded his staff considerable latitude, which "felt flexible."[894] Fortunately indeed, the sheer numbers of personnel, the good quality of some, and the high motivation in general made up for much of the qualification deficiencies. Still, recruitment and on-site training could have been much better and, in an ideal world, much better *suited* to the mandate. Even if that is not coping in the sense of enacting a counter-strategy, it was the sheer number of personnel and the motivation of the staff that helped contain pathologies.

4.2.3.3 Termination

In UNTAES' final months, pathologies of tight coupling emerged from the "outside," i.e. triggered by the local parties, as well as from "within," i.e. stemming from UN and member state policies, politics, and polities.

---

894 Telephone interview with a field officer, UNTAES, 10 January 2007.

Deadline Liability

The pathology that has been described above as a principal-agent problem of deadline manipulation might also be interpreted as a problem that results from the tight coupling of different processes and imperatives during a transition. When the timeframe is clearly set, there is not much digression as member states' clocks are ticking and the mission does not get extension. Along with this rigidity comes a decreasing the mission's political leverage – which becomes more and more prone to being exploited by local spoilers.

Recognizing this problematic trajectory, Klein took direct action and went straight to the US head level, suggesting the Secretary of State to link IMF loans to GoC compliance with UNTAES instructions. While political leverage declined, Klein made a good move in applying economic pressure. Faced with Serbian delay tactics, UNTAES took up a clear stance and unambiguously communicated that there would be no "Croatian Cypress."

Precariousness of Controlled Exit

Apart from the local spoiler difficulty, the design and the evaluation of a deadline as well as the timing and the strategic approach to the exit of the mission has to be crafted carefully. If this is done inadequately, that means neither responsive to the situation on-the-ground nor to the international sustainability, the overall achievements of a mission are put at risk.[895]

UNTAES approached its devolution with timely planning and started the mission's restructuring in early summer 1997, following resolution 1120.[896] It started the gradual and sector-wise devolution of administrative responsibilities while maintaining its ultimate executive authority "until the day we left,"[897] monitoring the joint Serbo-Croat local administration. That said, not all processes were conducted as thoughtfully, as the following observation proves.

---

895 Cf. UN Doc. S/2001/394.
896 UN Security Council, "Resolution on the Situation in Eastern Slavonia, Baranja, and Western Sirmium," UN Doc. S/RES/1120, 14 July 1997. The drawdown of the military component started in October 1997.
897 Telephone interview with Dr. Robert J.A.R. Gravelle, Head of the JIC Secretariat and Head of STACTA, 11 August 2007.

On the Leave

Since UN field contracts are only valid for six months, the deadline was clear, and since the system suffered a scarcity of personnel, the (good) staff left before the mission ended. Thus, what has been achieved so far was put at risk. There was not much to be done about this.

Still, some people could be hired for the follow-on OSCE mission though and stayed on, being offered attractive incentives in the form of consummate salaries.

Moving Chairs

The most crucial and harmful leave was that of the SRSG/Transitional Administrator: the sudden drop-out of Klein disappointed not only his staff but was a setback for the local population, particularly for the Serbs. In fact, they were shocked. As reports on reasons are ambiguous, there is only speculation. There are at least two interpretations on this: either, it was the Klein's preference – who thus must have underestimated the effect of his withdrawal; or it was the Secretary-General who desperately wanted him to take charge in a different high-profile position in Bosnia – which would reveal a notable shortage of suitable personnel for critical posts. The unfortunate consequence was that during the important last months, ultimate impetus was lacking and the mission lost much of its drive.

4.2.4 Path Dependence Deficiencies

Path dependence denotes the lock-in of a given non-conducive policy. In UNTAES, the inadequate policy was the technical focus of the JICs. Virtually living up to textbook suggestions, the SRSG stooped the lock-in from becoming virulent by enforcing a decisive redesign.

Lock-in of Inadequate Policies

The individual "tunnel visions" put success in a crucial area of administrative institution-building on the brink: foci were set on technical matters while important political issues were sidelined. Accordingly, the overall progress in the JICs was very low regarding both, their institution-building as well as their reconciliation purposes.

Fortunately, UNTAES did not succumb to a protracted lock-in of inadequate policies in the public sector. Recognizing that the present working speed would make the mission fail, Klein and his senior staff decided on a rigid and comprehensive redesign,[898] they identified a range of cross-cutting priority issues, and they changed the mission's general approach from a consensus-oriented to a hard-nosed negotiation attitude. Besides the very systematic nature of the review process, the following coping measures are particularly noteworthy. First, the JIC Secretariat was required to apply more micromanagement while also becoming more proactive in its coordination and support functions as superior agency. Second, citizenship was unambiguously identified as primary condition for multiethnic reintegration and the UNTAES leadership engaged in persistent top-level negotiations on the issue. Eventually, this led to a Croatian anti-discrimination law change. On the same matter, UNTAES started a proactive public information campaign that was in the main addressed at Serbs in order to build confidence in UNTAES policy. Third, UNTAES focussed very much on employment security rights and could eventually "rhetorically trap"[899] Croat negotiators on the issue: the international negotiators pointed to previous commitments of the GoC and made the future status of the GoC within Europe conditional upon its compliance with these commitments.

Table 4: Ill-Structuredness, Path Dependence, Accidents, and Coping Strategies

	Ill-Structuredness	Pathology	Accident	Coping
Transition	*Mandate Complexity, Local Hostility, Time Pressure (leading to individual cognitive biases and adding up to policy lock-in)*	*Lock-in of Inadequate Institution-building*	*Precarious Mandate Achievement*	*Rupture: Re-design of JIC Structure, accompanied by an Introduction of Cross-Cutting Deals, a Change of Negotiation Style, Public Communication, Rhetorical Trapping*

---

898 The makeover included the reduction of the number of JICs, pooling them so as to have a three-pronged approach and a review on general principles, on the reintegration and mediation process, on priority issues, on issues currently under discussion, outstanding issues, time frames for implementation of reintegration programs, and on processes by which meetings were conducted, agendas set, agreements reached and implemented, on issues mediated and on identified obstacles to mediation.

899 Cf. Schimmelfennig, Frank. 2001. "The Community Trap: Liberal Norms, Rhetorical Action, and the Eastern Enlargement of the European Union." *International Organization* 55:1, pp. 47-80.

4.2.5 Conclusion and Further Findings

The hypotheses about the existence of organizational pathologies could be confirmed. Various case study observations on dysfunctionalities could be interpreted as cognitive biases, tight coupling of complex interactions, path dependency, and particularly as principal-agent problems: the longest list of findings relates to the pathologies of principal-agent constellations. This finding is not exactly surprising as it is the analytically broadest pathology category. A differentiation in terms of the obstructer's locus reveals that most of these pathologies were caused by the agents of transition, i.e. the former local parties to the conflict who, for different motives, were often not willing to comply with the transitional administration's policies.

Analyzing the transitional administration's behavior, one comes across a range of "enablers" or important advantages for the invention and/or application of coping strategies, such as leadership, sufficient resources, and support of international actors. UNTAES could even flee its "tragic curse" and realize its chances of disentanglement from a knot of unfavorable constellations by putting advantages to good use and apply fit coping strategies. I will conclude this chapter by discussing one outstanding advantage of the transitional administration in Eastern Slavonia, namely the factor of leadership.

Paralleling the confirmation of my hypotheses about the presence of pathologies, I found as well evidence for successful coping. Many observations on the coping behavior of UNTAES go in line with academic recommendations on the adequate management of cognitive biases, principal agent problems, tight couplings, and path dependency.

For instance, cognitive biases were indeed coped with by acquiring experience and expertise (preparation for the JIC re-design), fluent communication within and by the organization (containment of international tensions and reduction of local mistrust), the sequencing of goal implementation (bridging of the gap between mandate and implementation), the creation of sufficient organizational slack (creating local revenues to pursue neglected economic reconstruction), and by vigilance. A vigilant attitude, defined as the thorough canvassing and balancing of alternatives, objectives and consequences while assimilating new information without bias,[900] helped the SRSG in giving up any sort of partisanship and deciding to have only genuine UN people in top positions. He thus reduced the risk of turf wars between US and other staff. Other approaches also helped in dealing with the cognitive bias pathology: efforts of cooperation and integration by means of hand-

900 Cf. Janis, Irving L. 1985. "Coping Patterns among Patients with Life-threatening Diseases." In: Charles D. Spielberger et al., eds., *Stress and Anxiety*, Vol. 9. The Series in Clinical and Community Psychology.

picking trustworthy locals and advancing civil society helped minimize the risk of non-commitment to the institutions to be.

Furthermore, I identified some advantages or basic capacities that turned out to be crucial for the invention and execution of "fit" coping across different issues. Giving coping strategies a second thought, one may note that apt coping can only occur if certain preconditions are in place. For UNTAES, these important preconditions were: clear end status, comprehensive support from member states and particularly from the United States and Australia, comprehensive authority including strong MoU on CivPol,[901] robustness,[902] abundant personnel,[903] abundant assessed budget, cooperation partnerships – particularly with NATO, but also with the UN family, particularly UNHCR, UNICEF, and WHO, the Council of Europe and the EU, the IMF and the Word Bank,[904] contact groups, bilateral agencies, e.g. JEN, ICRC, IOM, and international NGOs –, unity of command, and "good leadership." The latter is pivot as it is for the leader of a mission to coordinate the resources and the other governmental and non-governmental partners in the field, sustain the international support, seize the authority he is given by the mandate, and specify the latter's vagueness for the succeeding of the operation. In fact, "The success or failure of UN initiatives can rest on the SRSG's performance."[905]

From what could be observed in UNTAES, leadership was one of the crucial factors indeed. The leadership style and the persona of Klein have been described as proactive, charismatic, innovative and informed, as "getting the big picture" and being aware of the public image, of staff motivation.

---

901 The strong mandate was the basis for the Memorandum of Understanding on TPF, "which gave CivPol extensive rights to monitor and conduct investigations." Coleiro 2002, p. 100.
902 An observer to UNTAES' military robustness notes, "The military, in every mission, is critical. You don't even start any process before you have the military sites down and taken care of. UNTAES is a great example of how the military did a great job, and creating the environment for the civilian side to take over. And it's not always the case. UNTAES was able to achieve a huge and definitive military success and it eliminated all kinds of problems. Even though they're not the ones that in the end do transition, one cannot lose sight of the military." Interview with Dr. Christine Coleiro, UNITAR POCI, Washington, DC, 1 December 2006.
903 "It really made a difference that we – 6,000 people, including soldiers – were covering an area of maybe 2,600 square kilometres." Telephone interview with a field officer, UNTAES, 10 January 2007.
904 A special arrangement had been made with the World Bank since, normally, the Bank does not "do" regions.
905 Hooper, Rick and Taylor, Mark. 1999. *Command from the Saddle. Managing United Nations Peace-Building Missions. Recommendations Report of the Forum on the Special Representative of the Secretary General. Shaping the UN's Role in Peace Implementations.* Oslo: Fafo Institute for Applied Social Science, p. 29.

Proactiveness

Klein used to make a point of being on the go and as such promote an image of proactiveness, acting as a role model for his staff. For instance, he was constantly flying all over Europe, breezily playing his "ancestry card" with various governments, while sustaining his close contacts with NATO and Washington, too. These tightly knitted international contacts were the backbone of his daring "floor approach" to mandate implementation.[906]

Charisma

Klein has frequently been described as a charismatic SRSG. In the business, sociological, and political sciences literature, there is broad consensus to define *charismatic leadership* as a relationship between the leader and his/her followers that bases on specific leader behaviors on the one hand and favorable attributions made by the followers on the other.[907] According to Robert J. House and colleagues,[908] a charismatic leader acts as a role model, articulates an attractive vision of the future, shows determination and confidence, and exhibits high performance standards. As a result, followers are likely to perceive the leader as extraordinary and outstanding personality, attribute respect and strong admiration, and develop deep trust in both himself and his articulated vision.[909] Klein was working the mechanisms of both dimensions: he appeared charismatic by his very own personal traits and he was respected by his staff as well as by the local populace and leaders.

Innovation

Holding true for the SRSG as well as for the mission in general, an important asset for the success of UNTAES was its innovative drive. Particularly the mission leadership was going innovative ways in attracting voluntary funds, establishing various mechanisms and sources of on and off ground support.

---

906 As a prominent observer notes in a personal conversation, "There is gonna be more flexibility for the SRSG, for Jacques Klein, more willingness to be coercive, more credibility in terms of being threatening the use of forces." Personal conversation with Professor Stephen J. Stedman, political science professor at Stanford University and research director of the UN High-level Panel on Threats, Security and Change, Konstanz, 29 June 2006.

907 Cf. Gardner, W.L. and Avolio, B.J. 1998. "The Charismatic Relationship: A Dramaturgical Perspective." *Academy of Management Journal* 23, p. 32-58; The classic contribution to the issue is Max Weber's elaboration about the charismatic leader. Weber, Max. 1922. *Wirtschaft und Gesellschaft. Grundriss der verstehenden Soziologie.* Tübingen: Mohr, especially pp. 140-147.

908 Klein, K.J. and House, Robert J. 1995. "On fire: Charismatic leadership and levels of analysis." *Leadership Quarterly* 6, pp. 183-198; House, Robert J. 1977. "A 1976 Theory of Charismatic Leadership." In: J.G. Hund and L.L. Larson, eds., *Leadership: The Cutting Edge.* Carbondale: Southern Illinois University Press, pp. 189-207; Shamir, Boas et al. 1993. "The Motivational Effects of Charismatic Leadership." *Organization Science* 4:4, pp. 577-594.

909 Cf. Klein and House 1995.

236

Credibility

What made Klein particularly credible in the eyes of the local actors was his knowledge of the local situation. Klein would visit the place before the mission started and make a report about the local situation and his appraisal of it – which had not been a standard practice for SRSGs. Likewise, the way he immersed into the local customs and his toughness and determined impartiality in dealing with local leaders added to his status. In this regard, his links to NATO and to Washington and his perception, particularly by Tudjman and the Croats, as an American were fundamental for the way he executed the office of the SRSG.

Public Image Awareness

Klein seemed to be aware of the fact that his outer appearance may be important for being accepted by the locals. Thus, instead of wearing a chic diplomat suit, he showed up in a bomber jacket, melting in with the local population.

"Getting big picture" and Creating Synergies

In political science, there is the leadership-related concept of a political entrepreneur. Defined as an advocate to a specific cause, he or she is willing to invest resources – time, energy, reputation, financial resources – "in return for anticipated future gain in the form of material, purposive, or solidary benefits."[910] Such an entrepreneur is capable of linking available means and solutions to emerging problems and seizes windows of opportunity in order to match them. There is evidence that Klein – and his leadership team – are almost ideally fitting this concept as they were rather consistently trying to "get the big picture" and to create synergies by pursuing encompassing approaches and cross-cutting issues. It is said to be typical for the mission that successes like the one about the Djelatovci oilfield were immediately used to create credibility and to bring UNTAES in better negotiation positions. In this case, there was also the positive side-effect of generating cash money for reconstruction.

Motivation Skills

In managing his mission, Klein has been said to be a good role model, someone who by his own example animated his staff to work the extra hours and to invest the extra efforts. The UNTAES staff was said to be very motivated and proactive, literally taking people by their hands and accompanying them to offices. "Peacekeeping requires passion. It's not another job, peacekeeping can't be another job; it needs people that are highly motivated, with a burning desire to do good. And I think that's what it was in Eastern Slavonia. They felt they were part of it."[911]

---

910   Kingdon 1995, p. 179.
911   Interview with Dr. Christine Coleiro, UNITAR POCI, Washington, DC, 1 December 2006.

Learning Ability

Learning ability is a crucial feature of the textbook leader. With the non-risk-free restructuring initiative regarding the JIC process, Klein showed that he was adept for learning and willing to implement lessons learned. At the same time, a textbook leader should also promote the learning capability of the people around him. Under this aspect, too, the UNTAES leadership seemed to have acted just right. As a field staff officer remembers, "We had a good structure and a good leadership so that we were able to learn relatively quickly and adjust to new conditions."[912]

In sum, Klein's leadership style seems to coincide with many of the wishful traits of leading figures as stated by textbook literature on charismatic leaders. While charismatic leadership is the ideal type proposed for times of crisis and for complex organizations acting in dynamic environments – this describes nicely the context of a transitional administration – there are also "dark sides" to this kind of leader. In the first line,

> Highly charismatic leaders tend to overestimate their own abilities and have a rather self-centered attitude. Consequently, they may be less willing to see the viability of alternative approaches, neglect to regularly reflect on their organizational vision and objectives and thus miss out to timely adapt their vision to environmental changes. As a result, their organizational vision is more likely to become inappropriate and flawed, ultimately leading to reduced organizational performance.[913]

Second, teams led by highly charismatic and visionary leaders run the risk to fall into *group think*.[914] If this is the case, contrary viewpoints and doubts are not openly expressed within the group in order not to provoke disapproval and not to threaten the group atmosphere. Consequently, group decisions are likely to be of inferior quality.[915] Third, under highly charismatic leadership, followers may develop high levels of identification with and dependency on their leader, which might hinder their critical thinking processes.[916] "Hence, the single members of the respective top management team are less likely to question the leaders' vision and perspectives and providing him with diverging opinions. This missing feedback on the part of the followers might reinforce the negative effects of charismatic leaders' self-centrism."[917] Some of these negative traits seem to be reflected in the case of UNTAES indeed. Klein's overly determined and pushy leadership style – which often coincides with proactiveness and charisma – at times led to frictions with headquar-

---

912 Telephone interview with a field officer, UNTAES, 10 January 2007.
913 Eisenbeiß, Silke, "Thesen," unpublished document, on file with the author. See also Conger 1990.
914 Cf. Janis 1997; Conger 1999.
915 Cf. Janis 1997.
916 Cf. Kark, Shamir and Chen 2003; Kets de Vries 1988a.
917 Eisenbeiß, "Thesen."

ters, certain member states, or with cooperation partners in the field. In cases where such frictions culminate, the SRSG's dismissal becomes likely. In fact, there are narratives on the depositions of SRSGs that adopt this argument. Prominent cases include the suspension of Jan Pronk from the UN mission in Sudan after he was declared a *persona non grata* by the government of Sudan.[918] Another pitfall for leaders is the balance and the proper handling of private live and public duties. The maintenance of improper relationships can not only undermine the respect for the leader on part of his staff and on part of the locals, but it can also constitute a dangerous distraction from the work that needs to be done; he makes himself vulnerable, and on top of it all, accepts the risk of a security leak. There is evidence that this is what brought Jacques-Paul Klein to fall as SRSG in Liberia, revealed after the US had posted hundreds of highly confidential UN audits and investigations reports on a US government web site. According to the *Washington Post*,

> [The disclosure of the documents] shed light on some major UN mysteries, including the abrupt retirement of Jacques-Paul Klein, a former American diplomat who served as the U.N. special representative in Liberia until April 2005. A two-page document labelled 'strictly confidential' accuses Klein of an improper relationship with a local woman suspected of passing on secrets to Charles Taylor, the former Liberian president now on trial for war crimes. [...] Klein met Linda Fawaz, a 30-year-old Liberian-American woman whose uncle headed a major timber company. According to the report, Fawaz (identified as 'Local Woman') accompanied Klein (described as 'Senior Official') to diplomatic functions and regularly travelled on UN aircraft in violation of organizational rules. 'Senior Official has invited Local Woman to functions both with UNMIL staff and persons outside the UN, some of which have been of an official nature,' the report said. 'A number of staff interviewed by (U.N. investigators) expressed concern that the Local Woman was passing information which she had gathered from Senior Official to Mr. Taylor' and others.[919]

For Klein's tenure in Eastern Slavonia, no such stories have been told, but I make a point by striking that it is a crucial personality trait of a leader that he does not let his private affairs interfere with his duties and that he does not put the mission's integrity at stake by undermining it through personal misdemeanor.

In conclusion, UNTAES experienced various setbacks particularly in the form of principal-agent problems but did not allow the occurrence of virulent accidents. Being smart in the use of the advantages that they had at their disposal, the decision-makers in the transitional administration made up a range of useful coping strategies. They fell short, however, in establishing provisions that could have better served the long-term sustainability of their own achievements.

---

918 Cf., e.g., Osman, Mohamed, "Sudan Expels UN Envoy over Report of Losses in Darfur," *The Washington Post*, 23 October 2006, p. A13.
919 Lynch, Colum. 2008. "US Officials Divulge Reports on Confidential UN Audits", *The Washington Post*, 17 February 2008, p. 20.

V. Case Study on the United Nations Transitional Administration in East Timor

The second case study deals with the other relatively successful instance of a UN transitional administration. The UN operation in East Timor began a year and a half after the finalization of UNTAES. While the latter set out to reintegrate a region where there had been intense fighting into a greater entity, UNTAET's goal was to prepare the colonized and suppressed people of East Timor for independence of their newly created state. Governing the former Portuguese and Indonesian colony for an interim period of almost three years, the mission exercised executive and legislative authority and engaged particularly in institution-building. The most determined international drivers for a comprehensive engagement were Australia and Portugal, but the international community at large was supportive of the mission. Like UNTAES, UNTAET was a demonstration object. Maybe even more so than in Eastern Slavonia, the international community wanted to deploy a prestigious, successful mission. At the end of the day, the transition in East Timor could indeed be acclaimed as a relative success. The sustainability of UNTAET's performance, however, has been ambiguously discussed.

1. Background

East Timor's road to independence has been long, grievous, and traumatic. Previously colonized by the Dutch, Portuguese and Japanese, Indonesia invaded East Timor in 1975 and violently suppressed the populace for 25 years. Using the power of intimidation, and leaving 183,000 dead,[920] Indonesia exploited the East Timorese work force and the oil and gas resources of the East Timor Sea. In the course of the occupation, the majority of the Timorese population, which is ethnically and linguistically heterogeneous and spread over the mountainous island, was united behind the resistance movement and attempted to stand up to its tormentors. Yet, the international community remained silent. In fact, "World powers were accused of contributing to the subsequent calamity by turning a blind eye or by actively supporting the occupation by supplying weapons."[921]

---

920 Cf. East Timor Commission for Reception, Truth and Reconciliation, "Final Report." Available online at http://www.ictj.org/en/news/features/846.html, last access on 1 March 2009.
921 BBC, "Country profile: East Timor." Available online at http://news.bbc.co.uk/1/hi/world/asia-pacific/country_profiles/1508119.stm, last access on 1 March 2009.

1.1 Topography and History of the Region

The island of Timor is located at the Indonesian archipelago's eastern end, north-west of Australia. Colonial occupiers had split the island into West and East Timor.[922] Until September 1999, the island was a *de facto* province of the Republic of Indonesia.[923] Consisting of 15,007 square kilometres of mountainous territory, it is inhabited by a population of 1,067,000,[924] dominated by the Austronesian ethnicity.[925] Their largest sub-group of about 100,000 people are the Tetun or Tetum, who live primarily on the north coast and around Dili. The ethnic diversity evolved from the isolation of settlements due to the territory's geography and due to the poor infrastructure. Corresponding with the high ethnic diversity, various indigenous languages are spoken, with Tetum and its sub-dialects prevailing.[926]

> You have seven – some people say 30 – different languages spoken in this small country. Cultural differences arose because people have lived in isolation as transportation is so difficult. The biggest difference between the eastern area and the rest is that the language that is spoken here belongs to a completely different language family. It has no words in common; it's like the difference between Finish and German. East Timor has, for over thousand years, been sort of the edge where the two cultures, Asia and Indonesia,

---

922 East Timor also included the enclave of Oecusse (Ambeno) on the northwest portion of the island, and the islands of Pulau Atauro and Pulau Jaco. The districts are: Aileu, Ainaro, Baucau, Bobonaro, Cova-Lima, Dili, Ermera, Lautem, Liquica, Manatuto, Manufahi, Oecussi, and Viqueque. In 2002, the country has been named "Democratic Republic of Timor-Leste; for the remainder of the study, I will stick to the conventional term "East Timor".

923 Cf. figure 2. For details on the Indonesian institutional structures in East Timor 1975-1999 see Fox, James J. 2002. *East Timor: Assessing UNTAET's Role in Building Local Capacities for the Future.* Canberra: Council for Asia Europe Co-operation, pp. 2-6.

924 UN Department of Economic and Social Affairs, Population Division. 2007. *World Population Prospects: The 2006 Revision Population Database, UN Country Population Estimate of 2005.* Available online at http://esa.un.org/unpp/p2k0data.asp, last access on 1 March 2009. In the year 2000, the population estimate was as low as 819,000, marred with high uncertainty due to the unfavorable conditions for counting. Ibid.

925 They are also called Malayo-Polynesians. There are more than 270 million people belonging to the Austronesian speaking population, who inhabit Madagascar to the Easter Island, and from Taiwan to New Zealand. On Austronesian language history and anthropology, see e.g., Bellwood, Peter et al., eds. 2006. The *Austronesians. Historical and Comparative Perspectives.* Canberra: ANU E Press. Other groups living in East Timor consist of Papuans and a small Chinese minority. As of 2005 estimates, the overwhelming majority of the population adheres to the Roman Catholic faith (98 percent); one percent are Muslim, one percent Protestant. Cf. CIA World Fact Book, "Timor-Leste." Available online at https://www.cia.gov/library/publications/the-world-factbook/geos/tt.html, last access on 22 February 2009.
The official languages are Tetum and Portuguese, but English and Indonesian are also understood.

926 For an overview of the various language and ethnic groups in East Timor, see "The Joshua Project" by the US Centre for World Mission, which relies on 21 different data sources. It is available online at http://www.joshuaproject.net/countries.php?rog3=TT, last access on 1 March 2009.

overlap, long before the Europeans came. And some of these differences still exist, particularly in languages and customs.[927]

Portuguese and Bahasa Indonesia, the languages of the colonizers, are the other dominant languages in East Timor. Different languages have come along with social distinctions: the social cleavages that are most important today are those between *mestizos*,[928] i.e. the exiled Timorese-speaking Portuguese, who generally have a higher status in society; the Bahasa-speaking urban and younger people; and the indigenous Tetum and other dialect speakers who live in the island's rural areas.

The "modern" history of the island is characterized by foreign occupation.[929] The period of foreign rule began in the early 16th century when Portugal started trading with the island, and colonized it a couple of decades later. With the exclusion of two short interludes when East Timor was administered by the Dutch in the late 18th and early 19th century[930] and by Imperial Japan between 1942 and 1945,[931] East Timor was governed by Portugal as an overseas province until 1972. In the first few centuries of colonial occupation, Portugal exploited East Timor's natural resources and introduced the Portuguese language and Catholicism, but generally remained a "passive colonizer who did not invest much in the terri-

---

927 Interview with a representative of the Timor-Leste Institute for Reconstruction Monitoring and Analysis, New York, 27 November 2006.
928 "*Mestizos* people, who are of partly European ancestry, tend to disproportionally be in positions of authority. They are the people that the Portuguese gave land to. These are the rich families, like the Carrascalao family or the family of Ramos-Horta. They have land because their grandfathers came from Portugal. So, during the colonial time they were the upper class. And then their children were the ones who were more likely to get good education: the Portuguese only taught about 50 percent of the population. So, you have that division not just in government but in society in general: there is a disproportion of members of *mestizos* in influential positions while the number of *mestizos* in the population is probably less than 10 percent." Interview with a representative of the Timor-Leste Institute for Reconstruction Monitoring and Analysis, New York, 27 November 2006.
929 The "old" history of East Timor is marked by three waves of people coming into the country: Australoids, Melanesians, and 'Proto-Malays.' "Probably due to the mountainous nature of the country, these new arrivals did not mix with the former inhabitants, who withdrew to the interior mountainous regions." Government of Timor-Leste, "About Timor-Leste: History." Available online at http://www.timor-leste.gov.tl/AboutTimorleste/history.htm, last access on 1 March 2009.
930 "Skirmishing with the Dutch in the region eventually resulted in an 1859 treaty in which Portugal ceded the western portion of the island." CIA World Fact Book, "Timor-Leste."
931 "When World War II started, the Australians and the Dutch, aware of Timor's importance as a buffer zone, landed in Dili despite Portuguese protests. The Japanese then used the presence of the Australians as a pretext for an invasion in February 1942 and stayed until September 1945. By the end of the war Timor was in ruins. Approximately 50,000 Timorese had lost their lives as a result of Japanese occupation and the efforts of the Timorese to resist the invaders and protect Australia. People were also forced to give food to the Japanese, so when the Japanese finally surrendered the scene in Timor was one of human misery and devastation." Government of Timor-Leste, "About Timor-Leste: History."

tory."[932] In this period of neglect, the invaders did not severely penetrate the country and its socio-political structure. In the late 19th century, however, the Portuguese colonial approach changed from indirect to direct rule, and "in alliance with local chieftains, the Portuguese established an increasingly harsh regime of exploitation and *corvée* (forced) labor that by the turn of the twentieth century had swept up the entire able-bodied male population."[933] A grand, yet hopeless revolt for independence occurred from 1885 to 1912. The population's situation regressed from bad to worse when the Japanese landed on the island during World War II: their cruel occupation "spawned a resistance movement that resulted in the deaths of 60,000 Timorese or 13 percent of the entire population."[934] After war's end, Portugal retained control of the island, but the resistance against colonial rule intensified. In the decolonization context of the 1960s and 1970s, the Carnation Revolution in the Portuguese homeland eventually triggered the formation of the first independent East Timorese political organizations. That was in 1974.

1.2 Indonesian Occupation

The seeds of the conflict, which ultimately led to the international intervention and to the UN interim administration, were planted in the tumultuous years of 1974 and 1975. After East Timor's political dynamics unravelled in 1974, two diametrically opposed parties fought for dominance. The conservative Timorese Democratic Union (UDT) furthered the interests of the local elites, in the main being *mestizos* of Portuguese origin, who "supported continued association with Portugal within the context of a new federal association."[935] Fretilin, the *Frente Revolucionária do Timor-Leste Independente* (Revolutionary Front for an Independent East Timor), was a leftist party that promoted independence and was dominated by indigenous, rural people. An outburst of violence between the UDT and Fretilin, including the latter's military branch, Falintil (*Forças Armadas da Libertação Nacional de Timor-Leste*/Armed Forces of the National Liberation of East Timor), resulted in more than 2,000 deaths.[936] The victorious Fretilin quickly declared East Timor's independence on 28 November 1975. In those tumultuous times, independence did not last long: only nine days later, East Timor was invaded by Indonesian forces. Fretilin members had to escape, either seeking exile abroad, if they

---

932 Cf. Aid East Timor, "East Timor History and Activism." Available online at http://www.aideasttimor.org/history.html, last access on 1 March 2009.
933 Gendercide Watch, "Case Study East Timor (1975-1999)." Available online at http://www.gendercide.org/case_timor.html, last access on 10 July 2008.
934 Ibid.
935 Doyle and Sambanis 2006, p. 243.
936 Cf. Government of Timor-Leste, "About Timor-Leste: History."

had the financial means to do so, or retreating in the island's mountainous hideouts. The occupation proceeded with the assistance of former UDT supporters and under tacit international approval, most infamously by Portugal and the United States.[937] In 1976, *Timor Timur*, as the Indonesians came to call the region, was annexed as Indonesia's 27th province.[938] The mighty neighbor imposed a heavily militarized regime that was characterized by extreme violence.[939]

One of the most bizarre and gruesome [...] atrocities occurred within 24 hours of the invasion and involved the killing of about 150 people. This shocking spectacle began with the execution of more than 20 women who, from various accounts, were selected at random. [...] The women were led out to the edge of the jetty and shot one at a time, with the crowd of shocked onlookers being forced at gun-point to count [out] loud as each execution took place.[940]

Besides the violent acts of predation and discrimination, Indonesians exploited the East Timorese workforce at the bottom of the working chain, and systematically prevented them from seizing influential posts in the local administration as well as in the local economy. Except for pro-Indonesian co-operators, East Timorese could not assume most blue and virtually no white-collar positions. "The Indonesians took all the good jobs for themselves. Elementary-school teachers were Timorese, for example, but high-school teachers were Indonesian. Police clerks were Timorese, but the officers were Indonesian. East Timor was permitted neither a professional class nor a political one."[941] Another devastating statistic indicated that the

---

937 Cf. Doyle and Sambanis 2006, p. 244.
938 "According to Indonesian accounts, it was East Timor's elected government that made the decision to join Indonesia. Jakarta said its military response came at the behest of local leaders who needed outside assistance to quell internal violence. From there, the elected People's Assembly of East Timor reportedly submitted a resolution to Indonesia's House of Representatives asking to become a province. Foreign observers disagree, however, saying Indonesia forcibly steered East Timor into annexation. The United Nations and all western countries except Australia ignored the annexation altogether, and continued to recognize East Timor as a Portuguese possession. From either side, it is clear incorporation did not come easily." Barber, Greg. 2002. "East Timor: Under Indonesian Rule." *Online NewsHour April 2002.* Available online at http://www.pbs.org/newshour/bb/asia/july-dec99/timor_background.html, last access on 1 March 2009.
939 See, e.g., Anderson, Benedict. 1993. *Imagining East Timor.* Cepesa Working Papers. Lisbon: Cepesa.
940 Budiardjo, Carmel and Liem Soei, Liong. 1984. *War against East Timor.* London: Zed Books, pp. 128-129. The occupiers fortified their influence by the policy of *transmigrasi.* The term denoted a national relocation programme by which Indonesian President Suharto wanted to cope with the main islands' overpopulation while simultaneously controlling the population of annexed Timor. The policy was enacted in other occupied islands as well, such as the Molukkas or West Papua. Cf. Frey, Theo. 1999. "Ost-Timor: Teuflische Allianz." *Zeitschrift für Friedenspolitik* 5, p. 2.
941 Traub, James. 2000. "Inventing East Timor." *Foreign Affairs,* p. 2. "The development of East Timorese skills in the areas of administration and governance had been very limited during the years of Indonesian rule and the majority of the technical as well as senior and

244

population was 46 percent illiterate.[942] Indonesia had no interest in changing this.[943]

Faced with an oppressive Indonesian regime, Fretilin and its Falinitil phalanx launched a fierce resistance fight against Indonesian troops and pro-Jakarta militias. On another front, the Timorese exile diaspora started to raise international awareness: in 1982, the UN initiated talks on the situation in East Timor. However, nothing substantial happened. On the contrary, "Gradually, [...] the Indonesian army eliminated the resistance threat, reducing Fretilin from 27,000 to 5,000 people by 1978."[944] In 1987, there were only some 100 guerrillas left hiding in the mountains. It was not until 1998 that the East Timorese struggle for independence and cessation of the atrocities had a chance to succeed. In that year, former Indonesian president Suharto, who had previously resisted all efforts to find a political compromise, departed. His successor B. J. Habibie reopened negotiations, determined to resolve the issue of Timor-Leste for good.

Box 4: The East Timorese under Indonesian Occupation

"A particularly massive roundup of Timorese males was conducted as part of Operasi Keamanan ('Operation Security') in March/April 1981, when 'virtually the entire male population from the ages of 15 to 50 was pressed into service. In some places, boys as young as nine and men as old as 60 were ordered to join.' (Budiardjo and Liem, p. 41.). [...] 'The army marched into villages, ordered together all men and boys and took them to the region from which the [so-called] fence of legs was to begin. Once assembled, they were organized into small groups and forced to walk in front of units of soldiers, searching the countryside for Fretilin cadres. [...] Since they were forced to leave without any notice, they were unable to take with them supplies of food or clothing. Provided with the most meagre food rations, many died of starvation.' (East Timor: The Price of Freedom, p. 117.) Many thousands of Timorese, also overwhelmingly 'able-bodied' males, were rounded up for brutal torture and incarceration – although many younger women also suffered this fate, being exposed especially to sexual torture and rape. [...] Entire families of 'Fretilin suspects' were often annihilated together with the suspects themselves, or out of frustration at the Indonesian soldiers' inability to locate them. In many cases, whole village populations were targeted for savage atrocities."[945]

---

middle-level management positions in government had been occupied by Indonesian officials." UN Development Program. 2005. *Capacity-building Seminar.* Available online at *europeandcis.undp.org/files/uploads/CDF/Timor%20Leste-case%20study.doc*2005, last access on 15 March 2009.

942 Cf. Steele, Jonathan. 2002. "Nation Building in East Timor." *World Policy Journal* 19:2, p. 79. See also La'o Hamutuk. 2002. "East Timor Faces Post-UNTAET Challenges." *La'o Hamutuk Bulletin.* Available online at http://www.laohamutuk.org/Bulletin/2002/May/bulletinv3n4.html, last access on 5 March 2009; the latter source, however, indicates an illiteracy rate of 48 percent.

943 "The Indonesians invested quite a lot in infrastructure – but not much in political culture, and technical expertise," while the Portuguese had never invested much in the territory in the first place. Interview with a senior staff member of UNTAET, New York, 23 November 2006.

944 Doyle and Sambanis 2006, p. 244. See also Barber 2002.

945 Gendercide Watch, "Case Study East Timor (1975-1999)."

And on top of that, the "most destructive strategy of all was the starvation and heavy bombing inflicted on populations remaining in the 'liberated zones' outside the Indonesians' control, or in concentration camps set up, in classic counterinsurgency fashion, to separate the Fretilin guerrillas from their 'base of support.'"[946] In addition to general warfare, the Indonesian occupation was marked by frequent outbursts of extreme violence and brutality, the most prominent and woeful examples being the 1981 Aitana massacre where "[t]hey murdered everyone, from tiny babies to the elderly, unarmed people who were not involved in the fighting but were there simply because they had stayed with Fretilin and wanted to live freely in the mountains;"[947] the massacre of 1983 at Malim Luro, where Indonesian troops "after plundering the population of all "their belongings, firmly tied up men, women and children, [...] made them lie on-the-ground and then drove a bulldozer over them, and then used it to place a few centimetres of earth on top of the totally crushed corpses";[948] the 1999 Liquiçá Church Massacre, where an unconfirmed number of 200 were shot; and the 1991 Dili Massacre. The latter was committed at a cemetery where Indonesian troops murdered 270 mourners. It was a pivotal event since it triggered attention from the international community.[949] In the years of Indonesian occupation, an estimated 100,000 to 250,000 individuals lost their lives.[950]

1.3 Excursus: The Socio-Political System of East Timor

In East Timor, the traditional socio-economic order is still very significant, but it has become penetrated by administrative principles introduced by the Portuguese and the Indonesians, and supplemented by the structures and principles established by the resistance movement.

The consuetudinary East Timorese society is structured hierarchically, ordered by rules of kinship and marriage. The basic unit is a "House," i.e. a group of people "connected through 'blood relations,' who make up a lineage or extended family."[951] The Houses, in turn, are connected by an elaborate system of marriages. "New marriage relations between Houses are used to create a peaceful connection (for example, after war)."[952] A number of more or less coherently geographically located Houses form a strict hierarchically structured kingdom, headed by the king, the *liurai*.

Within the hierarchical order of Houses, a distribution of tasks and responsibilities exists. The oldest House, with its close connection to the land and the first ancestors,

---

946 Ibid.
947 Ibid.
948 Ibid.
949 In fact, the massacre was videotaped and spread around the world. See, e.g., Global Policy Forum, "East Timor Action Network: Justice Call on East Timor Massacre Anniversary." Available online at http://www.globalpolicy.org/intljustice/tribunals/timor/2005/0406justicecall.htm, last access on 1 March 2009; East Timor Action Network, "The Santa Cruz Massacre: November 12, 1991." Available online at http://www.etan.org/timor/SntaCRUZ.htm, last access on 1 March 2009.
950 See, e.g., the Reports by the Commission for Reception, Truth and Reconciliation in East Timor. Available online at http://www.easttimor-reconciliation.org/Documents.htm, last access on 1 March 2009.
951 Hohe, Tanja. 2002b. "The Clash of Paradigms: International Administration and Local Political Legitimacy in East Timor." *Contemporary Southeast Asia* 24:3, pp. 569-589, p. 571.
952 Ibid.

is responsible for fertility. [...] The first House, therefore, holds ritual power and plays the most crucial role in all ceremonial activities. In opposition to these ritual tasks stand political issues. The second, or one of the Houses lower in the hierarchy, thus provides the king or the political head of a settlement. The political authorities are responsible for defining the border of the land, for relations with other kingdoms, for conflict resolution, and all other political issues, such as conducting wars.[953]

Social anthropologist Tanja Hohe draws two conclusions from these habits. The first is the division between ritual and political tasks with the former having a dominant role and higher standing. The second is that where a leader comes from is more important than what he does or what his personal characteristics are. Hence, a political leader must derive his legitimacy through an ancestral agreement.

> If a political leader is not ancestrally legitimized (appointed by the ritual leaders), the population will suffer from ancestral punishment [...]. If a House cannot provide a political ruler, the ritual leaders have to find another House as a substitute. In a ceremony, political power is then handed over (mostly symbolized in a stick as an insignia of political rule) to the new House Ancestrally legitimized, the new House can exert political power without society having to fear ancestral punishment.[954]

The legitimized leader has the unitary support of the *whole* kingdom. This means that the persistent co-existence of multiple opinions or of peacefully opposing candidates, as is used in democratic systems, is not part of the way East Timorese people think. "Opposed elements must be in a hostile/violent relationship with one another or they must be reconciled in a blood or marriage tie,"[955] thus creating unity. In East Timorese perceptions, unity is the ideal. Similarly, decision-making is characterized by constant discussion and by reaching a consensus that everyone can agree to. "In this way no-one 'loses face.' The powerless people accept the result and do not question it."[956] The exception from the ubiquitous *ancestral* worshipping consists of the warrior cult, which strongly developed during the resistance fight under Indonesian occupation. "The backgrounds of the clandestine leaders reveal that the population, in their work and deeds, mostly trusted them. Here, another traditional idea of 'capacity as a warrior' comes into play. The character of the person was emphasized."[957]

How did the former occupiers, the Portuguese and the Indonesians, deal with these structures and principles? In the 19th century's second half, the Portuguese imposed an increasingly comprehensive administration. The country was divided into eleven districts, and a Portuguese commander "with civilian and military tasks,

---

953 Ibid. p. 573. "The legitimization for certain tasks derives from the 'old mythical times' when the ancestors created and ordered society." Ibid., p. 572.
954 Ibid., p. 573.
955 Cf. Hohe, Tanja. 2002a. "Totem Polls: Indigenous Concepts and 'Free and Fair' Elections in East Timor." *International Peacekeeping* 9:4, pp. 69-88.
956 Ibid., p. 82.
957 Hohe 2002b, p. 579. However, the "right" ancestral background remains a precondition.

and a small number of soldiers"[958] was put at the top of each. The internal societal structures were not yet affected, but became ever more co-opted. For instance, the head-tax system stopped the direct tributes from the population to the kings and lined the Portugueses' pockets. The kings, in turn, were paid by the Portuguese. As a result, the Portuguese positioned themselves between the population and the kings. Over time, it became obligatory to have a new king approved by the colonial administration, and eventually, the traditional power structures were officially abandoned.

> Districts were then divided into sub-districts (*posto*), and these again into villages (*suco*) and hamlets (*povação*). The Portuguese now appointed local village chiefs (*chefe de suco*) and hamlet chiefs (*chefe de povação*) and used them as their link to the local population at the sub-district level. In some cases, the sub-district covered the former area of a kingdom, in others they differed. The sub-district chiefs worked right down to the village chiefs. These had to be literate and speak Portuguese. Every week they would come to the sub-district to receive their orders from the colonial government regarding conduct and work in the villages and pass them on to their population. They were held responsible for their communities. The village chief was now called *liurai* in some areas. The hamlet chiefs were active at the lowest level. They collected and passed on the taxes in their respective hamlets and had to watch the workers to make sure they were working well.[959]

In some cases, the former kings were transformed into sub-district or village chiefs, while in other instances, the Portuguese *imposed* leaders that they had hand-picked. Informally, however, the traditional authorities were still adhered to. Possibly due to the Timorese ideal of unity,[960] the two systems were not working against each other or contradicted each other, but a parallel power structure was maintained. As the Portuguese learned how to co-opt the structures, they used them for their own good, particularly by taking advantage of marriage rules, "Through this strategy, some of the kings were tied into such strong relationships with the Portuguese that they had to help the Portuguese fight against other kings."[961] Importantly, "Under Portuguese rule, the concepts of descent and customary law, conduct of ceremonies or the position of ritual authorities were never challenged. Ritual life remained

---

958 Ibid., p. 573.
959 Ibid., pp. 573-574, italics from the original text.
960 "The important thing was that village chiefs and hamlet chiefs originated from the 'right' royal Houses and therefore had ancestral legitimization for their role. If new appointees were from the 'wrong' Houses, there was a way to ritually pass on the political authority to another family. If the person was from a 'commoner' family, the appointment would cause conflicts. In contrast, a person from another area who was still of 'royal' origin was still acceptable. In some areas, the Portuguese rulers let it up to the local leadership to appoint a person. In these cases, the ritual leadership chose the person of the right descent." Ibid., pp. 574-575. It was also important that this happened in an "appropriate ceremony."
961 Ibid., p. 575.

strong, as it was perceived to be the 'inside' of society, and had nothing to do with 'outside' political issues."[962]

Similarly, the Indonesians also tried to instrumentalize the local system in order to impose their rules. However, the social system they introduced was somewhat different from the integrated administrative structure that the Portuguese had established.

> At the sub-district level, the government was composed of a centrally-appointed sub-district chief and other administrative officers in charge of civil administration, personnel, welfare, rural development, finance, and village offices. Like the Portuguese, the Indonesians had an interest in finding loyal people for these positions. Nevertheless, they tried to make use of the local system to receive local recognition of official positions. This led to a diverse picture. In some cases, former kings were appointed for the position (even better if they were pro-Indonesian), or persons from 'royal' families who seemed loyal to the government were brought in from other districts. The local population often claimed that their ritual authorities were still involved in the appointments. The space that ritual leadership was given depended on how much resistance the governmental authorities faced in a specific area. If former leaders were replaced, they often still held informal power and acted in conflict resolution. Nevertheless, most people state that the Indonesians did not honour the kings and village chiefs any longer.[963]

In the villages, the traditional structures and principles remained valid, and the Timorese developed their own strategies for bringing the Indonesian approach in accordance with their own customs.[964] The establishment of a clandestine system of resistance during the Indonesian occupation, whose structures are still working today, is important to understand the more recent developments in East Timor. The main actors within the resistance were Fretilin and its military wing, Falintil. After

---

962 Ibid.
963 Hohe 2002b, p. 576.
964 "After [discussion and reaching of consensus on a candidate; ES], the people voted in the 'democratic' elections for the 'right' person. In their perception, the '*liurai* now became the village chief.' [...] The Indonesian Government and the armed forces then adjusted the election results to their own interests. In some of the politically sensitive areas, the Indonesian Government and the military are said to have put the village chiefs of their own choice in place. If this was the 'wrong' person according to the local perception, there were several local coping mechanisms. The elders could excuse a change in power by claiming that people 'just voted like that,' because they did not know who was the right person to be the village chief. However, the elders feared ancestral sanctions if the 'wrong' person sat on the *cadera manas* (hot chair). To avoid misfortune, the former leader had to keep his position in ritual functions. The new leader had to be ritually legitimized by the 'royal' family by entering their sacred House and asking the proper king for permission to rule on his behalf. The descendants of the 'royal' House would then pass on the rattan stick and appoint the member from the new family as their representative. [...] Nevertheless, these village chiefs did not enjoy much trust from their community. They needed the official governmental power behind them to exert their power. The population in these cases would explain that they were only 'transitional.'" Ibid., pp. 576-577. For the hamlet level, Hohe notes that the appointments here were even more traditional "since government interference here was not strong." Ibid., p. 577.

the extinction of Fretilin in late 1978, when most remaining "members of Fretilin's Central Committee [...] had fled overseas,"[965] the resistance of East Timor gathered under the clandestine umbrella of the CNRT, the National Council of Timorese resistance.[966]

> The resistance was organized in three parts: as a military front (Falintil), an internal clandestine structure, and a political and diplomatic front that operated from outside the country. [...] Through the clandestine structure, a large number of people supported Falintil and its struggle for independence after successful socialization. Falintil commanders were powerful and respected leaders in their communities. They set up a clandestine parallel system of governance to support the resistance fight. This network of key individual was composed of the head of the village (*nurep*) and the hamlet leader (*celcom*). Their main tasks were to organize the population to support the resistance fighters and to establish an information system for the population. [...] The designation of the clandestine 'power-holders' by Falintil at the local level was organized through a consultation process with community members. It took into account the relationship of the potential candidate with the population, his work performance, and particularly his trustworthiness. [...] How many *nureps* were actually from 'royal' families is another point. In many cases, the 'Indonesian' village chief filled the 'politically' classified positions in the village or hamlet anyway. Hence, on the political level, everything was in accordance with traditional requirements. Nevertheless, in some cases, the *nurep* was also from a 'political family' (for example, his older brother might be the village chief).[967]

The intertwined structure of traditional principles and resistance hierarchies was the one that UNTAET encountered when it arrived in the country. "Right after the Indonesians left there was only one power structure, which actually presented an ideal scenario for UNTAET."[968] The UN's presence was also favored by the high profile, yet moderate and cooperative, East Timorese integration figures, particu-

---

965 CNRT, "The History of CNRT." Available online at www.cnrt-timor.org/about/history/php, last access on 2 March 2009. CNRT is the organizations's latest name. From 1988 to 1998, the organization called itself Conselho Nacional de Resistência Maubere (CNRM).

966 For an exhaustive description of the CNRT and the parties of East Timor, see Walsh, Pat. 2001. *East Timor's Political Parties and Groupings*. Briefing Notes, Australian Council for Overseas Aid.

967 Hohe 2002b, pp. 578-579. "The clandestine movement during the occupation supported Falintil not as traditional political authorities but more in their capacity of warriors. "Even nowadays, Falintil fighters without a 'royal' background are honoured and respected by the traditional elders, but they deny them a position as political leaders. On the other hand, famous warriors with the appropriate family background can be expected to become the new political leaders of the country." Ibid.

968 Written interview with Dr. Tanja Hohe, former team member of UN Volunteers in East Timor, 30 September 2006. Dr. Hohe is a social anthropologist and author of "The Clash of Paradigms: International Administration and Local Political Legitimacy in East Timor" and "Totem Polls: Indigenous Concepts and 'Free and Fair' Elections in East Timor." Cf. "Bibliography.".

larly national hero and independence fighter Kay Rala, "Xanana,"[969] Gusmão, and Nobel Laureates Bishop Carlos Belo and José Ramos Horta.[970]

1.4 Summary and Assessment

"According to the 1999 GDP index, East Timor has the lowest ranking in Asia and was on par with Rwanda."[971] The unfavorable geographic location of the country as one of the driest regions in Southeast Asia and the heavy seasonal variations in rainfall contributed to this situation.[972] The other part was structurally induced: as a long-neglected and then suppressed Portuguese colony, East Timor had to struggle with a rudimentary logistical, economic, financial, and administrative infras-

---

969 His given name was José Alexandre. Gusmão's nick name is said to be derived from Sha Na Na, a 1970s American rock'n'roll band. Cf. Jolly, Joanna. 2002. "Ex-Guerilla leader wins East Timor presidency." *Milwaukee Journal Sentinel*, 17 April 2002. Available online at http://findarticles.com/p/articles/mi_qn4196/is_20020417/ai_n10777952, last access on 1 March 2009.

970 Belo and Ramos-Horta were awarded the Nobel Peace Prize in 1996 "for their work towards a just and peaceful solution to the conflict in East Timor", as the official press release announced. It continued, "Carlos Belo, bishop of East Timor, has been the foremost representative of the people of East Timor. At the risk of his own life, he has tried to protect his people from infringements by those in power. In his efforts to create a just settlement based on his people's right to self-determination, he has been a constant spokesman for non-violence and dialogue with the Indonesian authorities. Ramos-Horta has been the leading international spokesman for East Timor's cause since 1975. Recently, he has made a significant contribution through the 'reconciliation talks' and by working out a peace plan for the region." Official Website of the Nobel Foundation, "Peace Prize." Available online at http://nobelprize.org/nobel_prizes/peace/laureates/1996/press.html, last access on 22 February 2009.

971 Dobbins et al. 2005, p. 155. The index uses a combination of indicators on life expectancy, levels of education, and standards of living. See also Traub 2002, p. 2. East Timor's income per capita was around $300 and hence well below of most comparable Caribbean nations and small Pacific islands. Cf. Hill, Hal and Saldanha, Joao M. 2001. "The Key Issues." In: ibid., eds., *East Timor: Development Challenges for the World's Newest Nation*. Singapore: ISEAS, pp. 3-36, p. 3. And even worse, the situation is not likely to change soon, even with massive assistance from abroad, "Even with very rapid growth, of (say) 5 percent per capita GDP, it would take 12 years to catch up to Indonesia's current (and very depressed) level of GDP per capita and 53 years to Malaysia. Slower growth, of 2 percent per capita – higher than most of Timor's usual comparators – would stretch these periods to 55 and 131 years respectively." Hill and Saldanha 2001, p. 34. However, "Although East Timor remained Indonesia's poorest province the decrease in illiteracy rates from more than 90 percent in 1974 to approximately 46 percent in 1999 reveals an improvement in the standard of living as compared to the period under Portuguese rule." Doyle and Sambanis 2006, p. 244, drawing on Steele 2002 and Smith, Michael G. and Dee, Moreen. 2003. *Peacekeeping in East Timor: The Path to Independence*. Boulder: Lynne Rienner.

972 Cf. Booth, Anne. 2001. "Poverty, Equity and Living Standards in East Timor: Challenges for the New Nation." In: Hal Hill and Joao M. Saldanha, eds., *East Timor: Development Challenges for the World's Newest Nation*. Singapore: ISEAS, pp. 241-255, p. 252.

tructure,[973] and a devastating situation in terms of human capacity. The situation did not improve under Indonesian rule. When the occupation began in 1974/75, a large part of the literate population fled the island.[974] Apart from physical occupation, Indonesia prohibited the Timorese from education and access to higher-level positions; the great majority of the people worked in the low-profit yielding agricultural sector.[975]

As result, there were no local East Timor capacities, at least from what would be required from a Western perspective, to run the civil service, the judiciary, the police, or the health system in the independent state-to-come.[976] The same holds true for economic and commercial expertise, which are likewise important for quick economic reconstruction.

Furthermore, East Timor had no experience running a state, not to mention running a state democratically, "from which the UN administration [...] could have benefited."[977] This being said, the intricate socio-political system was both a challenge and an opportunity: there were multiple layers of principles and structures, all of which were closely intertwined and certainly unfamiliar with Western views on society and politics. At the same time, there were no rivalling structures, and the existing one offered potential starting points (*Anknüpfungspunkte*) for the international government. Besides, powerful and well-meaning leaders were ready to take on responsibility.

2. Negotiations, Mandate, and Planning for the Transitional Administration

The UN Administration in East Timor was based on a peace agreement between Indonesia and Portugal, supervised and mediated by the UN who had been active in the region for almost forty years and who had supported the cause of the East Timorese. The peace agreement provided for a popular consultation on integration

---

973 "Timor-Leste remained largely underdeveloped with an economy based on barter. Prior to World War II, the capital, Dili, had no electricity or water supply and there were few roads." Government of Timor-Leste, "About Timor-Leste." See also Garrison, Randall. 2005. *The Role of Constitution-Building Processes in Democratization*. Paper prepared for IDEA's Democracy and Conflict Management Programme. Stockholm: International Institute for Democracy and Electoral Assistance (IDEA), p. 11.
974 Cf. Hill and Saldanha 2001, p. 3.
975 "[A] combination of small average landholding sizes, low productivity per hectare and a dearth of off-farm employment opportunities meant that farm household incomes were very low." Booth 2001, p. 248.
976 Cf. Garrison 2005. "Timor-Leste found itself a society [...] that lacked indigenous skills and training in all areas essential to democracy and development. It faced independence as a nation bereft of entrepreneurial, technical, medical, educational, and administrative skills and experience." Cf. ibid., p. 6.
977 Croissant 2006, p. 6.

into Indonesia or independence after an UN-supervised transitional period. In what became a most ferocious retaliation, the pro-independence vote was met by Indonesian mass murder and burning of East Timor. The courageous and, in fact, non-rule conform actions of the UN staff in the country, the ones who had organized the referendum, could prevent an even greater humanitarian catastrophe. Eventually, an international peacekeeping force under Australian leadership could halt the mayhem, paving the way for UNTAET. Meanwhile, however, the UN's initial strategy of joint Indonesian-Timorese reconstruction had become obsolete and planners were under great pressure to craft suitable strategy and design. The ubiquitous time pressure triggered some unfortunate decisions.

2.1 UN Engagement for East Timor prior to 1999

The UN started dealing with East Timor in 1960 when the General Assembly put "Timor and dependencies" on its list of non-self-governing territories.[978] When in 1974, after Portuguese withdrawal and Indonesian occupation, civil war broke out, the UN Department of Political Affairs got more directly involved in the territory, and thus, in the resistance movement that was comprised under the umbrella organization CNRT. Not recognizing Indonesian authority of the region and claiming the status of a non-self-governing territory for East Timor, the UN Secretary-General started to concern himself with the region.[979] A major benchmark was set in 1982, when instead of passing the usual annual resolution calling on Indonesia to withdraw, "The General Assembly asked the Secretary-General to 'initiate consultations with all parties directly concerned.'"[980] Without much practical effect, as one should add. Still, since then, successive Secretary-Generals of the UN have engaged in talks with Indonesia and Portugal to try to resolve the region's status. The talks intensified in 1994, sadly triggered by reports of mass killings. A real opportunity for change eventually ensued with the collapse of the Suharto regime in Indonesia in 1998.[981]

---

978 UN Department of Public Information. 2000. *The United Nations and East Timor. Self-determination through Popular Consultation.* New York: United Nations, p. 62.

979 Under Chapter XI, Art. 73 (e) of the Charta of the UN.

980 Suhrke 2001, p. 3. Suhrke refers to UN Doc. A/37/30, the International Civil Service Commission Annual Report of 1982 – and not to A/37/39 as referred to in the article. In sum, the General Assembly had passed eight resolutions asking Indonesia to withdraw; without any effect though.

981 "It was the culmination of years of grassroots efforts, violent militia clashes and international diplomatic pressure on Indonesia to allow East Timor to choose its own destiny after decades as one of the vast archipelago's most unwilling member territories." Barber 2002. On the UN's policy in East Timor, there are also critical voices, "For 24 years the UN did essentially nothing. Occasionally, they passed resolutions: the General Assembly passed eight resolutions asking Indonesia to withdraw, the Security Council passed two, various

2.2 Negotiations to Reach the 5th May Agreement

In early 1999, Indonesia announced that it would reconsider East Timor's demands, including the possibility on independence,[982] which triggered a process that resulted in official negotiations between Indonesia, Portugal, and the UN over a peace agreement and over the further status of East Timor.

Under UN leadership, Indonesia and the *de jure* sovereign Portugal engaged in talks about an arrangement for East Timor. The East Timorese themselves were not officially involved in the negotiations. "Given strong opposition in the Indonesian military to relinquishing the territory, attempts to include the Timorese would probably have derailed the talks."[983] This being said, at least they were given the opportunity to utter their voice informally as the president of the CNRT, Gusmão, and the likewise prominent independence fighter Ramos-Horta, communicated closely with the Portuguese as well as with the UN delegation.[984]

On 5 May, an agreement was signed.[985] It entrusted the Secretary-General with organizing and conducting a popular consultation to ascertain whether the East Timorese people accepted or rejected special autonomy for East Timor within the unitary Republic of Indonesia. It further specified that the rejection of the autonomy package would lead to a UN administration pending a transition for the territory to independence.[986]

> The prominence of the UN reflected the existence of partial and conflicting authority claims: Indonesia had *de facto* but not *de jure* control, Portugal had *de jure* authority but none *de facto*, and the East Timorese independence movement, *Conselho National da Resistencia Timorense* (CNRT), had a wide international solidarity network and a

Secretary-Generals tried to negotiate – but not really that seriously." Interview with a representative of the Timor-Leste Institute for Reconstruction Monitoring and Analysis, New York, 27 November 2006.

982   The reason why Habibie took this step is unknown. What is known, however, is that, first, Indonesia suffered extremely from the Asian financial crisis of 1997-98 and was becoming increasingly dependent upon international debt relief and financial help, and, second, that with the Nobel Prize awarded to independence fighters Ramos-Horta and Bishop Belo in 1996, the international pressure grew for Indonesia to change its oppressive policy and violations of human rights in East Timor. It seems likely that the trade-off between holding on to the economically unprofitable and hard-to-reach island of East Timor and resisting the international pressure no longer paid off and that the new government appeared a diplomatic problem that eventually should be gotten rid of. Cf. Doyle and Sambanis 2006, pp. 255-256.

983   Suhrke 2001, p. 4.

984   Cf. Suhrke 2001, p. 4. The delegation was staffed mainly by DPA personnel.

985   Cf. UN Secretary-General, "Report of the Secretary-General on East Timor," UN Doc. S/1999/513, 5 May 1999.

986   Cf. Martin, Ian. 2001. "Self-Determination in East Timor: The United Nations, the Ballot and International Intervention." *Contemporary Southeast Asia* 22:1, pp. 8-20; Cotton, James. 2000. "The Emergence of an Independent East Timor: National and Regional Challenges." *Contemporary Southeast Asia* 22:1, pp. 2-6.

Nobel Prize winner among its leaders, but no formal international standing and only a one-man lobby at the UN. Between these claims the UN appeared as an impartial broker to carry out the referendum.[987]

The popular consultation was scheduled for 8 August 1999 and was supervised and monitored by the UN. In case of a vote for independence, the agreements provided for an interim period in which a UN transitional administration should prepare the Timorese for building a new state.[988]

2.3 Referendum and Renewed Outbursts of Violence

Following up on the peace agreement, the UN deployed the United Nations Mission in East Timor (UNAMET) in order to organize the referendum, which eventually paved the way for independence. Somewhat unexpectedly, Election Day passed peacefully; but even more unexpectedly, it was followed by unprecedented violence. All hell broke out over the following three weeks in East Timor. In an unusually quick fashion, an international peacekeeping force was mandated and deployed. At the end of the day, the Australian-led International Force for East Timor (INTERFET) was capable of getting the situation under control, witnessing the fleeing of hundreds of Indonesians and pro-Indonesian militias. Two days after the agreement took effect, the Council adopted resolution 1236 (1999), welcoming the 5 May Agreements and the proposed United Nations involvement. In order to carry out the consultation, the Security Council set up UNAMET. On 11 June 1999,[989] Resolution 1246 established the mission and approved the modalities for the consultation, "a direct, secret, and universal ballot, to decide whether the East Timorese wished to accept special autonomy within Indonesia, or reject such autonomy, leading to East Timor's separation from Indonesia."[990]

---

987 Suhrke 2001, p. 3.
988 The agreement is available online on the East Timor and Indonesia Action Network site. East Timor and Indonesia Action Network, "Agreement between the Republic of Indonesia and the Portuguese Republic on the Question of East Timor." Available online at http://www.etan.org/etun/agreemnt.htm, last access on 2 March 2009.
989 For an account on the prominent problems, see Martin 2001, pp. 21-54. See also UN Secretary-General, "Report of the Secretary-General on East Timor," UN Doc. S/1999/803, 20 July 1999 and ibid., "Report of the Secretary-General on East Timor," UN Doc. S/1999/862, 9 August 1999. The original deadline was August 31, 1999.
990 UN Security Council, "Conflicts in Kosovo, Sierra Leone and Angola, Question of East Timor Key Elements of Security Council's Work for 1999," Press Release, UN Doc. SC/6784, 18 January 2000. "That resolution also stressed the Indonesian Government's responsibility to maintain peace and security in East Timor and to insure the integrity of the consultation and the security of international staff and observers. All acts of violence were condemned." Ibid. The mission's duration got extended two ties, eventually until November

Indonesia was put in charge of referendum security – a decision that incurred the resentment of the East Timorese and many observers, since that very same military that had suppressed the people of East Timor for 24 years. "If they had been consistent with their decisions, they would have said that there shouldn't be any Indonesian troops here, there shouldn't be any Indonesian police here, and that they will come in with UN personnel to take care of security."[991] And indeed, the Indonesian troops did not seem to take their engagement too seriously, prompting a rebuke by the president of the Security Council.[992]

On 30 August 1999, about 98 percent of the East Timorese registered with UN-AMET and voted in the popular consultation. "On September 4, 1999, anxious Timorese gathered around their television sets and radios to hear Ian Martin, the head of the UN elections mission, read the results. Many wept joyously when the local radio and television reporters translated Martin's announcement: 78.5 percent of Timorese had voted for independence,"[993] and thus, for an UN-operated interim administration.

Election Day passed by relatively peacefully,[994] but it turned out to be the quiet before the storm. Following the announcement of the results and the implementation assignments, hell broke out in East Timor. "Within an hour of the announcement of the results, the sound of gunfire and screams abruptly halted Timorese celebrations."[995] Over three weeks, the situation deteriorated completely. Pro-Indonesian militias looted and burnt houses and attacked, killed, and forcibly displaced large numbers of the population.[996] "The actions were calculated to destroy

---

30. Security Council Resolution on the Situation in East Timor, UN Doc. S/RES/1262 (1999), 27 August 1999 furthermore authorized an expansion of UNAMET's civilian police component to 460, and its military liaison component to 300 personnel, in anticipation of the post-consultation phase of the operation.

991 Interview with a representative of the Timor-Leste Institute for Reconstruction Monitoring and Analysis, New York, 27 November 2006.

992 Following an attack on a UNAMET regional office on 29 June, another presidential statement was issued by the Council stressing Indonesia's responsibility for maintaining peace and security in East Timor. Furthermore, "It endorsed the Secretary-General's decision not to begin the operational phase until UNAMET was fully deployed, and his decision to postpone the ballot date for two weeks beyond the 8 August date." Ibid.

993 Power, Samantha. 2008. *The Man for Dark Times. Sergio Vieira de Mello and the Fight to Save the World.* New York: Penguin Press, p. 287.

994 This was, however, with the woeful exception one East Timorese UN employee who was stabbed in the western town of Ermera. Cf. Barber 2002.

995 Power 2008, p. 287.

996 "A preliminary United Nations inter-agency assessment of the humanitarian situation in East Timor [...] estimates that, of the total pre-ballot population of 890,000, over 500,000 people have been displaced by the recent violence, including some 150,000 to western Timor." UN Secretary-General, "Report of the Secretary General on the United Nations Transitional Administration in East Timor," UN Doc. S/1999/1024, 4 October 1999, para.

Timor's survival."[997] Approximately 1,200 civilians were murdered, three quarters of the population displaced, and "anything of value"[998] destroyed.[999]

The main logistical infrastructure – transport, water, power, telecommunication, and housing – was heavily damaged,[1000] the financial system had cracked,[1001] and public administration was factually non-existent, "In the wake of the post-ballot violence, the civil administration in East Timor was no longer functioning [...] and essential services were on the brink of collapse."[1002] The Secretary-General noted in his report that large parts of the Indonesian military and police forces were involved in the violence.[1003] He condemned, "The Indonesian authorities were either unwilling or unable to provide the proper environment for the peaceful implemen-

19. See also Dobbins et al. 2005, pp. 155-156, "The violence that followed the [...] referendum displaced close to 90 percent of East Timor's total population of 967,000. Approximately 265,000 East Timorese became refugees, and 500,000 East Timorese escaped to the interior of the island. Roughly 265,000 refugees were transported under Indonesian and militia control to West Timor and neighboring islands in ships and trucks."

997 Power 2008, p. 288.
998 Doyle and Sambanis 2006, p. 248.
999 "Between the referendum and the arrival of a multinational peacekeeping force in late September 1999, anti-independence Timorese militias – organized and supported by the Indonesian military – commenced a large-scale, scorched-earth campaign of retribution. The militias killed approximately 1,300 Timorese and forcibly pushed 300,000 people into West Timor as refugees. The majority of the country's infrastructure, including homes, irrigation systems, water supply systems, and schools, and nearly 100 percent of the country's electrical grid were destroyed." CIA World Fact Book, "Timor-Leste." "Following ballot day the security situation in East Timor deteriorated, and after the announcement of the results there was an eruption of violence, as has been well documented. Pro-integration militias conducted organized, coordinated operations through population centres, ransacking towns and forcibly displacing hundreds of thousands of East Timorese to the hinterlands and to West Timor. There were consistent reports, from UN staff, credible international observer groups and the media, of the direct involvement of TNI and police personnel in this campaign. UNAMET was forced to evacuate all of its offices except for Dili headquarters, where the remaining staff were besieged along with some 2,000 East Timorese who had taken refuge there." UN General Assembly, "Question of East Timor: Progress Report of the Secretary-General," UN Doc. A/37/30, 13 December 1999, especially para. 32.
1000 During the Indonesian occupation, "only 48 percent of all households had access to clean water and only 38 percent to sanitation." The situation worsened after 'Operation Clean Sweep' as "[t]hree quarters of all clinics, hospitals, and doctor's offices in East Timor were damaged, senior medical staff evacuated the island, and most medicines and medical equipment were looted or destroyed [and] telecommunications transmission towers, switchboards, and telephone cables were heavily damaged." Dobbins et al. 2005, pp. 156-157.
1001 "Following the breakdown of the banking and payments systems, all transactions in Timor were conducted in cash." Ibid., p. 157.
1002 UN Doc. A/37/30, para. 37. Dobbins et al. 2005, p. 157, "[T]he provision of public services stopped." Cf. also UN Doc. S/1999/1024, para. 12, 13.
1003 Cf. UN Doc. S/1999/1024.

tation of the 5 May Agreement [...]."[1004] The presumably well-prepared and systematic policy of murder and destruction during the *Operasia Sapu Jagad* (Operation Global Clean-Sweep) "aimed at preserving Indonesian control over the territory, or at least a substantial portion of it."[1005]

Box 5: International Reactions to *Operasia Sapu Jagad*

"On September 5, after an American policeman was shot in the stomach, Martin ordered the withdrawal of UN election staff from rural areas. Timorese and international UN workers flocked to the capital, Dili, gathering at the UN base here. They saw that many terrified Timorese with no connection to the UN had taken shelter at a high school that abutted the UN compound. As night fell, a mob of militiamen hacked one man to death in the school yard and then began firing homemade guns – welded pipes packed with nails and gunpowder that were set off with cigarette lighters – at the Timorese, who fled toward the UN compound. UN security officers guarding the base initially fended of the desperate Timorese. But fearing that the militia were closing on them, others began hurling their children over the concrete wall separating the high school from the UN complex. [...] As UN staff saw parents begin to follow their children over the wall, they formed an impromptu assembly line, passing the Timorese from one pair of hands to the next, until they were safely inside the UN building. [...] By the end of the evening more than fifteen hundred Timorese had joined foreign journalists and UN Timorese and international staff in the UN compound [...]. With corpses lining the streets, the sound of gunfire echoing through the night, and bare-chested militiamen brandishing large machetes outside the UN gate, UN staffers feared that the mob would storm the compound. [...] [Designated SRSG; ES] Vieira de Mello watched events unfold from New York, and still Under-Secretary-General for Humanitarian Affairs, he attempted to coordinate the UN's humanitarian response. [...] But while the militia were on the loose, he knew it would be very difficult to reach those in greatest need. He believed the crisis was so severe that military intervention, that rare and risky measure, was necessary. [...] Although the evidence indicated that Indonesian armed forces were committing and abetting the massacres, Western diplomats continued to point to the original referendum agreement. [...] When Sandy Berger, the national security adviser to President Clinton was asked why the United States had not stepped up to try to stop the violence, Berger said, 'You know, my daughter has a very messy apartment up in college; maybe I shouldn't intervene to have that cleaned up. I don't think anybody ever articulated a doctrine which said we ought to intervene wherever there's a humanitarian problem' (Sandy Berger, 'Special White House Briefing, Subject: President Clinton's Trip to APEC Meeting in New Zealand,' September 8, 1999). None of the major powers seemed inclined to rescue the Timorese. [...]

1004 Ibid., p. 2, referring to the Report of the Security Council Mission to Jakarta and Dili, UN Doc. S/1999/976, para 19, 14 September 1999. An article by Theo Frey in the journal "Zeitschrift für Friedenspolitik" comments what happened as follows, "Verteidigungsminister General Wiranto rechtfertigte die Passivität des Militärs mit dem Argument: 'Wenn die Soldaten auf die Milizen schiessen, haben wir einen Bürgerkrieg.' Die UNO glaubte ihm, dass er gleichzeitig auch die timoresische Bevölkerung vor den Milizen schützen werde. Als Kontrast zur Gutgläubigkeit der UNO sah man zur gleichen Zeit die Fernsehbilder der letzten ReporterInnen in Dili, in welchen sich indonesische Soldaten mit dem für die Armee typischen Kurzhaarschnitt Langhaar-Perücken überziehen und zu zweit oder zu dritt, auf dem Motorrad schiessend durch die Strassen fahren." Frey 1999, p. 1. On the involvement of the Indonesian military in the violence see also The Carter Center, "Pre-Election Statement on East Timor Elections." Available online at http://www.carter-center.org/news/documents/doc267.html, last access on 2 March 2009.
1005 Gendercide Watch, "Case Study East Timor (1975-1999)."

Martin was worried both about the bloodshed in the country and about the people gathered at the compound. [...] The UN had a policy of never evacuating civilians, but Martin urged New York to lobby member states to do something to protect all Timorese (UN and non-UN alike) at the compound. Hearing nothing, on the evening of September 8, Martin felt he had no choice but to follow the advice of Alan Mills, the head of UN civilian police, and his security advisers, and recommend to New York that the Secretary-General declare a 'Phase V' emergency (the UN system uses five escalating security phases to describe the prevailing conditions in a country and the commensurate requirements for staff: Phase I, precautionary; Phase II, restricted movement; Phase III, relocation; Phase IV, program suspension; Phase V, which can be declared only by the secretary-general, evacuation). Annan reluctantly accepted the recommendation and ordered the withdrawal of all UN staff. [...] Most Timorese made no attempt to hide their emotions. They grew so panicked that they wailed in agony. [...] 'We must stop the UN from leaving. The bald man cannot leave the compound,' said one Timorese man, referring to Martin. UN security staff began preparing to depart, burning UN documents and removing the hard drives from computers. Throughout the compound groups of UN staff members clustered together to discuss their predicament. Many were sure a Rwanda-style massacre would commence if they withdrew. Some [...] suggested that the staff resign so that nobody would have the authority to order their evacuation. 'We were trying not only to save the Timorese,' she recalls, 'but to save the UN from itself.' [...]

With reports of hundreds of Timorese already murdered, Vieira de Mello had the feeling of 'here we go again.' In Bosnia in 1993 and 1994, he, like other UN officials, had understood the major power to be unwilling to act to stop atrocities and had not pushed the matter. But a central lesson of the calamities of Rwanda and Srebrenica was that UN officials should, at a minimum, be on the record advocating solutions and challenging political constraints instead of simply deferring to them. When large numbers of lives were at stake, the smooth pragmatist had to exercise moral leadership. Doing so, he saw, was its own form of pragmatism. [...] Although his responsibilities towards East Timor were technically only humanitarian, he took a strong political stand. Just as the UN should not have trusted the Serbs to guarantee the Bosnians' safety in Srebrenica, he argued, the UN could not now trust the Indonesians. Since the UN had already rightly decided to evacuate Timorese UN staff, he endorsed a proposal that was gathering momentum at headquarters: to send a small Australian contingent to the UN compound to protect the non-UN Timorese who had sought shelter here. 'I appreciate there is a high likelihood that this will be unacceptable with the Security Council,' he argued in writing. 'However, I feel if we wish to avoid being a scapegoat, we should put the onus of rejecting solutions on others' (Vieira de Mello, "Note for Mr. Prendergast: Re: IDPs in UN Compound," September 9, 1999). He pressed the point. 'If we learned anything in the last five years,' he said, 'it is that we have to stop telling the Security Council what it wants to know, and instead tell it what it needs to know.' He added, 'We can't censor ourselves' (ibid.). 'For once,' he urged in a senior staff meeting, 'let's allow the states on the Council to make the wrong decisions instead of saving them the trouble by making the wrong decisions for them.' [...]

The two parts of the UN – UN career staff and UN member states – were responding differently. While UN staff were repulsing to leave Dili with the Timorese and UN senior staff in New York were pressing Western governments to act, the governments themselves were still resisting sending troops to rescue either the Timorese at the UN compound or the imperilled population as a whole. [...] But not all Western countries were alike. Portugal [...] joined the push for intervention. Portuguese prime minister António Guterres telephoned President Clinton and pleaded with him to bring the issue before the Security Council. In Australia, the first UN member state to have recognized the legality of Indonesia's occupation, the political left pressed Prime Minister John Howard to make up for the country's past sins, while conservatives argued that something had to be done to stave off the flood of Timorese refugees who would end up in Australia. In his boldest statement of the crisis, Secretary-General Annan warned that what he called 'crimes against humanity' would be punished. On September 9, 1999, [...] Clinton announced that the United States was suspending a $2.5 million military assistance program to Indonesia, as well as $40 million in commercial sales. [...] The Indonesians, Clinton said, 'didn't like the results and they're trying to undo it by running people out of the country or into the grave.' He continued, 'We expect the authorities to live up to their word and their responsibilities. [They] must invite' – Clinton repeated himself for effect – 'must invite the international community to assist in restoring security.'"[1006]

1006 Power 2008, pp. 288-296.

All non-essential UNAMET staff had been relocated out of the territory, and only 86 international personnel remained in the headquarters compound in Dili. On the background of the developments described in box 5, the UN Security Council decided to deploy a multinational peacekeeping force. On 15 September 1999, ultimately with the consent of Indonesia, the Security Council authorized a multinational force. Acting under Chapter VII of the UN Charter, INTERFET had no minor task than to restore peace and security.[1007] Resolution 1264 also charged it with the protection and support of UNAMET personnel and the facilitation of humanitarian assistance operations. The first elements of the multinational force arrived in East Timor as early as 20 September. "[T]he speed of deployment was achievable only because INTERET was not a 'blue helmet' force, instead the leadership was 'subcontracted' under a UN mandate to Australia."[1008] The quick and massive deployment advanced immediate results: the Indonesian Armed Forces and most militias, but also the entire caste of the Indonesian administrative officials fled across the border.[1009] In mid-October, UNAMET re-established its headquarters in Dili and began to restore its logistical and personnel capacity, while other organizations of the UN system were starting a "large-scale emergency humanitarian relief effort, including airdrops of food, aid convoys, and the provision of shelter and basic services."[1010]

1007 INTERFET was financed by a Consolidated Inter-Agency Appeal of $199 million, coordinated by the United Nations. Cf. Salomons and Dijkzeul 2001, p. 92.
1008 Ryan, Alan. 20002. "The Strong Lead-nation Model in an Ad-hoc Coalition of the Willing: Operation Stabilize in East Timor." *International Peacekeeping* 9:1, pp. 23-44, p. 30.
1009 Cf. Doyle and Sambanis 2006, p. 248. Australian forces expert Alan Ryan identifies two major reasons for INTERFET's success: fit of the strong lead nation model of the mission and absence of a more determined opposition that could have used the coherence weaknesses of the multinational operation. "In large part, the success of INTERFET was due to the troop-contributing nations' acceptance of the imperfections inherent in such a disparate force. Operational responsibility was distributed according to the capabilities of the forces assigned to the mission. The need for a robust command-and-control architecture was realised in the strong lead-nation model that INTERFET adopted. [...] As the mission was faced by only a low level of opposition the lack of preparation and internal coherence did not prove critical. However as General Roméo Dallaire found in Rwanda and General Cevik Bir discovered in Somalia, there is no guarantee that the security situation will not rapidly deteriorate. The transition period during a handover/takeover is when forces are most vulnerable both tactically and operationally. A more committed and professional opposition could have targeted this vulnerability." Ryan 2002, pp. 30, 32. In addition, "The pro-Indonesian militia lacked sufficient arms command and control capabilities, and discipline to pose a significant insurgent threat. Some militia possessed modern semi-automatic assault rifles and hand grenades, but most carried decrepit bolt-action rifles, shotguns, pistols, homemade pipe guns, machetes and knives." Dobbins et al. 2005, p. 154.
1010 UN Department of Peacekeeping Operations, "East Timor: UNTAET Background." Available online at http://www.un.org/peace/etimor/UntaetB.htm, last access on 2 March 2009. "Relief workers and supplies were deployed incrementally as the security situation improved. At the same time, increasing attention was paid to the voluntary repatriation of

2.4 Mandating UNTAET

Events were piling up in the second half of October. Following the 5 May Agreements and the referendum results, the Indonesian People's Assembly revoked the law that integrated East Timor within Indonesia, finally recognizing the result of the popular consultation. The domestic legal framework for East Timor's separation from Indonesia was thereby created.[1011] In Dili, Xanana Gusmão, former rebel leader, national hero, and long-time Indonesian detainee, "made a triumphant return [...] as an unquestioned leader of the pro-independence movement."[1012] The Timorese expected Gusmão to become the leader of the new state. At the same time in New York, pre-mandate planning was speeding up. The Secretary-General had brought forward his recommendations to the Security Council that eventually established the most comprehensive UN peace operation ever. The negative side of this decisiveness was that the East Timorese themselves were sidelined from the transition plan.

Mandate Goals

On 25 October, acting along the recommendations stated by the Secretary-General in his report of 4 October,[1013] the Security Council unanimously adopted resolution 1272 on the establishment of the UN Transitional Administration in East Timor to maintain security, provide interim governorship of the territory, and prepare the country for the transition to independence. The strong mandate rested upon unani-

---

some 250,000 East Timorese from West Timor and other areas in Indonesia and the region. To finance the relief effort, a Consolidated Inter-Agency Appeal for $199 million was launched on 27 October 1999." Ibid.

1011 Cf. Doyle and Sambanis 2006, p. 248. See also UN Department of Public Information 2000, p. 68. Dobbins et al. 2005, p. 154 add, "The pro-Indonesian militia lacked sufficient arms command and control capabilities, and discipline to pose a significant insurgent threat. Some militia possessed modern semi-automatic assault rifles and hand grenades, but most carried decrepit bolt-action rifles, shotguns, pistols, homemade pipe guns, machetes and knives." In addition, "They also agreed that ad hoc measures were required to fill the gap created by the early departure of the Indonesian civil authorities." Ibid.

1012 UN Department of Public Information 2000, p. 56. "Gusmão's poetry and letters from prison, as well as South African president Nelson Mandela's meeting with him in 1997, had made him a national hero and an international cult figure." Power 2008, p. 298.

1013 UN Doc. S/1999/1024. The 21-day delay was due to the US Government requiring the Security Council to wait three weeks to act on the report as it had to consult Congress first. Cf. UN Department of Public Information 2000, p. 56.

mous consensus within the Council.[1014] The mandate entailed peacekeeping as well as comprehensive peace- and state-building elements. Specifically, the objectives were

(a)   To provide security and maintain law and order throughout the territory of East Timor;
(b)   To establish an effective administration;
(c)   To assist in the development of civil and social services;
(d)   To ensure the coordination and delivery of humanitarian assistance, rehabilitation and development assistance;
(e)   To support capacity-building for self-government;
(f)   To assist in the establishment of conditions for sustainable development.[1015]

UNTAET was "to put together institutions that form a country."[1016] The Security Council entrusted the mission with full-fledged governing authority in the executive, legislative, and judicative branches. The SRSG/Transitional Administrator was even given the power to sign international treaties on behalf of the East Timorese.[1017] Applying the terminology used by Michael W. Doyle, UNTAET was endowed with the maximal "supervisory authority"[1018] that allowed it to take all

---

1014   "Unlike ever before or since, from May to October 1999, there was a flurry of activity regarding East Timor in the Security Council, with the Council holding eight discussions, and passing six resolutions. All resolutions were passed unanimously, in light of Indonesia's consent for INTERFET, as well as the follow-on peacekeeping operations. There was consensus as to the basic nature of the problem, and debates were not acrimonious. We can therefore determine that there was consensus around Security Council action toward East Timor, both for INTERFET and UNTAET." Howard 2008, pp. 271-272.

1015   UN Security Council, "Resolution on the Situation in East Timor," UN Doc. S/1999/1272 (1999), 25 October 1999, para. 2. As Aurel Croissant puts it, "In other words, 'UNTAET would have to invent a functioning state in East Timor.'" Croissant 2006, p. 7.

1016   Saldanha 2003, p. 161.

1017   "The United Nations will conclude such international agreements with States and international organizations as may be necessary for the carrying out of the functions of UNTAET in East Timor." UN Doc. S/1999/1024, para. 35.

1018   For a debate on different stances on the UN taking over governing authority, cf. Goldstone, Anthony. 2004. "UNTAET with Hindsight: the Peculiarities of Politics in an Incomplete State." Global Governance 10, pp. 83-98, pp. 91f. "At the conceptual level, there is considerable uncertainty over the sovereign status of an interim administration such as East Timor' […]. Suzannah Linton notes that 'the view that the UN cannot have territorial sovereignty is a well-established one. However, she adds that 'together, Security Council Resolution 1272 and [UNTAET] Regulation 1999/1 vest what appears to be sovereign authority over a territory and its inhabitants in UNTAET. This power has enabled it, inter alia, to legislate and enter into international agreements on behalf of East Timor. This transfer of sovereign power has not occurred in other UN transitional administrations' (fn. 15: Linton Suzannah. 2001. "Rising From The Ashes: The Creation Of a Viable Criminal Justice System in East Timor." Melbourne University Law Review 5. Online Journal available at www.austlii.edu.au/au/journals/MULR/2001/5.html, last access on 3 March 2009). [Also,] Matthias Ruffert takes the view that UNTAET did not have sovereign powers, 'There is no effective performance of autonomous government and thus one of the elements

necessary measures to fulfil its mandate. Established under Chapter VII of the UN Charter, it was granted the use of force,[1019] and was planned as an integrated, multidimensional mission.[1020] A deadline of two years was set, following the recommendations of the Secretary-General that he had outlined in his report to the Council.

> The report stated Annan's view that [...] 'the process will take two to three years' [...]. None of the reports to the Security Council had given any insight into the reasoning behind his selection of this timeframe. Nevertheless, the view of most observers is that this interval was selected based on the Secretary-General's assessment of how much time and attention the Security Council and donor nations would be willing to devote to Timor-Leste [...]. This in fact is the only possible explanation for adopting such a short time frame given the task at hand and resources available.[1021]

The highly comprehensive mandate and endowments were the result of the strong international interest in a prestigious, successful mission. After Indonesia had signalled its consent,

> Involvement in Timor-Leste was an opportunity for the international community to demonstrate what it could do, in contrast to its shameful abandonment of Rwanda five years earlier. International enthusiasm for involvement was particularly mobilized by

---

of Statehood is absent.' He argues from the absence of a clear legal category in which to place the territory of East Timor under transitional administration that its legal personality was also in doubt or at the very least ambiguous. [...] By contrast, Paulo Gorjao, echoing Chopra, asserts that 'for the first time, the UN had sovereign control over a trust territory, and UNTAET was a 'trusteeship administration' preparing a territory for independence' (fn. 17: Gorjao, Paulo. 2002. "The Legacy and Lessons of UNTAET." *Contemporary Southeast Asia* 24: 2, pp. 313-336, p. 314). Chopra himself bases his own case for UNTAET's sovereign powers heavily on an agreement between UNTAET and the International Development Association (IDA, a World Bank affiliate) on the Trust Fund for East Timor signed in February 2000, which because it was a treaty was, in his words, 'nothing less than the first ever act of UN sovereignty' (fn. 18: Chopra 2000, p. 30). The agreement [...] was a treaty, but only because the UN felt constrained to accept the World Bank's argument that IDA rules required that the agreement have the status of a treaty. It highlights the fact that conceptual confusion was mirrored by a similar practical confusion."

1019 Chapter VII allows the Security Council to take non-military as well as military measures "to maintain or restore international peace and security." Charta of the United Nations, Chapter VII, Article 39. Crucial is Article 42 which says, "Should the Security Council consider that measures provided for in Article 41 would be inadequate or have proved to be inadequate, it may take such action by air, sea, or land forces as may be necessary to maintain or restore international peace and security. Such action may include demonstrations, blockade, and other operations by air, sea, or land forces of Members of the United Nations." The peacekeeping responsibilities were to be shared with INTERFET in the first few months. Cf. UN Department of Public Information 2000, p. 56.

1020 By definition, this refers to a mission structure where all components of the operation, especially also the humanitarian component, are under the leadership of the SRSG or Transitional Administrator or Head of the UN's office for the Coordination of Humanitarian Affairs. Cf. Eide et al. 2005, p. 9.

1021 Garrison 2005, p. 8.

Australia, which used diplomacy and its alliances to galvanize support for Timor-Leste.[1022]

Early Timorese Disappointment

The other side of the all-comprehensive authority was the marginalization of East Timorese – who had been waiting for centuries to govern themselves – in involving them in the transition process. While the mandate stated the need for UNTAET "to consult and cooperate closely with the East Timorese people in order to carry out its mandate effectively with a view to the development of local democratic institutions,"[1023] Timorese leaders were severely disappointed by the arrangement. "Gusmão, who had favored a central UN role but not outright UN rule, was livid."[1024]

2.5 Planning Process

The mission's planning met opposition on two fronts: first, pre-mandate planning was obstructed by Indonesians who apparently tried to stall the transition process, claiming that the UN must remain neutral and must not engage in mission planning prior to the referendum. Second, operational planning could not proceed due to post-ballot violence, which not only left many victims but also much uncertainty about the transition phase.

2.5.1 Pre-Mandate Planning

The planning process at headquarters faced a high level of uncertainty and adversity. Indonesia was formally obstructing the process at the international level by requiring the UN not to begin with planning prior to the referendum. It also obstructed to the international efforts by secretly allowing brutal assaults by Indonesian and pro-Indonesia Timorese militias on-the-ground. Furthermore, Indonesian administrators and other officials, who were supposed to work with UN personnel during the transition period, were fleeing the country.

1022 Harston, Julian, 2005. *United Nations as Ambivalent Administrator in the Balkans and East Timor*. Manuscript for UNITAR Conference in Hiroshima, March 2005, on file with the author, p. 4.
1023 UN Doc. S/1999/1272, para. 8. "A top priority of UNTAET is the establishment of close consultation and liaison with the East Timorese." UN Doc. A/37/30, para. 41.
1024 Power 2008, p. 300.

Conventional mission planning of UNTAET was put on hold. "The Indonesians made it politically very difficult for us to plan for a transitional administration. They said, 'The UN is guaranteeing a free and fair popular referendum – so why are you planning for one outcome?' And this was a very sensitive political point, from a very influential member state."[1025] Official involvement of East Timorese leaders prior to the referendum would have been tantamount to acknowledging that the occupation of the territory was illegal. Following Indonesia, other member states refused to allow any planning to take place before the ballots were counted.

> Core Group countries were […] reluctant to engage in any sort of planning for after the ballot without the participation of the Indonesian Government. In early August, for example, US State Department officials told an official of the UN Department of Political Affairs that, with Congress in recess until the following month, the administration would feel more comfortable if detailed planning were deferred until after the result of the referendum was known.[1026]

For the Security Council and member states, it was a priority that Indonesia would not be offended.[1027] Adding to the Council's rubber-stamp stance, "There was concern that at that stage a mission that smacked of peace-building would run into opposition from member states, particularly from the US."[1028] However, "The people at DPKO were pretty confident that the real popular opinion would run against the Indonesians."[1029] At the end of the day, the Security Council did not allow any mission planning to take place until after the referendum. This situation increased time pressure on planners in the Secretariat, even before chaos broke out on-the-ground.

1025　Interview with a senior staff member of UNTAET, New York, 23 November 2006.
1026　CSDG, "East Timor Report," para. 14, 15. "The plan set out for Phase II in the Secretary-General's Report of 9 August was, according to a person involved in drafting it, the 'weak' one of a modified UNAMET. This was not just the position that prevailed within the UN Secretariat. Perhaps more important, it also held sway among the Core Group of countries (Australia, Japan, Portugal, the United Kingdom and the United States). Up to the time of the ballot and beyond, Australia was saying that it would not sanction a major troop deployment until Phase IIIB and that it was not disposed to contribute to a peace enforcement exercise under any circumstances. Any contribution that it might eventually make would have to be at the request of the UN and with the agreement of Indonesia. Other Core Group countries were also reluctant to engage in any sort of planning for after the ballot without the participation of the Indonesian Government. In early August, for example, US State Department officials told an official of the UN Department of Political Affairs (DPA) that, with Congress in recess until the following month, the administration would feel more comfortable if detailed planning were deferred until after the result of the referendum was known." Ibid., para. 13-15.
1027　"[I]n deference to Indonesian sensibilities, the East Timorese resistance movement was to keep a low profile in the governing structures of the transitional state." Suhrke 2001, p. 3.
1028　CSDG, "East Timor Report," para. 26.
1029　Interview with a senior staff member of UNTAET, New York, 23 November 2006.

Before the burning of East Timor by militias supported by the Indonesian military, we were dealing with the country on the basis of good faith diplomacy. The understanding was that whatever the outcome, we would need a period of interim preparation between the vote and the implementation of the outcome. So, if the Timorese voted for independence, there would be a period where we would go on the ground, where we would get the files from the Indonesian administrators, where we could talk to the Indonesian administrators about who would stay and who could stay for a while, et cetera. – We would work out a transition.[1030]

Chaos in East Timor

The international community had planned to manage the transition in cooperation with the Indonesians. But after the looting, the original transition plan became obsolete: there were no more Indonesians because they all had fled, and Indonesia was even less trustworthy cooperation partners than before. In addition, "Operation Global Clean Sweep" involved a massive loss of information as all public records were destroyed or taken by the Indonesians. "Now, of course, what happened is all of that planning went up in smoke. We didn't actually have the space to plan that we would have liked to have, or the information – which was all in the hands of the Indonesians."[1031] While there had been "some thinking in the UN Secretariat about what should be done if the Indonesian Government failed to live up to its commitments under the 5 May Agreements"[1032] and some unofficial worst-case planning by individual governments, none of these scenarios were as bad as what eventually happened. Besides, those scenarios had remained rather general and concepts were not concretized so that there was "no way of feeding them into UN Secretariat planning mechanisms – which, on that note, a diplomat closely involved in the process described as 'rather incompetent.'"[1033]

1030 Ibid. The original plan had envisaged a phased approach with phase A being the referendum, phase B with the UN checking on the situation on-the-ground, "Phase C was going to be the results of the referendum, and phase D was going to be us working with the Indonesians." Ibid. For the original UN scheme see also Chopra 2002, p. 983. In the opposed case, if they voted to remain as part of the Indonesian Republic but with autonomy, "we were gonna hit the ground, we were gonna talk with the Indonesian administrators and ask them how they plan to set up these structures to create the autonomous unit of East Timor. We would monitor to make sure these things were happening." Ibid.
1031 Interview with a senior staff member of UNTAET, New York, 23 November 2006.
1032 CSDG, "East Timor Report," para. 14.
1033 Ibid., para. 12. "I think they didn't expect the magnitude of the problems at the referendum. They didn't do anything to plan for transitional government, such as to identify people who would be in it, to look for an SRSG, to figure out the structure, to allocate the resources, any of that. Because they said, 'If we do that Indonesia is gonna say we're biased, we were prejudging the result of the vote.' That's ridiculous! You can't sacrifice the whole country because you're worried about offending the government that's been illegally occupying the territory for 24 years." Interview with a representative of the Timor-Leste Institute for Reconstruction Monitoring and Analysis, New York, 27 November 2006.

Faced with catastrophe, the official planning for UNTAET started when the Security Council invited "the Secretary-General to plan and prepare for a UN transitional administration in East Timor [...] and to make recommendations as soon as possible to the Security Council."[1034] This was one month before the mandate was eventually issued. Following-up on a tripartite meeting among the UN, Indonesia, and Portugal on 28 September, *ad hoc* measures were identified. "Urgent measures were taken to address the vacuum left in civil administration, legal and judicial systems, and law and order, using the available assets of INTERFET and UN personnel on-the-ground."[1035] In his follow-up report to the Council, the Secretary-General outlined his recommendations for mission planning.[1036]

The Fight over Turf at UN Headquarters

At UN headquarters, a rivalry between the small but traditionally influential and politically well-versed DPA, which had supervised the referendum and had been the major UN agency in East Timor for decades, and the then ascending DPKO, which had been broadening its sphere of responsibility from military peacekeeping to operations of a more complex and political nature, became virulent. Eventually, the planning and implementation of the transitional administration in East Timor was operated by DPKO. DPA, which had been enjoying the trust of leading East Timorese, was sidelined.[1037]

While DPKO is an agency genuinely concerned with peacekeeping and conflict resolution tasks, it does not have much expertise in political and social aspects of missions as they are implied by state-building ventures.[1038] With strong peacekeeping elements prominently entering the mandate of UNTAET, DPKO claimed

---

1034   Security Council Resolution, UN Doc. S/RES/1264 (1999), 15 September 1999, para. 11.
1035   UN Doc. A/37/30, para. 37.
1036   Cf. UN Doc. S/1999/1024.
1037   The East Timor Report of the Conflict and Security Development Group at King's College cites a letter from Xanana Gusmão to Kofi Annan of 15 September 1999, stating, "[UNAMET's] knowledge of the East Timorese political process, their understanding of the conditions on-the-ground and, most important, of our people, leads me to make a very special, yet bold, request: to include the participation of this DPA team in the designing of the future UN mission to East Timor." CSDG, "East Timor Report," para. 25. Furthermore, it was also DPA that had participated in the World Bank-led needs assessment process foregoing the intensified international efforts. The needs assessment had been done mainly by the World Bank and DPA. Telephone interview with a staff member of the Post-UNTAET Planning Team, UNTAET, 15 October 2006. For similar criticism see, e.g. Pippard undated, pp. 5-6, "The DPKO's subsequent adoption of control meant that the entire operation was staffed and organised by a department with little experience of 'governance missions,' limited country knowledge of East Timor, and operating procedures designed for short-term operations. UNTAET's structure was therefore unsuitable for long-term administration responsibilities."
1038   Cf. Suhrke 2001, p. 6.

that the mission would fall into their resort – despite shortage in personnel for planning support thumped its demand.[1039] Matter of fact, DPKO had proposed that it be responsible for co-ordinating planning for the scenario of East Timorese independence option since early July. It also argued strongly that planning should be New York-based. Ultimately, the Secretary-General's decision to put DPKO in the lead was inevitable given the UN's internal procedural logic.[1040] However, the ruling was heavily disputed and DPA continued to fight a rearguard action in an attempt to establish a role for itself in the process, proposing that the lead department concept be bypassed through the creation of an interdepartmental/inter-agency East Timor Task Force.[1041] There is evidence that those in the DPA were somewhat blamed for the violent outbursts following the Timor referendum. "The UN officials who had helped arrange the referendum believed Annan's planners were shunning them as if they were responsible for the carnage. Ian Martin, who had organized the vote and remained in East Timor afterward, was rarely canvassed for advice."[1042] Discussions were consistently "reinforced by personality clashes, especially at the top level."[1043]

Timorese (Non-)Involvement

The fact that DPKO led UNTAET had implications for the mission's future politics and polity. Decisions were made that appeared *ex post* inadequate, inappropriate, and eventually counterproductive to the mandate's implementation, especially with regards to the "ownership" imperative that all transitional administration are required to adhere to.

Having DPKO operate the transition had particular consequences for the status of the East Timorese during the transition process. At the beginning of the mission's planning process, there were two schools of thought within the Secretariat about the CNRT's status:

> One school was that the CNRT is the sort of legitimate holder of Timorese wishes and sovereignty. The other view was that the Timorese themselves had voted on a simple

---

1039 Cf. Pippard undated, p. 6.
1040 The decision was made after the September 1999 violence and the deployment of the INTERFET peacekeeping force. "In mid-September, a decision in the Secretary-General's office settled the matter: while the planning team drew its staff from both departments and was assisted by a wider agency cast, the DPKO was to be in charge." Suhrke 2001, p. 7.
1041 East Timor Task Force. Cf. CSDG, "East Timor Report," para. 20-21.
1042 Power 2008, p. 300. "He pleaded with officials in Headquarters to move their planning base to Darwin, Australia, so that Gusmão and other Timorese leaders could be consulted. But New York paid no heed and gave no guidance to Martin, who was told to bide his time until his successor showed up." Ibid.
1043 Suhrke 2001, p. 6.

question: do you want a transition to independence or do you want autonomy? They hadn't voted for Xanana Gusmão as their president, they hadn't voted for the government to be formed. And so we didn't actually have the legitimacy to hand that over to them. And there was a bit of a debate within the UN about that.[1044]

The proponents of the latter view finally won – not least because their perspective was backed by the traditional DPKO principles and experiences. An observer reflects,

Since the CNRT was not a sovereign authority, in UN peacekeeping thinking it was automatically a faction. As a faction, the CNRT had to be kept at a distance and therefore ideas such as power-sharing or dual governance structures could not be considered. The refusal of UNTAET to deal with the CNRT as a partner denied the organization a viable role in the transition.[1045]

The CNRT would have been the obvious choice. It represented "pro-independence political perspectives,"[1046] enjoyed broad legitimacy,[1047] was "led by charismatic, eminent individuals,"[1048] and disposed over a working infrastructure throughout the territory. However, the political and legal considerations at UN headquarters prevailed. In fact, they prevailed so intensely that a virtual "*terra nullis* assumption" could emerge, conceptualizing East Timor as a political and administrative vacuum.[1049] Without much information or insight into East Timorese socio-political structures and with the East Timorese resistance leaders excluded from the planning process, the physical destruction of government institutions and the perceived lack of local capacities led DPKO to conclude that there were no structures to build upon. While the capacity issue might have been correctly judged in terms of technical or administrative skills, in terms of political capacities, DPKO and its mission

1044   Interview with a senior staff member of UNTAET, New York, 23 November 2006. "Almost 20 percent of the electorate had voted the other way. And so, you know, they hadn't voted on the assumption that if they lost a government would be formed, they had also voted on certain assumptions – and that was important to take into account." Ibid.
1045   Garrison 2005, pp. 8-9.
1046   Chopra 2000, p. 28.
1047   "There was a very strong feeling among the East Timorese – the 'real' Timorese – that Gusmão and friends had earned that recognition and legitimacy." Interview with Professor Dirk Salomons, Director of the Program for Humanitarian Affairs at the School of International Public Affairs, Columbia University, New York, 20 September 2006.
1048   Interview with Professor Michael W. Doyle, former UN Assistant Secretary-General, New Haven, 11 September 2006. "The CNRT had existed since 1998 as a broad popular front representing all political factions and in 1999 served as the umbrella for those who worked together to achieve a victory in the referendum campaign. [...] An active civil society existed as well, with the Catholic Church as the prime example." Garrison 2005, p. 8.
1049   See, e.g., UNIS Press Release of 29 Januar 2001, "In September 1999, East Timor had been 'knocked back to year zero.'" UN Information Service, "East Timorese Leader Commends UNTAET's 'Timorization' Policy in Day-Long Security Council Debate on Territory." UN Press Release, UN Doc. UNIS/SC/1307, 29 January 2001. Available online at http://www.unis.unvienna.org/unis/pressrels/2001/sc1307.html, last access on 3 March 2009. See also Goldstone 2004, p. 85.

got it wrong. A well-informed observer criticized the process, "There was too much colonial paternalism at work."[1050]

2.5.2 Operational Planning

Parallel to the drafting of the mandate, operational planning started at a time when DPKO was more than busy. Given a considerable constraint on time and facing unprecedented tasks, planners were looking for some guidelines and "best practices" to use. They found them in the UN's transitional administration in Kosovo.

Kosovo Blueprint

In the planning process, the template that was used for guidance was the recently deployed UN interim government in Kosovo. "Lacking familiarity with Timor itself, UN officials in New York took the plans they had developed for the Kosovo administration and virtually transposed them onto East Timor. UN staff who felt sidelined joked that Security Council Resolution 1272 was a 'delete Kosovo, insert East Timor' resolution."[1051] Soon it showed that this was an inadequate, stereotyping design.

Structurally, the UNMIK blueprint was most visible in the pillar structure of UNTAET.[1052] The mission's three pillars were:

First, a military component with up to 8,950 troops and up to 200 military observers:

[T]he multinational force should be replaced as soon as possible by a United Nations peacekeeping operation [...], [i]ncorporated into UNTAET and [forming] the military component of the mission. It will consist of two complementary elements, the United Nations force, and a military observer group. The tasks of the United Nations force would be to maintain a secure environment throughout the territory of East Timor, to provided direct security for United Nations personnel

---

1050 Interview with Professor Michael W. Doyle, former UN Assistant Secretary-General, New Haven, 11 September 2006.
1051 Power 2008, p. 300. "Annan asked Lakhdar Brahimi, the former foreign minister of Algeria and UN negotiator in Afghanistan, to become the head of UNTAET. Brahimi declined on the grounds that an international administration was unnecessary now that the Indonesians had left. He also argued that it was wrong to assume that what suited Kosovo would fit East Timor. 'I know nothing about either Kosovo or Timor,' Brahimi told Annan, 'but the one thing I'm absolutely certain of is that they are not the same place.'" Ibid., pp. 300-301.
1052 UN Doc S/1999/1272, para. 3. By and large, the set up corresponded to standard DPKO mission set ups. Telephone interview with a staff member of the Post-UNTAET Planning Team, UNTAET, 15 October 2006. On the military component see UN Doc. S/1999/1024, para. 73-78.

and property, to monitor the prompt and complete withdrawal of any remaining Indonesian military and security personnel, to take measures to disarm and demobilize armed groups and to assist humanitarian activities as appropriate, including the safe return of refugees and internally displaced people.[1053]

Second, a humanitarian assistance and emergency rehabilitation component:

> The Deputy Special Representative for Humanitarian Assistance and Emergency Rehabilitation will oversee the provision and coordination of humanitarian and emergency rehabilitation assistance. [...] The responsibilities of the Deputy Special Representative will be to ensure the comprehensive delivery of multisectoral humanitarian assistance to all those affected by the recent conflict; to extend protection to and facilitate the voluntary return and reintegration of displaced persons and refugees; and to undertake emergency rehabilitation of critical infrastructures and services to promote social well-being and the restoration of civil society. In the performance of these functions, the Deputy Special Representative will build upon and strengthen humanitarian structures currently operating in East Timor, and ensure that the work of the United Nations agencies is fully incorporated into the mission and that there is full collaboration with the international organizations and non-governmental organizations.[1054]

Third, a governance and public administration component, including an international police element:

Contrary to the Kosovo mission, however, the heads of the different divisions "did not include representatives of other international organizations [...], but merely different geographic regions (in line with UN practice),"[1055] and there was also no separate division for institution-building and reconstruction – tasks of utmost importance for East Timor's specific situation.[1056] While these were deliberate decisions, it was a blunt mistake of the planners to omit a unit responsible for customs: heavily relying on the model of Kosovo, where it was not necessary to establish a customs unit, the planners for East Timor simply forgot it.[1057]

The crucial GPA pillar had a "curious structure."[1058] It represented a new and unknown design of the international staff's work environment: following from its dual mandate, UNTAET's structure on public administration initially consisted of three functionally different arrangements. One set was designed to administer the mission itself (e.g., the procurement section), a second was established to perform the immediate tasks of government, and a third set functioned as a precursor to

---

1053 Ibid., para. 73-75.
1054 Ibid., para. 70-72.
1055 Suhrke 2001, pp. 7-8. Vgl. UN Doc. S/1999/1024, para. 70-72.
1056 The planners conceived of these tasks as being part of GPA. Cf. ibid.
1057 It was later on improvised. Cf. Harland, David. 2005. *UN Peacekeeping Operations in Post-Conflict Timor-Leste: Accomplishments and Lessons Learned. UNTAET Governance and Public Information: 1999 to mid-2000*. New York: United Nations Department of Peacekeeping Operations, pp. 8-9.
1058 Interview with a senior staff member of Civil Affairs, UNTAET, New York, 18 September 2006.

agencies of the future independent East Timorese Government (e.g., the Department of Economic Affairs) right from the beginning. The second portion was the largest, with five separate divisions: judicial affairs, civilian police, the division for economic, financial and development affairs, the public services division, and electoral operations.[1059] The complex design notwithstanding, the planners did not specify how the various mission components were to work together: the organizational structure "did not define crucial relationships."[1060] And while the decentralized structure of UNTAET was an innovative and welcomed feature which formally deferred considerable latitude to the district administrators,[1061] the relationship be-

---

1059 Judicial affairs' responsibilities were the reform and the "administration of courts, prosecution services and prisons, development of legal policies, the review and drafting of legislation for the goals and purposes of UNTAET, the assessment of the quality of justice in East Timor, including training requirements." S/1999/1024, para. 50. See Whittington, Sherrill, "The UN Transitional Administration in East Timor: Gender Affairs." Gender Affairs Unit UNTAET. Available online at http://devnet.anu.edu.au/online%20versions %20pdfs/53/20Whittington53.pdf, last access on 3 March 2009. The civilian police had the goal of providing "the provision of interim law enforcement services, the rapid development of a credible, professional, and impartial East Timor police service." S/1999/1024, para. 57. The Division for Economic, Financial and Development Affairs was to plan and monitor the economic and social reconstruction of East Timor, in close consultation with the East Timorese, to prepare and evaluate policies and to set up institutions in the economic, social and financial fields, to coordinate with the various donors and international financial institutions the resource mobilization efforts of UNTAET. S/1999/1024, para. 60. It also included the set up of a new tax system. It is noteworthy that, unlike in many other missions, the tasks of development and of humanitarian aid were separated. The public services division set out to "establish governmental structures necessary for the sustainable delivery of public services, including in the realms of health, water, sanitation, public information, post and telecommunications, port and airport management, social protection and education. [...] In the districts, Division staff will oversee the implementation of policy directives, report on the effectiveness of local bodies, and exercise executive authority where necessary." Ibid., para 65-66. The responsibilities of electoral operations consisted of "institutional capacity-building and organizing and overseeing the next elections." Ibid., para. 67. It also was in charge of overseeing the work of the district administrators. The latter were the heads of administration in the 13 provinces. In addition, GPA was supposed to set up an Environmental Protection Unit, a Land and Property Commission, as well as a Civil Service Commission; it was responsible for the support of agricultural affairs. This included fisheries and forestry, food and agriculture, agricultural research and extension. Cf. Whittington, "The UN Transitional Administration in East Timor: Gender Affairs." Finally, there were some staff doing "Research and Census." Ibid.
1060 CSDG, "East Timor Report," para. 28.
1061 "In a striking departure from previous UN experience, District Administrators were to have 'full executive powers,' with district-level personnel reporting directly to the District Administrator rather than to their department superiors in the central administration (fn. 36: Memorandum from Jarat Chopra, UNTAET head of District Administration, to Sergio Vieira de Mello, UNTAET Transitional Administrator, 17 November 1999, 2 (copy on file with author). For a fuller discussion of district administration, cf. Chopra 2002, pp. 985-989." Caplan 2005, p. 97. See also Beauvais 2001, p. 1142, "One of the innovative aspects of the mission's planned structure was the adoption of a decentralized structure in which District Administrations would function as discrete governmental units (fn. 161). District-level personnel would report directly to the District Administrator, rather than

tween the central and district levels was left undefined. The most concretely defined aspect was the staffing table. The very table was created for UN personnel only though. It did not provide for Timorese integration into it. "Proposals from the Timorese regarding their role during the transitional period were ignored."[1062] A subsequently drawn organizational chart for UNTAET obliquely indicated Timorese consultative bodies at the national and district levels, but "purposely did not specify what they might be."[1063] The chart was drawn up, however, only in 2001. In 1999, no such provisions were made.

This observation seems typical of the overall approach towards East Timorese participation. The mandate stipulated that "East Timorese [are] to serve in positions inside the administrative structures together with international counterparts and deliver sufficient training and capacity-building to enable these persons gradually to replace international staff."[1064] Yet, this stipulation was not put into practice in the initial structure. In fact, with DPKO in the lead, "UNTAET 'had to be neutral, impartial as if it was going to operate in a classical peacekeeping context, rather than a transitional administration with a government in waiting.'"[1065] The rationale behind it was that legally, East Timor was not a sovereign state, and there was no government to be recognized as a legitimate negotiation or cooperation partner.[1066] Hence, DPKO's imperatives of neutrality and impartiality denied an actor that had the formal status of a party to the conflict cooperation. "[DPKO] assumed that you were dealing with a liberation force in East Timor that should not be adopted as the sole interlocutor in this place."[1067] Accordingly, the option to include the CNRT or to acknowledge its proposal for transition, was taken off the negoti-

vertically on a department-by-department basis to central administrators. This was intended to overcome the cumbersome and uncoordinated efforts that had characterized the UN Transitional Authority in Cambodia (fn. 162)."

1062   Interview with Professor Shepard L. Forman, Director of the Center on International Cooperation, New York University, New York, 20 September 2006. From 1973-74, Professor Stedman lived with his family in East Timor where he conducted anthropological studies and has remained a close observer of the political developments on the island.

1063   Chopra 2002, p. 990.

1064   S/1999/1024, para. 47.

1065   CSDG, "East Timor Report," para. 26. The report quotes an UNTAET official.

1066   "In East Timor, there was no state or regime, as both vanished in flames and ashes after Indonesia had drawn back its troops." Croissant 2006, p. 6.

1067   Interview with Professor Shepard L. Forman, Director of the Center on International Cooperation, New York University, New York, 20 September 2006. Consistent with this position, suggestions by the CNRT leader Gusmão for a Transitional Council were neglected. "In September 1999, the then President of CNRT, Xanana Gusmão, presented a document detailing a proposal by the Timorese leadership about the transitional period and its organs. In the document, the Timorese leadership proposed the establishment of a Council of East Timor Transition to work in partnership with the UN." Rodrigues, Ruben. 2003. "Introductory Remarks and Keynote Address: There is No Success without Shared Responsibility." In: Nassrine Azimi and Chang Li Lin, eds., *The United Nations Transitional Administration in East Timor (UNTAET): Debriefing and Lessons*. Boston: Martinus Nijhoff Publishers, pp. 28-29.

ating table altogether.[1068] The Kosovo blueprint had some impact on these considerations as well:

> In the Balkans, there were lots of political parties, and lots of groups who were fighting amongst each other. So, the idea was you should not give any local group any power until there had been elections. And that was one of the reasons why people like Gusmão were kept out of the decision-making process by the UN, thinking that they could not hand-over anything to the nationals until there had been elections to give them legitimacy.[1069]

At the same time, the strong mandate provided UNTAET with the ability to operate the transition process on its own, holding off on local ownership.

> There would be a government formed out of international technocrats, and their job would be to steadily hire and train and have themselves replaced by East Timorese. It would be kind of a bottom-up model. And in order to have political buy-in we would have a National Consultative Council, NCC, to provide guidance on the political side, to the SRSG – while the functioning of the government would be a technocratic exercise, steadily being 'timorized', but starting with internationals. That was basically the model.[1070]

The Kosovo experience affected staffing as well. "Many of the UNTAET personnel, including the SRSG, came directly from the UN Mission in Kosovo."[1071] While the personnel had mission experience, they were, unlike UNAMET staff, not familiar with the territory.

> UN inefficiencies were also on evidence when the transition from UNAMET to UNTAET did not involve the retention of expertise by the latter from the former. While

1068 During the planning stage, CNRT representatives elaborated a proposal for Timorese participation. The modus operandi in this proposal was to be a dual-desk system where the Timorese were put in charge of the administration while at the same time there would be "accompanying consultants from the UN – really necessary – to help and give advice." Interview with Professor Shepard L. Forman, Director of the Center on International Cooperation, New York University, New York, 20 September 2006. Also, an action plan was included in the document, with a timeframe for each target. Cf. Rodrigues 2003, pp. 28-29. However, "The UN didn't want to empower CNRT." Ibid.

1069 Interview with Professor Dirk Salomons, Director of the Program for Humanitarian Affairs at the School of International Public Affairs, Columbia University, New York, 20 September 2006. "DPKO very much had Kosovo on its mind and assumed that you were dealing with a liberation force in East Timor that should not be adopted as the sole interlocutor in this place, which I think was a mistake because, in fact, the CNRT was a very broad umbrella group and the UN knew it had to deal with Xanana Gusmão because of his legitimacy on part of the Timorese population." Interview with Professor Shepard L. Forman, Director of the Center on International Cooperation, New York University, New York, 20 September 2006.

1070 Interview with a senior staff member of UNTAET, New York, 23 November 2006. "There was also the technocratic issue that they don't have the technical capacity the Indonesians had in the civil service – all or a lot of the technocrats had gone to West Timor, either fled or in a sense pushed to West Timor. So, there was also the technocratic kind of thinking of 'We have to do it before others can take over the reign.'" Ibid.

1071 Garrison 2005, p. 8. See also Chesterman 2004, p. 64.

UNAMET was under DPA-lead, UNTAET was placed under the aegis of the DPKO. DPKO did not utilize the personnel, and thus the experience, of the UNAMET operation in what can only be seen as rigid territorialism within the UN bureaucracy. It is inevitable that mistakes will be made as a new UN mission, like East Timor itself, undertakes its work from 'scratch.'[1072]

Thus, instead of personnel with knowledge (of East Timor), personnel who were involved in previous missions (especially in Kosovo) were chosen. A recruitment mechanism to find people with knowledge of government and administration was simply not in place, and neither country-specific knowledge, nor training skills were used as selection criteria.

You rarely have many people in the mission who have extensive mission experience. And almost no one of these people knows local languages, local culture, nor are they rewarded for identifying local capacity. Their idea is to get things done – and you don't get things done by training, you get things done by doing as much as you can yourself.[1073]

Strong SRSG

The task of integrating the various mission components as well as the specification of how to have the East Timorese participate was passed on to the SRSG.

In *"Personalunion,"* the SRSG was going to be the head of the mission and the administrator of East Timor. "The Special Representative will be the Transitional Administrator, and will be responsible for all political, managerial, and representational functions of the mission."[1074] In effect, he was "the proconsul, that's the only expression for it. He had all powers."[1075] Correspondingly, he had all the responsibilities, too: he needed to define the mission structure and to delegate the resulting tasks, as well as having to manage political relationships with the Timorese, donors, with the troops, police, and contributing countries.

1072 Smith, Anthony. 2001. "The Role of the United Nations in East Timor's Path to Independence." *Asian Journal of Political Science* 9:2, pp. 25-54, pp. 43-44.
1073 Interview with Professor Dirk Salomons, Director of the Program for Humanitarian Affairs at the School of International Public Affairs, Columbia University, New York, 20 September 2006.
1074 UN Doc. S/1999/1024, para. 39.
1075 Interview with a senior staff member of Civil Affairs, UNTAET, New York, 18 September 2006.

Recruitment

The recruitment of a complex peace operation proceeds at different levels and according to different imperatives. The top-level positions are filled on political grounds and are partly handpicked by the Secretary-General, particularly concerning the SRSG. The SRSG, in turn, may have a say in who is going to be in his or her leadership team. The mid- and low-level staff of the civilian components proceed via the usual – and in particularly complex missions, usually inadequate – departmental roster, while police and military recruitment (which I do not focus on) are both run via the respective member states, which implies a considerably time consuming process.

At the top level, Sergio Vieira de Mello was asked by Secretary-General Kofi Annan to become his SRSG in East Timor.[1076]

> Vieira de Mello was the only UN official who brought fluent Portuguese, extensive experience in Asia, and, after his second stint in Kosovo, the spirited backing of the Clinton administration, which would foot a large portion of the UN bill. He was the UN official best suited to performing tasks as varied as overseeing the drafting of a constitution, planning elections, and facilitating the return of Timorese refugees.[1077]

He was ready to quit his job as Under-Secretary General for humanitarian affairs in New York immediately.

> The Special Representative will be assisted in these responsibilities by two Deputy Special Representatives, and a Chief of Staff. The two Deputy Special Representatives will head the governance and public administration and the humanitarian assistance and emergency rehabilitation components. The Special Representative will also be assisted by the Force Commander who will head the military components.[1078]

Box 6: Sergio Vieira de Mello
The Brazilian career diplomat used to be the UN's trouble-shooter and the man for difficult cases. Polyglot, dapper, accessible, un-bureaucratic, hard-working, and extremely smart, he has been described as "the ultimate trouble-shooter, the ultimate diplomat."[1079] He spent his entire professional life at the UN and dedicated himself to humanitarian and conflict issues.

1076 Annan had been turned down by Lakhdar Brahimi at first. See fn. 1051. For background information on Sergio Vieira de Mello, see box 6.
1077 Power 2008, p. 301.
1078 UN Doc. S/1999/1024, para. 39.
1079 Governor Bill Richardson, former US Ambassador to the UN, in an interview with Larry King. Larry King Live, "An Analysis of Bombing of UN Headquarters in Iraq." Transcript available online at http://transcripts.cnn.com/TRANSCRIPTS/0308/19/lkl.00.html, last access on 15 March 2009.

Born in Rio de Janeiro in 1948 as the son of a Brazilian diplomat, Sergio Vieira de Mello was a "prototypical global cosmopolitan."[1080] He joined the UN as early as 1969 while studying philosophy and humanities at the Sorbonne in Paris.[1081] He started his UN career at UNHCR, which sent him to Bangladesh, Cypress, Mozambique, Peru, and Southern Sudan. "He assumed his first high-profile post in 1981, when he was appointed Senior Political Adviser to UN forces in Lebanon. He then occupied several high-level posts at UNHCR: Chef de Cabinet for the High Commissioner, Director of the Regional Bureau for Asia and Oceania, and Director of the Division of External Relations."[1082] Increasingly known as the man for hard times, de Mello engaged in post-conflict territories, be it Cambodia, Bosnia, Kosovo, or eventually East Timor and Iraq.[1083] In early 1999, he was earning much credit for his work in Kosovo where he assumed his post as Acting SRSG on an interim basis. "He rose swiftly, shedding his youthful idealism for an increasingly pragmatic approach. He struggles to relieve humanitarian crises while maintaining his organization's neutrality and preserving his access to political leaders, a balancing act that occasionally requires compromising contortions."[1084] Allegedly, it was his very ability to suspend moral judgment that made him such an effective leader.[1085] As his biographer, Professor/Pulitzer-winning journalist Samantha Power argues, the evolution of the UN and his personal evolution were going hand in and. Similarly, Francis Fukuyama notes, "More than anyone else at the United Nations, he embodied the organization's idealism, as well as its limitations."[1086] As much as he had been dedicated to the purpose of the UN, as much was he frustrated with the organization's red-tape and the political manoevering of member states. At the time he was asked to take over as SRSG/Transitional Administrator in East Timor, de Mello was UN Under Secretary-General for Humanitarian Affairs and head of OCHA. Rumor had it that he was even on the road to becoming the next Secretary-General of the UN. Yet in September 1999, de Mello left his Geneva and New York offices behind in order to comply with the strong wish of the Secretary-General to take charge of the new operation. Taking off to East Timor, he was about to find himself in the role of a "benevolent dictator."

On 19 August 2003, Sergio Vieira de Mello – and 22 colleagues – were brutally killed in a coward assault at the UN office in Baghdad. Xanana Gusmão, his closest partner in East Timor, remembered him as a "unique and unforgettable friend," emphasizing how much he "endeared himself to the people of East Timor with his common touch, sensitivity, sense of humor and charisma."[1087]

1080 Fukuyama, Francis, "The Internationalist," *The New York Times*, 17 February 2008. Available online at http://www.nytimes.com/2008/02/17/books/review/Fukuyama-t.html?_r=1, last access on 15 March 2009.

1081 Office of the High Commissioner for Human Rights, "Sergio Vieira de Mello." Available online at http://www.ohchr.org/EN/AboutUs/Pages/Vieira.aspx, last access on 15 March 2009.

1082 Ibid.

1083 "Between 1991 and 1996, Vieira de Mello served as Special Envoy of the High Commissioner for Cambodia, Director of Repatriation for the United Nations Transitional Authority in Cambodia (UNTAC), Head of Civil Affairs of the United Nations Protection Force (UNPROFOR), and United Nations Regional Humanitarian Coordinator for the Great Lakes Region of Africa. In 1996, he was appointed United Nations Assistant High Commissioner for Refugees." Ibid.

1084 Tarnoff, Ben. 2008. „Power Memorializes Mello in 'Flame,'" *San Francisco Chronicle*, 10 February 2008. Available online at http://www.sfgate.com/c/a/2008/02/10/RVD1UF5R8.DTL, last access on 15 March 2009.

1085 "If he had refused to meet with the Khmer Rouge or had denounced the American invasion of Iraq, he would have forfeited the access he needed to reduce human suffering." Ibid.

1086 Fukuyama, Francis. 2008. "The Internationalist." *The New York Times*, 17 February 2008. Available online at http://www.nytimes.com/2008/02/17/books/review/Fukuyama-t.html?_r=1, last access on 15 March 2009.

1087 Associated Press, "East Timor Mourns Loss of UN Envoy Vieira de Mello." Available online at http://www.etan.org/et2003/august/17-23/20adiplo.htm, last access on 15 March 2009.

The DSRSG for GPA was French ex- *préfet* Jean-Christian Cady.[1088] His mandate was "to lay the foundations for sustainable institutions of an independent East Timor and to design an agenda for sustainable economic and social development."[1089] In addition, he would also be responsible for capacity-building:

> In all elements of the functioning of the governance and public administration elements of UNTAET, the United Nations will work on the basis of the principles of participation and capacity-building. This will involve assigning East Timorese to positions within the transitional administrative structures to be established, where qualified individuals are available and can be identified. Where such persons are not available, UNTAET will nevertheless assign East Timorese to serve in positions inside the administrative structures together with international counterparts, and deliver sufficient training and capacity-building to enable these persons gradually to replace international staff. This will allow for the development, throughout the duration UNTAET, of a cadre of well-trained East Timorese capable of performing the administrative and public service functions necessary to support an independent East Timor.[1090]

The maximum allotted strength of the mission included 9,150 military staff, 1,640 civilian police, and about 900 civilian staff.[1091] Soldiers and policemen were made available by the respective troop- and police-contributing member states.[1092]

1088 "[…] In addition to serving as UNTAET's Deputy SRSG, Mr. Cady was also UNTAET's Cabinet Member for Police and Emergency Service. Among his many responsibilities as the Deputy Head of Mission, he was responsible for setting up a functioning East Timorese Police Force, the East Timorese Defense Force and an independent judiciary. Prior to his experience with the United Nations, Mr. Cady served as Inspector General of Administration in the French Ministry of Interior. From 1993 to 1999, he was Préfet of the Departments of Aveyron and Hautes-Alpes, that is, the sole representative of the State and the Government, supervising the Departments' police force and central government agencies. Overall, he has 29 years of experience with the French civil service in various senior positions. From 1975 to 1977, he also served abroad as Commercial Attaché in the French Embassy in Iran." United Nations, "UNMIK, Jean-Christian Cady (France): Deputy Special Representative, Police and Justice." Available online at http://www.un.org/peace/kosovo/pages/kosovo9.htm, last access on 3 March 2009. In July 2001 replaced by Dennis McNamara from New Zealand, who earlier on had served as Deputy Special Representative for humanitarian assistance in UNMIK together with de Mello.

1089 UN Doc. S/1999/1024, para. 46.

1090 Ibid., para. 47.

1091 Cf. Smith 2001, p. 43 and UN Department of Peacekeeping Operations, "East Timor: United Nations Transitional Administration in East Timor." Available online at http://www.un.org/peace/etimor/etimor.htm, last access on 3 March 2009.

1092 The main contributors were Australia, Jordan, Korea, Philippines, Portugal, Thailand, and New Zealand. For more insights on the military operations see, e.g., Col, Mark Koh. 2001. "UNTAET. A Military Insight." *Journal of the Singapore Armed Forces* 27:4. Available online at http://www.mindef.gov.sg/safti/pointer/back/journals/2001/Vol27_4/1.htm, last access 22 February 2009. Police recruitment faced similar difficulties as those depicted in detail in Chapter IV.3.2.1.1 for UNTAES.

The recruitment of civilian staff, processed by DPKO, was characterized by one observer as "a nightmare,"[1093] and by another as "disgusting."[1094] These devastating judgements are due to the inter-crossing of different factors. First, DPKO was overstrained, "Recruitment for this hugely expensive mission depended on one P2 or P3 staff member, on junior people who had huge piles of CVs and said, 'This one to Timor, this one to Congo, this one to Timor…'"[1095] Second, in late 1999, mission staff was an extremely scarce resource: at that time, DPKO was running as many as 16 operations,[1096] with the 17th, in Congo, in the making. As the already tiny staff had been cut by a quarter in the aftermath of the setbacks of UN peacekeeping in the mid-1990s, running so many missions at one time was clearly overstretching capacities. "The department was so thinly staffed that it could commit just one professional staff member per operation."[1097] Third, there does not seem to be a well thought-out recruitment *system* in general. A revealing anecdote dates back to December 2006, when a DPKO staff member called an intern at UNV to ask how they organized their personnel roster.[1098] Corresponding to this observation, the deficit in matching was criticized by a senior UNTAET official, elaborating on a case in point,

> There were two people of the Comoros Islands who had applied to go on missions with the UN. One of them was an English speaker, the other one was a French speaker. They sent to East Timor the French speaker, which is completely useless; and the English speaker they sent to Congo, which is a French speaking country. A good example.[1099]

1093 Telephone interview with a senior UN official, 27 October 2006.
1094 Interview with a former UNTAES staff member, Washington, DC, 1 December 2006. The harsh statements are met by further confirmative comments.
1095 Interview with a senior staff member of Civil Affairs, UNTAET, New York, 18 September 2006. Beauvais makes a similar cause. "[D]uring the course of UNTAET's deployment, a single staff person in the DPKO was charged with recruiting over four thousand civil servants for Kosovo and East Timor simultaneously." Beauvais 2001, p. 1124.
1096 These were UNTSO, UNMOGIB, UNFICYP, UNDOF, UNIFIL, UNIKOM, MINURSO, UNOMIG, UNMOT, UNMIBH, UNMOP, MINOPUH, MINURSA, UNAMSIL, UN-MIK. See UN Department of Peacekeeping Operations: List of Operations.
1097 Power 2008, p. 301.
1098 In a personal talk with a UNV staff member, I was told that just the day before, she got a call from a DPKO employee who inquired about UNV's recruiting standards and best practices. "Ich hatte schon den Eindruck, dass er etwas lernen wollte. Er war sehr interessiert an unserem Raster. UNV hat ein Raster, in dem 6000 Volunteers gespeichert sind, und das nach Qualifikationen geordnet ist – was ein gutes Matching von Aufgabe und Person möglich macht." Personal conversation with a UNV intern, New York, December 6, 2006.
1099 Interview with a senior staff member of Civil Affairs, UNTAET, New York, 18 September 2006. See also Rodrigues 2003, p. 28, "[A] majority of the UN personnel did not speak any of the languages that were crucial to communicate with the local population."

Fourth, just like the UN itself, DPKO's recruiting system is a "bureaucratic bottleneck,"[1100] serving many masters. "UN personnel come from different countries with different systems. There are more than 50 countries involved in the UN Mission in East Timor. Each country, and for that reason individual, has a different perception of what should be done in East Timor."[1101]

In the recruitment of staff for the G&A pillar, the "nightmarish system's" faults were even compounded. Adhering to its routine roster-recruiting process, DPKO still had no category or mechanism to include personnel with administrative capacities or skills related to building and running a state.

> The machinery for peacekeeping personnel for peacekeeping missions has seven well-known categories, such as people who can deal with UN budgets, or people who can deal with UN finance or UN logistics or they are political officers et cetera. But there was no real mechanism for recruiting people who can run a government. So we had a shortage of people who could run a national budget office, or who could run a cabinet office, or who could even run a traffic control system. The mission was planned on the assumption – it seems – that there would be a functioning local administration, that the airports would run, that there would be a budget office, that there would be teachers, and that there would be mechanisms for paying them, and that you would simply require some international personnel to be able to provide interim guidance and direction to the structure. In fact, in no area was that really true. That was, largely, true in Eastern Slavonia and in Kosovo, but in Timor there were almost no doctors, there were almost no legal professional, almost no finance professionals, and there were no people with extensive senior civil service experience and so on. So, the UN found itself lacking a mechanism to identify and deploy the right skill sets in a timely way. That was one of the major problems.[1102]

The kind of people that were needed for this task was simply unavailable. "It requires people from development or from actual governmental work. And that kind of people usually don't work in peacekeeping. And that was the problem."[1103] A related difficulty is that member states do not easily delegate their good people:

> Most government functionaries who are good are in demand in their home countries. So, when we went to governments and said, 'Could you send us good justice people?' – 'Well, good justice people are needed throughout the justice system in our country.' We did ask member states. We also advertised, and did different other things. The problem with that idea is that, you know, it assumes that we can run a country; but we

---

1100 Cf., e.g., Shravanti, Reddy. 2002. *Watchdog Organization Struggles to Decrease UN Bureaucracy*. Availabe online at http://www.globalpolicy.org/ngos/ngo-un/rest-un/2002/1029watchdog.htm, last access on 15 March 2009.
1101 Saldanha 2003, p. 162.
1102 Interview with a senior staff member of UNDPKO PBPS, New York, 15 September 2006. "We don't have people who have been justice ministers et cetera." Interview with a senior staff member of UNTAET, New York, 23 November 2006.
1103 Telephone interview with a staff member of the Post-UNTAET Planning Team, UNTAET, 15 October 2006.

were also very green at doing that. We were learning as we went along. And in some cases we did better, in some cases we did not so well.[1104]

Thus, the recruitment process turned out to be hit or miss. "Some people were good, some people were bad."[1105] Over and above personnel's lack of qualifications was the inability to train and transfer capacities. "In most cases, they did not possess the skills to transfer their knowledge,"[1106] a skill that was, in fact, assiduously emphasized by the mandate. Summing up with a quote by Jonathan Steele,

> UN missions always have a high share of incompetence, partly because of the speed with which they have to be set up. Individual members come from a variety of nations and take time to gel. And UNTAET had to run a government, which meant providing more than the standard peacekeeping package of improving human rights, organizing refugee returns, and conducting elections. 'I got a bunch of generalists,' de Mello complained.[1107]

Reporting on staff *qualification* can be done somewhat more objectively than evaluating staff *attitude*. Sources are also more readily available when it comes to their qualifications. That being said, one UNTAET staff member who, in observation of the following, resigned from his position, reports hubristic and insolent traits of some mission staff. "De Mello brought with him an inner circle from the Balkans, whose members projected a blunt, bullying style, when both the veterans of UN-AMET and the traumatized Timorese would have responded better to modesty and genuine concern."[1108] In fact, "the unprecedented powers to be assumed by the UN attracted the very type of individual who would be intoxicated by that thought."[1109]

Financing

As with UNTAES and complex peace operations in general, UNTAET's budget was split into an assessed budget and voluntary contributions.[1110] While the former

---

1104   Interview with a senior staff member of UNTAET, New York, 23 November 2006.
1105   Ibid.
1106   Rodrigues 2003, pp. 28-29.
1107   Steele 2002, p. 84. Steele continues by saying that "[i]t was partly as a result of the UN-TAET mess that Brahimi proposed that member governments help the UN Secretariat compile an internet-based roster of candidates for civilian posts." Ibid.
1108   Chopra 2000, p. 32. He also quotes Mark Todd of the "Sydney Times" complaining about the very issue and even using the term "UN czars." Dodd, Mark. 1999. "To Market, To Market, With a Fistful of Useless Cash." *Sydney Morning Herald*, 3 December 1999, p. 10; ibid. 2000. "Digging In." *Sydney Morning Herald*, 1 January 2000, p. 23; ibid. 2000. "Bank, UN Fight Over Timor Cash," *The Age*, 22 February 2000, p. 9; ibid. 2000. "UN Staff Battle Over Independence Policy." *Sydney Morning Herald*, 13 March 2000, p. 10.
1109   Chopra 2002, p. 981.
1110   Cf. Chapter II.2.3.

were rather abundant, the latter turned out to be insufficient for many of the consummate list of projects which should have been on UNTAET's list.

The assessed budget paid "expenses related to the UN involvement in East Timor which include the peacekeeping forces, civilian police, UN buildings, UN vehicles, UNTAET staff, and communications."[1111] It was comparatively large.

> At the start of UNTAET, ACABQ had released $50 million, and on 23 December 1999, the General Assembly decided to apportion an advance of up to $200 million, in accordance with the flexible arrangements set out in its resolution 49/249. By April, a first budget had been reviewed by ACABQ and the Fifth Committee, covering the period from 1 December 1999 to 30 June 2000 (again adjusting to the special budget cycle established for all peacekeeping missions), and a sum of $341 million net was appropriated including the advances released earlier.[1112]

As described in Chapter II.2.3, there is not much digression vis-à-vis the budgeting ACABQ,[1113] and there is, obviously, not much influence that the local actors could exert in developing or modifying it.[1114] On the contrary: if anyone had some influence, it was only the member states. Among themselves, they "very hotly" contested about where to use assessed money.[1115] While some states are fonder of using assessed money for state-building tasks, "others were not at all keen on using assessed money for state-building. And a great part of the mission was state-building."[1116]

For the development, reconstruction, and peacebuilding-oriented tasks, a range of tools for raising these contributions was established.[1117] The arrangements for UNTAET represented a network of different "pots," consisting of the Consolidated Inter-agency Appeal Process (CAP), the Trust Fund for East Timor Trust Fund (TFET), the future domestic revenues of East Timor, direct bilateral funding, the

1111 La'o Hamutuk. 2001. "External Funding: Sources and Uses." *La'o Hamutuk Bulletin* 2:1,2, part 1, April 2001. Available online at http://www.laohamutuk.org/Bulletin/2001/Apr/bulletinv2n1.html, last access on 7 March 2009, p. 3. See also Scheye, Eric. 2002. "Transitions to Local Authority Executive Policing." In: Renata Dwan, ed., *Enforcing the Law in Peace Operations*. New York: Oxford University Press, pp. 102-122, p. 107.
1112 Salomons and Dijkzeul 2001, pp. 92-93.
1113 "[U]nder the General Assembly's 'assessed budget' for UNTAET, the mission was not permitted to finance health, education, or other public services. 'The money can only be spent on ourselves,' de Mello told me. At roughly $600 million a year, the assessed budget covered everything from peacekeeping forces and a helicopter fleet for UN use to international civilian staff salaries and the 29,000 bottlers of imported Indonesian water the mission consumed every day." Steele 2002, p. 83.
1114 Cf. La'o Hamutuk 2001, p. 3.
1115 Telephone interview with a staff member of the Post-UNTAET Planning Team, UNTAET, 15 October 2006.
1116 Ibid.
1117 The most important ones are trust funds, cost-sharing projects, and parallel financing and especially the multilateral pledging conference, which is "[t]he traditional mechanism for raising funds for humanitarian and development activities linked to political missions or peacekeeping operations." Salomons and Dijkzeul 2001, pp. 14-15.

funding for UN agencies,[1118] for NGOs and for INGOs.[1119] Most noteworthy, the TFET was a result of a so-called Joint Assessment Mission, led by the World Bank and IMF. The first funds that flowed into this structure, $147 million, was collected at the December 1999 Tokyo Donor Conference. The TFET was subsequently managed by the World Bank and the Asian Development Bank. Likewise established early on was the so-called CAP, which is a UN instrument to raise funds for international emergencies and which is usually coordinated by the UN Office for the Coordination of Humanitarian Affairs:

> OCHA's proposed budget for humanitarian operations called for $183 million for East Timor and $15 million for humanitarian needs in West Timor. In response, foreign government representatives committed $156 million in voluntary contributions to the CAP [...]. [...] UN agencies such as the United Nations Children's Fund, the United Nations Development Program, the United Nations High Commissioner for Refugees, the World Food Program, and the World Health Organization were involved in the effort. International agencies such as the International Organization for Migration and the International Committee of the Red Cross also participated.[1120]

The World Bank took a leading role at its launching in Geneva on 27 October 1999, two days after the resolution was adopted.

When UNTAET deployed, most of these pots were in a rudimentary state or had not yet been established. Later on, to coordinate the diverse funds, a Donor Coordination Unit (DCU), in close cooperation with the World Bank, was created. There was a strong willingness by foreign governments to donate. "At the top of the list in spending were Portugal, Japan, the United States, the EU, and Australia, followed by 19 other countries."[1121] As for their motivation, an observer notes,

> Political concerns led to enough money on the table. Donors got very scared when they saw the level of violence at the time of the Indonesian pullout: for the Australians this was very close to home and for the Americans, Indonesia is a key element in their idea

---

1118 The agencies financed their activities by using their own budgets. Usually, their budget is composed of voluntary contributions from member states and by the regular UN budget, which is itself funded by assessed contributions. "In East Timor, the agencies, particularly in the initial phase, also received money through the CAP. A few agencies also receive support from other areas (i.e. UNICEF receives significant non-governmental support and the WFP receives significant multilateral and bilateral support) [...]. [Finally; ES], bilateral monies funded some of the East Timor-specific activities of some agencies." La'o Hamutuk 2001, p. 4. The report continues, "These agencies do a wide range of work especially in the areas of relief and development. While it is difficult to calculate their combined spending in East Timor, it runs into the tens of millions of dollars."

1119 Almost all of the money that supports the work of [them; ES] originally comes from outside East Timor. All of the contributions to local and international NGOs are voluntary and include some foreign government monies. In some cases, monies also come from UN agencies and supranational bodies," but also from "individuals, community, activist/solidarity and church groups; foundations [...]." In addition, "some local NGOs have income-generating activities." Ibid., p. 5.

1120 La'o Hamutuk 2001, p. 3.

1121 Steele 2002, p. 83.

of how to stabilize South-East Asia. So, regional stability, for Americans and Australians, was a key consideration. And the Brits: they still see Australia as part of the broader British condominium. British, American, Australian, and Japanese interests as well were focused on stability in the region. There was also great fear that this would lead to a new flaring up of the conflict in Aceh. People feared that a lot of ethnic conflicts in South-East Asia could rekindle.[1122]

At the end of the day, "[f]unding was adequate although there was pressure from the beginning to 'downsize' the operation to minimize costs."[1123]

2.6 Summary and Assessment

UNTAET's crucial advantage was that it could be established on the basis of a comprehensive international peace agreement,[1124] including an explicit role for the UN. Similarly conducive, the East Timorese population and the resistance movement's leadership supported the international intervention,[1125] providing for a high amount of input-legitimacy.[1126] Although there was no significant experience with democratic rule, the international administration was warmly welcomed as a facilitator of independence. Finally and most importantly, as Indonesian troops and related militia had fled the region, the security situation staggeringly improved and Australian-led INTERFET was left in control of the territory.[1127] In this regard, the East Timor operation was different from other post-conflict situations since one party to the conflict had completely withdrawn from the territory, and there were

1122   Interview with Professor Dirk Salomons, Director of the Program for Humanitarian Affairs at the School of International Public Affairs, Columbia University, New York, 20 September 2006.
1123   Howard 2008, p. 272.
1124   "UNTAET was operating in a political environment that was relatively favorable and that conferred on it a degree of legitimacy not routinely available to an interim administration. Meanwhile, the vast majority of East Timorese living in the territory regarded the UN intervention as essentially benign, at worst as an uncomfortable interregnum that was the necessary precursor to independence." Goldstone 2004, p. 85.
1125   Steele 2002, p. 79. "It has frequently been pointed out that UNTAET was operating in a political environment that was relatively favorable and which gave it a degree of legitimacy unusual for an interim administration. By the time that UNTAET came into existence, hard-line 'pro-integrationists' had fled over the border into Indonesia, and the PKF's robust Rules of Engagement were able to ensure that neither they nor their allies in the Indonesian military (the TNI) ever posed more than a minor security threat." CSDG, "East Timor Report," para. 290.
1126   Cf. Scharpf, Fritz W. 1999. Regieren in Europa. Frankfurt a.M.: Campus.
1127   See also Goldstone 2004, p. 85.

no "proxy conflicts"[1128] within East Timor, at least not at that time.[1129] Nonetheless, after the September violence, East Timor was "a territory nearly bereft of infrastructure or basic services,"[1130] and faced a devastating GDP situation.[1131] This implied that "the daunting task of rebuilding a nation was placed squarely on the shoulders of a limited pool of qualified people who had been affected by the legacy of malpractices during the Indonesian rule."[1132] The population of East Timor did not only have low formal education and capacities – which are essential factors when it comes to establishing and running their own, newly created state – but was also traumatized and still mourning their dead. Even more, some decisions made during the planning process started to thwart some relatively favorable starting points, paving the way for pathologies to emerge. Besides, "The management cadre of the former civil service as well as its corporate memory – human and physical – was [...] largely destroyed." [1133]

Typically, a complex UN mission requires six months to be planned and prepared.[1134] Planning for UNTAET was done within one month.

> Our planning was done in the midst of chaos. We were already managing the UNAMET operation, which was under attack and all of that. And it had itself a very difficult mandate. And then the same people who were involved in trying to make that happen also have to think about what the interim administration might be like, and they had to think about it while the whole place was going up in smoke. So, I think the major thing I wish would have been different is the opportunity to plan more, to think more, to talk more to Timorese, and that's... that's hard. That's just kind of wishful thinking. It wasn't the case. But that would have changed things a lot.[1135]

The scope of the tasks and the power conceded to UNTAET were unprecedented, which did not make planning any easier. The mandate implied that the UN was to

---

1128   Cf. Maull, Hans W. 2001. *Task Force: Comparing Experiences with Post-Conflict State Building in Asia and Europe: The Cases of East Timor, Bosnia and Kosovo.* Report on the Task Force Meeting in Bali, Indonesia, 15-17 October 2001, p. 4. "Notwithstanding the political tensions, we are not going to see an Angolan-style civil war erupt." Hill and Saldanha 2001, p. 4.
1129   New divisions and conflicts have meanwhile developed. They will be discussed below.
1130   Beauvais 2001, p. 1124.
1131   Over 200,000 refugees fled during the September violence, i.e. around 75 percent of the total population. Cf. Doyle and Sambanis 2006, p. 248. In May of 2001, "[a]bout 10 percent of the country's pre-1999 population [...] [still resided] abroad, mostly in squalid refugee camps across the border in West Timor." Hill and Saldanha 2001, p. 3. See also Steele 2002, p. 79, "When de Mello arrived in Dili in November 1999 he found a level of destruction far worse than what he had seen in Kosovo."
1132   UN Development Program 2005.
1133   Ingram, Sue. 2003. "Mission Implementation: Developing Institutional Capacity." In: Nassrine Azimi and Chang Li Lin, eds., *The United Nations Transitional Administration in East Timor (UNTAET): Debriefing and Lessons.* Boston: Martinus Nijhoff Publishers, pp. 85-94, p. 88.
1134   Suhrke 2001, p. 14.
1135   Interview with a senior staff member of UNTAET, New York, 23 November 2006.

build a state from scratch. This was a task that the UN had never taken on before. Furthermore, while the mission's end-state and the timeframe were neatly defined, the mandate remained ambiguous in most other areas. This is often unavoidable for Security Council mandates, as they reflect a political compromise. Hence, most decisions on specifics, particularly on capacity-building, were left to the SRSG to elaborate upon.[1136] However, neither the SRSG nor other designated senior leaders were involved in the policy formation phases.[1137] As a senior UNTAET official put it, he felt that the basic action framework of the mission was "imposed" on them.[1138] Concerning the mission's design, rather than tailoring a model that suited the East Timor case, "[t]he structure for UNTAET was virtually a carbon copy of the arrangements for Kosovo."[1139] Yet, the Kosovo arrangement reflected fear of a resumption of hostilities between warring parties. It thus did not provide mechanisms for closer consultation and coordination with the East Timorese. Instead, participation was to be "provided through unspecified 'mechanisms of dialogue.'"[1140] Fortifying this uncertainty, UNTAET "did not have a detailed roadmap to follow *en route* to its end-state. It was provided with no clear formula for East Timorese participation. It was not given clear guidelines on the status of potential interlocutors."[1141]

The decision to apply the Kosovo model was made at DPKO. There was no alternative to putting DPKO in the driver's seat, given the departmentalization within the UN. Nonetheless, this had very specific implications for the "local ownership" of the process. It also triggered a turf war with DPA, resulting in the preemptive isolation and exclusion of DPA – and DPA's knowledge and local exper-

---

1136   Interview with Joseph Andrews, Special Adviser to the Deputy Special Representative of the Secretary-General, UNTAET, and to the Foreign Minister, ETTA, Washington, DC, 9 September 2006.

1137   They had also not been involved in the negotiations and initial mission planning. Cf. Subianto, Landry H. 2002. *A State in the Making: Role of UNTAET in East Timor*. Project report to be submitted to the Council for Asia and Europe Cooperation. London, October 2001, p. 18. To my knowledge, there is only one person who was involved in the entire UNTAET process, from planning in DPKO to implementation on-the-ground.

1138   Interview with a senior staff member of Civil Affairs, UNTAET, New York, 18 September 2006. See also McNamara, Dennis. 2002. "Introductory Remarks and Keynote Addresses." In: Nassrine Azimi and Chang Li Lin, eds., *The United Nations Transitional Administration in East Timor (UNTAET): Debriefing and Lessons*. Boston: Martinus Nijhoff Publishers, pp. 33-44, p. 44.

1139   Garrison 2005, p. 8. "[...] UNTAET drew directly upon the institutional and personal knowledge of the UNMIK. The planning staff were, it seems, told to 're-jig' the Kosovo plan for East Timor." Chesterman, Simon. 2005. *Building Up or Building Down the State: State-Building and Humanitarian and Development Assistance*. Paper presented at the SSRC Humanitarian Action Seminar, New York, p. 8.

1140   Martin, Ian and Mayer-Rieckh, Alexander. 2005. "The United Nations and East Timor: From Self-Determination to State-Building." *International Peacekeeping* 12:1, pp. 125-145, p. 136.

1141   CSDG, "East Timor Report," para. 329.

tise – from the transition in East Timor. Furthermore, as the peacekeeping department was also in charge of recruitment and staffing, "The mission risked assembling the wrong skill sets and operating from the wrong mindset."[1142] Combined with the overload of work and inadequate personnel, finding the right people for state- and capacity-building was a crucial weakness of the mission, recognized by senior DPKO officials.[1143]

The mission's resource equipment "enjoyed an exceptional degree of international support financially and politically – certainly higher per capita than any comparable operation."[1144] That being said, the budget faced the usual constraints. The assessed budget was subject to strict[1145] and often inadequate[1146] allocation rules; the voluntary contributions needed to be raised on an ad hoc basis, providing for a high level of uncertainty with regards to the resources of the mission's civilian parts. In addition, the gap between the abundant assessed and precarious voluntary contributions was hard to communicate with the local population. In fact, "For every voluntary dollar spent administering the country, ten assessed dollars are spent on the mission itself."[1147]

In conclusion, taking into account the serious constraints of time, resources, and politics, as well as the complexity and novelty of tasks, the policy structure that was eventually produced by the planning team in early November might be a creditable result. Still, the planning process was considerably flawed. The late Sergio Vieira de Mello stated:

> The UN, to put it mildly, is rarely accused of excessive or premature planning. [...] To be effective, planning requires internal cohesion within the United Nations, effective and regular contacts with other international organizations and key member states, and an end to bureaucratic territoriality. It also requires effective consultation with local actors. Failure to do so means that we will not hit the ground running. Failure to hit the ground running means that we risk, from the outset, failing to earn legitimacy with the populations we have come to assist. Final on this point, it is vital that we develop the systems required to draw on the requisite personnel and assets for the tasks before us, and that we do so in a timely fashion.[1148]

1142 Garrison 2005, p. 8.
1143 Interview with a senior staff member of UNDPKO PBPS, New York, 15 September 2006.
1144 McNamara 2003, p. 37.
1145 Babo Soares 2001, p. 1.
1146 Cf. Harland 2005, p. 3, "[T]here [was] a lack of rigour in determining the resources required to carry out the mission – the 'troops-to-tasks' function."
1147 Steele 2002, p. 83, referring to a statement by de Mello.
1148 Vieira de Mello 2001, p. 17-18.

> As his Red Cross plane landed in the Dili darkness of November 16, 1999, Vieira de Mello had two thoughts. The first was, 'This time you've got to do it right.' He, like all senior UN staff, knew that the UN's reputation for competence had plummeted in the 1990s. His second thought was, 'How do we do this? We've never done anything this big before.'[1149]

UNTAET was not well planned and started to operate with a carbon copy of UNMIK that closed off Timorese participation. The technocratic approach was ill-suited to Timorese needs and expectations. Misinterpretation and ignorance occurred frequently during the first months and contributed to mismanagement – as did the necessarily tight coupling of the diverse processes that the transition involved. Inadequate monies and insufficient and unqualified staff were a point in case. At the end of the day, the decision-makers of UNTAET could cope with pending failure and redirect the transition towards more Timorese participation. Again, much credit apparently has to be given to the SRSG who proved to have the right diplomatic skills to customize the "benevolent dictatorship" of UNTAET to the Timorese requirements.

3.1 Deployment

While favorable security conditions prevailed, an enormous amount of people were still displaced, the majority of public buildings and private housing was destroyed, and all public administration activities lay idle. Accordingly, the logistical and organizational processes absorbed much time, resources, and in the end, legitimacy. The overload of substantial tasks of deployment, mission set up and ongoing humanitarian and demilitarization activities were compounded by the so-called "mandate – implementation gap." In the beginning, the meaning of the core mandate imperative of governing was unclear and could not be tackled instantaneously. UNTAET appeared increasingly as a self-focused mega-organization that, at the same time, was still unable to improve the lives of the Timorese.

3.1.1 Arriving in East Timor

The good progress in the security sector through INTERFET was enhanced by the comparatively efficient deployment of the UN Peacekeeping Force

---

1149 Power 2008, p. 303. She quotes an interview of de Mello with the *Washington Post* of May 19.

(UNPKF).[1150] After about four months, UNPKF became operational, marked by the transfer of command for the military operations from INTERFET to UNPKF on February 23. The deployment of the civilian police forces (UNTAET CivPol) and of the international civilian staff, however, proceeded sluggishly: by 28 January 2000, only 387 police officers had been deployed, compared to a projected total strength of 1,640, and only around 400 international civilian staff of the expected 1,200 had arrived.[1151] The recruitment was still ongoing.

3.1.2 Demilitarization

Demilitarization of former warring parties is a crucial first step in any peace operation – much of its future development depends on the success of this measure. In UNTAET's early stages, military and policing tasks were conducted by INTERFET, who was running the vacant law and order structures. When UNPKF came in, its top priority was to disarm, demobilize, and reintegrate the pro-Indonesian militias and the Falintil, in order to build a new East Timorese army and police force. However, this process encountered various hurdles.

> The UN peacekeeping force attempted to implement a search-and-seize campaign to disarm militia and checked returning refugees for weapons at border crossings. These efforts were undermined by the Indonesian government's refusal to disarm militias based in West Timor. Consequently, the militias were never disarmed. In January 2001, the Falintil High Command and UNTAET agreed on a disarmament plan for Falintil fighters. However, many never gave up their weapons. Those weapons that were surrendered were made available to the East Timor Defense Force. The Falintil Reinsertion Assistance Program, funded by USAID, the World Bank, and Japan, assisted in the reintegration of Falintil fighters. A number of dissatisfied ex-Falintil members nevertheless turned to robbery, extortion, and other crimes.[1152]

Diverse militia groups continued to attack international peacekeepers, killing several of them. In retaliation, UNTAET peacekeepers launched two major counterattacks, cooperating closely with CivPol and other UNTAET divisions. At the same time, Security Council members kept on pressuring Indonesia to assist in militia control.

1150 UN Doc. S/1999/1024, 4 October 1999, para. 75. 70 percent of the INTERFET Force were supposed to stay and join the UN Peacekeeping Force. Cf. UN Department of Peace Operations, "Brochure on UNTAET," UNTAET/OCPI IC/01E 5,000, January 2000. Available online at http://www.un.org/peace/etimor/untaetPU/WUntaet.pdf, last access on 6 March 2009.

1151 Cf. UNTAET Public Information Office, "Law and Order Initiatives," 28 January 2000. Available online at http://www.un.org/peace/etimor/DB/br280100.htm, last access on 4 March 2009. "[T]he limited capacities of the UN Secretariat were fully stretched in the second half of 1999 [...]." Martin and Mayer-Rieckh 2005, p. 142.

1152 Dobbins et al. 2005, p. 163.

In January 2001, the two sources of pressure came together to produce joint UNTAET-Indonesian patrols in problem areas on the border between East and West Timor, greatly reducing the ability of the militias to infiltrate. [...] As Vieira de Mello explained later, 'Our ability, on-the-ground, to modify our military's rules of engagement – quickly – as the security situation warranted was vital. Only by doing so were we able, effectively, to address the serious militia incursions of mid-2000 and fulfil one of our core responsibilities: ensuring peace in East Timor.'[1153]

3.1.3 Humanitarian Action

The stabilizing security situation notwithstanding, the pressing humanitarian needs in East Timor were still ubiquitous. In some disclosed districts, people were starving and the health care system was close to non-existent. Likewise, the return of refugees and displaced persons was an urgent issue, as people had fled in masses from Indonesian assaults.

> Access to and protection of displaced persons and their return to their homes remain primary concerns of the ICRC/International Federation of Red Cross and Red Crescent Societies, and the United Nations High Commissioner for Refugees, who visited the region from 18 to 21 September. In the medical and water and sanitation sectors, relief efforts will concentrate on restoring primarily health-care services and the re-establishment of the central hospital in Dili under the auspices of ICRC, the United Nations Children's Fund and the World Health Organization. The World Food Programme has initiated regular food drops of humanitarian daily rations to provide emergency sustenance to concentrations of internationally displaced persons.[1154]

UNTAET tackled these tasks in comprehensive cooperation arrangements with other governmental, intergovernmental, and non-governmental partners. When UNTAET deployed, UNHCR, ICRC, UNICEF, WHO, the WFO, and various NGOs had already taken up humanitarian relief work, steered by OCHA.[1155] Gradually, OCHA's activities were integrated into UNTAET's humanitarian assistance

---

1153 Howard 2008, p. 285.
1154 UN Doc. S/1999/1024, para. 20.
1155 A Humanitarian Coordinator had also been appointed. "A Humanitarian Coordinator for the East Timor crisis was appointed on 11 September. He and other humanitarian relief partners are working in close cooperation with the multinational force to ensure that relief operations are carried out with appropriate logistic and security support. Civilian-military coordination units have been established in Darwin and Dili. A Humanitarian Operations Centre has been established in Dili to support the activities of United Nations agencies, non-governmental organizations and ICRC, which are all active in East Timor." UN Doc. S/1999/1024, para. 18.

and emergency rehabilitation pillar,[1156] "learning on the second level from the UN peacekeeping operation in Mozambique, where humanitarian assistance had not been centrally coordinated."[1157]

Cooperating closely with the Humanitarian Coordinator and the UN field agencies, UNTAET's early priorities were security, emergency relief, and humanitarian assistance tasks.[1158] The return of refugees and IDPs was particularly important. "A preliminary United Nations inter-agency assessment of the humanitarian situation in East Timor [...] estimates that, of the total pre-ballot population of 890,000, over 500,000 people have been displaced by the recent violence, including some 150,000 to western Timor."[1159] With these pressing humanitarian issues, the mission has been acknowledged to have done a good job.[1160] One of the respondents related this to the fact that top-level UNTAET staff came from the emergency relief "business:"

> Many of the mission leadership were people that came out of UNHCR: de Mello, Dennis McNamara, for instance. And UNHCR does crisis response: they go in when there is a

---

1156   "On 1st January 2000, OCHA was integrated into UNTAET in financial terms, and by April 2000 OCHA identity had been formally incorporated into the UNTAET system." Hurford, Chris and Wahlstrom, Margareta. 2001. *OCHA and the Timor Crisis, 1999. An Independent Study for OCHA*. Available online at ochaonline.un.org/OchaLinkClick.aspx?link=ocha&DocId=100399, last access on 15 March 2009, p. 50.

1157   Howard 2008, p. 287.

1158   Cf. Chesterman 2004, p. 64. "Zu Beginn [musste die Mission] aufgrund der lokalen Gegebenheiten [die Priorität der humanitären Hilfe, Polizei, Justiz] setzten [...]." Forster, Michael. 2005. *Nation Building durch die internationale Gemeinschaft: Eine völkerrechtliche Analyse der Vereinten Nationen im Kosovo und in Ost-Timor*. Göttingen: Cuvillier, p. 94. "The situation in East Timor is critical. [...] The civil administration is no longer functioning. [...] Essential services, such as water and electricity, are in real danger of collapse. [...] There are no medical services and hundreds of thousands of displaced persons are in dire need of emergency relief. These are critical issues, which must be addressed *even before the full deployment of the United Nations Transitional Administration*" [emphasis added]. UN Doc. S/1999/1024, para. 22.

1159   UN Doc. S/1999/1024, para. 19.

1160   Interview with a representative of the Timor-Leste Institute for Reconstruction Monitoring and Analysis, New York, 27 November 2006. "There was a general consensus, among representatives of agencies, funds and programmes, interviewed in the field for this report, that coordination among them was exemplary, [facilitated by] OCHA during the emergency phase, and consolidated by other factors, including the leadership exercised by the United Nations Resident Coordinator as well as by the sheer hardship and difficulty which all aced at the outset and which forced them to seek each other's support. Coordination in Dili was formalized very quickly as a normal country team was established soon after the resumption of UN operations through UNTAET in December 1999. Weekly meetings were held for heads of agencies (also attended by the World Bank representative), and theme groups were set up. The Resident Coordinator was the main channel of contacts and communication between the agencies and the SRSG, although they all had direct access to the SRSG if required." Duque Gonzáles, Armando et al. 2002. *Evaluation of United Nations System Response in East Timor: Coordination and Effectiveness*. Geneva: United Nations, p. 16. They also stated that the emergency help financing especially via CAP was effective. Cf. ibid., p. 14.

flood, when there is a war. Their job is to make sure that people don't starve, that they don't have epidemics. And they do a recently good job at that. But that's all short-term emergency response, it's not thinking about what happens after that – that's not their job. So when you have people who have no experience or to whom this is not even part of their consciousness: that was the case in East Timor.[1161]

That said, the refugee problem continues to persist nowadays. In fact, UNTAET was never able to completely fulfil this part of its mandate.[1162]

3.1.4 Installing the Mission: Drop a Brick

The set-up of UNTAET was challenged by constant clangers. Besides humanitarian needs, the mission had its hands full taking care of itself, i.e. arranging staff arrival, finding staff offices and lodging, and setting up the internal administration, communication, and infrastructure capacities for mission maintenance. Owed in large part to this overload of tasks, the international staff did not establish early contact with the locals, making them feel marginalized, nor was it able to fulfil a range of pressing issues. This "mixture" seriously damaged UNTAET's reputation. Already during those early days, the mission's initially high legitimacy started to decrease.

While UNTAET could rely on SOPs and experience for the humanitarian challenges, "neither the Secretary-General's Report nor the subsequent Security Council Resolution 1272 set out any specific plans for achieving either the timetable or the goals"[1163] of the *civilian* mandate. "Developing a strategy to accomplish the goals within the time frame was left to the SRSG."[1164] The strategy that was eventually developed envisaged four integrated phases.

> Phase 1: The mission would set administrative structures, deploy international civilian police, provide emergency assistance for returning refugees and displaced people, restore public services, and train local police and judiciary. In addition, with close cooperation with relevant institutions, it would also develop a phased economic recovery plan and reconstruction, and therefore seek to establish and develop a self-sustaining economy. Phase 2: UNTAET would finalise preparations and conduct elections, as well as necessary political arrangements to ensure the success of elections. Phase 3: based

---

1161 Interview with a representative of the Timor-Leste Institute for Reconstruction Monitoring and Analysis, New York, 27 November 2006.
1162 Cf. Howard 2008, pp. 287-288, "Upon independence, the problem became one for the new East Timorese government, which, while professing an interest in reconciliation with Timorese who were opposed to independence, was not prepared to put a lot of effort into trying to repatriate the remaining people who were the most reluctant to return. [...] In other words, UNTAET did not completely fulfil its mandate of overseeing refugee return before its end, and the problem remains one that the East Timorese and Indonesian governments must sort out."
1163 Garrison 2005, pp. 7-8.
1164 Ibid.

on the outcome and result of elections, UNTAET would help setting up the institutions necessary for democratic and autonomous self-government. In this regard, UNTAET would transfer its remaining administrative responsibilities while supporting the consolidation of East Timor post-election institutions. Phase 4: as the institutions (especially the legislative-like one) reach a substantial decision on the date of independence as well as the state system and its supporting arrangements, thus, as an exit-strategy, the UN mission will be downsized to a very minimum scale, both, in terms of personnel and responsibilities.[1165]

Still, the flawed policy formation phase had negative effects on deployment. "From the perspective of time, the presence of UNTAET was […] not well planned. This could be seen from the beginning, when UNTAET did not know what to do."[1166] Particularly the slow take-up of the international administration staff was a major constraint. The inefficiencies were even compounded by unfortunate signals towards the East Timorese. A case in point was the way UNTAET's staff was accommodated: they lived either at luxurious boat hotels or in the few buildings in East Timor that had not been razed. "It was like, 'East Timor is so distasteful I couldn't even sleep in the country,' they had to sleep in a boat, in the harbor."[1167] At the same time, many Timorese were still without shelter and the UN "squatters" raised hairs.[1168] "The ships would become such a headache for Vieira de Mello that in July 2000 he ordered the nightclub on the ship to be closed at midnight. But by then the damage had long been done."[1169] Similar signals were given with other deployment activities, for instance the way telecommunication was set up. "They brought in satellite dishes so they could have phone service; they brought in this Australian telephone company that had no interest in being in East Timor after they finished their work for the UN. A lot of stuff like that, where they just created their

1165 Subianto 2002, pp. 4-5.
1166 Saldanha 2003, p. 162. Still half a year into the mission, UNTAET "was groping to determine what to do since the mission was not quite well defined." Ibid.
1167 Interview with a representative of the Timor-Leste Institute for Reconstruction Monitoring and Analysis, New York, 27 November 2006. "In late 1999, when the first groups of UNAET personnel arrived in what used to be Indonesia's 27th province, Hotel Olympia was the only place to stay for most of the expatriates. With no competition, Olympia charged an exorbitant $200 for a 3 x 2 meter room a night. The floating hotel, owned by an Australian, had been in operation prior to the rioting in the wake of the 1999 referendum and escaped the fire which destroyed most government buildings and hotels in the city. In its one year of operation under contract with UNTAET, Olympia is believed to have made at least $40 million in profits – eight times the amount UNTAET spent in salaries to its local employees during the same period." Tempo Magazin, "Timor's Floating Hotels." *Tempo Magazin* 30, October – 5 November 2001. Available online at http://members.pcug.org.au/~wildwood/01novhotels.htm, last access on 4 March 2009.
1168 "They took over all the left buildings. You know, in 1999, when UNTAET came in, 70 percent of the buildings were destroyed, but there were a few buildings that were not totally destroyed – so, the UN took those and used them for their offices and stuff." Interview with a representative of the Timor-Leste Institute for Reconstruction Monitoring and Analysis, New York, 27 November 2006.
1169 Power 2008, p. 312.

own infrastructure for the functioning of the mission without thinking about."[1170] Further enhancing the appearance of double standards, UNTAET was operating under a secret Status of Mission Agreement[1171] that put its staff above the very laws they were about to establish.

> The Status of Mission Agreement is not so much an agreement, it's a policy. In UNTAET's case, it said that the UN personnel had no legal responsibilities in the country: they don't have to follow local laws, they can't be prosecuted, they can't be obliged to testify even if they're witnesses, all of that. There are reasons for that maybe in a military peacekeeping operation, but there is no justification for it in a transitional government in a peaceful time. But once you have that, it leads to all kinds of violations to the law – violations of common sense, drunk driving, and things like that. It's also a ridiculous model to impose if you're trying to create a democracy to have this class of people who don't have to follow the law. That's something that could be changed.[1172]

Ultimately, a special health care system was created exclusively for international personnel while the local system remained in shambles.[1173] Summarizing the problem, a senior official acknowledges, "We arrived with that car, our radio, our own salary, a salary line to hire a few local staff – but we had no money as the government. And yet we were the government."[1174] The budget for government tasks had to come from donors. And that took time. "You go to the donors, you get the money, and you have to create the budgeting authority, create the budget system, and create a system to pay people, decide who you are going to pay... Months! And in the meantime there are all of these white cars running around."[1175]

1170 Interview with a representative of the Timor-Leste Institute for Reconstruction Monitoring and Analysis, New York, 27 November 2006. Another often-cited example is the bottled water consumption. "By the end of UNTAET, the mission had probably spent 15 million dollars on importing bottled water. For 15 million dollars they could have re-built the water system for Dili that would have not just met their own staff's need but would have served the whole population and had lasted forever." Ibid.

1171 "Even the existence of this agreement was secret. We [local NGOS; ES] got a copy of it. In fact, someone from the UN gave us a copy. We never published it but we should have. Anyway, a couple of times we asked UN people at press conferences and things like that and they would always sort of hedge around and not admit that it existed. For example, I remember an instance where I had a copy in my hand and said, you know, 'This is the mission agreement and it says this and that.' And someone from the UN said, 'I don't know what you're holding here.' You know, it's like... it's not dishonesty but maybe arrogance. They think people are so stupid that they believe these fictions. Another example is a seminar where I touched the issue and asked a UN official, 'The UN is here teaching the East Timorese about transparency, why is there a secret agreement about what laws apply to the UN staff?' And he said, 'I'll have my legal adviser answer that.' And his legal adviser then, maybe 15 minutes later, came and said, 'It's not a secret agreement, it's just not public' [laughs]." Ibid.

1172 Ibid.

1173 Interview with a representative of the Timor-Leste Institute for Reconstruction Monitoring and Analysis, New York, 27 November 2006.

1174 Interview with a senior staff member of UNTAET, New York, 23 November 2006.

1175 Ibid.

In January 2000, the first major demonstration against the UN was staged.

Box 7: "Hoarding Power, Hoarding Blame"[1176]

"The arrival of the UN had raised expectations that, thanks to familiar UN funding structures, the mission could not deliver. [...] 'Something clearly is not right if UNTAET can cost $692 million, whereas the entire budget of East Timor comes to a bit over $59 million,' Vieira de Mello declared before the Security Council. 'Can it therefore come as a surprise that there is so much criticism of United Nations extravagances, while the Timorese continue to suffer?' (Vieira de Mello, "The Situation in East Timor," presentation to the Security Council, June 27, 2000). [...]

An even more remarkable UN rule held that UN assets could be used only by mission staff. This meant that, although the UN was there to assist in 'state-building,' owing to liability concerns, the Timorese technically could not be transported in UN helicopters or in UN vehicles. UN staff eventually had more than five hundred vehicles, but Vieira de Mello had to break the rules in order to get a dozen of them released for the top Timorese leaders who would one day be running the country themselves. 'This is ridiculous,' he exclaimed during one of many arguments with the UN official in charge of administration. 'I have the authority to order troops to open fire on militia leaders, but I don't have the authority to give a computer to Xanana Gusmão!'

Since New York was thirteen hours behind East Timor, he could rarely get the authorization he needed in a timely fashion. [Staff member] Prentice explains, 'There will always be that tension, with headquarters thinking we are all a bunch of Colonel Kurtzes, and the field people thinking, 'These guys who just sit behind their nice desks don't understand anything.' 'The rules,' Vieira de Mello wrote in a 'lessons learned' paper, 'make the UN appear arrogant and egoistical in the eyes of those whom we are meant to help' (Vieira de Mello, "How Not to Run a Country: Lessons for the UN from Kosovo and East Timor," 2000, unpublished)."[1177]

Pull towards Centralization

Giving in to various dynamics, UNTAET did not pursue the decentralized governance approach – as was, in fact, requested by the mandate – but ended up with the usual centralized model of mandate implementation. The idea of the decentralized design rested on the assumption that UNTAET should function as the nucleus for the government-to-be.[1178] In theory, the intention was to set up offices at the district level by making use of the administration system "inherited" from Indonesia, with its 13 districts, 65 sub-districts and 448 villages (*sucos*), themselves subdivided into hamlets (*aldeias*).[1179] In practice, however, the mission staff's focus was not

---

1176 Power 2008, p. 303.
1177 Ibid., p. 314.
1178 Cf. Beauvais 2001, p. 1142.
1179 This structure in fact entirely reflected the views of the local resistance people inside the territory, "because they had organized the resistance according to administrative areas. You had a competition for influence at the local level between three types of people. One was the old rulers, and the Portuguese, the noble families of East Timor. Secondly, the *chefes de suco* or *chefes de aldea* who'd been appointed by the Indonesians; some of them were competent, and some of them were also part of the first structure, those who were the original ruling class. And thirdly you had the resistance leaders. So, you had a competition for influence at the local level of who is actually going to be the dominant political force." Interview with a senior staff member of Civil Affairs, UNTAET, New York, 18 September 2006.

on local-level administration, even less on local level consultation or capacity-building.[1180] The envisioned model "was not implemented during the first nine months of the mission and only to a limited extent thereafter."[1181] What was more, UNTAET moulded into a *de facto* centralized institution.[1182] Anthropologist and former UN volunteer Tanja Hohe gave a vivid narrative of the developments in the early post-conflict time:

> The early post-conflict days in the field were a story in itself. Imagine nothing highly professional and functional. It was completely chaotic and everybody was just trying to survive. [...] staff quality can be very low, logistics are a nightmare, and you are basically left with yourself and a couple of maybe smart colleagues to deal with what is chaos – but that is normal, not UNTAET-specific. Imagine in early December 1999, we were six UNVs (because the professional staff only joined much later, when everything was set up, because their recruitment takes so long. Also, don't imagine professional staff being more professional than UNVs. I knew people who were not taken by UNV, but got a professional position later on.). Most of us had worked for UNAMET, so we at least knew the environment. The town of Maliana was completely destroyed, 80 percent of the houses were burnt, hardly any people were left, and there was zero food. We had chosen a random building that was empty and that still had a roof and we were camping in our tents inside. One room we had dedicated as 'office space.' We worked closely with the military observers, the police, and INTERFET. INTERFET was our lifeline, as army they were the only ones that were fully equipped and had the logistics to make things work. UNTAET looked completely pathetic in comparison. Anyway, there was one of the early days, when the six of us sat on the veranda and decided to split tasks. It was like playing monopoly, one colleague wanted to take on coordination of education, one humanitarian aid, one infrastructure etc... I opted for land and property. I never had anything to do with that, but there was need because the first land disputes had already come to us. That is how the sectoral offices of the Bobonaro district administration were established! In reality, everyone did everything. We had Timorese staff as drivers and translators. The CNRT and Falintil commanders lived next doors. We only hesitantly went over and started contact with them – having had orders from headquarters that the CNRT is no official power to be cooperated with. However, the CNRT was the only available and well-organised authority on-the-ground. Without them, we could have packed up and gone home. However, some fool in New York had decided that the referendum had not been about the CNRT – but that is another story. Otherwise, we had hardly any connection to headquarters in Dili. We could only communicate via satellite phone, and that is arduous. We basically ran our own show, with a computer or a chair sometimes making its way to us from Dili. At six in the morning, the night was over, because the first people were gathering in front of our office. We got up and there was often no time for breakfast. We basically had a 16 hours day, just responding to emergencies. People would come with all kinds of

---

1180 Telephone interview with a program officer of the Donor Coordination Unit, UNTAET, 7 October 2006.
1181 Beauvais 2001, p. 1142. The structure went no further down than the sub-district. Cf. CSDG, "East Timor Report," para. 312.
1182 "The original UNTAET structure was quite centralized." Interview with a senior staff member of UNTAET, New York, 23 November 2006.

issues, land conflicts, children were starving, and they wanted this and that. People were without anything and were trying to rebuild their lives. They had thousand requests to us about what they needed. They also, of course, did not understand who we were and what our role was. And we, in turn, did not know what they required to rebuild their lives – not that we could have put in request to headquarters anyway... So, the first agricultural cycle was lost, because nobody in UNTAET would have thought of ordering seeds, for example. The food aid delivered was not what many children were used to eat. They rejected the food therefore. People came down from the mountains to tell us that they only live of mangos, and that people had died of starvation already. So we would need to go out there (which was partly extremely difficult terrain, especially in the rainy season), and check. I had no clue what malnourishment looked like. I was not an expert, but people were dying." Meanwhile at the central level, the focus was on "the technical establishment of building proper western institutions."[1183]

One part of the problem was that the staff allocated to the districts had only very rudimentary operative instructions. "As for planning, there was absolute chaos. Everything was very improvised, and compounded by scarce financial resources for the districts."[1184] A former district administrator immediately started to laugh when asked if he had been given some kind of implementation plan. "I was just told, 'Go there.'"[1185] In the beginning, "everyone was doing their own thing."[1186] At the same time, DPKO did not push for a coherent decentralization approach. On the contrary, as stated above, the decentralization model outlined by the mandate was an innovation, while the centralized, top-down model was DPKO's routine approach.[1187] At the end of the day, despite the mandate instruction, the standard model was chosen. "UN missions run their structures very much in line with UN hierarchy. In itself, it is a very nice system, but not necessarily a model which meets local requirements and which the nationals simply can take over and inherit."[1188]

Adding to the problems of availability and a shortage of quality staff, the deployment of the international personnel was delayed. "[T]he UN's complex recruitment procedures and the Secretariat's understaffed personnel section, under increasing pressure from other new or expanding missions, failed to expedite the

1183 Written interview with Dr. Tanja Hohe, former team member of UN Volunteers in East Timor, 30 September 2006.
1184 Interview with a district field officer, UNTAET, New York, 15 September 2006.
1185 Ibid. The description of the situation was confirmed by a senior UNTAET staff member as "unfortunately true", adding that there was not much supervision from Dili Headquarters. Interview with a senior staff member of Civil Affairs, UNTAET, New York, 18 September 2006.
1186 Written interview with Dr. Tanja Hohe, former team member of UN Volunteers in East Timor, 30 September 2006.
1187 Interview with Professor Michael W. Doyle, former UN Assistant Secretary-General, New Haven, 11 September 2006. However, even this routine approach does not work well still.
1188 Interview with Professor Dirk Salomons, Director of the Program for Humanitarian Affairs at the School of International Public Affairs, Columbia University, New York, 20 September 2006.

recruitment of well-qualified international staff."[1189] There were just not enough people to do heavy staffing at the district and sub-district level. In that situation, quite a large share of the civilian personnel that were deployed was of questionable technical expertise and work practice. "To be very honest, a lot of people who we had working with us were completely unsuitable for mission life, people who did not make a significant contribution to the live there. On the other hand, people who wanted to make progress and get better jobs preferred to be in Dili, in the head-quarters, rather than going out to the districts."[1190] Besides, the personnel only had limited skills in the relevant local languages.

> Very few of the people spoke either Portuguese or Bahasa. This was a big problem indeed since UNTAET officers in the districts and sub-districts were dependent totally on their translators – when we had translators at all. Then, there was no means of com-municating with the people he or she was supposedly responsible for. Big problem. It meant that in practice, the contacts of most Timorese with the foreigners, the 'malai,' which is a Timorese expression for the foreigners, were very superficial. What they saw were people who were completely incompetent, people who had no idea about their situation, and who could not deliver anything for them, whether it be improving a road to go there, or building a schoolroom, anything like that. The people we sent out didn't have the tools, they didn't have the money that they needed to be able to give the Timorese what they wanted – clinics, schools, road tracks. We couldn't do any of those things.[1191]

And they could not communicate it properly. "This put an unreasonable burden on the few staff in the mission and contributed to UNTAET's loss of credibility during its first months of operation."[1192] Finally, UNTAET faced "enormous logistical challenges in mobilizing an operation of this scale in a territory nearly bereft of infrastructure or basic services,"[1193] and the numbers and levels of capacity of the local people was even lower in rural areas than the average in East Timor.

Participation Put on Hold

The early ending of the formal involvement of the CNRT as an interlocutor and transition partner and the inadequate and inappropriate assumption on a local power vacuum (*terra nullis*) had their repercussions. Not only did UNTAET soon struggle

1189 Martin and Mayer-Rieckh 2005, p. 134. "[T]he limited capacities of the UN Secretariat were fully stretched in the second half of 1999 [...]." Ibid., p. 142.
1190 Interview with a senior staff member of Civil Affairs, UNTAET, New York, 18 September 2006.
1191 Ibid.
1192 Martin and Mayer-Rieckh 2005, p. 134.
1193 Beauvais 2001, p. 1124. Reasonable infrastructure was only available in Dili and imme-diate surroundings; it was very difficult and took a long time to get out and built institutions up out in the districts.

with a drop of local support, but it was also gambling away synergies that would have resulted from the use of the CNRT-structures.

UNTAET would have had a much easier start had it availed itself of the CNRT structures that were "the only available and well-organized authority on-the-ground."[1194] Instead, the *terra nullis* policy cut this option short. "UNTAET had no awareness of any traditional power structures. The country was assumed to be in a 'vacuum,' which was complete nonsense."[1195]

This stance, however, was hardly contested among international staff during UNTAET's first months, resembling the discussions that had taken place during mission planning:

> There had been desperate attempts in the early months of UNTAET amongst its staff, in the capital and in the districts, to convince the mission leadership to confront the question of internal political dynamics. There were differing views. One view felt that the CNRT should be broken up as soon as possible. But anyone who had been in Somalia was horrified by the thought of the loss of a single interlocutor and its fragmentation into disparate, perpetually shifting factions and the World Bank also strongly opposed this idea. Thus, at the other extreme were those who believed there should be recognition of the CNRT as the *de facto* local authority, an argument made more possible with the essential absence of pro-integrationist forces in the political arena. Yet it was hindered by the underlying assumption from New York that the August 1999 vote was for independence, not for the CNRT as the government. [...] [A]nother position held that elections should be conducted at the beginning of the mission, and not in the middle or at the end. Still others somehow thought the issue and the CNRT itself could be ignored, just as the Timorese should be excluded.[1196]

The neglect of CNRT as an official partner resulted also in tensions at the district levels between UNTAET and the indigenous structures. "You had a competition for influence at the local level of who is actually going to be the dominant political force. And that emerged with UNTAET and there were quite a lot of tensions."[1197] They were exacerbated when the World Bank launched a program for Community Empowerment – which UNTAET took issue with.[1198]

1194 Written interview with Dr. Tanja Hohe, former team member of UN Volunteers in East Timor, 30 September 2006. "East Timorese leaders were keen to take charge and tackle the enormous problems. The National Council of Timorese Resistance (CNRT), a collation of the pro-independence, groups, and the Armed Forces for the National Liberation of East Timor (Falintil) moved into the vacuum of local authority, and in some places asserted a security role. The situation improved as José Alexandre (Xanana) Gusmão, President of the CNRT [...] began to play an effective leadership role." UN Secretary-General, "Report of the Secretary-General on the United Nations Transitional Administration in East Timor," UN Doc. S/2000/53, 26 January 2000, para. 2.
1195 Interview with a representative of the Timor-Leste Institute for Reconstruction Monitoring and Analysis, New York, 27 November 2006.
1196 Chopra 2002, pp. 996-997.
1197 Interview with a senior staff member of Civil Affairs, UNTAET, New York, 18 September 2006.
1198 See box 8.

Box 8: The Community Empowerment Programme (CEP)

The thirty-months-long project that cost $22.5 million was intended to provide for the establishment of representative village and sub-district councils in charge of allocating World Bank and Asian Development Bank (ADB) development funds.

"The CEP's objective is to establish transparent, democratic, and accountable local structures in rural areas to make decisions about development projects in a decentralized fashion. The local CEP councils will allow communities to rehabilitate basic infrastructure and revive local economies. On a longer-term basis, the Bank presents the councils as a vehicle for expressing their development needs and desires, and for implementing projects. In this regard, they are a form of local governance and structures for a 'bottom-up' approach to development. The CEP would thus seem to be a good example of the Bank's new face. Jarat Chopra, the former UNTAET head of the Office of District Administration describes the CEP as 'an introduction to local democracy, as well as a functioning form of self-determination in the reconstruction process.'" [1199]

However, it was rejected by UNTAET twice, on the basis that the councils would provide for a "premature politization of the environment." – "[O]ur concern is that elections under the community empowerment programme, which are intended to elect local representatives who will decide on the allocation of funds for development projects at the community level, should not be confused with local elections-local political elections for the establishment of local political bodies.' (Daily Briefing, UNTAET, Transcript of Remarks by SRSG Sergio Vieira de Mello After the Signing Ceremony of a Grant Agreement by UNTAET, CNRT and the Wold Bank) [...]." [1200] Apart from that, UNTAET reportedly feared that it "would not have control over the significant amount of funding, and that CEP would set up decision-making bodies circumventing UNTAET's governance structures." [1201] Indeed, there "have also been tensions between CEP structures and traditional decision-making mechanisms. It also appears that the CEP has unintentionally served to reinforce power relations in some areas as the relatively powerful have been best positioned to take advantage of the opportunities offered by the project. Because of insufficient communication within localities and between villages and the district levels, there is also a problem of CEP projects duplicating projects by NGOs, UNTAET, or UN agencies." [1202]

When UNTAET finally agreed to adopt the program, under pressure from UN Secretary-General Annan, World Bank President Wolfensohn, and the Timorese CNRT, it deliberately used the term "election" in the respective regulation. Later on, UNTAET set up District Advisory Boards to help link sub-district CEP councils with district administrations. [1203]

Overall, CEP was rated a successful project. [1204] Still, the CEP councils are creations of the international community. In this regard, they are not as legitimate and vibrant as socio-political structures that have emerged out of local, long-term processes. As the resulting Joint Donor Report noted, "[A]t present the talent and energy at village level is more likely to be found around the *chefe* and the old clandestine structures than within the council." [1205] It is such structures that the report contends "must be built upon if the country's urgent rural development problems are to be solved." At the same time, what the report calls their "control mentality and gender bias" runs counter to international notions of democracy, as well as to the official positions of the CNRT." [1206] All that being said, the CEP was a more coherent and successful approach than that what UNTAET was able to deliver at the district level at that time. [1207]

1199 La'o Hamutuk. 2000. "Evaluating the World Bank's Community Empowerment Project." *La'o Hamutuk Bulletin* 1:4, 31 December 2000. Available online at http://www.etan.org/lh/bulletin04.html#CEP, last access on 5 March 2009.
1200 Beauvais 2002, p. 1126.
1201 La'o Hamutuk 2000.
1202 Ibid.
1203 Ibid.

3.1.5 Summary and Assessment

The mission's early deployment and its set-up proceeded within the usual timeline
– and with the usual shortcomings. While humanitarian relief efforts and military
stabilization were implemented rather successfully, UNTAET was not able to live
up to the praise it received. It nearly gambled away the local population's acceptance, support, and its own legitimacy.

The secure and supportive environment was not readily adjusted to by the mission. Due to problems with logistics and recruitment, the deployment proceeded
sluggishly. The situation was the worst about civilian aspects and much of the
governance work needed to be deferred. Besides, the focus was almost exclusively
on the mission set-up and the central level. Matter of fact, UNTAET was planned
and deployed "first and foremost as a peacekeeping operation."[1208]

Since sufficient voluntary funds for civilian peacebuilding measures were not
available from the outset, such programmes needed to be deferred; hence, the provision of services to the districts was also delayed. Programmes and services were
developed later on, mostly on-the-ground, in a "back and forth" process.[1209] "It is
probably correct to say that there was no, at the beginning, no real strict template
or guidelines. So, the individuals who got the tasks had to make it up as they went
along. There wasn't a recipe. Over time, we began to build the framework."[1210]
Possibly its biggest fault during the early implementation phase was UNTAET'
poor communication of the procedural necessities and of its financial constraints.
"We looked very powerful and people came to us and said, you know, 'Can you
come and fix my broken house?', and we said, 'No, we don't have any earth-moving
equipment. The only earth-moving equipment we have is to fix our headquarters.
That's what has been budgeted.'"[1211] Still, the immediate priorities of security and

---

1204 417 village-level development councils were formed and 60 sub-district-level councils.
"The project has funded over 600 local projects. The Bank reports that 43 percent of
projects are for the construction of community meeting halls, 25 percent for small roads
linking up to larger ones and for the repair of agricultural infrastructure, 15 percent for the
restoration of household assets (such as pots, pans, plates, cups, and/or spoons shared by
villagers) and productive equipment (such as communally-owned low-tech farm equipment, lathes, or saws) destroyed in the post-referendum violence, 10 percent for repair of
water supply infrastructure, and seven percent for schools or clinics." Ibid.
1205 Ibid.
1206 Ibid.
1207 Interview with a representative of the Timor-Leste Institute for Reconstruction Monitoring
and Analysis, New York, 27 November 2006.
1208 Chesterman 2004, p. 64. "East Timor is technically a peacekeeping operation, de Mello
reports to Under Secretary-General Bernard Miyet, the head of UN peacekeeping." Traub
2002, p. 5.
1209 Interview with Joseph Andrews, Special Adviser to the Deputy SRSG, UNTAET, and to
the Foreign Minister, ETTA, Washington, DC, 9 September 2006.
1210 Interview with a senior staff member of UNTAET, New York, 23 November 2006.
1211 Ibid.

emergency relief were carried out relatively well. In these areas, better routines and expertise was more readily available.

3.2 Implementation of the Mandate

On the grounds of the mandate and based on the *terra nullis* assumption, UNTAET's institution-building approach was to establish administrations across sectors to be run by international staff and, once they were functional, to hand them over to the East Timorese. The pitfall of this approach was fourfold: one, international staff were themselves, for the most part, not well-versed administrators and had no experience in setting up institutions. Two, Timorese felt that they were excluded from the beginning. Three, capacity-building was no priority. Four, the modus of the hand-over of responsibility from the internationals to the locals had not been specified. Step by step, the transitional administration, increasingly pushed and led by its SRSG, tried to make up for these shortcomings by identifying administrative priorities and involving the East Timorese on political and implementation levels. Still, UNTAET moved slowly, whereas Timorese discontent increased exponentially. In a radical and, in fact, innovative move, the SRSG eventually decided to end UNTAET's original institution- and state-building approach. That probably saved the mission from becoming a failure.

3.2.1 The Technocratic Approach

The big question was, when building a state from scratch, how does one prioritize?

> I wish I knew the answers to that question, because since I arrived here [...] everything we touch, everything we see, everything we hear is a priority. So what we've been trying to do is to prioritize among the priorities, and what we have decided to focus on is infrastructure – that is, very basic public services that the population requires. The second priority would be institution-building, starting with justice first, because you cannot build a new society... a new country... unless you lay the foundations of state based on the rules of law.[1212]

Thus, the sectoral priorities were infrastructure, basic public services, and administration. The "vertical" priority in terms of government levels was on the central level.

1212 Foreign Correspondent. 2000. *Transcript of a broadcasted interview with SRSG Vieira de Mello on February 20, 2000. Sergio Vieira de Mello – East Timor transitional administration.* Available online at http://www.abc.net.au/foreign/s225290.htm, last access on 5 March 2009.

The first *formal* participative mechanism was decided on in December 2000. It was an important first step, but it soon turned out to be insufficient. Triggered by the increasing displays of dissatisfaction by the population,[1213] UNTAET created the National Consultative Council (NCC). Established by UNTAET regulation 1999/2, the NCC consisted of seven CNRT representatives,[1214] three members other than CNRT, i.e. members of pro-integration parties, one representative of the Catholic Church in East Timor, three UNTAET members, and the Transitional Administrator/SRSG who presided over the body.[1215] The low number of fifteen members was set deliberately.

> [...] UNTAET had accepted that no new political parties would be admitted to the NCC – giving exclusivity to the voice of the CNRT. This had been accepted in a spirit of conciliation – and frankly without any careful thinking behind it – but partly also because the negotiated formula included representatives of women's groups, youth organizations, traditional leaders and others. Somehow, these categories were discarded in the finalization of the terms of the NCC between the Transitional Administrator and Gusmão, on the pretext that lower numbers would make for a more workable body.[1216]

The possibility to include more local representatives was denied, citing legitimation deficits:

> The involvement of local leaders is a pre-requisite for stability and sustainability of the UN administration. But in the absence of elections, on what basis are leaders to be chosen? Difficulties arise not only in the choice of local representatives but also in the delegation of authority to them. The more powers conferred on local representatives, the closer power is to the people, and thus the more legitimate the nature of the administration. But cornering power on non-elected local representatives can also have the undesired effect of furthering a particular party. The inclination of the UN is thus to be cautious about delegating power in the interest of avoiding furthering any particular political part. There is consultation, but all essential decision making and executive authority remains with the UN.[1217]

This design made some local key figures restrain from it. "José Ramos-Horta, East Timor's eventual foreign minister, laughed off the UN's invitation to join the NCC, 'I was powerless outside of East Timor for long enough,' he told Vieira de Mello,

1213 Cf. Chopra 2002, p. 990.
1214 The seven CNRT seats corresponded to the number of its parties. Cf. Beauvais 2001, p. 1119.
1215 The mechanism of setting up non-elected councils is a conventional one in post-conflict situations or system transformations where elections are not yet appropriated. Cf. Shain, Yossi and Linz, Juan J, eds. 1995. *Between States: Interim Governments and Democratic Transitions.* Cambridge: Cambridge University Press; Ottaway, Marina and Kumar, Krishna, eds., 1998. *Postconflict Elections, Democratization and International Assistance.* Coulder: Lynne Rienner.
1216 Chopra 2002, p. 990. The same argument is made by Beauvais who, referring to a senior UNTAET official, states that the limited number facilitated "swift decision-making during the 'emergency phase' in which it was established." Beauvais 2001, p. 1120.
1217 Statement by SRSG de Mello, quoted in Beauvais 2001, p. 1120.

'the last thing I need is to be powerless inside Timor.'"[1218] At last making use of its new status, the CNRT came up with a timeline for the transition period.[1219] De Mello, who knew about the importance of giving the Timorese a feel of ownership[1220] and of offering them a fixed transition deadline, signed the timeline on 23 February 2001.

> The proposed political transition calendar included steps to the creation of a Constituent Assembly (Constituent Assembly) entrusted with the task of drafting and adopting a Constitution. The steps were as follows: political party registration; civil registration; publication of an electoral law; establishment of an independent electoral commission; creation of national constitutional commissions; launch of a civic education program; start of the electoral campaign for the Constituent Assembly; publication of official results; swearing-in ceremony of Members of the Constituent Assembly; proclamation East Timor's Constitution and transformation of the Constituent Assembly into the National Parliament by December 15, 2001.[1221]

The rationale of the approach was a technocratic idea, "There would be a government formed out of international technocrats, and their job would be to steadily hire and train, and to have themselves replaced by East Timorese."[1222] Politically,

---

1218   Power 2008, p. 307.
1219   Cf. Baltazar, Alipio. 2004. "An Overview of the Constitution Drafting Process." *East Timor Law Journal* 9. Available online at http://www.eastimorlawjournal.org/ARTI-CLES/2004/constitution_drafting_process_east_timor_alipio_baltazar.html, last access on 8 March 2009, p. 5. In fact, it was Gusmão who presented the Council with its own timetable for independence, sparking, however, dissension since he had not consulted with many of his CNRT colleagues on the issue; threatening to resign, he managed to force approval of it. Furthermore, it very much resembled the plan that de Mello had himself presented to the Security Council in June 2000. Cf. Garrison 2005.
1220   "In a November 27 brainstorming session with staff, [Vieira de Mello] argued, 'The current goodwill of the East Timorese toward the mission is and expendable asset. The longer UNTAET stays, the greater the chances that it will be perceived as a competing power.'" Power 2008, p. 308.
1221   Baltazar 2004, p. 1. The elaboration of details was referred to the Political Affairs Unit of UNTAET which came out with several regulations on the issues touched by the timetable. Also, Political Affairs engaged in a public consultation process on the constitution; the results were to be presented to the Constituent Assembly to be elected. On December 23, 2000, the Political Affairs Unit sent a letter to all political parties, district administrators, NGOs, members of cabinet and National Council and church representatives to stimulate debate on the political transition calendar. From 18 through 23 January, 2001, the Political Affairs Unit held a number of public hearings. The outcome of the public hearings showed that most of civil society organizations (such as SAHE, LAIFET, Human Right Commission, Yayasan Hak) and political parties (Apodeti, PDM, UDC PST, KOTA) objected to the transitional calendar, arguing a lack of preparation to participate in the process. Prior to the consultation process, the Political Affairs Unit benefited from extensive oral briefings of constitutional and electoral experts. Issues such as the type of electoral system, number of constituent assembly members, and the period of time for completion of the constituent assembly mandate were exhaustively analyzed during a two month period. As a result of the consultation process, a regulation on the election of a Constituent Assembly was adopted." Baltazar 2004, pp. 1-2. The results of these activities will be presented below ("Elections").
1222   Interview with a senior staff member of UNTAET, New York, 23 November 2006.

the buy-in would be through the NCC, to provide guidance on the political side. Capacity-building would be bottom up, "Ceding senior positions to local control only in the latter phases."[1223] Yet, efforts to fill even junior positions with Timorese or to give them more voice opportunities remained low. Soon, the NCC came under "increasing scrutiny for not being representative enough of East Timorese society, and not transparent enough in its deliberations."[1224] UNTAET, once again, did nothing to develop these civil society elements further. Nor was the NCC strong enough of an institution to mitigate the growing intra-East Timorese developments; with frequent shifts in the CNRT's major bodies and with some important political figures still acting from abroad, tensions within the CNRT emerged.[1225]

Red-lined

Timorese were eager to participate in the new structures but were not allowed to. Possibly, they did not have the capacity to do so either, at least in Western per-specitves. Under Indonesian rule, the majority of Timorese worked in the civil service, but in very low ranked positions. It was nonetheless important that they *had* an income at least. With the civil service going up in smoke and the new one not yet in place, unemployment rose sharply.[1226] In addition, the end of the East Timorese resistance struggle also implied that there was now an out-of-work military force, implying a security problem.

> Falintil had been sidelined during the UN consultation by being placed in containment near Baucau in attempt to avoid clashes with the Indonesian military. After the arrival of the international peacekeeping force and UN civilian police, Falintil was excluded from any security role in Timor-Leste. The UNTAET assessment of defense needs called for a Timor-Leste Defense Force (FDTL) for an independent Timor-Leste of only 1,500. This meant that in the first round of recruitment, only 650 of more than 1,300 ex-Falintil fighter found a place in the FDTL. This recruitment took place before independence and selection of members was left in the hands of Gusmão loyalists in Falintil. As most of the ex-combatants had low levels of education and lacked skills necessary

---

1223 Dobbins et al. 2005, p. 168.
1224 Viera de Mello, "Address to CNRT Congress," quoted in Beauvais 2001, p. 1124. See also Ingram 2003, p. 87, "The mechanism for selection of members of the NC was widely criticised by NGOs and some political parties, and similar interests strongly opposed the transformation of the Constituent Assembly into the parliament, seeing it as cementing the position of Fretilin as the dominant party."
1225 "The CNRT leadership was not stable in the immediate post-conflict phase, leading to frequent shifts in designated interlocutors for particular policy areas. Several of the CNRT leaders were not in the territory of East Timor on a consistent basis and the relatively few recognized representatives of East Timorese civil society were not organized yet to provide consultation on policy issues." Beauvais 2001, p. 1121.
1226 As of January 2000, the UN estimated that "80 percent of the population is currently without visible means of support" UN Doc. S/2000/53, para. 43.

to take up paid employment, the situation of those excluded quickly become dire despite some modest material assistance to demobilised veterans under an internationally funded program. Renaming the force Falintil-FDTL did little to address the concrete problems faced by veterans.[1227]

Sporadic attempts to deal with the issue were undertaken by UNTAET as well as by internationally funded assistance programs for demobilized veterans.[1228] A group that calls itself "the real Fretilin," the People's Defense Committee of the Democratic Republic of East Timor (CPD-RDTL), took up the veteran cause. But as it rejected UNTAET's authority and opposed powerful representatives of Fretilin, it marginalized itself.[1229]

While unemployment rose, UNTAET staff not only displayed wealth, "like cars, trucks, computers, or satellite phones,"[1230] but they also created a double or "bubble economy."

> The extent and nature of foreign investment, which is not subject to social or environmental guidelines, is a cause for great concern. The influx of foreign investors and comparatively wealthy UN and aid workers has led to the creation of a double economy and the perception of the UN as the new colonialists in East Timor.[1231]

This tension that results from a display of "wealth in the midst of extreme poverty"[1232] holds for nearly every international peace operation. Plus, UNTAET's fight against the World Bank's CEP "alienated much of the CNRT leadership, which felt the stance of many UNTAET officials on the CEP was unnecessarily hostile to East Timorese participation in decision-making at the local level."[1233]

UNTAET also harbored some individuals that did considerable harm to the mission by behaving like land lords, not acting in the best interests of the East Timorese people. In this context, the UNTAET Head of District Administra-

---

1227 Garrison 2005, pp. 24-25.
1228 Cf. ibid., p. 25.
1229 "Clashes between CPD-RDTL and Fretilin youth occurred before the 2001 elections [...]. The anti-Fretilin riots which broke out in Baucau and Dili in March 2002 were widely seen as having been incited, if not organised, by the CPD-RDTL. In Dili rioters targeted the residences of Prime Minister Alkatiri and his family, as well as the mosque (fn. 8: The attack on the mosque is generally seen as a result of the fact that PM Alkatiri is a Muslim, rather than as an ethnic clash)." Ibid.
1230 Donini, Antonio. 1996. *The Policies of Mercy, UN Coordination in Afghanistan, Mozambique, and Rwanda.* Providence, RI: Watson Institute, Brown University, p. 89.
1231 Denton, Jenny. 2001. "East Timor Suffers under Weight of World Plans," *The Canberra Times*, 14 April 2001 Saturday Final Edition. Available online at http://www.etan.org/et2001b/april/15-21/14etsufr.htm, last access on 5 March 2009. While SRSG Vieira de Mello tried to contain this development, he could not quite succeed though, "I served in Cambodia, where our record in that respect left much to be desired. I have been very clear with my colleagues here and with New York, that I woul like to keep the UN civilian and military presence here to the minimum, so as to also reduce to the minimum the negative social and economic impact of our presence." Foreign Correspondent 2000.
1232 Donini 1996, p. 89.
1233 Beauvais 2001, p. 1126.

tion[1234] infamously stood out, "Jesudas Bell, who led to opposition to the CEP, was criticized both by UNTAET officials and by CNRT president Xanana Gusmão as protecting a personal bureaucratic fiefdom without regard to the interests of the East Timorese."[1235]

This behavior and the undisputedly poor record of decentralized governance and Timorese involvement caused severe discussions amongst UNTAET staff on the fundamental mandate implementation approach. The internal disputes culminated when the Head of District Administration quit his job.

Overstrained

While UNTAET harbored some "positively dangerous" people, it is only fair to state that most staff tried to give their best. They had to face enormous challenges in terms of tight time frames and extremely complex tasks as well as in terms of the "newness" of the tasks they were asked to fulfil.

The pretensions for international staff were extreme, "'Suddenly the UN became formally responsible for everything, and yet it had zero capacity for anything.'"[1236] Personnel were mixed as well. Some excellent people were around but also a lot of "deadwood" and even vice and opportunistic people.

> It's hard to find people with expertise in government. The UN can find a few different types of people quite well: we had a track record for human rights, monitoring, political/ diplomatic types, humanitarians, support people... The task of setting up a government is not something we do all the time, and what you want there is people who have been in government and in the civil service. And, as I said, the good ones usually are needed at home. So you don't always get the best ones when you ask governments anyway. Point one. Point two is that there is a difference between being, let's say, a very good finance ministry director in the governments of the UK or Switzerland, and being able to set up a finance ministry out of the burnt building in Dili that you find yourself in. That's the question of cultural adaptability: as a technical expert, you have to act in an environment that is not your own and where you have to act in a completely independent way. We needed expertise that can organize and work in a development and post-conflict context where infrastructure has really been destroyed. And we had some very bad people and poor people who I think made decision that set Timor back. And we had some excellent people who I think the Timorese really remember with great respect and which contributed to success.[1237]

1234   This was the successor to Jarat Chopra who had quit because of the very centralized and detached policy.
1235   Ibid. See Mark Dodd, "UN Peace Mission at War with Itself," *Sydney Morning Herald*, May 13, 2000, p. 19.
1236   Power 2008, p. 308.
1237   Interview with a senior staff member of UNTAET, New York, 23 November 2006.

In parts, the frustrations and tensions with UNTAET's shortcomings and mistakes could be tempered "by reference to the uncontested aim of independence and a timetable within which this was to be achieved."[1238] Still, the pressure on UNTAET continued to grow.[1239]

3.2.2 Redesign and Expansion of the State-Building Approach: Timorization

The technocratic approach of institution-building and the hand-over of functions produced some working institutions, but except for very low positions, they were almost exclusively run by international staff. In terms of local support and legitimacy, the technocratic policy brought the mission on the brink of collapse. "'Our vision was we'd administer the place and we'd consult with the Timorese. Then, after elections we'd hand over the keys to the Timorese and be on our way [...] The Timorese, who had been waiting centuries to govern themselves, understandably had different ideas.'"[1240] In this situation, Vieira de Mello made a critical decision. Against resistance from headquarters as well as from many of his staff who did not want to "serve under" East Timorese, he decided to radically redesign the transition approach. He installed a co-government where international ministers acted together with East Timorese cabinet members. Likewise, he asked for a more representative and more powerful legislative organ to be established. "Vieira de Mello [...] came to see that he would need to bend the UN rules in order to save the mission. The most effective way for him to exercise power in East Timor would be to surrender it."[1241]

1238   Chesterman 2004, p. 240.
1239   "It is clear that the formal conditions of freedom of speech, freedom of assembly and personal security were met very quickly be UNTAET, but the question of social inclusion proved more problematic. The Secretary-General reported to the Security Council that UNTAET had managed to establish general conditions of freedom of movement and personal security by January 2000 (Secretary-General 2000, para. 14). Though Indonesian law remained in place on Timor-Leste, those sections which had restricted personal freedoms and political activity were declared vid by Vieira de Mello in his capacity as the Transitional Administrator (UNTAET Regulation 1999/1)." Garrison 2005, p. 11. See also Beauvais 2004, p. 1124.
1240   Power 2008, pp. 321-322.
1241   Ibid.

In early 2000, the mission made some crucial decisions for the further course of the transition.[1242] A new legislative council, the National Council (NC), and an executive body, the Transitional Cabinet, were created. They endorsed the Timorese with more political participation. The Transitional Cabinet soon, however, merged with UNTAET's GPA pillar to form the East Timorese Transitional Administration. In an exceptional and unprecedented move, the Administration was even granted its own, un-earmarked budget.

A staff member recalls, "There were plenty of reasons to say, 'Look, you know, this is not the right model given the situation and the New York-made plan has to adapt quite a bit.'"[1243] The speed and scope of re-adjustment was considered almost revolutionary by UN standards:

> If you think that, you know, Sergio hit the ground with his all-encompassing, near dictatorial – although benign – powers in October of 1999, already in May/June, we were discussing how to re-structure this to make it more of a shared political endeavor and how to make it more acceptable to the Timorese. And then come August we had discussed it with the Timorese and set up these new transitional structures. Then there was the election on the all-Timorese Council under the presidency of a Timorese Prime Minister. And then there was independence. So, I think the total transition was probably 28 months. We only kept the original structure for about eight months, if you think about it. And then we immediately began to devolving and delegating and trying to restructure. So, it was a very quick learning process in some respects: the original plan had reflected the Kosovo model, I think, and then it had to adjust according to realities.[1244]

On 30 May 2000, the new policy of "co-government" was officially announced. With the new approach, UNTAET tried to make more use of the opportunities it had on-the-ground, particularly that there *was* relatively homogenous support for comparatively moderate leaders. The first step was the criticized NCC's replacement by the more representative East Timorese NC, now comprising 36 members. It also included representatives from the district level and it had the authority "to initiate, to modify, and to recommend draft regulations" as well as "to amend reg-

---

1242 "In a way, it was a lose-lose-situation: they didn't feel satisfied, we didn't feel satisfied. And so all of those reasons, I think, led up to the belief that we really needed to begin to share the political ownership much more." Interview with a senior staff member of UN-TAET, New York, 23 November 2006. "The SRSG admitted that the approach adopted from the outset would not work. He actually planned to 'Timorize' only the civil service with the delay on political transition just until the election or well before independence. Meanwhile, consultation with a selected few would suffice. It became clear, however, that consultation was insufficient, and thus, the mission accelerated the Timorization process." Subianto 2002, p. 18.

1243 Interview with a senior staff member of UNTAET, New York, 23 November 2006.

1244 Ibid.

ulations"[1245] by the SRSG. The SRSG also no longer chaired the body.[1246] Furthermore, "ordinary" East Timorese and the formerly ignored Falintil were allowed in the quasi-parliament NCC as observers.[1247] The CNRT continued to provide the lion's share of the Council and Gusmão was its leading figure. That said, ultimate legislative authority remained with the Transitional Administrator/SRSG.[1248]

Secondly, the new executive organ was the Transitional Cabinet. Established by UNTAET Regulation No. 2000/23, the Cabinet was

> (a) to formulate policies and programs for the government of East Timor; (b) to supervise the East Timor Administration; (c) to recommend regulations for consideration by the National Council [...]; (d) to recommend to the Transitional Administrator the approval and promulgation of regulations as adopted by the National Council or to return draft regulations to the National Council with the Cabinet's recommendations for further consideration; and, (e) to recommend to the Transitional Administrator the approval and promulgation of directives.[1249]

Taking up work in September 2000, the Transitional Cabinet comprised nine cabinet posts: Internal Administration, Infrastructure, Economic Affairs, Social Affairs, Foreign Affairs, Police and Emergency Services, Political Affairs, Justice, and Finance. While the last four minister posts needed to be assigned to international staff, Timorese were in charge of the remaining ones.[1250] The ministers were appointed by the SRSG. The filling of positions was an "extremely political"[1251] process, and Fretilin, which was in the process of regaining its strength and confidence, was regularly interfering.

> There was a lot of consulting with the parties and key players involved, looking at the balance of people – gender balance, balance in terms of geographic representation, of skills sets – and finding a candidate that everybody was happy with. So, that was mostly

---

1245 UNTAET Regulation No. 2000/24 On the Establishment of a National Council, UN Doc. UNTAET/REG/2000/24, para. 2, 14 July 2000.
1246 By vote of the NC members, this post went to Gusmão. Cf. Beauvais 2001, p. 1128. "Its composition was divided as follows: seven representatives of the CNRT and three representatives of other political parties; three additional representatives of the CNRT or other political parties to be selected by the Transitional Administrator; one representative each from the Catholic Church, the Protestant church denominations, the Muslim community, the women's organizations, the student/youth organizations, the Timorese NGO Forum, the professional associations, the farming community, the business community, and the Labor organizations; and one representatives from each of the thirteen districts." Ibid.
1247 Cf. Beauvais 2001, p. 1121, fn. 70.
1248 This fact caused the East Timorese ministers of the ETTA to complain that it would give them little power to act independently. Cf. Baltazar 2004, p. 5.
1249 UNTAET Regulation No. 2000/23 of 14 July 2000, para. 4.1.
1250 The Foreign Affairs post was only added in October, being assigned to Ramos-Horta. See UNTAET, "Daily Briefing," 19 October 2000. Available online at http://www.un.org/peace/etimor/DB/DB191000.HTM, last access on 5 March 2009.
1251 Telephone interview with a senior staff member of UNTAET, 9 October 2006.

what Sergio had to do, as the administrator, and he consulted with Ramos-Horta, the Prime Minister and others on who those candidates would be.[1252]

Rupture: A New Transitory Structure

Once the Transitional Cabinet was complete, it was combined with UNTAET's GPA pillar. The resulting executive structure was titled the East Timor Transitional Administration (ETTA). The organizational structure is displayed below. At the top of the joint international-local hierarchy sat the SRSG/Transitional Administrator, retaining full executive authority.[1253]

It was essential in terms of reconstruction and development capabilities that ETTA obtained its own budget, sustaining reconstruction and capacity-building for the future East Timorese ministries and their civil service.

> Once we established ETTA, we created a budget for it. It was separate from the UN Transitional Administration that was funded by the headquarter structures and had a funding model like a peacekeeping operation. The Timorese ministers and the Timorese staff of the ETTA were funded by Timorese National Government budget, which was formed totally in East Timor, without any reference back to any of the budgetary committees, because they weren't paying for it. We opened it up to donors to fund and we tried to also begin funding it through local tax revenue. ETTA was the national government.
>
> And we insisted on no earmarking. 'If you wanted to support this, you were giving one dollar into the treasury fund, and the treasurer and the government through its own budgetary process would decide how it would be allocated.' Of course, there was the potential for these countries to influence us, to say, 'We will only give it to you if you don't set up an X, or you do set up a Y,' or, 'We believe this is important.' So, that's part of that kind of influence which people try to give. But there was no earmarking of the funds: once you give it into the treasury, the treasury is to spend. A dollar is a dollar. That was how we approached it. And that was actually an innovation – because there is a tradition within the development community of not funding the recurrent budget on the development country but only funding development assistance. And East Timor was one of the first times when that changed in a way – because what we explained to the donors was, 'It doesn't matter if you come here and build fifteen wells if there is no ministry that can manage the overall water resource, it doesn't matter if you go and build a road here and put a Japanese flag on it if there is no infrastructure system which is part of a national plan that makes sense. So, you can do these projects, but in this

1252 Ibid.
1253 In order to check and balance the comprehensive competences of UNTAET, the Office of the Ombudsperson – "where decisions of the transitional administration could be challenged" – and the Office of the Inspector General – "to verify the use of the funds from the World Bank-administered TFET" – were created. Cf. UN Secretary-General, "Report of the Secretary-General on the United Nations Transitional Administration in East Timor (for the period 27 July 2000 to 16 January 2001)," UN Doc. S/2001/42, 16 January 2001, para. 38; Pippard undated, p. 6.

particular case, this project of East Timor is setting up a state, and a state can't function without a government. If you don't want to fund the recurring budget of this government you might as well forget your separate donor funds, it's just a waste of time.' And they actually agreed to that.[1254]

Figure 2: Organizational Chart of UNTAET

Source: UN Doc. S/2001/42, p. 11.

1254 Interview with a senior staff member of UNTAET, New York, 23 November 2006. "In fact, since that East Timor experience there has been much more readiness within the donor community to do this kind of thing, to fund the recurring budget of governments in post-conflict countries, because they realized this is really the centre. One of the problems they don't like to hear of course is the recurring budget is as it's called: recurring. There is no end in sight. But the idea that you need to kick-start to get the centre going and then what you hope is that that state begins to ascertain authority and moves towards own taxation revenue and becomes self-sufficient – that's what you hope." Ibid.

With this substantive change, the ties with East Timorese improved. "Gusmão recalls the sense of relief within his party, 'This was the time we started to believe that Sergio was committed to the Timorese,' he says. 'The Security Council had given him all of the power, but he said, 'No, I need you.'"[1255] Not all reactions, however, were positive. UN headquarters in New York saw the SRSG breaking the rules and discredited his decision. Some staff on the ground heavily confronted the SRSG, as they were not willing to serve under Timorese. But Vieira de Mello got his way, "Sergio knew that he was trying to do something revolutionary in the UN system,' recalls Prentice. 'His attitude was, 'If you want to deny the Timorese power, then have the guts to fucking say it to them yourself.'"[1256] Presented with a *fait accompli*, headquarters reluctantly gave in. The SRSG decided to talk to the uneasy international staff up front, letting them decide to stay or to leave.

> He assembled the entire UN staff – some seven hundred people – ailing with the four new Timorese cabinet ministers, in the auditorium of the parliament building. He spoke from the dais and, pointing to the Timorese sitting in the front row, said, 'These are your new bosses.' When one UN official objected that there was no provision in the UN Security Council resolution for what UNTAET was doing, he was defiant. 'I assume full responsibility,' he said. 'You either obey, or you can leave.'[1257]

The bold remaining challenge for UNTAET consisted in creating government structures while simultaneously identifying and building local capacities to run these institutions ("Timorization"). The following paragraphs give an illustrative overview of the developments in the different public sectors.

3.2.3 Building Public Authorities

UNTAET built most public service institutions from scratch and only punctually built on Indonesian legacy. Under the new co-government paradigm, East Timorese were supposed to be more involved in the institution-building process, but participation was far from satisfying. It was also biased in favor of exiled Timorese and members of Fretilin. At the same time, UNTAET was still struggling with the challenges' complexity and would succumb, time and again, to inevitable pathologies such as: the politicalization of critical decisions, e.g. on the size and payment of civil service employees; neglect of sectors that did not seem crucial to mandate achievement; shrinking from "hot potatoes," i.e. particularly the presumption of (urgent) legal decisions; or having malfunctions in one sector affect the progress in others, for instance with regards to the re-integration and re-employment of for-

---

1255 Power 2008, pp. 328-329.
1256 Ibid., p. 329.
1257 Ibid., pp. 329-330.

mer combatants. That said, in other sectors, success stories emerged. Particularly in the health sector, they were owed to good cooperation networks that bundled expertise.

Civil Service

The (re-)building of the civil service, specifically the Civil Service and Public Employment section (CSPE), was the GPA's responsibility. The head of CSPE had to make a range of difficult decisions that strongly affected the transition process and the sustainability of the public institutions. He was constantly challenged by local and international actors, particularly the IMF, when it came to the design and allotment of money within the public service. Due to the slow deployment of civilian staff, the CSPE initially consisted of only eight people, and the eight different departments that were created under its direction started out with "not more than a total of a hundred and fifty staff altogether."[1258]

Box 9: UNTAES' Government and Public Administration Unit
The subjects of GPA were divided into political and other civilian matters: "The structure created some differences between those, like myself and Jean Cady, who were working for the new government but who were part of the UN structure, and those around Sergio Vieira De Mello, who were part of the political structure of the UN and were managing the political relationships."[1259]   That meant that as SRSG, de Mello was "responsible for all the political side and the foreign relations and the security side, relations with the peacekeeping forces for example,"[1260] while the "responsibility for the basic running of the territory, all the smooth running of the territory – on the civil side"[1261] was assigned to the DSRSG Jean Cadis[1262] and his staff. Specifically, the design of the CSPE section and the planning of its transformation into what was to become the future East Timorese public administration,[1263] fell in the responsibility of the Director of Civil Service.

When the calls for Timorization intensified, the CSPE faced a "rush to fill the recruitment rolls and to fill the payroll, and to create a structure."[1264] When this process started, a hitherto sidelined challenge emerged, "It was very clear in our minds that we needed to get some kind of endorsement from some people, but the question was: by whom?" At the top-level, the CSPE team made the obvious choice

---

1258 Interview with a senior staff member of Civil Affairs, UNTAET, New York, 18 September 2006.
1259 Ibid. See also CSDG, "East Timor Report," para. 320.
1260 Interview with a senior staff member of Civil Affairs, UNTAET, New York, 18 September 2006.
1261 Ibid.
1262 In June 2001, Australian diplomat Dennis McNamara succeeded the disputed Jean Cady.
1263 "This office was the nurturing body, the incubator for the future civil service." Interview with a senior staff member of Civil Affairs, UNTAET, New York, 18 September 2006.
1264 Ibid.

and "initially started working with Xanana and his own immediate team."[1265] On the mid- and low-levels, however, it showed that there were only "few competent people to deal with."[1266]

In fact, "It would have taken ten years to train these people."[1267] Nonetheless, the enormous time pressure brought about a situation in which "a lot of people were pushed into the government positions who really were completely unsuitable, who had no idea what they were doing at all."[1268]At the same time, relevant and potentially useful groups of people were neglected, most notably some former *chefes do suco,* and the *chefes do aldeia*, they had left because they were collaborators, or were still in refugee camps in West Timor.

When it came to the institutional set up and orientation of the service, important "threshold" questions were unveiled, "such as how large should it be, how centralized should it be or decentralized should it be?"[1269] Discussions of these issues were held between the international team, representatives from other international organizations, especially the World Bank, IMF, and UNDP, and about eight to ten Timorese, most of them Fretilin-affiliated expatriates. Only a few of them – those who had been in exile in Portugal or Australia – had experience with the fundamental requirement of the UN, namely with a system based on democratic rationales. Some of the former émigrés, in particular those that had been granted asylum in Mozambique, even suggested Marxist models. Partly wed to these stances, an UN official admitted that at the end of the day, "The dialogue did not go into a great deal of depth"[1270] and that it was not very well informed.

> We had neither the time nor the expertise to deal with it. We had neither the people nor the documents, nor did we have any very good sense of what was the ideal model. I cannot say that we had any particular manual to go on. We were feeling our way as we went along. And you have to remember we were only a very small number of people who were involved in this.[1271]

In order to create at least some generic benchmarks for the civil service structure, CSPE began to elaborate guidelines. While being "far from scientific precision,"[1272] one central criterion identified was finance, i.e., how much can the East Timorese government afford to pay?

1265 "One of the people most directly involved was a lady called Emilia Pires. Emilia was the person who was designated as my first contact point. And Emilia arranged a representative group of people. Some of them were exiles, who had just returned, and some of them were people who'd been part of the resistance, local people in the area." Ibid.
1266 Ibid.
1267 Ibid.
1268 Ibid.
1269 Ibid.
1270 Ibid.
1271 Ibid.
1272 Ibid.

When you're planning the structure, you have to think about, first, what is the purpose of government, and secondly, how much can a poor small island developing country which has got very few resources apart from international assistance, going to be able to afford to pay? So, one very basic decision that we, i.e. all the foreigners there – UNDP, IMF, the World Bank – took early on was that the previous Indonesian model was not the best one to follow. The obvious reason for this was that the Indonesians had taken a model that suited them in terms of securing their control, which meant that they had a large civil service, but a poorly paid one. Civil Service positions used to be positions which were able to buy loyalty to the government. For the efficiency of the civil service, this meant that you would have many people on the payroll that did very little. You had far more people employed, particularly in the districts, than you really needed, because these were people who were the eyes and ears of Jakarta. These were the people whose loyalty was to the Indonesian regime – because they were on the government payroll. Our view, at the start, was to do the reverse, was to have a small, well-qualified, un-corrupt civil service where the people were responsive – and not corrupt. We wanted to have a civil service and an administrative structure that was relevant to the needs of East Timor.[1273]

Hence, the salary structure became one of the key issues in civil service planning. It was a fiercely contested one though.

The public sector wage bill was a function of two things: the number of people and the level of salaries. We had many discussions and I can remember some heated discussions with Sergio in the chair, when I made presentations and the IMF made presentations in different ways… You look at the overall model and you say, 'This is how much money you've got, you can afford to have 15,000 people but you pay them an average of this much. Or you can afford to have 10,000 people and you pay them that much.' And then the question is how do you divide that pay bill between the different levels of people? I was involved with designing a salary structure and I worked together with the Timorese and we started to look at comparable structures. And we looked first of all at what other small island developing counties had done, at how much did they get paid. Secondly, we looked at regional governments, and the Philippines I remember being one of them. And then we wanted to have a quite simple pay-scale. We didn't want to make it too detailed and complicated. But we did a job classifications system and we did get some professional manuals for this from UNDP, which assisted us with this task of designing and classifying public functions. So we would have some arguments about whether a head teacher in a school should be paid on this rate compared with an engineer over here, and so on. We were definitely in favor of a small but well-paid and well-qualified service. However, the IMF took the view, very early on, that the country could not afford more than a certain amount of money for the civil service budget, and there were tensions and arguments between myself and the IMF representatives over how much we should be paying.[1274]

In the end, the "low salaries–large civil service"-model prevailed. "The Timorese were rightly complaining that they couldn't afford to live on the public sector salary

1273 Ibid.
1274 Ibid. The Civil Affairs official adds, "And I regret that, personally, because I felt that a lot of the efforts that I had made were undermined as a consequence of that."

scales"[1275] that UNTAET preliminarily set. The IMF was in charge of paying a large part of the salaries, but it "gave more importance to keeping down the public sector wage bill than it did to creating a corruption-free, competent, qualified civil service."[1276]

The dispute over the salary structure was intertwined with the question of whom to put in the civil service's senior positions, people in the well-educated diaspora "from the outside" or people "from the inside," who stayed on the island during Indonesian occupation.

> Here again you have a very important factor that you have to keep in mind when thinking about this, which is that we had different paradigms, different models of how you should look at the subject. There were those who said we have to create a structure that is fair and open to everyone, both to those people inside and outside. Others said we must do whatever it takes to bring good people back. Because we realized early on that one of the critical problems that Timor was going to face – and which is the case until today, and I regret it very much – is a shortage of skilled, experienced manpower in the public service. It was *the* critical question.[1277]

Bringing in expatriates had the advantage of them being able to speak English, having better formal education and more work experience than most Timorese.[1278] Some of them also had experience with democratic political systems. UNTAET actively set incentives for them to come back to their home country.

> In the first weeks, when we were designing this and thinking about it, obviously most of the Timorese in the exile community had not made up their minds on what they

---

1275 Ibid. "I think here you have the gap between the theoretical hopes and aspirations of the international community and the reality, which is that almost all the people who joined the civil service saw it as a means for personal benefit. With the high rates of unemployment, this is totally understandable. Besides, they were used to the Indonesian model of a government where by the government is looked after everyone, even if they paid you badly." Ibid.

1276 Ibid.
"This is very important [insisting]. Because we realized early on that one of the critical problems that Timor was going to face – and which is the case until today, and I regret it very much – is a shortage of skilled, experienced manpower in the public service. It was *the* critical question. Cost is becoming increasingly a factor because under the United Nations, East Timor became very expensive. East Timor always was expensive for Indonesia because of its geographical position, and because it was a society that had benefited from a lot of subsidies, for instance by all the Indonesian army officers who went to East Timor. So, it was a relatively expensive place, compared to West Timor where costs were much cheaper, or other islands nearby in the Indonesian archipelago. And under the United Nations, for these simple economic facts, i.e. that there was a lot of money chasing too few goods, the costs went up." Ibid.

1277 Ibid.

1278 "Many of them were the middle-class people – even before the Indonesian invasion – they were the more affluent people. Even their parents had more education: They were among the 15 percent people that were of Portuguese descent." Interview with a representative of the Timor-Leste Institute for Reconstruction Monitoring and Analysis, New York, 27 November 2006.

wanted to do. It was still too difficult to come back. You have to put yourselves in the position of people who've been in exile, made new lives for themselves, with their children, be it in Australia or in Portugal. But these were the qualified people who'd done well and who, potentially, were available to come back and serve the new country. So we had to create incentives for them to do this. One incentive is patriotism: you are going to come in order to be able to help build your new country. A second incentive might be status: you are given a job, let's say you are a medical technician in Australia and you are given the change to set up a new medical laboratory, for instance. The third, important incentive is financial. And that's why the whole question of the level of the salary scale was very important. Because you have to create the conditions for people to be able to say, it was worthwhile giving up their comfortable job in Sydney or in Lisbon to be able to return to Dili. And this was really a key issue because you have to fill the administrative positions adequately, to the right level.[1279]

The downside of this policy was that people in the diaspora did not have much legitimacy with the majority of local East Timorese, who had suffered long under oppression.

The Timorese in exile now come back and of course, for UNTAET and for any kind of administrative or government position, they were much more qualified than East Timorese who hadn't left. But from a more political or human rights point of view, it was rather reverse. In the eyes of the 'resident Timorese,' the others ran away, they weren't part of the struggle – so why should they get the good jobs now. They also don't understand the society because they had left half a century ago. And now they come back and the UN especially wants to put them on their Consultative Council and in better positions in the government.' On paper, it's true, they were more qualified, and they started from a more advanced level. But from a point of view of somebody who choose not to go in exile and instead to live in the jungle for fifteen years to fight for the freedom of their country, and who then becomes marginalized: it's not a way to get people to feel that they are respected.[1280]

While UNTAET officials realized this problem indeed, the dilemma was that assigning senior posts to "local" East Timorese was risky, too. "They had been kept down by the Indonesians. And suddenly, people with very limited experiences are now given the chance to make big decisions about their country – but they're not in the position to do that. In fact, it's unfair to them in some ways."[1281] In the end, the "outsiders" prevailed.

The result was owed mainly to intense Fretilin pressure: they pushed the transition process forward, opting for a centralized system, and making enormous direct

---

1279 Interview with a senior staff member of Civil Affairs, UNTAET, New York, 18 September 2006.
1280 Interview with a representative of the Timor-Leste Institute for Reconstruction Monitoring and Analysis, New York, 27 November 2006.
1281 Interview with a senior staff member of Civil Affairs, UNTAET, New York, 18 September 2006.

and personal efforts to staff the administration with their own followers.[1282] These efforts went down to the district and sub-district levels: once Fretilin's power increased, they tried to replace the district administrators with their own personnel. This was not always well accepted, though.[1283]

Established in order to counterweight the development of a Fretilin auto-recruitment, two safeguards were created upon a decision by the Director for Civil Service: the Public Service Commission (PSC), and the Public Service Academy (PSA). "The PSC was supposed to be an independent body that would be outside of the government, and which would determine high-level appointments, and in fact determine most appointments including the high-level ones" while the PSA was "meant to be providing a basic training so that the new civil servants could have an understanding" of how to run a efficient administration.[1284] "The two institutions were supposed to establish a system that would allow *all* East Timorese to join the civil service, not only those affiliated with a certain party. However, the PSC could only rudimentarily live up to its purpose, "because the decisions for the highest appointments were taken on political grounds,"[1285] still. The PSA struggled with similar problems: leading Fretilin representatives strongly argued "that it was natural that the winning party of government should be able to acquire its own people."[1286] Furthermore, the training was not allegedly held often enough and classes were "not tailored to the right audience."[1287]

As of mid-2001, the transitional staff structure consisted of four different "clusters:" international UNTAET staff, local staff working in the UNTAET structure, local staff working in the ETTA structure, and expatriates working as experts in the UNDP's so-called TOKTEN (Transfer of Knowledge through Expatriate Nationals) program. These structures ran on different salary scales. The international

---

1282 "Efforts were made particular by Anna Pesoa as the minister responsible for the civil service and a close aid to Mari Alkatiri, trying to ensure the rewards of independence for people who are considered to be loyal to Fretilin." Interview with a senior staff member of Civil Affairs, UNTAET, New York, 18 September 2006.

1283 Written interview with Dr. Tanja Hohe, former team member of UN Volunteers in East Timor, 30 September 2006.

1284 Interview with a senior staff member of Civil Affairs, UNTAET, New York, 18 September 2006. PSA provided training for all levels, from entry level, which included things like training in English language, to training in comparable models of government. Our resources were quite small, but we made a serious effort to build the PSA through an open recruitment process. This was quite important because we wanted to introduce the Timorese to a new model of government. And that meant a model of government in which the public service was genuinely at the service of the state. We wanted the public service to be people who were concerned, who were experts, or at least qualified in their own particular field, and able to execute their responsibilities without regard for political considerations. Not an easy thing to create over night!" Ibid.

1285 Ibid.

1286 Ibid.

1287 Interview with Joseph Andrews, Special Adviser to the DSRSG, UNTAET, and to the Foreign Minister, ETTA, Washington, DC, 9 September 2006.

staffs on the UN payroll were obviously at the high end. Then there were the Timorese who worked for UNTAET in the realm of civil administration, likewise obtaining above-average pay, although not as high as the first group. Third, the Timorese who were part of ETTA were on another salary scale, obtaining far less money than those working for the UN mission – who did the same job, essentially. That was a "big problem, it created a lot of tensions."[1288] The tensions emerged not only among the Timorese but also for the UN mission: since they had recruited the most capable people for the UN in the first place, there were not much qualified local people left to work in the public administration of the future government.[1289] The fourth group of personnel were the experts – expatriates in the TOKTEN program that brings expats back for short-term assignments in order to train "their" people. They also earned a comparatively high salary.

The big difference between the salary scales and the extreme poverty in the country fuelled discontent. The "solution" that was found consisted of employing more and more people in UNTAET, mostly as guards.[1290] But here again, they were recruited under different salary scales, continuing the vicious cycle. "Then you have more demonstrations about that they wanted more money. So, this was a constant headache, which was really a result of the strange situation whereby you have an international organization running the country for a couple of years on a transitional basis."[1291]

Police

As is usual for a complex mission, UNTAET was in charge of a large CivPol component, staffed by officers of diverse contributing UN member countries, and required to restore stability and the rule of law, as well as to create and train a new local police force to which they gradually hand over police functions. The authority,

1288 Interview with a senior staff member of Civil Affairs, UNTAET, New York, 18 September 2006.
1289 "In practice we had difficulties filling a lot of the positions because we just didn't have enough qualified people." Ibid.
1290 "They had no qualifications and they did not speak Indonesian and only little Bahasa. So you give them jobs as guards. So at one stage we had a huge job creation programme which was by the way completely contradictory to the goals that we had previously, namely of limiting the civil service. So we had a job creation programme to deal with an immediate political issue which was that we were faced with daily demonstrations for jobs. Because the ordinary Timorese thought, well, 'UNTAET is here in order to give us jobs.' So I had to hire a lot of people under a fast-track recruitment programme to be building guards. We had far more people than we needed actually guarding the buildings to stop them being attacked." Ibid.
1291 Ibid.

however, remained in the hands of CivPol and thus of the member states, until the transition was complete and the UN administration withdrew.

[L]ittle was left of the Indonesian police and justice system in East Timor. Indonesian military, police, and judicial personnel left the country en masse following the referendum; few East Timorese had worked in these institutions. When Indonesian civil administrators, judges, and lawyers fled, East Timor was without a justice system. The courts and legal buildings were heavily damaged. Because of the legacy of distorted justice left by the Indonesians, the public had no confidence in the judiciary. Remaining police were poorly trained. They lacked community-based policing skills, did not know how to handle weapons or how to manage civil disturbances. The militia had destroyed barracks, police stations, and equipment used by the military, police, and judiciary. The UN had to fill the immediate security void while building a police force, military, and justice system from scratch.[1292]

Concurring with the mission's unprecedented governance authority, the CivPol was the first international police force to assume "full responsibility for law enforcement in pending the establishment of newly formed local police forces."[1293] Holding executive enforcement functions, the major tasks of UNTAET's police was the maintenance of law and order, the establishment of a new East Timor police force, including its recruitment and training, and the monitoring and assisting of IDP and refugee return.[1294] There were as many as 39 CivPol member states contributing to the authorized 1,640 officers – which made it difficult to set up coherent approaches "UNTAET's police from close to fifty countries had little guidance in criminal procedure in the intervening months and often operated according to the procedures they knew from home."[1295] For example, "There were as many sets of traffic rules as there were contributing CivPol nations!"[1296] This was not the only problem, though:

Recruitment was agonizingly slow, and the overall quality of those recruited was low. Most CivPols were recruited for three-month tours of duty, hardly enough time to understand the place or the people. Almost none spoke a language intelligible to the East Timorese, and interpreters were scarce, leading to a reliance on informal security forces

---

1292 Dobbins et al. 2005, pp. 154-155.
1293 Caplan 2005, p. 46.
1294 Cf. UN Doc. S/1999/1024.
1295 Human Rights Watch. 2001. *World Report 2001: East Timor*. Available online at http://www.hrw.org/wr2k1/asia/etimor.html, last access on 5 March 2009. The civilian police contributors were: Argentina, Australia, Austria, Bangladesh, Benin, Bosnia & Herzegovina, Brazil, Canada, China, Egypt, Gambia, Ghana, Jordan, Kenya, Malaysia, Mozambique, Namibia, Nepal, Niger, Nigeria, Norway, Pakistan, Philippines, Portugal, Russian Federation, Samoa, Senegal, Singapore, Slovenia, Spain, Sri Lanka, Sweden, Thailand, Turkey, Ukraine, United Kingdom, United States, Vanuatu, and Zimbabwe.
1296 Smith 2001, p. 43.

set up by the CNRT, whose activities CivPol had almost no capacity to monitor or control.[1297]

The result was a large number of officers who lacked basic capabilities, be it English proficiency or the ability to drive a car.[1298] When, in December 1999, UNTAET decided on an international panel of the Dili district court to investigate international crimes – crimes against humanity and all serious offences committed, such as murder and rape – that occurred from 1 January 1999 to 25 October 1999, CivPol had a low capacity to assist with the process.

> None of the CivPol who were legally empowered to investigate the 1999 crimes [...] received any training in investigating crimes against humanity until late June. Most CivPol treated each case as a routine homicide investigation, with no attention to the role of the Indonesian state or to the links among the different crimes. The short tours of duty meant that every new investigator coming in tended to start the questioning of witnesses from scratch.[1299]

In addition, the lack of institutional infrastructure and untrained CivPol officers, as well as the bureaucratic divisions within UNTAET slowed the investigation process down.

1297 Human Rights Watch 2001. See also Call, Chuck and Barnett, Michael. 1999. "Looking for a Few Good Cops: Peacekeeping, Peacebuilding, and CIVPOL." *International Peacekeeping* 6:4, pp. 43-68.
1298 Cf. Caplan 2005, p. 56. According to CivPol officials, the problem is known as "slippage." Ibid.
1299 Human Rights Watch 2001. "Authority for investigations changed repeatedly. In late November 1999, a special five-member commission appointed by UN High Commissioner for Human Rights Mary Robinson arrived in Dili to hear testimony from over one hundred eyewitnesses to murder, rape, and arson. Known as the International Commission of Inquiry on East Timor (ICIET), the group issued a report on January 31, 2000, recommending, among other things, that an international tribunal be set up to prosecute those responsible for the abuses. In his letter forwarding the report to the Security Council, Secretary-General Kofi Annan did not endorse the recommendation for a separate tribunal, stressing that full cooperation should be given to Indonesian efforts to investigate the crimes, but recommended that UNTAET capacity for coordinating investigations be strengthened. From November to late March, CivPol alone had full authority for investigations. Its investigation unit, however, was responsible not just for investigating the 1999 violence but for all ongoing crimes as well. As law and order concerns in East Timor increased, attention to the 1999 crimes was often diverted. On March 22, a war crimes/human rights investigations unit was set up within CivPol to be headed by an investigator from the Office of Human Rights Affairs. The change was only on paper; the new unit had no investigators other than CivPol. In early June, a prosecution service was set up under UNTAET's judicial affairs department, separate both from CivPol and from the Office of Human Rights Affairs (OHRA). On July 20, 2000, UNTAET formally shifted from its original peacekeeping structure to a coalition government with the CNRT. Among the eight 'ministries' created was a Ministry of Judicial Affairs to which the investigation unit was formally moved in August. In the meantime, six different agencies concerned with accountability for the 1999 crimes – judicial affairs, human rights, political affairs, legal affairs, CivPol, and the East Timorese courts – went ahead with their efforts, sometimes tripping over each other in the process. East Timorese witnesses to these crimes grew resentful over repeated questioning without any obvious progress in bringing the perpetrators to justice." Ibid.

The recruitment of the new East Timorese Police Force, the future National Police of East Timor (PNTL), started in early 2000. Basic training commenced on 27 March of that year. "On August 10, 2001, the East Timor Police Service was officially established alongside U.N. Civilian Police, later changing its name to the Timor-Leste Police Service, before finally adopting its current title of the *Polícia Nacional de Timor-Leste*."[1300] In late January 2001, a police academy was founded. The graduates were supposed to "[join] UN CivPol officers on-the-ground and gradually replace them."[1301]

> Around twenty thousand application forms for the future police officers will be distributed in all regions of East Timor. The applicants will compete for 3,000 available positions in the future force. The training will consist of an intensive four-month course followed by eight months of on-job supervision and training. The course will be conducted at the East Timor Police Academy in Comoro. (The first class will have 40 recruits to be followed by another class at the third month of first class' course). During the course, candidates will be trained in the basics of criminal law, police techniques, traffic rules, investigation techniques, and driving.[1302]

The primary selection criteria for the Academy were the level of education and "skills related to the police function."[1303] Apart from the general problem that the educational situation posed in East Timor, the latter criterion – as straightforward as it seems – bore the potential of creating conflict with the military. The East Timorese who *did* have police experience were "the ones that had been in the Indonesian police,"[1304] which meant that they had likely been collaborators. They mostly came from the island's Western part "because this is where the Indonesians had better control."[1305] At the same time, the future East Timorese military was designated to be a transformed Falintil, the former independence fighters who resided more in the rural Eastern parts of East Timor. Thus, a situation resulted where the police force became "dominated by people who are considered by some as collaborators during the occupation"[1306] while the military consisted of people previously involved in the resistance. This constellation implied a strong conflict potential between the police and the military.

1300 Human Rights Watch, "East Timor: Torture and Mistreatment by Police." Available online at http://www.hrw.org/english/docs/2006/04/19/eastti13223.htm, last access on 5 March 2009.
1301 Vieira de Mello, UNTAET Public Information Office 2000.
1302 Ibid.
1303 Ibid.
1304 Interview with a representative of the Timor-Leste Institute for Reconstruction Monitoring and Analysis, New York, 27 November 2006.
1305 Ibid.
1306 Ibid. Differentiating the picture, some of the "collaborators" were in fact "double agents," officers officially working for the Indonesians but clandestinely helping their fellow East Timorese, "And people in the local community know who support the East Timorese community and who was for Indonesia. But the UN internationals don't know." Ibid.

Police was one of the more decentralized sectors, but policing remained a core competence of the international personnel until UNTAET ended. There was no way that they would run under East Timorese command since the police forces are entrusted to the Secretary-General by the member states.[1307] Thus, "Timorization" of the police sector began rather late. The same logic applied to the hand-over of the military responsibilities.

Military

Similar to the tasks of the CivPol, the peacekeeping force of UNTAET was in charge of providing security in the region as well as of the establishment of a new defense force. Never having been a state entity, East Timor did not dispose of a regular military. Hence, the UN took on a completely new challenge as it was supposed to build a new military force from scratch. "Although the UN had often supported the development of new or reformed police forces, this was its first foray into building a military."[1308] International assistance was in abundance, from Australia and Portugal in particular, who were involved heavily in funding and training.

> There were some initial problems, such as UNTAET's failure to publicly articulate the criteria for including some Falintil fighters in the force but not others. However, the construction of the East Timor Defense Force proceeded relatively smoothly. Nevertheless, in 2002, Secretary-General Annan concluded that the East Timor military forces were still not capable of handling growing militia threats on their own.[1309]

Technically, the challenge was met rather smoothly. Still, UNTAET/UNPKF did not appropriately consider the repercussions following the exclusion of a high number of former Falintil combatants. On 1 February 2001, Falintil was retired and the new force, Falintil-FDTL, was established in fact and law. However, there were two pitfalls – one external and one internal. One, there was the ongoing threat of pro-integration militias in the West of the island as well as an increasing problem with gangs.[1310] Secondly, the new East Timorese military did not absorb all of the former Falintil combatants:

> This shocked many who had understood that simply by being Falintil they would become F-FDTL. It is important to note that the UNTAET-shepherded process whereby it was decided who would join the first F-FDTL battalion and who would be demobilized under the Falintil Reinsertion Assistance Program (FRAP) – implemented by the International Organization for Migration and funded by the United States Agency for

1307   Interview with a senior staff member of UNTAET, New York, 23 November 2006.
1308   Dobbins et al. 2005, pp. 163-164.
1309   Ibid., p. 164. The report that is referred to is UN Doc. S/2003/243.
1310   Cf. Power 2008, p. 293.

International Development and the World Bank – was the key turning point in the development of East Timor's security sector – and the key mistake.[1311]

Health

The most successful reconstruction efforts and the smoothest transfers of responsibility were accomplished in the health sector.[1312] "Health benefited from a combination of a strong international health advisor of the WHO and good Timorese leadership alongside him. That partnership was crucial."[1313] Plus, the cooperation with NGOs was fruitful.[1314] That said, Health was "a relatively simple sector to reconstruct"[1315] since the goals were rather unambiguous and the equipment was provided quite easily. Sufficient funds were available as health was one of the "sexier" sectors in which donors were keen to spend.[1316] Yet, a fundamental means-ends dilemma persisted:

> Particularly when the UN itself assumes a governing role, there is a temptation to demand the highest standards of democracy, human rights, the rule of law, and the provision of services. Balancing these against the need for locally sustainable goals presents difficult problems. A computerized electoral registration system may be manifestly ill-suited to a country with a low level of literacy and intermittent electricity, but should an international NGO refrain from opening a world-class clinic if such levels of care

1311 Rees, Edward. 2003. *The UN's Failure to Integrate Falintil Veterans May Cause East Timor to Fail.*" Available online at http://www.onlineopinion.com.au/view.asp?article=666, last access on 6 March 2009. "In response to the establishment of the F-FDTL, there was an increase in paramilitary security groups across the country (involving disaffected former Falintil and Clandestine activists) operating throughout the country. These groups were loosely connected under the umbrella of the Association of Ex-Combatants 1975 (AC75), headed by the now Minister for Internal Administration, and include among others Sagrada Familia and the Committee for the Popular Defense of the Democratic Republic of Timor-Leste (CPD- RDTL). While most are politically oriented, others have motivations that are more criminal. Under the patronage of a lead Fretilin Central Committee member and one-time Minister of Defense (Rogerio Lobato) from 2001 until 20 May 2002 these groups challenged the legitimacy of the F-FDTL. This process culminated on 20 May 2002 after a series of veteran marches across the country with the appointment of the political patron of these groups to the portfolio of Minister of Internal Administration – the political master of the police service." Ibid.
1312 "In the Secretary-General's final report on UNTAET, he explained that five hospitals and 64 communal health centres had been built." UN Secretary-General, "Report of the Secretary-General on the United Nations Transitional Administration in East Timor," UN Doc. S/2002/432, 17 April 2002, para. 43-57.
1313 Interview with a senior staff member of Civil Affairs, UNTAET, New York, 18 September 2006.
1314 Written interview with Dr. Tanja Hohe, former team member of UN Volunteers in East Timor, 30 September 2006.
1315 Interview with a senior staff member of Civil Affairs, UNTAET, New York, 18 September 2006.
1316 Telephone interview with a program officer of the Donor Coordination Unit, UNTAET, 7 October 2006.

are unsustainable? An abrupt drop from high levels of care once the crisis and international interest passes would be disruptive, but lowering standards early implies acceptance that people who might otherwise have been treated will suffer. This was the dilemma faced by the ICRC, which transferred control of the Dili National Hospital to national authorities in East Timor almost a year before independence (note 34: Lise Boudreault, 'Official Handover Speech Given by ICRC East Timor Head of Delegation' (Dili, ET, 29 June 2001); Report of the S-G on the UNTAET (for the period from 25 July to 15 October 2001), UN Doc S/2001/983 (18 Oct. 2001), para. 53-4).[1317]

Agriculture

East Timor had been a society of farmers and fishers, and hence, advancing the agricultural sector would have been an important measure for stimulating the local economy. Like in many missions, however, economic reconstruction was made a low priority.

Despite progress being made,[1318] compared to other sectors, the lack of international emphasis on agricultural support measures made itself sorely felt by common Timorese.[1319] Although some foreign investment was attracted and plans were in the making, they did not finally materialize due to the uncertain legal situation,. "We tried to attract some foreign investment but the laws were not clear at that time and no serious foreign investment will come in if you don't get a clear legal structure."[1320] Capable individuals were available, though:

> There were some competent people on the international side in both agriculture and fisheries, I can remember them well. And there was a good East Timorese who was involved in agriculture and who had degrees from Indonesia. In fact, this was one of the areas that the Indonesian universities were good in, agricultural expertise. And so therefore you had available quite a number of people who had been trained in Jakarta or Bali in agricultural economics, in agricultural science. And I know that they were capable people who'd come back and who were available.[1321]

1317 Chesterman 2004, pp. 247-248.
1318 See Howard 2008, p. 288.
1319 "The problem was that agriculture was ignored or, at least, it was not made as much a priority as health or education." Interview with a senior staff member of UNDPKO PBPS, New York, 15 September 2006. The staff numbers were also relatively small, at the beginning only comprising four to five members. See also Fox 2002, esp. pp. 10-11.
1320 Interview with a senior staff member of Civil Affairs, UNTAET, New York, 18 September 2006.
1321 Ibid.

Justice

Some crucial institutions could be set up in the justice sector. However, decisions that would have been important for a quick improvement of the Timorese economic situation were deferred due to political considerations, despite the fact that the reconstruction of the justice system was made a priority. This concerned decisions on land rights in particular. Another problem was the shortage of locals with a legal education.

> UNTAET found that only about 70 East Timorese who had graduated from law school were actually living in East Timor. None had been practicing law when East Timor was under Indonesian control. Severe shortages of prosecutors, investigative police, bailiffs, and judges resulted in delays in the administration of justice. So did the absence of courtrooms, holding facilities, and prisons.[1322]

Early on, UNTAET's leadership

> took several steps [...] to try to re-create a legal system, including reinstating the primacy of the pre-August 1999 law (minus the elements threat contravened basic human rights [...]); setting up a UN-run incarceration facility; and establishing a joint UN-East Timorese Transitional Judicial Service Commission. A joint UN-East Timorese Serious Crimes Unit was also established, and it indicted many high-ranking officials for crimes against humanity during the September 1999 rampage [...]. The unit began handing down serious indictments for regular crimes, as well as crimes against humanity, in December 2000. In the same month, the Transitional Cabinet approved of a Commission for Truth, Reception, and Reconciliation, which forwarded its first convictions for crimes against humanity in December 2001. In general, UNTAET's strategy in judicial affairs was to train Timorese staff quickly, and turn over the administration of justice to the East Timorese as rapidly as possible. But as one observer noted, 'There is no quick way to set up a justice system.'[1323]

As for substantial decisions on jurisdiction, however, Vieira de Mello's stance was that the justice sector was "entirely outside his sphere of power"[1324] and delegated exclusive judicial authority to East Timor's courts. This caused a new challenge for the courts since they were now required to proceed on the "imposed" high international standards. Obviously, applying the highest judicial standards in a post-conflict territory nearly bereft of lawyers and judges is close to absurd. Thus, the discrepancy between means and ends became virulent in the justice sector, too.[1325] Complicating matters, it was not even clear which law should be applied:

1322 Dobbins et al. 2005, p. 169.
1323 Power 2008, pp. 283-284, referring to Dunn, James. 2003. A Rough Passage to Independence, 3rd ed. Double Bay: Longueville Books, p. 370.
1324 Ibid.
1325 See "Health," p. 293.

there was Portuguese law, Indonesian law, as well as the new UN regulations; and at the rural level, traditional institutions were being acted out as well.[1326]

A particularly contentious issue was land rights.[1327] There was a cacophony of claims by various people on the same piece of land, because different people owed it under different regimes. By and large, UNTAET deferred the issue. It reasoned that this would be something that East Timorese had to deal with themselves.

> The transitional administration recognized land and property as a pressing issue on more than one occasion, but it felt unable to act before a democratically elected government was in place [...]. UNTAET did seek to regulate the use of public and abandoned land and property by setting criteria for issuing temporary agreements governing their use. But this approach created new facts on-the-ground that further bedevilled the issue. By limiting itself to temporary allocations of public and abandoned land while avoiding the quagmire of private ownership (not even feeling able to facilitate a debate on the issue that might conceivably have created some momentum for its resolution), it fostered a presumption that the latest round of land occupations, whether sanctified by temporary use agreements or not, was in fact giving rise to new claims based on the fact of possession.[1328]

Politically, this might have been the right decision, but it affected UNTAET's ability to do a great deal in the way of economic reconstruction. Not making things any easier, justice was also one of the "unsexy" sectors for donors, "None of them wanted to put their money into unsexy sectors, you know, such as justice or labor. That was always an issue."[1329]

Economic Reconstruction

East Timor was far from being a prosperous economy under Indonesian rule and conditions even worsened after the deteriorations of September 1999.[1330] Compounding the already poor economic situation of the local people, (some) UNTAET staff added to Timorese frustration by appearing as wealthy Westerners but who, at the same time, did not much to improve Timorese lives. An important achievement that UNTAET *could* eventually bring about was the so-called Timor Sea

---

1326   Cf. Goldstone 2004, p. 93.
1327   "The land and property issue was exceptionally complicated and politically fraught." Ibid.
1328   Ibid., pp. 93-94. See also Steele 2002, p. 80.
1329   Telephone interview with a program officer of the Donor Coordination Unit, UNTAET, 7 October 2006.
1330   For exact figures see the World Bank. 1999. *Timor-Leste: Building a Nation. A Framework for Reconstruction and Development.* Available online at http://web.worldbank.org/WB-SITE/EXTERNAL/COUNTRIES/EASTASIAPACIFI CEXT/TIMORLESTEEXTN/0,,contentMDK:20878086pagePK:141137piPK: 141127theSitePK:294022,00.htm, last access on 8 April 2007.

Arrangement, which placed 90 percent of the oil and gas revenues coming from the Timor Sea at East Timor's disposal.

Large parts of the economic reconstruction work was done by international partners; mainly the World Bank, the Asian Development Bank, and the IMF. UNTAET, through its mandate, was given the task of assisting "in the establishment of conditions for sustainable development" and preceded over important matters, such as the Timor Sea Agreement.[1331] It also raised funds for economic reconstruction through the channels introduced above. A crucial shortcoming, however, was the reluctance to make decisions that would have strengthened the infrastructure conducive to the economy in rural regions, where the most part of the Timorese lived. "I think we should have done much more to support the rural economy, particularly because if you do that then you keep the people in the countryside. And then they don't come in to Dili, sitting there looking for jobs and eventually creating trouble."[1332]

A major obstacle for economic development was the uncertain investment situation. Potential foreign investors were afraid that "after independence, the laws will be changed, the taxation could go up, and the whole basis under which they invested money in this risky little country will change. And it was a very legitimate concern."[1333] Hence, nearly every business plan that had been in the making was dropped.[1334] To what extent it would have been wise for UNTAET to bring about all of these laws, particularly on land issues, is a question that yields ambiguous answers. That being said, more time, more technical expertise, and more efforts to improve rural roads[1335] may well have attenuated the negative effects.

A similarly ambiguous aspect, that also had negative effects for UNTAET's perception and legitimacy, related to the provision of commercial buildings:

> The reality of life in Timor throughout almost the entire time that we were there is that the reconstruction, the physical reconstruction of the destroyed homes was largely the result of the personal efforts of the international staff who were there and of the money that they brought in, while the Timorese owners who were there had very little money to be able to do it themselves. Therefore, we lived with a great deal of destroyed build-

---

1331 The text of the Timor Sea Treaty is available online at http://www.austlii.edu.au/au/other/dfat/special/etimor/index.html, last access on 15 March 2009.

1332 Interview with a senior staff member of Civil Affairs, UNTAET, New York, 18 September 2006. "Which is precisely what happens today with all the fights between the gangs going on, gangs consisting of unemployed young people who come from different districts, who have nothing to do." Ibid.

1333 Ibid.

1334 "There were some Chinese business men, Australian business men, Portuguese men and there were some big plans. But none of it was realized essentially because the political and the legal environments were so uncertain. And I think that's totally understandable from a business point of view." Ibid.

1335 "[...] which was an expensive programme but necessary in a country like Timor where the roads are very bad and washed away by the rains every year." Ibid.

ings around us, both commercial buildings and residential buildings. And we lived there the entire time, which created a very bad image. But it was also very bad in terms of economic activity: many governments use reconstruction as a means of generating employment. It's a normal activity to do. The reason why we did not do as much as we could have done goes back to the question of land rights, and it goes back to the question that most of those who had the money had fled the country. So, it goes back to the political problem which is that the former civil servants, who would own the property, or the former owners of these properties, were Indonesian companies or East Timorese who had fled to West Timor. And we had the whole question of whose property was this? And it goes back to a really big issue – and I don't know if it's being resolved, yet – which was: how far do you go back in terms of the dispute of legality over the rights of these lands. What should be the role of the United Nations in trying to resolve these deep-rooted historical land disputes which is a big source of problems?[1336]

This catch-22 was attenuated by the relatively abundant funds for East Timorese development. Their allocation, however, remained controversial:

> Unfortunately, coordination among the various aid vehicles was poor. [...] The separation of recurrent cost financing (provided through the Consolidated Fund for East Timor) and reconstruction financing (provided from the Trust Fund) posed the most difficult problem. This arrangement made it difficult to incorporate funding from multiple sources into East Timor's budget because the funds could only be used for specific purposes. There arrangements also made it challenging to synchronize reconstruction efforts. East Timorese civil servants needed to be recruited to manage the various projects, but project funds could not be used to pay their salaries, creating the difficult problem of finding funding for steps that needed to be taken before major reconstruction projects could begin.[1337]

An important measure for the good of the economic development of East Timor was the signing of the so-called Timor Gap Treaty, an oil-sharing agreement with Australia. Based on the paper "The Timor Gap Treaty vs. an Exclusive Economic Zone: Economic Independence for East Timor" by UNTAET's senior economic advisor, ETTA/UNTAET's Minister for Political Affairs, Peter Galbraith, began talks with the Australian Petroleum Production and Exploration Association. In April,

> Fresh from the second round of negotiations with Australia, Galbraith calls for scrapping the Timor Gap Treaty and negotiating boundaries with Australia based on inter-

1336 Ibid.
1337 Dobbins et al. 2005, p. 174. "East Timor [...] demonstrates the inappropriate complexity of aid financing for post-conflict countries with low capacity [...]. These differing and complex modes of aid provision crated barriers to national ownership of the reconstruction planning process in the initial period, and prevented the integration of all funding sources into the national budget." Rohland, Klaas and Cliffe, Sarah. 2002. *The East Timor Reconstruction Program: Successes, Problems and Trade-offs.* CPR Working Paper No. 2. Washington, DC: World Bank, p. ii, quoted in Dobbins et al. 2005, p. 174.

national law. He urges that an agreement be reached before 15 July to avoid possible complications from East Timor's soon-to-be-elected government.[1338]

On 5 July, Galbraith, ETTA's Economics Minister, Alkatiri, and two Australian Ministers signed a Memorandum of Understanding, called the Timor Sea Arrangement.

> Under this Arrangement, which replaces the February 2000 MOU, East Timor will receive 90 percent and Australia ten percent of oil and gas revenues from the JPDA. The JPDA inherits the ZOC from the 1989 Timor Gap Treaty, altering only the division of revenues. The largest gas field, Greater Sunrise, is deemed to lay 20 percent in the JPDA and 80 percent in Australian territory.[1339]

It was the first time that the UN had negotiated a bilateral treaty on behalf of a "government in waiting."

3.2.4 Summary and Assessment

As de Mello later explained, "Faced as we were with our own difficulties in the establishment of the mission, we did not, we could not involve the Timorese at large as much as they were entitled to."[1340] The difficulties resulted from the complex mandate, the heavy time pressure, the inadequate funding, and the insufficient staff and experience. UNTAET did not manage to come up with a "fit" implementation strategy in the first place.

To the contrary, "UNTAET built institutions based on the assumptions that there were no strong concepts and ideas existing on the local level and that the population just had to be 'taught' democracy [and] [...] local perception of practices was per-

---

1338 La'o Hamutuk. 2002. "Chronology of Oil and Gas Developments in the Timor Sea." *La'o Hamutuk Bulletin* 3:8, part 2. Available online at http://www.etan.org/lh/bulletins/bulletinv3n8b.html, last access on 6 March 2009.

1339 Ibid. While the treaty has been beneficial for East Timor, there are some critics claiming that UNTAET could have negotiated even better conditions. "None of the discussions between UNTAET and Australia covered areas outside the ZOC/JPDA, which has allowed Australia to continue to develop seabed resources that should rightfully belong to East Timor. Although the Timor Sea Treaty and other agreements say they are 'without prejudice' to a future maritime boundary settlement (and they become null and void once boundaries are agreed to), there is no incentive for Australia to settle the boundaries, which could end its lucrative maritime occupation, until all the petroleum has been extracted." La'o Hamutuk 2003. "Timor Sea Historical Background." *La'o Hamutuk Bulletin* 4:3-4. Available online at http://www.laohamutuk.org/Bulletin/2003/Aug/bulletinv4n34.html, last access on 6 March 2009.

1340 Vieira de Mello, Sergio, "Address at the First CNRT Congress, Dili, August 21, 2000." Available online at http://members.pcug.org.au/~wildwood/cnrt.htm, last access on 2 March 2009.

ceived as cultural 'folklore' and was not accorded much significance."[1341] Likewise, capacity-building for those who were supposed to run the future public institutions experienced many setbacks. There was a lack of time and peacebuilding funds, and of good personnel to train. A fundamental mismatch of expectations existed: the international community was about "to institute a certain system for which there was no capacity to really manage."[1342]

The first step of "Timorization" was done with the funding of the NC, but the really important step was the broadening of the state-building strategy with the establishment of the NCC and ETTA. For UN standards, this reorientation was remarkable; although criticism remained that it was done too late. An important step in creating the more consistent framework for public service reconstruction was common budgeting.[1343] The institution-building performance across the sectors of the ETTA varied according to different factors: local personnel, international personnel, NGO cooperation, and funding. The latter depended crucially on bilateral contributions, but donors' rationales were not always functional but rather guided by strategic or media interests. A crucial performance factor was the determinedness of the international senior staff to make important but delicate decisions. Especially the crucial issue of land rights latter was considered "too hot a potato" to be dealt with.[1344] This, however, created an uncertain environment for investment that was deerly needed to boost the local economy. More economic reconstruction would also have been a counterweight to a smaller and potentially more effective and sustainable civil service. In self-critical introspection, a former senior UNTAET official regretted this reluctance.[1345] Another prominent case of procrastination was the establishment of a rent payment system for the former Falintil fighters who could not make it into the new police and military. On this note, the ex-Falintil fighters played an infamous role in the summer 2006 clashes between the government troops and "rebel soldiers." On a final note, a crucial obstacle to more sustainability-oriented measures was Fretilin: increasingly regaining power,

1341 Hohe 2002b, p. 570. "To the local elite, UNTAET failed to provide access to power, while to the general population it was unable to improve their daily lives." Gorjao 2002, p. 320.
1342 Telephone interview with a senior staff member of UNTAET, 9 October 2006.
1343 "Once we had the budget law that determined what all the sectors would have to do in order to form that budget. So, that's one kind of framing device that creates uniformity of input and process. Once we had a transitional cabinet we had a cabinet manual; it created a kind of uniformity about how a law had to be drafted and was the consultation process was. So, over time we began to build in frameworks which created uniformity of input and some kind of commonality in terms of the way in which issues were approached." Interview with a senior staff member of UNTAET, New York, 23 November 2006.
1344 Interview with a senior staff member of Civil Affairs, UNTAET, New York, 18 September 2006.
1345 Ibid.

it began to try to take over the process.[1346] As UNTAET's legitimacy decreased, the more would it concede power to Fretilin. But this was an ambiguous venture since a large part of the diaspora was not well accepted by a large part of the local population.

3.3 Running the Mission

So far, I have reconstructed the efforts of UNTAET in implementing the mandate, focussing on the (re-)building of government institutions. I will now turn to the description of the style of UNTAET's external and internal transitional management, referring to its relationship with the Timorese population and to how the mission leadership handled its staff and its relationship with New York headquarters. In both "arenas," dynamics were unfolding. In East Timor, old and new divisions occurred increasingly while Fretilin was gaining power. Within the mission, staffs were arguing about the degree of Timorese participation, and the high percentage of underperforming personnel represented another headache for the mission leadership. In his dealings with headquarters, de Mello tried to play political games as much as he could, such as to cope with the stalling transition process. And he was good at it. With regards to raising and coordinating voluntary funds, UNTAET had set up a specialized Donor Coordination Unit that had oversight of the varying progress of the different sectors and tried to win over and "steer" donors to commit to previously neglected issues.

3.3.1 Local Dynamics

The status in the independence struggle still mattered enormously to East Timorese. A tripartite differentiation existed, building on the "remembered effort and service in the civil war in 1974 and 1975. Back then, there were three parties – one which was loyal to Portugal and wanted Portugal to return to govern here in the transitional period, those who had wanted independence, and those who wanted Indonesian sovereignty."[1347] The latter were primarily located in the western parts of East Timor; after independence, "Westerners" were generally suspected to be collabo-

---

1346 "Once they were in power, they exchanged administrators with loyal Fretilin personnel," which was not always well accepted with the population. "I heard, for example, Bobonaro is fully boycotting their District Administrator, who was selected by Fretilin." Written interview with Dr. Tanja Hohe, former team member of UN Volunteers in East Timor, 30 September 2006.
1347 Interview with Professor Shepard L. Forman, Director of the Center on International Cooperation, New York University, New York, 20 September 2006.

rators with Indonesia by the population in the eastern parts of the island that had traditionally functioned as retreat area for Falintil.[1348] Hence, latent divides between inhabitants of the eastern and western parts of the island, between the independence fighters and the collaborators, and between the Tetum- and the Bahasa-speaking East Timorese, emerged.[1349]

The conflict about the staffing of the positions in the new government and public services fuelled further discontent. It even mounted to the filing of a claim by the NC that "those who hold dual citizenship should be barred from standing as condition for the Constituent Assembly."[1350] Fretilin regained power and a high profile throughout the territory, increasingly separating itself from CNRT and Gusmão.[1351] When developments cumulated, a divide between Fretilin, which was increasingly dominated by exile Timorese,[1352] and other groups, who were more or less coherently united in CNRT, became inescapable.[1353] After the split, two major political forces consolidated. "Those were not necessarily two power structures, but political opposition. Hence, the Fretilin leader in the village would start undermining the CNRT village chief."[1354] All of this is not to say, however, that Fretilin purported bad-intentioned politics – there were many competent people who were needed for the reconstruction of the country and who cared about it.[1355] It continuously enjoyed broad support as the resistance party, which was its major asset.

Still, Fretilin was determined in its grip for power, and it adopted the role of an opponent rather than a partner of UNTAET.[1356] UNTAET's reaction was to grant Fretilin a stronger position in the transition: feeling that they were losing legitimacy, UNTAET's senior staff, especially de Mello, deemed the collaboration with the

1348   Ibid.
1349   In 2006, this division became virulent.
1350   Garrison 2005, p. 24.
1351   The political rivalry between Alkatiri-Fretilin and Gusmão started in 1987, "When Gusmão, as leader of the Resistance Armed Forces, known as Falintil [...] had broken with Fretilin's Central Committee." King, Dwight. 2003. "East Timor's Founding Elections and Emerging Party System." *Asian Survey* 43:5, pp. 745-758, p. 749.
1352   "Fretilin itself is dominated by individuals from the diaspora who know how to hide behind the local Fretilin heroes." Written interview with Dr. Tanja Hohe, former team member of UN Volunteers in East Timor, 30 September 2006.
1353   The split came after Fretilin's refusal "to participate in the Permanent Council since the August 2000 Congress due to dissatisfaction with some congress processes and decisions." Walsh 2001, p. 11. Cf. also Garrison 2005, p. 24.
1354   Written interview with Dr. Tanja Hohe, former team member of UN Volunteers in East Timor, 30 September 2006.
1355   "Most of them were well-intentioned, too. You know, they came back because they wanted to be part of re-building their country." Interview with a representative of the Timor-Leste Institute for Reconstruction Monitoring and Analysis, New York, 27 November 2006.
1356   A senior UNTAET official credits this attitude to the party's history: the major – or sole – topic of their political agenda had always been independence and resistance. Interview with a senior staff member of UNTAET, New York, 23 November 2006.

strongest party a good way to save the mission's standing. While this procedure was a possibility to increase "Timorization," it forestalled political developments and furthermore impaired UNTAET's control of the transition process.

3.3.2 "Dead Wood" in the Districts

Although UNTAET's mandate required the mission and the institution-building processes to be decentralized, the opposite was the case. After the sluggish deployment of DFOs to the more rural areas of the country, i.e. all but Dili, a push towards centralization began. The Dili-focused transition approach was brought about by the interplay of UNTAET's small territory assumption, the centrally designed UNTAES civil service division, and Fretilin's like of centralized government.[1357]

On-the-ground, orientation rapidly changed to a more pragmatic view, focusing on "do-able" central level institution-building. One argument for centralization advocates that Timor is too small a country for reasonable federal structures.[1358] While this was a correct statement considering the square kilometres of the country, it was based on too little information or understanding: it neglected the island's very poor infrastructure. For instance, it can take several days to get from Dili to Los Palos with local means of transport. And in these terms, East Timor is an extremely large country.[1359]

The district administration became more organized after the initial mess, but capacity-building in the districts continued to depended much on the people involved, with the quality of district officers and field staff varying considerably. While there were very good and ambitious people who opted to work in remote rural areas, "many of the people who were assigned to being district administrators had very little administrative talent themselves and very little administrative experience."[1360] This was one of UNTAET's general problems. But there were even worse cases: useless and lazy staff, "Who were simply there trying to collect their next salary and who had no contact with the locals at all."[1361] The "strategy" to

---

1357 Fretilin knew also how to use, for its own good, the traditional ideal of unity. Accordingly, there was also no consultation with *the chefe do suco* and the *chefe do aldea* in this matter. Interview with a senior staff member of Civil Affairs, UNTAET, New York, 18 September 2006.

1358 Ibid.

1359 The argument also ignores the fact that the kingdoms of East Timor had been indeed self-governing entities for centuries: the Portuguese rule was only superficial and still in Indonesian times, the locally acting *chefe de suco* and *chefe de aldeia* had enormous leverage.

1360 Ibid. "So, unfortunately, the UN appointed people who were quite unsuitable because they had not had any previous experience of being administrators." Ibid.

1361 Telephone interview with a staff member of UNTAET, 9 Oktober 2006.

cope with this "dead wood"[1362] that soon developed at UNTAET headquarters was to place them in far-away districts. Since it is very difficult to fire people within the UN system, a continuous shuffling of – very well paid – personnel materialized. "Staff was being moved around who no one wanted in the mission. [...] There was a game of musical chairs."[1363]

The successive replacement of the international DFOs by Timorese started hesitantly in late 2000.[1364] Still, "The way Timorese were selected for the positions in the districts was either after the gusto of the district administrator, or we had some weird western criteria and selected people that had no authority."[1365]

3.3.3 Relation to Local Population

The issue of deciding on the local interlocutors was straightforward *and* loaded with intricacies at the same time. On the one hand, CNRT and its leaders enjoyed broad legitimacy in the eyes of the East Timorese and presented themselves as moderate transition partners, yet the UN did not accept them formally as interlocutors due to their status. Recognizing the absurd nature of this contradiction, SRSG Vieira de Mello tried to handle the situation by building close informal ties with the former resistance leadership.

Brushing Off

The obvious candidate for cooperation was the CNRT as the umbrella organization of the resistance movement. However, formal participation was put on hold and built up slowly through the NCC/NC.

"Contrary to most post-conflict situations where you have completely dysfunctional structures and where integer counterparts are hard to find,"[1366] in East Timor there *was* a trustworthy interlocutor. The CNRT had been the main organizational

---

1362 Interview with a senior staff member of Civil Affairs, UNTAET, New York, 18 September 2006.
1363 Ibid.
1364 Interview with a senior staff member of UNTAET, New York, 23 November 2006.
1365 Written interview with Dr. Tanja Hohe, former team member of UN Volunteers in East Timor, 30 September 2006. When the CNRT split, however, a new dynamic started, with Fretilin starting to turn against the umbrella organization by using and partly manipulating the grassroots.
1366 "In countries in transition you often have a completely dysfunctional structure. You have either no government at all or a government which is the core of the problems." Interview with Professor Dirk Salomons, Director of the Program for Humanitarian Affairs at the School of International Public Affairs, Columbia University, New York, 20 September 2006.

driving force for the pro-independence vote during popular consultation, and enjoyed considerable *de facto* legitimacy.[1367] Besides, DPA, UNAMET and other international agencies, such as the World Bank and UNDP, had already acknowledged them as their local cooperation partner and had worked with them previously. In addition, the CNRT had "quickly reorganized its nationwide structures"[1368] and held a working infrastructure. Despite these well-known facts – at least the knowledge would have been easily accessible via DPA[1369] – there was a political dynamic of rejecting the formal involvement of indigenous East Timorese from the very beginning.[1370] Most interactions between UNTAET and East Timorese took place where the latter worked as drivers or translators for the international staff.

The Gusmão – Vieira de Mello Link

With CNRT's *non grata* status and "[no] clear guidelines on the states of potential interlocutors,"[1371] the interaction with the local leadership in the early days was sketchy and far from formalized.[1372] UNTAET made a very bad first impression. "I won't deny that there was a situation where one could think that doors for dialogue were closed. Yes, I admit that this existed," Gusmão stated as early as November 1999.[1373] Realizing the precariousness of the situation, it was only hours after his arrival that de Mello visited Gusmão in Aileu, and only three days later when a meeting between high-ranking UNTAET and CNRT leaders first took place.

> We discussed two aspects of this question. One at the highest level, how we bring the CNRT and possibly the other protagonists to a mechanism of consultation and decision-making on the many priority issues that lie ahead of us in the short and medium term. So, this would be the political consultative body. The other aspect is how we articulate

---

1367   CSDG, "East Timor Report," para. 293.
1368   Ibid.
1369   "The choice of interlocutors was obvious and known to the UN for a long period of time because the UN, for 27 years, had had to deal with the question of the occupation in East Timor, then with the referendum. The Department of Political Affairs, which had been responsible for East Timor, had long dealt with a set of East Timorese in exile, in Portugal, and to some extent in Mozambique. But when UNAMET became a peacekeeping mission and the mandate switched to DPKO, there was a really serious breakdown because DPKO isolated DPA." Interview with Professor Shepard L. Forman, Director of the Center on International Cooperation, New York University, New York, 20 September 2006.
1370   Suhrke 2001, p. 5.
1371   CSDG, "East Timor Report," para. 329.
1372   Cf., e.g., Saldanha 2003, p. 162.
1373   UNTAET Public Information Office, "Gusmão at a press conference on November 19, 1999. Briefing by Ian Martin, Sergio Vieira de Mello and Xanana Gusmão, 19 November 1999." Available online at http://www.un.org/peace/etimor/DB/br191199.htm, last access on 6 March 2009.

the work of the transitional administration of the UN and of this embryonic Timorese civil service that we are here to nurture and to develop and train on the day-to-day execution of the policies defined at the highest level.[1374]

An effective consultation and participation "mechanism" that *was* put in place was the personal tie that quickly developed between de Mello and Xanana Gusmão. Indeed, it was reported that later on, de Mello would not make any major decision without Gusmão's consent. However, throughout UNTAET's lifespan, the mechanism was never formalized. In fact, the SRSG had

> [s]truggled to decide how much preferred status to give to Gusmão. UN officials in New York urged him not to play favorites and to treat Gusmão as the head of one party among many. But it did not take Gallup pollsters or a formal election to confirm Gusmão's hallowed local status. Vieira de Mello appreciated New York's concerns. If he relied on Gusmão to gauge 'the will of the people,' he would alienate anybody who did not follow Gusmão. Plus, even of doing so meshed with overall Timorese sentiment, it would send the wrong signal to the Timorese about how leaders would be chosen in the new democratic East Timor. In advance of presidential elections, he would try to walk a fine line, respecting Gusmão's *de facto* authority without formally enshrining it.[1375]

To sum up, at the early stages, UNTAET had a mediocre image with the locals and their interaction evolved on an informal and strongly personal basis; later on, their relationship did technically improve but there was not much interaction with the "commoners" or civil society.

3.3.4 Capacity-building

The competence to build Timorese capacity was not spread widely among international staff. At times, even the willingness was lacking. Yet, staff quality was mixed and there were many UNTAET officers who tried to convey their knowledge and expertise. But then again, their enthusiasm was cut short by the language obstacles as well as by the immense gap between demands and available knowledge and education of Timorese, who had been kept by the Indonesians from receiving good education. An obstacle to having more contact and exchange with locals was also the language barrier.[1376]

1374 UNTAET Public Information Office, "De Mello at a press conference on 19 November 1999. Briefing by Ian Martin, Sergio Vieira de Mello and Xanana Gusmão, 19 November 1999." Available online at http://www.un.org/peace/etimor/DB/br191199.htm, last access on 6 March 2009.
1375 Power 2008, pp. 306-307.
1376 See below.

Proper hiring was the first obstacle to capacity-building. It was the hardest at the mid- and lower-levels, where it "took forever."[1377]

> That sort of working levels was the hardest to deal with. I mean: where are you going to get them? I mean there is certainly that tier of people that were a part of the bureaucratic structures during the Indonesian time, right. So, some of those people were still around, many of them had fled, but some were still around, so we would try to find them because they had some basic skills. Everyone knew who they were, everyone knew where they were. It wasn't a secret. But there weren't so many of them either. So, we would also look to universities, people connected somehow to universities; you know, people who were just graduating or people we knew who graduated at least the last five or ten years, and people with at least some basic skills, some basic writing skills and communicating skills. But they were usually *very* basic. They weren't so specialized in all these different areas of government.[1378]

What would have been needed in that situation were qualified capacity-building skills on parts of the international staff, such as to train East Timorese to do the required specialized tasks. But, despite the mandate's explicit requirements on mission staffing, stressing the importance of qualified personnel as well as of its ongoing training,[1379] the UN did not have much personnel with pertinent administrative capacities, nor were people prepared for their capacity-building jobs. "The UN does not usually work that way. You're not usually working in a way to replace yourself. You're just doing your job."[1380] The "mechanism" by which skills were transferred was "See-and-Learn" and then to gradually hand-over duties to local staff. Normally, this took several months, "In most sectors international UN staff members were put in charge so as to mentor and train the Timorese and to restore services. Unfortunately for Vieira de Mello, UN staff performed neither tasks well."[1381] There were also no formal capacity-building guidelines, "No one of the international staff had a clue."[1382] There were no guidelines. In addition, Asian culture as well as the Timorese experience under Indonesian rule took its toll: there was no attitude of asking, insisting, or taking initiative at the work place. "They were very quiet" and possibly "intimidated by this work they've never done before."[1383] Vice versa, "In the minds of a lot of the UN staff, there was never really a competent, capable Timorese counterpart with who to work to transfer those

---

1377   Telephone interview with a senior staff member of UNTAET, 9 October 2006.
1378   Ibid.
1379   Cf. UN Doc. S/1999/1272, para. 15, "[The Security Council] [u]nderlines the importance of including in UNTAET personnel with appropriate training in international humanitarian, human rights and refugee law, including child and gender-related provisions, negotiation and communication skills, cultural awareness and civilian-military coordination.".
1380   Telephone interview with a senior staff member of UNTAET, 9 Oktorber 2006.
1381   Power 2008, p. 308.
1382   Interview with a UNTAET staff member, Washington, DC, 10 September 2006.
1383   Ibid.

skills."[1384] That often led to "a lot of frustration"[1385] for the international staff. Thus, efforts of capacity-building were relatively low. Not making things any better, there are some reports on international staff individuals that behaved even counterproductively, obstructing their Timorese counterparts from taking over their jobs – because *they* wanted to keep them as long as possible.[1386]

Another huge issue for capacity-building was language. "The fact that the UN official language was English was really devastating – because no Timorese could read or write English."[1387] Most people spoke Bahasa Indonesian. Tetum and Portuguese were only spoken by elderly people in the rural areas and by the expats, respectively. Yet, UNTAET official documents were produced in English. For their translation of the latter, there were simply no capacities, "Who's gonna do that, with every single document, with every single e-mail. It's not possible."[1388] Thus, giving the East Timorese written instructions was a difficult issue. It also played out during the final hand-over.[1389] The language problem was even exacerbated when the Transitional Government, under Fretilin, proclaimed Portuguese and Tetum as the official languages, "Although everybody knew that 75 percent of the country wasn't going to speak their language and this was going to create a lot of torments for the newly graduates."[1390] But particularly Fretilin leader Mari Alkatiri was very adamant about it and ignored the concerns.[1391] It also implied that the relatively poorly skilled people had to cope with an extremely heavy workload: not only bound to learn how to run an administration, the mostly Bahasa-speaking Timorese had to study Tetum, Portuguese, *and* English at the same time. Obviously, the new regulation favored expat Fretilin as well as younger people.[1392] While UNTAET uttered protests against this policy, it did not do so decisively, and accepted Fretilin's decree.

1384 Ibid.
1385 Ibid.
1386 Ibid. See also Beauvais 2001.
1387 Telephone interview with a program officer of the Donor Coordination Unit, UNTAET, 7 October 2006.
1388 Interview with Joseph Andrews, Special Adviser to the DSRSG, UNTAET, and to the Foreign Minister, ETTA, Washington, DC, 9 September 2006.
1389 Telephone interview with a program officer of the Donor Coordination Unit, UNTAET, 7 October 2006.
1390 Ibid.
1391 And for political reasons, UNTAET did not push the matter which, in the eyes of several former UNTAET officials was a devastating mistake.
1392 "The question of language became a major issue of division in that those who had been in exile were from a generation educated in Portuguese and had continued to function in Portuguese, whether they had been in Mozambique, Portugal, Macau, or Brazil. The original Fretilin draft of the constitution designated Portuguese alone as the official language of Timor-Leste. Making Portuguese the official language limited participation in the constitution building process where documents and debate were often conducted in a language

A different aspect of UNTAET's underperformance in capacity-building was UNTAET's poor promotion of East Timorese civil society. The conditions of a working civil society were not put in place. Again, this is related to the dual nature of the mission/interim administration: while in other contexts the UN in post-conflict territories focuses much more on the establishment of a political space that balances the power of the government, in the case of East Timor it *was* the government. With a high workload and a novelty of tasks, UNTAET reportedly focused much more on this side of the mandate.

3.3.5 Cooperation with International and Local Organizations

For capacity-building – but for other purposes too – UNTAET cooperated with international, local, governmental, and non-governmental actors. UNTAET was designed as a fully integrated mission, i.e. all UN components in the country were merged into one structure; in addition, non-UN actors were requested to cooperate closely with UNTAET and be coordinated by their SRSG by the mandate. Cooperation went rather smoothly in the sense that there was not much friction. In terms of adequateness and efficiency, however, a range of services and resources that were rendered to the mission were not very useful.

In the realm of capacity-building, training courses were offered by different member countries – far from coherent though. For instance, Sweden made an offer to have some East Timorese flown over to get basic training in foreign diplomacy. "It wasn't like, 'OK, here is what we got, here are all the people we got, here are those skills, here is what we need, here's the training that we need.' It wasn't like that. It was like, 'Member state x is willing to do that – so fit it in.'"[1393] Another field for cooperation between member states and UNTAET was the contribution of voluntary funds.[1394]

that only few members of the Assembly were comfortable with (Schulz). More importantly for the young, making Portuguese a requirement for employment in government jobs limited access to paid positions for a generation literate only in Bahasa Indonesia (ABC). The constitution only recognises Bahasa Indonesia as transitional working language alongside English. As a result many younger Fretilin supporters shifted their support to the PD, while others opted for a more radical version of Fretilin re-founded as the ASDT by Amaral." Garrison 2005, p. 24.

1393 Interview with a UNTAET staff member, Washington, DC, 10 September 2006.
1394 See next chapter. An interesting point to mention is that, opposed to other comparable missions, the number of international organizations and other member states directly involved on-the-ground was rather low. More experienced actors might have contributed to generating more alternatives to contested issues or issues with whom UNTAET was overstrained. For a similar argument, see Chesterman 2004, p. 64.

3.3.6 Raising and Managing Resources

Donor's willingness to contribute to statebuilding in East Timor was relatively high. The downside of it was that the strong donor position had an impact on the different performances across sectors.[1395] UNTAET tried to manage the fundraising, coordination, and allocation using a separate office, the Donor Coordination Unit (DCU). With the change of the transition strategy to more "Timorization," East Timorese ministers gained a voice in the workings of the DCU, too. The ultimate "principals" remained the donating member countries.

> A lot of the donors were ready to put in money into the infrastructure sector, health, education – but none of them wanted to put their money into other, unsexy sectors, you know, such as justice or labor. Another issue was the geographical equity: a lot of the money came in to the central, the national level, and to strategically important areas, such as the borders or the regional centres, but then there were the mid-inland districts that were completely forgotten because they were inaccessible and strategically unimportant. No money was flowing in there. So we were always trying to convince the donors to put money into other areas, but also we were trying to convince them to put money into the Trust Funds where the Timorese government had the authority to allocate the money wherever they wanted it to.[1396]

The rationales behind these variances trace back to donors' strategic interests as well as to considerations of symbolic policy.[1397] For instance, the Japanese were said to never put in money into the trust fund, "They always stuck to highly visible, large-scale infrastructure projects."[1398] Other cases in point were Australia and Portugal, "The Australians were almost a 100 percent financing the Ministry of Finance. And the Portuguese were financing large parts of the police and justice."[1399] Towards the end of the mission, civil administration became an even more important issue, "There was hysteria among the UNTAET personnel as well as the World Bank to get some money for the civil administration. And we succeeded in having the donors strengthen the civil service administration, but it was not satisfactory."[1400]

The coordination and allocation of the newly founded monies was executed by the DCU,[1401] in close cooperation with the World Bank and, later on, with the East

---

1395 This does not relate to the un-earmarked funds for ETTA.
1396 Telephone interview with a program officer of the Donor Coordination Unit, UNTAET, 7 October 2006.
1397 Ibid.
1398 Ibid.
1399 Ibid.
1400 Ibid.
1401 The Unit itself consisted of about ten people. Ibid.

Timorese National Planning and Development Agency.[1402] The DCU coordinated the funds via four strategic mechanisms: the first and most prominent one was donor conferences, organized by the World Bank in close coordination with UNTAET and with participation of Timorese officials. The first conference was held in Tokyo in December 1999. It was followed by four other donor meetings in Lisbon, Brussels, Canberra, and Oslo in 2000 and 2001. The second mechanism was the donor coordination meetings chaired by DCU and the World Bank in East Timor on a monthly basis. They were also arranged *ad hoc*, "whenever we had guests coming from overseas, or whenever we had the Timorese authorities, or the UNTAET officials coming over to see."[1403] The participants in these meetings, apart from DCU and the World Bank, included UNDP as the UN coordinator representing the UN agencies; the minister of the trust fund; some major donors, including the multilateral ones; the Minister of Finance; the Head of the East Timorese Planning Agency; and certain other ministers whenever there was a specific agenda.[1404] The NGOs involved were predominantly interested in human rights, geographical equity, people's involvement, and corruption. They were selected by the NGO coordination body.[1405] However, a DCU member concedes that, for the sake of efficiency, they were often sidelined:

1402 "In mid 2000, a National Planning and Development Agency (NPDA) was established under UNTAET and with a Timorese head. Gradually and under close mentorship of both UNTAET and the World Bank, the East Timorese began to take on the role of donor coordination and mobilization of donor support." An important result was the elaboration of a National Development Plan (NDP) which "was prepared in 2001/2002 [...]. Participatory consultations were held with about 40,000 people throughout the territory under the leadership of Xanana Gusmão, who was to later be elected as the first President of Timor-Leste. Several sector working groups with government and civil society participation were actively involved in formulation of the Plan. The NDP was adopted by the National Parliament on the eve of the Restoration of Independence and has served as the guiding beacon for the independent Timor-Leste and its development partners since 20 May 2002." Hasegawa, Sukehiro. 2004. *Beyond Cold Peace: Strategies for Economic Reconstruction and Post Conflict Management.* Speech at the Conference "International Donor Coordination, Civil Society and Natural Resource Management", 27-28 October 2004, organized by the Foreign Office of the Federal Republic of Germany. Available online at http://www.unmit.org/UNMISETWebSite.nsf/e4899f58093d136749256f0a00 3f1073/cb0d674b2e83c6fa49256f3a0081dbb7?OpenDocument, last access on 7 June 2007.

1403 Telephone interview with a program officer of the Donor Coordination Unit, UNTAET, 7 October 2006.

1404 "For example when we needed to boost the civil administration we would have the Head of Civil Service Administration come in and make a presentation; and sometimes the chief minister would be present, and we had some sectoral ministers come in." NGOs participated "from time to time." Ibid.

1405 There was an umbrella NGO where all the Timorese and the international NGOs had registered themselves. Cf. The International Forum of National NGO Platforms, "FONGTIL-Forum NGO Timor-Leste." Available online at http://www.ong-ngo.org/ spip.php?page=article_base&modele=capitalisa-tion&id_rubrique=323&pfn=323&lang=en, last access on 2 March 2009.

There was a dilemma because at times, you know, we were trying to make some major decisions, and then the NGOs would come from a different perspective – and rightfully so – but that could kind of stifle the discussions a little bit. Like, for example, when we were talking about civil service administration and the need to strengthen the military and the police, one NGO would say, 'Look we have to address the human rights violation part.' Again, it's an important issue but there might have been a different, better form to discuss that kind of issue. So it got a bit contentious, and sometimes, you know, the ministers saw it as derailing the discussions a little bit. So, there were times when the ministers actively tried not to have NGOs involved, just for the sake of efficiency.[1406]

Paralleling the strong donor influence on the allocation of funds from the bi- and multilateral development funds,[1407] the ministers of the transitional cabinet ascertained their voice on the ETTA funds, provided by the development budget of the Reconstruction Trust Fund and the recurrent budget paid from this pot.[1408] With the World Bank and the DCU only making suggestions,

The ultimate decision-making lay with the Cabinet members and every line minister would come up with their own budget of what needed to be done, including the recurrent and the development budget, and then they would discuss and trying to allocate. And that decision very much depended on the political leverage of each minister.[1409]

3.3.7 Leadership Style and Relationship with New York Headquarters

If Vieira de Mello revealed an important quality in East Timor, it was not his wisdom so much as his adaptability. As early as the spring of 2000 he felt that his mission, which outside of East Timor was seen as a rare UN success, was on the brink of failure. Physical security was breaking down, the economy was in ruins, and the Timorese had begun to view the UN as a second 'occupier.' Desperate to recover, he aggressively cracked down on security threats and attempted to give the Timorese a meaningful say in their own affairs. In order to regain momentum, he realized, he would have to pay more attention to Timorese dignity and welfare than to UN rules.[1410]

As it was in UNTAES, the central figure was the SRSG/Transitional Administrator. Both were strong charismatic leaders, Mello's style differed considerably from the

---

1406 Telephone interview with a program officer of the Donor Coordination Unit, UNTAET, 7 October 2006.
1407 "That is the money that is funded 100 percent by bilaterals or multilaterals. So they come in with a specific road project, and the governments, let alone the NGOs, had no say in how the money was used. We could advocate for something but the ultimate decision lay with the bilateral donors." Telephone interview with a program officer of the Donor Coordination Unit, UNTAET, 7 October 2006.
1408 "Later on, when ETTA was created, also daily discussions with the East Timorese Minister of Finance, and weekly meetings with all the different ministers of the transitional cabinet so that they had a voice in deciding on where the funds would go." Ibid.
1409 Ibid.
1410 Power 2008, p. 323.

patterns of behavior Klein displayed. While Klein had a proactive military persona, Vieira de Mello has been described as a very political animal.[1411]

> He had gaiety, a lightly worn cosmopolitan charm, chiselled good looks, and a Clinton-like knack of making even someone he barely noticed feel as though they had his undivided attention. He used those assets to cut compromises, by no means always to his credit or that of the UN, with such hideous characters as the Khmer Rouge's Ieng Sary and the Serbian President, Slobodan Milosevic.[1412]

He could point to a long list of records as a UN diplomat, but was still ready to bend New York headquarters rules for the sake of on-the-ground progress, willing to learn *and* implement lessons he had internalized.

In UNTAET, however, he had a difficult start. From the beginning, the mood in the mission was somewhat tense due to the local conditions.

> The heat (90 degrees daily, with humidity between 60 and 90 percent) was withering. Most of the UN staffers lied off rice and Indonesian noodles. Those UN staff who worked in the districts, far from Dili, felt particularly cut off, unable to procure desks, computers, or even pens and paper. Following their boss' lead, UN staff worked nineteen-hour days and on weekends.[1413]

The most challenging moment for his internal leadership occurred after his decision regarding ETTA. A lot of his international staff argued that "[t]hey had not come all the way to East Timor to answer to Timorese" and that their "contracts said that they worked for the UN Secretary-General."[1414] In this situation, de Mello decided to talk to them up front. "He assembled the entire UN staff – some seven hundred people – along with the four new Timorese cabinet ministers, in the auditorium of the parliament building. He spoke from the dais and, pointing to the Timorese sitting in the front row, said, 'These are your new bosses.' [...] 'You either obey, or you can leave.'"[1415]

Towards headquarters, de Mello knew the system by heart and he knew how to play it, though he often despised it. He was able to bend the constraining rules on occasion, particularly concerning funding, which forbade him from rebuilding Timorese infrastructure. For instance,

> After a long struggle Vieira de Mello succeeded in getting permission to donate eleven percent of UN assets – about $8 million worth of equipment – to the new government of East Timor. By claiming that East Timor's ravaged roads were damaging UN vehi-

---

1411 Interview with a senior staff member of Civil Affairs, UNTAET, New York, 18 September 2006.
1412 Righter, Rosemary. 2008. "The brilliant Sergio de Mello," *Times Online*, 28 April 2008. Available online at http://entertainment.timesonline.co.uk/tol/arts_and_entertainment/the_tls/article4020096.ece, last access on 6 March 2009.
1413 Power 2008, p. 321.
1414 Ibid., p. 329.
1415 Ibid., pp. 329-330.

cles, he also managed to get a portion of his budget used for road repair. This was a major victory.[1416]

3.3.8 Summary and Assessment

UNTAET had enormous tasks to solve and it produced respectable achievements in institution-building. Important factors that contributed to this success included the good financial equipment and the learning ability of key international staff, particularly de Mello, who not only had the power to initiate a change of approach, but also understood that a shift was necessary if the mission was not to be put at risk. Still, the outcomes could have been even better, had the mission engaged in comprehensive participatory policies earlier and had it put a greater emphasis on capacity-building.

For nearly two years, the mission was almost exclusively staffed by international personnel and overloaded with the difficulties of its internal dealings. As a consequence, local ownership was foreclosed. This triggered not only frustration[1417] but also created a precarious situation where time was running out to build up the capacities needed for running the new democratic state. The issue comes down to not being able to cope with the dual mandate of running a state and doing capacity-building at the same time. That should have been incorporated into the design of the mission – including structuring, staffing, funding, and timelines – and a more culturally sensitive planning of the mission in general.[1418] Although the mandate stated it, the mission was not designed to be an issue of training and hand-over. All of these considerations, however, refer to assets which the UN simply did not seem to be able to mobilize. Most importantly, staff was not selected on their ability to train, "They also often are not given the opportunity to train because there is nobody to train, there is no overall plan."[1419] A private remark by de Mello to one of his senior staff was that "the mission was effectively run by about ten percent of the people. Maybe 50, 60 percent of people were simply collecting their salary and not doing any great harm. The rest were positively dangerous: people who you had to

---

1416 Ibid., p. 332.
1417 "People who had been involved in an independence struggle do not like the idea that when they finish that struggle they do not get to take over control." Interview with a senior staff member of UNTAET, New York, 23 November 2006.
1418 For example, considering the history of a Timorese working for the suppressor Indonesia in the administration. The theme of the resistance was "Give them your bodies but not your minds." For the Timorese working in the Indonesian run administration this meant just sitting around, doing close to nothing, and getting the salary. UNTAET apparently did not do anything about transforming this kind of behavioral pattern.
1419 Interview with Professor Dirk Salomons, Director of the Program for Humanitarian Affairs at the School of International Public Affairs, Columbia University, New York, 20 September 2006.

keep out.'"[1420] Meanwhile, the rest of the mission tried to "get things done" and the best way to get things done is not by long-term training but by doing as much as you can yourself, such as to achieve short-term goals. What was done in capacity-building was focused too much on technocratic issues.[1421] Only incrementally did ambitious staff learn to "feel their way."[1422] All of these constraints, routines and the following necessities and automatisms were, however, only poorly communicated and led to irritation and discontent with the local population. The East Timorese expectations were not well managed.[1423]

As for political consultation, the mission officially adhered to the *terra nullis* policy. Having had closer and official ties with the readily available CNRT right from the beginning would have enabled UNTAET to get control of the power structure in the rural areas, where 80 percent of the population lived. Instead, it created a parallel structure triggering confusion and rivalries and rendering international attempts a failure ore left them with only marginal impact.[1424] Increasingly realizing the necessity for more exchange, informal consultation relationships were established, and there was an extremely close link between de Mello and Gusmão. While these relationships were important, they did not respond to the public protests for more consultation though.

In addition, some UNTAET staff even opposed a World Bank programme[1425] that was intended to help reconstruct the rural areas – a reluctance which had to be perceived unfavorably by the local population but also with other senior UNTAET officials. In fact, this dynamic led to intra-UNTAET fights, with the political-pragmatic view winning over. Closing on a more positive note, UNTAET's DCU could provide for some organizational slack by convincing donors to put their money into un-earmarked general funds.

1420 Interview with a senior staff member of Civil Affairs, UNTAET, New York, 18 September 2006.
1421 Cf. Interview with a senior staff member of UNDPKO PBPS, New York, 15 September 2006. "In general, if I had to make a criticism of our own work in capacity-building. The problem was that it was too technically focused."
1422 Cf. Interview with Joseph Andrews, Special Adviser to the DSRSG, UNTAET, and to the Foreign Minister, ETTA, Washington, DC, 9 September 2006.
1423 "[T]hey tried to reinvent the will of the people." Saldanha 2003, p. 162.
1424 Cf. Hohe 2002b. Opposed to the mandate instruction, the mission was centralized with district level issues becoming second or third order things. The establishment of the civilian governance parts of the mission were still deferred; at the central level and particularly in the rural areas. The DFOs that were out there received only sketchy instructions if at all. And over one and a half year into the interim administration, it remained staffed almost exclusively with international personnel.
1425 There were other similar programs, for instance, the Quick Impact Programme of UNHCR or USAID's TABS. While these programmes may have not been the ultimate solution to all the problems of Timorese, the good thing they did was, "They got some money in circulation, to give people something to live on, so they're not just dependent on welfare." Interview with a representative of the Timor-Leste Institute for Reconstruction Monitoring and Analysis, New York, 27 November 2006.

3.4 Termination

In its final stage, UNTAET engaged in three parallel and complementary processes. First, it prepared the hand-over of authority and government functions to the Timorese in the run-up to an independent Timor-Leste, based on elections of a Constituent Assembly and of a president, following the drafting of the new state's constitution. Second, it prepared the hand-over of specified military, police functions and of some civilian matters to its successor. Third, it engaged in controlling its own end, focussing on the deadline of 20 May 2002. The drawdown processes were operated by a "special force," a team headed by a high UN official that had not formerly been part of the mission.

3.4.1 Elections and Constitution-Building

The elections were won by the favorites, Fretilin and Xanana Gusmão, and occurred peacefully, with a high voter turnout. It was, however, questionable if the common Timorese population knew what they were eventually voting on. UNTAET seemed to have focussed too much on technical voter education issues rather than teaching people the essence of their new political system. Likewise criticized was the inadequacy of the highly sophisticated, computerized registration system that was difficult even for UN staff to handle. Likely to further long-term repercussions, the semi-presidential government system implied a constitutionalized rivalry between the majority in the parliament and the president, and that meant between Fretilin and Gusmão, who had already established personal rivalries.

On 30 August 2001, East Timorese voted for a Constituent Assembly to elaborate the constitution for the new state was *the* major milestone on the road to independence.

> In order to implement the decision of the people of East Timor in the popular consultation of August 1999 and so as to protect the inalienable human rights of the people of East Timor including freedom of conscience, freedom of expression, freedom of association and freedom from all forms of discrimination, there shall be a Constituent Assembly to prepare a Constitution for an independent and democratic East Timor.[1426]

According to UNTAET Regulation No. 2001/2 of 16 March, the Constituent Assembly comprised 88 representatives, divided into 13 representatives for each of

---

1426 UNTAET Regulation No. 2001/2, "On the Election of a Constituent Assembly to Prepare a Constitution for an Independent and Democratic East Timor," UN Doc. UNTAET/REG/ 2001/2, 16 March 2001, para. 1.1.

East Timor's 13 districts,[1427] and 75 representatives elected on the basis of a single, nation-wide proportional representation system.[1428] The UNTAET regulation also stated, "If required by the Constitution, the Constituent Assembly will become the Legislative Assembly of East Timor."[1429] The election was scheduled for 30 August 2001.[1430] The date represented on the two-year anniversary of the vote for independence. There were arguments in favor of an even earlier election, but this possibility was ruled out since "elections potentially would have been very destabilizing in the aftermath of the bloody 1999 referendum and might well have invited further violence from pro-Indonesian elements."[1431] The timeframe was tight anyway: once elected, the Constituent Assembly was to adopt a constitution within ninety days of its first meeting.

The UN took on the election tasks without much experience. In the past, they had observed elections and provided technical support, but actually managing elections and designing the overall election framework were new tasks, "They made it up as they went along."[1432] The only clear guideline for UNTAET was that elections, as a prerequisite for independence, had to take place before its relatively short mandate ended.

Multi-Party Election System

The votes were supposed to be cast on two separate ballots, one for national parties and independent candidates, and one for district-level parties and independent candidates. Yet, the idea of competition among different factions did not fit the realities on-the-ground: it was juxtaposed with the East Timorese ideas on social order, and it resulted in a bit of a joke because "there was really one major dominant par-

---

1427 They were elected on a majority basis; the candidate with the highest number of votes is the district representative.

1428 Parties win seats in the Assembly in proportion to the share of votes they receive in the election for National Representative. Cf. De Sousa, Lurdes Silva-Carneiro. 2001. "Some Facts and Comments on the East Timor 2001 Constituent Assembly Election." *Lusotopie* 2001, pp. 299-311. The regulation further elaborated on the competences of the CONSTITUENT ASSEMBLY to be elected, the establishment of an Independent Electoral Commission, the process of party registration, specifying the eligibility criteria and forms of candidacy, and seats allocation rules.

1429 De Sousa 2001, p. 2. The regulation also said that "with the consent of the Special Representative of the Secretary-General in East Timor, the Constitution or provisions in it may go into effect prior to independence." Ibid.

1430 UNTAET, "Daily Briefing," 12 June 2001. Available online at http://www.un.org/peace/etimor/DB/Db120601.htm, last access on 6 March 2009.

1431 Beauvais 2001, p. 1133. In addition, a period of stabilization following conflict can be "crucial in securing the preconditions for genuinely pluralistic and competitive elections." For an argumentation in favor of early elections see Della-Giacoma 2000.

1432 Interview with a representative of the Timor-Leste Institute for Reconstruction Monitoring and Analysis, New York, 27 November 2006.

ty,"[1433] Fretilin. Still, UNTAET was bound to hold multi-party elections. While there is evidence that the cultural incompatibility did not go unnoticed,[1434] there was apparently just no alternative to the multi-party paradigm.[1435] At the end of the day, the approach was accepted, "The East Timorese also knew that all this money was coming to them, and that all the donors were lobbying for certain things and were stressing certain things. And one is multi-party."[1436]

During the registration process of the parties, some irregularities cropped up. For instance, in a number of districts, political parties with significant local support bases were unsuccessful in placing their district-level candidates on the ballot. Likewise, application errors occurred rather often, for instance registering the same person for national and district elections or selecting someone with an address outside the district. Despite a one-week extension of application deadlines by the Independent Electoral Commission (IEC), last-minute submissions made it impossible for some parties to correct their errors in time. "Although most parties have accepted their errors in registration, the lack of local candidates in some districts may have exacerbated party tensions."[1437]

Fretilin had started to elect its party representatives in March 2001. In many places, Fretilin was the only party people had ever heard of, and thus got support from a large majority of the population. The dynamic of the increasing opposition between Fretilin and CNRT increasingly affected the political climate in the villages and hamlets.

> [I]n some places a new Fretilin representative at the village level suddenly emerged as an opposition to the former CNRT candidate. Traditionally opposed groups would then support different leaders; this increased local tensions. Some Fretilin representatives misunderstood the idea of a multi-party system and requested the UNTAET district administration to stop working with the former CNRT representatives and to co-ordinate with them 'as the whole village is Fretilin anyway.'[1438]

1433 Interview with Professor Shepard L. Forman, Director of the Center on International Co-operation, New York University, New York, 20 September 2006.
1434 Transitional Administrator and SRSG Vieira de Mello even at one point proposed a government of unity which, however, was not enforceable. "[I]t would have been a quick fix." Written interview with Dr. Tanja Hohe, former team member of UN Volunteers in East Timor, 30 September 2006.
1435 Personal conversation with Professor Simon Chesterman, Global Professor and Director of the New York University School of Law Singapore Programme and author of various books and articles relevant for the topic of the present thesis, in particular concerning the transitional administration in East Timor, Konstanz, 24 July 2009.
1436 Telephone interview with a senior staff member of UNTAET, 9 October 2006.
1437 The Carter Center 2001.
1438 Hohe 2002b, p. 583.

At the end of the process, sixteen parties were registered for elections.[1439]

Civic and Voter Education

Since the vast majority of the population had no experience with democracy,[1440] UNTAET set out to teach them the basics about democratic elections. At least, this was the intention.

The person in charge of UNTAET's Civic Education Unit ("CivEd") was Peter Galbraith, formerly US ambassador to Croatia. Starting on the wrong foot from the start, his original education program was rejected by the East Timorese Non-Governmental Organization Forum "because of the non-involvement of East Timorese civil society."[1441] He was confronted with some sharp criticisms.[1442] After a turnaround – which tightened the schedule even more – the program entailed a first round of training for East Timorese "multiplicators," supposed to create constitutional commissions in each of East Timor's 13 districts.[1443] In addition, civil society organizations, such as NGO FORUM, the women's network REDE, CNRT, and

1439 The parties were registered along with five independent candidates at the national level and eleven independent candidates spread throughout East Timor's districts. Fourteen of them signed a so-called pact of national unity, committing them to respect the results of the election.

1440 "The Asia Foundation conducted a survey in the period from February to March 2001 that found some confusion about the purpose of the elections to be held in August (Asia Foundation)." Garrison 2005, p. 17.

1441 "A Popular Challenge to UNTAET's Achievemens." *Back Door Newsletter on East Timor*. Available online at http://members.pcug.org.au/~wildwood/01seppopular.htm, last access on 6 March 2009. See also Beauvais 2001, p. 1132: "They [the NGO Forum; ES] objected to not having been consulted on the project, as well as to the enormous expenditure of funds on foreign staff for which it called." A local NGO worker confirms, "Nobody in East Timor has ever lived in a democracy – apart from a few who came back from Portugal and Australia, but for the great majority of the population, they have never experienced any kind of democratic government." Interview with a representative of the Timor-Leste Institute for Reconstruction Monitoring and Analysis, New York, 27 November 2006.

1442 "I mean, Galbraith had also no governmental experience. He was a diplomat – of the US, which is already a problem. And when it came to... You know,he was the head of the political section during the time when they were preparing for the Constituent Assembly elections, and he created this civic education structure that was totally useless. It was basically rejected by all the civil society people that they asked to be part of it, and they had to scrap it and had to do something different." Ibid.

1443 UN Department of Peacekeeping Operations, "East Timor – UNTAET News. Civic education programme ends in East Timor." Available online at http://www.un.org/peace/etimor/news/01apr27.htm, last access on 5 March 2009. See also Garrison 2005, p. 19, "UNTAET had suggested the creation of a Constitutional commission in each of Timor-Leste's 13 districts to operate in the run up to the Constituent Assembly elections. These mini-commissions were to be tasked with conducting civic education on the transition process and with gathering input to content for a constitution from citizens in each district (UNTAET Regulation 2001/2). The input from the district commissions would then be made available to the Constituent Assembly when it was elected (Carter Centre, 44)."

the Students Solidarity Council, got involved formally.[1444] Yet, people were primarily taught about the mechanics of voting,[1445] which implied that people would not learn "what it meant to have an elected government, that politicians have to be accountable to the people, what are you voting for."[1446] Whereas in 1999 "the choice was a clear cut decision between staying with Indonesia and opting for independence, in 2001, the East Timorese had a far more complex decision on who would be the best party to represent them in a Constituent Assembly and make decisions on the future political system of their country."[1447] Observers attribute the CivEd shortcoming to the intense time pressure.

Furthermore, CivEd was also weak in its rural outreach. Transport, translation, and technical problems posed the major challenges here.[1448]

> As far as Dili is concerned, and to some extent Baucau, people had a variety of chances to participate in civic education events and were in a much more privileged position to have access to information on the elections in general. But the things were quite different in the countryside. OETA observers heard that some people did not know that the election was for the Constituent Assembly, and that people were confused about the 16 political parties. Some political party leaders complained to OETA observers that the facility prepared by the UN was totally not enough for their campaign to cover the country side. In Letefoho, Ermera District, a civic education concert was planned for a mid-August day. The plan was to have a concert with a band and after that to show a civic education video to people who gathered. The concert began at 5 PM as scheduled, but the civic education team from Gleno arrived too late. As a result, the video was not shown. The organizers in Letefoho were angry. OETA observers were there but did not know why the team arrived too late. In Manatuto District, OETA observers heard that the number of the cars allocated for a three-person UN civic education team was reduced from two to one when the program was at its peak. It was feared that they could not fully implement the planned program.[1449]

An unintended negative side effect of the civic education programme was the deterioration of the village structures.

> The spontaneous idea people got after some civic education campaigns was that, 'We have democracy now, and therefore do not need to listen to our village chief anymore.'

1444 Baltazar 2004, p. 3.
1445 "Analysis of voting results by US political scientist Dwight Kong showed that voters in fact cast their ballots in quite sophisticated ways, taking full advantage of the opportunities offered by a mixed member system (Kong, 756)." Garrison 2005, pp. 17-18.
1446 Interview with a representative of the Timor-Leste Institute for Reconstruction Monitoring and Analysis, New York, 27 November 2006.
1447 Smith 2001, p. 46. "[…] due to the time constraint the campaign focused mostly on voter education. Given the short time frame, CivEd was not able to disseminate information throughout the country and matters related to the process of election of the Constituent Assembly […]." Baltazar 2004, p. 3.
1448 The Carter Center 2001.
1449 Osaka East Timor Association 2001, p. 2. See also Azimi and Li Lin 2003, p. xxxii: "[…] voter education and communication of information to the districts/rural areas could have been better."

These statements led to village-level anarchy and were used whenever convenient by any person who wanted to act independently without the agreement of the village chief or any local authority.[1450]

The voter registration process struggled with various technical problems as well. Starting out with the rolls from the 1999 ballot, the organizers soon found out that the system was no longer of any use as the discrepancies in counting were too significant – people were missing on the list or could no longer be identified.[1451] Even after the dismissal of the 1999 ballots the set-up of the registries was confronted with problems of over- and under-coverage, i.e. a person is counted more than once or is not counted at all.[1452] A huge factor for under-coverage was that voting places were sometimes far-away, "One criticism from observers was that forcing people to vote in one of the 350 registration sites meant that some people who were unable to travel were disenfranchised."[1453] Furthermore, the voter registration would be built in tandem with the registration. While this might have been opportune at this stage, it also complicated the process of voter registration and created a high workload. In order to support the registration process, a sophisticated computer system was flown in from Germany that set up a completely computerized voter registration structure. It was completely inadequate for the Timorese context though.

> Such a system might work fine in Germany but it didn't work in a country where communication and infrastructure and illiteracy and a lot of other things were big problems. In addition, the documentation for the computer system was written in German, and only very few people in the mission and nobody in East Timor spoke German. And there was no plan for translating.[1454]

Involving more East Timorese in its design might have attenuated some of the difficulties. One observer notes,

---

1450   Hohe 2002b, p. 583.
1451   "According to information from the various IEC district officials, this discrepancy or shortfall ranged from 3 percent to 18 percent." The Carter Center 2001.
1452   People appear on the count more than once, for example due to multiple names for the same person, in Tetum or Portuguese, or people are registered that do not belong to the target population "East Timorese residents" any longer, for example due to false refugee or death accounts (over-coverage). On the other hand, people may also be missed out because they could not be identified under their former addresses or because of, for instance, poor reach out to the districts due to bad infrastructures (under-coverage). A case in point is the IEC's attempt to use the Indonesian identity card holders as the selection population. However, "people who were in the clandestine resistance had ten different Indonesian identity cards because they were playing different roles. And people who were in exile hadn't any." Interview with a representative of the Timor-Leste Institute for Reconstruction Monitoring and Analysis, New York, 27 November 2006.
1453   Smith 2001, p. 46.
1454   Interview with a representative of the Timor-Leste Institute for Reconstruction Monitoring and Analysis, New York, 27 November 2006.

If East Timorese who knew how the society works had been in positions of authority while the consultants were designing the system, they would have told them, 'Hey, wait a minute, if you don't have manuals in languages we can read, this is not good enough!' That was all stuff that, you know, if somebody had a one-hour orientation, they would know that, or had read one book about East Timor, they would know.[1455]

At the end of the day, with a lot of manpower from UNV, the registration process was able to be finished in a reasonable manner.[1456] By the end of July, the IEC had reinstated approximately 20,000 voters that could be added to the list of voters. The latter eventually comprised some 420,000 East Timorese.[1457]

In the run up to the elections, the split within East Timorese leadership, "based on divisions stretching back to the 1980s but one which had been kept under wraps in the interest of unity in the struggle against Indonesia,"[1458] deepened. On the one side was Gusmão, the charismatic figure of the independence struggle, who advocated a broad, united front of equal parties. He increasingly opposed the stance of Fretilin, the party of the independence fight, whose members saw themselves as the only legitimate party that could lead East Timor.[1459] Finally, in June 2001, the CNRT dissolved itself in order to pave the way for truly multi-party elections.[1460] In turn, the dissolution of the CNRT triggered the emergence of new factions. These new parties often resembled former traditional entities – and they

1455   Ibid.
1456   UN Volunteers. 2001. *UN Volunteers complete civil registration in East Timor.* News Release. Available online at http://dynamic.unv.org/Infobase/news_releases/2001/01_06_25TMP_reg.htm, last Access on 6 March 2009.
1457   It was made available for viewing as of August 23, "To ensure that all voters clearly understand where they must go to vote." The Carter Center 2001.
1458   Garrison 2005, p. 24.
1459   "Gusmão split openly with the Fretilin leadership in March 2001 when he resigned as National Council President over the issue of consultation during the constitution building process." Garrison 2005, p. 24. "From this point on Gusmão tried to assume a neutral position above the competition among political parties. For Gusmão, Fretilin, and the other political leaders in Timor-Leste the constitution building process had become a question not only of how best to create the conditions for sustaining democracy and independence, but also a question of whether to legitimise Freilin's claim to leadership." Ibid.
1460   "At their Congress in Dili, the idea of dissolution created confusion among all the CNRT district and sub-District representatives who had travelled to the capital. There was opposition and a lack of understanding for the dissolution. This was not surprising as the traditional concept of 'unity' was very important for the maintenance of peace and stability. Finally, the CNRT president, Gusmão, gave the order to dissolve, to which nobody protested, as it was an order from the top. Yet, representatives went back to their districts to pass on the new order without understanding the reasons. The message caused even more confusion at the village level, where the CNRT-appointed village chiefs lost their 'legal' basis of power. Yet, backed by their traditional legitimacy or because of the transitional character of the period, most village chiefs remained, although in some cases the village chief's authority was questioned because of the loss of the 'legalizing' umbrella to work under. He was still asked to work for his community and frequently used by international actors, while opponents started to use the new 'legal' vacuum to undermine his position." Hohe 2002b, p. 582.

adopted ancient divisions such as those between traditional kingdoms.[1461] The re-emergence of old frictions in the shape of new parties propelled political dynamics at the village and hamlet level.[1462] The party that best knew how to manipulate these local power structures was Fretilin.[1463] Although the party agendas were relatively differentiated across diverse issues, the one crucial issue of interest to the population was independence. And the faction that occupied this issue was, again, Fretilin.[1464] "People voted for Fretilin to honor the resistance."[1465] In districts where other political considerations were gaining importance, Fretilin agents allegedly "assisted" people in making up their minds; there were reports of defamation and intimidation by some Fretilin proponents.[1466] That being said, other parties did not consistently live up to the standard of being "free and fair" either, using "inflammatory or provocative language in their campaign speeches that raise[d] serious questions about the parties' adherence to the Pact."[1467] Fortunately, only minor irregularities occurred on polling day.[1468]

1461 "Relationships between kingdoms were defined either through kinship or marriage relations, or through hostility. With the 'loss' of the importance of kingdom borders, social rifts appeared along other lines, yet on a similar structural basis. During the resistance movement, for example, some hamlets were pro-Indonesian while others supported Falintil. These hostilities partly confirmed former entities that were entangled in a hostile relationship under Portuguese rule." Ibid., p. 583.

1462 "Often, these rifts seem to occur along the lines of hamlets (confirming a family), or other traditional entities, and so there seems to be a strong dialectic between traditionally opposing parts that 'naturally' entangles with opposing groups. In the wake of the unity brought by the CNRT, factions now had the opportunity to revive. As a result, local communities stopped respecting the 'unwanted' village chiefs, or one faction would work against him. Factions were also disguised as representatives of political parties or organizations." Ibid.

1463 "Fretilin used traditional symbols to manipulate the Constituent Assembly elections." Ibid., p. 584.

1464 "Fretilin was a dominant party with a lot of popular support. Again, support from the people who didn't have the experience of being part of complex political issues and in which you have multiple different positions or multiple different issues. There was one major issue for the resistance – and that was resistance, and independence. And Fretilin represented that." Interview with a senior staff member of UNTAET, New York, 23 November 2006.

1465 Written interview with Dr. Tanja Hohe, former team member of UN Volunteers in East Timor, 30 September 2006.

1466 "The party has completed a national registry of all militants and sympathisers. Some citizens felt there was a high degree of intimidation in this process." Walsh 2001, p. 12.

1467 The Carter Center 2001. The report continues, "References to opponents as 'communists' or 'traitors' are unfortunate examples. The most troubling statements involve references to 'sweeping up,' a phrase in the local Tetum language reminiscent of previous Indonesian military and militia threats." Ibid. It was reported that there were instances where people indeed "expressed fears of post-election retribution toward political parties, their leaders and supporters and that a number of parties cite these instances of intimidation as affecting their ability to campaign, causing them to scale back planned campaign activities, and in some cases party members have resorted to meeting in secret," further diminishing the information available to the public. Ibid.

The full and final results of the election were presented to the Chief Electoral Officer of the IEC on September 6.[1469] In the districts, Fretilin received 12 of the 13 available seats. At the national level, the results looked somewhat more differentiated but still displayed a majority for Fretilin.[1470] The numbers were not surprising. In fact, some Fretilin members had expected an even clearer victory, speculating that they would win over 80 percent of the vote.[1471] A noteworthy remark is the poor result of Apodeti, the party that had formerly favored integration into Indonesia; compared to receiving 22 percent of the vote in 1999, the support dropped to 0.6 percent. This result possibly indicated "that many of those who support integration into Indonesia are not participating in the political system, whether through lack of trust or through intimidation."[1472] The controversies over the consultation process and the tight timetable did not seriously affect voter participation.

As 91 percent turned out to vote, one could argue that the public demonstrated high levels of support for the constitution building process based on their participation in the

1468　Cf. Osaka East Timor Association 2001. A few polling centres in Dili and Liquica start-edthe voting of ordinary voters one to two hours later than the planned time 7 a.m. One problem seemed to be a lack of smooth communication between DEOs and local polling officials partly because DEOs did not understand Indonesian or Tetun or because there was only one or few translators. Another reason was a lack of training of local officials. At one polling centre, local officials were making so many procedural mistakes that the DEO him/herself had to handle the opening procedures at all polling stations. At one polling centre, because the opening of the polling centre for ordinary voters delayed almost two hours, OETA workers observed voters who were waiting in queues were not well controlled. They were not properly informed about the reason of the delay that they packed at the gate of the polling centre. "It seems that the identification procedure took much more time than had been expected. One reason for this was that voters had been told to go to a voting centre which is far from their residence. OETA observers heard that this was caused by some confusion at the civil registration process. The IEC wanted to compile a voters registration list but the UNTAET requested to make the civil registry to avoid the over wrapping of the work. This decision is understandable, but it is our question why the necessary information for the voters list was not systematically included in the civil registry." Ibid.

1469　The total valid votes summed up to 363,501 – with a total vote cast of 384,248 and 20,747 invalid ones. Cf. De Sousa 2001, p. 307.

1470　Frente Revolucionária do Timor-Leste Independente (Fretilin): 57.3 percent of the vote, 43 seats; Partido Democrático (PD): 8.7 percent, 7 seats; Partido Social Democrata (PSD): 8.1 percent, 6 seats; Associação Social-Democrata Timorense (ASDT): 7.8 percent, 6 seats; União Democrática Timorense (UDT): 2.3 percent, 2 seats; Partido Nasionalista Timorense (PNT): 2.2 percent, 2 seats; Klibur Oan Timor Asuwain (KOTA): 2.1 percent, 2 seats; Partido do Povo de Timor (PPT): 2 percent, 2 seats; Partido Democrata Cristão (PDC): 1.9 percent, 2 seats; Partido Socialista de Timor (PST): 1.7 percent, 1 seat; Partai Liberal (PL): 1.1 percent, 1 seat; Partido Democrata-Cristão de Timor (UDC/PDC): 0.6 percent, 1 seat. Cf. ibid.

1471　Cf. Garrison 2005, p. 19.

1472　Ibid., p. 26.

elections for a Constituent Assembly. As well, international observers certified the election results as meeting international standards for being free and fair.[1473]

Still, the result conveyed indicators that the rationale for a large portion of the population in the election related "more to local ideas of leadership and not to the modern concept of elections as a means of choosing the most capable leadership."[1474]

On the same day the results were officially announced, the Transitional Cabinet met for the last time. It was to be replaced by the all-East Timorese Council of Ministers of the Second Transitional Government, with Fretilin's Mari Alkatiri appointed as Head of Cabinet.

Constitution-Building in the Constitutional Assembly & Public Consultations

The Constituent Assembly was established on 15 September. In its inaugural session, the Transitional Administrator handed over the constitutional reports that UNTAET's Political Affairs Unit had drafted in the follow-up of public hearings through its Constitutional Commission (see Box 10).[1475]

However, the reports, "which were meant to feed the Constituent Assembly with the opinions of the people on the future constitution,"[1476] were not discussed at all.[1477] This early boycott indicated that the constitution-building process was completely in the hands of Fretilin, who interpreted their majority position as "a clear mandate to proceed with writing a constitution and with governing the new country."[1478] Likewise, Fretilin's constitutional draft became the text that the discussion was based on; the proposals by UDT, PSD, KOTA, and PPT were sidelined.[1479] The ensuing discussion of the text of the constitution was organized by

1473   Ibid., p. 17.
1474   Written interview with Dr. Tanja Hohe, former team member of UN Volunteers in East Timor, 30 September 2006.
1475   Cf. Baltazar 2004.
1476   Ibid., p. 2.
1477   "Although members of the Constitutional Commissions requested to participate in the sessions and brief members of the Constituent Assembly on the outcomes of the public hearings, Fretilin rejected their proposal, invoking a lack of legitimacy of the Commissions – it was not an elected body." Ibid.
1478   Garrison 2005, p. 20. "Fretilin then dominated the constitution and drafted it in their own favor." Written interview with Dr. Tanja Hohe, former team member of UN Volunteers in East Timor, 30 September 2006.
1479   In fact, Fretilin had the draft adopted already in 1998 at its party congress in Melbourne.

way of four Thematic Commissions,[1480] which were bound to hold public hearings for civil society organizations and other institutions. This requirement eventually led to an extension of the tight constitution-building time-frame.

Box 10: The Constitutional Commission

"A Constitutional Commission (CC) was established in each of the thirteen administrative districts of East Timor to solicit the views of the people on the future Constitution. In fulfilling its mandate, each CC should take note of civil society initiatives carried out in the district in relation to constitutional issues and coordinate with them to ensure that the people were informed on the constitutional development process.

Each CC was composed of between five and seven members appointed by the Transitional Administrator; all of them East Timorese. The members of each CC were selected from a broad section of civil society organizations. Their main tasks were to inform the people in each of the concerned sub-districts about the constitutional consultation process and to conduct and facilitate public hearings in each sub-district.

There were two phases in the selection process; nomination and appointment of candidates. Candidates were nominated after a consultation process conducted by each District Administration in collaboration with the District Advisory Council was completed. Each District Administration submitted a list of 10 candidates to a selection panel. Candidates should be respected people in the community, show willingness, and commitment to serve as well as impartiality and ability to conduct public hearings as well as be fluent in Tetum and Indonesian with good communication skills.

The Constitutional Commissions were charged with conducting at least one public hearing in each of the administrative sub-districts of every district. The constitutional consultation process was organized to take place in five phases: public information campaign to inform all East Timorese about the public hearings; training of constitutional advisors, commission members, and administration staff; constitutional consultation preparatory phase; public hearings and reporting.

The Constitutional Commissions conducted more than 200 public hearings in each of East Timor's 65 sub-districts in which around 38,000 East Timorese participated between the launch of the Constitutional Commissions on March 15 and July 14, 2001."[1481]

The consultations took place from 24 February to 2 March 2002, but were marred with many irregularities:

> During the consultations, each district team held meetings with the local people for a week to listen and gather their recommendations and views on the draft constitution. Given the limited availability of time, late distribution and dissemination of information, often people were not informed in advance to the public meetings, not informed of the contents of the draft constitution, and so people were not prepared to discuss substantive matters of the constitution. Another constraint faced was the fact that the original constitution was written in Portuguese making it difficult for most of the East Timorese people who speak Tetum and/or Indonesian to understand the text. Translations were made to Tetum and Indonesian, but prior to the consultations some districts (Lautem) were only given Portuguese versions of the constitution. Leaders like Bishop Belo and President Xanana expressed their concern with the short period given for public consultation. President Xanana wrote to Mr. Kofi Anan requesting an extension

---

1480 These were: Thematic Commission I on Rights, Duties, and Liberties/Defense and National Security, Thematic Commission II on Organization of the State/Organization of Political Power, Thematic Commission III on Economic Social and Financial Affairs, and Thematic Commission IV on Fundamental Principles/Guarantees, Amendment of the Constitution/Final and Transitional Provisions. In addition, a Systematization and Harmonization Commission was formed "to organize and harmonize the drafts produced by every Thematic Commission." Baltazar 2004, p. 3.
1481 Ibid., pp. 2-3.

of time for the public consultation. The lack of a scientific methodology for analyzing the information gathered raised the concern that political parties might try to influence or manipulate the opinions and views of people. In this regard, the Deputy-Speaker of the Constituent Assembly Mr. Arlindo Marcal said, 'It will not make a difference if just one person is objecting to a provision in the constitution, but if the same issue would be raised in all districts, then Constituent Assembly members will take note of that point and discuss it later during the plenary session after returning to Dili.'[1482]

Besides, time pressure persisted and biased the political process to advantage Fretilin.[1483] In the end, only twenty-one of forty-five amendments[1484] were adopted for revision by the plenary, and eventually, only four of them were adopted in the draft of the constitution. "Nearly all of them came from institutions rather than from the public."[1485]

The constitution itself contained essential good governance principles but also some whose adequacy and utility to the territory was questionable. International experts included constitutional principles that did not meet East Timor's traditional values and principles while Fretilin infused principles that suited its one-party system claim. The provision for the Constituent Assembly's transformation into the

---

1482 Ibid., p. 4.
1483 First, there was "no time for an alternative model for drafting such as the use of a broadly representative Constitutional Commission as had been proposed by the NGO Forum." Garrison 2005, p. 12. Second, time pressure "ruled out the idea of adopting an Interim Constitution to allow for more extensive civic education and consultation as some in the NGO community had suggested." Garrison 2005, p. 12. See also Babo Soares 2001. Third, "The short time frame also assumed that the Constituent Assembly would transform itself into the first national parliament without further elections," putting Fretilin straight into the 'driver's seat' of the future government. Garrison 2005, p. 12. "Given the short time frame, CivEd was not able to disseminate information throughout the country and matters related to the process of election of the Constituent Assembly and of drafting the constitution took priority. As a result, important topics like the decision on the transformation of the Constituent Assembly into the first independent Parliament of the country were not communicated to the people. Criticism and widespread public outrage arose when the announcement was made once the constitution was drafted. Only the political elite had access to all the information during the entire transitional process." Baltazar 2004, p. 3. See also Goldstone 2004, p. 90, "Armed with its large majority, Fretilin was also a convert to the controversial plan to transform the Constituent Assembly into the National Parliament on independence, thus obviating the need for a second election."
1484 They included eight recommendations from the East Timorese people and thirteen from different organizations.
1485 Baltazar 2004, p. 5. "There was a general perception that many suggestions made by the people were neglected by the Constituent Assembly. Also, attempts by some minority parties (UDT, PSD, PD, PDC, PST) to advance the concerns of the people during the final debates did not succeed. The most polemic issues discussed during the consultation process were related to the following provisions of the Constitution: Article 1 Section (2) Independence Day, 13 (1) Official Languages, 17 Equality of Women and Men, 15 (1,2) National Flag, 39 (3) Family, Marriage and Maternity, 42 (2) Freedom of Demonstration, 146 National Defense and Security, 150 Abstract Review of Constitutionality and 167 Transformation of the Constituent Assembly into a Parliament." Ibid.

national parliament was especially problematic, leaving a legacy of unresponsiveness and (one) party centrism.[1486]

On 31 January 2002, the Constituent Assembly (with the large Fretilin majority) voted to transform itself into East Timor's first legislature. "The overwhelming vote for the transformation [...] ended a heated debate on whether or not legislative elections should be held in concert with the 14 April presidential election or shortly after East Timor marks its independence on 20 May."[1487] The vote also represented the apex of Fretilin's increase in power. While the party was still enjoying broad generic support, the way it pushed its agenda made many East Timorese feel that "political decision making about the transitional process only took place at the level of the political elite."[1488]

Presidential Election

The constitution envisioned a semi-presidential system of government, implying that the elected president has the power to dismiss the prime minister and veto legislation, but in a framework of strong checks and balances. The presidential elections were dominated by Xanana Gusmão, who insisted on "running as a candidate endorsed by nine opposition parties, rather than as an independent candidate as urged by the Fretilin leadership."[1489] In the run up to the presidential elections on 14 April 2002, the split between Gusmão and the Fretilin leadership grew further. "Mari Alkatiri, Fretilin General Secretary and Prime Minister in the Transition Administration, announced that he would be casting a blank ballot and senior Fretilin leaders were seen lending their support to Francisco Amaral, Fretilin's first

1486 "The transformation of the Constituent Assembly into the national Parliament has left another legacy in terms of the character of the relationship between elected officials and the electorate. [...] In planning the electoral structure for the Constituent Assembly, several factors came into play, including technical considerations related to the creation of electorates, and a concern to ensure a degree of pluralism. A consequence of the predominantly 'closed list' electoral model is limited accountability of parliamentarians to the people. Because members of Parliament are in the main not elected locally, they do not have a local presence and local communities have no easy access to them. Rather, because they owe their election to their position on a party ticket, the party rather than the people becomes the principal arbiter and reward of their performance. The effect is remote government, physically and politically isolate from the eighty percent of the population who live outside the major urban areas. It is perhaps no coincidence that recent political unrest has had its genesis in the districts, with marches on Dili and demands for inclusion in the political process." Ingram 2003, pp. 87-88.
1487 UNTAET, "Daily Briefing," 31 January 2002. Available online at http://members.tip.net.au/~wildwood/02janassembly.htm, last access on 6 March 2009.
1488 Baltazar 2004, p. 5. "East Timorese people had limited involvement in the transitional administration itself." Ibid.
1489 Garrison 2005, p. 24.

president and Gusmão's only opponent in the Presidential race."[1490] As expected in this vote based on personalities, Gusmão gained an overwhelming majority, 83 percent of the vote. Despite the council and the presidency in place, UNTAET retained its law-making authority, and thus maintained its influence up until the end. "That was pretty fundamental."[1491]

3.4.2 Extension of the Mandate

From the start, UNTAET operated under two axiomatic parameters: first, there was comprehensive international support for a giant mission; second, the support was strictly limited by time. Going in line with this stance, the Secretary-General outlined a deadline of two to three years for the achievement of UNTAET's mandate. Eventually, the mission started on the premise of an initial period of up to 16 months and two further Security Council resolutions extended it for another 16 months.

The Secretary-General's report of 4 October 1999 envisaged that the transition to independence would take two to three years, and UN resolution 1272 established the mission "for an initial period until January 31 2001."[1492] This formulation entailed a rather short but still vague deadline for UNTAET, implying some leeway for the ultimate withdrawal.

There had been different views on the timeframe for the mission. The preference of East Timorese leadership had initially been for a much longer timeframe:

> In the mid-1990s, the East Timorese resistance body, the National Council of the Maubere Resistance (CNRM), the precursor to the CNRT, had proposed a UN-supervised transition to independence lasting as long as eleven to thirteen years. This extended timescale was not in any sense regarded by the East Timorese leadership as optimal, but rather as a negotiating position developed in the light of what seemed feasible in the unpromising political context of the time. But in the wake of the Popular Consultation, some in the CNRT leadership (including its president, Gusmão) were still envisaging a relatively long, five-year transition to independence.[1493]

In fact, when a small but high-ranking UNTAET delegation in December 1999 met with Mario Carrascalao, one of East Timor's important political figures, to consult on the international transition strategy, "he laughed at us when we told him that our plans were to leave after two to three years and he said, 'It will take you ten years at least until you get to know this society, never mind winning their trust and

---

1490   Ibid.
1491   Interview with a senior staff member of UNTAET, New York, 23 November 2006.
1492   UN Doc. S/1999/1272, para. 17.
1493   Goldstone 2004, pp. 87-88.

gaining the ability to help them.' He understood the limitations of his own people."[1494]

Such a long timeframe was not in consideration in the Security Council, though. On the contrary, this body generally prefers short missions. Except for cases where political deadlock prevails, such as it has been the case in Kosovo, it is unrealistic to expect the Council to engage in long-term, comprehensive engagements that relate to peacebuilding; as soon as the security situation is stable and the mandate deemed fulfilled, it withdraws its missions. However, when the realities on-the-ground ridiculed the parameters fixed at headquarters, discussions on seizing the interpretive leeway of the deadline ensued. In spring 2001, a decisive meeting was held in Bacao among eight UNTAET officials – senior people in charge of civil service, ETTA, justice, and infrastructure. There were two stances: one was the pragmatic, politics-guided view that the targets and goals had to be adjusted to the timetable, which had become concretized and "Timorized" by Gusmão with its proposal of December 2000,[1495] to the timing of elections and the hand-over. In line with this argument were Gusmão, Fretilin, most member states whereby the United States and Australia were particularly important, the Security Council, which was determined to finalize the mission in the first half of 2002, and also the SRSG.[1496] De Mello and the international community wanted – and needed – a quick success, in addition to avoiding anything that seemed neo-colonial.

> And certainly it was easier for him to go through with the elections for the Constituent Assembly and then the hand-over to the independent government – and not to worry too much, for instance about the details of the fact that the Public Service Commission. With all its kinds of nice sentiments about independence and neutrality and public service ethics, it was not working as well as it should do – because it started to be politicized by the new Fretilin people who were brought into the transitional government.[1497]

A senior UNTAET official adds, "It's also important to know that Sergio, who was a very political animal himself, was under pressure from the Fretilin people to stick to the timetable and not to delay it."[1498] The other view was that East Timor would not be in the condition to run itself soon after the UN's withdrawal. In reality, UNTAET did not have the 32 months it was given on paper to prepare the country

---

1494   Interview with a senior staff member of Civil Affairs, UNTAET, New York, 18 September 2006.
1495   As stated above, this timetable largely coincided with what de Mello had presented to the Security Council in June 2000.
1496   The preferences were expressed in the Security Council and the Friends Group for East Timor. Telephone interview with Julian Harston, senior UN official and Director for Post-UNTAET Planning, UNTAET, 26 October 2006. Mr. Harston served as the Director for Post-UNTAET Planning in the United Nations Transitional Administration in East Timor.
1497   Interview with a senior staff member of Civil Affairs, UNTAET, New York, 18 September 2006.
1498   Ibid.

for independence but rather "maybe 18 months because there was a slow time at the beginning because everything was destroyed. And then we had difficulties, and then there were the quarrels within the different Timorese groups."[1499] Within UNTAET, mostly civil affairs staff supported this viewpoint. But also member states that were affected were in favor of an extension, most importantly Portugal.[1500] Locally, the most visible proponents were UDP, the people around Bishop Belo, and some NGOs[1501] – but their voices and those of the more sustainability-oriented UNTAET officials were no longer heard. Hence, the stance that won out in the end was the political one, which had more powerful supporters.

Eventually, UNTAET was extended twice. By the end of 2000, the important capacity-building benchmark for the development of political institutions had not been met, and thus Security Council resolution 1338 of 31 January 2001 extended the mandate in consideration of "the possible need for adjustments related to the independence timetable"[1502] for another year. Given the abundant mission equipment and the promising security situation, the Security Council expressed its expectation *and* demand for a quick and successful mandate accomplishment. The second mandate extension of 31 June 2002 was a reaction to the lack of consultation during the constitution-building process, granting UNTAET a few more months to catch up with it.[1503] The resolution determined that the definitive hand-over be on 20 May 2002. Fretilin proposed the day: it was a symbolic date, commemorating the declaration of independence in 1975, and the Timorese wanted *that* date very much.[1504]

1499   Ibid.
1500   Another major member state supporting mandate extension was Brazil. As said, the preferences were expressed in the Security Council and the Friends Group for East Timor. Telephone interview with Julian Harston, senior UN official and Director for Post-UN-TAET Planning, UNTAET, 26 October 2006.
1501   "[…] Bishop Carlos Ximenes Belo, […] expressed concern that the political timetable was too short to prepare what was assumed to be a highly volatile electorate for a peaceful election, while others, primarily from the local nongovernmental organizations, were ambivalent, on some occasions arguing that the UN had outstayed its welcome and on others echoing Bishop Belo's view." Goldstone 2004, p. 88.
1502   UN Department of Peacekeeping Operations, "UNTAET." Available online at http://www.un.org/peace/etimor/docs/UntaetDrs.htm, last access on 20 March 2007.
1503   UN Doc. UN/Res/1392 (2002).
1504   Cf. interview with Joseph Andrews, Special Adviser to the DSRSG, UNTAET, and to the Foreign Minister, ETTA, Washington, DC, 9 September 2006. The date was in accordance with a Constituent Assembly recommendation that UNTAET hand over sovereignty to elected Timorese government institutions on 20 May, 2002.

In hindsight, a range of former UNTAET officials saw a mistake in not having dared to stand up to Fretilin and opt for a re-negotiation of the timetable.[1505] While a multiple-year extension would have been as ideal as it was idealistic,[1506] the officials are convinced that the country would have already benefited a great deal from a mere one-year extension. Possibly such an appeal would have had good chances of success if it presented the Security Council the right arguments.[1507] At the end of the day, major stakeholders made the decision, and after the election date was announced, everyone got involved in the preparations, the "Timorization" process in the ministries accelerated, and the discussions abated. "The overwhelming momentum was toward independence. This was the big thing. This was what everybody wanted."[1508]

1505 "Internationals understood towards the end that one needed a much longer involvement to achieve the tasks and not just drop a half finished country. However, at that point, UNTAET had been such a dramatic experience for the locals, that they just wished for them to go. Equally, senior staff such as Sergio must have known that they look much better if they left now instead of waiting until things break down. Also, remember that there were follow up missions, and many internationals actually remained in place. All that changed was decrease in international authority." Written interview with Dr. Tanja Hohe, former team member of UN Volunteers in East Timor, 30 September 2006. The same opinion is expressed in various interviews by different actors involved in the transition, ranging from program officers and political advisers to senior staff members of UNTAET and DPKO officials.

1506 "Ideally, there would have been six to seven years for the mission but for political reasons that was not possible. The Timorese fiercely wanted to be independent." Interview with Joseph Andrews, Special Adviser to the DSRSG, UNTAET, and to the Foreign Minister, ETTA, Washington, DC, 9 September 2006.

1507 "Most of the time, the Security Council adopts most or all of the Secretary-General's recommendations, and, you know, we don't pay much attention to that. Why would we? We think that's option one. The exception is probably when the Council reacts negatively to the Secretary-General's recommendation – either rejects or rewrite or changes. That does happen sometimes. The biggest disputes between the Council and the Secretariat – no surprises here – tends to be over resources. We tend, as the Secretariat, to give a hard-headed assessment of what's needed and of the resources required to carry that out, because we want to be in a position to succeed as the Council adopts our recommendations. And the Council, at least some members of the Council, in some of the cases, seem to be more concerned about saving money than accomplishing the task. I'm overstating it a little bit for clarity's sake but there are different interests. That said, obviously, the case at hand is a big priority for all Council members. Then they're much more likely to just adopt the recommendations and not cripple over the details." Interview with a senior official of the UN Department of Political Affairs, New York, 12 December 2006.

1508 Telephone interview with Julian Harston, senior UN official and Director for Post-UN-TAET Planning, UNTAET, 26 October 2006. "As you know, independence came up and there was going to be a big party, nobody wanted to be a 'Spielverderber,' you know." Telephone interview with a staff member of the Post-UNTAET Planning Team, UNTAET, 15 October 2006. See also Caplan, pp. 217-218, "The UN decided to accelerate the political transition process, allowing only three months for the Constituent Assembly, elected on 30 August 2001, to draft, debate, and approve a constitution. In the event, the deadline was extended by another three months but as the date for independence had by then already been established, there was now very little time for the assembly to adopt the considerable amount of legislation that the new state would require." A high-ranking DPA official

3.4.3 Devolution and Arrangements Following UNTAET's Withdrawal

Phasing-out the mission comprised two procedural measures: planning and organizing the withdrawal of UNTAET, while at the same time preparing the follow-up mission. Both processes were operated by the so-called "axe men," a delegation from New York that was specifically deployed for these tasks. The team worked rather efficiently and met its tasks but in preparing the mission's withdrawal, they faced various hitches that were induced by UNTAET staff who did not want to lose their jobs; by headquarter regulations that barred the hand-over of mission assets to Timorese institutions; by local Timorese themselves who increasingly packed themselves into planning processes even when this might have been counterproductive; and by the very complex structure of UNTAET, which was difficult to disentangle.

The "Axe Men"

Because of Vieira de Mello's insistence,[1509] the organization of the mission withdrawal and the planning for the next step were built around two crucial parameters: the planning process was to take place on-the-ground – which is considered an unusual practice for the UN[1510] – and an external team was to be set up particularly to phase out management.[1511]

The external planning team[1512] started its work around May 2001, headed by an expert with international experience, Julian Harston.[1513] The task was to work "with Sergio and his team to develop a plan for the down-sizing of UNTAET, and then

assents, "This was one of those cases where some of the members in the Council were ready to be done, to draw down. There was a lot of pressure to reduce." Interview with a senior official of the UN Department of Political Affairs, New York, 12 December 2006.

1509 "You got to remember this all overwhelming person of Sergio Vieira de Mello who was more or less able to get what he wanted right up to the last minute." Telephone interview with Julian Harston, senior UN official and Director for Post-UNTAET Planning, UNTAET, 26 October 2006.

1510 "He wanted the planning to happen in the mission; because, as you know, in New York you're at headquarters, with politics – and you're far away from the needs." Telephone interview with a staff member of the Post-UNTAET Planning Team, UNTAET, 15 October 2006.

1511 Interview with Joseph Andrews, Special Adviser to the DSRSG, UNTAET, and to the Foreign Minister, ETTA, Washington, DC, 9 September 2006.

1512 Harston and his team had not been previously part of the mission but were 'flown in.' "Julian Harston left again in September 2001, but his team stayed on and continued the transition planning." Telephone interview with a staff member of the Post-UNTAET Planning Team, UNTAET, 15 October 2006.

1513 He was an experienced ASG level person who had been involved in many UN peacekeeping missions, for instance in Bosnia, but also in the decolonization experience of the United Kingdom in the 1960s.

to work with in New York and Washington and elsewhere on a resolution and a plan for the new mission."[1514] Having the exceptional status of "external but on-the-ground," the reason they were "brought in from outside was precisely because the UN wanted an outsider since then, you can be more rigorous."[1515]

In its first weeks, the team consisted only of international staff – especially people from mission support and from political affairs, Harston, and his direct assistant. Soon, however, the group had to be re-designed. Since Timorese, that basically means Fretilin, "were really pissed off"[1516] for not having been included, they complained to de Mello. As a result, to-be Timorese officials entered the team. Apart from the fact that the group became inappropriately large,[1517] this political decision by de Mello was diametrically opposed to the team's more functional agenda.

> They brought in East Timorese much earlier than we wanted them to. Because the moment you did that you knew that you virtually handed over the process to them. And my view, which I still hold to this day, was that the people we were talking to very largely didn't represent the people of East Timor. *We* did. We actually did it. We had a better view than they did. But the moment you let them in, in this sort of Cabinet process, which was run by the Deputy SRSG, it became almost impossible to take tough decisions. I just think we should have gone on governing longer than we did. Because of the hang-ups that people have – most people have sort of colonial baggage, of one kind or other, me included – and I think when you're dealing with Australians, New Zealanders, Pakistanis, Brazilians and so on, I think they are very uncomfortable in the role of a colonialist. Therefore, the hand-over to local personalities developed power because it makes them feel better – not because it's necessarily the best thing to do.[1518]

Even worse, the enlarged team "didn't meet very often and the meetings were horrible because there was all that bad faith. And whatever that was decided in this team was not really implemented."[1519] In incremental steps backwards, the tasks could be redistributed across smaller teams, which worked "much better."[1520]

1514 Ibid. "Decisions on phasing-out provisions are a bargain between the Security Council and the Secretariat. The Security Council is certainly weary about the continuing commitment and drain of resources." Personal conversation with Professor Stephen J. Stedman, Senior Fellow at the Center for International Security and Cooperation at Stanford University, Konstanz, 29 June 2009. In 2003, Professor Stedman was recruited to serve as the research director of the UN High-Level Panel on Threats, Challenges and Change.
1515 Telephone interview with a staff member of the Post-UNTAET Planning Team, UNTAET, 15 October 2006.
1516 Ibid.
1517 It eventually comprised up to 20 people.
1518 Telephone interview with a staff member of the Post-UNTAET Planning Team, UNTAET, 20 October 2006.
1519 Telephone interview with a staff member of the Post-UNTAET Planning Team, UNTAET, 15 October 2006.
1520 Ibid.

At the beginning, there was a dominant focus on activities related to withdrawal.[1521] On this aspect, "there was quite a lot of guidance,"[1522] and member states got involved, too. The plan that ensued included a table with milestones and timelines, and a detailed and rigid cutback matrix. The focus for the milestones was very much on the central level and on civilian aspects: legislators, the Cabinet, and central support.[1523] While some of the decisions were hard to accomplish, it was decisive that the team was in the agenda-setting position.[1524] Each week, the "axe men,"[1525] as they came to be called, made "key decisions, and it came down to getting rid of people, like, 'OK, by the end of September, we're gonna have to get rid of five more UN staff.'"[1526] Thus, pushing people to make deadlines, the mission size went decreased by about ten percent within a period of six to seven months.[1527] "Pretty brutal but it worked."[1528] The rationale for communication was, "'Listen, we have to leave. So what we want to make sure is that there is a gradual pull-out' – and not that on one day you wake up and we're all out, and then things were gonna fall apart."[1529]

The cutbacks proceeded according to considerations of stability and of functions. The general rule of thumb was that the sectors and districts that were least stable and had the fewest capacities in place were handed over last.[1530] That said, the police and the military were definitely the last functions to downsize: international police and military were directly under member states' command, and there was no hand-over until formal independence, as member states would obviously not allow their personnel to be put under the command of another state, especially not

1521 "What New York was talking mostly about, at the outset, was just the draw down, i.e., drawing down to the numbers of personnel on the UN mission; smaller and smaller and smaller so that at the end there was no one left and it was handing it over completely to the government with only a hundred consultants and a small administrative support mechanism to the UN mission." Interview with Joseph Andrews, Special Adviser to the DSRSG, UNTAET, and to the Foreign Minister, ETTA, Washington, DC, 9 September 2006.
1522 "And there was plenty of experience for that after all. You know, other missions had been downsized before. So we just did it mechanically." Telephone interview with Julian Harston, senior UN official and Director for Post-UNTAET Planning, UNTAET, 26 October 2006.
1523 Telephone interview with a staff member of the Post-UNTAET Planning Team, UNTAET, 15 October 2006.
1524 "And that was the trick. *We* had to come up with the draft." Telephone interview with a senior staff member of UNTAET, 9 October 2006.
1525 "That's why we were essentially there: we're axe people, we were referred to as the axe men." Telephone interview with a staff member of the Post-UNTAET Planning Team, UNTAET, 15 October 2006.
1526 Interview with a UNTAET staff member, Washington, DC, 10 September 2006.
1527 Telephone interview with Julian Harston, senior UN official and Director for Post-UNTAET Planning, UNTAET, 26 October 2006.
1528 Ibid.
1529 Telephone interview with a staff member of the Post-UNTAET Planning Team, UNTAET, 15 October 2006.
1530 Ibid.

of one that was not yet in existence. These hand-overs proceeded after independence with specific restrictions and in a very gradual manner.[1531] In local public administrations, the UN commissioners "would retain executive authority over the entire country until the last district was handed over."[1532] Oddly enough, as all the other functions were reduced, the internationally run public administration got even slightly bigger. This had to be readjusted.[1533] The *in situ* downsizing and replacement were handled by interdisciplinary teams – with staff from the justice sector and the public administration, and East Timorese from the police and the military. "We'd always make sure that the Timorese police commissioner to be was there and his staffs were there. The same on the military: a team with the Deputy Force Commander, with the future East Timorese commander, with administration, legal people and so on."[1534]

The "axe men" encountered major setbacks. There was much confusion about the different structures the UN had created.

> What was difficult, at least at first when I arrived, was this whole loss and confusion of what's UN and what's not UN. There are two planning processes here. One is the future UN mission – that's one thing, that's a purely UN thing. But the second is the future East Timorese government. And how are we going to divide these two things? And we have six months to do it. And it took forever for people to understand. They were confused, they didn't understand. You know, that they were working for what was going to become a government; many people just thought of it as another UN mission, where you just fill out your forms and write your daily reports. Not like, you are working towards two different things. I found this a huge constraint, just conceptually getting this through to people.[1535]

In this chaotic situation, UNTAET's flawed public communication system did not help much. What was helpfgul was that UNTAET tried to use symbolic measures such as little ceremonies that were held for each hand-over – "so that it would be clear what it means."[1536]

1531 "It was not until May 20, 2002, Independence Day, that an agreement was signed outlining the terms and timetable for CivPol to hand over full policing duties to the PNTL. The handover of policing duties for the final district, Dili, took place on December 10, 2003, when the PNTL assumed responsibility for general day-to-day policing for the whole country." Human Rights Watch 2001.
1532 Telephone interview with a staff member of the Post-UNTAET Planning Team, UNTAET, 15 October 2006.
1533 "I remember I went to the UN in New York, having asked for their plan for downsizing, and when I came back I noticed that during the time when everybody else was downsizing, the administration was actually getting bigger." Telephone interview with Julian Harston, senior UN official and Director for Post-UNTAET Planning, UNTAET, 26 October 2006.
1534 Telephone interview with a staff member of the Post-UNTAET Planning Team, UNTAET, 15 October 2006.
1535 Ibid.
1536 Ibid.

The second challenge was the sheer time pressure and workload: there were only a couple of months left, and "most people in the mission went like, 'How are we ever gonna finish by that... It's impossible.'"[1537] A planning team member recalls, "We had to force ourselves to meet certain milestones; and that's why it became really technical within this transition body. Because we had to meet very specific goals, we had to meet these goals at all costs – because we had to meet the May 20th deadline."[1538]

Third, the increasing integration of high-profile East Timorese as well as the intensified consultation with international civil administration officials hampered the decision-making progress, "We had done a lot of consultation with the East Timorese themselves – too much in my view – and with our own civil administration people and so on, and we were slowly withdrawing our presence from these places, and handing-over locally."[1539] In addition, problems at the individual-level emerged occasionally, for instance, with the police.

> When we arrived, basically, the UN police commissioner was not talking to anyone, any civilians in the rest of the mission. So, there was a huge divide. He was unwilling to do any planning with us. And when we arrived – because Julian and I used to work on police a lot, in Bosnia – we spent a lot of energy in building up a relationship with this guy, trying to work together on plans; and this came to fruition only later, after Julian left. But the seeds were planted then.[1540]

Frictions developed vis-à-vis international staff, too. One the one hand, the very idea of downsizing, withdrawal, and post-mission planning was difficult to get through, as staff had to live up to their own challenging daily schedules, "'We have our daily shit to do here and you're talking about six months or even two years from now – we don't have time for that.'"[1541] The other aspect was that there were many people who clung desperately to their jobs. When detailed withdrawal schedules with name lists were published,[1542] staff began to complain immediately – "and that was a nightmare. Our office was like a psychiatrist's office. How many people came crying into my office crying, 'My family, I have to care for my family... I don't understand... Why me...?'"[1543]

1537 Ibid.
1538 Interview with Joseph Andrews, Special Adviser to the DSRSG, UNTAET, and to the Foreign Minister, ETTA, Washington, DC, 9 September 2006.
1539 Telephone interview with Julian Harston, senior UN official and Director for Post-UN-TAET Planning, UNTAET, 26 October 2006.
1540 Telephone interview with a staff member of the Post-UNTAET Planning Team, UNTAET, 15 October 2006.
1541 Ibid.
1542 "What we had to do was to collect names from line officers, and then they would say, 'OK, in this first couple of points: these people should be cut, in the next couple of points: these people.' So that slowly, we were drawing down. So, we would collect these names and then eventually pass it on to the administration." Ibid.
1543 Ibid.

Obviously, the devolution is a genuinely tricky issue:

> Nobody wants to give up power. That's just I think human behavior. So, some people understood very well, especially people who came with a development background. But other people who came from different kinds of training just insisted that "they're not ready, they're not ready, they're not ready." But that's just not how it works: time is running out and money is running out – we're going to have to prioritize. And you're going to have to make sure – it's not going to be perfect – that at least you get the very essential things across. And then you have to leave.[1544]

The final cumbersome issue concerned the hand-over of *assets*.

> What we wanted to do was when UNTAET would end we would hand-over assets to the East Timorese government, meaning cars, computers. So, we wanted to write them off – as a gift. And I think they also did an assessment that it would be more expensive to ship all this stuff to another place because Timor is so far away from everything. Anyway: it was not economically very sound to move everything from Timor. And anyway, Timor needed this stuff. And our argument was that this was part of our mandate to establish a viable state. Again, it was blocked, in New York, by the General Assembly, because they were saying, 'The UN does not hand over assets to a government' – only to NGOs or something like that. But we said, 'Yes, but Timor is an exception, it's different because the UN is government right now, and it is part of our mandate'… I don't remember how exactly it was solved, but in the end, if I remember correctly, it was a compromise. Still again, this took months and months and months and everyone had to get involved. But at the end, we managed to hand over some of our computers and cars and furniture. Otherwise, they would have taken everything up. Can you imagine?[1545]

Follow-up Arrangements

Harston and his team were also in charge of the planning of the succeeding UN Mission of Support in East Timor (UNMISET). "I made it up as it came along, and I mean I have a fair amount of experience in peacekeeping, so it wasn't that difficult."[1546] That being said, however, there was not much guidance and the issue was politically contested, "It was clear from the beginning that we would need another mission – but even that, at the beginning, wasn't a given in New York, particularly not in the Council. People said, 'This is a success, we're going to declare a victory and leave.' And so it was quite a tough battle."[1547] First, the Americans – whose support was essential – were initially against a successor mission "that smacked of

---

1544 Ibid.
1545 Ibid. See also Power 2008, p. 314.
1546 Telephone interview with Julian Harston, senior UN official and Director for Post-UN-TAET Planning, UNTAET, 26 October 2006.
1547 Ibid.

peacebuilding."[1548] Luckily for the UN, however, the chairmanship of the US committee in charge changed at that time, "And we finally persuaded the Americans to support a resolution and a plan for the mission, which included civilian experts, to stay in vital places in the new administration."[1549] Still, the Americans were not the only ones who had to be convinced. Other key players – the Council, the Australians – "all wanted different things at the end of the day. We were arguing about whether we would continue to have an executive police force, we were arguing about the size and nature of the military force that would stay, and we were arguing about the judicial system and how many judges there would be."[1550] On the Timorese side, too, discussions about the scope and competences of the successor mission unfolded:

> Some Timorese, mid-level Timorese, were concerned that everything would collapse when the internationals left. So, there was a group of middle-class Timorese that were very, very concerned about what would happen after we left. And then there was another group of Timorese that really hated internationals, for personal reasons. and they wanted us out.[1551]

But these extreme voices did not win over: it was acknowledged that UNTAET had not been able to live up sufficiently to its mandate of capacity-building,[1552] and that without continued assistance, much of the work that *had* been done would be put at risk. "So, for UNMISET, the main mission was to build a capacity of the Timorese government"[1553] – but in a much smaller and scaled-back version of UNTAET.

The initial planning approach entailed a detailed inquiry with the line managers, i.e. the international as well as Timorese ministers of ETTA. They were asked what they thought would be essential for the stability of the future government. "And then when I arrived, we were collecting these plans, and they were totally not compatible because they did not include any parameters. So anybody wrote what they

---

1548 Ibid. "When we first mentioned the need for continued assistance to the Americans, they simply said, 'No, we're not going to involve ourselves.' And then, you know, we came across the sort of religious debate on the difference between peacekeeping and peacebuilding." Ibid.

1549 "It reflected a change in the American position in Washington away from this ideological view that you couldn't mix peacebuilding and peacekeeping to a compromise. ... Well, it wasn't even a compromise, because it was what we wanted in the end." Ibid.

1550 Ibid.

1551 Telephone interview with a program officer of the Donor Coordination Unit, UNTAET, 7 October 2006.

1552 "I think the biggest failure for UNTAET was that we did not provide enough capacity-building. And we all knew that. But again, from our part, there was so much to do that we really did not have enough resources or the time to allocate as much." Telephone interview with Julian Harston, senior UN official and Director for Post-UNTAET Planning, UNTAET, 26 October 2006.

1553 Ibid.

kind of thought. It was useless."[1554] As a reaction to that, "Julian decided to sit down with each and every line manager and go through their wish list and make it what he considered realistic."[1555] This framework was based on functional goals, not on institutional ones, "And we had the different institutions then to agree to these objectives and then to think about how they were going to implement it – something that we thought was quite cool for the UN."[1556]

However, as in other areas, Fretilin wanted a stronger voice in follow-up planning, complaining that it had been ignored. In that situation, de Mello decided to re-do the planning, and to include a so-called Integrated Mission Tasks Force (IMTF). The IMTF was an institution that came out of the Brahimi process, composed of representatives of different UN agencies and chaired by DPKO. That "was a smart move,"[1557] since it added legitimacy without adding much extra work: the local actors were explicitly consulted in the composition of the report while international agenda-setter's ideas remained, basically, unchanged. The IMTF team was integrated into the interdisciplinary working groups on-the-ground, "And they wanted to see what is happening with our plan, and then they went back to New York, and they agreed to the objectives in the plan."[1558] As a result, the DPKO/ IMTF list looked almost the same as the one the Harston team developed, "In fact, they had downloaded it from my computer. But the droplet was accepted – because they went and consulted everyone. And the Timorese wanted to feel consulted. And that's fair enough, it's their country. And then the list was finally agreed to by the Timorese."[1559]

Eventually, one hundred civilian posts were agreed upon.[1560] They related to strategic departments such as the Ministry of Finance and the National Planning Agency. A major success of the planners was the *financing* of the advisors: for the first time in UN history, a strict division between peacekeeping and peacebuilding assets was made and the advisors were paid for by assessed contributions. "It was so important first to do this on assessed contributions. Because if you rely on voluntary contributions, the donors... It doesn't happen, because the international fo-

1554 Telephone interview with a staff member of the Post-UNTAET Planning Team, UNTAET, 15 October 2006.
1555 Ibid.
1556 Ibid.
1557 Ibid.
1558 Ibid. They proceeded one major modification: the numbers of both police and especially military went up.
1559 Ibid.
1560 The first result of the planning process included about 300 civilian posts, but due to political and resource constraints, the original number was subsequently reduced to 100, "which is still a lot of people" for UN standard. Interview with Joseph Andrews, Special Adviser to the DSRSG, UNTAET, and to the Foreign Minister, ETTA, Washington, DC, 9 September 2006.

cus moves on."[1561] The crucial argument made to the Security Council was that these were crucial for the stability and security of the country.[1562]

Obstacles remained though. For instance, the job descriptions of the advisors had to be based on the UN Personal Management Report Services – "because we had to, that's the rule."[1563] But the rule did not fit the case:

> Then, you know, we wanted to say 'Portuguese language required.' But then the UN said, 'No, you can't do that, because Portuguese is not an official UN language. So, you cannot say 'required' [laughs].' But they said, 'OK, you can say *desirable*.' So, we wanted New York to somehow advertise and recruit in a targeted way so we could attract Portuguese speaker, for example. And they didn't. They did it the same old way which was putting it on the UN website. And we said, 'We are not gonna find these people with very specific skills with, you know, I told you, road work for example – these people are not gonna go on the UN website.' So, we had the same old applicants, we had no Portuguese speakers. In the end we couldn't get the right people.[1564]

In fact, a large number of positions in government and civil service remained vacant and difficult to fill: hiring and training continued to be a challenge.[1565] "How I saw it, as we got closer and closer to the hand-over, and even after the hand-over – and I was there for a couple of months after… that was everyone's frustration, like, 'How can the UN just pull out when the skills are not really there on-the-ground?'"[1566]

Eventually, on 20 May 2002, UNTAET's government authority was formally handed-over to the newly independent Republic of Timor-Leste. The Constituent Assembly was transformed into the first parliament of Timor-Leste and the Council of Ministers turned into the government of the youngest independent nation. On the same day, UNMISET was established.[1567]

1561 Telephone interview with a staff member of the Post-UNTAET Planning Team, UNTAET, 15 October 2006.
1562 "We argued that there was some core issues which they were not taken care of properly, the state itself would fail. And if the state failed that was a peace and security issue. And what's more, it meant the failure of the original mandate which the Council had found of essence for of international peace and security." Interview with a senior staff member of UNTAET, New York, 23 November 2006.
1563 Telephone interview with a staff member of the Post-UNTAET Planning Team, UNTAET, 15 October 2006.
1564 Ibid.
1565 "We would also look to universities, to people connected somehow to universities like people who were just graduating or people we knew who graduated at least the last five or ten years. Generally, we looked for people with at least some basic skills, some basic writing and communicating skills. But they were usually *very* basic; they weren't so specialized in all these different areas of government." Interview with Joseph Andrews, Special Adviser to the DSRSG, UNTAET, and to the Foreign Minister, ETTA, Washington, DC, 9 September 2006.
1566 Ibid.
1567 Howard 2008, p. 291.

3.4.4 After UNTAET

Towards the end of UNTAET's mandate, everyone was waiting for independence,[1568] but not everyone or everything was ready for it.

A range of crucial polity issues remained unresolved and presented the not-yet consolidated state with a huge burden. In its last report on UNTAET, Secretary-General Annan set it straight, "A number of issues that present challenges to the short and longer-term security of the new State have not yet and could not have been fully resolved."[1569] In the first place, these were: the integration of refugees and former pro-integrationists, the handling of serious crimes,[1570] the establishment of a Serious Crimes Unit, and the very "coming to terms with the violence of the recent past."[1571] Furthermore, the capacities for running an effective state were not sufficiently in place, and the economic situation, poverty, and unemployment – related to the unsettled issue of land rights and the poor investment in agriculture – required quick action. The East Timorese capacity situation remained precarious, too. After an initial phase of dedication, a brain drain set in. "A lot of the exiles who came back didn't like it. They came back for a year and then went back to Australia. […] So whatever the UN did in terms of training them didn't help East Timor, it helped their career in Australia."[1572]

Making matters worse, some UNTAET regulations had some unintended negative consequences. For instance the discussion of applicable law: one of the first UNTAET regulations made an ambiguous statement on the laws applicable in East Timor during the interim period;[1573] although it was obvious to everyone on-the-ground that the statement referred to Indonesian law, the ambiguous formulation made it possible for a witty lawyer to reinterpret the passage to the Portuguese law if that suited his client.[1574] For the development of the East Timorese jurisprudence, it was fatal.

On a self-critical note, a former official in charge of planning reflects,

---

1568 "Everybody was in this mood for independence. And the Independence Day celebrations became a huge part in the, you know, international community. And the whole world was watching. And there was no one who said, 'Hey, wait…' – everyone was looking forward to the party." Telephone interview with a staff member of the Post-UNTAET Planning Team, UNTAET, 15 October 2006.
1569 UN Doc. S/2002/432, para. 3.
1570 There were more than 600 cases outstanding. Cf. Garrsion 2005, p. 25.
1571 Ibid.
1572 Interview with a representative of the Timor-Leste Institute for Reconstruction Monitoring and Analysis, New York, 27 November 2006. He continues, "It's sort of a pattern that is repeated over and over again.".
1573 UNTAET Regulation on the Authority of the Transitional Administration in East Timor, UN Doc. UNTAET/REG/1999/1, Section 3, 27 November 1999.
1574 The lawsuit was a non-political, penal case. Interview with a representative of the Timor-Leste Institute for Reconstruction Monitoring and Analysis, New York, 27 November 2006.

One thing we missed in our planning was to put in positions that monitored the implementation of planning. We did manage to get a post into the future mission that would work on planning –which is already good. But we should have already, as we were reporting to the Security Council on the plans, we should have probably offered suitable mechanisms to the monitoring of the implementation of plans, you know, maybe a team of ex-people who will meet once every x months and who will report specifically on that. We didn't do that – and we should have done that.[1575]

The period was dictated by political considerations at the international level:

UNTAET was formally and legally accountable to the Security Council, which exerted indirect control over the mission via the Secretariat and DPKO. The Security Council's primary interest was to keep UNTAET's involvement 'as brief and tidy as possible' and to avoid the re-emergence of hostilities (note 266). The emphasis, as with prior peace operations, was to resolve major security issues and move toward 'free and fair' elections as an exit strategy within a defined time period. The concerns of donor countries, particularly Portugal and Australia, were somewhat more complex, but focused primarily on the achievement of visible reconstruction results within a relatively short timeframe (note 167). Each of these constituencies provided incentives for UNTAET to minimize the short-term risks of failure (in the form of overt conflict or crisis) and maximize visible returns on donor investments. These interests militated strongly in favor of central control and allocation of resources to direct service provision.[1576]

This, however, also had implications on the evaluation of the UNTAET mission, because "[e]xactly what success entailed was unclear, except that it placed a premium on speed and concrete results."[1577]

The question of to what extent Timor-Leste was to be called a democratic state is still an open one. With Fretilin having established something close to a one-party state, and with many villages remote from the political processes, some basic principles were not met. As an expert on East Timorese society observes, the spirit of national community that prevailed around independence began to dispel. The East Timorese government committed a range of failures, concerning in particular its multiple shortcomings at providing services, its management of the growing urbanization, and the related increase in unemployment.[1578] Tensions were exacerbated in last three years, when the divisions of the military and the police forces and between inhabitants of the East and West of East Timor became virulent, the increasing urbanization dynamics fuelling the unrest. The actions of rebel soldiers cumulated in the assault on East Timor's new president José Ramos-Horta in February 2008. "Many are wondering what's next for the tiny impoverished coun-

1575   Telephone interview with a staff member of the Post-UNTAET Planning Team, UNTAET, 15 October 2006.
1576   Beauvais 2001, p. 1166.
1577   Suhrke 2001, p. 14.
1578   Interview with Professor Shepard L. Forman, Director of the Center on International Cooperation, New York University, New York, 20 September 2006.

try, which has been dogged by political instability – and violence – since it became independent in 2002 [...]."[1579]

UNMISET was designed to mitigate the birth pain of the new state: its mandate required the mission "to provide assistance to core administrative structures critical to the viability and political stability of East Timor; to provide interim law enforcement and public security and to assist in the development of a new law enforcement agency in East Timor, the East Timor Police Service; and to contribute to the maintenance of the external and internal security of East Timor."[1580] However, UNMISET did not perform ideally. "It took UNMISET almost a year to get up to its staff numbers and they hired people of debatable competence in some cases."[1581] After UNMISET, three other missions followed: In May 2005, the remaining blue helmets left and the former UNMISET structures were remodelled in the small political mission that succeeded UNTAET, the UN Office in Timor-Leste (UNOTIL). The mandate was originally to end in May 2006, but after violence broke out again, UNOTIL morphed into the more comprehensive UN Integrated Mission in Timor-Leste (UNMIT) in September 2006.[1582] The mission is ongoing, as are local tensions.

From a scientific point of view, establishing a straightforward causal connection between UNTAET's management of the hand-over and the current situation would not have methodological validity. Its further discussion is outside the analytical focus of this paper.

1579 National Public Radio, February 21, 2008, "In East Timor, Tension over Violence Continues." Available online at www.npr.org/templates/story/story.php?storyId=19242931, last access on 15 March 2009.
1580 UN Security Council, "Security Council Resolution on the Situation in East Timor," UN Doc. S/RES/1410 (2002), 17 May 2002.
1581 Interview with a representative of the Timor-Leste Institute for Reconstruction Monitoring and Analysis, New York, 27 November 2006. It was known several months ahead of the termination date that the contracts of international UNTAET staff ended on May 20th, and so the most capable ones made timely efforts to get good jobs in other places. Thus, UNMISET could not simply take over UNTAET personnel. "In some cases there were people re-hired, that had worked in UNTAET but there were a lot of new people." Ibid.
1582 Interestingly enough, after the 2006 deteriorations, many of the same government officials who spearheads in the calls for the UN to leave, now wanted them desperately back. "That's crazy – these are the same people who wanted us out." Telephone interview with a staff member of the Post-UNTAET Planning Team, UNTAET, 15 October 2006.

Box 11: Situation in East Timor after the Exit of UNTAET

"East Timor gained its independence on 20 May 2002 and became the 191st member of the United Nations on 27 September of the same year. [...] As the newest nation of the new millennium, East Timor is also one of the poorest in the world, with three of every five Timorese earning below \$2 per day. [...] Unemployment is rife, particularly amongst the young, and there is a significant urban drift by young people in search of work, partly caused by the systematic destruction of agricultural infrastructure by the militias following the ballot in 1999. Life expectancy is 50-58 years with high infant mortality. The major prevalent health problems are malaria, dengue, and TB and the system of health care is rudimentary. The Indonesians significantly improved education and health services from the former Portuguese rulers, but East Timor remained their poorest province.

Significant revenue from oil and gas in the Timor Sea will not commence for a few years, until which time the Government's budget deficit will continue to be bridged by donor grants. A decision on entitlements in relation to the Timor Sea is being hotly contested by Australia and East Timor as a matter of international law, representing a significant hurdle in an otherwise close relationship between the two countries. The outcome will have significant financial implications for the economy of East Timor.

East Timor has no manufacturing industries and its infrastructure is underdeveloped and tenuous. The power supply, systematically destroyed in the post-ballot violence, is unreliable in the towns and non-existent in much of the countryside. The road network is fragile. Outside Dili, telecommunications coverage is poor in urban areas and nonexistent for most of the rural population. There are no rail services, government-owned public transportation, or internal air services (other than restricted flights provided by the United Nations). International air services are normally restricted to Dili, which also provides the main port facility. There are a number of rudimentary ports along the north coast, including in the Oecusse enclave, but there are none on the south coast. The projected rate of development indicates that East Timor's infrastructure is likely to remain in a rudimentary state for many years.

Since the post-ballot violence of 1999 – and in all measures – East Timor has been a relatively safe place to live. Unlike many other post-conflict environments, the level of security in East Timor has improved [...]. Despite this rosy assessment, security concerns exist along the border with Indonesia, where about 25,000 refugees remain encamped in West Timor, including some hard core militia leaders who continue to be tolerated by the Indonesian Government. The fledgling East Timorese border police and defense force would be unable to counter a resurgence in militia activity – their combined capabilities being significantly less than the Peacekeeping Force. [...] Another major concern with external security is the inability of East Timor to effectively patrol and police its coastal waters, thereby increasing the threats of the spread of communicable diseases as well as criminal activity – the latter including people trafficking, smuggling, drug and gun running, money laundering, and piracy. [...] Of more immediate concern, however, is the potential for internal unrest, partly fuelled by historic political differences and partly by high levels of youth unemployment and unfulfilled expectations in the aftermath of independence. We know that the 1975 invasion by Indonesia was preceded by acts of politically motivated violence. I am not suggesting that these events would necessarily be repeated, but equally it would be foolish to ignore that a core of disaffected and influential militia remain in West Timor, and that they have connections with individuals and political groups in East Timor.

Thinking more domestically, and as demonstrated during the internal unrest of December 2002, the community can quickly be incited to riot. The "rule of law" is not yet firmly established: the local police force remains underdeveloped, and the judicial system and correctional service still has a long way to go. These were weak and largely unsuccessful components during the transitional administration and will take many years to mature, requiring assistance from the international community.

Another issue of security concern is the distrust between the newly created defence force (comprised mainly of former Falintil resistance fighters who remain loyal to their former leader and now President, Xanana Gusmão), and the nascent police force (the leaders of which tend to be more supportive of the Prime Minister, Mari Alkatiri). The defense force has significant respect within the community, but the mechanisms to ensure civilian control remain ambiguous and underdeveloped. The defense force has little faith in the police force and (despite the President's recent warnings against such action) could be persuaded to take a leading role in any internal security disturbances, rather than assisting the police force in situations of last resort."[1583]

1583   Smith, Michael G. 2004. *East Timor: Some Peacebuilding Lessons.* Paper presented at the JIIA-UNU Symposium, 24-25 February 2004, UN University Center, Tokyo, pp. 2-3.

3.4.5 Summary and Assessment

The Constituent Assembly and presidential elections were considered major benchmarks of UNTAET's exit strategy: they legitimized the Timorese in charge via democratic elections, and new political leaders were to take over the newly created institutions. With a high turnout, a calm election day, and the process having been deemed "free and fair,"[1584] the Constituent Assembly elections have been called a success. However, the sluggish dealings with technical difficulties and the insufficient delivery of information to the population were some major flaws of the processes of voter registration as well as civic education. People voted according to traditional ideas and values that they thought specific parties would represent.

> Although the elections were declared to be 'free and fair' and the democratic drama played out, the exercise was rather a 'totem poll, in which voters expressed their honour and respect towards their history and cultural values. The Constituent Assembly hence reflected the will of small elite, the diaspora, and overseas-educated individuals who knew how to exploit local beliefs. Fretilin as the main party employed traditional ideas and relied on earlier 'resistance-socialization' of the population rather than developing a democratic understanding (note 52: They had 'socialized' the village populations for the resistance fight during the last decades to win their support. The Fretilin election outcome confirms that its socialization had a great impact. A campaign that was more based on party programmes and the future could contribute to civic education, but this did not seem to be one of Fretilin's main concerns). Other politicians still adhered to the local paradigm themselves and had their own 'traditional' political agenda instead of party programmes that aimed to build a democratic state. [...] This should question electoral assistance as the ultimate way of creating popular participation and democratization. The focus of the international community has to shift from the electoral event to long-term assistance in nation building with full attention to paradigmatic differences between liberal-style democracy and local concepts.[1585]

The constitution-building process was dominated by Fretilin, which knew how to use the political leeway that had been provided by UNTAET. At the same time, their preferences of centralization and a tight time schedule met that of the head of UNTAET as well as those of UN headquarters and donors. The constitution itself would score high on "good governance" criteria, but low on the "fit" with Timorese social and cultural principles.

1584 "[...] the Independent Electoral Commission had announced the final certified results and declared that the criteria for a free and fair election had been met." UN Security Council, "Security Council Hears Details of Free and Fair Elections in East Timor." UN Security Council Press Release, UN Doc. SC/7139. Available online at http://www.un.org/News/Press/docs/2001/SC7139.doc.htm, last access on 6 March 2009.

1585 Hohe 2002a, pp. 83, 69. See also Chesterman 2001, p. 4 and The Carter Center 2001. "[I]ts approach to the Civic Education Project gave evidence that the need for local participation still had not yet penetrated UNTAET's approach. In any event, the administration remained deep in the political thicket until the very end." Beauvais 2001, p. 1133.

With the Timorese successors in place, UNTAET engaged in downsizing. The timeframe that had been set for UNTAET's ultimate withdrawal was extended twice, but it might have been valuable for sustainable institution and particularly capacity-building indeed if the mission would have stayed longer. However, there was threefold pressure to withdraw: the Security Council's attention started to fade,[1586] donors' clocks were ticking faster, and the Timorese, particularly Fretilin, were impatiently waiting for independence to be declared.[1587]

> When the relations between the Timorese and the internationals became increasingly estranged, the honeymoon was over. I mean, this happens in every mission, so this is not unusual. But the Timorese at that time were very keen to get the UN out, as quickly as possible. And there was a lot of bad faith between the UN, the internationals, and the Timorese.[1588]

One great advantage the UN enjoyed in meeting its pre-set deadline was its unambiguous end state, celebrated wholeheartedly by the nationals.[1589]

The "technique" of outsourcing the management of mission withdrawal proved to be a valuable tool, particularly for the cutbacks of *UN personnel*. The team had considerable latitude to make: there was no overall strategy particularly for post-mission planning. While it was an advantage that the cutbacks were conducted by people from the outside – they did not know the other staff very well and the process was less influenced by emotions – the downside of it was that Harston's team was not familiar with local and intra-mission dynamics.[1590] The successor arrangement in the form of UNMISET had a hard time getting international and local support, but eventually, it even represented a seminal innovation in UN post-conflict peace-building missions: for the first time in UN history, it could use *assessed* contributions to finance *civilian* consultants.

1586 The UN were determined to finalize its interim administration mission in the first half of 2002.
1587 "One consequence of the dynamics of the relationship between UNTAET and its East Timorese counterparts was a broadening consensus among the East Timorese in favor of a quick transition. By April 2000, six months into the mission, voices in the East Timorese leadership were calling for the UN's prompt withdrawal, and by early 2001 a consensus seemed to be forming that the relationship was not a healthy one and should be terminated as soon as possible (fn. 12: The strongest statement of this position was Gusmão's New Year's speech of January 2001, available online at http:/www.tip.net.au/~wildwood/ JanYear.htm)." Goldstone 2004, p. 87-88. "The forming of the East Timorese preference to have UNTAET leave soon happened later as frustrations grew with the presence, as Timorese felt isolated by the mission. But the initial premise was they needed more time – not less." Interview with Professor Shepard L. Forman, Director of the Center on International Cooperation, New York University, New York, 20 September 2006.
1588 Interview with a senior staff member of UNTAET, New York, 23 November 2006. See also King 2003, p. 756.
1589 See, e.g., Goldstone 2004, p. 87.
1590 Telephone interview with a staff member of the Post-UNTAET Planning Team, UNTAET, 15 October 2006.

4. *Analysis: The Transitional Management Process*

Resembling the procedure in the first case study, this chapter analyzes the descriptive material about the transition process in East Timor and assorts ill-structured conditions, pathologies, and – where observable – successful coping strategies. I will be able to show that particularly cognitive biases and pathological phenomena of tight coupling became virulent. Furthermore, an obstructive path dependent trajectory almost got the mission on its brink. Benefiting from the advantage of a vigilant and powerful SRSG as well as from abundant resources, UNTAET was able to contain and attenuate many pathologies to a reasonable degree. A radical redesign of the transition approach turned out to have been crucial.

4.1 Ill-Structured Conditions: Challenges, Constraints, Dilemmas

In comparison to the Balkan mission, UNTAET met sort of opposite conditions on the ground: hostility levels were rather low while the local capacity situation was disastrous. But just like UNTAES, the transitional administration in East Timor met consummate support by the international community who, again, were in need of a success and wanted to create a demonstration object. At the same time, support remained inherently ambiguous as reflected in the tight schedule; structures of financing and recruiting had not changed either. The mandate was highly comprehensive and complex: it called for the building of a new state.

Local Hostility

As done in the case of UNTAES, I make a distinction between those aspects that relate to the "hostility among parties" and those which relate to "hostility towards the mission."

The security situation in East Timor was changing rapidly during 1999. Before the ballot, there were two major factions, both highly coherent, and with a long history of hostility: the colonial occupier Indonesia on the one side and the suppressed East Timorese and their Falintil independence fighters on the other. With the 5 May Peace Agreement, Indonesia consented to the possibility of independence but immediately after the ballot, the situation deteriorated, and the level of hostility reached a new high. The quick interference by INTERFET restored security and forced the Indonesian troops and militia out of the country. At the time UNTAET deployed, the situation had recovered tremendously.

There was *one* political faction with comprehensive legitimacy and reach-out throughout the population, namely the umbrella organization of the resistance, the CNRT. When elections approached, no extremist parties appeared on the scene: the formerly pro-Indonesian parties had either dissolved or transformed their agendas. Yet, the traditional rivalry between Fretilin and more conservative forces emerged again, with Fretilin perceiving itself as the sole legitimate party of East Timor. Fretilin displayed the same attitude vis-à-vis UNTAET. Associated with the CNRT, there were strong and integrative leading figures, such as ex-Falintil leader and resistance icon Gusmão, and the Nobel Prize laureates Bishop Belo and Ramos-Horta. They were politically moderate and supportive of the UN.

There was, at least at the outset, comparatively high input-legitimacy for the international administration, homogenously spread throughout the general population and the local elite. UNTAET symbolized the transition to longed-for independence and hence enjoyed a high degree of *ex ante* endorsement.

Local Capacity

In 1999, East Timor was a poor region, and it still is today. It has had one of the lowest GDPs in the world, difficult climatic conditions, and low living standards and life expectancies. The East Timorese were a colonized society – with all the implied traumas: years of oppression and incapacitation, loss of family members, rape, and exploitation. The traces of recurrent atrocities were deep-seated features of the identity of the collective and of the psychology of the individual. The refugee and IDP situation was devastating: about three quarters of the population were displaced, which compounded the human capacity situation.

The formal education and working capacity of the East Timorese were low, as the Indonesians had systematically prohibited them from blue- and white-collar positions and invested almost nothing into the education system. There was a lack of skilled, trained people in Timor. "This country did not have very many people available who were competent. Nothing you can do about that. It was not, in government terms, a viable territory at that time."[1591] Timorese, 80 percent of whom were living the traditional life in the rural areas of the island, did not dispose over the required capacities to build and run a new state.[1592] This being said, the evaluation is relative to the standards applied: the international community strived to impose role-model Western institutions in East Timor.

1591 Interview with a senior staff member of Civil Affairs, UNTAET, New York, 18 September 2006.
1592 Written interview with Dr. Tanja Hohe, former team member of UN Volunteers in East Timor, 30 September 2006.

Compounding the situation, institutional and corporate memory had been lost:

> 95 percent of the previous administrative structure had been wiped out. Not just the buildings which you didn't have, you didn't have any manual at all. The only manual people had, was the memory of the Indonesian structures. Memory! You didn't even have papers! You didn't even have an organigram, an organizational chart of how the Indonesians used to do it. They didn't leave it and they didn't hand us over anything. They destroyed all the documents. All of the basic administrative papers were burnt.[1593]

Overall, the local capacity situation was rather unfavorable. The vast majority of people were at a low education level, there was a high uncertainty on the possibilities for development, and high time pressure to put the needed capacities in place. At the same time, there were the educated diaspora elite, most of them Fretilin-associated, which came back into the country, ready to take over high-level posts.

Concerning infrastructure, it is important to know that East Timor is an extremely mountainous island. Combined with the poor transportation infrastructure, this feature makes for a highly segregated topography: most rural places are extremely hard to reach. As a consequence, the small territorial size of East Timor is an illusion: anyone who does not have access to helicopters or private jets may need several days to get from one side of the island to the other. The deficient infrastructure – transportation, buildings, communication, and public services – even deteriorated after "Operation Global Clean Sweep." These deficiencies resulted in grave constraints for the organizational set-up of the UN mission.

Although I dealt with the topic only superficially, the Timorese socio-cultural paradigm is an essential aspect when it comes to understanding the inadequacy of UNTAET's initial approach. Due to the segregated topography, a vast range of different ethnic, cultural, and lingual diversity were able to develop. Still, there was a unifying socio-cultural paradigm common to all Timorese tribes. Moreover, the Timorese were united in their fight against the Indonesian occupiers. Accordingly, the political agenda of the Timorese used to be a single-issue agenda: the fight for independence. But politics is not at the core of Timorese society anyway: the "inside of society" is made up of rituals, not politics.

Likewise, after more than 400 years of foreign occupation, there was hardly any experience with being a state, least of all with being a democratic one. This non-experience of statehood notwithstanding, a well-established socio-political structure did exist. It certainly followed a different paradigm than that of a Western style liberal-democracy, but it was a valuable – if not indispensable – starting point for state-building.

1593 Interview with a senior staff member of Civil Affairs, UNTAET, New York, 18 September 2006.

International Support

UNTAET enjoyed generally high political support, indicated by its unprecedented state-building mandate with supervisory authority,[1594] as well as by the robustness granted to the mission. Likewise, the financial support for UNTAET was high. The international community wanted to have a success. In the words of an UNTAET official, "We were given Mission Possible."[1595]

That being said, the support of the member states was ambiguous. This was already obvious in the reluctant dealings with Indonesia. By keeping the Timorese out and refusing to tolerate "premature" planning, the regional hegemon could obstruct the planning process and the generation of other planning alternatives, such as the transition schedule presented by Gusmão. Indonesia's obstructionist role was even exacerbated with the September blast. Furthermore, Indonesia's preferences had a multiplying effect: other member states and eventually the Security Council decided on a non-compensatory political rationale against the formal involvement of the Timorese, since any other move would have offended Indonesia, "a very influential member state."[1596] Against the backdrop of these events, one has to keep in mind that the UN is a political, intergovernmental organization and its activities are conditioned by the interests of its member states. At the end of the day, the consequence was that options for more comprehensive preventive planning were ruled out, and worst-case scenario planning was not included in the UN Secretariat's planning mechanism. Time was wasted.

United Nations Capacities

UNTAET's goal was to build a state from scratch. Although the UN "had some experience in transitional administration, [...] it had no experience on the scale of what was required of it in [...] Timor Leste."[1597] After the staggering rise of complex peacekeeping in the 1990s, capabilities and resources did not catch up quickly enough to the new tasks. At the Secretariat and DPKO, there was only a marginal ability to deal with operational demands and to engage in policy reflection.

1594 "Sovereignty was being transferred completely to the international community." Interview with Professor Michael W. Doyle, former UN Assistant Secretary-General, New Haven, 11 September 2006.
1595 "'We were given Mission Possible,' says Galbraith, [...]. 'The mission was completely congruent with people's wishes. We had adequate security resources. No countries opposed Timorese independence, including Indonesia [...].'" Steele 2002, p. 79. Also, East Timor had the "inestimable benefit, unique to countries scourged by modern war, [namely that; ES] [l]and mines were never used." Ibid.
1596 Interview with a senior staff member of UNTAET, New York, 23 November 2006.
1597 Harland 2005, p. 2. Cf. Kelly and McCormack undated, p. 12.

The effort to take a step and say, 'Let's develop guidance for all of this,' requires both consensus that this is a business you're in and support to professionalize it, distance to learn the lessons, and enough personnel so you just stop running around like chickens without their heads and say, 'OK, how do we conceptualize what we've learned and turn it into guidance?' That's something that's happening now – when I was doing it, it certainly was not the case.[1598]

"Doing" transitional administration was an exception to the rule of peace operations and it was not – and probably is not – expected that this is an operational mode to institutionalize.[1599] Accordingly, institutionalized knowledge and expertise were low.

Furthermore, an overstrained and under-resourced DPKO dealt with the demanding recruitment process under high time pressure. Junior staff members were charged with staff recruitment, whereby committing mistakes, such as mismatching language abilities and country assignments. The DPKO's involvement in other parts of the world, combined with the UN's institutional inertia that had failed to re-structure DPKO came to affect the agency's planning ability.

United Nations Rules and Funding

The politically conditioned and organizationally cemented separation between assessed and voluntary contributions divided peacekeeping, mission set-up, and maintenance from administration, peacebuilding, and reconstruction tasks. Although institution-building and capacity-building figured prominently in the mandate, their financing was precarious and their approach to this part of the mandate was likewise pending.

The rules and principles by which UNTAET was designed were rigid, and East Timor experts had already expected problems with mandate implementation and the legitimacy of the mission. Indeed, major problems emerged.

1598 Interview with a senior staff member of UNTAET, New York, 23 November 2006. "So, sadly that was an ad hoc-period. So, the chance to take a look and think about what guidance was needed and what peacekeeping was about was really happening around that time with the Brahimi report; that was almost at the same time as we were doing all of this stuff, you know. So, we really hadn't yet reached the point where, I think, we have both the agreement of the international community that UN peacekeeping was here to stay, and the space taken to have a look at what that meant and what the requirements were." Ibid.
1599 Interview with a senior staff member of UNTAET, New York, 23 November 2006.

Time Pressure and Mandate Complexity

Per definitionem, a transitional administration faces an enormous challenge and the colossal mandate of UNTAET was just overambitious.[1600] "You don't establish a new state over night. And nobody would deny that is completely unrealistic. Other state formations in other places in the world took place over centuries. There is no way the UN could have done that."[1601] The inherent tension of UNTAET's dual mandate was exacerbated by the fact that the mission had to build a new local government from scratch. As of day one, a huge political and financial pressure was exerted by the Security Council and the donor community, while local expectations were piling up as well. As the facilitator of the transition to independence, UNTAET enjoyed consummate acceptance, but the high input legitimacy could be expected to decrease the longer the mission stayed.

4.2 Pathologies and Coping

At times, UNTAET must have seemed to Timorese like the blind cyclops of Greek mythology: very powerful and mighty but blind to what was going on around him at the same time. Occasionally, UNTAET caused harm rather than relief. The "blindness" and other cognitive biases resulted from a mix of trying hard to live up to a very complex yet ambiguous mandate, of inadequate routines, views and blueprints, low and inadequate UN capacities, and of the sheer time pressure on a venture that would have required five to ten years but was squeezed into 32 months. The ill-structuredness also caused dilemmatic principal-agent interactions – between the member states as principals and their agent, the UN; UN headquarters and the mission on-the-ground; the mission's leadership and field staff; and between the mission and the local Timorese. Even more virulent were pathologies of tight coupling of complex interactions – induced by the tightly knit knot of ambiguous member state support, rigid financing provisions, inadequate and slow recruitment, and conflicts between goals within the complex mandate – and a path-dependent trajectory that was about to put the success of the mission at risk.

In the following chapters, I present the observed trajectories of pathologies, accidents, and, where observable, coping strategies.

1600   Cf. Maull 2001, p. 6. "[T]he mandate is too big because it involves nation-building, economic reconstruction, and promote peace and stability." Saldanha 2003, p. 161.

1601   Telephone interview with a staff member of the Post-UNTAET Planning Team, UNTAET, 15 October 2006. "[I]t is impossible to establish a new administration, democratic institutions, restore public services and revive an economy in just over two years' (fn. 8: As quoted from UNTAET and the World Bank Press Release, East Timor Moves from Emergency Reconstruction to Development Mode, 15 June 2001)." Subianto 2002, p. 4.

4.2.1 Cognitive Biases

Instances of cognitive biased decisions occurred frequently. They were particularly virulent during the first half of the transition. Behavior of un-conflicted avoidance, decision-making using analogies, and focussing on known and controllable factors and procedures occurred frequently.

4.2.1.1 Deployment

During deployment, three different patterns of cognitive biases persisted: a mix of standard operating procedures and reversions to predetermined alternatives, exacerbated by the scant overlap between planners and implementers; ignorance, manifesting itself in the scarcity of pathological information; and a reliance on known alternatives, generating few and insufficient alternatives, materializing as inappropriate peer recruitment. In this early phase, UNTAET was not able to cope well.

Gap between Planners and Implementers

When the mission started to become operational, it suffered from the effects of poor overlap between planners and implementers. In line with common DPKO practice and compounded by the high time pressure, the staff who were supposed to implement the mandate on the ground had hardly been involved in the planning process. The time pressure even increased after the September blast. As a consequence, the structural set-up and procedures missed the pragmatic view of mission personnel. Besides, the implementers needed time to become familiar with the complex construction. They even felt that the structure was "imposed"[1602] on them.

Incrementally coming to terms with their situation, the field staff "learnt as we went along."[1603]

Pathological Information Deficits

Not only was information about the mission processed inadequately, but so was the territory of East Timor. For instance, in 1999, no seeds were ordered for the upcoming season and thus the first agricultural cycle was lost. If the information

1602 Interview with a senior staff member of Civil Affairs, UNTAET, New York, 18 September 2006.
1603 Ibid.

had been available, it was either ignored or omitted amidst the multitude of challenges during the early, confusing stages of the mission. The distressing consequence was that people were starving and some died from the lack of food in rural districts.

Inappropriate Peer Recruitment

Like UNTAES, the transitional administration in East Timor struggled with staff shortages. They were particularly severe when it came to expertise in civil administration and institution-building. The reaction to these well-perceived constraints, however, made the situation worse: DPKO started to recruit civilian personnel that had formerly served on UNMIK. While this might appear to be a straightforward procedure intended to ensure expertise, the personnel transplanted strategies and lessons learned in Kosovo that did not fit the situation in East Timor. Garrison describes this as "assembling the wrong skill sets and operating from the wrong mindset."[1604] Compounding the situation, no former UNAMET staff were brought over to the UNTAET mission due to "rigid territorialism within the UN bureaucracy"[1605] at the Secretariat. In sum, the cognitive bias of relying on known alternatives and generating insufficient alternatives was aggravated by internal obstructionist dynamics, with DPKO using its *de facto* veto power.

4.2.1.2 Mandate Implementation and Mission Management

UNTAET suffered pathologically from cognitive biases that resulted from the complex and the new mandate, and from deficient information gathering and processing much more than did UNTAES. The latter was partly self-inflicted. During the main implementation period, over twenty pathological episodes were observable.

1604 Garrison 2005, p. 8.
1605 Smith 2001, p. 44.

Table 5: Ill-Structuredness, Cognitive Biases, Accidents, and Coping Strategies

	Ill-Structuredness	Pathology	Accident	Coping
Deployment	UN Routines, UN Capacities, Time Pressure	Gap between Planners and Implementers	(Implementers not "Owning" Mission)	Incremental Learning by Individuals
	UN Rules and Routines, Time Pressure	Pathological Information Deficits	Humanitarian Catastrophe	-
	UN Capacities, Time Pressure	Inappropriate Peer Recruitment	Wrong Skill Set for Mandate Implementation	-
Implementation	Mandate Complexity, Local Capacities and Demands	"Everything a Priority"	Overload	Decision Staggering
	UN Capacities, Time Pressure	Pull towards Centralization	Marginalization of Rural Residents	-
	UN Capacities, Time Pressure, Poor Local Infrastructure	Deficient Public Communication	Loss of Legitimacy	-
	Time Pressure, UN Capacities	Misperception of Local Challenges	Marginalization of Rural Residents	Incremental Learning by Individuals
	Time Pressure, UN Capacities, UN Routines	Blueprint	No Hand-over and Training Provisions, Precariousness of Mandate Achievement	-
	UN Rules, Time Pressure	Simplifying Terra Nullis Assumption	Precariousness of Mandate Achievement	-
	UN Rules, Time Pressure	Endorsement Confusion	Pending Local Ownership	Informal Relationships at Senior Level
	Time Pressure, Local Capacity, UN Expertise	Harum-Scarum Capacity-building	Unsuitable People in Government Positions	Setting Incentives for Diaspora to Return
	Local Capacity, Time Pressure	UN-inflicted Rivalry between Diaspora and Residents	Curbing Division in Timorese Society	-
	UN Rules, Time Pressure	Neglect of Local Dynamics	Allowing for New Division in Timorese Society	-
	UN Rules, Time Pressure	"Too Hot a Potato"	Pending Economic Development, Allowing for Opportunistic Occupation of Zones of Uncertainty	-
	Mandate Complexity, Time Pressure, Local Capacity	Individual Procrastinations	Loss of Legitimacy, Insufficient Capacity-building	-

	UN Rules and Routines	Construction of Parallel Structure	Risk of Creating Unsustainable Institutions	-
	Local Capacity, Time Pressure	Inappropriate Staff Selection and Allocation Rationales	Risk of Creating Unsustainable Institutions	-
Termination	UN Capacity, Time Pressure, UN Rules	"Square Peg in Round Hole:" Election	Waste of Time, Political Biases	Creating Time Slack
	Time Pressure, Mandate Complexity, UN Capacity	Deficient Consultation Planning	Omission of Civil Society Perspective	-
	UN Capacities, Time Pressure, Loss of Local Acceptance	Pull towards Centralization in Post-UNTAET Planning	Marginalization of Rural Residents	Mission Deadline Extension by Appealing to Security Concerns of UNSC
	Time Pressure, Mandate Complexity and "Newness"	Waste of Time in Planning for Successor Mission	(Delay)	-

"Everything a Priority"

Even after the immediate deployment stage, the mission's leadership kept on struggling with the multitude of challenges and had a hard time tackling the high expectations on-the-ground. "Everything was a priority."[1606] The immediate reaction to the overload of demands was a defensive adherence to more manageable humanitarian tasks. They were more manageable because expertise was readily available. In this situation, UNTAET's reputation faced early blowback and the mission came under increasing time pressure. Trying to cope with its disastrous public image, de Mello prioritized the justice sector and staggered decisions. Generally, the SRSG was the linchpin of the mission, a strong role model and integrative figure who not only disposed over diplomatic and negotiation skills and knew how to act one-on-one with Timorese leaders. Besides, he also knew how to play the UN's political games.

Pull towards Centralization

When UNTAET started to set up its structures, it did so in strongly contracting moves. The mandate's instructions to decentralize were ignored and the focus was more on the "controllable" central level. This development was compounded by the poor guidance of district field officers. As a result, the people living in the rural

---

1606 Vieira de Mello, quoted in Foreign Correspondent 2000.

districts of the island were marginalized. This consequence was particularly severe since the appropriate procedure for East Timor would have been bottom-up institution-building so that people could become familiar with the new practices, and then get ready for the next level.[1607]

Deficient Public Communication

As Timorese discontent increased, the policy of the so-called Status of Mission Agreement, which had put the international staff beyond the law, added to their mistrust of UNTAET. While this policy is common practice in all UN missions, it was very badly communicated to the locals in this case. In fact, UNTAET tried to defensively avoid the topic and keep it secret – which evoked even more suspicion. UNTAET's initial acceptance was tarnished once again. Besides hardly getting its own messages across, UNTAET continued to suffer from deficient information gathering. Aggravated by the deliberate exclusion of the DPA perspective, it seems that further important pieces of information about necessities on-the-ground were either not collected or they were wrong. As a consequence, there was a huge element of waste in East Timor, a waste of (inadequate) resources as well as of equipment.

Misperception of Local Challenges

UNTAET misperceived the situation and had a narrow focus of seeing East Timor as a "small" island, yet the relatively few square kilometres belied the bad infrastructure and the circumlocutory terrain. Matter of fact, East Timor can be a very large country. The effect of this mispercetion was defunct outreach, thus neglecting people in the districts as well as the expansion of the rural roads network.

Blueprint

Concerning the basic mission structure, processes, and even personnel, UNTAET resembled the transitional administration in Kosovo. Given the high time pressure, the capacity overload, and the non-existence of a mechanism for how to apply lessons learned, planners at DPKO fell back on the analogy of the Kosovo mission,

---

1607 For this argument on bottom-up and top-down approaches in institution building, see Chopra, Jarat and Hohe, Tanja. 2004. "Participatory Intervention." *Global Governance* 10:3, pp. 289-305.

which had started just a few months earlier, as well as on other "bits and pieces" of the system.

> One of the things which happened and which was a mistake in hindsight, is that for the East Timor mission we naturally drew quite a lot from the Kosovo model. That was the very latest. So of course we said, 'What do we have in terms of guidance?' And people said, 'Well, what we have is the experience we got in Kosovo.' So, we had a few people, quite a few core people who came with Kosovo experience to the mission, and a few who came for planning to New York. And so we sort of used that template – which was itself not yet tested by the Kosovo experience, itself not yet evolved by the Kosovo experience. But it was the guidance we had. There are bits of pieces of guidance, of course, that we used to set up a political section or a human rights section. They came from other parts of the system. But overall, I would say, the guidance was quite sketchy.[1608]

While the procedure might appear warrantable,[1609] the isomorphistic dynamic[1610] of adopting the UNMIK model analogy sent UNTAET on the wrong track. It did not fit the local Timorese conditions. Time, trust, and resources were wasted. In addition, the UNMIK lense made planners omit certain elements of their mandate, such as the customs unit, and neither was the mission designed as to pursue hand-over and training issues, nor was the government's pillar design suited to be inherited by local Timorese. Compounding the matter, there was no early adjustment.

1608 Interview with a senior staff member of UNTAET, New York, 23 November 2006. See also Pippard undated, p. 6, "[There was an; ES] absence of any planning guidance or established model for transitional administration from which UNTAET could draw lessons. As a result, the mission drew heavily on the institutional and personal knowledge of UNMIK, with planning staff effectively told to take the Kosovo plan and reconfigure it to fit East Timor. While Kosovo provided the most recent and relevant experience of a governance mission undertaken by the UN, its use as a model meant UNTAET proved slow to adapt to the specific conditions on-the-ground." In this context of lack of experience by UN DPKO, another option was briefly considered. "Since the UN essentially assumed a trusteeship role in East Timor as part of decolonization, it would seem logical to legally anchor the mission in the UN Charter's provisions for trusteeship (fn. 11: The UN Charter specifies that 'one or more states or the Organization itself' may administer a territory placed under the trusteeship system (Art. 81, italics added). East Timor might fit under Art. 77 (c): territories that are voluntarily placed under the system by states responsible for their administration.). Politically, this might be a liability in that the trusteeship model was associated with colonialism [...]. On the other hand, basing the mission on a specific Charter provision for direct UN rule might pre-empt critics who questioned the legitimacy of the UN's unprecedented authority in East Timor (fn. 12: See Chopra 2000, pp. 27-39. Whichever the case, the trusteeship model was briefly considered and quickly discarded." Suhrke 2001, pp. 7-8.
1609 "The criticism is unfair because when the UN entered East Timor it was reasonable to assume that it was entering an area of potential conflict. Kosovo represented the most relevant experience in pacifying territory that had come under UN control [...]." Chesterman 2004, p. 64.
1610 For the concept of institutional isomorphism in organizational theory, see DiMaggio, Paul J. and Powell, Walter W. 1983. "The Iron Cage Revisited: Institutional Isomorphism and Collective Rationality in Organizational Fields," *American Sociological Review* 48, pp. 147-160.

It was not until mid-2001 that the pressure apparently reached a threshold value that encouraged UNTAET to begin to restructure its transition approach.[1611]

Simplifying Terra Nullis Assumption

The Indonesian pressure to put planning on hold, the exclusion of DPA expertise, DPKO principles and routines, and the UNMIK blueprint produced a transitional administration that operated under a simplifying *terra nullis* assumption. This assumption implied that the international mission would operate the transition on its own, and that there would be nothing to build upon. This narrow focus had a bearing on the entire transition period and culminated in a virulent path dependent trajectory.[1612]

Confusion about Local Endorsement

When the inadequacy of the *terra nullis* assumption became more and more obvious, UNTAET's civil affairs unit in particular solicited local endorsements. However, the question was: endorsements *from whom*? Due to the previous policy of ignorance, it was unclear where to turn to. In reaction, they turned to de Mello's confidant Gusmão and his immediate circle. This decision implied a biased cooperation though: other pertinent groups, such as the *chefe de sucos* and *de aldeias*, remained neglected.

Harum-Scarum Capacity-building

Time pressure of "Timorization"[1613] led to an acceleration of actions. People were pushed into government positions "who really were completely unsuitable."[1614] They were unsuitable either in terms of education, social acceptance – the educated students were too young and were not accepted by traditional society – or they were politically unsuitable, as many professionally experienced Timorese had previously been associated with the Indonesian occupiers.

1611 This restructuring will be elaborated in Chapter V.4.2.4.
1612 See Chapter V.4.2.4.
1613 After in the first year, time was wasted, the time pressure for capacity-building steadily increased.
1614 Interview with a senior staff member of Civil Affairs, UNTAET, New York, 18 September 2006.

Coping with this harum-scarum situation, UNTAET actively created positive incentives for Timorese living in Diaspora, e.g. with status and salaries, but also by appealing to their patriotism. While this policy had the advantage of bringing in well-educated people, the negative effects were probably underestimated and ignored.

UN-inflicted Rivalry between the Diaspora and Timorese Residents

Faced with difficulties finding suitable local personnel to take over in the new government, UNTAET fell back on Timorese living in Diaspora in Portugal, Mozambique, and Australia. In fact, it actively set incentives for them to come back. This was also the fastest and most convenient method, since most of them spoke English and had enjoyed higher levels of (Western) education than those who had remained on the island. This sidelined the "resident" population who felt discriminated against. Thus, by unconflictedly adhering to its Diaspora policy, UNTAET was creating a new social division.

Neglect of Local Dynamics

UNTAET could not develop sufficient sensitivity towards the divisions and differing loyalties within Timorese society. First, the need for experienced Timorese in the police and in the military led to a conflict between the two institutions because experienced Timorese policemen were associated with the Indonesian occupation, and experienced military had been Falintil fighters. Second, structural effects were neglected when many ex-Falintil fighters were denied their requests to join the new force, and the frustration of veterans smouldered. The issue was not approached with much diligence, and the plan for a small military force was adhered to unconflictedly. Since the majority of Timorese males had been active in the resistance fight, there was now an army of disillusioned and unemployed people, producing a considerable potential for conflict and a security risk for the new state. UNTAET did not follow-up on these aspects. Unwittingly, a serious division within the new state was created.

"Too Hot a Potato"

Some crucial issues were "too hot a potato" to be touched by the mission at all.[1615] Property rights were a point in case. A clear legal situation would have been important for Timor's economy but the SRSG decided to defer the tricky question to the new government. The same rationale applied to the justice sector in general. In a situation where hardly any qualified lawyers or court buildings were available, and where it was not clear which law should actually be applied, the SRSG delegated judicial authority to the (future) courts, arguing that jurisdiction was "entirely outside his sphere of power."[1616] While it might have been the right decision politically, the deferral created uncertainty, especially for foreign investors. The consequence was that Timorese economic growth could not take off. Besides, the legal uncertainty allowed backdoors and feints, and it allowed for some unfortunate decisions regarding the applicable law to be made. UNTAET's focus remained on controllable and politically less ambiguous issues.

Individual Procrastinations

The shortage of proper information and proper handling of the local dynamics was a feature of the entire mission, and as such, was also observable with individual staff. On the part of the majority of the international staff, insensitivity of Timorese culture and their inexpertness in dealing with a colonized society caused individual deferrals and only incremental Timorization. In the short run, this had a backlash on UNTAET's legitimacy. In the long run, insufficient capacity-building negatively affects the sustainability of the new institutions.

Construction of Parallel Power Structure

The *terra nullis* policy that UNTAET continued to adhere to had negative effects. UNTAET did not recur on the existing local governance structures. To the contrary, it established a completely new power structure that worked parallel to the traditionally, locally accepted structures on the ground.

1615   Ibid.
1616   Dobbins et al. 2005, p. 169.

Inappropriate Selection and Allocation Rationales for Local Staff

The selection of local district administrators proceeded "either after the gusto of the district field officer, or we had some weird western criteria and selected people that had no authority"[1617] within the local community, reflecting a narrow focus on pre-preferred alternatives and the use of familiar criteria. The staffing of the civil administration at the mid and low levels took extremely long. Eventually, UNTAET just took "what was there," in order to stay on track. Thus, as Timorese staff was not chosen according to qualification or fit, i.e. local acceptance, the decisions risked becoming unsustainable. The poor capacity situation took its toll, and low institutional performance was to be expected.

4.2.1.3 Termination

The cognitive biases that occurred during the termination phase related to poor and narrow planning of the elections, of the preparation of the schedule for the Constituent Assembly, and of the successor mission.

"A Square Peg in a Round Hole:" Elections

Managing elections on that comprehensive scale was a new task for the UN. Some mistakes occurred almost necessarily. The flawed civic and voter education was a case in point: it focussed too much on technical issues, unsuitable computerized voting rolls were used, technical errors in data collection were committed, and much of the informational duties of objective party profiles were inappropriately delegated to the parties themselves. Compounding this pathology of focussing on controllable factors and un-reflected adherences to familiar practices, UNTAET was not able to control parties' foul play. The major consequences were that time was wasted, but also that political biases were produced, as well as traditional social institutions neglected.[1618]

There was only *ex post facto* corrective action, such as the extension of the schedule, which created at least some time slack.

1617 Written interview with Dr. Tanja Hohe, former team member of UN Volunteers in East Timor, 30 September 2006.

1618 "The spontaneous idea people got after some civic education campaigns was that, 'We have democracy now, and therefore do not need to listen to our village chief anymore.' These statements led to village-level anarchy and were used whenever convenient by any person who wanted to act independently without the agreement of the village chief or any local authority." Hohe 2002b, p. 583.

Deficient Planning for Consultation on Constitution

The organization of the public consultations for discussions on constitutions had its flaws, too. "Wrong" languages were used (e.g. Portuguese where only Tetum was spoken), and the time frame for consultation was ridiculously short. Important aspects were ignored. As the different election-related processes were tightly coupled, these shortcomings interacted and exacerbated each other. In reaction, Fretilin blocked public consultation inputs, justifying this strategic move by referring to the procedural flaws. Thus, the perspective of the civil society did not make its way into the political process.

UNTAET extended the timeframe for discussion. In order to do that, the deadline for the mission had to be extended as well. De Mello was able to convince the Security Council by framing the challenges on-the-ground as threats to international security. That being said, "Had UNTAET had a culture of Timorese inclusion in the first place, civic education would have had the time to complement the political process undertaken by Timorese people themselves."[1619]

Another aspect questioning the adequacy of the constitution was the presidential system. Implicating a rivalry between the president and the government, it did not fit the Timorese political culture of unity. The presidential system even institutionalized the personal tension between long-term rivals, President Gusmão and Prime Minister Alkatiri.

Pull towards Centralization

During the termination phase, the mission once more succumbed to a centralization dynamic. The heavy workload forced the devolution planners to focus on the central level. Again, this implied a marginalization of the people and political processes in the districts.

Waste of Time: Planning for the Successor Mission

For the follow-up planning, line managers were asked to write down what they thought would be essential for the stability of the future government. But these compilations were useless because they turned out to be crude wish lists – no

---

1619   "A Popular Challenge to UNTAET's Achievements." *Back Door Newsletter on East Timor*. Available online at http://members.pcug.org.au/~wildwood/01seppopular.htm, last access on 6 March 2009.

guidelines or parameters had been set for this process. Subsequently, the list had to be done all over again. Obviously, this was a waste of precious time.

4.2.2 Principal-Agent Dilemmas

The transitional management in East Timor witnessed different forms of commitment deficits: intentional and unintentional defection by agents, as well as by principals, but also commitment overkill in the form of overachieving international staff.

4.2.2.1 Deployment

During the first months of the transition, ill-structured conditions translated into difficulties in demilitarization, the deployment of inadequate staff, a lack of guidance, and in providing deficient information. The latter was due to an ongoing departmental turf war at headquarters.

Demilitarization on Hold

Resulting from the ambiguous support of the powerful neighbor state Indonesia, demilitarization was put on hold. The Indonesian government refused to disarm its militias based in West Timor. A security risk persisted on East Timor's western border.

Bureaucratic Territorialism

The turf war that ensued between DPA, which had formerly been responsible for East Timor, and DPKO, which now had become the "principal" on the issue, prohibited the flow and good use of essential DPA information regarding local dynamics and expertise. The consequence was that the DPA's perspective was excluded altogether and an inadequate *terra nullis* assumption and "colonial paternalism"[1620] could prevail.

1620 Interview with Professor Michael W. Doyle, former UN Assistant Secretary-General, New Haven, 11 September 2006.

Table 6: Ill-Structuredness, Principal Agent Problems, Accidents, and Coping Strategies

	Ill-Structuredness	Pathology	Accident	Coping
Deployment	Ambiguous Intern. Support	Demilitarization on Hold	(Pending Security Situation on Border)	Stabilization through INTERFET/UNPKF, CivPol
	UN Rules and Rivalries, Time Pressure	Bureaucratic Territorialism at HQ	"Colonial Paternalism" on-the ground	-
	Member States Interests, Time Pressure, UN Capacities	Politization	Imbalanced Mandate Implementation	Setting Clear End Status and Timeframe Plus Mandate Ambiguity
	Time Pressure, Mandate Complex., UN Capacities	Dead Wood	Precarious Mandate Implementation	Rolling-out Under-performing Staff
	Time Pressure, Local Capacity	The Ten Percent Pathology	Overload for "Good" Staff, Precarious Mandate Implementation	-
	Time Pressure, UN Capacities	Impatience and Frustration of International Staff	Insufficient Capacity-building	-
	Local Capacity, Time Pressure	Over-performance	Precarious Local Ownership	(Capacity Limits)
	Time Pressure, Lost of Local Acceptance	Opportunism	Political Bias, Marginalization of Non-Portuguese Speakers	-
	Ambiguous Intern. Support, Mandate Complexity	Loss of Coordination Synergies	Precarious Mandate Achievement	-
	Ambiguous Support, UN Rules, Mandate Complexity, Local Necessities	Incoherent Contributions and Inadequate Investments	Precarious Mandate Implementation	Vigilance on Available Resources, DCU Creating Transparency and Turning Pledges into High-Profile Issues
	Ambiguous Support, Mandate Complexity	Effects of Mandate Ambiguity	Uncertainty, "Organized Hypocrisy"	Delegation to Strong Leadership
	UN Capacities, UN Rules, Ambiguous Intern. Interests	Unpreparedness for Institution-building	Precarious Mandate Achievement	Incrementalism, Identifying Comparative Benchmarks, Using UNDP Expertise
	UN Rules, Mandate Complexity, Ambiguous Support	Exclusive Political and Financial Considerations for Institution-building	Creation of Inefficient, Corruption-prone Public Service	-
Termination	UN Rules	"Glued to Their Seats"	(Insufficient Capacity-building, Procrastination)	"Axe Men"
	Ambiguous Support	Deadline Exogeneity	Precarious Mandate Implementation	Comprehensive Follow-On Arrangement
	Local Capacity, Time Pressure	Opportunism in Post-UNTAET Planning	Political Bias in Favor of Fretilin, Hurry	Small Working Groups
	Member State Interests	Ambiguous Support for Follow-On Mission	-	Organizational/Financial Slack through Security Appeals

4.2.2.2 Mandate Implementation and Mission Management

During the course of the mission, UNTAET faced problems that resulted from its double role as an agent – namely of member states and headquarters – and a principal – namely of the local actors and other international and non-governmental cooperation partners. But frictions between the mission leadership and the other staff emerged within the mission as well: UNTAET struggled with many defective staff who were there just to collect a salary, or who even misbehaved towards their local counterparts to protect themselves from being replaced. On the other hand, a diametrically opposed phenomenon was also observable, namely overly motivated staff doing just too much, and thus keeping local counterparts from owning the transition process.

Politization

There were different views on UNTAET's approach towards mandate implementation and, at times, these diverging interpretations unleashed serious internal fights, dismissals, or resignations. Consistently, the results of such discussions were biased in favor of political considerations. These political interests were essentially those of the Security Council and relevant member states. The consequence was a loss of good, idealistic people that might have induced a better balance in the emphasis between short-term and long-term goals.

Dead Wood: Incompetent and Insufficient Staff

Under considerations of sovereignty and resource obligations alike, member states did not want the UN to routinely engage in state-building and, particularly, in state-*running* missions. For the recruitment system at DPKO, this meant that there was not a suitable roster that could identify human capacities to maintain post-conflict administrations. Specifically, the roster did not identify civilian, especially administrative, skills, it did not select according to cultural or country knowledge, and it did not identify training capabilities. Staffing proceeds according to the necessities of the UN system, e.g. country proportions and their willingness to contribute, and only in second place to functions. Trying to amend the recruitment process, DPKO made specific requests to member states that they send administration specialists. But states were very reluctant to delegate their good people. "Except for the peace-keeping element, the UN does not have experience in running a country as such. Therefore, it is not surprising that the UNTAET personnel recruit did not fit the job qualification for public administration or economic reconstruction."[1621] The result was a hit or miss of people. Unfortunately, the system produced a lot of "dead wood," i.e. staff which was neither qualified nor motivated to do the job[1622] or which was even "positively dangerous."[1623] Individuals can make it or break it. Accordingly, there was a high degree of uncertainty in the mission's performance.

Obviously, the inclusion of roster criteria of qualifications that suited transitional administrations' challenges would have been a straightforward solution. However, it is an intricate question of whether it makes sense to formally establish such a mechanism: as member states are often hesitant to approve of such extensive mandates, it is likely that the "tool" of transitional administrations would not be applied too often in the future. Anyway, it is recommended that the system be made more flexible, such as to be able to include further categories on demand, depending on the respective mandates. Or, as suggested by de Mello himself,

> One simple measure would be the development of stand-by arrangements (similar to those we have with troop contributors) with member states for the provision of pre-specified assistance at virtually short notice. This could either be in the form of essential equipment or, crucially, through making available self-contained sectoral teams (e.g. in areas such as banking, budget management, taxation, immigration, civil service re-cruitment, customs, penal services, veterinary services, roads, parts, electricity, health services and so on). In other words, all the skills actually required to run a government. We need to be able to roll up our sleeves and get down and dirty at the coal face of administration. This must be coupled with ensuring that our administrative rules and regulations facilitate – rather than impede – the implementation of the mandate. Monies, including from assessed funds, must be made quickly available to allow the mission in question to perform the tasks required of it.[1624]

Coping with the situation, "useless" personnel were expelled from the central level and sent to the districts where their attitudes were less harmful to the performance of the mission. Thus, the district staffing problem was "alleviated", but only in numbers, not in quality.

Further measures that, *prima facie*, could have been useful are: retaining key UNAMET personnel, recruiting externally, providing more training for administrative and governmental functions within the UN, or creating a standing group of support staff for peace operations with large civilian components. However, none of these could be implemented, due to various institutional, legal, and political

---

1621   Saldanha 2003, p. 161.
1622   "Peacekeeping can't be another job, it needs people that are highly motivated, with a burning desire to do good." Interview with Dr. Christine Coleiro, UNITAR POCI, Washington, DC, 1 December 2006.
1623   Interview with a senior staff member of Civil Affairs, UNTAET, New York, 18 September 2006.
1624   Vieira De Mello 2001, p. 18. At present, a revision of the DPKO recruitment and planning system is being worked on. Cf. Interview with a senior staff member of UNTAET, New York, 23 November 2006.

barriers. First, efforts to hire good personnel from UNAMET were limited, possibly due to the turf war going on between DPA (UNAMET) and DPKO (UN-TAET).[1625] Secondly, the option of external recruitment is difficult legally.

> The UN has in general problems with outsourcing personnel recruitment. Most of the private companies to which you could outsource personnel are from a very small number of Western countries. And so the budget committees, which have to approve the arrangement, generally don't approve of it, because it is not representative enough of the world. In fact, it *has been* occasionally applied, like in UNPROFOR where they outsourced a lot of the personnel. But it's always been looked at relatively negatively by our own intergovernmental committees, by the finance, budget committees. So, it's not easy.[1626]

Third, the possibility of having more intra-UN training for international administration personnel is unrealistic, since member states – different states with different reasons, but united in their reluctance – are unwilling to institutionalize efforts to prepare the UN to run countries. "They say that Kosovo and Timor and Eastern Slavonia were sort of exceptions, and that we should not develop a dedicated capacity in that area."[1627] Eventually, the idea of a standing civilian force is a straightforward one. And in fact, the UN used to have a professional group of field staff, guaranteeing that every mission would have a "baseline" of good people to could provide general support, quickly and reliably, to the mission. This service, however, was abandoned ten years ago.

While some decision-makers in the mission reflected about the mentioned approaches, at the end of the day, they were not put into practice. This was due to inter-departmental fights, legal and political constraints, as well as to overall institutional inertia.[1628]

The Ten Percent Pathology

UNTAET pathologically suffered from what I call the Ten Percent pathology. "The mission was effectively run by about ten percent of the people."[1629] As a consequence, there was not only an overload of work for these ten percent, but it also meant an enormous waste of resources: after all, the oterh 90 percent were being paid, too.

1625 Beauvais 2001, p. 1124.
1626 Interview with a senior staff member of UNDPKO PBPS, New York, 15 September 2006.
1627 Ibid.
1628 For an overview of contributions about UN reform and its hurdles, see Global Policy Forum, "UN Reform." Available online at http://www.globalpolicy.org/reform/index.htm, last access on March 2, 2009.
1629 Interview with a senior staff member of Civil Affairs, UNTAET, New York, 18 September 2006., remembering a remark by de Mello.

Impatience and Frustration of International Staff

When it came to training Timorese, international staff was often impatient, as Timorese did not match their (mistaken) expectations. Language gaps compounded the difficulties, as did the different social behavior of the Timorese, which most international staff was not able to interpret. There were many sources of misunderstanding. As a consequence, the motivation of the international staff was decreasing. This implied another setback for capacity-building.

Over-performance

At the other extreme, some UNTAET staff was over-performing. The transitional administration was under high time pressure to succeed from day one. At the same time, it had the power, the resources, and the capacities to do it alone.

> The reality of life in Timor throughout almost the entire time that we were there is that the reconstruction, the physical reconstruction of the destroyed homes was largely the result of the personal efforts of the international staff who were there and the money that they brought in. I myself was involved in that and so were many of our colleagues.[1630]

Warranting visible short-term results, it seemed that the rationale for the staff of the interim administration was to "get things done." And they seemed to assume that things would not get done by training others to do them, but by doing as much as they could by themselves. This procedure, however, ended the participation of lower-skilled Timorese. Over-performance was most severe at the beginning of the mission and was only gradually reduced with the introduction of the time schedule and the co-government approach.

UNTAET's over-performance prevented Timorese from owning the operative processes. "Coping" with over-performance was, at the end of the day, a self-regulating process: the challenges were so manifold and quality of the international mission's civilian capacities were so mixed that over-performance did not exceed a certain threshold.

Opportunism

Making up for its initial ignorance, UNTAET occasionally moved towards the other extreme, and increasingly displayed some sort of opportunistic behavior. For in-

---

1630   Interview with a senior staff member of Civil Affairs, UNTAET, New York, 18 September 2006.

stance, the issue of the official languages was "solved" in line with the preferences of the most influential party. Portuguese was established as first language, Tetum as the second, and the widely spoken Bahasa Indonesian was omitted; its speakers did not figure into Fretilin's major constituencies. Despite knowing about the effects of this policy, UNTAET did not oppose it, as Fretilin had meanwhile put itself in a position where UNTAET needed its endorsement. The consequence was that large parts of the population were excluded from political life. The policy also created a heavy workload for the mostly Bahasa speaking civil servants in mid-level positions: not only did they have to find their way in their new positions, but they also had to learn Portuguese and Tetum, as well as, for the transition period, English.

Loss of Coordination Synergies

UNTAET suffered from partly self-induced turf-ism with other organizations that were supposed to help with the implementation of the mandate. NGOs were often excluded from the "real" decision-making. Thus, potentially useful information on allocation needs was disregarded. Frictions occurred with international organizations, too: the most virulent case was the discussion of the World Bank's CEP. The mission fought against the project on the grounds that it avoided "premature politization of environment."[1631] Having an interest in the failure of a cooperation partner, UNTAET wanted to be the one to set the rules of the game. Thus, instead of integrating a project with a huge amount of money, UNTAET put it on hold and obtained the worst of two worlds, i.e. poor influence on local structures and a fight with an essential international financial organization.

Incoherent Contributions

As peacebuilding activities are operated through voluntary financial and in-kind contributions, the shares of member states were rather inconsistent. At times, they were even inadequate. The mission depended on what member states are willing to offer, be it fireworks from China or high-level diplomat training seminars in Sweden, resulting in a scattered state-building approach.

The lion's share of the money for reconstruction was not invested according to local needs, but instead for strategic and media considerations, i.e. member states invested in areas important to their geopolitical interests, in projects of symbolic value, or in those with high visibility, such as high profile government offices in

1631   Statement by SRSG de Mello, quoted in Beauvais 2001, p. 1126, fn. 94.

Dili. Therefore, the rural, decentralized areas of East Timor, as well as "un-sexy"[1632] sectors, e.g. rural infrastructure and agriculture, were marginalized. Another negative side-effect was that urbanization increased, and with it, related social problems.

UNTAET's DCU engaged in intense communication with donors, providing them with as much information as possible, so that they were at least aware of what was needed. Their hope was that they would change their minds. DCU's efforts were met with occasional success, and at least the civil service administration got a boost. "But it was not satisfactory."[1633] The DCU also arranged that at least one high-ranking UNTAET official and, later on, the respective Timorese minister attended every donor conference.

Effects of Mandate Ambiguity

Vagueness and ambiguity of the mandate are common features of UN resolutions. The wording of the mandate, particularly about "East Timorese participation, issues of accountability, UNTAET's own political role, the scope for governmental action available to an administration that was interim in nature, and the priority to be given to the mission's sometimes competing objectives,"[1634] was ambiguous and did not undergo further concretization. Furthermore, the mandate was imprecise on questions such as,

> How much of his plenary power should the Transitional Administrator devolve and how quickly? Could the SRSG/Transitional Administrator reconcile being simultaneously accountable to the people of East Timor and to the Security Council? To what extent was UNTAET political player and to what extent political arbiter? Given its interim and semi-legitimate nature, how could it avoid pre-empting the decisions of the coming independent East Timorese government? Could East Timorese aspirations be satisfied during the transitional period without prejudging the outcome of the political process that it was committed to completing? How should a balance be struck between the short-term requirements of coping with a humanitarian emergency and providing basic government services, and the longer-term needs of capacity- and institution-building?[1635]

1632 Telephone interview with a program officer of the Donor Coordination Unit, UNTAET, 7 October 2006.
1633 Ibid.
1634 CSDG, "East Timor Report," para. 329.
1635 Ibid., para. 330. Similar Martin and Mayer-Rieckh 2005, p. 133, "The mandate left several key questions unanswered, including the roadmap leading to self-government, the relationship of the governance and public administration component to the future East Timorese government, and the mechanisms for consultation with the East Timorese."

While ambiguous language can, in fact, help to cope with the precariousness and fragility of member states' commitments, it becomes a problem when it results in poor guidance.[1636] "A mandate is gonna be two or three pages – which is fine. I mean, the Security Council should be taking strategic decisions, not micromanaging. But then, that leaves the big gap of the operational planning right down to the technical level."[1637] Ambiguity creates uncertainty for a mission and a lack of clear guidelines also implies a higher risk for mission creep. Besides, the mandate called for the highest standards of the involvement of East Timorese in state-building efforts, and created high expectations. Wasting time and trust, the mission remained far from obtaining these goals, pointing to a gap between rhetoric and action.[1638]

Counterbalancing the ambiguity, strong mission leadership was imposed upon the mission and policy specification was supposed to be delegated to the SRSG.[1639] In fact, the Secretary-General chose one of the most experienced candidates as SRSG. He made him the head of an integrated mission structure, ensuring unity of command under the SRSG's lead.

Mandate ambiguity implies evaluation ambiguity as well. The manipulation of performance criteria becomes easier: ambiguous wording and a lack of specification create space for interpretation of whether the mandate has been accomplished, and whether the mission needs additional time and resources or not.

Unpreparedness for Institution Building

Expertise and manpower that the mission would have needed to match the governing mandate were hardly available.

UNTAET staff coped by steadily readjusting to the precarious situation. "We were feeling our way as we went along."[1640] Benchmarks and orientation points were identified, by means of analyses of comparable states or regions or by using UNDP classifications and public functions designing tools. For highly specialized issues, falling back on institutionalized knowledge turned out to be useful along the incremental learning processes.

1636 The CSDG report puts it in a somewhat more optimistic way: "it did require considerable political creativity and flexibility of a transitional administration facing a range of other pressing priorities." CSDG, "East Timor Report," para. 330.
1637 Interview with a senior official of the UN Department of Political Affairs, New York, 12 December 2006.
1638 This phenomenon has already been identified by Michael Lipson and labelled "organized hypocrisy." Lipson, Michael. 2007. "Organized Hypocrisy." *European Journal of International Relations* 13:1, pp. 5-34.
1639 While this might have indeed been a valuable a good decision, it does not seem that this was due to deep reflection.
1640 Interview with a senior staff member of Civil Affairs, UNTAET, New York, 18 September 2006.

Exclusive Political and Financial Considerations for Institution-building

Institution-building was subject to political and financial primacies, less so to considerations of the sustainability of an efficient system. During Indonesian rule, many Timorese worked in the civil service. They were low paid, but earned an income at least. Being the one who signed the pay checks, Indonesia intended to co-opt the local population. As a consequence, the civil service had been far from efficient and struggled with corruption. UNTAET continued that "tradition" as it follwed the IMF's and Fretilin's financial and political preferences. Being dependent upon their money and their political support, UNTAET created a large public service system. This implied that it eventually opted out for a more efficient, smaller, and better educated civil service as was proposed by its civil affairs staff. At the same time, the general population favored this option too, as the many unemployed and under-qualified people were looking for government jobs.

4.2.2.3 Termination

An interesting phenomenon that evolved during the termination phase was the change in the relationship between UNTAET and the Timorese. Fretilin gained power and claimed a position of being the "principal" of the transitional administration. UNTAET complied with most of its requests. While this is, in principle, an important and warranted development, it was still unfortunate for the transition. "Ownership" was overly biased in the direction of one single party. Overall, I observed five different pathological episodes during the termination phase.

"Glued to Their Seats"

In a transitional administration, the primary task is to hand jobs over to the locals, letting them take over. The contracts of international staff are short-term, resulting in internationals' perception of their employment situations as precarious. Personnel from developing countries, who are supporting entire families by their income, may be especially "glued" to their jobs. This job precariousness is likely to be the reason behind the reported obstructions of international staff to their Timorese counterparts, whom they were supposed to train. Whatever the reasons, intentionally poor capacity-building resulted, and the transition process procrastinated.

When withdrawal approached, many internationals would not want to leave, for both egoistic and idealistic reasons. The mission's staff complained about being "sorted out" and the "axe men" had a hard time dealing with those complaints. In addition to the loss of time, internal frictions occurred in UNTAET.

Deadline Exogeneity

The deadline was set deliberatively, according to political and resource considerations of the sponsoring "principals," the member states, and not according to the situation on-the-ground. As a matter of fact, UNTAET withdrew before it had implemented its mandate. Contributing to a transitional administration's generic precariousness, a premature withdrawal can thwart sustainable results.

Attenuating the negative effect of interrupted institution-building, a comparatively comprehensive successor mission was agreed upon.[1641] For UN standards, it was very comprehensive.

Opportunism

In the drawdown and hand-over planning, the functional ideas of the "axe men" were soon co-opted by political demands. This time, the "principal" was Fretilin. While this added legitimacy to the process, Fretilin pushed the process with great hurry.

The head of the planning team and his people designed a range of small teams in which effectiveness could continue to be the imperative.

Similarly, the planning process for the successor mission was criticized, and eventually started all over again, by the increasingly powerful Fretili´n. Their argument was that they had not been appropriately involved. As a result, the follow-on planning was put on hold.

De Mello decided to do the process all over again, this time, however, under the aegis of the IMTF which had been sent in by UN headquarters. That being said, he basically stuck to the parameters of the old approach, and hence, merely applied a new label to it. This procedure added to the legitimacy of the planning phase. However, it did produce much extra-work.

1641   For a similar argument, see Hampson, Fen Osler. 1996. *Nurturing Peace – Why Peace Settlements Succeed or Fail.* Washington, DC: United States Institute of Peace Press.

Ambiguous International (and Local) Support for Successor Mission

UNTAET encountered external objections, i.e. from member states, and some local objections, i.e. from Fretilin, against the scope and content of the successor mission. For quite some time, it was unclear what kind of mission would be designed, and the implementation of the remaining transition tasks was precarious.

Coping with the ambiguity of support for its successor, UNTAET's leadership argued that UNMISET and particularly its civilian posts would be essential for the security of East Timor. With this argumentation, even the civilian UNMISET posts could be financed via the assessed budget. This was an innovation.

> We argued that there was some core issues which they were not taken care of properly, the state itself would fail. And if the state failed that was a peace and security issue. And what's more, it meant the failure of the original mandate which the Council had found to contribute to international peace and security, namely a transition to an independent and stable East Timor.[1642]

4.2.3 Tight Coupling of Complex Interactions

The tight procedural and organizational alignments of a multidimensional peace operation make it prone to situations that can be likened to a traffic jam: implementation processes have to start where preconditions are not yet in place, negative results in one area trigger problems in other fields, or inflexible institutional structures, such as the discussed recruiting provisions, bind resources for adequate problem management. In the case under scrutiny, I have observed pathological links between interests, rhetoric, and mandated goals, organizational and procedural structures, decisions at multiple levels, and between different actors: member states, headquarters, the mission and its staff, and local spoilers.

4.2.3.1 Deployment

Due to member states ambiguous support, caused by their reluctance to come into conflict with Indonesia, the deficient mission design and recruitment, aggravated by the extreme time pressure in the planning phase, resulted in an inability to hit the ground running. In addition, the rigid financial provisions did not allow for early measures to be taken in the non-peacekeeping realm, and demilitarization was dealt with half-heartedly, thus planting the seed of future unrest.

1642 Interview with a senior staff member of UNTAET, New York, 23 November 2006.

Failure to Hit the Ground Running

For the first six months, UNTAET had its hands full setting up of the mission. As soon as money and adequate expertise were available, it became a natural priority to take on peacekeeping and humanitarian challenges first. But this also meant that the core task of UNTAET, its executive mandate, was postponed. Failing to hit the ground running, it did not tackle its reconstruction, governmental, and training tasks until a year into the mission. At the same time, the local elite did not have their fair share of the process; even more, the lives of the general population did not improve.

> The contacts of most Timorese with the *malai* [foreigners; ES] were very superficial and what they saw were people who were completely incompetent, who had no idea about their situation, and who could not deliver anything for them. We were, from the outset, failing to earn legitimacy with the population we have come to assist.[1643]

Necessarily, the mission had to develop an implementation strategy and the mechanisms to implement it for themselves, on-the-ground, in a back and forth process. "We learnt as we went along."[1644] An important element of this learning process was the early establishment of informal consultations with local Timorese leaders. Dealing with the constraining rules on the relationship with local interlocutors and with the fading local support, de Mello built a strong, yet informal relationship with Gusmão.[1645] These informal relationships were crucial. Still, the strong influence of informally singled-out leaders bore a generic risk of political bias.

Occasional actions by individuals, particularly by experienced UNVs who co-operated informally with CNRT and Falintil, attenuated Timorese frustration as well.

It also helped mitigate the tense climate that the mission could point to its goal of East Timorese independence, and frame itself as the "good broker" of the transition. Good communication would have helped to multiply this advantage, but the communications unit was already delayed at the start of the mission. International staff were literally not able to reach out to the people, and translators were rare.

No Money, No Action

Voluntary contributions for peacebuilding tasks needed were not available from the start. They needed to be raised ad hoc. Hence, the finanicial shortages prevented UNTAET from reacting quickly to in the early stages of the transition process. The

---

1643 Interview with a senior staff member of Civil Affairs, UNTAET, New York, 18 September 2006.
1644 Ibid.
1645 Both, by the way, were native Portuguese speakers.

situation was particularly severe at the district levels. As the communications unit was not yet in place during the first couple of months, the mismatch between high expectation and hardly visible action went largely uncommented upon and furthered local Timorese frustration. This sharply reduced the original high input-legitimacy of the transitional administration.

UNTAET was able to construct a network of diverse pots with many cooperating actors who came together at various donor conferences. The flexible East Timor Trust Fund created particular financial slack.[1646] That being said, civilian-administrative tasks were still delayed considerably. In some cases, good cooperation with international organizations and local NGOs helped, as could be seen in the health sector. Nonetheless, shortages persisted. A case in point was the gap in treatment standards that remained when the ICRC handed the Dili National Hospital over to the local government.

Table 7: Ill-Structuredness, Tight Coupling, Accidents, and Coping Strategies

	Ill-Structuredness	Pathologies	Accidents	Coping Strategies
Deployment	UN Capacity, UN Rules, Mandate Complexity	"Failure to Hit the Ground Running"	Loss of Time and of Legitimacy, Precarious Mandate Implementation	Incremental Learning, Establishing Informal Relationships, Organizational Slack (UNVs), Positive Framing
	UN Rules	No Money, No Action	No Early Reconstruction.	Establ. Funding Network
Implementation	Mandate Complexity Local Capacity, Member State Interests/Ticking Clocks	Dual Mandate Tension	Overload, Necessary Shortcomings in Mandate Implementation	-
	Mandate Complexity, Local Capacity, Member State Interests/Ticking Clocks, UN Rules	Tension between External Legitimacy and Internal Legitimacy Needs	Bias towards External Legitimacy, Loss of Internal Legitimacy, Precarious Mandate Implementation, Inconsistent Transition Approach	(Relying on Diaspora and Fretilin)
	Mandate Complexity, Local Capacity Type, UN Rules	Tension between (Benevolent) Autocracy and Promotion of Democratic Values	"Do as I Say Not as I Do"	Gradual Involvement of Timorese
	Mandate Complexity, Local Capacity Type, UN Rules	Imposition Trap	Questionable Sustainability	Intern./Local Co-operation (IOs, NGOs)

1646 The necessary condition for the high commitment was geo-political concerns. "Purely political concerns led to enough money on the table." Interview with Professor Dirk Salomons, Director of the Program for Humanitarian Affairs at the School of International Public Affairs, Columbia University, New York, 20 September 2006. He points at regional stability considerations, which intensified after the September violence.

	Member State Interests, UN Rules, Time Pressure	Accountability Deficits	Decrease of Local Legitimacy	-
	Time Pressure, Uncertainty about Local Infrastructure, UN Rules	Inevitable Waste	Loss of Local Legitimacy, Waste of Resources	-
	UN Rules (comes automatically with interventions)	Bubble Economy Pathology	Precarious Economic Stability	Promoting Cooperation, Timor See Agreement
	UN Capacities, Ambiguous Support, Mandate Complexity	Inadequate Expertise	Precarious Mandate Implementation	-
	UN Rules	Heterogenity in CivPol	Credibility Problems	-
	UN Rules, Local Capac.	Payroll Deltas	Confusion, Social Tensions	-
	Ambiguous Support, UN Rules, Mandate Complexity, Local Capacity	Earmarking Effects	Preventing Timorese Ownership	-
	UN Rules and Routines, Local Capacity, Mandate Complexity	Mismatch of UN Routines and Mandate Challenges	Insufficient Capacity-building and Integration of Timorese into State-building Process	See-And-Learn Capacity-building
	Local Capacity, UN Capacities	Persistence of Communication Difficulties	Deficient Interaction with Timorese, Legitimacy Loss, Prohibiting Ownership	-
	Mandate Complexity, Time Pressure, Local Capacity	Role Conflict	Civil Society Neglect	-
Termination	Time Pressure, Loc. Cap.	Precariousness of Controlled Exit	Precarious Sustainability	Outsourcing to External Planning Team
	UN Rules, Local Capacity	Pathological Impeding Regulation	Precarious Mandate Achievement and Sustainability	Obstinate Negotiations with SC/GA, Appeals to Security Considerations
	Time Pressure, Local Capacity	Not Yet Finished	Precarious National Legitimacy of New Timorese Administrators	Making Use of Tradit. Rite with Symbolic Hand-Over Acts

4.2.3.2 Mandate Implementation and Mission Management

Again and again, UNTAET struggled with its contradicting yet interwoven mandate imperatives and had a hard time implementing them in a balanced way. Tensions arose between the ubiquitous questions of legitimacy, democracy promotion, accountability, and efficacy. They were compounded by inadequate expertise, routines, and money allocation. Altogether, I witnessed almost twenty different pathological episodes concerning to the implementation of the mandate and mission management.

Dual Mandate Tension

The mandate of the transitional administration was simply enormous and conveyed inherent conflicts between goals and trade-offs that turned into pathological problems for the transitional management. The "dual mandate tension"[1647] has already been identified by Joel Beauvais, but I argue that it can be further differentiated: while Beauvais identified the "UN- governorship" and the "local self-government" mandate that collide in terms of decision-making control and resource allocation,[1648] there are additional tensions that ensue from the multiple mission duties. They concern the generic approach to peace operations, chronological priorities, being a political role model, and (at least) two constituencies of an international interim administration in a conflict-ridden territory.

Tension between External Legitimacy and Internal Legitimacy

Stemming from its dual mandate, UNTAET had to answer to its international and local constituencies. The resulting imperatives contradicted each other regularly.

More and more, UNTAET manoeuvred itself into a situation where its official policy of impartiality contradicted its legitimacy needs. Officially still adhering to its impartial and neutral stance, it was not able to succeed in thorough Timorization. In need of legitimacy, it relinquished enormous power to certain political groups, especially Fretilin, letting them dispose over financing decisions. Calls for more

---

1647   Beauvais 2001.
1648   "UNTAET is mandated to establish itself as the *de facto* government of East Timor, but also is charged with preparing the East Timorese for democratic self-government. The overall 'state-building' mandate thus breaks down into two distinct aspects, which might be termed the 'UN governorship' mandate and the 'local self-government' mandate, respectively. While conceptually compatible, in practice these two mandates are in deep tension with one another, particularly with control to decision making and allocation of resources." Beauvais 2001, p. 1108. See also, e.g., Vieira de Mello, Sergio. 2001. *How Not to Run a Country. Lessons for the UN from Kosovo and East Timor.* Paper for the UNITAR-IPS-JIIA Conference to Address the Report on UN Peace Operations, Singapore, February 2001, "Thus, compared to many other UN missions in peacekeeping, UNTAET had to shoulder the extremely delicate task of building a new government structure, which should be in accordance with international standards, on the basis of ownership on the part of the local population, in partnership with the international community. In parallel, UNTAET had had to engage in the establishment of a community equipped with improved social infrastructure and other necessary conditions for sustainable development in East Timor, with full support from other UN organs and programmes as well as with the help from international financial institutions such as the World Bank and the Asian Development Bank."

sustainability-orientation remained unheard.[1649] Often enough, the consequence was an incoherent transition approach, combining the worst of both worlds.

Tension between (Benevolent) Autocracy and Promotion of Democratic Values

UNTAET operated under the tension of its imperative to promote democratic values, while at the same time being a *de facto* autocracy, although a largely benevolent one. Still, the means of the UN interim administration contradicted its ends.[1650] The tight grip of the powerful mission and its deficits regarding accountability mechanisms vis-à-vis the Timorese were diametrically opposed to the goal of democracy promotion, resulting in what Chesterman termed the governance of "Do-as-I-Say-Not-as-I-Do."[1651]

The gradual involvement of Timorese via the NC/NCC and eventually ETTA attenuated the difficulty.

Imposition Trap

External state-building is problematic *per se*, since it implies the imposition of a non-indigenous blueprint; the blueprint of the UN is the Western liberal-democratic state model. For all interim administrations, this imperative constitutes what I call the "imposition trap." They are running the risk of failure when they try to apply the highest standards of democracy, human rights, the rule of law, and provision of services[1652] in a context where "material" preconditions such as infrastructure and capacities are low to non-existent, where the basis of democratic experience is by and large missing, and where Western standards just do not fit the local patterns. Thus, the sustainability of the newly created institutions is precarious: a persistent tension emerged between trying to "impose a little Switzerland,"[1653] as one observer called it, and balancing these standards against the "need for locally sus-

---

1649 Cf. International Commission on Intervention and State Sovereignty. 2001. The Responsibility to Protect. Report of the International Commission on Intervention and State Sovereignty. Available online at http://www.iciss.ca/pdf/Commission-Report.pdf, last access on 15 March 2009. "[I]ntervention must be directed towards returning the society in question to those who live in it." Ibid.

1650 Cf. Chesterman 2004. Besides the risk of not living up to being a role model, what might be even more is that "[p]olitical values cannot simply be transfused or imposed." Traub 2000, p. 80.

1651 Chestermann 2004, p. 150.

1652 Cf. ibid., p. 247.

1653 Written interview with Dr. Tanja Hohe, former team member of UN Volunteers in East Timor, 30 September 2006.

tainable goals."[1654] In addition, UNTAET was supposed to be an international protectorate with all powers centralized in the hands of the SRSG/Transitional Administrator. He was allowed to take "all necessary means to fulfil the mandate"[1655] with the goal of establishing a Western-style state construct.[1656] At the end of the day, the state-building template in combination with UNTAET's comprehensive governing authority triggered criticisms of neo-colonialism.

Accountability Deficits

Like its predecessor in Kosovo, UNTAET suffered from severe accountability deficits.

> The stated aim of the United Nations Transitional Administration in East Timor is to effectively administer the country during the period of transition to a popularly elected government. However, effective, let alone democratic, administration is impossible while so little decision-making power is being given to East Timorese community and political organizations. Even the highest East Timorese body, the seven-member Transitional Council, has only a consultative role with UNTAET.[1657]

UNTAET is accountable only to the UN Secretary-General and the Security Council. While this does not automatically preclude it from implementing policies desired by the East Timorese people, it was still hard for the mission to meet local accountability.

The primary mechanism that had been established to cope with this deficit was ineffective:

> [A]n Ombudsperson was appointed in September 2000, but only became operational around May 2001 – even then without an UNTAET regulation establishing the institution's mandate. It engaged in some formal inquiries but [it lacked; ES] [...] both the mandate to investigate human rights and the institutional support of being part of an organization like the OSCE. It was generally seen as ineffective.[1658]

1654   Chesterman 2004, p. 247.
1655   UN Doc. S/1999/1272.
1656   "The mission was criticized, both from the inside and from the outside, for being a sort of neo-colonial power." Interview with a senior staff member of UNDPKO PBPS, New York, 15 September 2006. For the basic comparability of historic colonialism and UN interim administration, see Owen 2002.
1657   Green Left Weekly, January 19, 2000.
1658   Chesterman 2004, pp. 149-150.

Inevitable Waste

While a mission often faces shortages, there is also an element of waste, since the windows of time for fundamental information gathering and procurement overlap. The enormous and inappropriate expenses for drinking water of the mission staff represented one of these cases.

Not only money is wasted, but in this particular case, it resulted in a backlash against UNTAET's reputation yet again.

Bubble Economy

As it is the case with any international mission in a post-conflict territory, UNTAET created a parallel or bubble economy as the relatively wealthy mission personnel triggered the development of their own economic infrastructure. This negative influence worsened the prospects of Timorese economic sustainability.

Inadequate Expertise

UNTAET asked member states for (top level) administration experts. However, being an expert for, say, administration, in say, France, does not mean that this person is a good administrator in a post-conflict country if he or she lacks cultural adaptability skills. Templates and standards were applied that did not fit Timorese conditions.

Heterogeneity in CivPol

The international police officers, inexperienced as they were, applied the rules and laws that they knew from their home countries. Thus, the recruitment process was slow and did not function well, and the accelerated deployment took its tolls as the police officers interacted in an unfavorable way. Similarly, the due investigation of war crimes was severely slowed down because of poor institutional infrastructure, untrained CivPol officers, and bureaucratic divisions within UNTAET. As a consequence, a confused police force and an inert mission furthered their fair share of credibility problems.

Payroll Discrepancies

Due to the various goals and the comprehensiveness of UNTAET, it entailed, under
its aegis, a wide range of functions to be staffed and set up diverse terms of employment.[1659] These differences were a gateway not only for confusion but also for
social tensions.

Mismatch of UN Routines and Mandate Challenges

There was a pathological mismatch between UN routines and mandate challenges.
The capacity-building mandate could not be implemented by UNTAET, as "the
UN does not usually work that way."[1660] Inevitably, UNTAET witnessed short-
comings of Timorese training and integration.

UNTAET's training approach was a simple see-and-learn method, which did
not give the Timorese much responsibility or ownership, as did, for instance, the
"dual-desk approach" of joint decision-making in Eastern Slavonia or Kosovo.[1661]

Persistence of Communication Difficulties

Throughout the mission, UNTAET struggled with communication and translation
shortcomings. Due to the scarce translation capacities of the mission, official documents were at least initially published only in English. As a result, UNTAET could
not create transparency or even interact with the local population, which decreased
the prospects of ownership and the mission's legitimacy.

Effects of Earmarking

As with many complex peace operations, UNTAET suffered from "earmarking
effects".

1659 There was the international staff of UNTAET; Timorese working in the UNTAET struc-
      ture, mostly as translators, drivers, guards; locals, i.e. particularly exile Timorese working
      in the ETTA structure; and expats in TOKTEN. Those Timorese that were working in the
      most crucial functions, in ETTA, were given the lowest payments.
1660 Telephone interview with a senior staff member of UNTAET, 9 October 2006.
1661 Cf. National Democratic Institute. 2003. *Government Within Reach: A Report on the Views
      of East Timorese on Local Government.* Washington, DC: National Democratic Institute.
      The report is available online at http://www.ndi.org/node/13125, last access on 2 Novem-
      ber 2008.

The separation of recurrent cost financing (provided through the Consolidated Fund for East Timor) and reconstruction financing (provided from the Trust Fund) posed the most difficult problem. This arrangement made it difficult to incorporate funding from multiple sources into East Timor's budget because the funds could only be used for specific purposes. It was also a challenge to the synchronization of the reconstruction efforts. East Timorese civil servants needed to be recruited to manage the various projects, but project funds could not be used to pay their salaries. Thus, there was a dilemma in getting money for steps that needed to habe been taken before major reconstruction projects could begin.[1662]

The complex funding, dynamic post-conflict environment, and uncertainty of capacity-development were a bad match. "These differing and complex modes of aid provision created barriers to national ownership of the reconstruction planning process in the initial period, and prevented the integration of all funding sources into the national budget."[1663]

Role Conflict

Trying to live up to its role as a government, UNTAET omitted its responsibility of fostering Timorese civil society. Capacities to assume *both* roles were not sufficiently available. As a result, the promotion of civil society was neglected. The underdevelopment of a civil society resulted in a backlash on the prospect of a sustainable democratic political system.

When increasingly confronted with the realities and protests on-the-ground, internal discussions about the timeframe ensued. Proponents of this view were civil affairs staff, in particular, and they suggested a minimum one-year extension. Again, political considerations won out, complying with the preferences of the Security Council and member states, as well as with the pressure from Fretilin. In fact, each of UNTAET's international constituencies "provided incentives for UNTAET to minimize the short-term risks of failure and maximize visible returns on donor investments."[1664] The UN hazarded the consequence, namely the *de facto* failure to accomplish certain aspects of the mandate at the time of the mission's withdrawal.

1662   Dobbins et al. 2005, p. 174.
1663   Rohland and Cliffe 2002, p. ii, quoted in Dobbins et al. 2005, p. 174.
1664   Beauvais 2001, p. 1166.

4.2.3.3 Termination

Under the perspective of "tight coupling," UNTAET's termination was marred by the discrepancy between having to be finished and not having finished yet. The most innovative step in coping with the overall precariousness of a controlled exit consisted of outsourcing the planning of the termination process to an external team of experts.

Precariousness of a Controlled Exit

UNTAET's exit was precarious at all times. The devolution of the mission and the personnel cutbacks were expected to be a daunting task, as was the complex planning of the successor mission, UNMISET. Not only was there considerable time pressure, but the sensitivity towards internal and external obstructers increased: member states were impatient to finish their commitments, and local actors increasingly claimed that they should take over.

Vieira de Mello requested that the post-UNTAET planning be "outsourced" to an experienced team of experts who were operating directly on-the-ground. They operated the planning processes in a relatively clear, consistent, and functional manner.

Impeding Regulations

During the termination phase, UNTAET struggled with some unfortunate regulations. When it came to the job descriptions of the civilian advisers for UNMISET, bureaucratic provisions from headquarters had to be applied. This delayed the announcement process.

Such instances added up to be a considerable waste of time, particularly if they had to be corrected *ex post facto*. Better standard operating procedures for information processing, for instance, could have helped here.

The same interpretation holds for the handing over of assets from UNTAET to local administrators. Formal UN rules forbade this transfer, implying not only an interruption of Timorese reconstruction, but also high transportation costs for the UN in bringing these assets back to its material reserves. Fortunately, obstinate UNTAET staff were able to compromise with headquarters: they framed the need for these assets as essential to continued and controlled reconstruction.

Not Yet Finished

Many of the local Timorese who worked in the future administration were not yet ready to run the institutions, implying a state of precariousness.

The low level of local capacity was a fact and the low performance in capacity-building was one of UNTAET's major shortcomings. At least, however, UNTAET staff regularly organized inauguration rites, known from Timoerese traditions, when they formally handed over authority to their local coutnerparts. This added legitimacy to the new institutions and to those who were supposed to run them.

4.2.4 Path Dependence Deficiencies

UNTAET's "original sin" was the early end of formal East Timorese participation, triggered by Indonesian pressure and reinforced by UN rules, routines, and internal turf wars. These dynamics were locked into an inadequate technocratic policy of Timorese non-participation, which discredited the mission enormously. In a rigid move that did not conform to the rules, SRSG de Mello altered the course dramatically and established a structure of international-local co-governance.

Lock-in of Inappropriate Technocratic Implementation Approach

The imposition of DPKO as the lead agency was consistent with the institutional framework and previous assignments. However, the mission's strong civilian emphasis, the capacity-building requirements, and the calls for East Timorese involvement did not correspond to the genuine principles and capacities of the agency, assuming a Timorese *terrra nullis*. In line with this assumption, UNTAET devised an incremental technocratic approach. The vision for Timorese integration resembled one of "unconflicted change."[1665] Starting with a technocratic international administration, East Timorese had to gradually "buy in" to the structure. While the idea was a rational one as such, it conveyed an unrealistically overconfident view, while not fitting the conditions on-the-ground. Nearly every stage of the implementation process encountered problematic constraints, be it in international staff running the administration, international staff hiring locals, international staff training locals, or international staff having themselves replaced. The management of the complex interactions of these various elements was underesti-

---

1665 Cf. Chapter III.2.2.1.

mated.[1666] In the end, a policy path that deferred the integration or participation of East Timorese was locked in.[1667] The technocratic approach did not work and Timorese frustration cumulated.

De Mello recognized early on that the Timorese were reluctant to accept the UN transition approach, and started dealing intensely with local leaders. Yet, the increasing frustration of the Timorese called for further measures if failure wanted to be averted.

Only de Mello's fiercely contested decision to go for a power-sharing arrangement via the ETTA could put an end to the inadequate policy. In a "critical juncture," UNTAET brought about a *rupture* from its state-building approach. "The original plan had reflected the Kosovo model, and then it had to adjust according to realities."[1668] A radical redesign and expansion of the state-building approach ensued, at least structurally, with the NC becoming more representative and wtih the creation of ETTA. It was a particularly valuable move – after intense efforts to convince donors to pay the recurrent budget – to grant ETTA its own budget, without earmarks, which created considerable financial slack for the future governmental bodies. That being said, the SRSG/Transitional Administrator retained full authority.

Table 8: Ill-Structuredness, Path Dependence, Accidents, and Coping Strategies

	Ill-Structuredness	Pathology	Accident	Coping
Transition	*UN Rules, UN Capacities, Time Pressure; Accumulation of Cognitive Biases*	*Default Non-Participation Policy and Adherence to It*	*Loss of Legitimacy, Precarious Sustainability*	*Rupture: Re-design of Technocratic Approach, Co-Government (against UN Rule)*

1666   Thus, the combination of cognitive biases with the tight coupling pathology aggravated the difficulties.

1667   "CNRT participation in the planning process would only have complicated a process that had to be completed in the shortest possible time. One member of the planning team said that he was aware that the East Timorese would have preferred some form of parallel structure that would have given them a formal consultative role, but stressed the difficulty of coming up with a formula that would have met this desire in such a short period of time. [...] An informant who was close to the process noted, 'With hindsight the lack of consultation is really shocking; but it also would have been impossibly complex to bring all the different Timorese interests to the table as well. In a way, the fact they were inaccessible made it much easier. It was hard enough to deal with the existing [...] variety of views among Member States [...]. It was almost easier for UNTAET to set up from this ground zero position with little local politics to worry about.'" CSDG, "East Timor Report," para. 26.

1668   Interview with a senior staff member of UNTAET, New York, 23 November 2006.

4.2.5 Conclusion and Further Findings

Nor aught so good but, strain'd from that fair use,
Revolts from true birth, stumbling on abuse.
Virtue itself turns vice, being misapplied [...].[1669]

Just like a cure turns to poison with the wrong dosage, a less ambitious mandate and less exclusive implementation approach might have better served the purpose of a transition to independence in East Timor. UNTAET had more authority than necessary; international staff did too much on their own instead of involving the Timorese; it was a well-equipped mission but it took it an awful lot of time until they could be allocated and distributed relatively coherently and adequately; it had enough personnel, yet the quality of its staff was low and the mission struggled with underperforming, and, at times, destructive staff behavior. With time, UNTAET came to terms with its deficits in information gathering and processing. SRSG Vieira de Mello can be given particular credit for approaching critical situations with unconventional means. At the end of the day, UNTAET displayed more pathologies and less coping capacity than UNTAES. An obvious part of the explanation is that the mandate and the undertaken activities were more encompassing in East Timor than in Eastern Slavonia. Still, more interaction with the Timorese "would have changed a lot."[1670]

It took the mission a rather long time until it started to cope in a comprehensive way, but at the end of the day, UNTAET prevented pathologies from becoming so virulent as to provoke major accidents. Coping strategies of vigilance and incremental learning, of proceeding analytically and setting priorities, "playing" the UN system, creating organizational and time slack, increasingly building-up informal relationships with local leaders, and of daring a decisive *rupture* of the initial transition approach eventually proved crucial. Partly, the coping strategies that I have observed represent semblances of textbook recommendations. However, one could also obersve coping approaches that have not yet been covered systematically by the existing theories and which may contribute to inductive theory-building.[1671]

Cognitive biases were fairly virulent and could not always be coped with sufficiently. Where they existed, the textbook recommendations of vigilance and decision-staggering had positive effects. Furthermore, expertise was assembled by involving the capacities of the diaspora. However, a negative side effect emerged.

1669 Shakespeare, William. 2000. *Romeo and Juliet*. Edited by Jill L. Levenson et al. Oxford: Oxford University Press, Act II, Scene 3. I quote these paragraphs remembering the analogy to the classic tragedy that I proclaimed in the "Introduction."

1670 Interview with a senior staff member of the UN DPKO and former Cabinet Minister in ETTA, New York, 23 November 2006.

1671 Cf. Chapter III.2.3.

Unfortunately, but characteristic of the mission, the textbook recommendation of coping by communication was not adopted.

Concerning principal-agent problems, the recommendation of more control was realized, for instance, by establishing small working groups during the termination phase. Most problems of deficient agent behavior – and this concerned mostly mission personnel – were solved by marginalizing them, for instance by relocating them to the districts. One could say that, in an interim administration, there is just not enough time to create a culture of common goals and values. This might have indeed been the case in East Timor. On the other hand, I would say that peace operations have a tremendous potential to appeal to idealistic goals, and that there may be apt opportunities to create a "common vision."

The creation of slack and incremental learning were, where applied, useful strategies for coping with tight coupling of complex interactions – as suggested by the literature. Vigilance and framing actions of the decision-makers also contributed to positive results.

Certain assets were important for the application of coping strategies. Parallel to my observations of the UN mission in Eastern Slavonia, UNTAET also disposed over some crucial advantages. Prior to the implementation of the civilian mandate, the existence of a leading nation for peacekeeping, namely Australia, was important to reinstall security as a precondition for all further actions. A clear end status along with the consummate backing of the international community, as well as the mission's abundant financial resources was also an advantage. Furthermore, its cooperation with a range of international actors helped to cope with the overwhelming mandate; UNTAET benefited greatly from the UNV work force, and from their understanding of the situation on-the-ground. Eventually, de Mello's leadership and the leverage he had with the UN system were extremely useful. Not only did he adapt to the difficult impositions placed on him in East Timor by developing his own coping strategies, but he was also able to bring the UN to commit to genuine innovations in peacebuilding that saved the entire venture at a precarious turning point.

De Mello's leadership quality rested, I argue, in his capacity as a "boundary spanner" within the UN system and towards local actors and as an "institutional entrepreneur" who managed precarious trajectories. A boundary spanning unit is a structured link or point of contact between a given organization and other actors in its environment.[1672] While the original conceptualization of boundary spanning roles, as developed by Thompson and Aldrich, refers to organizational units, I apply it to the leader of the mission as am organizational entity of its own right. The SRSG of a transitional administration fits the definition of a boundary spanner, as he

---

1672 Cf. Aldrich, Howard E. 1979. *Organizations and Environments*. Englewood Cliffs: Prentice-Hall; Thompson 1967.

occupies a crucial position within the mission and is its main link to headquarters, other states, other organizations, and to local actors in the "host" territory. Sergio Vieira de Mello enacted his position particularly well, using his knowledge about the UN system and the surrounding political processes to get the latitude he needed to operate a challenging redesign. By determinedly occupying so-called zones of uncertainty, where guidelines were ambiguous or where diverging perspectives on one issue needed to be handled, he successfully resolved dilemmatic situations. He did the same vis-à-vis his own staff, when he and his senior leadership team specified a highly complex and ambiguous mandate by identifying priorities, and elaborating upon a transition schedule at the beginning of the mission. In fact, many of his best decisions required him to bend or break bureaucratic rules.[1673] De Mello also acted as an institutional entrepreneur: he recognized UNTAET's legitimacy problem with the locals early on, used his diplomatic skills and experience to deal with people, and established a close relationship with CNRT leaders, thus attenuating the negative effects of the *terra nullis* policy. De Mello understood that he had to leave known paths and develop a new, a more suitable design for the transition. On the background of this consideration, learning in East Timor also implied "un-learning:" the routines and standard operating procedures of a peacekeeping mission, as well as the personal experience of senior staff were gathered in contexts that were (very) different to the challenge on this island. As, by definition, routines equal human memory at the organizational level,[1674] the revision of their former routines was a crucial competence.[1675]

1673 Cf. Seibel, Wolfgang. Forthcoming. *Internationale Politik und lernende Verwaltung: UN-Friedensmissionen zwischen politischer und bürokratischer Logik.* Unpublished manuscript, on file with the author.

1674 Cf. Pawlowski, Peter and Neubauer, Katja. 2001. "Organisationales Lernen," in: Weik, Elke and Lang, Rainhart, eds., *Moderne Organisationstheorien – Eine sozialwissenschaftliche Einführung.* Wiesbaden: Lang, pp. 253-284.

1675 A more consummate involvement in un-learning would have benefited the mission even more: the internal staffing structure of an interim administration resembled that of UN headquarters itself which makes it questionable if such a system can produce the nucleus of an administration that a post-colonial development country is able to inherit. What should have been done is develop a civil service model – with respective salary and benefit structures, work planning and evaluation tools, career patterns et cetera – that has good prospects of being sustainable. Here, however, known standards and procedures were adhered. On this note, un-learning is extremely difficult. Cf. Weick, Karl E. and Westley, Frances. 2003. "Organizational Learning: Affirming an Oxymoron." In: S.R. Clegg et al., eds., *Handbook of Organization Studies,* London: Sage, pp. 440-458, p. 440, "Organization and learning are essentially antithetical. [...] to learn is to disorganize and to increase variety. To organize is to forget and to reduce variety."

VI. "Success Against the Odds": Findings

The transitional administrations under scrutiny found themselves in the midst of an "intrinsicate knot" of complex and often conflicting requirements and goals, suffering from uncertainty and time pressure. This thesis aimed to decompose the diverse ill-structured conditions and their pathological consequences. It also explored sensible approaches of coping and could identify crucial advantages required for "fit" coping. By systemizing, contrasting, and synthesizing the vast amount of observations discovered in the case studies, the following chapter delivers the answers to the research questions posed in the introduction.

1. Contrasting the Transitional Managements of UNTAES and UNTAET

There are patterns of pathologies that appear in both cases. We see that all of the hypothesized pathologies operate and trigger accidents in UNTAES as well as UNTAET. Likewise, similar general patterns of problems and dilemmas appeared in both cases under scrutiny: the tension between short-term and long-term goals, the "dual mandate dilemma," the "democracy trap," the vulnerability of the transitional government, the dilemma between efficient governance and legitimate governance, the precariousness of controlled exit, and the risk of inadequate policy lock-in persisted in UNTAES as well as in UNTAET.

In complex peace operations, there is a tension between short-term and longer-term considerations. The proponents of a short-term "getting-things-fone" approach may clash with the supporters of a longer-term, sustainability approach. While the perspectives are not fundamentally contradicting, a basic difficulty consists of the diverging views on the available time horizon and on the allocation of resources. Incalculable extensions of the intervention that may undermine a mission's legitimacy needs and a premature withdrawal that thwarts sustainable results are two problems that may follow from "solving" this dilemma in a biased way.[1676] Both scenarios contribute to the transitional administration's precariousness and fragility.

A similar tension arises when a complex peace operation takes on government duties (and becomes a "transitional administration"). The operational requirements and the legitimization needs become opposed to each other, creating a so-called "dual mandate tension."[1677] In acting as a mission, a transitional administration executes its power through agenda-setting, decision-making authority, and its veto

1676 Cf. Hampson 1996.
1677 Cf. Beauvais 2001.

capacity.[1678] As a government, it is responsible for the population of the war-torn territory and needs their support to implement the mission's comprehensive mandate, thus relying much more on participative, interactive, and accountability-ensuring procedures. The tension is usually "solved" in favor of the first imperative. The resulting phenomenon has been called the policy of "Do-as-I-Say-not-as-I-Do."[1679]

Third, the imperative of building democratic government institutions implies a much more political approach than "normal" peace operations usually entail. Resulting questions are,

> Whether to hold elections, and on what basis; which currency to adopt; whether to consult with local interlocutors, and how widely; whether to promote the re-integration of ethnic communities or to accept the *de facto* division; what role to give women in the reconstructed polity; which curriculum to teach in schools; whether to allow public ownership of enterprises; what limits, if any, to place on the content of party manifestos.[1680]

There is no alternative to "importing" democracy: resting on the background of the changes in the international politics paradigm after the Cold War, democracy promotion has established itself as a means to further the goals of the UN Charter.[1681] The policy conveys inherent pitfalls though. One, there is the clash with the fundamental rationale of common peace operations, which is to not get involved in political matters. Two, a one-size-fits-all model may not suit all regions, as political traditions may not be complementary with the notions of, say, individualism or open controversy. In the most extreme cases, "importing" the ideals of foreign political systems may be perceived as neo-colonialism.[1682] Here, the transitional administration runs the risk of losing its legitimacy in the eyes of the host population, which may not only leave the UN with a tarnished reputation, but may also prevent political institution-building since the key actors, i.e. the locals, will not be participating.[1683] I called this hitch the "democracy trap." Three, while a transitional administration has *de jure* all-encompassing governing authority in the territory, it

---

1678   Cf. ibid., p. 7.
1679   Chestermann 2002b.
1680   Caplan 2005, p. 3.
1681   In fact, neither the UN Charter nor its preamble does mention the word "democracy." However, the post-Cold War rationale of the UN has become that the three basic purposes of the world organization – as declared in the preamble to the Charter – can best be attained by promoting democracy: the "scourge of war" may be avoided in a democratic political system; the "faith in fundamental human rights" is theoretically and empirically linked to democratic practices; and a democracy is "fitter" to "promote [...] social progress and better standards of life." Cf. Rich and Newmann 2004, p. 9.
1682   For a historical review of imports of domestic institutions as an instrument of power politics, see Owen 2002.
1683   For differentiated discussions about the external promotion of democracy, see Newman and Rich 2004; for a historic contextualization of the phenomenon, see Owen 2002.

is still reliant on the support and participation of the host population in order to have a chance at success. This reliance, however, bears a risk that a highly interdependent and thus vulnerable governance system will be created. As Seibel points out:

> *Die Störung oder gar Unterbrechung der Verwaltungsleistungen bleibt einfach und kann für die lokalen Konfliktparteien gerade wegen der auf die internationale Ebene „durchschlagenden" Wirkung attraktiv sein. Virulent wird dieses Problem, wenn die neuen, in der Regel fragilen zivilgesellschaftlichen Strukturen unterschiedlicher ethnischer, religiöser oder politischer Gruppen in Zusammenhang mit derjenigen Krise stehen, welche die internationale Intervention ausgelöst hat. Die gut gemeinte Förderung zivilgesellschaftlicher Strukturen kann dann Machtzentren stabilisieren, die den Zielen des internationalen Mandats und den Zwecke der Interimsverwaltung eher abträglich als zuträglich sind.[1684]*

Fourth, a dilemma concerning the participation of multiple international actors exists.[1685] The necessity to assemble diverse skills and resources and the need for wide political legitimacy counterveils efficient governance and accountability.

> *Die Beteiligung zahlreicher Nationen auf der einen Seite und die Verflechtung von Ordnungs-, Hilfs- und Dienstleistungsaufgaben bei Förderung des lokalen Potentials zur Selbsthilfe erzeugt eine beträchtliche organisatorische Vielfalt. „Im Feld" sind militärische und zivile, staatliche und nicht-staatliche, ausländische und inländische Organisationen tätig, die starke Unterschiede im Hinblick auf Organisationskultur, Ressourcen und Professionalität aufweisen. Auch hier stellen sich erhebliche Steuerungsprobleme, die wiederum mit Problemen der Ressourcenmobilisierung und der Legitimation verknüpft sind.[1686]*

The dilemma is repeated within the UN peacekeeping system itself. The UN needs to obtain infrastructural and military resources from a diverse range of member states in order to ensure broad legitimization and sufficient capacities. The multinationality and heterogeneity of this support system produce political as well as administrative coordination problems, though. They might – and often do – result in inefficient governance.

Fifth, UNTAES as well as UNTAET lacked controlled exit strategies: local spoilers tried to exploit and manipulate the deadline to serve their ends, while the international staff in the transitional administrations struggled with the organization of post-mission planning.

Eventually, both missions experienced dysfunctions resulting from a policy lock-in. Fortunately, both missions were able to cope with it by means of a rigid change of course, initiated by their SRSGs.

1684 Seibel, Wolfgang. 2006. International Interim Administration: Binding Bounded Rationality. Internal Working Paper, on file with the author.
1685 Cf. UN Department of Peacekeeping Operations, Lessons Learned Unit 1999.
1686 Seibel 2006.

That said, other elements of the transition processes differed considerably. Three aspects are particularly striking. First, UNTAET exhibited more susceptibility towards the cognitive bias pathology, especially during the first half of the mission. I hypothesize a connection between this observation and the overly ambitious mandate. Secondly, the lock-in of an inadequate policy was more severe in UN-TAET: the *terra nullis* assumption produced a range of further pathologies and persisted comparatively long. Generally, UNTAET exhibited more pathologies and a stronger portion of cognitive biases than UNTAES, which was probably related to the more consummate complexity of its mission. On the other hand, UNTAES had a harder time dealing with principal-agent pathologies. The latter may be explained by the higher hostility level. Based on this observation, one might hypothesize that more thorough *ex ante* mediation and peacekeeping efforts would have made the peacebuilding environment more conducive to the transitional administration, as such actions are designed to reduce the level of hostility and make the former conflict parties comply more consistently with the international mission. At the end of the day, UNTAES seems to have a more comprehensive record of (successful) coping. The following paragraphs delve deeper into these issues.

2. Ill-Structured Conditions

No two missions are the same. Nonetheless, a range of pathology-inflicting conditions were similar for the two multidimensional peace operations under examination. These are the dysfunctional infrastructure, the nationals' lack of experience with liberal democratic political institutions, shortfalls in planning and in early peacebuilding financing, limited headquarters support structures, rules that could countervail the mission's efficacy, and ambiguous member state support. The latter was particularly eminent in the East Timor case. UNTAET also struggled with lower levels of local capacity, a more alien socio-cultural system, an extremely ambitious yet ambivalent mandate, and more resource allocation ambiguities than did UNTAES. A precarious security situation was less of an issue for UNTAET though – compared to UNTAES, where security concerns prevailed.[1687] On the other hand, UNTAES was not severely challenged by a virtual lack of local capacities. Eventually, just as UNTAES was constantly challenged with spoiler attacks, the most crucial challenge in East Timor rested in *adequate* political and administrative institution and capacity-building. Table 9 summarizes the ill-structured conditions under which both missions had to operate.

1687   In fact, the comparison holds for the majority of peace operations where security is often *the* most serious challenge.

Table 9: Ill-Structured Conditions of UNTAES and UNTAET

		UNTAES	UNTAET
Local Conditions	**Local Hostility**	Two major ethnic factions, with populist national leaders, long history of conflict, and high coherence; ongoing recalcitrance but peace agreement signed Serb paramilitary groups displaying open hostility towards mission; reluctance by "official" leadership and population, Croats and Serbs alike vis-à-vis UNTAES	Rapidly changing security situation: from Indonesian colonial suppression of East Timorese population and independent fighters to peace agreement to post-ballot deterioration to INTERFET intervention/Indonesians and pro-integration militias taking flight to eventual pacification of East Timor. Only one coherent faction left, with strong and integrative leading figures High input-legitimacy and support for UNTAET as the agent of East Timorese independence by population and leadership alike. Uncertainty on internal Timorese divisions and dynamics
	Local Capacity	Sharply decreased GDP and living standard Severely damaged infrastructure, particularly transport and electricity Crucial refugee challenge Brain drain Comparatively high education and capacity, yet no experience with democratic, liberal rules and weak local political personae, particularly at the Serb side	One of the world's lowest GDPs and living standards; agriculture and fisheries prevailing; extremely limited formal education; destruction of the anyway scarce infrastructures Devastating refugee and IDP situation; traumatized colonized society Given destroyed records and Indonesian flight: UNTAET uncertainty about available capacities and local governance structures Segregated topography, diversity of ethnicities and languages One-issue political agenda, no experience with democracy or "statehood," but entrenched local socio-cultural system Well-educated diaspora elite
International Political-Institutional Conditions	**Member State Support**	High international support for Balkan crisis resolution, yet clear emphasis on short-term mandate and success, given UNSC's limited attention span and donors' ticking clocks	High international support for what was supposed to become a UN success story, yet Indonesia remained ambiguous in its support and had other member states and the UNSC comply with its inert stance—in line with UNSC's limited attention span and donors' ticking clocks, and member states generic reluctance to UN state-building/-running activities
	UN Capacity	UNTAES most comprehensive mission at that time Discrepancy between personnel capacity, expertise, and challenges on-the-ground	Most comprehensive mission at that time Personnel shortage Discrepancy between personnel capacity, expertise and challenges on-the-ground No meta-approach
	UN Rules, Funding	Rules of impartiality and neutrality Narrow (Chinese) definition of Chapter VII Comprehensive funds from the assessed budget, but owing peacebuilding resources, particularly for quick reaction projects for reconciliation	Rules of impartiality and neutrality Indonesian impairment of planning on the horizon Comprehensive funds from the assessed budget, but owing peacebuilding resources, particularly for quick reaction projects for providing basic services
	Time Pressure, Mandate Complexity	One plus one year for demilitarization, refugee return, security maintenance, establishment of multiethnic police force, minority protection, elections, institution-building- and transformation, and reconciliation	Two and a half years for building a state from scratch High local expectations for quick managing

I modify the initial conceptualization of ill-structured conditions, as described in Chapter III, to include the "local socio-economic system" dimension, and to differentiate "local hostility" into "hostility among factions" and "hostility towards the international mission," because to what extent hostility exists between parties to the conflict or is directed at the international administration makes a difference for the transitional management. Similarly, "local capacity" conditions ought to include the socio-cultural system of the post-conflict territory, as it proved to be decisive for the development of pathologies, particularly in the case of UNTAET.

3. Pathologies and Accidents

Ill-structured conditions create a stressful environment where organizational pathologies for the mission are likely to emerge. Given the virulent condition of hostility in the Eastern Slavonian case, the dominance of both principal-agent pathologies and negative spillover, resulting from the tight coupling of complex interactions, is not exactly surprising, whereas pathologies of cognitive bias were most frequent[1688] in the Timorese transitional management, and a path dependent development set the mission on the brink of collapse.[1689] Specifically, UNTAET suffered from insufficient generation of information and action alternatives, and it also regularly applied inadequate analogies. They were particularly prominent during the initial delineation phase; adding up to each other, they caused the mission's path dependence deficiency at its later stages. The dominance of UNTAET's cognitive bias pathology can be attributed to its greater scope, its even more complex mandate, and the very "newness" of state-building from scratch.

The principal-agent perspective is relevant to understanding deficient behavior, and deserves closer examination in both cases. A typical lack of commitment is observable in diverse arenas, by diverse actors, with diverse impacts. The member states' ambiguous support of UN state-running operations furthered the consequences of inadequate and under-qualified staff, and their considerateness of Indonesia's wishes impaired proper mission planning. Not only was the international support ambiguous, but it was also conditional. Sponsoring member states are more likely to spend their money on visible, symbolic projects, which are not necessarily the most essential ones. Third, the mission can be ambiguous itself, as the feud over the CEP between UNTAET and the World Bank indicated. On the other hand, the different international and local agencies, acting as "agents" to the SRSG during the transition, all had their own agendas, and accordingly, may have counteracted the goals of the transitional administration. Some of the observations about the

---

1688   The frequency measure is relative to the total of observations.
1689   Cf. Chapter V.4.2.4.

principal-agent pathology could be specified by the veto player concept. This theorem describes actors who are indispensable for the implementation of the mandate, contributing competences and resources, and creating legitimacy or ownership, but who, at the same time, purposefully obstruct the interim administration's transition agenda.[1690] Results become biased towards the preferences of the veto players or the decision-making becomes deadlocked. That also means that the theorem may likewise be a sensible starting point for the analysis of obstructions that are not enacted by local spoilers, but by players related to the UN intervention itself. Within the UN system there might be actors who seem to have an interest in impeding (parts of) the transition process, or who do so unintentionally. In the chapter on the "Outlook of Future Research," I will elaborate a bit more on this thought.

There are two additional observations that broaden the concept of the principal-agent dilemma, namely overperformance as well as the phenomenon of agents becoming principals. First, while principal-agent problems conventionally denote a lack of commitment, an overperforming actor displays a high level of commitment that may be valuable for short-run accomplishments, but that impairs long-term interests, such as the sustainability of political and social institutions by apt local "owners." Secondly, however, the very requirement of ownership can lead to unfavorable results if it is confused with abandoning the steering wheel and ceding too much power to seemingly legitimate actors, such as Fretilin in East Timor whose vested interests often differed from those of the international mission. As consequence, the transition policy looses coherence. In Eastern Slavonia, the agents of the transition often acted as spoilers, obstructing the implementation of the mandate. Most of the UNTAES' principal-agent dilemmas related to the necessity of Croat involvement and agreement – which basically brought the "fox to watch the geese." Yet, peace processes will always be dependent upon the involvement of at least some of the former malefactors in order to bring about a sustainable arrangement.[1691]

The pathologies furthered two patterns of accidents, respectively. UNTAET had lots of trouble retaining its local support, and, for a long time into the mission, failed to provide adequate institutions. It experienced many setbacks in its schedule, mainly resulting from internal flaws such as the *terra nullis* assumption. As delays cumulated, so did Timorese frustration, decreasing the mission's initially high input-legitimacy. In UNTAES' case, the most pertinent observations were the delays and procrastinations that resulted from purposeful obstructions of the mission's transition policy.

1690   I discuss this idea in fn. 1720.
1691   In turn, it will always be a worthwile act to analyze the coping behavior of the "international custodians of peace." Cf. Stedman 1997.

4. Coping, Coping Fit, and Advantages

The ill-structured conditions of complex peace operations are not to be expected to change anytime soon, and they will keep on suffering from pathological patterns. They will remain precarious ventures, resembling a situation of constant crisis. A crisis, defined as a "non-desirable situation which might in fact be created and perpetuated by the same organizational actors who try to solve it,"[1692] is no static phenomenon though. It moves between the extremes of complete failure and relative stability. Thus, when one interprets complex and pathology-prone peace operations in terms of dynamic crises, three conclusions can be derived. First, pathologies make an already critical venture worse, and move it towards failure. Second, a crisis is not doomed to result in failure, but relative stability can be achieved if pathologies are met by what I call coping or contingency strategies. Third, from a meta-theoretical perspective, the above interpretation of complex peace operations as dynamic crises implies a specific ontological position, namely that structural factors and factors of agency are mutually dependent and influence each other. That means that the conditions and the structure of a critical venture set the parameters in which pathologies and coping strategies develop, while the latter can influence the structure of the crisis – towards failure or relative stability – in turn. In a longer-term perspective, although not covered by this study, pathologies and coping strategies can also change the ill-structured conditions under which they operate, by, for instance, changing the conflict structure on-the-ground, building new institutions in the conflict-ridden territory, convincing member states to spent more time, money, and pay more attention, or by triggering organizational learning on standard operating procedures. This phenomenon of "structuration"[1693] could be a fruitful research topic for future studies.

Coping

In this study, I have examined how ill-fated peace operations were able to succeed against the odds. Both of the missions under scrutiny were able to redirect a critical venture into relative stability. I suggest that fit coping made this possible.

In the transition of Eastern Slavonian, the buy-in provisions and people-orientated actions, in combination with determined leadership action, credible threats, and a proactive "floor approach" to the mandate's implementation, contributed to the positive result. The actions listed created slack. Importantly, the radical redesign

---

1692   Thiétart, Raymond-Alain and Forgues, Bernard. 1997. "Action, Structure and Chaos." *Organization Studies* 18, pp. 119-143, p. 120.
1693   Cf. fn 128.

of the tranistional institutions helped UNTAES to live up to the tight transition schedule.

UNTAET also brought some effective coping strategies to the table. Resembling UNTAES' experience, a radical *rupture* with the initial technocratic, over-performing approach saved UNTAET from failure. The effectiveness of this measure was decreased, however, for it was put into action too late. Similar to Klein's actions in Eastern Slavonia, de Mello had to break rules in order to lower the chances of failure. Yet, while Klein and his senior staff choose to "seek forgiveness rather than permission," de Mello decided to present the UN Secretariat with different options and consequences, trying to convince and push them in a particular direction at the discussion table. It was helpful that he knew the system and its rules. In UNTAET's termination phase, the outsourcing of the liquidation and follow-on planning by a team of experts not formerly part of the mission was a smart move, as it furthered effective downscaling and results-oriented planning. Another important coping feature was based on UNTAET's very purpose of jumpstarting Timor's transition to independence. Despite recurrent and often self-inflicted setbacks, UNTAET was still the facilitator of independence and this was its trump card in gaining local support. In fact, a framing of the mission in even stronger terms would have been a commendable act.

The various strategies observed with the two transitional administrations can be grouped according to two aspects: according to their mode of operation, and along the dimension of structure and agency.

First, the modus operandi of the coping strategies allows for a categorization into nine different sets. These are: analysis, negotiation, control, cooperation and integration, communication, change, slack enhancement, framing and symbolic action, and self-regulation.

Analytical coping strategies increase decisions' rationality and their "informedness." Looking at both, UNTAES and UNTAET, successful analytical coping strategies were vigilant planning, vigilant use of available resources, vigilant readjustment, use of external expertise, analysis of comparative cases, setting priorities and decision staggering, benchmark setting, and the establishment of small working groups.

Coping strategies that consist of negotiation tactics are designed to force obstructers into compliance, potentially implying a threat. In specific, agenda-setting, browbeating (backed by inter-organizational linkage or by the international community), using political leverage granted by local leaders against lower-level spoilers, playing spoilers off one another, cross-cutting deals, creating a win-win situation, blaming, issue linkage, and the bridging of stalemate situations through interim solutions proved to be useful in the cases under scrutiny.

Coping by control denotes mission behavior where external as well as internal spoilers were eliminated or reversed based on the authority and the hierarchical power position given to the mission leadership. The following coping strategies can be abstracted out into this set: physically enacting robustness, eliminating provocative local figures, dismissing delinquents, excluding spoiling NGOs, rolling-out under-performing staff, and gradual mission downsizing while retaining authority.

Coping strategies of integration and cooperation operate by including diverse actors in a given policy, making them co-operate, and thus, creating synergies and cohesion among various actor groups. In this category of strategies belong: co-opting local leaders, hand-picking trustworthy locals, triggering positive spillover through cooperation with local key figures, preserving continuity of institutions, adopting a facilitator role and transforming structures incrementally, providing extensive information and consultation with the local minority, providing local minority buy-in in the transition process, institutionalizing minority representation in future political structures, pacifying unemployed veterans through a large police service, providing for informal get-togethers with former political contestants, evoking a sense of community, establishing economic measures at the communal level, coordinating international mandate extension support, convincing staff to change hats and to work in the successor mission), and promoting cooperation with international organizations and NGOs.

Communicative coping strategies avoid or attenuate pathologies by spreading sufficient information about certain issues. Vis-à-vis the local population, a mission could attenuate unfavorable developments by a plain, open communication style, establishing a public information campaign, and institutionalizing talks between the parties to the conflict. Internally and vis-à-vis cooperation partners, the following behavior proved fruitful: establishing regular staff and interagency meetings at all working levels, playing the transparency card vis-à-vis cooperation partners, openly communicating within the mission, maintaining good informal relations with officers at headquarters, and maintaining an open reporting style towards the Secretariat and the Council.

Coping strategies of change denote innovative, discontinuing or even disruptive actions, thus correcting a previously inadequate course of decision-making and action taking. Observations included: re-designing the transition approach, changing negotiation style (in the sense of becoming more strict), creating a transition-supporting agency with the local counterparts, establishing external training and reconciliation workshops (for civilian administrators and the transitional police force), re-framing policies as more transparent, and incremental learning.

Coping strategies of slack enhancement consist of increasing the mission's financial, temporal, or organizational leeway. It is the largest category of coping and should thus be included in any recommendation on how to improve the performance of complex peace operations. For convenient reading, the list of successful coping behavior is organized in bullet points:

- Designing flexible "Janus deadline"
- Falling back on UN personnel and equipment that had been present in the region
- Outsourcing troop transport
- Adopting a "floor approach" to mandate implementation
- "Seeking forgiveness rather than permission"
- De-coupling from headquarters
- Creating "surprise slack" through non-compliance with formal rules
- Raising local revenues
- Furthering inter-organizational linkages
- Creating economic leverage, e.g. through the backing of powerful member states
- Donor conferences
- Including new and able donors
- Establishing funding network
- Creating transparency and turning pledges into high-profile issues, e.g. by establishing a Donor Coordination Unit
- Creating time and financial slack through security appeals, e.g. by extending mission deadline using appeals to security concerns vis-à-vis the Security Council
- Direct lobbying of the SRSG/TA
- Informal handling of resource shortages by drawing upon SRSG/TA connections
- Informal deals on conflict issues
- Establishing informal relationships with local leaders
- Enhancing enforcement credibility, e.g. by having armed Special Forces mingle with unarmed CivPol
- Circumventing impeding regulations, e.g. by re-labelling "treaty" to "affidavit"
- Mission leadership promoting pro-activeness and hands-on attitude of international staff
- Mission leadership promoting generic people-orientation with outreach efforts
- Creating work slack through the use of UNVs
- Establishing and communicating a clear political end status for the territory
- Extending election deadline flexibly by falling back on governing authority

- (Maintaining mandate ambiguity)
- (Using diaspora capacities)

"Maintaining mandate ambiguity" and "using diaspora capacities" are put in brackets since they had only partial success.

Coping by framing and symbolic actions consists of appeals to salient norms of the respective constituency and thus make decisions accepted and resonated positively with the relevant audience. In specific, UNTAES and UNTAET were successful by making commitment visible for the locals, by framing the mission positively by remembering locals that the UN is the agent of independence (in East Timor), by framing actions that do not comply with the rules as being conducive to the overall transition goal towards headquarters, by triggering a comprehensive successor mission arrangement by appealing to security concerns, and by making use of traditional rituals through symbolic a hand-over of the mission.

The capacity shortage of a mission had a also a positive side-effect: it contained virulent over-performance. This final *"coping strategy" of self-regulation* stands apart, though, as it denotes a structural automatism and not a deliberate decision.[1694]

The second categorization results from a consideration of the duality of agency and structure. Coping strategies are *eo ipso* an agency phenomenon as they describe the decisions and actions by a (boundedly rational) actor to deal with a difficult situation. One can, however, differentiate the coping strategies of an actor *per comparationem ad aliquem effectum,* i.e. by means of a comparison of the respective strategy's effect and related emergent phenomena. If they are targeted at particular individuals or single institutional actors, such as the exclusion of certain spoilers or counteractive NGOs, we can talk about agency-related coping strategies. If a coping strategy affects a new structural arrangement that has direct effects on the transition process, for instance resulting in a negotiated agreement, we talk about structural coping strategies.

The typology that results from the application of both grouping rationales is presented below.

1694 In future studies, more observations might be added to these sets.

Table 10: Coping Strategies

		Agency	Structure
Analysis		Vigilant planning	Establishing small working groups
		Vigilant use of available resources	
		Vigilant readjustment	
		Using external expertise	
		Analysis of comparative cases	
		Setting priorities and decision staggering	
		Benchmark setting	
Negotiation		Browbeating (backed by inter-organizational linkage or by the international community)	Agenda-setting
		Using political leverage granted by local leaders against lower-level spoilers	Cross-cutting deals
			Creating a win-win situation
		Playing spoilers off one another	Bridging through interim solutions
		Blaming	Issue linkage
Control		Physically enacting robustness	Gradual mission downsizing while retaining authority
		Eliminating provocative local figures	
		Dismissing delinquents	
		Excluding spoiling NGOs	
		Rolling-out under-performing staff	
Cooperation and Integration		Co-opting local leaders	Triggering positive spillover through cooperation with local key figures
		Hand-picking trustworthy locals	
		Providing extensive information/consultation for minority	Preserving continuity of institutions
		Evoking a sense of community (with clothes and socializing)	Adopting facilitator role and transforming structures incrementally
			Providing local minority buy-in in the transition process
			Institutionalizing minority representation in future political structure
			Pacifying unemployed veterans through a large police service
			Providing for informal get-togethers with former contestants
			Establishing economic measures at the communal level
			Coordinating international mandate extension support
			Convincing staff to change hats (successor mission)
			Promoting cooperation with IOs and NGOs
Communication		Plainly communicating vis-à-vis the population	Institutionalizing talks between the parties to the conflict
		Establishing a public information campaign	Establishing regular staff and interagency meetings at all working levels
		Playing the transparency card vis-à-vis cooperation partners	
		Openly communicating within the mission	Maintaining good informal relations with officers at HQ
		Maintaining open reporting style towards Secretariat, SC	
Change		Changing negotiation style (becoming more strict)	Re-designing the transition approach
		Re-framing policies as more transparent	Creating a transition-supporting agency with local counterpart
		Learning incrementally	Establishing external training and reconciliation workshops (for civilian administrators and the transitional police force)

436

	Agency	Structure
Slack Enhancement	Falling back on UN personnel and equipment present in the region	Designing "Janus deadline"
	Direct lobbying of the SRSG/TA	Outsourcing troop deployment to local contractors
	Informal handling of resource shortages by drawing upon SRSG/TA connections	Adopting a "floor approach"
	Informal deals on conflict issues	"Seeking forgiveness rather than permission"
	Establishing informal relationships with local leaders	De-coupling from headquarters
	Enhancing credibility by having armed Special Forces mingle with CivPol	Creating "surprise slack" (non-compliance on formal rules)
	Circumventing impeding regulations, e.g. by re-labelling "treaty" to "affidavit	Raising local revenues
	Promoting pro-activeness and hands-on attitude of international staff	Furthering inter-organizational linkages
	(Using diaspora capacities)	Creating economic leverage through backing of powerful member states
		Donor conferences
		Including new and forceful donors
		Establishing funding network
		Creating transparency, turning pledges into high-profile issues (DCU)
		Creating time and financial slack through security appeals
		Promoting generic people-orientation with outreach efforts
		Creating work slack through UNVs
		Establishing and communicating a clear political end status for the territory
		Extending election deadline flexibly using authority
		Extending mission deadline by appeals to security concerns
		(Maintaining mandate ambiguity)
Framing and Symbolic Action	Making commitment visible for the locals	
	Framing the mission positively by emphasizing that mission is agent of independence	
	Framing actions that do not comply with the rules as being conducive to the overall transition goal towards HQ	
	Triggering a comprehensive successor mission arrangement by appealing to security concerns	
	Making use of traditional rituals for hand-over	
Self-regulation	(Capacity limits)	

A descriptive-analytical result from this typology lies in the distribution of the coping strategies: most strategies of "negotiation" aim to have a structural impact, coping strategies of "control" and of "framing" affect the behavior of agents directly, and coping strategies that effect "change" and "slack enhancement" do so via structures.[1695] It is a remarkable observation that coping strategies of structure

---

1695 For the sets of analytical, cooperative/integrative, and communicative coping strategies, no well-defined distribution is observed.

and of agency are, in sum, balanced. Hence, one might conclude that a mix of strategies is best suited to deal with pathologies.[1696]

Coping Fit

"Coping strategies" have been defined as successful actions to avoid, reduce, or contain pathological developments. "Fit coping" has been defined as a phenomenon to be specified *ex post facto* according to its positive impact: *eis ipsis*, the listed observations of pathology-coping combinations are "fitting" combinations.

Comparing my empirical findings with the textbook suggestions of fit coping, as have been outlined in Chapter III.2.3, the picture is mixed. On the one hand, many recommendations that I found in the literature go in line with what I have observed as fit coping. On the other hand, various empirically oberved coping strategies had not been covered by the literature. That said, recommendations for coping meet some limits in the specific context of peace operations indeed. These limits have their cause primarily in the temporary nature and the time pressure of these ventures.

On Coping with Cognitive Biases: From the textbook perspective, cognitive biases ought to be coped with by acquiring experience and expertise, communication, sequential pursuing of goals, and vigilance. In UNTAES and UNTAET, we observed the application of these strategies – in the forms of changing and replacing personnel, accessing knowledge from agencies with specialized knowledge, outreach efforts, prioritizing, benchmark setting, self-criticism, and revoking previous decisions. Additionally, I observed diverse coping strategies that created slack. The transitional administrations needed to create organizational, financial, and time slack in the first place as it relaxed the condition of time pressure and the procurement of time and opportunities in order to develop experience and expertise, as well as measures of communication and vigilance.

On Coping with Principal-Agent Problems: Similarly, I do not only observe the textbook strategy of incentive setting when it comes to coping with principal-agent problems. In Eastern Slavonia, for instance, the right negotiation tactics, as well as setting clear changes and brining about innovations that transformed problematic relationships between principals and agents were of the essence, particularly between the mission and the local communities. These supplementary strategies became necessary because of the tight time limit of transitional administrations: the

---

1696 Due to the case-focused design of the study, no solid conclusions can be drawn on the relative quality of the different strategies when it comes to comparing them, neither can one extrapolate from these results to other cases. That said, one could deduce plausible working hypotheses for future research.

textbook recommendation of incentive setting is often not enough. Incentives are of good use when a "shadow of the future" is present, but in a transitional administration, this can hardly be the case.

The complex, ambiguous, and dynamic nature of the roles and of the relationships between principals and agents in peace operations contributes to the limited applicability of conventional textbook recommendations to this kind of setting. It is important to note that the transitional administration and its pivotal decision-makers can be the agent (of the principal Security Council or of the Secretariat) and it can as well assume the role of the principal (vis-à-vis local "agents of transition"). At the same time, the imperative of any interim administration is to hand-over its administrative and governmental functions to local actors for them to "own" the process. As a conclusion of these observations, the roles of the principal and the agent should ideally start to revert towards the end of the mission. For the coping behavior of the decision-makers in the peace operation, that means that they must be able to apply coping strategies in their role as the principal as well as in their role as an agent. Both UNTAES and UNTAET could succeed in this intricate task by involving the national actors gradually (UNTAES) and in a co-government (UNTAET), while retaining ultimate authority until the date of its exit.

Eventually, a useful textbook recommendation that was applied in both cases, but particularly sucessfully in UNTAES, consisted in the creation of transparency. The mechanism by which it was established consisted of the establishment of structures for communication and cooperation.

On Coping with Problems of Tight Coupling: Both missions performed well in producing slack – i.e., time, resources and leverage – and also started to learn at individual and organizational levels. This was crucial. Another important coping approach towards the pathology of tight coupling consisted of accessing external capacities and resources. UNTAES did particularly well in benefiting from synergies of cooperation and inter-organizational linkage.

On Coping with Path-Dependence Problems: The resolution of path-dependence pathologies rested on one recommendation that we also find in the literature, namely the determined action of a leader who acts as a political or institutional entrepreneur, investing power and resources in order to change an inadequate course.[1697] A radical *rupture* furthered positive results in both missions.

1697 Cf. Bauer, Michael. 2006. Politikbeendigung als policyanalytisches Konzept." *Politische Vierteljahresschrift* 47/2, pp. 147-168.

Advantages

Favorable preconditions or capacities set the framework for coping options. Their advantages were essential to the missions' ability to successfully generate contingency strategies.

In Eastern Slavonia, a clear end status, comprehensive support and political will of member states (from the United States in particular), as well as comprehensive authority with a strong MoU on CivPol[1698] and Chapter VII robustness[1699] represented favorable assets. They empowered the transitional administration with the preconditions for success. Furthermore, abundant personnel and financial resources, plus organizational linkages – particularly with NATO, but also with the UN family,[1700] the Council of Europe and the EU, the IMF and the World Bank, contact groups, bilateral agencies, international NGOs – were helpful in putting the mandate into practice. They provided for leverage – diplomatically, politically, militarily, and economically. On top of all, the leadership factor was of crucial importance: only with a determined and vigilant leadership, the above listed assets could be put to good use.

In East Timor, important preconditions for fit coping also included its clearly set end state, the will of the international community to craft a success story, the determinedness of Australia to take on a leadership role with regards to the peacekeeping forces, Chapter VII robustness, abundant financial resources, and the personal leadership style and the political and managerial skills of the Transitional Administrator/SRSG who was able to move the mission forward.[1701]

For both peace missions, it was key to their success that they were transitional administrations, i.e. that they had authoritative power. This said, transitional ad-

---

1698 The strong mandate was the basis for the MoU on TPF, "which gave CIVPOL extensive rights to monitor and conduct investigations." Coleiro 2002, p. 100.

1699 An observer to UNTAES' military robustness notes, "The military, in every mission, is critical. And I think UNTAES is a great example of how the military did a great job, and creating the environment for the civilian side to take over. They were able to achieve huge, definitive military success. And that was a great foundation; it eliminated all kinds of problems. So, I think, one can't lose sight of the military – even though they're not the ones that in the end do the transition, but they're really important." Interview with Dr. Christine Coleiro, UNITAR POCI, Washington, DC, 1 December 2006.

1700 Particularly WFP, WHO, UNICEF, UNCHR, UNHCR.

1701 As said, these findings hold for the case studies only (internal validity); externally valid findings on the most determining factors could only be furthered by a comprehensive large-N exploratory factor analysis. Cf., e.g., Thompson, Bruce. 2004. *Exploratory and Confirmatory Factor Analysis. Understanding Concepts and Applications.* Washington, DC: American Psychological Association. Plausibly, the different advantages are also not independent of each other: abundant resources are more likely to be available if it is a strongly supported mission with much political authority, leaders may act stronger if they can act confidently on a broad base of authority and if they can build their actions on thorough expertise–while experts may help delineate an adequate mission design that helps build interorganizational linkages as well as local ownership.

ministration missions are no silver bullets *per se*, nor can they be applied in all contexts. Obviously, they cannot be put in a place where there *is* a government. In addition, a venture as comprehensive and expensive as an interim administration should be deployed in cases where the political end status is clear; the fragility and frustration that can result from reverse scenarios have been observable in Kosovo. Accordingly, one would argue in favor of a short mandate when designing such a peace operation: besides the aspect of cost, there is the aspect of legitimacy, because if a transitional administration stays too long, it transforms into a neo-colonial structure (at least as perceived by many locals). UNTAET was a case in point. Nonetheless, the exceptional authority that a transitional administration is being granted represents a highly valuable advantage. Particularly in Eastern Slavonia, success would have been beyond imagination if UNTAET had not had ultimate governing power.

The "leadership factor" deserves a closer look also. Leadership was crucial in both missions; their SRSGs had completely different styles though. UNTAES's Jacques-Paul Klein featured a range of characteristics that the management literature attributes to a "charismatic leader," such as acting as a role model, articulating an attractive vision of the future for their staff[1702] and for the local population as well, showing determination and confidence as well as enthusiasm and persistence, and exhibiting high performance standards.[1703] Specifically, Klein's proactive personality and extensive foreign policy and leadership experience was combined with innovative potential, knowledge about the local situation, the ability to "get the big picture" and to create synergies, image awareness, and the capability to learn. The latter was indicated by his initiation of the JIC redesign. Klein was result-oriented and displayed a "can-do" attitude. Ultimately, he incorporated one important lesson from previous peace missionsm, namely that they should never make promises that cannot be kept and not make threats that cannot becarried out. "A UN mission will always have limitations of resources in money or capability, or military force, and therefore should guard against giving a local authority or local populace a false impression of what can be achieved."[1704] By being straightforward in his messages to the local population, he averted the risk of losing credibility. To the contrary, he earned himself a reputation of an honest broker.

The leadership style of de Mello differed from that of Klein, as much as their personalities and appearances were allegedly different. While Klein had a reputation as a bold *enfant terrible*, de Mello, likewise charismatic, excelled because of his diplomatic and political genius. He has been described as a "charming diplomat,

---

1702   "They felt they were part of it." Interview with Dr. Christine Coleiro, UNITAR POCI, Washington, DC, 1 December 2006.
1703   Cf. House 1977; House and Klein 1995; Shamir et al. 1993.
1704   Written interview with Derek G. Boothby, Deputy Special Representative of the Secretary-General and Deputy Transitional Administrator, UNTAES, 5 February 2007.

a canny politician and an inspiring leader" capable of handling the many crises and dilemmas he had to manage with flexibility and pragmatism. He was in hot spots like Rwanda, Cambodia, Kosovo and Bosnia, where he served as senior UN official and got used to managing an incredible amount of tasks and challenges. He had also already gained experience in running a conflict-ridden territory when he was appointed SRSG of UNMIK. "In each posting, he [confronted] a hydra-headed monster of communal violence and poverty, plus difficulties compounded by UN red tape, miserly budgets and uncaring Western governments."[1705] In East Timor, his greatest dilemma was the modus of transitional governance. First and foremost, de Mello came to terms with the conundrum of participation and time pressure by sensitively establishing informal links to the local leaders and by making a passionate cause for a transitional co-government, while being well aware of the need to break UN rules and the risk of losing the loyalty of some of his own staff. At the end of the day, he most likely saved UNTAET from becoming a failure – just as the determinedness, bold negotiation style, and the gutsy efforts on re-design of Jacques-Paul Klein had been crucial for UNTAES to succeed.

The two leaders had to characteristics in common: they were able to act as boundary spanners and as institutional entrepreneurs. Both Klein and de Mello displayed internal and external boundary-spanning capacities in mission management and external boundary-spanning capacities in their relationships with headquarters and in their cooperation with other international organizations; and both were able to initiate and implement critical junctures for the good of the mission. In addition, both SRSGs disposed over important, yet indeed different, social skills. Whereas Klein had the ability to strike the right tone with military leaders and crafted a mission that was strongly people-oriented, de Mello had the smooth skills of a diplomat and was able to communicate sensitive matters consummately; crucially, he knew the UN system well and how to deal with headquarters, such as to accomplish what he thought was best for UNTAET and East Timor. At the end of the day, one could conclude by saying that both SRSGs were a blessing to the two different missions. Reflecting on a counterfactual idea, a different appointment might very possibly have led to very different mission performances.

In conclusion, leadership was an important factor for both missions in dealing with the vulnerabilities of the complex transition,[1706] a finding that is in line with textbook explanations of political and management science.[1707] In leadership, "in-

1705 Publishers Weekly, "Review of Samantha Power, 'Chasing the Flame,'" 6 March 2008. Available online at http://www.amazon.ca/Chasing-Flame-Samantha-Power/dp/1594201285, last access on 15 March 2009.

1706 Cf., e.g., Boin, Arjen and t'Hart, Paul. 2003. "Leadership in Times of Crisis: Mission Impossible?" *Public Administration Review* 63:5, pp. 544-553; Kingdon 1995.

1707 Cf. Doyle and Sambanis 2006. See also Essens, Peter et al., eds., 2001. *The Human in Command: Peace Support Operations*. Amsterdam: Mets & Schilt.

dividuals matter greatly."[1708] That being said, it seemed like the UN does "not take care of their people" and does not put particular effort into the sustaining the thin pool of people that might be able to be future SRSGs. Jacques-Paul Klein recalls his experience with the system:

> When he came to Sarajevo in October 1997, I asked the Secretary-General, 'Kofi, how long do you want this mission to stay open? I can run it easily for another year, and kind of do final touches and all that.' And he said, 'No, we need the money, we have so many other priorities, get it done. When do you think you can get it done?' I said that we can probably have it done until February 2003, and he responded, 'Yes, do it.' But then you realize that suddenly in February 2003 you're without a work. I mean the UN didn't say, 'Oh, you did a wonderful job, here is another mission.' I mean I was in Virginia waiting to go to Princeton, when suddenly Kofi called up and asked if I wanted to do Liberia. Otherwise, I would have had nothing. So, they don't take care of their people, they really don't.[1709]

In general, a more holistic and considerate treatment of senior field staff can contribute to easier staff identification and smoother recruitment processes. It is also likely to increase the loyalties and intrinsic motivations of leader personae which are of essence to the success of a mission.

Conclusion

The fundamental stipulation of the study could be substantiated: throughout the transitional process, ill-structured conditions of complexity, uncertainty, ambiguity, and time pressure made UN missions prone to pathologies and ensuing accidents. As the cumulative effects of cognitive biases and principal-agent dilemmas indicated, the frequency of pathologies made accidents more likely. The accumulation of accidents, in turn, increased the risk of mission failure, as one could observe well in the case of UNTAET, where the negative effects added up to an inadequate policy lock-in that brought the mission close to the brink of failure. What the East Timor case also illustrates is that the early stages of a complex peace operation may be particularly prone to the pathology of cognitive biases. This, in turn, can lead to a lock-in of inadequate policies. Besides, the tight coupling of transition processes in the narrow schedule allows for manipulation and exploitation particularly by the parties to the conflict who are still pursuing agendas that are not compatible with the peace process – and who, nonetheless, still need to be involved in the transition. It further seems that complex peace operations with governing authority face inherent trade-offs between short-term and long-term ori-

---

1708   Hooper and Taylor 1999, p. 29.
1709   Telephone interview with Ambassador Jacques-Paul Klein, SRSG and Transitional Administrator, UNTAES, 19 July 2007.

entation, government role and civil society support, and between security goals versus economic and social policies. In the cases under scrutiny, I observed a bias of "solving" these dilemmas in favor of short-term goals, government role, and security issues. Generally, social and economic considerations are put second. These biases may convey a precarious sustainability of the international efforts. In the case of UNTAES, some of these shortcomings could be attenuated through the creation of a legal framework. This is not to say that a UN mission should become even more complex and should also take care of economic growth: such a design is likely to produce even more pathologies of the tight coupling type. Still, international peace operations, and especially such powerful ones as transitional administrations, are in the unique position of having the authority to make crucial decisions for the future economic and social development of the territory and its people. They should seize this opportunity.

Preventing the mission from major accidents and failure, the coping capability of the transitional administration is key. I identified a wide range of coping strategies and abstracted them into categories of action theory ("*handlungstheoretische Kategorien*"): vigilant analysis, adaptive negotiation, inclusive cooperation and integration polices, comprehensive internal and external communication, the ability to change flawed policies and structures, the ability to enhance the slack for the mission concerning time, finances, organization, or attention, and the capability to frame itself vis-à-vis other actors and to make good use of symbolic action. From a generic ontological perspective, coping materializes in the form of influence on individuals or groups of individuals or they resemble emergent phenomena that influence the structural constellation of the transition. The two successful cases under scrutiny showed a relatively balanced distribution of actor-centred and structural coping strategies.

Specifying these generic propositions, the observations on coping fit allow for the following statements. The application of "analysis" coping strategies makes the containment of the cognitive biases pathology more likely; the application of "analysis" and "change" coping strategies makes the containment of the cognitive biases pathology more likely; the application of "negotiation," "control," "cooperation and integration," "communication," and "framing and symbolic action" coping strategies make the containment of the principal agent pathology more likely; the application of "slack enhancement" coping strategies makes the containment of the tight coupling pathology more likely; the application of "change" coping strategies makes the containment of the path dependence pathology more likely; and organizational, financial and time slack is generally conducive for the containment of pathologies. The causal mechanisms accounting for the latter is that more slack gives decision-makers more time for considering decision alternatives, it makes deficient commitment by principals and by agents less necessary, it relaxes tightly coupled systems, and it provides leeway for re-evaluating and re-designing established structures.

Furthermore, the coping capacity of a mission is dependent upon the availability of certain advantages, such as the availability of supervisory or executive authority, robustness, abundant resources, cooperation partnerships, expertise, and qualified personnel.

The SRSGs of both missions were crucial as initiators and coordinators of coping strategies. On the backdrop of the case studies, I found that leadership qualities of being a boundary spanners and a political entrepreneur are conducive for successful achievement of the mandate. The mechanism that operates this hypothesis is that a leader of such qualities is an initiating and catalyzing force: only with a vigilant and determined leadership, the comprehensive authority and abundant resources of transitional administrations will be put to good use and enable successful coping. Bringing together my case study observations with Boothby's conceptualization of "floor" and "ceiling" approaches to mandate implementation, I can also state for the cases under scrutiny that with a leader who disposes over the qualities of a boundary spanner and political entrepreneur, the application of a floor approach makes success more likely than a ceiling approach would do.

At a more abstract level, one would hypothesize the performance of a complex UN peace operation as an emergent structuration phenomenon. The constellation of the constructs lends itself to the interpretation of transitional administrations as phenomena of structuration: they act within given structures that make the mission prone to develop pathologies ("ill-structuredness"), but that may also enable to mission to enact coping strategies ("advantage structure"). At the same time, decision-makers within UN missions are not determined by these structures, but dispose over latitude and the room to manoeuvre. This scenario was observable in both cases under scrutiny. The structuration concept is also likely to apply to a longer-term perspective on the system that operates complex missions. *Per definitionem*, peace operations are supposed to transform local conditions in the conflict-ridden territory. But, in principle, they are also capable of transforming their own ill-structured political and institutional conditions by the mechanism of mission staff reporting on the experience on-the-ground, the ensuing widening of organizational memory, and the resulting greater pool of routines and standard operating procedures. Furthermore, drastic experiences in war-torn territories may raise more member state awareness of the consequences of their ambiguous and inconsistent support. However, this structuration effect may also result in a diametrically opposed scenario, when member states start to back out of supporting large-scale peace operations because of their many pitfalls. In conclusion, the concept that constitutes the fundamental mechanism of structuration is double-loop learning at headquarters. Only if the decision-makers in the planning agencies at headquarters change their "theories-in-use," learned lessons can be put into practice. However, while the strategic landscape in which peace operations are located is astonishingly well elaborated and consistent across the most influential actors – particularly the UN, NATO, the EU, and the US[1710] –, the operative landscape still lacks this consistency. A similar gap exists between strategic pledges and their implementation. Thus, the prospects of changing the ill-structuredness of peace operations towards more comprehensiveness, consistency, adequacy, and clarity are mixed. "First, it is always hard to change things. Secondly, there are the interests of the member states."[1711] An intergovernmental organization like the UN can only be as good as its members will allow for.

5. Excursus: An Alternative Concept of "Success"

On the backdrop of my explanation of the success or failure of complex UN peace operations, I would like to elaborate a thought on a new conceptualization of the dependent variable *success/failure.*

As noted by many scholars who have reflected on the issue, the specification and operationalization of peace operations' performance, used synonymously with "effectiveness,"[1712] is a challenging task. Contrary to the tenor of the peacekeeping and peacebuilding literature, I suggest a specification of *performance* in terms of efficiency instead of effectiveness, because such a measure would be able to take into account the different conditions under which different missions operate. In the peacekeeping literature, two general measures of success are discussed: mandate achievement and sustainability of peace.[1713] There are obvious problems with each of these.

1710   The recent strategy papers of the UN, the EU, as well as of the United States resemble each other in many ways. Cf. United Nations, "Report of the Secretary General's High-level Panel on Threats, Challenges and Change, A More Secure World. Our Shared Responsibility;" European Union, "Report of the European Council on a Secure Europe in a Better World;" United Nations, "Report of the Panel on United Nations Peace Operations;" United States of America, "The National Security Strategy of the United States of America," September 2002. Available online at http://www.acq.osd.mil/ncbdp/nm/docs/Relevant%20Docs/national_security_strategy.pdf, last access 2 March 2009.

1711   Interview with Professor Michael W. Doyle, former UN Assistant Secretary-General, New Haven, 11 September 2006.

1712   See Downs, George and Stedman, Stephen John. 2002. "Evaluation Issues in Peace Implementation." In: Donald Rothchild et al., eds., *Ending Civil Wars.* Boulder: Lynne Rienner, pp. 44-54.

1713   Cf., e.g., Bratt, Duane. 1996. "Assessing the Success of UN Peacekeeping Operations." *International Peacekeeping* 3:4, pp. 64-81; Page-Fortna, Virginia and Howard, Lise Morjé. 2008. "Pitfalls and Prospects in the Peacekeeping Literature." *Annual Review of Political Science* 11, pp. 283-301; Downs and Stedman 2002.

On the one hand, mandate achievement is an endogenous approach, as the mandate and its goals are defined by the UN in the first place. This means that the measure allows for proclaiming success by lowering the standards or by setting low standards from the beginning. In addition, problems of comparability surface necessarily: it is difficult to compare missions if one is *mediocre* in fulfilling an *ambitious* mandate, while the other is doing *great* in fulfilling a comparatively *thin* mandate. Compounding matters, the purposes and substance of peace operations vary to a great extent, and the phrases in mandates are often extremely ambiguous.[1714]

On the other hand, evaluation approaches that are detached from mandate comparison and take on a longer time-horizon can escape the endogeneity problem. That said, these sustainability-focussed approaches suffer from comparability intricacies, too, since the concepts on sustainability are diverse, using different indicators and different combinations thereof. Some evaluators may be even tempted to apply unrealistically high standards for success. This means that the capacity of these measures to differentiate among different grades of sustainability success is very much reduced. Obviously, this diminishes the usefulness of these measurements. Besides, the longer the time-horizon that is taken into account, the more difficult it becomes to trace and confirm a relation between the UN operation in a given territory at time t_1 and the situation of the territory at time t_n: as time passes, a problem of "noise" develops. This means that the potential influence of exogenous factors grows and the quality of inferences declines.[1715]

While I do support (a combination of) the said measures of mandate achievement and sustainability, I have two points to add to this generic debate. First, I argue for a measure of efficiency, not effectiveness. The reason for this rests in the sensitivity of the efficiency concept to variance in "inputs:" efficiency is defined as the relationship between inputs and outputs. Thus, the success of a mission can be evaluated in terms that are relative to advantages, such as international willingness and investments, as well as to ill-structuredness, such as hostility or overly complex mandates. For instance, this perspective allows for the control of biases in well-equipped and high-profile missions as they have been observed for operations de-

---

1714   This was particularly virulent in UNTAET. One last difficulty that Stedman and Downs identify with this evaluation approach is that it might be instrumentalized by member states and the Security Council who set highflying objectives intended to signal their commitment and willingness and who are at the same time secured for the case of non-achievement as they can blame implementing agencies for the result.

1715   "The passage of time introduces the equivalent of noise in the form of a growing number of influencing factors that are not directly associated with the peace mission." Downs and Stedman 2002, pp. 48-49.

ployed in Europe, contrary to, say, Africa, where great power interest is more elusive.

Secondly, the discussion about the evaluation of peace operations iterates, in a surprisingly uninformed way, an old *sujet*. The difficulties that are outlined and elaborated upon closely resemble the research on the performance of generic public institutions, as has been discussed by Herbert A. Simon in his seminal *Administrative Behavior* of 1945. The bottom line is identical, and refers to the inherent vagueness of public policy goals, such as stability or public welfare. Contrary to goals of commercial organizations, public policy goals are neither measurable in monetary terms, nor are they value-free. The point on monetary assessment ought to be straightforward,[1716] the problems emanating from value attachment possibly less so. So, for example, if a certain health care policy aims at providing better preventive services, it is, for instance, relevant when this health care policy dominantly inures those in the upper income bracket. Likewise, if peacebuilding aims at reconstructing infrastructure, it is a relevant issue when buildings are only set-up in the center of a conflict-ridden territory, thus marginalizing large parts of the rural population. Furthermore, a given policy may have to pursue several goals: the infrastructure imperatives of a complex peacebuilding mission do not only include the provision of new buildings, but also the reconstruction of streets, electricity, schools, and businesses. This implies that scarce resources need to be weighed and split among these values accordingly. Assuming an *ex ante* identification of the ranking of the preference/value attribution, the measurement of the efficiency of a peace operation would increase both validity and reliability.

For Simon, the important benchmark for the evaluation of the performance of a given public policy is its efficiency, defined as the relation between the observed outcome and the maximally possible outcome, given the input.[1717] I suggest proceeding in kind with the evaluation of complex UN peace operations.[1718] The efficiency measure is the more appropriate evaluation standard since it can take the ill-structured conditions into account explicitly, and hence, be sensitive about pathologies, as well as considers the assets of a mission and hence its chances of good coping.

On the background of these thoughts, the standardized question on the dependent variable "performance" should be: what is the best alternative to the performance achieved given the mission's scope conditions? The answer can then be given in a descriptive-analytical way and start from the givens, or normatively and include suggestions for institutional change, such as to alter the constraining parameters

---

1716 For whom it is not, I recommend a reading on measurement theory, e.g. Schnell, Hill and Esser 1999, chapter 4.3.

1717 Cf. Simon 1981, p. 201.

1718 This suggestion holds for all discussed evaluation rationales, be it the evaluation imperative of mandate achievement, achievement sustainability, or a combination of both.

for a mission, for instance discussing the advantages of institutional reform at the UN.

With the efficiency approach, the adequate method of studying performance would be *counterfactual* reasoning.[1719] Possibly, the ratio between ill-structuredness and advantages might allow for predictions of performance – the smaller the ratio, the more likely a successful outcome might be.

6. Conclusion

Despite the wide-ranging interest in *explananda* for successes and failures of peace operations, the research focus of mainstream literature has been narrowly placed on static variables instead of dynamic processes. The thesis has explored an alternative explanation for their success and failure. It has built a theoretical framework that focuses on causal processes from an organizational-theoretical and behavioral perspective. The suggested causal mechanisms can usefully supplement explanations that emphasize macro-variables with a behavioral micro-foundation, as well as provide a systemizing framework for idiosyncratic qualitative case studies. The proposed theoretical and analytical framework would also allow for a more differentiated conceptualization of the dependent variable.

I started with the assumption that peace operations in general, and the "extreme type" of UN transitional administrations in specific, operate under unfavorable, ill-structured conditions: they are constrained by political considerations of member states, by often inadequate institutional rules and capacities, and they face adverse on-the-ground conditions. I argued that, under these conditions, UN missions develop organizational pathologies. The more virulent these pathologies become, the more likely failure is. I argued further that fit coping behavior of the decision-makers in the mission can attenuate these pathologies, making a mission succeed "against the odds." I specified my argument by falling back on concepts from organizational theory, organizational psychology, and research strands of administrative science and deduced four hypotheses on the existence of pathologies and coping strategies. These generic hypotheses were examined by analyzing the UN transitional administrations in Eastern Slavonia and in East Timor. Since both were successful missions, observations of coping behavior were possible.

1719   See Tetlock, Philip E., ed., 1996. *Counterfactual Thought Experiments in World Politics Logical, Methodical, and Psychological Perspectives*. Princeton: Princeton University Press. On the background of my argumentation on the dependent variable, one might also consider a re-evaluation of the transitional administration in East Timor: the case reconstruction has furthered evidence on various virulent pathologies and ensuing accidents that UNTAET suffered from, thus biasing the balance sheet of the comprehensive and comparatively well-resourced mission into a more negative direction.

In the first place, I was able to demonstrate pathologies of cognitive biases, commitment deficiencies of agents as well as of principals, tight coupling, and path dependency. Principal-agent problems were most striking and occurred regularly in both cases. Similarly, both transitions resembled a tightly coupled system, and both missions locked in an inadequate transition policy. Differing from UNTAES, UNTAET showed significant cognitive biases too, particularly during its initial stage. At the end of the day, both missions applied "fit" coping strategies and could mitigate pathologies, thus confirming the general argument of the study.

Putting the method of process tracing to good use, I categorized the explored coping strategies and their fit to the four forms of pathologies. Successful coping with cognitive biases is related to analytical action; for principal agent problems, strategies of cooperation, integration, and slack enhancement are prominently suggested; the negative effects of the tight coupling of complex interaction may likely be attenuated by slack enhancement, and path dependent deficiencies require rigid change. Slack enhancement, in addition, seems to be a coping strategy that has the potential to attenuate the pathologies of UN transitional administrations in general: it has found broad application as slack not only de-coupled tightly intertwined processes, but also provided time to re-evaluate decision-making, produced leverage vis-à-vis spoiling or free-riding agents, and helped finding alternative leverage when principals would or could not provide it. A final result was that fit coping depended on the availability of certain advantages, particularly authoritative power and resources, and on the existence of vigilant and determined leadership to put these advantages to good use.

As in any scientific treatise, this thesis has been subject to a range of research strategic decisions about the theoretical lenses applied, about the research design and methods, about the reconstruction of the empirical cases, and about their analysis and interpretation. Each of these decisions incorporates certain trade-offs: just as there is no *one* truth in depicting and interpreting reality, there is no *right* way in setting up a study, and the researcher needs to decide on consistent argumentation and procedure, and be clear about the pitfalls and benefits of his or her chosen path. In concluding this study, I will make the study's most crucial trade-offs explicit.

Alternative Theories: I selected four theoretical lenses for the study of the hypothesized ill-fated missions with the following reasons and considerations in mind: they represent the best-proved explanations of organizational failure in the disciplines of organizational theory and organizational psychology; they are complementary; and their complementary use allows for a balanced consideration of structure and agency factors. There might have been other potential "candidates," the theory of groupthink for example, but I excluded them from the above quadrivium either because they are absorbed by them or because they would have required different forms of data collection and analysis. For instance, the application of

450

groupthink would have called for a reconstruction of interactions within different complete leadership teams and implied a different method of data collection. Another likely rival explanation for inter-agency dynamics, which challenges the principal-agent theorem, would have been the veto player approach. Some observations that fall into the category of principal-agent pathologies might be indeed specified, and thus re-interpreted, by means of the veto player explanation.[1720] I

1720 Obstructing a given policy, veto players are self-interested individual or collective actors that use institutional or partisan veto power for their own good. A transitional administration of the United Nations is a venture where a multitude of actors is involved. Their functions vary between mandating agents, resource (also human resource) providers, deniers, allocators, addressees and cooperation partners. The most pivotal actor is the UNSC, which is itself a collective veto player: a transitional administration needs the unanimous consent of all of the Security Council members. At the headquarters level, the Secretariat and its Secretary-General, the ACABQ, DPA, and DPKO are important players in planning, financing, and maintaining the mission. In the field, a mission constitutes a highly heterogeneous entity in itself, and simultaneously relies on other organizations – international and regional, governmental and non-governmental – to see its mandate through. Eventually, the participation of and cooperation by the parties to the conflict and the population at large is key to a controlled transition. A transitional administration is subject to concerted decisions and the actions of multiple and diverse actors, at different levels, who are parts of the transition facilitating structure. If an actor does not "play in tune," this may constrain the chances of the entire venture's success. Thus, the structural conditions of complex UN peace operations is characterized by various points of access, and even a veto for actors who might all have independent and partial rationales and interests. In this perspective, the more veto points and thus veto players are involved, the smaller the probability of achieving the stated organizational goal. One may consider the introduction of a two-dimensional analytical scheme which captures veto players in transition processes. The first dimension would be the degree of veto power, the second, the veto player "locus." See Stedman 1997. First, actors may have *de jure* veto power or *de facto* veto power, and access capability: The only actors to have *de jure* veto power are the five permanent members of the Security Council. All of the actors who are necessary for implementing that mandate may have *de facto* veto power, for instance, other powerful member states that have an interest in the matter, agencies assisting in implementation, or local leaders. This differentiation is close to Tsebelis idea of "institutional" and "partisan" veto players, the former describing institutionalized, constant actors, and partisan veto players representing actors that become relevant only in certain situations. Cf. Tsebelis, George. 2002. *Veto Players*. Princeton: Princeton University Press. For a good discussion of the veto player concept, see also Ganghof, Steffen. 2003. "Promises and Pitfalls of Veto Player Analysis." *Swiss Political Science Review* 9:2, pp. 1-25. Secondly, the "locus" of the veto actor can refer to spoiling parties to the conflict or it can be "within" the international community. The local veto players or obstructers comprise the conventional spoiler concept, but enlarge it, insofar as defective non-participation is also included, for instance, we think of a population's refusal to get involved in the transition policy that was proposed by an international administration. An "obstructer from within" is, however, an actor or a group of actors that form part of the "international custodians of peace" – as a member state, a UN organ, field staff, or other cooperating organizations and their employees. Thus, as an analytical concept for the study of UN-managed transitions, "veto players" could be defined as actors who actively and intentionally obstruct the transition process with the effect of putting it on hold, at least temporarily. For instance, the Chinese addendum on the mandate of UNTAES may be interpreted as an "obstruction from within." China, the *de jure* veto player, used its power in the Security Council to pursue its separate interests. See also Seibel, Wolfgang. 2008. *'Coping with Spoilers from Within': Die Obstruktion von Friedens-*

have chosen, however, the perspective of principals and agents, as phenomena captured by the veto player perspective are falling into the broader conceptual category of principal-agent relationships.

Alternative Interpretations and the Ambiguity of Interpretation: The reflections on the principal-agent and veto player perspectives[1721] point to a second thought about the very interpretation of the phenomena observed. Interpretation means the transmission of one specific image of reality. We are not able to produce objective images of reality. However, we shall strive for making this incapacity explicit, and delivering a consistent interpretation of it. Consistence is reached by using a systematic procedure; the tool that helps us in becoming systematic is theory. At the same time, this implies that the use of alternative theoretical perspectives would lead to different interpretations of pathological patterns, using different categories and terms. If other theoretical perspectives than the ones used here are better at accurately describing and explaining, this would be conducive for scientific progress. For the time being, I have tried to make the study's perspectives and the selection of my interpretive schemes explicit and open for discussion.

Also concerning the interpretation of observations, I have to be explicit about the ambiguity potential of the schemes of pathologies and coping: occasionally, they can in fact coincide. A point in case is the matter of vague mandate phrasing. Especially for UNTAET, the language of the mandate remained ambiguous. While

operationen durch politisierte Bürokratien. Project Proposal, Deutsche Stiftung Friedensforschung, on file with the author. Similarly, the ambiguous support of Indonesia resembled a *de facto* "veto from within" that put UNTAET's planning process on hold. Likewise "from within" but of a structural nature is the inadequacy of the recruiting system that inherently obstructs efficient planning authority of the state-building, and particularly, state-running "business." The veto player idea also applies to the obstructive actions of the "agents of transition" in Eastern Slavonia. Boycotts (by the local minority), waiting games (by the local majority), and deadline exploitation are spoiling actions by local actors, who are key to the implementation of the mandate and who use their access either to maintain the UN-guarded status quo (the minority) or to sit out the transition until the UN has left again (the majority), which would be synonymous with Croatia's coming into power. Eventually, the concept might also be suitable to analyze the hidden agendas of NGOs who pursue interests different than the UN mission's transition agenda.Deutsche Stiftung Friedensforschung, on file with the author. Similarly, the ambiguous support of Indonesia resembled a *de facto* "veto from within" that put UNTAET's planning process on hold. Likewise "from within" but of a structural nature is the inadequacy of the recruiting system that inherently obstructs efficient planning authority of the state-building, and particularly, state-running "business." The veto player idea also applies to the obstructive actions of the "agents of transition" in Eastern Slavonia. Boycotts (by the local minority), waiting games (by the local majority), and deadline exploitation are spoiling actions by local actors, who are key to the implementation of the mandate and who use their access either to maintain the UN-guarded status quo (the minority) or to sit out the transition until the UN has left again (the majority), which would be synonymous with Croatia's coming into power. Eventually, the concept might also be suitable to analyze the hidden agendas of NGOs who pursue interests different than the UN mission's transition agenda.

1721   Cf. fn. 1720.

this conveys pathological potential of poor guidance and uncertainty for the missions' personnel particularly at the early stages of the transition, mandate ambiguity is in fact "normal" as well as it is purposeful: the Secretary-General is using a noncommittal language and diplomatic formulas that the members can agree to. Ambiguous language increases interpretive slack and hence the probability of member state support.[1722] Besides, it may also imply more latitude for the mission in formulating its policy for transition.[1723]

Fragmentary Character of the Reconstruction: The data collected is fragmentary. As a matter of fact, it is impossible to reconstruct complex processes consummately; empirical reconstructions necessarily reflect only a part of reality. And they may do so in a biased way.[1724] In particular, the observations about pathologies and coping are fragmentary and cannot claim to be a complete list of all pathological patterns and coping strategies that were "really" going on in the missions. I tried to find a reasonable and sincere way of dealing with this obvious problem by getting as much different information on the same processes as possible, and by sticking to the grand lines of policies and politics. I did so by triangulating data – using primary sources from the UN, but also from other actors, such as NGOs, secondary literature, and conducting expert interviews with people involved in the transition – and by focussing the interviews on a group of staff that were in key decision-making positions. Furthermore, I focused on the reconstruction of the main policy trajectories of both UNTAES and UNTAET, and I tried to systematically scrutinize events in line with the theoretical perspectives. Occasionally, tracing the complex and often overlapping phenomena and processes of interest may have led to redundancy – but it did so inevitably.

Implications of Case Selection: The selection of cases was discussed in Chapter III. At this point, I want to emphasize the critical point that both missions represented "demonstration objects." The reason for this is that one must assume that the positive outcome of these missions is somewhat biased as international support was over average. This observation raises the question of how comparable their successes are to performances of missions that do not enjoy this advantage. This perspective calls for a reflection upon the performance evaluation of peace opera-

---

1722 Cf. CSDG, "East Timor Report," para. 329, "This lack of clarity is not necessarily in itself grounds for criticism. In view of the lack of planning, the obscure political landscape which the mission confronted on its arrival in East Timor and the novelty of the task it was mandated to carry out, the open-endedness of the mandate may be seen as inevitable and even advantageous in so far as it did not close off options."

1723 "A lot of these strategic decisions should be done in the mission, of course with headquarters reviews, but that's the place to do it, on-the-ground, as they face reality day to day." Interview with a senior official of the UN Department of Political Affairs, New York, 12 December 2006.

1724 We are never free of theories, of a precast picture or idea of reality. Cf. Chapter II.

tions, and I have attempted to argue for conceptualizing "performance" not in terms of effectiveness but via the efficiency criterion.

Academic Analysis versus the "Real World": Finally, I would like to add a thought about a certain discrepancy between academic analysis and the "real world flavor" of the topic under scrutiny. Social science studies are about human beings, and this particular study has been about human beings in an environment full of tension, where human beings suffered tremendous horrors and pain, where they worked hard to help rebuild a conflict-ridden territory, and where they were required to make difficult decisions. I am aware that I could not always capture and account for the complications and dramatic fates that were involved in the stories of Eastern Slavonia and East Timor. The "cold eye perspective" of scientific work is not tailored to do so. In an attempt to reach a kind of middle ground, I inserted several "boxes" in the reconstruction of the cases, where I dug a bit deeper into some of these developments and events. They were not necessarily of essence to the analytical goals of the study, but hopefully provided for a better understanding of the situation on-the-ground.

7. Resumé

The thesis built and examined by means of two case studies an alternative theoretical framework for the analysis of complex UN peace operations and for the explanation of their performance: the suggested causal processes can usefully supplement explanations that emphasize macro-variables with a behavioral micro-foundation, as well as provide a systemizing framework for idiosyncratic qualitative case studies. Organizational theory is suitable and fruitful for the analysis of complex peace operations.

The findings of the study may also be relevant for practitioners and decision-makers who design and lead such operations: raising systematic awareness of cognitive, commitment-related, structural, or path dependent pitfalls may help in coping with them. What the UN can do to improve its chances of success relates to advantages and coping capacities: it should make sure that crucial advantages are in place even before the mission starts, but also promote and support individual and institutional analytical capacities, negotiation skills, know-how of enforcement and control actions, skills of cooperation and integration, framing techniques, and symbolic action.

I see three general directions for future research. They refer to applying the framework and the hypotheses to other empirical observations, further developing the theoretical framework, and studying specific aspects of the suggested approach separately. The most obvious starting point for future research would be the examination of the theoretical-analytical framework with other cases. The pathology-coping nexus is a concept that can explain the performance of a complex mission, and it does so from a hitherto under-explored angle. The model has demonstrated its analytical and explanatory potential, but will certainly benefit from further empirical studies that may futher develop the identified causal processes and mechanisms. Cases under scrutiny do not necessarily have to be extreme cases as are transitional administrations: for this explorative study, transitional administrations were the "best bet" to observe pathologies, but the theoretical framework applies to complex peace operations in general. Nor do further studies need to be purely qualitative.[1725] Shifting perspectives, a focus on the dependent variable promises valuable insights as well. For instance, the conceptualization of the dependent variable in terms of efficiency renders itself to counterfactual analysis, and a re-evaluation of missions that uses this methodology might be a due and interesting consequence. Second, elaborations on the theoretical framework could look at the four approaches in a concurrent rather than a complementary perspective. A possible result might be a more parsimonious explanation. Another direction for future refinement of the theoretical framework would be a specification of the broad analytical categories used. As mentioned, the principal-agent perspective might be specified by means of the veto player theory. Another potentially fruitful useful concept would be Robert Putnam's theory of two-level games. It could serve as a useful device in specifying the concept of "successful failure" as his idea of small win sets could inform the argument about insufficient mandates.[1726] The third strand of future research would start from a selection of single aspects of the study. For instance, studying coping behavior of different SRSGs across cases might reveal useful insights into how "good" or "bad" leadership qualifies and how it influences a peace operation. While I indicated some relevant, and what I deemed useful, concepts for categorizing and understanding the different leadership styles observable with UNTAET and UNTAES, the large body of management literature implies that there could be much more to say about how leaders succumb to pathological behavior and how they come to terms with it.

At the end of the day, no one can provide a recipe for success. In fact, peace operations cannot but move in the realm of the palliative, and in the introduction I stressed the "tragic" character of the challenge of transitional management. While they certainly reflect a constitution of permanent crisis and precariousness, the way

---

1725 Considering the limits of case studies regarding extrapolarization, the findings I have made in the examination of the cases apply to the UN missions in Eastern Slavonia and East Timor only.
1726 Cf. Putnam, Robert D. 1988. "Diplomacy and Domestic Politics: The Logic of Two-Level Games." *International Organization* 42:3, pp. 427-460.

the mission and its leadership manage and organize a transition can make a dramatic difference. At the end of the day, UN missions will have a chance of succeeding against the odds.

Bibliography

Monographies, Articles, and Conference Proceedings

Aall, Pamela et al. 2000. *Guide to IGOs, NGOs, and the Military in Peace and Relief Operations*. Washington, DC: United States Institute of Peace Press.

Ackerloff, Russell L. 1970. *A Concept of Corporate Planning*. New York: Wiley.

Adorno, Theodor W. e. a. 1950. *The Authoritarian Personality*. New York: Harper.

Aiken, Michael and Gerald Hage. 1968. "Organizational Interdependence and Intraorganizational Structure." *American Sociological Review* 33:6, pp. 912-930.

Aldrich, Howard E. 1979. *Organizations and Environments*. Englewood Cliffs: Prentice Hall.

Alutto, Joseph and Belasco, James A. 1972. "A Typology for Participation in Organizational Decision Making." *Administrative Science Quarterly* 17:1, pp. 117-125.

Anderson, Benedict. 1993. *Imagining East Timor*. Cepesa Working Papers. Lisbon: Cepesa.

Arkes, Hal and Blumer, Catherine. 1985. "The Psychology of Sunk Cost." *Organizational Behavior and Human Decision Processes* 35, pp. 124-140.

Ascher, William. 2001. "Coping with Complexity and Organizational Interests in Natural Resource Management." *Ecosystems* 4:8, pp. 742-757.

Axelrod, Robert. 1984. *The Evolution of Cooperation*. New York: Basic Books.

Azimi, Nassrine and Li Lin, Chang, ed. 2003. *The United Nations Transitional Administration in East Timor (UNTAET): Debriefing and Lessons*. Leiden/Boston: Martinus Nijhoff Publishers.

Babo-Soares, Dionisio. 2001. "Success, Weakness, and Challenges of the Political Transition in East Timor." In: Hadi Soesastro and Landry Haryo Subianto, eds., *Peace Building and State Building in East Timor*. Jakarta: Centre for Strategic and International Studies, pp. 12-38.

Bacharach, Samuel B. and Baratz, Morton S. 1962. "The Two Faces of Power." *American Political Science Review* 56:6, pp. 947-952.

Bailey, Sidney and Daws, Sam. 1998. *The Procedure of the UN Security Council*. Oxford: Clarendon Press.

Ball, Nicole. 2002. "The Reconstruction and Transformation of War-Torn Societies and State Institutions: How can External Actors Contribute?" In Tobias Debiel and A. Klein, eds., *Fragile Peace, State Failure, Violence and Development in Crisis Regions*. London: Zed Books, pp. 33-55.

Bardach, Eugene. 1977. *The Implementation Game. what Happens After a Bill Becomes a Law*. Cambridge: MIT Press.

Barnard, Chester I. 1938. *The Functions of the Executive*. New York: Wiley.

Barnett, Michael N. and Martha Finnemore. 1999. "The Power, Politics, and Pathologies of International Institutions." *International Organization* 53:4, pp. 699-732.

Ibid. 2004. *Rules for the World: International Organizations in Global Politics*. Ithaca: Cornell University Press.

Barton, L. 1990. "Crisis Management: Selecting Communications Strategy." *Management Decision* 28:6, pp. 5-8.

Bauer, Michael. 2006. Politikbeendigung als policyanalytisches Konzept." *Politische Vierteljahresschrift* 47/2, pp. 147-168.

Baumgartner, Ilse and Baumgartner, Wolfgang. 1997. *Der Balkan-Krieg Der 90er. Fakten, Hintergründe, Analysen, Zukunftsperspektiven.* Berlin: Verlag für Wissenschaft und Forschung.

Bazerman, Max. 2002. *Judgement in Managerial Decision Making*, 5th ed. New York: John Wiley & Sons.

Beach, L. R. and Mitchell, T.R. 1978. "A Contingency Model for the Selection of Decision Strategies." *Academy of Management Review* 3:3, pp. 439-449.

Beauvais, Joel C. 2001. "Benevolent Despotism: A Critique of UN State-Building in East Timor." *International Law and Politics* 33, pp. 1101-1178.

Behn, Robert D. 1976. "Closing the Massachusetts Public Training Schools." *Policy Sciences* 7:2, pp. 151-171.

Ibid. 1977. "The False Dawn of the Sunset Laws." *Public Interest* 49, pp. 103-118.

Ibid. 1978. "How to Terminate a Public Policy: A Dozen Hints for the would be Terminator." *Policy Analysis* 4:3, pp. 393-413.

Bellamy, Alex J. et al. 2004. *Understanding Peacekeeping.* Cambridge: Polity Press.

Bellwood, Peter et al., eds. 2006. *The Austronesians. Historical and Comparative Perspectives.* Canberra: ANU E Press.

Benner, Thorsten et al. 2008. "Learning to Learn? UN Peacebuilding and the Challenges of Building a Learning Organization." *Journal of Intervention and State-building* 2:1, pp. 43-62.

Bennett, Andrew. 2003. "A Lakatosian Reading of Lakatos: What can we Salvage from the Hard Core?" In: Colin Elman and Miriam Elman, eds., *Progress in International Relations Theory. Appraising the Field.* Cambridge: MIT Press, pp. 455-494.

Bennett, Andrew and George, Alexander L. 1997a. *Research Designs Tasks in Case Study Methods.* Paper presented at MacArthur Workshop, 17-19 October 1997, Harvard University.

Ibid. 1997b. *Process Tracing in Case Study Research.* Paper presented at MacArthur Workshop, 17-19 October 1997, Harvard University.

Ibid. 2001. "Case Studies and Process Tracing in History and Political Science: Similar Strokes for Different Foci." In: Colin Elman and Miriam Fendius Elman, eds., *Bridges and Boundaries: Historians, Political Scientists, and the Study of International Relations.* Cambridge: MIT Press, pp. 137-166.

Ibid. 2005. *Case Studies and Theory Development in the Social Sciences.* Cambridge: MIT Press.

Berdal, Mats and Caplan, Richard. 2004. "The Politics of International Administration." *Global Governance* 19/1, pp. 1-5.

Beyme, Klaus v. 1992. *Theorie Der Politik Im 20. Jahrhundert: Von Der Moderne Zur Postmoderne*, 2nd ed. Frankfurt a.M.: Suhrkamp.

Binnendijk, Hans et al. 2006. *Solutions for Northern Kosovo: Lessons Learned in Mostar, Eastern Slavonia, and Brcko.* Washington, DC: National Defense University.

Blatter, Joachim et al. 2007. *Qualitative Politikanalyse.* Eine Einführung in Forschungsansätze und Methoden. Wiesbaden: VS Verlag für Sozialwissenschaften.

Blitz, Brad K. 2003. "Refugee Returns in Croatia: Contradictions and Reform." *Politics* 23:3, pp. 181-191.

Blom, Hans J. C. and P. Romijn. 2002. *Reconstruction, Background, Consequences and Analyzes of the Fall of a Safe Area.* Amsterdam: Netherlands Institute for War Documentation.

Bogner, Alexander, Beate Littig, and Wolfgang Menz. 2002. *Das Experteninterview. Theorie, Methode, Anwendung.* Opladen: VS Verlag für Sozialwissenschaften.

Boin, Arjen and 't Hart, Paul. 2003. "Leadership in Times of Crisis: Mission Impossible?" *Public Administration Review* 63:5, pp. 544-553.

Bonacker, Thorsten. 2008. *Sozialwissenschaftliche Konflikttheorien: Eine Einführung.* Wiesbaden: VS Verlag für Sozialwissenschaften.

Booth, Anne. 2001. "Poverty, Equity and Living Standards in East Timor: Challenges for the New Nation." In: Hal Hill and Joao M. Saldanha, eds., *East Timor: Development Challenges for the World's Newest Nation.* Singapore: ISEAS, pp. 241-255.

Boothby, Derek G. 2003. "The Successful Application of Leverage in Eastern Slavonia." In: Jean Krasno et al., eds., *Leveraging for Success in United Nations Peace Operations.* Westport: Praeger, pp. 117-140.

Ibid. 2004. "The Political Challenges of Administering Eastern Slavonia." *Global Governance* 10:1, pp. 37-51.

Bratt, Duane. 1996. "Assessing the Success of UN Peacekeeping Operations." *International Peacekeeping* 33:4, pp. 64-81.

Breen, Bob. 2003. "Lessons for the Future." In: Nassrine Azimi and Li Lin Chang, eds., *The United Nations Transitional Administration in East Timor (UNTAET): Debriefing and Lessons.* Leiden/Boston: Martinus Nijhoff Publishers, pp. 205-228.

Breul, Rainer. 2005. *Organizational Learning in International Organizations: The Case of UN Peace Operations.* Konstanz: University of Konstanz.

Brewer, Garry D. 1978. "Termination: Hard Choices – Harder Questions." *Public Administration Review* 38:4, pp. 338-344.

Brockner, Joel. 1992. "The Escalation of Commitment to a Failing Course of Action." *Academy of Management Review* 17, pp. 39-61.

Bryman, Alan. 1992. *Charisma & Leadership in Organizations.* London: Sage Publications.

Budiardjo, Carmel and Liem, Soei L. 1984. *War Against East Timor.* London: Zed Books.

Bunge, Mario. 1974. *Treatise on Basic Philosophy, Vol. I.* Dodrecht: Reidel Publishing Company.

Butler, John K. 1996. "Two Integrative Win-Win Negotiation Strategies." *Simulation & Gaming* 27:3, pp. 387-392.

Cain, Kenneth et al. 2006. *Emergency Sex and Other Desperate Measures. True Stories from a War Zone.* New York: Miramax.

Call, Chuck and Barnett, Michael. 1999. "Looking for a Few Good Cops: Peacekeeping, Peacebuilding, and CIVPOL." *International Peacekeeping* 6:4, pp. 43-68.

Caplan, Richard. 2002. *A New Trusteeship? The International Administration of War-Torn Territories.* Adelphi Paper No. 341. Oxford: Oxford University Press for the International Institute for Strategic Studies.

Ibid. 2005. *International Governance of War-Torn Territories. Role and Reconstruction.* Oxford: Oxford University Press.

Chandler, David. 2000. "Western Intervention and the Disintegration of Yugoslavia, 1989-1999." In: Hammond and Edward S. Herman, eds., *Degraded Capability: The Media and the Kosovo Crisis.* London: Pluto Press, pp. 19-30.

Checkel, Jeffrey T. 2005. *It's the Process, Stupid!* Working Paper No. 26. Centre for European Studies, University of Oslo.

Chesterman, Simon. 2002. *Justice Under International Administration: Kosovo, East Timor and Afghanistan.* New York: International Peace Academy.

Ibid. 2004. *You, the People. the United Nations, Transitional Administration, and State-Building.* Oxford: Oxford University Press.

Ibid. 2005. *Building Up Or Building Down the State. State-Building and Humanitarian and Development Assistance.* Paper presented at SSRC Humanitarian Action Seminar, New York.

Ibid. 2006. *Shared Secrets: Intelligence and Collective Security.* Lowy Institute Paper 10. Sydney: Lowy Institute for International Policy.

Chopra, Jarat. 1999. *Peace-Maintenance – the Evolution of International Political Authority.* London: Routledge.

Ibid. 2000. "The UN's Kingdom of East Timor." *Survival* 42:3, pp. 27-39.

Ibid. 2002. "Building State Failure in East Timor." *Development and Change* 33:5, pp. 979-1000.

Chopra, Jarat and Hohe, Tanja. 2004. "Participatory Intervention." *Global Governance* 10:3, pp. 233-246.

Ćirković, Sima. 1999. "Zur Ethnogenese Auf Dem Gebiet Des Ehemaligen Jugoslawien." In: Dunja Melčić, ed., *Der Jugoslawien-Krieg. Handbuch zu Vorgeschichte, Verlauf und Konsequenzen*. Opladen: Westdeutscher Verlag, pp. 14-27.

Cohen, M. D. and March, James G. 1974. *Leadership and Ambiguity: The American College President*. New York: McGraw-Hill.

Coleiro, Christine. 2002. *Bringing Peace to the Land of Scorpions and Jumping Snakes: The Legacy of the United Nations in Eastern Slavonia and Transitional Missions*. Clemensport: Canadian Peacekeeping Press Publications.

Collier, David et al. 2003. "Qualitative Versus Quantitative: What does this Distinction Mean?" *Qualitative Methods, Newsletter of the American Political Science Association, Organized Section on Qualitative Methods* 1:1, pp. 4-9.

Ibid. 2004. "Sources of Leverage in Causal Inference: Toward an Alternative View of Methodology." In: David Collier and H.E. Brady, eds., *Rethinking Social Inquiry: Diverse Tools Shared Standards*. Lanham: Rowman & Littlefield, pp. 229-266.

Conflict Security & Development Group at King's College (CSDG). 2003. *A Review of Peace Operations: A Case for Change. East Timor Report*. London: King's College.

Conger, Jay. 1999. "Charismatic and Transformational Leadership in Organizations: An Insider's Perspective on these Developing Streams of Research." *The Leadership Quarterly* 10:2, pp. 145-180.

Corbin, Juliet and Strauss, Anselm. 2008. *Basics of Qualitative Research: Techniques and Procedures for Developing Grounded Theory*. 3rd ed. Los Angeles: Sage.

Cotton, James. 2000. "The Emergence of an Independent East Timor: National and Regional Challenges." *Contemporary Southeast Asia* 22:1, pp. 2-6.

Crozier, Michel and Friedberg, Erhard. 1977. *L'Acteur Et Le Système: Les Contraintes De l'Action Collective*. Paris: Seuil.

Cyert, Richard M. and March, James G. 1963. *A Behavioral Theory of the Firm*. Englewood Cliffs: Prentice Hall.

Daase, Christopher. 1999. "Spontaneous Institutions: Peacekeeping as an International Convention." In: Helga Haftendorn, ed., *Imperfect Unions: Security Institutions Over Time and Space*. Oxford: Oxford University Press, pp. 223-258.

Daniels, Mark Ross. 1977. *Terminating Public Programs: An American Paradox*. Armonk: Sharpe.

Ibid. 1995. "Closing the Oklahoma Public Training Schools." *Policy Sciences* 28: pp. 301-316.

Danziger, James N. 1976. "Assessing Incrementalism in British Municipal Budgeting." *British Journal of Political Science* 6:3, pp. 335-350.

DeLeon, Peter. 1978a. "Public Policy Termination: An End Or a Beginning." *Policy Analysis* 4, pp. 369-392.

Ibid. 1978b. "A Theory of Policy TerminationThe Policy Cycle." In: Judith May and Arron Wildavsky, eds., *The Policy Cycle*. Beverly Hills: Sage, pp. 279-300.

Ibid. 1987. "Policy Termination as a Political Phenomenon." In: Dennis Palumbo, ed., *The Politics of Program Evaluation*. San Francisco: Sage, pp. 173-202.

De Sousa, Lurdes S. 2001. "Some Facts and Comments on the East Timor 2001 Constituent Assembly Election." *Lusotopie*, pp. 299-311.

Dessler, David. 1989. "What's at Stake in the Structure-Agency Debate?" *International Organization* 43:3, pp. 441-473.

Ibid. 2003. "Explanation and Scientific Progress." In: Colin Elman and Miriam Fendius Elman, eds., *Progress in International Relations Theory. Appraising the Field.* Cambridge: MIT Press, pp. 381-404.

Deutsch, Karl. 1963. *The Nerves of Government: Models of Political Communication and Control.* Glencoe: The Free Press.

Diehl, Paul F. 2008. *Peace Operations.* Cambridge: Polity Press.

DiMaggio, Paul J. and Powell, Walter W. 1983. "The Iron Cage Revisited: Institutional Isomorphism and Collective Rationality in Organizational Fields." *American Sociological Review* 48, pp. 147-160.

Dobbins, James et al. 2005. *The UN's Role in Nation-Building. from the Congo to Iraq.* New York: Rand Corporation.

Donini, Antonio. 1996. *The Policies of Mercy: UN Coordination in Afghanistan, Mozambique, and Rwanda.* Providence: Watson Insitute, Brown University.

Dörner, Dietrich. 2004. *Die Logik Des Misslingens. Strategisches Denken in Komplexen Situationen,* 2nd ed. Reinbek: Rowohlt.

Doyle, Michael W. 2002. "Strategy and Transitional Authority." In: Donald Rothchild et al., eds., *Ending Civil Wars: The Implementation of Peace Agreements.* Boulder: Lynne Rienner, pp. 71-88.

Ibid. 2007. "The John W. Holmes Lecture: Building Peace." *Global Governance* 13:1, pp. 1-15.

Doyle, Michael W. and Müller, Jan. 1998. "Anatomie Eines Erfolges. Die UN-Mission in Ostslawonien." *Internationale Politik* 53:6, pp. 34-38.

Doyle, Michael W. and Sambanis, Nicholas. 2000. "International Peacebuilding: A Theoretical and Quantitative Analysis." *American Political Science Review* 94:4, pp. 779-801.

Ibid. 2006. *Making War and Building Peace. United Nations Peace Operations.* Princeton: Princeton University Press.

Dunn, James. 2003. *A Rough Passage to Independence,* 3rd ed. Double Bay: Longueville Books.

Duque Gonzáles, Armando et al. 2002. *Evaluation of United Nations System Ressponse in East Timor: Coordination and Effectiveness.* Geneva: United Nations.

Eide, Espen B. et al. 2005. *Report on Integrated Missions: Practical Perspectives and Recommendations.* Independent Study for the Expanded UN ECHA Core Group, May 2005.

Eisenbeiß, Silke, "Thesen für die mündliche Doktorprüfung," on file with the author.

Eisenhardt, Kathleen M. 1989. "Agency Theory: An Assessment and Review." *Academy of Management Review* 14:1, pp. 57-74.

Elges, Reinhold. 2004. *International State-building – Time to Reconsider.* Paper presented at POWI 04, Graduiertenkonferenz: Neue Impulse für die Politikwissenschaft in Österreich.

Elster, Jon. 1992. "Arguing and Bargaining in the Federal Convention and the Assemblée Constituante." In R. Malnes and A. Underdal, eds., *Rationality and Institutions. Essays in Honour of Knut Midgaard.* Oslo: Universitetsforlaget, pp. 13-50.

Ensign, Prescott C. 2001. "The Concept of Fit in Organizational Research." *International Journal of Organizational Theory and Behavior* 4:3/4, pp. 287-306.

Entman, Robert M. 1993. "Framing: Toward Clarification of a Fractured Paradigm." *Journal of Communication* 43:4, pp. 51-58.

Essens, Peter et al., eds., 2001. *The Human in Command: Peace Support Operations.* Amsterdam: Mets & Schilt.

Etzioni, Amitai. 1968. *The Active Society a Theory of Societal and Political Processes.* New York: The Free Press.

Ibid. 1989. "Humble Decision Making." *Harvard Business Review*, pp. 122-126.

Evans, Gareth. 2008. *The Responsibility to Protect: Ending Mass Atrocity Crimes Once and for All*. Washington, DC: Brookings Institution Press.

Fama, Eugene F. 1980. "Agency Problems and the Theory of the Firm." *Journal of Political Economy* 80, pp. 288-307.

Festinger, Leo A. 1957. *A Theory of Cognitive Dissonance*. Stanford: Stanford University Press.

Ibid. 1964. *Conflict, Decision, and Dissonance*. Stanford: Stanford University Press.

Fielding, Nigel G. and Lee, Raymond M. 1998. *Computer Analysis and Qualitative Research*. London: Sage.

Findlay, Trevor. 1995. *Cambodia—the Legacy and Lessons of UNTAC*. Stockholm: SIPRI.

Fligstein, Neil. 2001. "Social Skill and the Theory of Fields." *Sociological Theory* 19:2, pp. 105-125.

Forster, Michael. 2005. *Nation Building Durch Die Internationale Gemeinschaft. Eine Völkerrechtliche Analyse Der Vereinteen Nationen Im Kosovo Und in Ost-Timor*. Göttingen: Cuvillier.

Fox, James J. 2002. *East Timor: Assessing UNTAET's Role in Building Local Capacities for the Future*. Canberra: Council for Asia Europe Cooperation.

Frantz, Janet E. 1992. "Reviving and Revisiting a Termination Model." *Policy Sciences* 25:1, pp. 175-186.

Frey, Theo. 1999. "Ost-Timor: Teuflische Allianz." *Zeitschrift für Friedenspolitik* 5. Available online at http://www.efriz.ch/cgi/sfc.pl?a=/sys/htm/menu.html&b=/archiv/995/a-1.html, last access 16 March 2009.

Fröhlich, Manuel e. a. 2006. "Mapping UN Presence. A Follow-Up to the Human Security Report." *Die Friedenswarte. Journal of International Peace and Organization* 81:2, pp. 13-23.

Fukuyama, Francis. 2004. *State-building—Governance and World Order in the 21st Century*. Ithaca: Cornell University Press.

Funke, Joachim. 1991. "Solving Complex Problems: Exploration and Control of Complex Social Systems." In: Peter A. Frensch and Robert J. Steinberg, eds., A *Complex Problem Solving. Principles and Mechanisms*. New Jersey: Lawrence Erlbaum Assoc, pp. 185-222.

Ganghof, Steffen. 2003. "Promises and Pitfalls of Veto Player Analysis." *Swiss Political Science Review* 9:2, pp. 1-25.

Gardner, W. L. and Avolio, B.J. 1998. "The Charismatic Relationship: A Dramaturgical Perspective." *Academy of Management Journal* 23, pp. 32-58.

Garrison, Randall. 2005. *The Role of Constitution-Building Processes in Democratization*. Paper Prepared for IDEA's Democracy and Conflict Management Programme. Paper prepared for IDEA's Democracy and Conflict Management Programme. Stockholm: International Institute for Democracy and Electoral Assistance (IDEA).

George, Alexander. 1974. "Adaptation to Stress in Political Decision Making: The Individual, Small Group, and Organizational Contexts." In: D.A. Hamburg, G.V. Coelho, and J.E. Adams, eds., *Coping and Adaptation*. New York: Basic Books, pp. 176-245.

George, Alexander L. and McKeown, Timothy K. 1985. "Case Studies and Theories in Organizational Decision Making." In: Robert Coulam and Richard Smith, eds., *Advances in Information Processing in Organizations*, Vol. 2. Greenwich: JAI Press.

Gerring, J. 2004. "What is a Case Study and what is Good for?" *American Political Science Review* 98, pp. 341-354.

Geva-May, Iris. 2004. "Riding the Wave of Opportunity: Termination in Public Policy." *Journal of Public Administration Research and Theory* 14:3, pp. 309-333.

Gibbs, Graham. 2002. *Qualitative Data Analysis: Explorations with NVivo*. Buckingham: Open University Press.

Giddens, Anthony. 1984. *The Constitution of Society. Outline of a Theory of Structuration*. Cambridge: Polity Press.

Gigerenzer, Gerd and Todd, Peter M. 1999. "Fast and Frugal Heuristics—the Adaptive Toolbox." In: Gerd Gigerenzer, Peter M. Todd, and the ABC Research Group, eds., *Simple Heuristics that make Us Smart*. New York: OUP, pp. 3-36.

Gigerenzer, Gerd. 2001. "The Adaptive Toolbox." In: Gerd Gigerenzer and Reinhard Selten, eds., *Bounded Rationality: The Adaptive Toolbox*. Cambridge: MIT Press, pp. 37-50.

Gläser, Jochen and Laudel, Grit. 2004. *Experteninterviews und Qualitative Inhaltsanalyse Als Instrumente Rekonstruierender Untersuchungen*. Wiesbaden: VS Verlag für Sozialwissenschaften.

Goffman, Erving. 1959. *The Presentation of Self in Everyday Life*. New York: Double Day.

Goldberg, Victor P. 1976. "Regulation and Administered Contracts." *Bell Journal of Economics and Management Science* 7, pp. 426-448.

Goldstone, Anthony. 2004. "UNTAET with Hindsight: The Peculiarities of Politics in an Incomplete State." *Global Governance* 10, pp. 83-98.

Gorjao, Paulo. 2002. "The Legacy and Lessons of UNTAET." *Contemporary Southeast Asia*, 24:2, pp. 313-336.

Gravelle, Robert J. A. R. Undated. *The United Nations Transitional Administration in Eastern Slavonia, Baranja, and Western Sirmium (UNTAES): A Successful Mission*, on file with the author.

Haas, Ernst B. 1990. *When Knowledge is Power. Three Models of Change in International Organizations*. Berkeley: University of California Press.

Hall, Richard H. 1972. *Organizations—Stucture and Process*. Englewood Cliffs: Prentice Hall.

Hampson, Fen O. 1996. *Nurturing Peace – Why Peace Settlements Succeed Or Fail*. Washington, DC: United States Institute of Peace Press.

Harland, David. 2004. "Legitimacy and Effectiveness." *Global Governance* 10, pp. 15-19.

Ibid. 2005. *UN Peacekeeping Operations in Post-Conflict Timor-Leste: Accomplishments and Lessons Learned. UNTAET Governance and Public Information: 1999 to Mid-2000*. New York: UN Department of Peacekeeping Operations.

Harston, Julian, 2005. *United Nations as Ambivalent Administrator in the Balkans and East Timor*. Manuscript for UNITAR Conference in Hiroshima, March 2005, on file with the author

Heiner, R. A. 1983. "The Origins of Predictable Behavior." *American Economic Review* 73, pp. 560-595.

Heisig, Ulrich and Littek, Wolfgang. 1995. "Wandel von Vertrauensbeziehungen im Arbeitsprozess." *Soziale Welt* 46, pp. 282-304.

Herrhausen, Anna. 2007. *Coordination in United Nations Peacebuilding. Discussion Paper SP IV 2007-301*. Berlin: Wissenschaftszentrum Berlin für Sozialforschung.

Hill, Hal and Saldanha, Joao M. 2001. "The Key Issues." In: ibid., eds., *East Timor. Development Challenges for the World's Newest Nation*. Singapore: Institute of Southeast Asian Studies, pp. 3-36.

Hohe, Tanja. 2002a. "Totem Polls: Indigenous Concepts and 'Free and Fair' Elections in East Timor." *International Peacekeeping* 9:4, pp. 69-88

Ibid. 2002b. "The Clash of Paradigms: International Administration and Local Political Legitimacy in East Timor." *Contemporary Southeast Asia* 24:3, pp. 569-589.

Holbrooke, Richard C. 1998. *To End a War*. New York: Random House.

Hollingworth, Larry. 2003. "Resolutions, Mandates, Aims, Missions, and Exit Strategies." In: Kevin McCahill, ed., *Emergency Relief Operations*. New York: Fordham University Press, pp. 267-283.

Holsti, Ole R. 1979. "Theories of Crisis Decision Making." In: Paul Gordon Lauren, ed., *Diplomacy. New Approaches in History, Theory, and Policy*. New York: The Free Press, pp. 99-136.

Hooper, Rick and Taylor, Mark. 1999. *Command from the Saddle. Managing United Nations Peace-Building Missions. Recommendations Report of the Forum on the Special Representative of the Secretary General. Shaping the UN's Role in Peace Implementations*. Oslo: Fafo Institute for Applied Social Science.

House, Robert J. 1977. "A 1976 Theory of Charismatic Leadership." In: J. G. Hund and L. L. Larson, eds., *Leadership: The Cutting Edge*. Carbondale: Southern Illinois University Press, pp. 189-207.

House, Robert J. and Klein, K. J. 1995. "On Fire: Charismatic Leadership and Levels of Analysis." *Leadership Quarterly* 6, pp. 183-198.

Howard, Lise M. 2008. *UN Peacekeeping in Civil Wars*. Cambridge: Cambridge University Press.

Howlett, Michael and M. Ramesh. 2003. *Studying Public Policy. Policy Cycles and Policy Subsystems*, 2nd ed. ed. New York: OUP.

Ikenberry, G. J. 1994. *History's Heavy Hand: Institutions and the Politics of the State*. Paper Presented at Conference on New Institutionalism, University of Maryland.

Ingram, Sue. 2003. "Mission Implementation: Developing Institutional Capacities." In: Nassrine Azimi and Li Lin Chang, eds., *The United Nations Transitional Administration in East Timor (UNTAET): Debriefing and Lessons*. Leiden/Boston: Martinus Nijhoff Publishers, pp. 85-94.

Ivory, Chris and Vaughan, Roger. 2008. "The Role of Framing in Complex Transitional Projects." *Long Range Planning* 41, pp. 93-106.

Janis, Irving L. 1972. *Victims of Groupthink. A Psychological Study of Foreign-Policy Decisions and Fiascoes*. Boston, Mass: Houghton Mifflin.

Janis, Irving L. 1985. "Coping Patterns among Patients with Life-Threatening Diseases." In: Charles D. Spielberger et al., eds., *Stress and Anxiety, Vol. 9*. The Series in Clinical and Community Psychology.

Ibid. 1989. *Crucial Decisions—Leadership in Policymaking and Crisis Management*. New York/ London: The Free Press/Collier Macmillan Publishers.

Janis, Irving L. and Mann, Leon. 1977. *Decision-Making—A Psychological Analysis of Conflict, Choice, and Commitment*. New York: The Free Press.

Jones, Bruce and Charif, Feryal. 2004. Evolving Models of Peacekeeping – Policy Implications and Responses. New York: United Nations Peacekeeping Best Practice.

Junne, Gerd and Verkoren, Willemijn, eds., 2004. *Postconflict Development: Meeting New Challenges*. Boulder: Lynne Rienner Publishers.

Kahn, R. L. and Boysiere, P. 1992. "Stress in Organization." In: Marvin D. Dunette and L. M. Gough, eds., *Handbook of Industrial and Organizational Psychology*, Vol. III, 2nd. Palo Alto: Consulting Psychologists Press, pp. 571-650.

Kark, R., B. Shamir, and Chen, G. 2003. "The Two Faces of Transformational Leadership: Empowerment and Dependency." *Journal of Applied Psychology* 88:2, pp. 246-255.

Kaufman, Herbert. 1976. *Are Government Organizations Immortal?*. Washington, DC: Brookings Institution Press.

Ibid. 1987. *Time, Chance, and Organizations: Natural Selections in a Perilous Environment*. Chatham: Chatham House.

King, Dwight. 2003. "East Timor's Founding Elections and Emerging Party System." *Asian Survey* 43:5, pp. 745-758.

King, Gary et al. 1994. *Designing Social Inquiry: Scientific Inference in Qualitative Research*. Princeton: Princeton University Press.

Kingdon, John. 1995. *Agendas, Alternatives, and Public Policies*, 2nd ed. ed. New York: Harper Collins.

Klein, Gary. 1998. *Sources of Power. How People Make Decisions*. Cambridge, Mass: MIT Press.

Klein, K. J. and House, Robert J. 1995. "On Fire: Charismatic Leadership and Levels of Analysis." *Leadership Quarterly* 6, pp. 183-198.

Kogut, B. and Zander, U. 1992. "Knowledge of the Firm, Combinative Capabilities, and the Replication of Technology." *Organizational Science* 3, pp. 383-397.

Kramer, Roderick M. and Tylor, Tom R. 1995. *Trust in Organizations. Frontiers of Theory and Research*. Thousand Oaks: Sage.

Laffont, Jean-Jacques and Martimort, David. 2002. *The Theory of Incentives. the Principal-Agent Model*. Princeton: Princeton University Press.

Lakatos, Imre. 1970. "Falsification and the Methodology of Scientific Reserach Programmes." In: Imre Lakatos and Alan Musgrave, eds., *Criticism and the Growth of Knowledge: Proceedings of the International Colloquium in the Philosophy of Science, London 1965*. Cambridge: Cambridge University Press, pp. 91-196.

Lawson, M. 2001. "In Praise of Slack: Time is of the Essence." *Academy of Management Executive* 15:3, pp. 125-135.

Lazarus, R. S. et al. 1974. "The Psychology of Coping: Issues of Research and Assessment." In: G. V. Coelho et al., eds., *Coping and Adaptation*. New York: Basic Books, pp. 249-315.

Lindblom, Charles E. 1959. "The Science of Muddling Through." *Public Administration Review* 19, pp. 79-88.

Ibid. 1965. *The Intelligence of Democracy*. New York: Macmillan.

Lipson, Michael. 2005. "Transgovernmental Networks and Nonproliferation: International Security and the Future of Global Governance." *International Journal* 61:1, pp. 179-198.

Ibid. 2007a. "Peacekeeping: Organized Hypocrisy?" *European Journal of International Relations* 13:1, pp. 5-34.

Ibid. 2007b. "A 'Garbage can Model" of UN Peacekeeping.'" *Global Governance* 13:1, pp. 79-97.

Little, Daniel. 1991. *Varieties of Social Explanation: An Introduction to the Philosophy of Social Science*. Boulder: Westview Press.

Lyons, Terrence. 2002. *Postconflict Elections: War Termiantion, Democratization, and Demiliarizing Politics*. Working Paper No. 20, Institute for Conflict Analysis and Resolution. Fairfax: George Mason University.

MacGrimmon, Kenneth R. and Taylor, Ronald N. 1983. "Decision Making and Problem Solving." In: Marvin D. Dunnette, ed., *Handbook of Industrial and Organizational Psychology*. New York: John Wiley & Sons, pp. 1397-1453.

Magas, Braka. 2007. *Croatia through History. The Making of a European State*. London: Saqi Books.

Mahoney, James and Goertz, Gary. 2004. "The Possibility Principle: Choosing Negative Cases in Comparative Research." *American Political Science Review* 98, pp. 653-669.

Marais, Karen et al. 2004. *Beyond Normal Accidents and High Reliability Organizations: Lessons from the Space Shuttle*. ESD External Symposium, March 2004, Cambridge.

March, James G. 1978. "Bounded Rationality, Ambiguity, and the Engineering of Choice." *The Bell Journal of Economics* 9:2, pp. 587-608.

465

Ibid. 1978. "Bounded Rationality, Ambiguity, and the Engineering of Choice." *The Bell Journal of Economics* 9:2, pp. 587-608.

March, James and Olsen, Johan. 1986. "Garbage Can Models of Decision Making in Organizations." In: James G. March and Roger Weissinger-Baylon, eds., *Ambiguity and Command. Organizational Perspectives on Military Decision Making.* New York: Longman, pp. 11-35.

March, James G. and Olsen, Johan P. 1976. *Ambiguity and Choice in Organizations.* Bergen: Universitetsforlaget.

March, James G. and Simon, Herbert A. 1958. *Organizations.* New York: Wiley.

Martin, Ian and Mayer-Rieckh, Alexander. 2005. "The United Nations and East Timor: From Self-Determination to State-Building." *International Peacekeeping* 12:1, pp. 125-145.

Martin, Ian. 2001. "Self-Determination in East Timor: The United Nations, the Ballot, and International Intervention." *Contemporary Southeast Asia* 22:1, pp. 8-20.

Maull, Hanns W. 2001. *Report on the Task Force Meeting.* Paper presented at Task Force: Comparing Experiences with Post-Conflict State-Building in Asia and Europe: The Cases of East Timor, Bosnia and Kosovo, Bali, Indonesia.

Mayring, Philipp. 1993. *Qualitative Inhaltsanalyse. Grundlagen und Techniken.* Weinheim: Deutscher Studien Verlag.

Mazower, Mark. 2000. *The Balkans. A Short History.* London: Random House.

McDonald, Brian. 2001. *On the Road to Peace: The Implementation of the EU Special Support Programme for Peace and Reconciliation.* Monaghan: ADM/CPA Peace Programme.

McNamara, Dennis. 2003. "Introductory Remarks and Keynote Adress." In: Nassrine Azimi and Li Lin Chang, eds., *The United Nations Transitional Administration in East Timor (UNTAET): Debriefing and Lessons.* Boston: Martinus Nijhoff Publishers, pp. 33-44.

Meyer, John W. and Rowan, Brian. 1977. "Institutionalized Organizations: Formal Structure as Myth and Ceremony." *The American Journal of Sociology* 83:2, pp. 340-363.

Meyer, Marshall W. and Zucker Lynne G. 1989. *Permanently Failing Organizations.* London: Sage.

Milgrom, Paul and Roberts, John. 1988. "An Economic Approach to Influence Activities in Organizations." *American Journal of Sociology* 94 (Supplement), pp. 154-179.

Monteiro, Antonio. 2003. "Additional Remarks." In: Nassrine Azimi and Chang Li Lin, eds., *The United Nations Transitional Administration in East Timor (UNTAET): Debriefing and Lessons.* Report of the 2002 Tokyo Conference. Boston/Leiden: Martinus Nijhoff Publishers for UNITAR, pp. 235-241.

Moravcsik, Andrew. 1997. "Taking Preferences Seriously. A Liberal Theory of International Politics." *International Organization* 51:4, pp. 513-553.

Ibid. 2003. "Liberal International Relations Theory. A Scientific Assessment." In: Colin Elman and Miriam Fendius Elman, eds., *Progress in International Relations Theory. Appraising the Field.* Cambridge: MIT Press, pp. 159-204.

Mortimer, Edward. 2004. "International Administration of War-torn Societies." *Global Governance* 10/1, pp. 7-14.

Newmann, Edward and Rich, Roland, eds., 2004. *The UN Role in Promoting Democracy. between Ideals and Reality.* New York: United Nations University Press.

Nietzsche, Friedrich. 1990. *Menschliches, Allzumenschliches, Vol. 1,* 8th ed. Friedrich Nietzsche: Werke. Leipzig: Naumann.

Olk, Thomas. 1996. "Wohlfahrtsverbände Im Transformationsprozess Ostdeutschlands." In: R. Kollmorgen et al., eds., *Sozialer Wandel Und Akteure in Ostdeutschland. Empirische Befunde Und Theoretische Ansätze.* Opladen: Leske + Budrich, pp. 179-216.

Ottaway, Marina S. and Krishna Kumar, eds., 1998. *Postconflict Elections, Democratization and International Assistance.* Coulder: Lynne Rienner.

Owen, John M. 2002. "The Foreign Imposition of Domestic Institutions." *International Organization* 56:2, pp. 375-409.

Page-Fortna, Virginia. 2004. "Does Peacekeeping Keep Peace? International Intervention and the Duration of Peace after Civil War." *International Studies Quarterly* 48, pp. 269-292.

Ibid. 2008. *Does Peacekeeping Work? Shaping Belligerent's Choices After Civil War.* Princeton: Princeton University Press.

Page-Fortna, Virginia and Howard, Lise M. 2008. "Pitfalls and Prospects in the Peacekeeping Literature." *Annual Review of Political Science* 11, pp. 283-301.

Paris, Roland. 2004. *At War's End. Building Peace After Civil Conflict.* New York: Cambridge University Press.

Pauchant, T. C. and Mitroff, I. 1992. *Transforming the Crisis-Prone Organization. Preventing Individual, Organizational and Environmental Tragedies.* San Francisco: Jossey-Bass.

Pavlowitch, Stefan K. 2002. *Serbia: The History behind the Name.* London: Hurst

Pawlowski, Peter and Neubauer, Katja. 2001. "Organisationales Lernen." In: Elke Weik and Rainhart Lang, eds., *Moderne Organisationstheorien – Eine Sozialwissenschaftliche Einführung.* Wiesbaden: Lang, pp. 253-284.

Peck, Connie. 2004. "Special Representatives of the Secretary General." In: David M. Malone, ed., *The UN Security Council—from the Cold War to the 21st Century.* Boulder: Lynne Rienner, pp. 325-339.

Perrow, Charles. 1984. *Normal Accidents: Living with High-Risk Technologies.* New York: Basic Books.

Ibid. 1986. *Complex Organizations: A Critical Essay.* New York: McGraw-Hill.

Ibid. 1993. *Complex Organizations,* 3rd ed. New York: McGraw-Hill.

Ibid. 1999. "Organizing to Reduce the Vulnerabilities of Complexity." *Journal of Contingencies and Crisis Management* 7:3, pp. 150-155.

Peterson, Randall S. et al. 1998. "Group Dynamics in Top Management Teams: Groupthink, Vigilance, and Alternative Models of Organizational Failure and Success." *Organizational Behavior and Human Decision Processes* 73:2/3, pp. 272-305.

Picot, A. et al. 2000. *Organisation—Eine Ökonomische Perspektive.* Stuttgart: Schäffer-Poeschel.

Pierson, Paul. 2000. "Not just what, but when: Timing and Sequence in Political Processes." *Studies in American Political Development* 14, pp. 72-92.

Ibid. 2004. 2004. *Politics in Time.* Princeton: Princeton University Press.

Plümper, Thomas. 1996. "Entscheidung unter Unsicherheit und die Rationalität von Routinen." In Ulrich Druwe and V. Kunz, eds., *Handlungs- Und Entscheidungstheorie in Der Politikwissenschaft.* Opladen: Leske + Budrich, pp. 177-206.

Power, Samantha. 2008. *The Man for Dark Times: Sergio Vieira De Mello and the Fight to Save the World.* New York: Penguin Press.

Provan, Keith. 1982. "Interorganizational Linkages and Influence Over Decision Making." *The Academy of Management Journal* 25:2, pp. 443-451.

Pruitt, Dean G. 2001. "Achieving Integrative Agreements." In: Ira G. Asherman and Sandra Vance Asherman, eds., *The Negotiation Sourcebook.* Amherst: HRD Press, pp. 187-196.

Puchala, Donald J. 1993. "The Secretary-General and His Special Representatives." In: Leon Gordenker and Benjamin Rivlin, eds., *The Challenging Role of the UN Secretary- General. Making "The most Impossible in the World" Possible.* Westport: Praeger, pp. 81-97.

Pugh, Michael. 1995. "Peacebuilding as Developmentalism: Concepts from Disaster Research." *Contemporary Security Policy* 16:3, pp. 320-346.

467

Putnam, Robert D. 1988. "Diplomacy and Domestic Politics: The Logic of Two-Level Games." *International Organization* 42:3, pp. 427-460.

Radner, Roy. 1975a. "A Behavioral Model of Cost Reduction." *The Bell Journal of Economics* 6:1, pp. 196-215.

Ibid. 1975b. "Satisficing." *Journal of Mathematical Economics* 2, pp. 253-262.

Rathfelder, Erich. 1999. "Der Krieg an Seinen Schauplätzen." In: Dunja Melčić, ed., *Der Jugoslawien-Krieg. Handbuch zu Vorgeschichte, Verlauf und Konsequenzen.* Opladen: Westdeutscher Verlag, pp. 345-363.

Rauchhaus, Robert. 2006. *Principal-Agent Problems in Conflict Management: Moral Hazards, Adverse Selection, and the Commitment Dilemma.* Paper presented at Annual meeting of the American Political Science Association, Pennsylvania Convention Center, Philadelphia.

Reason, J. T. 1997. *Managing the Risks of Organizational Accidents.* Burlington, VT: Ashgate Publishing.

Rich, Roland and Newmann, Edward. 2004. "Introduction: Approaching Democratization Policy." In: ibid., eds., *The UN Role in Promoting Democracy. Between Ideals and Reality.* New York: United Nations University Press, pp. 3-31.

Rittberger, Berthold and Schimmelfennig, Frank. 2006. "Explaining the Constitutionalization of the European Union." *Journal of European Public Policy* 13:8, pp. 1148-1167.

Rivlin, Benjamin. 1992. "Regional Arrangements and the UN System for Collective Security and Conflict Resolution: A New Road Ahead?" *International Relations* 11:2, pp. 95-110.

Roberto, Michael A. 2002. "Lessons from Everest: The Interaction of Cognitive Bias, Psychological Safety, and System Complexity." *California Management Review* 45:1, pp. 136-158.

Roberts, Nancy and King, Paul. 1996. *Transforming Public Policy. Dynamics of Policy Entrepreneurship and Innovation.* San Francisco: Jossey-Bass.

Rockeach, Milton. 1960. *The Open and Closed Mind.* New York: Basic Books.

Rodrigues, Ruben. 2003. "Introductory Remarks and Keynote Address: There is no Success without Shared Responsibility." In: Nassrine Azimi and Chang Li Lin, eds., *The United Nations Transitional Administration in East Timor (UNTAET): Debriefing and Lessons.* Boston/ Leiden: Martinus Nijhoff Publishers for UNITAR, pp. 28-29.

Rohland, Klaas and Cliffe, Sarah. 2002. *The East Timor Reconstruction Program: Successes, Problems and Trade-Offs. CPR Working Paper No. 2.* Washington, DC: World Bank.

Rosamond, Ben. 2000. *Theories of European Integration.* Basingstoke: Palgrave.

Rose, Gideon. 1998. "The Exit Strategy Delusion." *Foreign Affairs*, pp. 56-67.

Ross, Stephen A. 1973. "The Economic Theory of Agency: The Principal's Problem." *American Economic Review* 63, pp. 134-139.

Rotberg, Robert. 2003. *When States Fail. Causes and Consequences.* Princeton: Princeton University Press.

Russo, J. Edward and Schoemaker, Paul, J.H. 1989. *Decision Traps: The Ten Barriers to Brillian Decision Making and how to Overcome them.* New York: Fireside.

Rust, Kathleen. 2002. *Organizational Slack and Performance: The Interactive Role of Workforce Changes.* Paper to be presented in the Strategic Management Track of the Midwest Academy of Management Conference.

Ryan, Alan. 2002. "The Strong Lead-Nation Model in an Ad Hoc Coalition of the Willing: Operation Stabilise in East Timor." *International Peacekeeping* 9:1, pp. 23-44.

Sackman, Sonja A. 1992. "Culture and Subcultures. An Analysis of Organizational Knowledge." *Administrative Science Quarterly* 19, pp. 140-161.

Saldanha, Joao M. 2003. "Mission Implementation: Developing Institutional Capacities." In: Nassrine Azimi and Li Lin Chang, eds., *The United Nations Transitional Administration in East Timor (UNTAET): Debriefing and Lessons*. Leiden/Boston: Martinus Nijhoff Publishers, pp. 161-168.

Salomons, Dirk. 2005. "Security: An Absolute Prerequisite." In: Gerd Junne and Willemijn Verkoren, eds., *Postconflict Development: Meeting New Challenges*. Boulder: Lynne Rienner, pp. 19-41.

Salomons, Dirk and Dijkzeul, Dennis. 2001. *The Conjurers' Hat. Financing United Nations Peace-Building in Operations Directed by Special Representatives of the Secretary-General*. New York: Center on International Cooperation, New York University and the Programme for International Co-operation and Conflict Resolution, Fafo Institute for Applied Social Science.

Scharpf, Fritz W. 1999. *Regieren in Europa*. Frankfurt a.M.: Campus.

Scheye, Eric. 2002. "Transitions to Local Authority Executive Policing." In: Renata Dwan, ed., *Enforcing the Law in Peace Operations*. New York: Oxford University Press, pp. 102-122.

Schimmelfennig, Frank. 2001. "The Community Trap: Liberal Norms, Rhetorical Action, and the Eastern Enlargement of the European Union." *International Organization* 55:1, pp. 47-80.

Ibid. 2006. "Explaining the Constitutionalization of the European Union." *Journal of European Public Policy* 13:8, pp. 1148-1167.

Schnell, Rainer et al. 1999. *Methoden Der Empirischen Sozialforschung*, 6th ed. München: Oldenbourg.

Schöndorf, Elisabeth. 2005. *Der Vergessene Hegemon. Die Vereinigten Staaten Und Die Europäische Integration*. Konstanz: University of Konstanz.

Schreyögg, Georg. 1999. *Organisation. Grundlagen Moderner Organisationsgestaltung*, 3rd ed. Wiesbaden: Gabler.

Schulz-Hardt, Stefan. 1997. *Realitätsflucht in Entscheidungsprozessen. Von Groupthink Zum Entscheidungsautismus*. Göttingen: Verlag Hans Huber.

Seibel, Wolfgang. 1992. *Funktionaler Dilettantismus. Erfolgreich Scheiternde Organisationen Im 'Dritten Sektor' Zwischen Markt Und Staat*. Baden-Baden: Nomos (published Habilitationsschrift).

Ibid. 1996. "Successful Failure. an Alternative View on Organizational Coping." *American Behavorial Scientist* 39, pp. 1011-1024.

Ibid. 2007. *The 'Responsibility to Protect' and Modern Protectorates – UN Peace Operations as Successfully Failing Venture*. Paper Prepared for the Conference "The New Protectorates: International Administration and the Dilemmas of Governance," Cambridge University, 6-8 June 2007, on file with the author.

Ibid. 2008. *'Coping with Spoilers from Within': Die Obstruktion von Friedensoperationen durch politisierte Bürokratien*. Project Proposal, Deutsche Stiftung Friedensforschung, on file with the author.

Ibid. 2008. "Moderne Protektorate Als Ersatzstaat: UN-Friedensoperationen Und Dilemmata Internationaler Übergangsverwaltungen." *Politische Vierteljahresschrift*, special issue, pp. 499-530.

Ibid. Forthcoming. *Internationale Politik und lernende Verwaltung: UN-Friedensmissionen zwischen politischer und bürokratischer Logik*. Unpublished manuscript, on file with the author.

Ibid. "Das Deutsche Regierungssystem," Power Point Presentation for BA-seminar at the University of Konstanz, on file with author.

Seibel, Wolfgang et al. 2006. *Discourse at the Juncture: The Explanatory Power of Discourse Theory and Policy Analysis for Understanding Peace Operations and Humanitarian Intervention*. Konstanz: University of Konstanz.

Shain, Yossi and Linz, Juan P. 1995. *Between States. Interim Governments and Democratic Transitions.* Cambridge: Cambridge University Press.

Shakespeare, William. 1992. *The Tragedy of Antony and Cleopatra. Edited by Raimund Borgmeier.* Stuttgart: Reclam.

Ibid. 1998. *Hamlet. Edited by Holger Klein.* Stuttgart: Reclam.

Ibid. 2000. *Romeo and Juliet. Edited by Jill L. Levenson Et Al.* Oxford: Oxford University Press.

Shamir, Boas et al. 1993. "The Motivational Effects of Charismatic Leadership." *Organization Science* 4:4, pp. 577-594.

Shimura, Hisako. 2001. "The Role of the UN Secretariat in Organizing Peacekeeping." In: Ramesh Thakur and Albrecht Schnabel *United Nations Peacekeeping Operations: Ad Hoc Missions, Permanent Engagement.* Tokyo: United Nations University Press, pp. 46-56.

Shrivastava, P. 1993. "Crisis Theory/Practive: Towards a Sustainable Future." *Industrial & Environmental Crisis Quarterly* 7:1, pp. 23-42.

Silva-Carneiro de Sousa, Lurdes. 2001. "Some Facts and Comments on the East Timor 2001 Constituent Assembly Elections." *Lusotopie*, pp. 299-311.

Simon, Herbert A. 1957. *Models of Man. Social and Rational.* New York: The Free Press.

Ibid. 1976. *Administrative Behavior. A Study of Decision-Making Processes in Administrative Organizations*, 3rd ed. ed. New York: The Free Press.

Ibid. 1979. "Rational Decision Making in Business Organizations." *American Economic Review* 69, pp. 493-513.

Ibid. 1982. *Models of Bounded Rationality.* Vol. I and II. Cambridge: MIT Press.

Ibid. 1991. "Bounded Rationality and Organizational Learning." *Organizational Science* 2:1, pp. 125-134.

Smith, Anthony L. 2001. "The Role of the United Nations in East Timor´s Path to Independence." *Asian Journal of Political Science* 9:2, pp 25-54.

Ibid. 2004. *Timor-Leste: Strong Government, Weak State.* Singapore: Institute of Southeast Asian Studies.

Smith, Dan. 2003. *Getting their Act Together: Toward a Strategic Framework for Peacebuilding.* Synthesis Report of the Joint Utstein Study of Peacebuilding, The Royal Norwegian Ministry of Foreign Affairs.

Smith, Michael G. 2004. *East Timor: Some Peacebuilding Lessons.* Paper presented at the JIIA-UNU Symposium, 24-25 February 2004, UN University Center, Tokyo.

Smith, Michael G. and Dee, Moreen. 2002. *Peacekeeping in East Timor: The Path to Independence.* Boulder: Lynne Rienner.

Soares Babo, Dionisio. 2003. "Building a Foundation for an Effective Civil Service in Timor Leste." *Pacific Economic Bulletin* 18:1, pp. 108-114.

Stanbury, William T. et al. 1977. *Uncertainty in Policy Analysis: Perception, Specification, and Coping Strategies.* Discussion Papers 77-59. Berlin: Wissenschaftszentrum Berlin, Internationales Institut für Management und Verwaltung.

Staw, B. and Ross, J. 1989. "Understanding Behavior in Escalation Situations." *Science* 246, pp. 216-220.

Stedman, Stephen J. 1996. "Negotiation and Mediation in Internal Conflicts." In: Michael E. Brown, ed., *The International Dimensions of Internal Conflict.* Cambridge: MIT Press, pp. 369-371.

Ibid. 1997. "Spoiler Problems in Peace Processes." *International Security* 22:2, pp. 5-53.

Stedman, Stephen J. and Downs, George. 2002. "Evaluation Issues in Peace Implementation." In: Donald Rothchild, et al., eds., *Ending Civil Wars: The Implementation of Peace Agreements.* Boulder: Lynne Rienner, pp. 44-54.

Steele, Jonathan. 2002. "Nation Building in East Timor." *World Policy Journal* 19:2, pp. 76-87.

Steinberg, Paul F. 2004. *New Approaches to Causal Analysis in Policy Research*. Paper Presented for the Panel "Multi-Methods in Qualitative Research" at the Annual Convention of the American Political Science Association, Chicago.

Steinke, Ines. 1999. *Kriterien Qualitativer Forschung. Ansätze Zur Bewertung Qualitativ-Empirischer Sozialforschung*. Weinheim: Juventa.

Stoker, Gerry. 1995. "Regime Theory and Urban Politics." In: David Judge et al., eds., *Theories of Urban Politics*. London: Sage, pp. 54-71.

Subianto, Landry H. 2002. *A State in the Making: Role of UNTAET in East Timor*. Project report to be submitted to the Council for Asia and Europe Cooperation. London, October 2001.

Suhrke, Astri. 2001. "Peacekeepers as Nation-Builders: Dilemmas of the UN in East Timor." *International Peacekeeping* 8:4, pp. 1-20.

Tanner, Marcus. 1997. *Croatia—A Nation Forged in War*. New Haven: Yale University Press.

Taylor, Mark B. and Jennings, Kathleen M. 2004. *In Search of Strategy: An Agenda for Applied Research on Transitions from Conflict*. Fafo-report 480. New York: Fafo.

Tetlock, Philip E., ed. 1996. *Counterfactual Thought Experiments in World Politics: Logical, Methodological, and Psychological Perspectives*. Princeton: Princeton University Press.

Thelen, Kathleen. 1999. "Historical Institutionalism in Comparative Politics." *Annual Review Political Science* 2, pp. 369-404.

Thiétart, Raymond-Alain and Forgues, Bernard. 1997. "Action, Structure and Chaos" *Organization Studies* 18, pp. 119-143.

Thompson, Bruce. 2004. *Exploratory and Confirmatory Factor Analysis. Understanding Concepts and Applications*. Washington, DC: American Psychological Association.

Thompson, James. 1967. *Organizations in Action*. New York: McGraw-Hill.

Todorova, Maria. *Balkan Identities. Nation and Memory*. New York: NYU Press.

Traub, James. 2000. "Inventing East Timor." *Foreign Affairs*.

Tsebelis, George. 2002. *Veto Players*. Princeton: Princeton University Press.

Tversky, Amos and Kahnemann, Daniel. 1981. "The Framing of Decisions and the Psychology of Choice." *Science* 211, pp. 453-458.

UN Department of Peacekeeping Operations and UN Department of Field Operations. 2008. *United Nations Peacekeeping Operations. Principles and Guidelines. Capstone Doctrine*. New York: United Nations.

United Nations Task Force to Establish the Transitional Administration in Sector East. 1995. *Background Report on the Region of Eastern Slavonia, Baranja and Western Sirmium* Zagreb, December 1995, on file with the author.

United Nations. 1945. *Charter of the United Nations and Statute of the International Court of Justice*. New York: United Nations.

US State Department, "News Briefing," Wednesday, 2 July 1997, FDCH Political Transcripts.

Valenzuela, Carlos. 2003. "Towards Elections." In: Nassrine Azimi and Li Lin Chang, eds., *The United Nations Transitional Administration in East Timor (UNTAET): Debriefing and Lessons*. Leiden/Boston: Martinus Nijhoff Publishers, pp. 179-190.

Van de Ven, Andrew H. 1976. "On the Nature, Formation and Maintenance of Relations among Organizations." *Academy of Management Review* 1:4, pp. 24-36.

Varwick, Johannes, ed. 2006. *Die Reform der Vereinten Nationen: Bilanz und Perspektiven*. Berlin: Duncker und Humblot.

Velikonja, Mitja. 2003. *Religious Separation and Political Intolerance in Bosnia-Herzegovina*. College Station: Texas A&M Press.

Vieira de Mello, Sergio. 2001. *How Not to Run a Country. Lessons for the UN from Kosovo and East Timor*. Paper for the UNITAR-IPS-JIIA Conference to Address the Report on UN Peace Operations, Singapore, February 2001.

Walsh, Pat. 2001. *East Timor's Political Parties and Groupings*. Briefing Notes, Australian Council for Overseas Aid.

Walter, Barbara. 1997. "The Critical Barrier to Civil War Settlement." *International Organization* 51:3, pp. 335-364.

Walters, Francis P. 1952. *A History of the League of Nations*. London: Oxford University Press.

Weber, Max. 1922. *Wirtschaft und Gesellschaft. Grundriss der Verstehenden Soziologie*. Tübingen: Mohr.

Weick, Karl E. 1969. *The Social Psychology of Organizing*. Reading: Addison-Wesley.

Ibid. 1976. "Educational Organizations as Loosely Coupled Systems." *Administrative Science Quarterly* 21, pp. 1-19.

Weick, Karl E. and Westley, Frances. 2003. "Organizational Learning: Affirming an Oxymoron." In: S.R. Clegg et al., eds., *Handbook of Organization Studies*. London: Sage, pp. 440-458.

Weir, David. 1988. "The Structure of Man-made Organizational Crisis: Conceptual and Empirical Issues in the Development of a General Theory of Crisis Management." *Technological Forecasting and Social Change* 33, pp. 83-107.

Ibid. 2004. "Disaster Management After September 11: A 'Normal Accident' or a 'Man-made Disaster'? What did We Know, What have We Learned?" In: Gabriele S. Suder, ed., *Terrorism and the International Business Environment: The Security-Business Nexus*. Cheltenham: Edward Elgar Publishing, pp. 201-216.

Weiss, Thomas, ed. 1997. *Beyond UN Subcontracting: Task-Sharing with Regional Security Arrangements and Service Providing NGOs*. London: Macmillan.

Weitzmann, Eben A. and Matthew B. Miles. 1995. *Computer Programs for Qualitative Data Analysis: A Software Sourcebook*. Thousand Oaks: Sage.

Wesley, Michael. 1997. *Casualties of the New World Order: The Causes of Failure of UN Missions to Civil Wars*. Basingstoke: Macmillan.

Whetten, D. A. and Leung, T.K. 1979. "The Instrumental Value of Interorganizational Relations: Antecedents and Consequences of Linkage Formation." *Academy of Management Journal* 22, pp. 225-344.

Wilde, Ralph. 2001. "From Danzig to East Timor and Beyond: The Role of International Territorial Administration." *The American Journal of International Law* 95:3, pp. 583-606.

Yin, Robert K. 2003. *Case Study Research. Design and Methods*, 3rd ed. Thousand Oaks: Sage.

Zaum, Dominik. 2007. *The Sovereignty Paradox: The Norms and Politics of International State Building*. Oxford: Oxford University Press.

Zürn, Michael. 1992. *Interessen und Institutionen in der Internationalen Politik. Grundlegung und Anwendungen des Situationsstrukturellen Ansatzes*. Opladen: Leske + Budrich.

UN Documents, Reports, and Internet Sources

Aid East Timor, "East Timor History and Activism." Available online at http://www.aideasttimor.org/history.html, last access on 1 March 2009.

Associated Press, "East Timor Mourns Loss of UN Envoy Vieira de Mello." Available online at http://www.etan.org/et2003/august/17-23/20adiplo.htm, last access on 15 March 2009.

Baltazar, Alipio. 2004. "An Overview of the Constitution Drafting Process." *East Timor Law Journal* 9. Available online at http://www.eastimorlawjournal.org/ARTICLES/2004/constitution_drafting_process_east_timor_alipio_baltazar.html, last access on 8 March 2009

Barber, Greg. 2002. "East Timor: Under Indonesian Rule." *Online NewsHour April 2002*. Available online at http://www.pbs.org/newshour/bb/asia/july-dec99/timor_background.html, last access on 1 March 2009.

BBC, "Country profile: East Timor." Available online at http://news.bbc.co.uk/1/hi/world/asia-pacific/country_profiles/1508119.stm, last access on 1 March 2009.

Blair, Tony, "Speech of British Prime Minister Tony Blair to the Chicago Economic Club, 22 April 1999." Available online at http://www.pbs.org/newshour/bb/international/jan-june99/blair_doctrine4-23.html, last access on 6 November 2005.

Cady, Jean-Christian Cady (France): Deputy Special Representative, Police and Justice. Available online at http://www.un.org/peace/kosovo/pages/kosovo9.htm, last access on 3 March 2009.

Center for History, Democracy and Reconciliation (CHDR). 2008. *The Shared History and the Second World War and National Question in ex Yugoslavia*. International conference, Tres Culturas Foundation, Seville (Spain), 31 January-2 February, 2008. Available online at http://www.centerforhistory.net/index.php?option=com_content&task=view&id=22&Itemid=49, last access on 30 January 2009.

CIA World Fact Book, "Timor-Leste." Available online at https://www.cia.gov/library/publications/the-world-factbook/geos/tt.html, last access on 22 February 2009.

CNN, "Biography of Slobodan Milosevic." Available online at http://www.cnn.com/resources/newsmakers/world/europe/milosevic.html, last access on 30 January 2009.

CNRT, "The History of CNRT." Available online at www.cnrt-timor.org/about/history/php, last access on 2 March 2009.

Coicaud, Jean-Marc. 2007. *International Organizations as a Profession and Distribution of Power: The Importance of Human Resources Management for the Success of UN Reform*. Speech by the Head of United Nations University (4 January 2007). Available online at http://www.unitarny.org/mm/File/Presentation%20by%20Jean-Marc%20Coicaud.pdf, last access on 15 March 2009.

Col, Mark Koh. 2001. "UNTAET. A Military Insight." *Journal of the Singapore Armed Forces* 27:4. Available online at http://www.mindef.gov.sg/safti/pointer/back/journals/2001/Vol27_4/1.htm, last access 22 February 2009.

Commission for Reception, Truth and Reconciliation in East Timor, "Reports." Available online at http://www.easttimor-reconciliation.org/Documents.htm, last access on 1 March 2009.

Croissant, Aurel. 2006. "International Interim Governments, Democratization, and Post-Conflict Peace-Building: Lessons from Cambodia and East Timor." *Strategic Insights* 5:1. Available online at http://www.ccc.nps.navy.mil/si/2006/Jan/croissantJan06.asp, last access on 6 March 2009.

Domini, Mirjana. 2000. "National Minorities in the Republic of Croatia." *Central Europe Review* 2:19. Available online at http://www.ce-review.org/00/19/domini19.html, last access on 15 March 2009.

East Timor Action Network, "The Santa Cruz Massacre: November 12, 1991." Available online at http://www.etan.org/timor/SntaCRUZ.htm, last access on 1 March 2009.

East Timor and Indonesia Action Network, "Agreement between the Republic of Indonesia and the Portuguese Republic on the Question of East Timor." Available online at http://www.etan.org/etun/agreemnt.htm, last access on 2 March 2009.

East Timor Commission for Reception, Truth and Reconciliation, "Final Report." Available online at http://www.ictj.org/en/news/features/846.html, last access on 1 March 2009.

473

Eckert, Hugo. 1997. "Zur jugoslawischen Geschichte: Nur die Vergangenheit kann die Gegenwart erklären." Available online at http://www.politikundunterricht.de/3_97/puu973e.htm, last access on 30 January 2009.

Encyclopedia Britannica, "Hamartia." Available online at http://www.britannica.com/EBchecked/topic/253196/hamartia, last access 2 March 2009.

European Union, "Report of the European Council on a Secure Europe in a Better World," presented by Javier Solana, EUHR for CFSP – European Council, Thessaloniki, 20 June 2003. Available online at http://ue.eu.int/ueDocs/cms_Data/docs/pressdata/en/reports/76255.pdf, last access on 2 March 2009.

Foreign Correspondent. 2000. *Transcript of a broadcasted interview with SRSG Vieira de Mello on February 20, 2000. Sergio Vieira de Mello – East Timor transitional administration.* Available online at http://www.abc.net.au/foreign/s225290.htm, last access on 5 March 2009.

Frey, Theo. 1999. "Ost-Timor: Teuflische Allianz." *Zeitschrift für Friedenspolitik* 5. Available online at http://www.efriz.ch/cgi/sfc.pl?a=/sys/htm/menu.html&b=/archiv/995/a-1.html, last access 16 March 2009.

Gendercide Watch. "Case Study East Timor (1975-1999)." Available online at http://www.gendercide.org/case_timor.html, last access on 10 July 2008.

Global Policy Forum, "East Timor Action Network: Justice Call On East Timor Massacre Anniversary." Available online at http://www.globalpolicy.org/intljustice/tribunals/timor/2005/0406justicecall.htm, last access on 1 March 2009.

Global Policy Forum, "UN Reform." Available online at http://www.globalpolicy.org/reform/index.htm, last access on March 2, 2009.

Global Property Guide, "Croatia." Available online at http://www.globalpropertyguide.com/Europe/Croatia/gdp-per-capitaFehler! Hyperlink-Referenz ungültig., last access on 15 March 2009.

Global Public Policy Institute, "Learning to Build Peace? The United Nations, Transitional Administration, Strategic Planning and Organizational Learning. Developing a Research Framework, Research Project Abstract." Available online at http://www.bundesstiftung-friedensforschung.de/archiv/projektarten/kleinprojekte/ zusammenfassungen/reinicke.html, last access on 6 March 2009.

Government of the Republic of Croatia, "Report of the Republic of Croatia on the Implementation of the Framework Convention for the Protection of National Minorities, pursuant to Article 25, paragraph 1 of the Framework Convention for the Protection of National Minorities of the Council of Europe, COE Doc. ACFC/SR(1999)005, received on 16 March 1999" Available online at http://www.coe.int/t/e/human_rights/minorities/2._framework_convention_(monitoring)/2._monitoring_mechanism/3._state_reports_and_unmik_kosovo_report/1._first_cycle/PDF_1st_SR_Croatia_en.pdf, last access on December 1, 2008.

Government of Timor-Leste, "About Timor-Leste: History." Available online at http://www.timor-leste.gov.tl/AboutTimorleste/history.htm, last access on 1 March 2009.

Guéhenno, Jean-Marie. 2005. *Statement by Jean-Marie Guéhenno.* Statement by Under-Secretary-General for Peacekeeping Operations to the Challenger Project, 2 March 2005. Available online at http://www.un.org/Depts/dpko/dpko/articles/article020305.htm, last access on 4 December 2009.

Hasegawa, Sukehiro. 2004. *Beyond Cold Peace: Strategies for Economic Reconstruction and Post Conflict Management.* Speech at the Conference "International Donor Coordination, Civil Society and Natural Resource Management", 27-28 October 2004, organized by the Foreign Office of the Federal Republic of Germany. Available online at http://www.unmit.org/UNMISETWebSite.nsf/e4899f58093d136749256f0a003f1073/ cb0d674b2e83c6fa49256f3a0081dbb7?OpenDocument, last access on 7 June 2007.

Heaton, Janet. 1998. "Secondary Analysis of Qualitative Data." *Social Research Update* 22. Available online at http://www.soc.surrey.ac.uk/sru/SRU22.html, last access on 25 November 2008.

Huhn, Walter. 2006. *UN Peacekeeping – Entwicklungen und Tendenzen.* Available online at http://www.europaeische-sicherheit.de/Ausgaben/2006/2006_01/02_UN/2006,01,02,02.html, last access on 4 December 2008.

Human Rights Watch, "East Timor: Torture and Mistreatment by Police." Available online at http://www.hrw.org/english/docs/2006/04/19/eastti13223.htm, last access on 5 March 2009.

Human Rights Watch. 1997. *Crotia.* Available online at http://www.hrw.org/reports/1997/croatia/Croatia-02.htm#P134_26389, last access 29 January 2009.

Human Rights Watch. 2001. *World Report 2001: East Timor.* Available online at http://www.hrw.org/wr2k1/asia/etimor.html, last access on 5 March 2009.

Hurford, Chris and Wahlstrom, Margareta. 2001. *OCHA and the Timor Crisis, 1999. An Independent Study for OCHA.* Available online at ochaonline.un.org/OchaLinkClick.aspx?link=ocha&DocId=100399, last access on 15 March 2009.

International Commission on Intervention and State Sovereignty. 2001. *The Responsibility to Protect.* Report of the International Commission on Intervention and State Sovereignty. Available online at http://www.iciss.ca/pdf/Commission-Report.pdf, last access on 15 March 2009.

Jolly, Joanna. 2002. "Ex-Guerilla leader wins East Timor presidency." *Milwaukee Journal Sentinel*, 17 April 2002. Available online at http://findarticles.com/p/articles/mi_qn4196/is_20020417/ai_n10777952, last access on 1 March 2009.

Koinova, Maria. 1996. "Stoyanov: An End to a Divisive Political Culture?" *Pursuing Balkan Peace* 45, 12 November 1996. Available online at http://www.hri.org/news/balkans/pbp/1996/96-11-12.pbp.html, last access on 18 February 2009.

La'o Hamutuk. 2000. "Evaluating the World Bank's Community Empowerment Project." *La'o Hamutuk Bulletin* 1:4, 31 December 2000. Available online at http://www.etan.org/lh/bulletin04.html#CEP, last access on 5 March 2009.

Ibid. 2001. "External Funding: Sources and Uses." *La'o Hamutuk Bulletin* 2:1,2, part 1, April 2001. Available online at http://www.laohamutuk.org/Bulletin/2001/Apr/bulletinv2n1.html, last access on 7 March 2009.

Ibid. 2002. "Chronology of Oil and Gas Developments in the Timor Sea." *La'o Hamutuk Bulletin* 3:8, part 2. Available online at http://www.etan.org/lh/bulletins/bulletinv3n8b.html, last access on 6 March 2009.

Ibid. 2002. "East Timor Faces Post-UNTAET Challenges." *La'o Hamutuk Bulletin* 3:4, part 2. Available online at http://www.laohamutuk.org/Bulletin/2002/May/bulletinv3n4.html, last access on 5 March 2009.

Ibid 2003. "Timor Sea Historical Background." *La'o Hamutuk Bulletin* 4:3-4. Available online at http://www.laohamutuk.org/Bulletin/2003/Aug/bulletinv4n34.html, last access on 6 March 2009.

Linton Suzannah. 2001. "Rising From The Ashes: The Creation Of A Viable Criminal Justice System In East Timor." *Melbourne University Law Review* 5. Online Journal available at www.austlii.edu.au/au/journals/MULR/2001/5.html, last access on 3 March 2009.

Martin, Ian. 1998. "A New Frontier: The Early Experience and Future of International Hunan Rights Field Operations," *Papers in the Theory and Practice of Human Rights* 19, University of Essex. Available online at http://www.essex.ac.uk/rightsinacutecrisis/report/martin.htm, last access on 25 February 2009.

Mayring, Philipp. 2000. "Qualitative Content Analysis" *Forum Qualitative Social Research*, 1(2). Available online at http://www.qualitative-research.net/index.php/fqs/article/view/1089, last access on 25 February 2009.

Müller, Ragnar and Schumann, Wolfgang. Undated. *The Policy Cycle*. Available online at http://www.dadalos.org/politik_int/politik/policy-zyklus.htm, last access on 28 November 2008.

National Democratic Institute. 2003. *Government Within Reach: A Report on the Views of East Timorese on Local Government*. Washington, DC: National Democratic Institute. Available online at http://www.ndi.org/node/13125, last access on 2 November 2008.

Office of the High Commissioner for Human Rights, "Sergio Vieira de Mello." Available online at http://www.ohchr.org/EN/AboutUs/Pages/Vieira.aspx, last access on 15 March 2009.

Official Website of the Nobel Foundation, "Peace Prize." Available online at http://nobelprize.org/nobel_prizes/peace/laureates/1996/press.html, last access on 22 February 2009.

Osaka East Timor Association, "Observer Report Constituent Assembly Election in East Timor." Preliminary Report, 6 September 2001. Available online at http://www.etan.org/etan/obproject/docs/older/osaka09-01.htm, last access on 12 March 2009.

OSCE, "Report of the OSCE Mission to the Republic of Croatia on Croatia's progress in meeting international commitments since September 1998," 26 January 1999. Available online at http://www.osce.org/documents/mc/1999/01/1049_en.pdf, last access on 18 February 2009.

Ouellet, Julian. 2004. "Procedural Components of Peace Agreements." In: Guy Burgess and Heidi Burgess, eds., *Beyond Intractability*. Boulder: Conflict Research Consortium, University of Colorado. Available online at http://peacestudies.conflictresearch.org/essay/procedural_peace_agree/?nid=1397, last access on 15 March 2009.

Peace Implementation Network. 1999. *Command from the Saddle: Managing United Nations Peace-building Missions*. Fafo report 266. Available online at http://www.fafo.no/pub/rapp/266/266.pdf, last access on 15 March 2009.

Pippard, Tim. Undated. *East Timor and the Challenge of UN Transitional Administration*. Available online at: http://www.una.org.uk/UN%20and%20Conflict%20Programme%20Briefs/East%20Timor.htm, last access on 4 November 2008.

Publishers Weekly, "Review of Samantha Power, 'Chasing the Flame,'" 6 March 2008. Available online at http://www.amazon.ca/Chasing-Flame-Samantha-Power/dp/1594201285, last access on 15 March 2009.

Rees, Edward. 2003. *The UN's Failure to Integrate Falintil Veterans May Cause East Timor to Fail*. Available online at http://www.onlineopinion.com.au/view.asp?article=666, last access on 6 March 2009.

Richardson, Bill, "Governor Bill Richardson, former US ambassador to the United Nations, in an interview with Larry King. Larry King Live, 'An Analysis of Bombing of UN Headquarters in Iraq.'" Available online at http://transcripts.cnn.com/TRANSCRIPTS/0308/19/lkl.00.html, last access on 15 March 2009.

Richter, Bastian. 2008. "Planning and Deployment of UN Peacekeeping Operations – Interactive Guide." Präsentation, ZIF. Available online at http://www.zif-berlin.org/de/analyse-und-informationen/veroeffentlichungen.html, last access on 15 March 2009.

Rouleau, Linda et al. 2008. "Revisiting Permanently Failing Organizations: A Practice Perspective." *Les Cahier de Recherche du GéPS* 2 :1. Available online at web.hec.ca/geps/GePS-08-01.pdf, last access on 15 March 2009.

Shravanti, Reddy. 2002. *Watchdog Organization Struggles to Decrease UN Bureaucracy*. Available online at http://www.globalpolicy.org/ngos/ngo-un/rest-un/2002/1029watchdog.htm, last access on 15 March 2009.

Sito Sucic, Daria. 1996. "Bosnia's Presidency Members Disagree Over Cabinet..." *Pursuing Balkan Peace* 45:12. Available online at http://www.hri.org/news/balkans/pbp/1996/96-11-12.pbp.html, last access on 18 February 2009.

Sito Sucic, Daria. 1996. "Croatia Buys US Military Helicopters." *Pursuing Balkan Peace* 45, 12 November 1996. Available online at http://www.hri.org/news/balkans/pbp/1996/96-11-12.pbp.htm, last access on 18 February 2009.

Tansey, Oisin. 2004. *International Administration and Democratic Regime-Building.* Working Paper. Available online at http://users.ox.ac.uk/~nuff0270/-%20APSA%20Paper%20Final.pdf, p. 3, last access on 8 January 2009.

The Carter Center, "Pre-Election Statement on East Timor Elections." Available online at http://www.cartercenter.org/news/documents/doc267.html, last access on 2 March 2009.

The International Forum of National NGO Platforms, "FONGTIL-Forum NGO Timor-Leste." Available online at http://www.ong-ngo.org/spip.php?page=article_base&modele=capitalisation&id_rubrique=323&pfn=323&lang=en, last access on 2 March 2009.

UN Department of Economic and Social Affairs, Population Division. 2007. *World Population Prospects: The 2006 Revision Population Database, UN Country Population Estimate of 2005.* Available online at http://esa.un.org/unpp/p2k0data.asp, last access on 1 March 2009.

UN Department of Peacekeeping Operations. 1995. *Comprehensive Report on Lessons Learned from United Nations Operation in Somalia (UNOSOM), April 1992 – March 1995.* Available online at http://www.un.org/Depts/dpko/lessons/UNOSOM.pdf, last access on 16 March 2009.

Ibid. 1996, "United Nations Protection Force: Profile." Available online at http://www.un.org/Depts/dpko/dpko/co_mission/unprof_p.htm, last access on 30 January 2009. Ibid. 1997. *Croatia: UNTAES.* Available online at http://www.un.org/Depts/DPKO/Missions/untaes_b.htm, last access on 18 February 2009.

Ibid., Lessons Learned Unit. 1998. *The United Nations Transitional Administration for Eastern Slavonia, Baranja and Western Sirmium (UNTAES), January 1996-1998: Lessons Learned.* Available online at http://www.pbpu.unlb.org/pbu/library/UNTAES.pdf, last access on 10 January 2007.

Ibid., "Brochure on UNTAET," UNTAET/OCPI IC/01E 5,000, January 2000. Available online at http://www.un.org/peace/etimor/untaetPU/WUntaet.pdf, last access on 6 March 2009.

Ibid., "Croatia: United Nations Confidence Restoration Operation." Available online at http://www.un.org/Depts/dpko/dpko/co_mission/uncro.htm, last access on 30 January 2009.

Ibid., "East Timor – UNTAET News. Civic education programme ends in East Timor." Available online at http://www.un.org/peace/etimor/news/01apr27.htm, last access on 5 March 2009.

Ibid., "East Timor: United Nations Transitional Administration in East Timor." Available online at http://www.un.org/peace/etimor/etimor.htm, last access on 3 March 2009.

Ibid., "East Timor: UNTAET Background." Available online at http://www.un.org/peace/etimor/UntaetB.htm, last access on 2 March 2009.

Ibid., "Eastern Slavonia, Baranja and Western Sirmium: Facts and Figures." Available online at http://www.un.org/Depts/dpko/dpko/co_mission/untaes_p.htm, last access on 25 February 2009.

Ibid., "Eastern Slavonia, Baranja and Western Sirmium: Brief Chronology." Available online at http://www.un.org/Depts/DPKO/Missions/untaes_e.htm, last access on 25 February 2009.

Ibid., "List of Operations." Available online at http://www.un.org/Depts/dpko/list/list.pdf, last access on 21 December 2008.

Ibid., "Mission Statement." Available online at http://www.un.org/Depts/dpko/dpko/info/page3.htm, last access on 3 December 2008.

Ibid., "UNTAET." Available online at http://www.un.org/peace/etimor/docs/UntaetDrs.htm, last access on 20 March 2007.

UN Department of Political Affairs, "About DPA." Available online at http://www.un.org/Depts/dpa/about_dpa/fr_dpa_mission.htm, last access on 3 December 2008.

UN Department of Public Information. 1996. *United Nations Transitional Administration for Eastern Slavonia, Baranja and Western Sirmium. Information Package.* New York: United Nations

Ibid. 2000. *The United Nations and East Timor. Self-determination through Popular Consultation.* New York: United Nations.

UN Development Program. 2005. "Capacity Building Seminar." Available online at *europeandcis.undp.org/files/uploads/CDF/Timor%20Leste-case%20study.doc*2005, last access on 15 March 2009.

UN Economic and Social Council, "Final Report on the In-Depth Evaluation of Peacekeeping Operations," UN Doc. E/AC.51/1995/2, 17 March 1995.

UN General Assembly, "Question of East Timor: Progress Report of the Secretary-General," UN Doc. A/37/30, 13 December 1999.

Ibid, "Comprehensive review of the whole question of peacekeeping operations in all their aspects," UN Doc. A56/863, 11 March 2002.

UN Information Service, "East Timorese Leader Commends UNTAET's 'Timorization' Policy In Day-Long Security Council Debate On Territory." Press Release, UN Doc. UNIS/SC/1307, 29 January 2001. Available online at http://www.unis.unvienna.org/unis/pressrels/2001/sc1307.html, last access on 3 March 2009.

UN International Civil Service Commission. 1982. *Report of the International Civil Service Commission.* UN Doc. A/37/30.

UN Secretary-General, "Report of the Secretary-General pursuant to the statement adopted by the Summit Meeting of the Security Council on 31 January 1992," UN Doc. A/47/277-S/24111, 17 June 1992.

Ibid., "An Agenda for Development," UN Doc. A/48/935, 6 May 1994. Available online at http://www.un.org/Docs/SG/agdev.html, last access on 6 March 2009.

Ibid., "Report of the Secretary General on Croatia pursuant to Security Council Resolution 1025," UN Doc. S/1995/1028, 13 December 1995.

Ibid., "Report of the Secretary-General on the United Nations Transitional Administration for Eastern Slavonia, Baranja and Western Sirmium," UN Doc. S/1997/767, 2 October 1997.

Ibid., "Report of the Secretary General on the United Nations Transitional Administration in East Timor," UN Doc. S/1999/1024, 4 October 1999.

Ibid., "Report of the Secretary-General on the UN Observer Mission in Angola (MONUA)," UN Doc. S/1999/02, 24 February 1999.

Ibid., "Report of the Secretary-General on East Timor," UN Doc. S/1999/803, 20 July 1999.

Ibid., "Report of the Secretary-General on East Timor," UN Doc. S/1999/862, 9 August 1999.

Ibid., "Report of the Secretary-General on the United Nations Transitional Administration in East Timor," UN Doc. S/2000/53, 26 January 2000.

Ibid., "Report of the Secretary-General on the United Nations Transitional Administration in East Timor (for the period 27 July 2000 to 16 January 2001)," UN Doc. S/2001/42, 16 January 2001.

Ibid., "Speech of the Secretary-General, Dialogue 'Vital to Success of UN Missions, Says Secretary-General in Remarks to Seminar of Special Representatives." Press Release, UN Doc. SG/SM/7760, 2 April, 2001.

Ibid., "No Exit without Strategy: Security Council Decision-making and the Closure or Transition of United Nations Peacekeeping Operations," UN Doc. S/2001/394, 20 April 2001.

Ibid., "Report of the Secretary-General on the United Nations Transitional Administration in East Timor," UN Doc. S/2002/432, 17 April 2002.

UN Security Council, "Resolution on the Socialist Federal Republic of Yugoslavia." UN Doc. S/1991/713 (1991), 25 September 1991.

Ibid., "Resolution on the Socialist Federal Republic of Yugoslavia," UN Doc. S/1992/743 (1992), 21 February 1992.

Ibid., "Resolution on proposal for termination of the mandate of the UN Confidence Restoration Operation in Croatia," UN Doc. S/RES/1025 (1995), 30 November 1995.

Ibid., "Resolution on the Situation in Eastern Slavonia, Baranja, and Western Sirmium," UN Doc. S/1996/1037 (1996), 15 January 1996.

Ibid., "Security Council urges Completion of Preparation for 13 April Elections on Eastern Slavonia, Baranja, Western Sirmium." Press Release, UN Doc. SC/6334, 7 March 1997.

Ibid., "Resolution on the Situation in Eastern Slavonia, Baranja and Western Sirmium," UN Doc. S/RES/1120 (1997), 14 July 1997.

Ibid., "Resolution on the Situation in East Timor." UN Doc. S/RES/1264 (1999), 15 September 1999.

Ibid., "Resolution on the Situation in East Timor," UN Doc. S/1999/1272 (1999), 25 October 1999.

Ibid., "Conflicts in Kosovo, Sierra Leone and Angola, Question of East Timor Key Elements of Security Council's Work for 1999." Press Release, UN Doc. SC/6784, 18 January 2000.

Ibid., "Security Council Hears Details of Free and Fair Elections in East Timor." Press Release, UN Doc. SC/7139, 10 September 2001.

Ibid., "Resolution on the Situation in East Timor," UN Doc. S/RES/1392 (2002), 31 January 2002.

Ibid., "Resolution on the Situation in East Timor," UN Doc. S/RES/1410 (2002), 17 May 2002.

UN Volunteers. 2001. UN Volunteers complete civil registration in East Timor. News Release. Available online at http://dynamic.unv.org/Infobase/news_releases/2001/01_06_25TMP_reg.htm, last access on 6 March 2009.

United Nations Dag Hammarskjöld Library, "United Nations Documentation: Research Guide." Available online at http://www.un.org/Depts/dhl/resguide/symbol.htm last access on 2 March 2009.

United Nations, "Follow Up on the Report of the Panel on United Nations Peace Operations," UN Doc. A/55/502, 20 October 2000.

Ibid., "Follow Up on the Report of the Panel on United Nations Peace Operations," UN Doc. A/55/507, 27 October 2000.

Ibid., "Follow Up on the Report of the Panel on United Nations Peace Operations," UN Doc. A/55/977, 1 June 2001.

Ibid., "Follow Up on the Report of the Panel on United Nations Peace Operations," UN Doc. A/56/732, 21 December 2001.

Ibid., "Follow Up on the Report of the Panel on United Nations Peace Operations," UN Doc. S/2000/1084, 10 November 2000.

Ibid., "Meeting of the Security Council," UN Doc. S/PV.4223, 15 November 2000.

Ibid., "Report of the Panel on United Nations Peace Operations," UN Doc. A/55/305-S/2000/809, 21 August 2000.

Ibid., "Report of the Secretary General's High-level Panel on Threats, Challenges and Change, A More Secure World. Our Shared Responsibility," UN Doc. A/59/565, 2 December 2004. Available online at http://www.un.org/secureworld/, last access on 2 March 2009.

Ibid. 2003. "Handbook on UN Multidimensional Peacekeeping." Available online at http://pbpu.unlb.org/Pbps/library/Handbook%20on%20UN%20PKOs.pdf, last access on 15 March 2009.

United Nations Task Force to Establish the Transitional Administration in Sector East. 1995. Background Report on the Region of Eastern Slavonia, Baranja and Western Sirmium. Zagreb, December 1995, on file with the author.

United States of America, "The National Security Strategy of the United States of America," September 2002. Available online at http://www.acq.osd.mil/ncbdp/nm/docs/Relevant%20-Docs/national_security_strategy.pdf, last access 2 March 2009.

UNTAET Public Information Office, "De Mello at a press conference on 19 November 1999. Briefing by Ian Martin, Sergio Vieira de Mello and Xanana Gusmão, 19 November 1999." Available online at http://www.un.org/peace/etimor/DB/br191199.htm, last access on 6 March 2009.

UNTAET Public Information Office, "Gusmão at a press conference on November 19, 1999. Briefing by Ian Martin, Sergio Vieira de Mello and Xanana Gusmão, 19 November 1999." Available online at http://www.un.org/peace/etimor/DB/br191199.htm, last access on 6 March 2009.

UNTAET Public Information Office, "Law and Order Initiatives," 28 January 2000. Available online at http://www.un.org/peace/etimor/DB/br280100.htm, last access on 4 March 2009.

UNTAET, "Daily Briefing," 12 June 2001. Available online at http://www.un.org/peace/etimor/DB/Db120601.htm, last access on 6 March 2009.

UNTAET, "Daily Briefing," 19 October 2000. Available online at http://www.un.org/peace/etimor/DB/DB191000.HTM, last access on 5 March 2009.

UNTAET, "Daily Briefing," 31 January 2002. Available online at http://members.tip.net.au/~wildwood/02janassembly.htm, last access on 6 March 2009.

UNTAET, "Regulation on the Authority of the Transitional Administration in East Timor," UN Doc. UNTAET/REG/1999/1, 27 November 1999.

UNTAET, "Regulation on the Election of a Constituent Assembly to Prepare a Constitution for an Independent and Democratic East Timor," UN Doc. UNTAET/REG/2001/2, 16 March 2001.

UNTAET, "Regulation on the Establishment of a Defense Force for East Timor," UN Doc. UNTAET/REG/2001/1, 31 January 2001.

UNTAET, "Regulation on the Establishment of a National Council," UN Doc. UNTAET/REG/2000/24, para. 2, 14 July 2000.

US Centre for World Mission, "The Joshua Project." Available online at http://www.joshuaproject.net/countries.php?rog3=TT, last access on 1 March 2009.

US General Accounting Office, National Security and Internal Affairs Division, "United Nations: Limitations in Leading Missions Requiring Force to Restore Peace." Report to Congressional Committees, 27 March 1997. Available online at http://www.gao.gov/archive/1997/ns97034.pdf, last access on 25 February 2009.

US State Department, "News Briefing of Wednesday, 2 July 1997," FDCH Political Transcripts.

Van der Lijn, Jaïr. 2009. If only There Were a Blueprint! Factors for Success and Failure of UN Peace-Building Operations. Netherlands Institute of International Relations 'Clingendael,' Clingendael Security and Conflict Programme (CSCP). Available online at http://www.clingendael.nl/publications/2009/20090218_joup_lijn3.pdf, last access on 16 March 2009.

Vieira de Mello, Sergio, "Address at the First CNRT Congress, Dili, August 21, 2000." Available online at http://members.pcug.org.au/~wildwood/cnrt.htm, last access on 2 March 2009.

Walker, Christopher, "Conflict Continues to Simmer on the Eastern Side of Croatia." Conflict Resolution Journal. Available online at http://www.sipa.columbia.edu/cicr/research/journal/archive/features/croatia.html, last access on 18 February 2009.

Whittington, Sherrill, "The UN Transitional Administration in East Timor: Gender Affairs." Gender Affairs Unit UNTAET. Available online at http://devnet.anu.edu.au/online%20versions%20pdfs/53/20Whittington53.pdf, last access on 3 March 2009.

World Bank. 1999. Timor-Leste: Building a Nation. A Framework for Reconstruction and Development. Available online at http://web.worldbank.org/WBSITE/EXTERNAL/COUNTRIES/EASTASIAPACIFICEXT/TIMORLESTEEXTN/0,,contentMDK:20878086-pagePK:141137piPK:141127theSitePK:294022,00.htm, last access on 8 April 2007.

World Bank. 2007. Croatia – Living Standards Assessment. Available online at http://www.worldbank.hr/WBSITE/EXTERNAL/COUNTRIES/ECAEXT/CROATIAEXTN/0,,contentMDK:21192606~pagePK:141137~piPK:141127~theSitePK:301245,00.html, last access on 15 March 2009.